# THE PSYCHOANALYTIC PROCESS

# The Psychoanalytic Process

**A CASE ILLUSTRATION**

*Paul A. Dewald*

Basic Books, Inc., Publishers       *New York / London*

© 1972 by Basic Books, Inc.
Library of Congress Catalog Card Number: 72–76917
SBN 465–06615–1
Manufactured in the United States of America
Designed at The Inkwell Studio

to
My Father and Mother,
and
to all their surrogates,
my teachers

# FOREWORD

When I received an invitation to write a foreword for Paul Dewald's book on the process of psychoanalysis, I was somewhat overwhelmed. The subject, however, was extremely interesting, so I accepted the challenge. Reading the manuscript and thinking about it over a period of some six months was a stimulating experience. Unfortunately, my experience cannot be communicated in the space of a foreword. Nevertheless, I shall try to outline some of the significant contributions to be found here and make some suggestions about how the book can be used.

This book is an attempt to give an unabridged example of the psychoanalytic method of data collection and how that data is processed by the analyst on the spot in the psychoanalytic situation. It is a sample of the basic behavioral data provided by the interactions between patient and analyst by means of which therapeutic change can take place. It is an illustration of the kind of behavioral phenomena from which the psychoanalytic theories of psychopathology, therapy, and technique have been derived, and which lead on another level of conceptualization to theories of normal development and general psychology. The primary goal of this book, however, is to focus on the process of the psychoanalytic treatment method.

We see here an account of how psychoanalytic procedures establish a relationship between two people which sets the stage for the action of movement toward understanding the past, an understanding which gives the patient an opportunity to re-solve childhood developmental conflicts in a more currently adaptive way. We see here the unfolding of a person's intimate fantasy life and her struggle to master the stresses of childhood in her reach for maturity. But this book adds significantly more than similar stories found in novels or plays. It includes the "how" of the new solutions to old problems. This "how" is visible in the interaction with the analyst as the transference reliving of the past takes shape and then as the distortions in the transference neurosis are gradually corrected to free the patient of the compulsion to repeat the outmoded patterns of the past.

In the discussions after each verbatim hour and in his summarized formulations, the author adds a dimension to the data of an analysis which is not usually available in process form. He shares with the reader the operation of his "empathic understanding." He shows us the development of his tentative explanatory hypotheses. He demonstrates how these formulations lead the patient to further interpretations, as the analyst responds to the ebb and flow of resistances—now strong, now crumbling, so that something else shows through, enabling the patient to observe and understand more about herself. Her mastery is increased by the analyst's flexibility in his responsiveness, his increased pressure against resistances when indicated, and his relaxation of pressure when he senses that resistances must be kept high for the sake of maintaining a necessary equilibrium within the patient.

After reading the introduction, it may be helpful to turn to the final summing up before reading the verbatim material. The author's synthesis gives a valuable frame of reference within which to map the course of the analysis in conjunction with the story of the patient's development during childhood. Dewald stresses the significant "organizing fantasy" at various levels of development. This is an important concept which establishes a bridge between the history of events in childhood and their effect on the patient's psychic resources at the time. Childhood events and their intrapsychic impact were integrated for the sake of a homeostatic balance into a prevailing fantasy. Such an "organizing fantasy" by means of reinforcement or buffering operations influenced, in turn, the impact of subsequent events and subsequent intrapsychic structuring to produce the picture of her personality when the patient came for analytic therapy. The elaboration of the factors which contributed to the origins of these organizing fantasies is the chief work of the initial and middle phases of the analysis. Until this elaboration and identification of causal factors can be established, the corrective influence of interpretation and working through on the transference distortions cannot be accomplished. In the synthesis Dewald also defines what he means by the "process of psychoanalysis" and describes the various factors which facilitate its evolution.

The reader of this book may have a tendency to become impatient with the detail and repetitiveness of the verbatim record. This is a natural reaction for an observer who is outside of the analytic experience and not responsible as the analyst is for staying with the patient during the inevitable fluctuations of working through. Repetitiveness is part of the process of psychoanalysis. For the patient, it is protective. It prevents the therapeutic regression of the ego from occurring too fast and going too far.

It keeps the observing ego intact while at the same time allowing regressive experiencing to occur in small doses—small enough not to exceed the ego's integrative capacity of the moment.

The reader is in the position of analyst. He can "see" much farther than the patient both horizontally and in depth. He is aware of much that is coming, but he is also aware of the patient's need to stay within her ego tolerance. The analyst's problem is the timing and the dosing of his interpretations which take the patient's observing and experiencing ego a little further on the road of regressive re-experiencing. The performance of this task, appropriate for the analyst, assists him in maintaining his own tolerance of what often seems to be a slow spinning of wheels without forward movement in the analysis. The reader of this book is not involved in the same way as the analyst and is in danger of succumbing to his wish "to get on with it." If he succeeds in controlling his impatience, he will be rewarded as the process unfolds to a transference neurosis in the middle phase (hours 143–219). To be able to observe the steps leading to the regressive re-experiencing followed by the gradual reintegration to a new level of insight and self-confidence has a vicarious pleasure of its own in identification with the success of both patient and analyst. A second pleasure comes from the increment of understanding of the phenomena and the process of a psychoanalysis that the experience of reading this book can provide.

One cannot conclude the foreword to such a book without commenting on the courage of both patient and analyst in exposing their analytic interactions in as much detail as is done here. It is inevitable that the reader will make evaluative judgments as to the "correctness" of the formulations and the technique. But the reader must keep in mind that the measure of approval from colleagues is not the reason for publication of this document—neither in terms of the "correctness" of technique nor evaluation of outcome. Rather, publication is intended to provide material for observation of the phenomena of an analysis hour by hour and in the longitudinal perspective of the evolving process. A careful study of this material offers students of psychoanalysis a rare opportunity to follow the microscopic "psychic operations" as they are related to the more macroscopic development of structural change. Teachers of psychoanalysis will find a rich storehouse of clinical examples for various teaching objectives that will aid a student's understanding of the correlations between behavioral observations and the theoretical concepts that explain them. Much has been written about psychodynamics and psychopathology. Much has been written about transference and psychoanalytic technique, but the emphasis has usually been cross sectional and anecdotal, neglecting the data that indicate the winding path of change within the patient and the signs of the analyst's role in bringing that insightful change about. Dr. Dewald's record of an analyst as it was experienced by both patient and analyst gives us the evidence of such a process. The road is not marked by flashing lights or beeping signals. The trail is hard to follow, especially in the beginning, but persistent effort is rewarded in the end for the reader, as well as the patient and the analyst.

JOAN FLEMING, M.D.

*Department of Psychiatry*
*University of Colorado*
   *Medical Center*
*Denver, Colorado*

"Dear Dr. Dewald,

"Yes, you may certainly use any material from my sessions with you in your paper. I would feel honored to be helpful in the field of psychoanalysis.

"I am a little disappointed in my reaction to an hysterectomy, followed by my talk with your friend (Dr. E. James Anthony). I found myself regressing in thought but never acknowledging them. I have finally realized that I was searching for an excuse to have you help me with my problem. I am growing farther and farther from this thought but any communication with you causes me a little regression. I am confident that I will mature beyond these defensive thoughts as I now fully understand them.

"Thank you for your thoughtfulness in asking my permission to use your notes.

"I am a fulfilled and maturing woman due to your analysis. I am forever grateful.

Sincerely,
(Signed)"

ACKNOWLEDGMENTS

I want to express my deep appreciation to the former patient who is the subject of this study for her gracious permission to use the material of her analysis. To the extent that this volume adds to the understanding of psychoanalysis, its readers will be in her debt.

My secretary, Mrs. Ann Mounts, contributed much time and energy in typing the various drafts of the manuscript, and I am grateful to her for this.

My wife's role in this work was indispensable. Not only did she function as an editorial assistant and copy reader, but her moral support and encouragement were vital. And her willing acceptance of the inevitable inroads which this project made upon our time together allowed it to become a reality.

P. A. D.

# CONTENTS

# THE PSYCHOANALYTIC PROCESS

# INTRODUCTION

Psychoanalysis is under continuing and recurrent attack from a variety of sources within the fields of medicine and psychiatry, and also from people working in other disciplines. Its status as a science and scientific theory has been challenged repeatedly, as has its effectiveness as a methodology in the therapeutic management of patients with neurotic and personality disturbances.

Many of these criticisms and condemnations arise from the unique methodological issues which are part of the clinical psychoanalytic situation, and these are particularly highlighted when one attempts a scientific study of the phenomena of psychoanalysis. A further methodological problem is that of data collection and its subsequent utilization.

The interaction that occurs in the usual situation of therapeutic psychoanalysis is an intimately private one between the patient and his analyst. Much of the therapeutic process itself becomes focused around the issues of this particular interaction and its various elaborations, both for the patient and for the analyst. In the usual clinical situation the analyst is both a participant in the process and also the observer of those things that go on between himself and his patient. Although the analyst during his training has submitted himself voluntarily to personal psychoanalysis in an attempt to reduce the significance and impact of his own unconscious intrapsychic conflicts and to enhance his objectivity and capacity to assess the situation without prejudice or bias, this remains an ideal goal which for most analysts can only be approximated or partially achieved. Whatever his residual shortcomings, the analyst remains the one who not only participates in the ongoing analytic process, but also collects the data therefrom, evaluates the patient's role, as well as his own, and evaluates the final outcome of the treatment.

A number of experimental attempts have been made to minimize or offset the possibility of bias or selective repression in the analyst by introducing some type of third-party observer into the analytic situation and analytic process. This has been done by the use of tape recorders, one-way screens, video sound recording, or, as in the case of analysis while in training, the introduction of a supervisory relationship in which the student analyst reports regularly to a more senior supervising and training analyst. Whereas these methods introduce the greater objectivity of a more neutral third-party observer to the scene, the very introduction of this observer has a significant impact and modifying effect upon the analytic process itself. Furthermore, the observers have access directly only to the external interactions between analyst and patient, and they have no *direct* access into the mental processes of the analyst as he functions in his analytic role.

The primary goal of acquiring "scientific data" from such an analysis may add another dimension to the complexity of the situation. For the analyst it may at times promote conflict between his immediate therapeutic responsibility and his detached scientific objectivity if, during the course of an analysis, there are strong focus and attention to the scientific aspects of the case. And for the patient, the knowledge that he is the object of chiefly scientific interest from his analyst will have many repercussions and will make the analysis less representative of usual therapeutic work.

Another methodological problem is that not uncommonly a complete analysis may involve three, or four, or more years of analytic work. As a result, voluminous amounts of data and clinical material are accumulated and the raw presentation of this data in a scientific publication or discourse is at times extremely unwieldy or even impossible. Case reports that appear in the literature must, by necessity, represent selective excerpts or condensations of the primary analytic data. The selection of the data to be presented and the interpretations drawn from such clinical phenomenological data require a judgment and selectivity which can easily be influenced by the theoretical or personal set of the individual reporting the data. It becomes extremely difficult for someone else to examine such data and possibly draw other conclusions from them. Thus, the problem of validation and verification of the inferences that were drawn by the analyst who presented the material is seriously compounded.

Another complicating factor is that many, if not most, analysts prefer not to write notes during the analytic sessions. In this, they follow Freud's early warning that an attempt to record the data as the process occurs in the analytic session will interfere with the analyst's use of his own unconscious mental processes in associating to, and understanding, his patient's communications. Probably the best-recorded nonexperimental psychoanalyses are those done by candidates-in-training who write rather detailed process notes after the conclusion of the session with the patient, in order to be able to present their material to the supervisor at a later time. However, these analytic data are available only for analysis conducted by a relatively inexperienced student analyst who, furthermore, is subjected to the various contaminating factors produced by the situation of the supervision of his work. They therefore would not give a clear or accurate picture of the total process of an analysis conducted by a relatively senior or experienced analyst.

Furthermore, the recording of data after an analytic session has been concluded may involve a number of selective distortions and omissions by the analyst, subject again to his perceptions of the analytic process which, as mentioned above, will be influenced by a variety of personal and, at times, unconscious factors. Experienced analysts are generally able to conduct a therapeutic analysis without recording the specific details of the process, and they tend, therefore, to rely on summarizing notes. Where an analyst has a particular scientific research interest, he may in selective areas record the data of his work in much greater detail, but in the usual clinical situation this tends to be spotty and more project-oriented.

Most of the long clinical reports in the analytic literature, including Freud's original five case histories, therefore, tend to be somewhat anecdotal or to be selectively focused on a particular facet of the psychopathology or of the therapeutic process. A number of exceptions to this general rule exist (see the reference section), but these are the exceptions, rather than the rule. As a result, the clinical reports in the literature can be effective and convincing for those who have had some personal contact with the process of psychoanalysis, either as a patient or as the analyst. However, for the person who has not himself experienced the vicissitudes of the analytic process, the clinical data may remain unconvincing, and when taken out of context, they may at times appear to be ludicrous.

Each individual psychoanalytic treatment is in some respects similar to every other psychoanalytic treatment, but each is also specifically unique in certain characteristics relating to the specific personality and past experience of the patient, as well as to the particular characteristics of the analyst. Any study of the analytic material reported by a specific patient will, therefore, be in part applicable to the general understanding of psychopathology and the therapeutic process and, in part, restricted in its applicability to the particular case under discussion. However, there is a need for the sharing of primary data of analytic experience as one small step toward solution of the problems of verification and validation that beset the science of psychoanalysis.

It has been my custom, therefore, to attempt to record in writing, as nearly verbatim as possible during the analytic session itself, the interactions between the patient and myself as I conduct the usual therapeutic psychoanalytic treatment. If I find that the process of recording tends to interfere with my own functioning in the analytic situation, I discontinue the recording of notes during the sessions. But if I find that it does not act as an interference, I have attempted to maintain the complete record of the analysis as it occurred. The recording of the notes not infrequently comes up in the patient's associations during the analytic process, and when it does, it is subjected to analytic scrutiny and understanding as would occur with any other element of behavior in either the patient or myself. It has been my experience that at least in a number of my patients the recording of such notes has not proved to be a significantly disruptive or insurmountable factor.

The case to be reported here is unusual in the sense that the patient had a particularly highly developed aptitude for analytic work, and the entire analytic treatment was completed in slightly less than two years. I had no specific or organized research plans in mind when I undertook the analysis of this patient, and had no particular anticipation that it would be a relatively brief analysis. But in the latter half of the analysis the outlines for this current presentation began to take shape in my mind. However, I did not formally begin the investigation and presentation of this material until after the termination of the analytic treatment, but merely continued to function as her therapeutic analyst while at the same time recording the primary data as faithfully as I could as they unfolded. The happy circumstance that it was a relatively brief analysis meant that it would be possible to present an account of these data and of the inferences drawn from them in a manageably concise and expedient form.

The plan in this project is to present the detailed and nearly verbatim notes of the analytic process as it occurred during alternate months of the analysis, illustrating the beginning, middle, and termination phases. Following each verbatim session there will be a discussion of the significant features of that particular session as they relate to the therapeutic process in analysis and the specific psychopathology of this particular patient. I will attempt to reconstruct as closely as possible the thinking that occurred in my mind during the analytic sessions themselves, but some of the material in these discussions will inevitably be influenced by my subsequent knowledge of the case and also by the passage of time and my own development since the treatment was completed. The presentation of the material illustrating early, middle, and terminal alternate months is an attempt to keep the total amount of material presented within a manageable range. But, in order to maintain the sense of continuity in the total analytic experience, there will be a narrative section describing in summary form the analytic work for those months in between the months where the primary data are presented.

In the attempt to record the data as faithfully as possible during the sessions, it was necessary to develop a personal set of abbreviations and shorthand symbols, relating both to the communication of the patient and also to the interventions of my own. Therefore in preparing these notes for publication it became necessary to fill these out in detail. Wherever this has occurred, I have attempted as faithfully as possible to use the style of the patient as well as my own personal style of speaking, in order that sentence structures will be complete. I also recorded the patient's non-verbal communications, and these appear in the columns alongside of the verbal text. Silences which lasted for thirty seconds or longer were recorded and each dash in the text represents a thirty-second interval of silence. Each series of dots represents blocking, incoherence, or an incomplete thought.

The complete study of any analytic treatment process should include a follow-up which is undertaken after a considerable time interval following the termination of the treatment. The issues of who is best able to make such a follow-up study and the effects of such a study on the patient are matters that have received considerable attention in the literature. In this instance the patient was seen for follow-up by Dr. E. James Anthony, three and one-half years after the termination of her analysis, and the results of his examinations will be included as an epilogue.

I have a number of goals in mind in making this study. One is to provide primary data illustrating the phenomenology of mental functioning as it is studied during a clinical psychoanalysis. The attempt is to demonstrate analytic material for those readers unfamiliar with it, and to illustrate the observational data from which psychoanalytic theory and metapsychology are derived. I hope also to provide data which offset the frequent accusation against analysis that the material which occurs in the mind of the patient is the result of direct suggestion by the analyst.

Another goal is an attempt to demonstrate the nature of the therapeutic process itself, and to illustrate the central importance of the transference neurosis. The chronological presentation of significant portions of the entire analysis (rather than brief selected excerpts) should permit a view of the gradual development, deepening elaboration, and ultimate resolution of the transference neurosis and the therapeutic impact of this process.

I would also hope that the comments and critiques of the individual sessions will allow for a glimpse into the working mind of the analyst as he conducts and reflects upon a therapeutic analysis. It is likely that no two analysts would conduct an analysis in exactly the same way, nor would they interpret or conceptualize all the data in an identical fashion. The presentation of my own style, approach, activity, and understanding can thus serve as a basis of comparison, confirmation, or disagreement by other analysts in reacting to the primary data. Thus the hope is that this material may ultimately serve as a model for the pooling of primary psychoanalytic data in preparation for studies of validation and verification.

I am therefore hopeful that this study will be of use not only to those already familiar with the principles and phenomena of the analytic process, but also to students of psychoanalysis, and to those individuals from other walks of life who have an interest or curiosity in what actually occurs during the process of a psychoanalysis.

## References

BERG, CHARLES. *Deep Analysis: The Clinical Study of an Individual Case.* New York: W. W. Norton and Co., Inc., 1947.

FRENCH, THOMAS M. *The Integration of Behavior,* Vols. 2, 3. Chicago: University of Chicago Press, 1953, 1958.

KLEIN, MELANIE. *Narrative of a Child Analysis.* New York: Basic Books, 1961.

McDOUGALL, JOYCE, and LEBOVICI, SERGE. *Dialogue with Sammy.* New York: International Universities Press, 1969.

MILNER, MARION. *The Hands of the Living God: An Account of a Psychoanalytic Treatment.* New York: International Universities Press, 1969.

PARKER, BEULAH. *My Language Is Me: Psychotherapy with a Disturbed Adolescent.* New York: Basic Books, 1962.

PEARSON, GERALD, ed. *A Handbook of Child Psychoanalysis.* New York: Basic Books, 1968.

# Prologue

# THE PATIENT AND
# THE PROBLEM

The following material is the initial diagnostic work-up recorded when the patient first applied to the Psychoanalytic Foundation of St. Louis seeking a low-cost analysis.

*Patient is a 26-year-old, married, white housewife with two children ages 2½ years and 2½ months. She is referred by Mr. Harris of Family Counseling Service for psychoanalysis since he and his supervisor, Dr. James Davis, feel this patient needs intensive treatment. The major symptoms began in the last month of her first pregnancy and consist of acute attacks of free-floating anxiety accompanied by palpitations, sweating, a sense of dread and terror, and at times a fear of dying. Immediately after the delivery of the child, she had people helping her for two weeks and was free of the symptoms, but as soon as she was alone again there was a recurrence of the intermittent acute anxiety attacks which have persisted to the present time. She also has a variety of phobic symptoms particularly involving being alone, where she frequently has the fear that someone will break into the apartment. These symptoms are particularly acute when her husband is working at night. She has fears of various types of illness, and finds that she becomes anxious and panicky at seeing or reading about any type of illness. She has fears of death, although she has come to recognize that these are irrational. At times she has fears that she will not be able to breathe, and on one or two occasions insisted that her husband come home to reassure her on this score. She has had difficulty in falling asleep at night, and her sleep is broken at times by nightmares which are quite disturbing to her. The most recent one that she can recall involved, "A crazy man was loose and I was afraid he was going to break into the house. I was worried he would do something to my child. I went down into the basement and there I saw a toilet and I thought I saw my husband's arm in the toilet. I thought my husband was dead and was very upset. I ran back upstairs and told someone about it. They said to me that it was not my hus-*

band but it was just worms and I woke up." The patient has also had symptoms of difficulty getting along with her daughter, with at times conscious feelings of anger and rejection toward the child. She also has episodes of moderately severe depression in which she feels that everything looks bleak and unhappy and that at times she will not be able to continue functioning, but yet at the same time finds that she is always able to do so even though not feeling like it. She at times has the impulse just to go to bed but never does so, and has maintained her responsibility as a wife and mother in spite of her symptoms.

She and her husband moved to southern Illinois one year ago, and she began consulting with Mr. Harris. Shortly after beginning her treatment with Mr. Harris she found herself increasingly reluctant to participate in sexual relations with her husband. Previously their sexual adjustment had been satisfying, and even currently she finds that once involved in sexual activity with her husband she is excited and derives pleasure from the act. However, she finds that she is irritable and unhappy at her husband's initial approaches to her and would prefer not to participate, but feels a tremendous sense of pressure to do so and a fear that her husband will no longer love her if she refuses. In her treatment with Mr. Harris she has noted significant improvement in her overall symptomatology but feels that she wishes to uncover and deal with the basic issues involved in her problems, and both Mr. Harris and his supervisor feel that he is not the appropriate professional person to deal with these issues. The patient herself feels that she wants to get at the bottom of her problems; she would like to be analyzed, but at the same time is conscious of her anxiety about the unknown.

The patient is the second of three daughters, her older sister being one year her senior and her younger sister four years her junior. The father is a lawyer whom she describes as having been stern, rigid, strict, at times harsh and punitive, and emotionally somewhat unstable. As a young man he had begun a promising career in government and politics, but because of his emotional difficulties he had to resign and has since been in private law practice. The father had repeated extramarital affairs with other women throughout the patient's life, which resulted in much marital unhappiness and discord, with many accusations by the mother, who brought all the children up to "hate my father as a bad and wicked person." The mother is described as a more stable but cold and somewhat bitter woman, and the patient states that she and her mother always had considerable difficulty and tension between them until after her marriage, since which time their relationship has been a more friendly and cordial one. The patient says that her mother told her years ago that she was born at about the time the mother had made up her mind to leave the father, and that the patient's birth had prevented this and caused the mother to change her mind. There were many threats of divorce throughout the patient's childhood, and when she was sixteen the family left Chicago because of one of the father's extramarital affairs and moved to a nearby community. Since that time there has been a subsequent move, again for the same reason, but the parents are staying together and the father continues in his legal practice.

The patient describes herself as having been a fearful and anxious child with fears of being left alone, fears of death, of suffocation as an infant and child, and she remembers on one occasion during World War II as a small child having severe nightmares in which soldiers, tanks, guns, and trucks were all coming toward her in her room. After repeated crying and screaming she was able to get her mother to come into her room and lie down on the bed next to her, thereby relieving for the moment some of her anxiety. She had enuresis until the sixth grade, and also was a tense child with many feelings of inferiority and uncertainty about herself. She had an average academic and extracurricular record in high school. Socially she developed a pattern in which she would go out with only one boy at a time, often for as long as a year, and then in a brief flurry would quickly find herself another boy whom she would date steadily to the exclusion of everyone else. After graduation from college she met her husband who was working as an instructor in a summer course, and they were married after about a year's courtship. During this time, however, the husband was in law school and they actually saw one another only a total of one month. In the few weeks prior to the patient's marriage she found herself increasingly anxious to the point that her physician prescribed mild tranquilizers for her, but she states that she had no hesitations or doubts about her husband as the proper person to marry. Beginning in her sophomore year of high school, the patient had noted the onset of intermittent episodes of intense overeating, to the point that she might gain ten or fifteen pounds in a relatively short time. She would gorge herself at times, sitting down to eat an entire box of cookies or crackers, etc., and at times eating to the point of physical discomfort. This eating disturbance had recurred in the few weeks prior to her marriage and the patient had gained about fifteen pounds.

She describes her marriage as having been a satisfying and satisfactory one, and states that sexually she was extremely responsive and involved, enjoying sex very intensely, and at times being concerned that she might be "more sexually active and interested than my husband." As she thought about this phase of her life more carefully with Mr. Harris, she became aware however that in the first year or so of marriage she was extremely jealous of her husband and had constant preoccupation and fear that he might be having extramarital affairs with secretaries at the school or office. Repetitively he would come home to find her in tears about this. In the last two or three years of marriage these doubts and suspicions of her husband have subsided considerably and she has recognized them as being without foundation, and she feels that her marriage in other ways solidified and became more stable. She describes her husband as a supporting, kind, considerate, and reasonably warm person, points out that they share a number of interests, and in general considers her marriage to be a successful one. The husband has currently come to Belleville where he is a law clerk in a legal firm, and where he plans to remain for at least the next three years. In spite of the distances involved, the patient does not feel that driving from the east side of the city will be a major problem for her therapy.

On interview the patient is a tall, attractive young woman who talked freely and easily with considerable spontaneity and awareness, and who overall made a very favorable, appealing, and attractive impression. She is intelligent and has a considerable psychological awareness, some of which may have been developed as a result of her therapy with Mr. Harris once-a-week in the past year. Over and above this, however, she shows a capacity for a reasonable degree of introspection and psychological perceptiveness. Her flow of associations and material was at all times appropriate, reasonably free, and the affect likewise appropriate. She was able to make use of the interview effectively and indicated the capacity for establishing a meaningful and reasonable therapeutic relationship. She spoke of her improvement in the therapy with Mr. Harris, but also of her awareness of further need for deeper and more intensive therapy. There was no evidence of psychotic ideation or affect or likelihood of significant disruption. She has been capable of fulfilling her family and social obligations in spite of her symptoms, and there is no evidence of recent decompensation. She is well motivated for psychoanalysis.

This patient presents a mixed neurotic picture with primarily hysterical and phobic symptomatology as well as some free-floating anxiety and mild-to-moderate neurotic depressive symptoms. It is not possible to clearly delineate all the dynamic problems in a single interview, but from the material available it would seem that there is a classical hysterical and oedipal conflict with the major psychopathology revolving around her relationship to her father and her sexual conflicts around this. Whether or not this masks a significant element of prephallic attachment to the mother is unclear, but there is evidence of her eating disturbance, as well as the dream in which the husband's arm is seen in the toilet, which suggests that there may be a significant pregenital fixation. In any event, however, she seems capable of establishing an intense and meaningful object relationship and as such would probably establish a classical transference neurosis in an analytic situation. She appears to be well motivated and the ego processes appear to be intact; and in general, I feel that she would be eminently suitable as an analytic case.

The patient is interested in analysis and the possibility of arranging for this privately is not realistic unless she were to borrow heavily from her husband's family, which she feels would be against the ultimate goals of the analysis. She and her husband have a limited income and she would prefer to support analysis out of this if possible. I discussed with her the differences between private and Analytic Foundation Treatment Service care, and she is to consider them and discuss it with her husband and let me know of her decision.

## Diagnosis

Mixed psychoneurosis with phobic, conversion, and depressive symptoms and free-floating anxiety.

## Preanalytic Treatment

While waiting to find out whether or not she could have a low-cost analysis, the patient's symptoms gradually intensified. She became particularly depressed, with recurrent fantasies of slashing her wrists, and her anxiety and phobic symptoms also intensified. She called me on the telephone several times, saying she felt alone and helpless in the face of her symptoms, and asking that something be done to help her while waiting for definitive treatment.

I still maintained the opinion that she could benefit from an analysis and did not want to refer her for any other type of long-term treatment while the issue of psychoanalysis was still open. On the other hand, she needed some type of therapeutic intervention to keep from further psychological decompensation.

I therefore referred her to a woman staff psychiatric social worker for support and counseling while she was awaiting the decision regarding analysis. This was done with the expectation that it might provide some symptomatic relief, and that she would not be likely to develop a significantly contaminating transference reaction which might later interfere with analysis.

The following are the summary notes of their sessions made by the social worker.

---

## SESSION 1

"The patient, a very attractive, very uncomfortable young woman, came in to keep her appointment. She can hardly stand the waiting. She will have an analysis some way or other, although she does not know where they will get the money. She is most uncomfortable, has desires to slash her wrists, has terrible dreams. She started to work part-time as a secretary and receptionist for a not-so-good lawyer. Although he is completely unattractive, she knows she is sexually attracted to him. Since she cannot express this, she is now very hostile to her boss. She is frigid with her husband and hostile to him.

"The patient hates her mother. She cannot understand how her mother treated her. She spoke of having a distended stomach, like she was pregnant or like she wanted to be pregnant, even when she wasn't. She blames her for everything and what she really is most upset about is that she set up a relationship in her home exactly the same as she had with her parents. In other words, she treats her children as her mother did. She realizes this is horrible, and something has to happen to help it. The patient said that she felt that it helped to come here, although she really found that she was beginning to become dependent on me and she did not want to be. She knew she couldn't be dependent upon anyone as much as she wanted to."

---

## SESSION 2

"The patient came in to keep her appointment. She said that she had felt much better after our last interview, but now she had a real problem. It developed that she went to see Dr. Smith, her gynecologist, because of her periods being irregular. She stated that they had been irregular ever since she stopped seeing Mr. Harris. She last menstruated two months ago. Dr. Smith suggested that she might be pregnant and since she has seen him she has had morning sickness. She does not know whether she is pregnant or not. She is very disturbed, as she heard that if she were pregnant she could not be analyzed. She has all her hopes pinned to analysis as the only treatment that will help her. She is afraid of having to wait for her analysis, as when she was seeing Mr. Harris she had very vivid dreams, and lately the dreams have been less basic. They were full of hostility and now she does not know what they are full of. She is afraid if she has to wait too long that she will suppress too much. She groups Mr. Harris, Dr. Dewald, and Dr. Smith with her father and is always using one name for another.

"The patient then talked about crying. She formerly was a person who could cry. She doesn't cry any more but continuously feels like she wishes to cry. She again talked about analysis and how it was her one salvation, and about her great dependency needs. She has quit her job with the lawyer and is now attempting to do substitute teaching. She thinks that she would like this."

---

## SESSION 3

"The patient came in quite upset. She hasn't been this depressed for a long time. She finds that she doesn't want to do anything. She is all right when she is out, but she is very panicky when she is on the way home. When she is at home, she lies down and does the bare minimum of work. Last Saturday night, they planned to go out and had a babysitter, and the patient did not want to go. She also dreads going to sleep as she is again having terrible dreams. She wakes up and she has a terrible feeling that someone is standing over her with a brick. It is going to sleep that she just dreads. However, she does get to sleep about 11:00 and sleeps until 6:00. She feels that she hasn't been this depressed before; she does not know exactly what it is, but it has been ever since she has been coming to see me. She also doesn't know whether she is pregnant or not. The past week she has been extremely hostile. She has hardly any affection for the children, especially the baby.

"She has the feeling that nobody cares and that nobody wants to do anything for her. She formerly had a daydream where she would wake up happy and now nothing makes her happy. It could have something to do with coming to see me. Consciously, she cannot direct hostility to me, she said, and then she directed hostility all through the hour to me. She thinks 'maybe it might be that instead of going to my father, I could never do so, I had to come to my mother. It may be that that's the way I feel about you and Dr. Dewald; Dr. Dewald, my father, that I could never go to because of my mother, you. Although you really are nothing like my mother. Mother would not guide me in the right way.' Then the patient said that she wondered if she ever would have a father to go to. She feels that she is very much more openly hostile. She knows she wants something from her husband to whom she is very hostile, but he is not capable of sharing. She feels that no one really understands her, no one in the world. To her, the man is the center of her life, and a woman is a friend, but never can really help her.

"The patient said that she must have help and why didn't they tell her when she could start. Dr. Dewald had said two or three weeks and it was more than two or three weeks. She feels that if there were some certainty, that she could stand it even if she was told that she could have treatment in a few months, if she just knew what months. The patient thinks that she can get the money for private therapy and wants to start. I told her I would talk with Dr. Dewald. I had the feeling that she was really very angry, primarily at Dr. Dewald, and I simply stood between them. She was doing everything she could to manipulate me so she could get to Dr. Dewald. The patient was told I would talk with Dr. Dewald and would then talk with her when she came in next week."

It developed around this time that the final committee decision was that she could not be offered a low-cost analysis. By coincidence, I had analytic time become available just as the final decision was reached. I therefore told the social worker that if the patient was able to make the necessary financial arrangements for private psychoanalysis, I would be able to begin such treatment with her. This information was relayed to the patient, who accepted it eagerly and called me the next day to arrange for her first appointment.

She began the analysis nine months after her original diagnostic referral.

# The
# Beginning
# Phase

# 1

# THE FIRST MONTH

## SESSION 1

The patient came in prepared to begin analysis. While still sitting up in a chair, we discussed and set the times of her four hours per week, and also the financial arrangement in which I would give her the bill on the first session of each month and she was to bring the check in prior to the tenth of the month. I explained to her the basic rule of free association, after which she lay down on the couch and the analysis began.

**P:** What will I do if I'm pregnant?

**A:** In analysis there will be times when you will have questions that you want to ask. But before answering them it's important for us to try to understand what's behind the question and see if it has other meanings than the question itself.

**P:** I don't think I have any special reason to be pregnant, but I do wonder if maybe it would be detrimental to my treatment. If I am pregnant I also wonder whether maybe I did have a reason?

**A:** What comes to your mind?

**P:** There can't be any other reasons and yet maybe I wondered that if I were to get pregnant that I wouldn't have to do this. (Elaborates the conflict.) I know that I did get pregnant within a month after I started my counselling with Mr. Harris.

**A:** Rather than jump to conclusions as to whether or not there is a reason, let's just look and see what comes to your mind.

**P:** Maybe I had the wish that it would make me ugly. I think I have a desire for that.

**A:** What's the detail?

**P:** I'm not sure whether that's my own thought or whether it is something that I was told. But I think that it would be an escape from any kind of sexual feelings. If I were pregnant and ugly then no one would be sexually attracted to me. I think that that is my biggest problem. -----

**A:** You seem to have some fear of talking about it.

**P:** Yes, I can feel that. I've been completely frigid for the last three weeks and I can't even stand the thought of anything sexual. And yet, at the same time I've had a lot of dreams with orgasm. – – – –

**A:** What comes to your mind about the hesitation in your thinking?

**P:** I have a sense of fright about my feelings toward you. – – – I was hoping that you could do my analysis. (Elaborates.) Then. . . . . I felt as if I had found someone who cared and that somehow I would get a relationship here even though I know that that's ridiculous and that I'm just a patient. – –

**A:** Try to pursue what comes to your mind about this.

**P:** – – – – I have the feeling that you'll be mad at me if I don't say something, and so I just can't say anything. But the longer the silence lasts the worse it gets.

**A:** What comes to your mind about the idea that I would be mad at you?

**P:** I think of the way Mr. Harris used to react if I didn't say anything. It also makes me think of my father and the way he would say "jump" and I'd have to jump or else he would call me "stupid." – – I have a sense of hostility about it. I know when I'm feeling love but I don't know when I'm being hostile. And it scares me most to show my hostile feelings. But I wonder if maybe I have that turned around.

**A:** What comes to your mind?

**P:** Maybe I'm really afraid to show my love feelings. I have quite a bit of hostility that I'm aware of, and it's like my mother's. She takes it out on sales people. Last night I dreamed that I was going to do this but then I ran back to Harris instead of to you. Somehow I felt so sorry for you. The person in the dream had a mustache so I figured it must be you. In the dream I thought "I'm so sorry that I didn't go to him and when I didn't, he cried." But then in the dream I said to myself, "You're not the first one and he's probably been hurt before." –

**A:** Dreams are frequently useful in analysis, but we use them in a special way. After you've told me the dream itself, try to take each of the elements in the dream as it occurred and see what your associations are to each part.

**P:** The man in the dream somehow reminded me of a boy that I used to go with. He got upset when I left him but he also got over it almost immediately. Somehow there was a feeling of many women being in the dream and that reminds me of my father and all of his affairs.

**A:** What are the details of your thoughts about the boy that you went with?

**P:** That was really the worst time in my life and I turned into a terrible person. He was a horrible boy and he came from a very bad family but I would cling to him just as I clung to my life. I had lost all of my feeling of security when we moved to Springfield and so I grasped the nearest straw that I could find. I did lose that security that I had.

A: What was the detail?

P: My father had left us just before we moved and I always had the feeling that my mother and father didn't care about me. – – – I feel sick to my stomach just thinking of this. I grabbed hold of boys and I'd go steady but then we had to leave Evanston and I felt as if half of my life was gone. It was all something new for me but I felt so estranged and I also knew that what I was doing was wrong. I've never talked about this before. I would conquer something and then I would immediately start with some-one new but it always made me so tired. Every time I grasp hold of some-body he slips away from me. That's the reason I felt so upset this morning about Tom's mother. Tom is my only stronghold and he was really the only one who would go with me steadily and he was the only one ever to really love me.

A: What comes to your mind about the upset this morning?

P: I got the feeling that somehow she would think me an unfit mother and then the whole thing began to snowball. I felt as if I had to call her and be sure that everything was all right. I had to convince myself that no one could take my children away from me. – – I wonder if maybe it was my own fear. I hadn't even thought about it until she suggested that maybe she should take the children for awhile. I felt as if I wanted some-thing this morning, but I don't know what.

A: What comes to your mind?

P: I felt so anxious as if I couldn't stand it. – – I was afraid to start my analysis and I felt as if I was going to lose something.

A: What are your associations to your fear of the analysis?

P: (Laughs.) I felt as if through starting analysis that I'd turned my back on my family and that somehow I would never return to my old world and that I would be dependent for my whole life. It all frightens me. – – I'm on my own for the first time in my life and I have to do this all by myself. My family are really opposed to it and I've never had to do anything by myself before.

A: What was the detail of the fright itself?

P: I feel like crying. I wonder what I'm thinking of? – – It's so hard to do something that you're not sure of yourself, especially when everybody else is trying to talk you out of it. My parents object. I tried to break away from them but I haven't. But then they didn't even contact me about this.

I know that I'm going to be mad if they don't help me, but I also know that they won't help.

A: What's the detail?

P: I think probably I'm going to change in some way, but I wonder is this the right thing for me to do? I don't know anyone who has ever been through analysis, and I wonder what about the results of analysis. I can't run away and yet I think that maybe my parents are right. I just don't know. I feel as if I'm hanging and I'm being pulled by both sides.

A: Let's look at the details of your fears of analysis and your doubts about starting. What comes to your mind?

P: I just don't know anything about it and I keep wondering what am I going into? I wonder will I be able to take it? At the same time I wonder what can be so frightening? But I sure do get frightened. I feel as if I'm completely placing myself in your hands and I don't even know you. I know that I'll probably be very dependent on you. (Elaborates.) I'm not sure that I'm strong enough for this and I know that I got awfully upset even while I was waiting to start.

A: So you feel as if you are starting on something new that's completely unknown and frightening, and you are doing it with someone that you don't know.

P: I feel as if I'm in a vise and that I'm caught. It's as if there are all kinds of holes and I'm about to fall through and yet I really do know that this is the only way. I've tried religion and I've tried running away and neither of them works. I'm so easily suggested to. (Elaborates.) I just have no mind of my own. (Elaborates.)

A: We'll stop here for today.

### DISCUSSION

In this first session, my goal is to begin the establishment of a therapeutic situation between us and to help the patient understand what her role is. For this reason, I choose not to remain silent when the patient begins her analysis with a question about the pregnancy, but instead use the question to illustrate and explain to the patient how questions are dealt with in analysis. Because she is anxious over the prospect of beginning the analysis, I choose not to permit any lengthy silences. The same is true in regard to my requests for detail, and for further information, as well as to my statement regarding jumping to premature conclusions. I assume that the possibility of a pregnancy at this time has a variety of conscious and unconscious meanings, probably related to the analysis. However, to have questioned her about these directly, or to have guessed at an interpretation of them, or to have commented directly upon her own explanations would have tended to intellectualize the analytic process. Since I have no particular doubts about analyzing her even if she is pregnant, I assume the latent material about this will emerge later in the analysis.

The patient very quickly begins to speak of her thoughts about me, and I assume this is a carryover from her previous therapy. To discuss or interpret transference reactions this early would be unwise as it would intellectualize her role. However, to ignore her references to me might suggest that I am afraid of such material. I therefore merely acknowledge my willingness to accept such material by asking for conscious associations and elaborations.

In handling the dream, I likewise choose to introduce her to the technique of dream interpretation and to emphasize the need for specific associations, rather than attempt an interpretation of its meaning. In this context, it is my impression that the patient's subsequent associations to her father and his affairs are based on an intellectual knowledge derived from her previous therapy, and that this is possibly a wish to please me by presenting the kind of material she thinks I want to hear. For these reasons I choose to focus on the association to the boy as a means of illustrating to her the need for detailed associations to dream elements. The success of this maneuver is illustrated by the relatively greater freedom in describing that time in her life, and by her subsequent statement that she has never before been able to talk about this material.

When the patient mentions her upset of this morning, it is my own association that this is related to her intense anxiety about beginning analysis and I want to expose this anxiety and get her to elaborate upon it. I feel that her fantasies of being an unfit mother and of her mother-in-law taking the children away represent a displacement from me and an anticipation that I might be critical of her and her handling of her children, or that I might have doubts about her being an unfit patient for analysis. However, I feel that it is much too early to introduce such transference issues, and instead, choose only to help her elaborate on the fear of the analysis. In my handling of this, I want her to realize that I can recognize and tolerate her anxiety and uncertainty, and in this way help further the development of the rapport necessary to establish an analytic situation.

## SESSION 2

The patient is three or four minutes late.

**P:** – – I don't know whether to talk about my present problems or whether I should be talking about my emotional problems.

**A:** Let's look at your wish to try to separate them.

**P:** I just feel unsure about everything. I do have some new problems.

**A:** What's the detail?

**P:** We've decided that we're not going to borrow any money for this and instead we are going to try to get it on our own. (Elaborates plans.) We're going to have to cut our budget and Tom is going to take some extra jobs and I'll try to get a part-time job. I feel as if there are so many things to do and I'm not even sure that we are going to get them done. I know now that I'm going to have a baby in October.

**A:** What's your feeling about it?

**P:** I feel happy, but it also makes me mad. Somehow being pregnant makes me somebody. I'm thinking about the money and how I resent the children about this right now. We wouldn't have any worries about paying for the analysis without them. But I must have things worked out. I somehow expected everyone to give me what I ask for and no one is going to. There are only two people in the world who love me. I think of my mother's call and all she said was that they would investigate the idea of analysis. I have no one to turn to. I have one friend and she offered to loan us $4,000.

**A:** What's the detail?

**P:** She went to Mr. Harris and she got divorced. She's through with her treatment now. I'm thinking of how much I feel my resentment! (Elaborates.) I feel it toward my parents and toward my sister. I feel so jealous of her. I feel as if I'm tied to them with strings, and it has been that way all my life. I hate them. It all depresses me and I have to bat my head against the wall with them. I know that I want to be independent of them and yet emotionally I'm just like a child. It's almost as if I need my parents to feed me and to change my diaper. – – –

**A:** What's the detail of your feeling about your sister?

**P:** She's a junior in college and right now she's in Europe with my older sister. – – – – I've been through this feeling so many times I just want to be rid of it.

*Cry*

**A:** What are you referring to?

**P:** I feel so frustrated. There's nothing that I can do to elicit love from anyone. It makes me mad but there is nothing there. It's like dealing with a statue. I can't hurt it no matter how hard I kick. – –

**A:** What comes to your mind?

**P:** – – – I can't do anything so I might just as well not try. I hate them! What's the good of that? It's just not fair! I want to scream and yell but it wouldn't do anything!

**A:** You feel as if it's been this way all of your life. What are your associations?

**P:** It's always been this way. I was just born into a family and I just happened to come along. My mother resented me and my father didn't care about anything. If only I had some device! – –

**A:** You seem to be holding back some of your feelings and thoughts.

**P:** I get very anxious when I think about this. I'm thinking of my mother now and how much I hate her! – – There's no love for me in my mother, and yet I feel that maybe I'm wrong. I want someone to say to me, "Yes, your mother was a. . . . ." –

**A:** What did you stop at?

**P:** A bitch.

**A:** What comes to your mind that you didn't want to use the word?

**P:** One time my father called her that. If I ever let go I'll just explode. – –

**A:** What's the detail of the feeling that you might explode?

**P:** – I feel like killing her sometimes. I'd like to take a knife and stab her but I know that I can't, and I don't really want to. Really I'd like to hurt her more some other way. Maybe I could do that by killing myself. That's what she wanted in the beginning anyhow. So I'm not going to give her that satisfaction, but I do blame all of my problems on to my mother. I wonder why? I think it has something to do with my father because she caused him to do what he did and so it all hurt me.

**A:** Let's not jump to conclusions about why you feel this way. What are your associations to the thought of her causing him to do the things he did?

**P:** – Somehow I feel as if my father's fate was inevitable. She digs at him and she drove him out. (Elaborates.) She kept him a child. I don't blame my father for his affairs. He couldn't help it. But I do blame my mother for her problems. She's been thirty years trying to get my father under her thumb.

**A:** What's the detail?

*Cry*

**P:** If she says, jump, he does. He's not having any more affairs now. She mammas him in order to control him. (Elaborates.) He's not even a man any more. – – – It would be much better for me now just to run away from them now and have no communication with them. Why do I hate my mother? – – –

**A:** Let's go back to your fear of exploding if you ever let go of your feelings. What comes to your mind?

**P:** My hands feel paralyzed right now. I wonder if I want to kill her? I know that I do want to get back at her. I'd like to stand and scream. I did once, but she just sat there and looked at me! Something is holding me back.

**A:** What comes to mind?

**P:** – – (Sobs.) – – I see her lying on the floor and then she is crawling around and I'm standing over her, and I'm big and I'm in control and she's completely helpless. – – I can't stand this. –

**A:** What is it that you feel you can't stand?

**P:** I can't stand my thoughts. – –

**A:** I wonder if you aren't reversing the positions in this image, and if it is you who feels helpless at the moment.

**P:** I feel as if I'm incapable of handling myself. It's an old feeling that I have all of the time. I feel as if something terrible will happen. Maybe I'll black out or something that I don't know. So it is much easier to be controlled and to be told what to do. – – I'm thinking of my children. If this emotion ever gets out I'm afraid I'll go wild and uncontrollable.

**A:** I think that here you are not distinguishing between the thought or feeling on the one hand, and an action on the other.

**P:** Yes, yes. – (Sigh.) I feel afraid to go home now. I'm afraid that I'll hurt my children or do something else. I wish I could put my aggression onto the person that I feel it for, but somehow I can't.

**A:** What comes to your mind?

**P:** I took it all out on my little sister as I grew up and I do it now with my children. – – When I stopped seeing Mr. Harris I used to beat the baby and sometimes I felt as if I'd kill her. (Elaborates.) This is just what my mother did to me.

**A:** What was the detail?

**P:** Her hostility towards my father was directed to me. I was bad and I had a temper and sometimes I was uncontrollable and she used to say, "You're so much like your father." – – Sometimes I'm afraid to leave my children with my parents because I'm afraid that they may physically hurt them. My mother sometimes used to look at me as though she wanted to kill me. (Elaborates.) – – – I feel helpless now and I couldn't fight back and I feel so sorry for this little girl who is so helpless. – – –

**A:** There seem to be some gaps in your associations. It's as if you're afraid to talk without editing here.

**P:** Sometime I'll get back at her. I'm just waiting for the chance. – – This frightens me. – – – I feel as if it's crazy. I can't. . . . .when I get mad like this I get a sexual feeling. I've got one now. It happens whenever I get anxious like this. It's as if I'm masturbating. – –

**A:** What comes to your mind about the fear of mentioning it directly?

**P:** I'm afraid of my feelings anyway. I'm afraid that you'll think that I'm terrible if I tell you these things.

**A:** If I suggest to you that for the purposes of analysis you let down your usual barriers and say everything that comes to your mind, then what right do I have to have a reaction if you do just that? – We'll stop here for today.

### DISCUSSION

In this session my main goal is again to help the patient learn how to work in an analysis. It is this that leads to my initial intervention about separating "present problems" from "emotional problems," as well as the various requests for the details of information and of feeling. Her report of the plans she and her husband are making to support the analysis financially is reassuring in regard to her positive motivation for analysis, in spite of her anxiety about it. It is also an indicator of her frustration tolerance, and of her ability to work toward long-range goals, as well as her husband's support for the analysis. All these factors support the original good prognosis.

As the session progresses, the patient increasingly experiences stronger affects and my intervention concerning the word "bitch" is an attempt to encourage her to be spontaneous and not to "clean up" her thoughts, and the same is true in regard to my interventions concerning her fear of exploding. All these interventions are a way of my indirectly saying that it is appropriate for her to express her thoughts and feelings openly here. Her question as to why she hates her mother is oriented toward a premature closure regarding the content of her feelings and thoughts, whereas my intervention is designed to help prepare the situation so that at a later time she can express this content directly and with lessened resistances.

I feel that although the image of her mother helpless on the floor represents a wish, at the moment it is more importantly also a defense against her own sense of helplessness. It also seems likely that this image has some relationship to the starting of her analysis, to her position on the couch, to her anxiety over her own affects, and to her anticipation of the relationship with me. Since it is too early to comment directly on the transference implications, I choose to try to deal with her fear of affect, and therefore I offer her the interpretation regarding the reversal. This seems to make it possible for her more directly to express her feelings of helplessness in regard to her own affects and her lack of confidence in her own controls. However, it must be kept in mind that the interpretation might have been used by her as a suggestion to feel this way. Subsequently, my comment regarding the difference between thinking and action is an attempt to encourage the development of the capacity for self-observation, as well as to indicate the safety of the analytic situation. Indirectly, this intervention also indicates to her my confidence that she will be able to control her feelings and not act on them.

Toward the end of the session my comment about the gaps in her associations and her continuing fear of talking without editing is inappropriate and unnecessary, since it puts the patient under too much pressure at the moment to follow the basic rule. It represents a countertransference demand that she immediately behave the way I want her to, and it doesn't take account of the degree of anxiety she has at starting the analysis. My intervention and explanation at the end of the session represents an indirect form of reassurance in regard to my neutrality, as well as an intervention designed to further the development of a working alliance by an appeal to the patient's rational ego.

The flow of the patient's material in this session, the references chiefly to the mother and her reactions to the patient, and the anticipations about me and my possible reactions to her all suggest that she is beginning the analysis with a pre-formed maternal transference reaction. This may be one factor in her becoming pregnant at this time, but in circular fashion the confirmation of the pregnancy is also a force in accelerating the emergence of the transference responses.

---

## SESSION 3

**P:** (Five minutes late.) — — — — —

**A:** What comes to your mind about the trouble getting started today?

**P:** There's one thing that is bothering me. I feel so hostile towards you and I know that I'm not going to get anywhere until I get it out.

**A:** What's the detail?

**P:** You're the coldest man I ever met. I can't get anything out of you. I feel like a child and I hate it. You seem to expect so much. I guess I expect so much from you and it's never going to be.

**A:** What comes to your mind?

**P:** You just sit and you judge me and you expect me to be perfect and to get right into this and not to have any hesitations. I feel as if you are mad and as if you are fed up with me. I've come here two times now. I want sympathy from you and I feel that you don't care. But I'm afraid that if I show this you'll say, "Get out."

**A:** Your feeling is that if you say what is on your mind that I'll tell you to get out. What comes to mind about this?

**P:** I feel as if I need you and so I can't afford to show my hostility.

**A:** So we can see that you don't fully believe me about saying whatever comes to your mind. It's as if you think that feelings like this are an exception.

**P:** I believe you and yet I'm still afraid. I think it will happen. | *Cry*

**A:** What are your associations?

**P:** – – I think of the time that my father was teaching me how to drive the car. He told me to put on the brake and somehow I couldn't do it. He got furious and screamed at me, "Get out of my car." (Elaborates.) I have such hostility but I've never shown it. I think about my terrible temper when I was little. Mother had such pride that she was able to squelch it. (Elaborates.)

**A:** So we can see how hard it is for you to accept this basic idea of analysis. You expect me to react either as your father did and tell you to get out, or else as your mother did and try to squelch you if you show your feelings.

**P:** – – – – – – – I really think that you do feel this way. I think that it's in your tone of voice. It's as if you're saying, "Be perfect or else forget it."

**A:** Your feeling is that I expect you to be perfect here. What comes to your mind?

**P:** – – You expect me to be perfect and I'm not. I never will be. (Elaborates.) You can't control my mind and I want to express myself. It's just your tough luck.

**A:** I wonder if this thought doesn't really reflect your own fear about your feelings and your thoughts and your ideas, and your fear of the whole process of analysis?

**P:** – What happens if I can't accept my own imperfections? I could do that if my parents only had. I feel as if you are detouring me and you are making me direct my hostility towards myself.

**A:** What's the detail?

**P:** That's just like my mother. Any time I'd react she'd always say that it was my fault or that I was born mad. I don't feel that it's my fault. – – – I feel as if I must blame others and I couldn't stand it if all of this was in me. – – –

**A:** You feel as if I'm blaming you and as if something is your fault. What's the detail there?

**P:** I can't control my feelings and I can't get rid of them and I can't ever be happy. – – – I balk at any responsibility for myself for my children and yet I have a fit if someone suggests that I can't handle something.

**A:** What's the detail?

**P:** I'm thinking about the closet in the house in Springfield. I think of myself in there. –

**A:** What comes to mind?

**P:** (Sigh.) – I used to hide my cigarettes there. Mother found them there one day and my parents were trying to do everything right then, but it was just too late. They told me to smoke in front of them but I still felt that she was mad. They decided to be perfect parents and do what was right by me and it made me mad because they should have done it twenty years earlier. And I remember their talks with me. They would try to re-strain themselves but I know that my mother could kill me. But she would try to restrain herself and be a perfect mother. For two or three years we were hardly speaking as we moved to Springfield. (Elaborates.) There was only one time when I ever pleased my parents and that was when I mar-ried Tom. And I felt as if I had knuckled down.

**A:** What was the feeling?

**P:** I had gone with some wild boys. (Elaborates.) Mother made all kinds of attempts to try to stop me. These boys drank and they cussed and they were really wild. Tom was the only nice boy in my life. I wonder why I married him? He's so nice and mature and stable. They used to say that he was a fine boy and they used to compliment him. That was when mother and I finally started to get along. But my father didn't like Tom because Tom was so opposite from my father. – –

**A:** What do you mean?

**P:** My father tried to show that he was a man, and he used to have affairs and he'd drink and he'd cuss and he'd be tough. He was like the truck-driver type. He felt that Tom had a feminine character. (Elaborates.) He felt Tom was weak and had no backbone and my father even felt that he was queer. – – – All my life I've either done what they wanted me to, or done the opposite. I've never done anything in my life that I really wanted to do. – – –

A: What's the detail there?

P: I was always controlled as a child. (Elaborates.) But then I used to do the opposite of my parents' wishes, even if I didn't want to do these things myself. (Elaborates.)

A: So we can see that you went back and forth between the two extremes. What comes to your mind about this?

P: That was the way I got their attention. That was what I did for sixteen years, and it kept on when we were in Springfield. I got their attention! I wonder why I ever changed? It happened after I met Tom. That was the first time my mother ever praised me. I was good and I got positive attention but that was when the trouble started.

A: What do you mean?

P: It was after Sally was born, and my mother became all involved in religion, and somehow she was going to get some money on it. It was just not right! I finally went to see Mr. Harris. I thought about going to see a psychiatrist in Atlanta but it seems as if it was like trying to fly to the moon. – – I came in drunk one night in Springfield and I was planning to go to church the next morning and my mother screamed at me, "You'll get what's coming to you." I was just trying to get their attention. They were so dumb! Something was so wrong. I used to get drunk and I used to smoke and I would just go wild! She'd say, "You're an evil child and you're mad and you're just like your father." They can go to hell! Some day they're not going to affect my life! I'll just let them go by me! I really want it. I realize that my parents are still controlling my life and that they cause the biggest reactions in me. I accept myself no matter if others do or not, but I have so many wrong thoughts in me. I'm wondering if the analysis is going to get rid of something or do I have to accept what I am and what I do have? (Elaborates.) *Angry*

A: What's the detail of your thought about having wrong thoughts?

P: I'm really a bad mother and at times I hate my children and I could kill them. That goes for Tom too. And yet, I have no reason to. I have temper-tantrums and I act like a child and I just stand there and scream. But I hate it! I want to be free and mature and adult and stable without worrying about what others are going to think of me. I know that I have

been avoiding my sexual feelings and that they are important too. I sometimes think of sexual relations with my husband as horrible but I just have
to live with it. That's just the way my mother used to think.

A: We'll stop here for today.


## DISCUSSION

I break the initial silence after it has gone on for several minutes, because I do not want to put the patient under the undue pressure of a
prolonged silence this early in the analysis. In doing so I focus on the conscious resistance, which then leads to the patient's expression of her reaction to my countertransference pressures from the previous session. In the
early part of the session, I still do not fully appreciate the impact of my
countertransference, and I maintain my pressures upon her to follow the
analytic rule. I am apparently behaving toward her in a way reminiscent
of her mother, and this finally becomes clear to me in her saying that I
am making her direct her hostility toward herself.

Although her reaction is partially correct and appropriate, it also contains transference elements of her own, and it is this (along with my not
fully recognizing the countertransference) which leads me to focus with
her on the immediate interactions between us. This focus, directly and indirectly, indicates to her that the interactions between us should be dealt
with in the analysis. After I am able to indicate my recognition of her
anxiety about the analytic situation and to make a superficial transference
interpretation regarding her expectations of my reactions, the therapeutic
partnership is slowly reestablished. Apparently in this way I am able to
get across to her my acceptance of her current feelings that I expected her
to be perfect and that I was blaming her for her imperfections.

Following these early transference experiences and my acceptance of
them, and my encouragement for her to associate to them, the patient then
becomes appreciably more spontaneous and free in her communication,
with recall of earlier historical information. However, the theme of rejection, misunderstanding, and criticism by the parents, and her expressed
anger about this, is a continuing indirect expression of feelings in regard
to me and my pressures upon her, but it would have been premature to
point this out now.

The patient's self-appraisal and description of her neurotic behavior at
the end of the session, as well as her remark, "I know that I have been
avoiding my sexual feelings," are indications of a readiness for the thera-

peutic split between the experiencing and self-observing ego functions. This is another favorable prognostic sign.

---

## SESSION 4

**P:** I have no idea what I'm doing here. I expected it would be like it was with Mr. Harris.

**A:** What did you expect?

**P:** I felt as if I needed a front with him, and I'm much more anxious here with you. I played games with him and I know that I can't do that here.

**A:** What comes to your mind about needing a front?

**P:** I wanted him to like me, so I would act cute and feminine and coy and nice. I suppressed all of my hostility towards him. But I know that you'll see through me and so it is senseless. You will know what I'm doing so I can't hide.

**A:** What comes to your mind about wanting to hide here?

**P:** I could make Mr. Harris like me but I can't do that with you. So I'm not even going to try. I know that I can't. I feel very hostile towards you and I don't understand what I'm supposed to do.

**A:** I think that really you do understand what you're supposed to do here in analysis but you can't believe it.

**P:** –– I don't really understand this. Somehow we don't seem to be discussing things and it seems as if I'm doing all of the talking. –––– I think of Mr. Harris and the way he used to support me. But somehow we never really talked about me. –– I've felt anxious all day. (Elaborates symptoms.) I don't know why.

**A:** Let's see what your associations are without jumping to any conclusions about it.

**P:** I feel as if someone is trying to overpower me. As if they are trying to......

**A:** What is it that you're afraid to say?

**P:** As if you are trying to sit on me and squash me.

**A:** I think this is one of your fears about starting analysis. It's as if you fantasy that you're going to end up in my power and that you're going to be helpless.

**P:** Oh! –––––

**A:** What's going through your mind?

**P:** – – I have an awful fear that I'll end up in your power. It's as if you are a huge black bug that is ready to claw me. I can't really feel this though.

**A:** How do you mean?

**P:** I don't know. I have sort of a feeling. . . . . the feeling of indifference. I don't feel as if I can hold onto you. It's all put over onto me and I feel as if I can't do it.

**A:** So you feel as if you're on your own here and as if you are all alone. What are your associations to that?

**P:** I feel as if you can't help me, so I get a sense of panic. –

**A:** What's the detail?

**P:** – Before I began I felt that all of my anxiety would leave, and that I'd attach myself to you. I see now that I can't and I probably never will and so I feel lost. – – –

**A:** I think at the moment that you're frightened by a number of feelings that you're having towards me. Some of these are sexual and some of these are involved with your hostility. Yet in spite of your fear I think that you are feeling quite a lot and we have to look at these feelings as part of the analysis. You are afraid to express them and yet in analysis the basic rule is that you say everything that comes to your mind. That's what I meant when I said before that you understand what you are supposed to do but it is hard to do. And you're afraid of it.

**P:** – – I can't feel anything. – – I feel just like a child and I'm afraid that I'm going to stay this way. I don't feel as if I'm an adult and a woman and I can't stand it.

**A:** How do you mean a woman?

**P:** I want to feel equal with you. And that is what I'd like for this analysis to result in, but I'm afraid that it will never come. I feel so inferior to you. I came to *you* for help and you didn't come to me and I resent this feeling. I could never be accepted as a woman in this world.

**A:** What's the detail of the feeling?

**P:** I'd much rather be a tiny girl or else a grown man. As a grown man I'm equal and as a baby girl I don't have to worry. But as a woman I'm defenseless, that's why I feel that you don't like me. – – I'm aware that I have some sexual feelings and this hostility. But to talk about it would be as though I was masturbating. It would be like saying, "Look, I have a penis and I'm great." And yet I have a feeling that I would like to take every penis in the world and chew it up. – –

**A:** What comes to your mind?

**P:** – – (Sigh.) – Then I'd have just as much power as you do. I wonder why, if I feel so defenseless as a woman, that I get pregnant. Somehow that's the ultimate of womanhood! But it's when a woman *is* pregnant that's she's helpless and she needs a man the most. I don't know, this just doesn't make sense.

**A:** You're trying to find the answers without looking at your associations first. You're trying to use logic on this but as yet you can't see the meanings because you don't know your thoughts about it.

**P:** I don't know you well enough to tell you anything. Why should I tell you the secrets that I hide from myself?

**A:** That's a good question. Why should you?

**P:** You know all of these things anyhow and I need the help and this is the only way to get it. But that's the same reason why I'm so hostile.

**A:** What comes to your mind?

**P:** I don't feel that I want to tell someone that I'm hostile to anything about myself. If I liked you then I'd tell you. But I can't because you'll laugh and that's one of the reasons why it's so frightening. I just can't even face it myself.

**A:** So your feeling is that your anger and hostility keeps us apart and keeps you from talking intimately here about these frightening thoughts and feelings and ideas that you have.

**P:** (Nods.) – – – When I got older occasionally my father . . . . . would talk to me. – – Sometimes he would help me with something that was bothering me. That's why this bothers me so and frightens me. I've used this defense for years and suddenly I feel as if everything is the opposite and I have no defense. – – My father browbeat me all my life until I grew up. He'd laugh at me and tease me and be annoyed and angry at me. But he understood me more as I grew older. I didn't like this. I preferred him the other way. I have such a conflict about my father and I can't handle my hate for him or even my love. I can't handle any feelings of love. *Cry, Sob*

**A:** I wonder if that isn't also true here with me. In one sense you are more afraid that I *will* understand than that I'll laugh or be angry.

**P:** Suddenly I have such a very strong love for you and a feeling of warmth right now. I know that I'll feel depressed when I leave here today. I always have such a feeling of guilt and depression and it's not worth it. (Elaborates.) – – –

**A:** What did you stop at?

**P:** This whole idea of getting understanding. – – – I feel as if I'm less of a person and as if you've completely overpowered me and you've weakened me. I feel that I'm completely defenseless against this and like I'm not a person at all. I'm here and you're here and it's like with my father. If there is any understanding between us then we will come together and I'm really nothing. I want to be a person and I want to grow up to be a woman. — — — — I feel all repressed again right now. I can't understand what happened. This is an ideal situation, but something happens to me. — — —

A: We'll stop here for today.

## DISCUSSION

The patient begins this session with a continuation of the anxiety about starting analysis and a retreat from the step forward into the analytic situation which she had made yesterday. Based on her behavior in the analytic situation and also remembering the fact that she had reported a number of dreams about me during the time she was waiting to begin analysis, it is my impression that a mobilization of transference feelings has already begun, and that this is the chief source of her anxiety. Her statement that she had been anxious all day prior to coming here and that she felt that someone was trying to overpower her confirms this impression for me.

I do not feel it would be particularly helpful to permit silences to develop and I feel it necessary to deal with her anxiety about analysis. My intervention about starting analysis and about her fantasy about ending up in my power is therefore designed to help her express more clearly her anxiety about the analytic situation. Although this really represents only a rephrasing of material she has already volunteered, her response to the intervention with the fantasy of the black bug strikes me as being a submissive response to appease me and to give me the kind of material she thinks I want to hear. Subsequently, the material further demonstrates her inhibition and anxiety about the analytic relationship.

Since I have the impression that transference feelings have already begun to emerge into her conscious awareness, and because of her anxiety about this, I choose to offer her the rather lengthy generalized interpretation about her fear of such transference phenomena. The aim here is to provide her with some reassurance about the development of such transference feelings, but to do it without departing from an analytic position. It is also an attempt to show her that I am not anxious or surprised by the development of such feelings, and through this to try to further the establishment of an analytic situation. My tactical goal is not to foster the emergence of further transference material at this time, but rather to reduce the patient's anxiety about those transference feelings already mobilized. However, this is ineffective and the patient's response is to plunge into the intellectualized material about penises, masturbation, womanhood, pregnancy, etc. I again feel this to be a resistive attempt at compliance based on her previous therapy and on a transference wish to please me. My questions about the details of her associations to this material and of her wish for premature understanding indicate my willingness to listen to any of her associations and material. But my focus is not so much an interest in the content of the material itself, but rather in teaching her to associate more freely and to suspend her critical judgment.

My subsequent nonspecific transference interpretation regarding her anger keeping us apart, and keeping her from talking here, is confirmed by her immediate affective response of crying, as well as her spontaneous associations to the relationship with her father. These are suggestive indications that the transference is shifting from mother to father. Although the content of this material is interesting and important, the tactical aim of establishing the analytic situation takes precedence this time. This is the reasoning behind my focusing her attention back into the anxiety about analysis and about my understanding her. The level of the interpretation is away from the transference implications of the wish for love from the father, and is instead directed at the more immediate problem of the therapeutic alliance and my willingness to try to understand her and her communications. Her immediate affective response and associations again represent a confirmation of the correctness of the interpretation. But at the very end of the session, her defenses are again reinstituted and the brief affective response disappears.

## SESSION 5

P: – My parents are here for a visit. I've had no particular reaction to their coming, and it's funny because generally I have a tremendous reaction whenever they are here.

A: What's the detail?

P: I usually get so nervous. I had a dream about my visit here yesterday. We were living where we are now, and I was outside with my children and I kept losing them. They would go off and play with the neighbors. There was a crazy boy in the dream who is mentally. . . . . he attached himself to me. I was afraid and it was like a nightmare. He kept following me. He was nice and he liked me, but somehow I thought he was dangerous. And I kept losing my children all through the dream. I had such a sense of panic, but then Tom came home and even though it was dark, everything was all right. – – – That boy in the dream. . . . . I had one other dream of a crazy person once. Somehow I associate it with sex and maybe it was the thought that they would rape me. There was a boy who lived in my neighborhood when I was about eight who tried to rape a friend of mine.

A: What was the detail?

P: He was a huge boy. (Elaborates.) The boy in the dream was different. But the boy at home took her into the woods and threw her on the ground and tried to take her pants off. In the dream I had such a sense of panic about my children. Somehow I think it was me who was lost. It was like being a child in a department store and being lost and having that terrible sense of panic. – –

A: What comes to your mind about the feeling of yourself being lost?

P: I remember something from when I was two years old. We had a maid who took care of us and we were living in a house with some woods nearby. We went out one day and I turned around and I couldn't see the house. I felt terribly lost. I think of the time that I was in college and I was taking a psychology test and there was a picture of a cave in the woods, and I had a sudden lost feeling. I wonder if that could be a dream that I made up? Somehow I have an image of a child and a waterfall who is lost. I feel as if I want to call Mr. Harris and go back to see him.

A: I think that this dream and this lost feeling somehow represents the analysis and your feeling of "what am I doing here." And you compare this situation with the one with Harris where everything was structured and you felt you knew your way around and knew what you were doing.

P: I really *don't* know what I'm doing here. Whatever I'll do in here will be all me and I'll be the one who will have to reflect on it. It's all me and there's no one helping me. There are all my emotions and my fears and I'll have to feel them and it's going to be up to me to help myself. There's no one else really to help me. I wish that I could run away like I usually do or else have an affair or give a party or buy a dress and then everything would be all right. But I know that I have no choice.

A: What's your feeling about not having any choice?

P: If this doesn't work I know that I've *had* it. All of my old mechanisms don't work anymore.

**A:** You said earlier that you felt the dream was somehow related to the session here yesterday. What comes to your mind?

**P:** After I left I felt very warm and close to you. Somehow there was something sexual about it and I had the urge to run. I just can't stand that.

**A:** What was the detail of "something sexual?"

**P:** I feel as if I did, and yet at the same time, I didn't really feel them. But then I had the dream and I knew that it was my *own* fear. If I could be a child then nothing sexual would be expected of me. If I'm an adult then it's like being a woman and that means that you should have sexual feelings. I can't. I wonder why they frighten me so much? – – –

**A:** You mentioned that the dream expresses some of your own fears. What are your associations?

**P:** – – It was like the attachment of the boy to me in the dream. It's like that if a man ever does have a close relationship with me. It's like the few times that my father did. I'm afraid. . . . . – I can handle my sexual desires but if a man can't handle his, then something terrible will happen and I'll be completely lost.

**A:** So I wonder if the man who was behind you in the dream represents me, and that you're wondering whether I can control my own feelings.

**P:** – – My father touched me fondly only once in my life. But somehow I keep thinking about that time.

**A:** What comes to your mind about it?

**P:** It was before I was married, and I'd come home from school and I was eating constantly and I was in a terrible mess. I was so hysterical before I went back and my father put his arm around me that once and he said: . . . . . – – –

**A:** I think you are trying to blot it out of your memory.

**P:** – He gave me tranquilizers. That scene makes me so mad and I hate him for it. I had a dream about that room in Springfield just three weeks ago. That's funny! In the dream I had just gotten into the room and the furniture was all gone and the room was painted all white. Somehow I was depressed. There were 10,000 rugs over each window and I was trying to get them off. I tried to call daddy at the office because I wanted him to be there and I said to him that I was sorry. But at the same time I didn't want him there and he was at the office.

**A:** This is somewhat like your wish to see me as being cold and distant from you and to feel that you are all alone—that way you feel that there is less of a sexual threat.

**P:** Whenever I look at my father he regurgitates me. People say that I have sexual feelings for my father but that makes me sick to my stomach. If I could just do one thing I'd be all right. If I could. . . . . I've said it all before. When my parents made love it was as if the whole world cared. It was so sick. If I could only get it cleared and if it wouldn't panic me and make me sick or hysterical or make me want to scream and beat my head against the wall. --

**A:** What's the detail of the thought?

**P:** I can picture it and I can see it. That was the stupidest thing they ever did. I used to lie in my room and put my pillow over my head. Even when I was at college that happened. But there was nothing more horrible than that as a child.

**A:** How did you mean stupid?

**P:** They hurt me.

**A:** What was the detail of the feeling?

**P:** It was their making love. I can't think about it! I grew up feeling it was all so animalistic, and that my father was horrible, torturing my mother like this. --- Whenever Tom and I make love I always have the feeling that my children are going to hear us or that they may be able to see us. I always dream about it too. ----

**A:** Let's go back to the dream that you had about the room. The walls were all white. What are your associations to that?

**P:** It was all clean. The feeling was of getting rid of things and the furniture was all gone. They were old rugs and they weren't showing but they were there.

**A:** What are your associations to the rugs?

**P:** We never had rugs like that in our house. They were braid rugs and somehow I hate them. I feel as if I want to go back to that room and have it all disappear and I know I can't. There is always something and I feel as if I can't get rid of it. That dream really upset me. When I am upset like that I try to clean my house and hope that it will all be gone but I never can.

**A:** In the dream you called your father at the office. What are your associations?

**P:** When I woke up I felt as if I needed my father and he was just never there. Now I have a feeling that he *was* in the room in the dream and I wished that he wasn't. There's also a sense of dependency there. It's like my calling Tom at the office all the time. I didn't want to come today and I feel as if I want to leave right now and yet I don't *feel* afraid of anything. When I was first married I used to stay at home and cry all the time. I have an urge to run right now and just get on a plane and go where no one knows me.

A: What comes to your mind about this wish to leave right now?

P: I don't know. There is something that I can't stand, and I'm feeling very nervous. I have a feeling as if I'll explode and as if my head will come off. – – – Now I have a fear that I have to leave. I would really like to stay here. I'm not getting out of you what I want and it's driving me nuts.

A: What's the detail?

P: I want more of you than you are giving to me. It makes me so hostile and it depresses me. You just sit there and you don't say anything.

A: The feeling is that you want more of me than you are getting. What's the detail?

P: I don't know. There is something that I want from you. You somehow remind me of my father. He'd sit and smoke his pipe and not say anything. I'd have to scream to get some attention and to get some kind of a reaction.

A: We'll stop here for today.

### DISCUSSION

The patient's opening comments that she is less reactive than previously to her parents and their visit is a sign of the developing transference relationship to me. Drives and conflict over them are beginning to be directed toward me, as I come to psychically represent the parental figures of childhood. As a result, the parents of today are used less intensively as the objects of such outmoded response patterns, and she can then respond to them in behavior more appropriate to her present age and status. This is confirmed by her pattern of association in going directly from the material about the parents to the report of the dream "about my visit here yesterday." Even her use of the word "visit" is pertinent since she used it in the introduction about her parents, and since most patients use words like "my session," "yesterday's hour," "my appointment," etc.

Partly as a result of this shift, the patient is beginning to talk more freely and she presents more elaborate and involved dreams with her sexual associations to them. My use of these dreams, however, is in keeping with my tactical aim of continuing the establishment of an analytic situation, rather than of responding to the deeper levels of conflict expressed in the dream. After describing the dream and the associations to sexuality, rape, and feeling lost and alone, the patient's immediate association is to her wish to go see her previous therapist. To me this association represents a defensive maneuver to escape from the anxiety being mobilized in the analysis and in the developing transference relationship to me. It is this reasoning which leads to my first interpretation of the dream as an expression of her anxiety about analysis. The interpretation is an attempt to help her face in consciousness the situation from which she wants to retreat. The patient's elaboration of her uncertainty about analysis confirms the correctness of this intervention.

In introducing the dream, the patient had said, "I had a dream about my visit here yesterday," which must be then considered as part of the manifest dream. When I ask for her associations to this, the patient mentions that she had experienced a conscious sexual feeling after leaving the session yesterday. Ordinarily, this is very early in analysis for such feelings to appear in consciousness, but as mentioned earlier, it is my impression that a good deal of transference feeling had been mobilized during the months she was waiting to begin analysis. To have ignored this feeling or not commented upon it, would have left the patient to struggle with it by herself and might have suggested to her that I am afraid of such feelings. On the other hand, to interpret it or to attempt a deeper exploration at this time would be premature and would intellectualize the process. Therefore I compromise by a simple request for details without further elaboration.

In response to the patient's associations and experiences, and because in the analytic situation I am literally seated behind her, I feel justified in making the transference interpretation that I am the man behind her in the dream. However, the level of this interpretation is still aimed at her anxiety about the analytic situation, but this, in turn, leads by association to the recall of anxiety in the relationship to her father.

I feel that the patient's subsequent associations to possible sexual feelings about her father and about the primal scene are probably related to material that had been interpreted or that she had discussed in her previous therapy, and that it again represents an attempt to please me with material she thinks I want to hear. Because of this, and because this material does not seem to be evoking any undue anxiety at the moment, I make only a few inquiries about the details of her thoughts. I then decide to postpone further inquiry into the content of these memories and feelings, and instead to continue her education as an analytic patient by inquiring about some of her further associations to the other dream elements. The same line of reasoning holds true for my continuing attention to her anxiety and her expressed wish to leave the situation. By acknowledging the wish to leave, and asking her to associate to it, I am indirectly encouraging the therapeutic ego split into experiencing and observing ego functions. The aim here is to teach her to observe herself and to report the immediate responses she experiences while she is here.

Toward the end of the session, the patient complains that I just sit there and don't say anything. The aim of my intervention is to demonstrate my acceptance of this as a genuine feeling without critical or defensive response, but with analytic interest in elaborating and deepening our understanding of the experience. In actual point of fact, throughout these first sessions, I have deliberately been quite active in encouraging her associations and participation in the analysis, and in not permitting long silences to develop. However, in my activity I have chiefly maintained a neutral analytic posture and position, and have made few direct interpretations. My thought is that in her previous treatment the therapist may have been very active in interpreting the content of her material, and that she is comparing my technique to his at this time.

---

## SESSION 6

Between sessions the patient's husband, and later the patient's mother, had called me to discuss by phone their questions and concern about the patient beginning analysis. The husband had particularly asked for some estimate of how long analysis might last, and what the prognosis was. I was polite but evasive with both of them.

A: I want to let you know that your husband and your mother both called me on the telephone since you were here last.
P: I don't understand anything about it.
A: (Explains the reality of the calls.)
P: I guess they had a lot of questions on their minds about analysis.
A: What are your feelings about the calls?
P: It upsets me. (Elaborates.) Especially I feel angry about my mother calling you. I am so afraid that someone is going to talk Tom out of this. They always sneak around behind my back. (Elaborates.) That's really not like him to do that. I'm so frightened anyway.
A: (Explains the nature of his call and the specific questions he asked and the answers given.)
P: No one thinks I have a mind of my own. (Elaborates.) I can't

say, "Go to hell and I'm going to do it anyway." I knew that he wanted to talk to you and I actually told him to. (Elaborates.) But he did it while I was gone. But my mother calling is too much to take.

A: What's the feeling?

P: I wonder why she did it? (Elaborates.) There was no necessity for her to. It's like she was saying, "I want to check on my two-year-old." (Elaborates.) It makes me so mad! I feel as if I could go home and kill them both! It's like calling a friend's mother and saying "send her home." It's so stupid! I felt so embarrassed when you told me! Now I feel depressed. – – –

A: What's the detail of the feeling?

P: I'm feeling frightened and scared. I was saying to myself, "I can't do this." I've been thinking about Harris all through this and I feel as if I can't take this. It's unrealistic but I feel everything and I take it all to heart.

A: Let's look at the details of your fear of the analysis.

P: I feel scared to death. (Elaborates.) I feel as if I need supportive therapy. – – – – What will happen to me?

A: What do you picture?

P: – – I picture myself being shoved off all by myself with no one around and I wonder can I live or will I die? One time as a girl I touched a stove when it was hot. I was curious and it shocked the hell out of me. Mother picked me up and she was very loving to me and I felt as if she had never been that way before. It was so sincere of her and the whole thing was so frightening. I hate feeling like a child in here.

A: You felt a shock after touching the stove. What are your associations?

P: It's like the analysis where I feel very curious. I feel as if I want to touch it and I want to have the experience and I want to find out what am I. But I'm afraid of the shock and any time I ever do anything on my own it always turns out to be wrong.

A: So it's as if you feel it is wrong and dangerous to be curious about your own thoughts and feelings.

P: Yes, and I get hurt whenever I do.

A: I think at the moment that your main fear is of having any feelings about me and that you're worried that you may not be able to control them, and that they may erupt and everything will explode.

P: – – I'm afraid that you're not very strong.

A: What are your associations?

**P:** I'm thinking of the time that my father put his arm around me and showed me some love. It was like a break for him and it was like a weakness on his part. I'm afraid that your emotions are going to enter into here.

**A:** What's the detail of the fear?

**P:** I'm afraid that you're going to be hostile to me. If I were ever to be really mad and nasty here you'd explode and you'd degrade me. I couldn't stand that.

**A:** The time that you felt your father was so weak was the time that he put his arm around you. It must be that you are afraid that I'll respond sexually to you.

**P:** I've had a fantasy of living with you and that you'd always be there. (Elaborates.) I just had a funny thought. – –

**A:** What did you stop at?

**P:** The last weekend I met two men. I was so sexually attracted to them. Then I had a sexual dream with an orgasm. (Elaborates.) One of them was going to take me and love me. The fantasy was that I was in bed with one of them but I don't feel this about my husband, and I can't feel it about you either. That bothers me, because it should be about my husband.

**A:** What was the detail about the two men?

**P:** They were the best looking ones at the party. One of them was huge and sweet and so nice, and pleasant. I had a fantasy that I was in bed with him and that I was going to have him engulf me. I was going to lose myself and he would take care of me and I'd be completely helpless. The other one I was so sorry for because his wife is in a mental hospital. (Elaborates.) I felt like I do about my father with him. I felt hysterical but I also felt so sorry for him. I do want to be taken care of by a man but I also want to mother and take care of a man myself. But I prefer the other. And yet at the same time I hate to be helpless and controlled by a man even though I like it.

**A:** I wonder if the feeling of being helpless and controlled by a man and having him take care of you isn't part of this fantasy of living with me.

**P:** – – – – I don't want anything to do with anybody. I want to be all by myself and I won't have to feel anything. I have so much emotion and I have no place to put it and I don't know what to do with it. My mother and father won't take it and that makes it horrible.

**A:** I think this helps us to understand these fears about analysis. It's as if you're wondering will I be like your mother and father or will I be strong and be able to deal with your emotions.

**P:** I wish that I didn't need you.

**A:** I think you are asking the question, can you trust me really to be your analyst?

**P:** I wouldn't mind if I could say *anything* and have you take it in your stride. But there aren't many people who are capable of that and after all everyone is human. I think that I trust you more with my sexual feelings than with my angry feelings.

**A:** So the real question is did I really mean it when I told you that here you can say anything and everything?

**P:** It's going to be a long time before I can believe that. I guess that there is a 50–50 chance but I worry about the consequences. I have all kinds of visions of us arguing and I'd stand up and I wouldn't fall to pieces but I've never done this. Not even with Tom. I always have such fears that he'll leave me or I'll lose his love. If I ever do confide in you I'll probably fall madly in love with you and drown myself in you and that will really be worse.

**A:** How do you mean?

**P:** I feel as if you're disgusted with what I've just said.

**A:** Let's look and see why you would feel that?

**P:** With the thought of me . . . . . it's better that way. It's all silly.

**A:** I think the fact that there is no limit set here on what you can say or what you can feel is really frightening you.

**P:** It's like it's all not real. It can't really be so. You really have to love someone to let them see the inside of you and see every horrible part. And they have to love you too. Oh! I just couldn't stand it. I don't *want* to be understood. – –

**A:** What are your associations?

**P:** I see myself as a child and never loving anybody. I felt hostile and that way I could cover up. That was my wall and no one could see beyond it. It's all so ridiculous because it can't be helped. I can't do anything about it now. I see people throwing spears at me and throwing at that wall and I feel sorry for myself and guilty about it. I'm sad because you can't say, "I love you and you love me." It would be so free and open and airy and wonderful, but it just can't be. There must be some strings attached to all this. You're different than everybody else because you can see through the walls and that frightens me, and so I think you must hate me. There's no love in there, it's all hate. I think of myself as a body with an open door.

**A:** Your feeling is that if I can see through this wall then I'll have to hate you. What's the detail?

**P:** Because I hate you. I must have some terrible thoughts about you and yet it's all so silly and stupid. This isn't right. Why am I so afraid to show love? I've never shown my family any love at all. I did once and I felt that I was rejected. But that happened when I was older. My sister was always so loving and I'd feel it too but I couldn't show it even though I wanted to. And so I'd seem cold and indifferent. My father is this way. I just realized this. He'd love it if I loved him, but he is afraid to show it.

**A:** We'll stop here for today.

## Discussion

Ordinarily, the analyst waits for the patient to open the session, but because of the two telephone calls, I choose to mention this to the patient first before she could begin her session. This is done to establish experientially for her the fact that I will not have contact about her with anyone else without telling her about it myself. Had she known about either of these phone calls and mentioned them first, I would have acknowledged them, but this would have left the patient with the questioning doubt as to whether I would have mentioned anything had she not brought it up first. By my bringing it up immediately, I avoid this risk and thereby hope to help her take another step toward establishing a sense of trust in me, and therefore, a greater capacity to move into the psychoanalytic situation. And then by asking for her associations and feelings to the calls, I am attempting to use these incidents analytically and to demonstrate the analytic expectation that she will have reactions and associations to ongoing current experiences and incidents. The patient's initial response, "I guess they had a lot of questions . . ." is a defensive one seeking to cover her feelings by excusing the calls through rational thought. My question about her feelings interferes with this defense and permits the more detailed and negative responses to be verbalized.

The fact she did *not* know of the calls makes it all the more important that I brought them up. Had she learned about them later from either her mother or husband, it would have seriously influenced her ability to trust me.

The material about the calls leads toward her anxiety about analysis, and the defense of fantasy about her previous therapist. My therapeutic attempt is to make this anxiety explicit, so that it can be more rationally dealt with by the patient in the therapeutic alliance. The patient's associations lead from the present anxiety situation of analysis to the positive experience with her mother and then back to the analysis and her expectations of being hurt here. Since she has made a number of allusions to feelings toward me in the previous sessions, and since I know from her history that she had experienced a great many intense feelings toward her previous therapist, I feel it necessary to make the generalized interpretation of her anxiety about developing any feelings towards me, and her concern over controlling them. This intervention leads to an already-conscious transference perception of me being similar to her father, and to the conscious fear that my emotions will enter into the analytic situation.

In the usual analytic situation, this is very early for such fantasies about the analyst to emerge directly into consciousness. However, since I did the initial diagnostic evaluation, and since the patient has been waiting for nine months, and since my position as clinic director puts me in a stronger parental image for her, and because of her readiness to develop transference responses and her previous transference response to her former therapist, it seems clear to me that the patient has begun analysis with an already partially formed transference reaction. For these reasons, I elect directly to interpret her anxiety that I might have a sexual response to her, in order that she will again learn that I am willing to accept such feelings without evasion or anxiety. The patient's report of the fantasy of living with me, and associations to the sexual dream tend to confirm the correctness of this intervention. My own personal association is that the two men represent her previous therapist and myself. However, when I go on to point out her fear of helplessness with me, anxiety about the emerging transference and the fantasied danger in the analytic situation emerges further, and the patient begins to manifest her typical defense of anger, suspicion, and distance to ward off any possibility of positive feelings or attachments.

In order to combat this defensive resistance against the emerging transference, my next series of interventions represent attempts to help her distinguish between her expectations that I will reject her feelings as the parents did, and the reality of my role as her analyst. In other words, my interventions represent attempts to strengthen the therapeutic alliance, with the anticipation that as the alliance grows stronger, the patient will feel more able to permit the underlying transferences to emerge. Her subsequent associations to her fears of being understood and her defenses against close relationships confirm the correctness of these maneuvers. But probably the most significant factor in the establishment of the analytic situation is my demonstration of my willingness to discuss these issues openly and directly, and that I accept her having feelings about them. Hopefully this will eventually lead to a partial identification with my analytic attitude, thereby helping to further the development of the working alliance.

---

## SESSION 7

**P:** I've been arguing with Tom's mother. (Elaborates.) And it has put me into a panic. I had a dream which is like the kind I used to have after Sally was born. It was of the world ending. I woke up in the morning and predicted that the world was going to come to an end that day. It was all wonderful and the sun was shining and I felt happy in the dream and I thought maybe it wouldn't happen. It was in Evanston which was our home for sixteen years and we were in the backyard and there were a lot of people around. Suddenly there was a lot of smoke from the sky. I thought that we'd die somehow by the water but then I realized that it was going to be by fire. And then in the dream I said, "I'm turning my hostility in towards myself." – – – I used to have nightmares when all this business started after Sally was born. The dream was somehow related to that argument with Tom's mother and her trying to tell me that "We all love you." And yet I feel that they don't and that they feel that I'm being selfish. I'm afraid of Tom and I'm worried about his trust in me and in the analysis. I'm thinking of all the pressure that is being put on him by our parents and that maybe he is not going to be able to stand up. He says it's all right now but I hate him for it. (Elaborates.) I'm upset that he doesn't trust me. But I feel as if I'm not alone, if Tom is with me on this. And yet I *am* alone. His mother has always been fighting with me for his affection and I picture them saying, "Let's take him away from her." That has always been my fear.

**A:** What's the detail?

**P:** I've always been afraid that they are going to take him away from me. I want him to say, "We're going to do this analysis." (Elaborates.) I want him to be different and I see it as his weakness. – –

**A:** What about your associations to the dream elements?

**P:** – I think about my seventh-grade science class and a teacher telling us that a comet could run into the earth. She said it would just be the tail but that that would be the end of the earth. That's the way the feeling was in the dream. I think of Halley's Comet. In the dream I wondered if we were going to drown in water. That would be the most horrible death to me. – –

A: What comes to your mind?

P: The thought of suffocation. The idea of being conscious and not able to breathe. I love to swim but I can't be ducked because it sends me into a panic. I always think that I'm going to drown and I wonder what it's like to be conscious and still to know that you are going to die.

A: What are your associations to the smoke from the sky in the dream?

P: I just had a crazy thought. I'm thinking about your pipe and my father's and the smoke that comes out of them. And thinking that that's the way I'll die. It's as if the water somehow represents my mother and the smoke represents my father. I used to feel that I'd die by my mother but now it's going to be by my father. The men are going to kill me.

A: How do you mean?

P: It's like. . . . .I think of Tom and my father talking to Dr. Davis about analysis and talking to you and others about it. I don't like that. All these men are trying to ruin me and no one ever comes to me. These are all men who are over my head and they talk about how they'll ruin me. I can fight with women and I can win, but I can't fight men. I'm too afraid of losing them, and afraid that they'll turn against me. (Elaborates.) Men have too much of a hold over me.

A: And what are your associations to the backyard and Evanston?

P: All of my dreams take place there. My parents used to get up at night and one time my father came into my room with a gun in his hand and he said that there's a man in the backyard who is going from tree to tree. -- . . . . . -- Why don't I want to think about this? - . . . . . That crazy boy I told you about. We used to play ball with him in the backyard and I'd be scared and I'd be glad when mother called us in to dinner, so that we'd have an excuse to go inside.

A: What comes to your mind about your hesitation just now in bringing this up?

*Cry*

P: I wonder if maybe I could have been jealous of Karen? Maybe I was jealous that he wanted to rape her and didn't want to rape me. ---

A: And what about the fact that there were a lot of people in the backyard in the dream?

P: I don't know! --- I feel as if this is all wrong and that a child shouldn't feel this way and have these desires. I want a man of my own. If I can't have my father at least I can have one of the yardmen. I want to have *one* of them pick *me*. It's all so silly. I fight against women all of my life just like I fight Tom's mother for Tom. I used to fight my mother for my father. It's just like her call to you. She had to stretch out her tentacle and she couldn't stand the fact that *I* was the one who knew you.

A: Your thought is that a child shouldn't *have* such feelings. What comes to your mind about that?

P: These are sexual feelings and you are only supposed to have them as an adult. It's wrong! Why do I think this? Grown men are for grown women and not for little girls. I don't like that. I could scream!

A: What's the feeling?

P: Here's the point where I get scared. To actually scream and to be mad! It's easier to just sit and take it. I have a feeling of fear and I want to balk at the idea about children . . . . . that children don't love their fathers and they don't have sexual feelings and they don't want older men. It's much easier to be a child and forget all this. I wonder if this is the reason for my hostility? Is it possible that I actually got this? I feel scared now.

A: What's the detail of the feeling?

P: It's the thought of receiving love and sexual feelings. It's the thought that I'm capable of that and yet I know that I'm frigid with my husband right now. I couldn't get these things as a child. But now I'm grown up and I can get them, but I'd just as soon be a child again. -- And yet my relationships at home are not those of a child but . . . . .

A: What did you stop at?

P: (Sigh.) – If. . . . .I really don't want to be a child but I have to escape my sexual feelings. I guess I could be a mother to escape these sexual feelings. But I love Tom and I'm trying to give him everything. (Elaborates.) But I can't give him sex and I can't give him myself. I can be a child, or I can be a mother. . . . .a third alternative is to have sexual feelings and I don't know who that is. I wonder who I should be. – – –

A: You seem to associate sexual feelings with a danger situation.

P: – – I get a funny feeling which I associate with sexual feelings and I've got it right now. It comes on when I'm lying down. I used to get it in bed when I was in high school and it was as if I was thirsty. . . . .

A: What was the detail?

P: It was a feeling in my mouth and in my body and in my hips. I don't want it.

A: Instead of trying to understand this feeling right now, see if you can just describe it.

P: – It's like I'm a woman. – . . . . . It's like I've got to do something with my mouth. It's like my whole body is going wild! Now I'm thinking of my parents making love. – – – I'm lying there and I want my father to come in and make love to me. It's like this couch. I feel so vulnerable. – – I wonder why people lie down in analysis.

A: What comes to your mind?

P: It's so hard. I feel as if I'm wide open and this is a dangerous position. – –

A: What are your associations?

P: If I sit up then no one can touch me. I can't do anything about it if I'm lying down and I feel weaker and incapable and childish and I know it's silly. – – – I feel as if I can't face the world. I can't go back home to my children.

A: What's the feeling?

P: I feel just like a child. But I also feel so guilty about what I've thought and what I've said here. I'm afraid that everyone else will know and that you know.

A: I wonder if this is a connection with your fear and hesitation about looking at me as you leave here every day?

P: Yes, exactly.

A: What's the detail?

P: – It's as if I said that I want you to make love to me and you didn't. I feel so embarrassed that I could die. It's as if you are saying, "Who do you think you are?"

A: We'll stop here for today.


## DISCUSSION

The patient begins with a current situation of conflict in which she feels herself to be in competition with an older woman (mother-in-law) for the love and support of a man (husband). This is followed by the dream, the associations to which come somewhat later in the session and involve direct connections to childhood and to both of her parents. But the associations of the smoke with my pipe reveals that the dream also has a transference implication. But after initially reporting the dream, her spontaneous flow of association is once again back to the present competitive situation, and indirectly refers to her anxiety that the parents will interfere with her developing relationship to me.

This sequence of material can be understood as the conscious expression of a variety of derivatives of her oedipal relationships and her conflict about them. These derivative conflicts are being stimulated, in part, by the developing transference relationship toward me, and therefore represent a continuation of the material alluded to in the previous session. The references to her husband and father talking to another psychiatrist about her and about analysis, and later on the reference to her mother's call to me, further confirm these speculations. They also confirm the importance and effectiveness of the tactics I used in dealing with the calls. Another indirect reference to the developing transference to me is the patient's reference to "the crazy boy," since in a previous session he had represented me in a dream. This suggests that the emerging transference fantasy is sexual and involves my assaulting her, but it would be premature and intellectualizing to point this out now.

Instead, my interventions are aimed at helping her elaborate on the details of her thoughts; and the patient's associations are coming more freely with evidence of a spontaneous oscillation in the material between the past and the present. This development is nicely illustrated toward the end of the session where she associates lying in bed, fantasying about her father, with lying on the couch in the analysis. The defensive need to deny the significance of her childhood recollections, associations, and feelings is apparent toward the end of the session, accompanied by her sense of guilt.

The experience of tension in her mouth while sexually aroused illustrates the theoretical concept of displacement upwards, and the utilization of a regressive mode of behavior to contain and cope with a conflict from a more advanced level of psychosexual development.

Midway during the session, while referring to the oedipal material, the patient asks the question, "Is it possible that I actually got this?" followed by the experience of anxiety. This is an initial reference to a traumatic sexual event that will emerge later in the analysis and as such represents a derivative of the core of her neurosis. However, at this time in the analysis, it would be impossible to know this.

Toward the end of the session, I direct her attention to an observation I have made about her behavior in not looking at me as she leaves each session. This intervention evolves from my own association to her comment, "I can't face the world," and from the patient's material regarding her concern about people knowing what she thinks and feels. Although this confrontation will tend to focus her attention more directly on the transference situation, my main purpose in bringing the matter up is again to educate the patient toward an ability to observe herself and her own behavior as it occurs here in the analysis. The patient's response indicates that she had already been conscious of this, but that it had not occurred to her to include it in her spontaneous communications. The intervention, therefore, again becomes a tacit educational instruction to the patient regarding what is expected of her in the analysis.

## SESSION 8

P: – – – I can't understand myself and my reactions. Either I'm terribly suppressed or else things don't bother me the way I think they do. – – I had a letter from my father today and it made me so upset. – –

A: What was the upset?

P: All I did was cry after I read it. I don't know what was wrong. It was a nice letter and it sounded as if he really understood me. I've wanted such a letter for such a long time but now that I got it, it doesn't mean very much. I'm afraid to let it mean anything.

A: What's the detail of the fear?

P: It's like what we were talking about the last time. It's easier for me to be hostile, and I can't ever picture us being close. Somehow we are very alike, my father and I, and neither of us can let ourselves give in. – – I feel as if I have to hold myself off from the whole world, and I can't get involved with anybody, even my husband. Having distant relationships is really better for me. – – – My parents are not the real problem any more, neither mine or Tom's. My depression is here and I feel black and have a drowning feeling and it's as if I'm in a whirlpool. – – – – I come here for analysis every day and my parents are visiting and I have problems with my children and with Tom and yet I don't feel that I'm reacting. I feel as if I'm a dead fish.

A: What's the detail?

P: I feel as if I'm in a daze. These things really should upset me and yet they don't. This is unusual, because they generally do. (Elaborates.) My father's letter didn't relieve me. I wanted these things for so long but it's no help now that I've got them. – – – – I'm so afraid of having any emotional reactions toward you that I'll not feel them and I won't let myself feel anything.

A: What are your thoughts about this?

P: I just can't get used to you seeing through me. I can't stand that.

A: What are your associations?

P: I'm thinking about the time my mother called me on the phone. She talked about my father and how she feels that I manipulate him. I'm thinking about my father's feelings and how no one could ever see them before because no one tried. It's just like me. Most people feel that I'm cold and hateful. No one knew *me* or knows who I am. I'm afraid that you might get to know this person, and I don't know why I'm so afraid of that, but I am.

**A:** What are your associations to my getting to know this person?

**P:** If anyone ever really got to know me, they'd see how helpless I am. I'm so weak and they could step on me and I couldn't do anything and they could completely control me. That's why I feel as if I'm a dead fish. I'm worried that after the analysis I may turn out to be what you want and that you'll be able to mold me. If that's the case I'll be just as chained as I am now, and I'll still not really be me. – – Mother once told me, "I took the spirit out of you because I beat it out of you." I feel as if you are doing that to me.

**A:** What is the detail of mother beating it out of you and taking the spirit out of you?

**P:** She did that with every natural reaction I ever had as a child, if I felt any anger, or if I felt any love. I'd show myself and she wouldn't accept it. – –

**A:** How do you mean?

**P:** – I grew up feeling that any expression of anger is bad and evil and wrong, and if I'd show any love she wouldn't take this either. So I felt that every feeling that I have is bad and that nothing I can do is right.

**A:** I wonder if this isn't the same thing as your fear of feeling any emotional reactions towards me. It is as if you expect that I'll think that they are bad just as your mother did.

**P:** – What I fear the most is your indifference. If you'd yell at me or get angry then I could fight back, but if you don't say anything and if you ignore it all, then I can't stand it.

**A:** Which is like the feeling that you had yesterday when you felt that you were asking me to make love to you and then you felt afraid to look at me as you left.

**P:** I just can't stand any rejection. (Elaborates.) I've felt this way all my life and really I have been afraid, but that is why people think me cold and think that I'm a snob. Tom feels that way about me too. – – –

**A:** Let's go back to the idea that you have to block your feelings towards me. What are your associations?

**P:** What would happen. . . . . – if I. . . . .I've seen people do this . . . . . if they say, I love you, I'm yours, and I'll not fight against you, you can take me. You wouldn't do anything. (Elaborates.) I envy the girls who are showing their feelings about boys but I couldn't ever do it for all the money in the world. I'll never show you these feelings and you'll have to come to me to get them or else you'll never see them and I'll miss out. You'll have to show your feelings first because then I won't feel rejected. I finally put my faith in Harris and then he rejected me. For a long time I held off but towards the end I let him see my weakness and then he couldn't take it. It's been that way all of my life.

A: So we're back to the question of whether or not I can take your feelings.

*Cry*

P: Why should you be any different? Tom is the only man who has ever seen even a little bit of me and I'm still not sure about him. – – I feel that all men want a strong woman who doesn't need them and that's the way I have to be in order to get any love at all. But it's all a front. I'm really not this way. The only way that I can do this is to just go ahead and do it. I have to just take a dive. – Either I jump or I don't. It's a question of success or else being a coward. It's like the problem of showing you my feelings. I have to really know you before I can do this.

A: The feeling is that you really have to know me. What are your associations?

P: I don't think that I ever will. No matter what I feel your reactions will always be the same. You're not going to meet me half-way. All the power is in your hands and that frightens me. No matter what I do I can't penetrate your shell. I feel as if you are cold and indifferent and you are rejecting. So why should I make a fool of myself and jump around and be all emotional.

A: What are your thoughts about making a fool of yourself?

P: To feel any kind of sexual feelings or love or anything like that. To think that I want you or to tell you about it. And to really feel this. I could and I can really picture myself begging you for it.

A: What do you see?

P: I can see myself begging you to love me and to take care of me. I feel as if I am between the devil and the deep blue sea. If you ever did that I'd fall apart. And if you don't then I feel frustrated. I can't take either one. So I guess I can survive with my hostility.

A: Let's look and see what your associations are to each of the alternatives you mention.

P: I *have* to find a man who loves me and who can take care of me. Like in a father-child relationship. Because if we both give in to our emotions we just couldn't survive. If one of us is strong. . . . . – If you're strong you can save me from drowning, but if you're not, then we're both going to drown. I feel so depressed now. – – –

A: We'll stop here for today.

## DISCUSSION

The patient begins the session with associations that indicate a beginning therapeutic split and capacity to observe herself and her own reactions, as well as a continuity of her thoughts and feelings from the previous session. She also reports that external events and relationships no longer evoke the same intensity of response as previously, and that "my depression is here. . . ." This is a reflection of the increasing transference development and her further cathexis of me as the object of her unconscious strivings, with the result that there is less need to use other external objects in this way. All these are favorable prognostic signs and indicate that an analytic situation is developing.

However, her defenses against consciously experiencing these transference drives and derivatives are being maintained. What she is consciously aware of are her characteristic defenses against such drives and affects, as occurred earlier in the relationship with her mother. By making my interpretation of the defensive maternal transference, I am trying to help the patient recognize the difference between the current analytic situation and the original relationship with the mother, thereby again supporting the therapeutic alliance. The same is true in regard to the transference from her previous therapist who was unable to tolerate her feelings after she had finally trusted him. My intervention as to whether or not I can accept and tolerate her feelings helps further to focus her into this issue and into the necessity to begin to differentiate me from others in her life in the past.

The remainder of the session essentially involves her working over the issues of whether or not she can trust me. Much of the material regarding my indifference and lack of response to her is actually an attempt to reassure herself that I will *not* become emotionally uncontrolled or involved with her, and therefore that it is safe for her here to experience and express her feelings. At the very end of the session, however, the transference expectation that I will not be strong enough recurs again, leading to her feeling of depression.

The analysis, the establishment of the analytic situation, and the experience and expression of the defense transference are all progressing rapidly. In many other patients, this type of material might not occur for several months, but since it is already conscious to the patient, it must be dealt with directly and immediately. If I were to have remained silent about this material, the patient's interpretation might well have been that I was anxious or uncomfortable about it myself, and that this reflected my concern regarding the control of my own impulses. This, in turn, might have mobilized more conflict and anxiety for her, and resulted in an inhibition and delay in developing the analytic situation.

---

## SESSION 9

**P:** I've found out that I'm definitely pregnant. – –

**A:** You must have some feelings about this.

**P:** I don't know what they are. I suppose it is going to produce problems for the analysis, but I guess I can work it out. Ha, ha! I'm doing something that no man can ever do. No matter how hard they try, they can't do it.

**A:** What's the detail of your feelings?

**P:** I've been pushed around by my father and by men, and this is the one thing that I have. They can't live without women. You all have a penis, but we have the main thing, and that's the babies. I'm also beginning to get my sexual feelings back and I had a desire to make love, but I'm not sure that I can. I had a dream about that boy that I went with. He ran around with a bad crowd and he was definitely not a saint. I dreamed that I met him again and he was a priest. He kept trying to talk to me and I didn't want to talk to him. Then I woke up and then I went back to sleep and dreamed that I wanted Tom to make love to me, but we couldn't because there were a lot of people around and I thought that I was about to die. – – – –

**A:** What are your associations to the elements of the dream?

**P:** I think the boy who was the priest represents Harris. I had an urge to see him and to tell him that I'm pregnant and I felt that he will be happy to hear it. – –

**A:** What's the detail of your feeling?

**P:** I was afraid to tell you. I felt that you would probably be mad. But with Harris I can run back to him and he will hold out his arms to me and he is the only one to understand me. – – You and every man that I know are trying to keep me from being a woman and from being an adult. You are trying to keep me a child and now that I'm pregnant this is impossible.

**A:** What's the detail?

**P:** Here I feel as if I'm a worm and that you are a giant. I could never be your equal. – – Harris once said to me that women who go for analysis think that they are going to find what they want and that all they want is to be a man. – – – – – – That's why I'm afraid of you. – –

**A:** How do you mean?

**P:** If I do, then I have to tell you something that I've never told any-one in my life. No one knows this. This boy. . . . . – the boy that I saw who was a priest knows that I'm not a man. I'm ashamed right now. I let him try to make love to me. – – That's really not the reason.

**A:** What are you trying to get at?

**P:** – – – – – The first time that we tried making love I couldn't do it. I couldn't be a man, and I couldn't even be a woman. – – –

**A:** I think that you have a lot on your mind about this and that the silence means that you are consciously editing what you are saying.

**P:** – There's something about. . . . . his being a priest now. He's so clean and holy and I'm so dirty. I'm so scared of something, but I don't know what it is. – – I'm so frightened of being alone. – – – – – I feel com-pletely alone and I can't stand it.

*Cry, Sob*

**A:** I think you are reacting to this thing that you've never told any-body. What comes to your mind?

**P:** – – I feel as if I was forced to do it. I didn't want to but I was afraid that I'd lose him if I didn't. – – He's the only thing that I had to hang onto at the time. – – I hate him for making me do it. I don't know what to do, I have no place to go and nowhere to turn; I feel forced in any kind of a relationship. Nobody really cares no matter what I do. I just don't know what to do. I think maybe that's why I'm pregnant. At least Tom has to stay with me and he can't leave me because I am. There's nobody that I can trust. I feel as if all men are horrible. If I ever depend on you, you'll take advantage of me. It's always been that way and it's all you men want. You want to get me into the position of where I can't do anything.

**A:** This is somewhat like the dream where he wanted to talk but you didn't want to. I wonder if you don't feel that way about the analysis as well.

**P:** – Now that I've done this, I wonder if you will. I feel helpless but I don't even care. I'm just resigned now.

**A:** You wonder if I will. What are you referring to?

**P:** I'm dependent on you and I'm beginning to trust you. Now it's your turn to take advantage of me. – –

**A:** What's the detail of the thought?

**P:** It's all sexual and that's all that you want out of me. You want to get me just to this point. That's the only reason that you pay any attention to me. – – –

**A:** What are your associations to the second dream?

**P:** We were in a swimming pool and I had all kinds of sexual desires but there were too many people around. He was going away and we never could get to do it. I really wanted him! But he didn't give to me. It was all on my part. It was just like here. I give everything to you but you don't give anything to me. – –

A: What are your associations to a swimming pool?

P: It was like the one in Springfield. I had a lot of my sexual desires when I was around there and there were boys around and we used to play in the water. (Elaborates.) I hid all my feelings there. But I had gone wild in the dream. – –

A: What was the detail?

P: My hand was grasping the back of his neck and his head. I just realized that it wasn't Tom in the dream. The man had black hair which reminds me of you or of my father. – – – I'll have to go home soon and Tom isn't going to be there tonight and I'm scared. I'm going to be all alone. It's just like after that first dream. If there are people around nothing is going to happen. – – – – I keep wondering if I'm capable of handling myself if there's no one around with me.

A: We'll stop here for today.


## DISCUSSION

The confirmation of the patient's pregnancy poses something of a problem for me in terms of what its impact will be on the analysis, and whether or not the analysis should be interrupted because of the pregnancy. As the session continues part of my thinking and attention is involved in considering these issues.

A number of analysts advise interruption of analysis during pregnancy, partly because of the woman's normally occurring heightened narcissism during pregnancy, as well as her needs to cathect the fetus, and to prepare without emotional distraction for the delivery of the child and for her relationship to it. However, an opposing point of view emphasizes the issue that a psychiatric patient's symptomatic neurosis may seriously interfere with her ability effectively to cathect her baby in a healthy fashion if she is not in treatment.

A number of factors specific to this case also require consideration. The patient had become pregnant while waiting to begin analysis, and her initial associations in this session indicate clearly that it was a symptomatic acting-out with many neurotic determinants. In addition, her neurosis had begun during her first pregnancy, thus suggesting a causal connection, and so it might be possible that repeating the pregnancy while in analysis could allow us to uncover the specific precipitating neurotic mechanisms and associations. Furthermore, an analytic situation is being established, along with the preformed transference mentioned earlier, and the patient's subsequent associations in this session make it clear that to interrupt the analysis at this point would be felt by her as a significant transference rejection, and might jeopardize her ever returning to analysis in the future. In addition, I had previously analyzed another patient during her pregnancy and found that the analysis had significantly improved her capacity to invest in the baby. As a result of this reasoning I therefore did not seriously consider interrupting her analysis because of the pregnancy.

Throughout the session the patient makes direct references to the transference relationship which is developing rapidly. Both dreams are transference dreams, but in my handling of them, the attempt is to discourage any immediate dream interpretation and instead, to encourage the pattern of association to the various components. The effectiveness of this tactic is confirmed by the progressive filling in of the details of the manifest dream, and the final association about the black hair. The developing transference is evoking sexual responsiveness in her, but initially in the session she is projecting this to me through the transference fantasy that I am like all men who will only be interested in taking advantage of her sexually. Her complaint that in the second dream, "It was just like here. I give everything to you, but you don't give anything to me," is actually an expression of confidence and relief. Although she voices it as a complaint, it is only her evolving knowledge that I am different from other men in her life and that although I accept her verbalization of her sexual feelings, I will not be responding to her sexually, that permits her to experience these transference wishes in an increasingly direct fashion. In other words, in spite of complaining about it, the patient is reassured that her sexual wishes in the transference will not be satisfied.

Since the patient is increasingly involved in the analytic process and her associations are continuing freely, I can now intermittently begin to permit silences to develop somewhat longer than previously.

---

## SESSION 10

**P:** I've been reacting to my last meeting. I felt fine on Saturday, but then Saturday night and Sunday I had all kinds of thoughts of killing myself. I had a whole lot of nightmares last night and they were all about being left alone. – –

**A:** What was the detail of the nightmares?

**P:** There were so many of them. In one of them I was in a pasture and it was like an animal story. I think I was a horse or maybe I was a pony. I yelled at my father, or maybe it was some other man, and I kept saying, "Please don't leave me." Then the other dreams were about the house in Evanston and about being in college and sororities, and in all of them I felt so insecure and felt as if I wasn't wanted. – – – I had the feeling during the dreams that I can't stand it even though it doesn't seem so frightening now. – – Saturday I felt very loving towards you and I thought that you were wonderful and that you were so strong. But right now I hate you and I don't know why. – –

**A:** What are your associations?

**P:** I'm thinking of your wife. You can't be mine and you never will be. So why should I tell you any horrible things about me? – –

**A:** You mention thinking about my wife. What are your associations?

**P:** – – – – I come here every day and each time I tell myself, "Don't cry or get hysterical." I feel as if I have no control! It makes me so mad that you are doing this to me! – – – – – –

**A:** I think your silence is an attempt at getting control here. I think that you are afraid that you'll get upset if you talk.

**P:** Uhm! – – – – – – – – I have the feeling that you are trying to control me again. I'm afraid that I'm going to get myself into a position that I'm . . . . . If I can control the situation, then you can't. Why should you control it? Why not me? I feel that I'm on such a low level and as if I'm degraded to being a child every time that I come here. – – – –

**A:** What about your associations to the dreams?

**P:** – I'm thinking about my children and how horrible it would be if they didn't have both Tom and I. It makes me feel so sad! That's the way I feel myself. I never knew if I had parents or not. – –

**A:** What was the detail?

**P:** I was just never sure. I had two sisters and a family and so on, but I never knew if they loved me or needed me or if they cared. We used to have a lot of babysitters and we used to go to my grandmother's a lot. My father and mother were somehow never home. (Elaborates.) We used to go to school but then we'd come home and eat dinner by ourselves and it was a hell of a life. I would be in the house and my parents would be there occasionally. I used to get homesick for that house even when I was away with my parents, and I used to get a kind word occasionally from my parents but it was just to keep me dangling. – – I must have tried to fight this. (Elaborates.) – – – I feel as if you throw me back to that same childhood, and I get the same feelings with you. I think that you'll have me in your power and then you'll do anything you want to me just to keep me dangling. I felt as if I'd die when my parents went out, and they'd go out every single night. Each time I felt as if I'd die. – –

A: What are your associations to the pasture in the dream?

P: I used to visit a friend and her mother was always very nice to me. She cared about me more than my parents did, and they used to live on a farm and I'd go out there for weekends. We'd play and I felt secure with them when I was away from home. – – I feel as if I'm fighting a losing battle and as if it's all over. So why should I get mad and upset. – – I feel an awful lot of hostility but I just can't show it. – – –

A: What are your associations to the horse or the pony?

P: We used to ride horses out there. I think of the animal movies that I used to see and how sad they made me. I'm thinking of Lassie and of how the animals would sometimes be lost. – – The horse ran away with me twice when I was riding and I was petrified. – –

A: What was the detail of that?

P: I was about three or four and the horse ran back to the stable and I felt as if he were going to the end of the earth. My mother was there at the stable but she didn't know how frightened I was. – – – –

A: You didn't say anything about the other time the horse ran away with you.

P: That happened when I was older. I was with the horse trainer and I was with the Joneses. My horse started going into a river and the stupid trainer kept hitting him and kept saying, "come back," but the horse would just go into the river further. Finally I was able to get him out. – – I never had control of anything in my whole life. I couldn't control anybody and I couldn't control my feelings or my life or anything. And I have *no* control over you. – – –

A: What's going through your mind?

P: The situation here is like with the horses. I think that I'm going to be swept away, and that I'm so minute that I can't do anything about it. I'm going to be caught up in a whirlwind and I'm never going to get out, and it's going to happen any minute and there will be no one there to help me.

A: I wonder if you don't think that I'm like that stupid trainer and I'm letting you get in deeper and deeper here.

P: There's nothing I can do about it. The only thing I can do is hide *Cry* it but that makes me so mad. I have an urge to put my hand out and to hold onto you to get steady again, but I can't. So I just sit, and I'm the whipping post for anyone who comes along. If I show my hostility or fight then I lose the tiny bit of love that I'm getting now. It's funny but I realize now that this is what my father wanted me to do, and that he would have respected this. – – –

A: What are you referring to?

P: He wanted me to stand up for myself. He hated any kind of weakness. I'd try and I'd put on an act but I never really could. It was like with the horses. I would try to ride them, but I was scared of the damned things. It was all a huge front. I think of my father's face and how he would have looked if I had ever said to him, "Go to hell, you bastard." He'd just crumble, and I couldn't stand that. At least he seemed strong this other way, but if I turn on him then he falls to pieces. I have a great fear of doing this. I hate the thought of a woman destroying a man to the point of where he is a helpless child. It infuriates me. – –

A: What's the detail of your feeling?

P: My mother has done this and all her life she has tried to destroy my father and I think she finally has. Tom's mother once said, "He's not a man." I felt as if I would like to kill her. I just saw red! For her to insinuate that he wasn't *man* enough. I held such a fury. But she has done this to him. I need a strong man around me or else I'll fall apart. That's why I'm so afraid to get mad at my father.

A: I think that's also one of your questions here. Will I fall apart if you ever get mad at me?

P: That's why I'm so afraid to get mad at my father. Every man that I've ever known has. (Elaborates.) They all start crawling when you get mad at them.

A: What's the detail of your thought?

P: I'm thinking of a boy I went with. (Elaborates.) He scared me and somehow he reminds me of my father. We had a huge fight one night and he just crumpled, and I was so afraid of him. It was just like my father. I'm *not* afraid of him. He can't hurt me. I can hurt him though. – – If you're strong then you'll be able to hold me up, but if you ever fall then we are both going to fall. It's up to you. – – – – –

A: We'll stop here for today.

### DISCUSSION

The analytic situation continues to develop with the patient progressively learning to associate more freely. There is a developing continuity from one session to the next as illustrated in her opening remark about the last session, and there is evidence that she is aware of increasing responses and reactions toward me and of my increasing psychic importance to her. The feelings of being "degraded to being a child . . ." while here are an indication that the process of regression in the therapeutic situation has already begun, and that the analysis is mobilizing her childhood conflicts. Since the analytic process is now underway, I can more readily permit silences to occur for somewhat longer duration and in this session the total silence amounts to more than half of the total time. However, I do point out the defensive function of the silence early in the session.

The patient spontaneously associates to the developing transference reactions, as in the direct references to me and in her association to my wife. These associations, as well as the dreams that she reports, represent oedipal transference derivatives with probable sexual implications (i.e., the symbolism of the horse). In past sessions, I have already indicated my willingness to listen and accept her sexual fantasy, so there is no further need to do this at present, but she is not yet ready for any type of deeper interpretation of this material, since such an intervention would tend to intellectualize the analytic process. However, early in the session after the subject of my wife has come up, I do ask her for further associations to this issue. Although she does not respond to this directly or consciously, she later gets into the area of her parents and their relationship, and as she fills in more of her past history there is an ebb and flow between childhood experiences and the current analytic situation. Therefore, there is no need for me to intervene beyond asking for her further associations and the details of her thoughts, and this permits her to develop her own associations spontaneously without my influencing or distorting them.

Aside from the interpretation about her silence, the first interpretation that I make is in response to her association of the similarity between the experiences with the horses and the analytic situation. This interpretation is again focused at the current level of anxiety regarding the analysis and her continuing fear of it and of the relationship it implies. Her immediate affective response of crying, as well as the content of the material itself, confirms the interpretation, and again the patient returns to her anxiety in the transference about my tolerance for her affects and her drives. Her anger and aggression are serving a defensive function against an underlying positive attachment to me, but until the patient's anxiety about the transference responses is further reduced, she will not be ready or able to see this in an effective way. Therefore, toward the end of the session, I again acknowledge my awareness of her anxiety by pointing out her fantasy that I may fall apart if she ever gets mad at me. Although this intervention is focused at the level of her defense, rather than at the underlying positive attachment, this is the current level of her conscious awareness, and it follows the general principle of interpretation from the surface of the patient's conscious awareness. It encourages her again to struggle with her reality perceptions of me and my attitude, as contrasted with her transference expectations and the anxiety mobilized by them. The tactical goal is to permit her conscious, rational, participating ego to assess the fantasied danger in the light of her own personal experience with me and of her observations of my comfortable attitude toward her feelings and thoughts. As such, it is again aimed at strengthening the working alliance between us.

---

## SESSION 11

P: – – – I had a sudden sense of panic when I was coming here and I felt so scared.

A: What was the feeling?

P: – I wondered if this was really ever going to do me any good. It's a situation that I can't control and I have no way that I can control you, or myself, or the world. It's all so frightening. I kept wondering what's the object of all of this if I can't get anything out of you.

A: Your fear is that you can't get anything out of me and yet at the same time to you it means that I'm strong, so you are tempted to depend on me, but the more you are tempted to depend on me, the more scared you get.

P: I'm *not* going to depend on you because I don't know what you'll do.

A: What do you picture?

P: Sometimes I think you are just a robot. What would I ever depend on you for? – –

A: What's the detail of your feeling that you don't know what I'll do?

P: There are strings attached any time things like this come up. (Elaborates.) I don't know what your strings are. – – I think of you. . . . . misusing me sexually. – –

A: What did you stop at?

P: – – I think you are going to *force* me to do something. You've reduced me to being a child and I feel as if I've lost my identity and I'm nobody. I'll have to think and do what you want me to, and I don't want to be this way. But what do I have to do about it? It's a conflict that I can't solve. I can't function in my life unless I can control something. I feel the way my daughter does and that's the way I used to think of myself as a child. I used to kick and scream and have temper-tantrums and stuff like that and sometimes it worked. But I can't control you. I can try it through my dependency but you are not going to let me do that either.

**A:** How do you mean?

**P:** If I ever let myself depend on you, then you'll have an obligation to me. I hate it and yet that's what I want. I don't know why I have to fight against your control, because if you are not in control, then I'd be lost, but I feel as if I must have a *little* control.

**A:** So we can see that the feeling that you're having with me now is in a sense a partial repetition of some of the feelings and problems you felt about controlling things as a little girl.

**P:** I always used to be able to control them. I could make my mother react just the way I wanted. I could act bad with her and I'd always get the same reaction.

**A:** What would happen?

**P:** If I was hostile towards my mother then she'd be hostile towards me. It was always the same.

**A:** So you'd be upset because she was angry with you, but at the same time you'd be reassured since you caused it and so you wouldn't feel so helpless.

**P:** – This was all so weak. I used to be able to reduce my mother to acting just like a child. But a child can't depend on another child. –– I feel as if I hate everybody! No one treats me right and no one does what I want. I think of Harris and how much I hate him. *Cry*

**A:** What was the detail?

**P:** – There were two different things with him. He didn't give me what I wanted, but also he *was* weak at times and he showed his emotions. I hate you because you don't show me *any* emotion, and also you don't give me anything.

**A:** But you are also reassured by that.

**P:** Why can't I ever be satisfied? Why do I always have to feel so frustrated? I feel as if I'm caged up. Each time I'm here I can show only one emotion, but I keep wondering if you can be strong against my hostility? I want to show you how I feel but I can't because I don't know what you are going to do.

**A:** What do you picture?

**P:** You'll tell me to go to hell or to get out and that you don't care. You'll probably be frightened, and that frightens me. I have a sudden urge to kill you, and I wish that I had a knife and then I could turn around and stab you. I've got to be sure that you'd be able to stop me. I had a dream about killing a boy the other night. It was at school, I think it was grade school and the boy was older than I was and he wasn't a classmate. I think he was an idiot, because he couldn't talk. His mind didn't work right. I killed him and I think he was wearing a white jacket. – – –

A: What are your associations to the parts of the dream?

*Cry!*

P: I think the boy represents you. You just sit there and you don't say anything. You are incapable of any emotion and I hate you for it. You caused me to hate you and that was the reason I killed the boy because he turned on me and followed me. It would have been fine if he had just let me alone. What are you going to do next?

A: I think that you're afraid of your own hostility, and you think that I'm an idiot not to be afraid of it too. But the fact that I'm not showing any fear means that you are tempted to rely on me, but at the same time that temptation causes you to be afraid.

P: – – I get a sudden feeling that I *can* rely on you and I want to tell you everything but then I get a feeling that I *can't*. I've got to get mad, but if I do then I'm afraid that it will kill you. I suddenly have a feeling that I don't want to think of you as my father, because if I do then I know that you're weak. – – – I feel that panic again right now. – –

A: What are your feelings?

P: I'm afraid of my sexual feelings. But if I don't hate you then I have to love you and I'm afraid of that too. That's even worse. I feel as though I'm going to jump out of my skin. – – You're not going to be my father. Even Harris and all of the other men are *not* my father. This is just like a bomb and I feel as if I'll explode.

A: What's the detail of the feeling?

P: – I want you to sit beside me and put your arms around me. I picture a sexual explosion, and I'll fall apart and my arms and legs will come off and I'll just fall apart. – – It's as if I'm a child and I'm having all of this sexual feeling and I don't know about it and if it ever comes to a head I'll explode. I've never experienced this before and I'm afraid and I feel as if I'm never going to reach the end. *You* could cause this to happen to me and it would be the *end* of me and I'll fall apart. I feel like begging you not to do this to me. Let me have this feeling all by myself and please don't take advantage of me for having it.

A: So we can begin to see how terrified you've been much of your life about the intensity of your own feelings.

P: If I ever let them go, the end result will be something that I've never experienced before and it would be horrible. It's like the feelings of anger. I don't know if there is a man in the world who could ever stand up against my sexual feelings. I've never met one. Even when I was a child there were greedy old men who were after me sexually. It was like my uncle.

**A:** What was the detail of your uncle?

**P:** I used to sit on his lap and I'd play with him. He never understood why I stopped. He used to embarrass me. It was a relationship that I had to terminate because he was such a child and was so weak.

*Cry!*

**A:** I think that you're just alluding to something here that you're not facing directly.

**P:** – I used to think of him in the way that I wanted to think of my father. – – I feel frightened suddenly! My uncle was a nasty old man. I remember one time in the bathroom, when I was about seventeen, he had just finished. He said to me, "Go in there and smell it. It smells like roses." That was horrible! He's so sick! It was as if he was saying, "Look at my penis." But then I wonder if all of this was just in my own mind? Was he really not so bad but was it just me? He used to be so nice to me and he'd play with me when I was a child which my father didn't do. I want you to tell me what happened and what's going on. I keep wondering if all of this is in *my* mind? I'm so afraid of my own fears I just can't continue. That's what I'm afraid of with you. If you're nice and you allow me to have my feelings then I have to stop. I just can't allow this to happen. The yardman used to be like this too. He used to have nasty thoughts about me. I think maybe he was an alcoholic. I wonder why my parents never saw all of this. Why did they let these idiot people into the house?

**A:** We'll stop here for today.

### Discussion

Throughout the early part of the session the patient illustrates the typical conflict of most patients in analysis. On the one hand, she objects to the neutrality and affective control that I demonstrate, that I am in control of the situation, and to the fact that her wishes toward me in analysis will be frustrated. At the same time, however, there is a reassurance to her from this fact, and it is only her knowledge that she can rely on my maintaining my neutrality that permits her to undergo further regression, reduce her conscious editing and other controls, and experience the increasing transference pressures. As she says in reference to the mother, "A child can't depend on another child." And apparently she perceived some of the same tendencies in her former therapist.

My interventions in the first half of the session are aimed at helping her to recognize and elaborate on this conflict again. This stems from my realization that until this conflict has been further resolved and her confidence in the analytic situation increased, she will continue to have difficulties in permitting the optimal degree of regression to occur. In other words, the aim of my interventions is the fostering and further establishment of a firm therapeutic alliance between us. It is this line of thinking that leads to my first interpretation of the dream at the level of the more superficial defense transference elements, followed by my focusing on the conscious conflict between her wish for and fear of relying on me.

These efforts bear some fruit when she has a brief feeling that she *can* rely on me, followed by the increasing awareness and expression of her sexual fantasy and tension. This regressive experience in the transference, accompanied by my intervention regarding her lifelong fear of the intensity of her own feelings (an intervention again aimed at the therapeutic alliance), permits the recall and expression of some of the earlier sexual fantasies and allusions from childhood. At this point in the transference situation I represent the uncle, who in turn was an object of displacement from the father. This material regarding the uncle is another derivative allusion to an important traumatic experience which will directly emerge much later in the analysis. Although in the transference situation and in the recall of the material about the uncle she is beginning actually to experience her fears, at the end of the session she demonstrates the capacity for self-observation when she spontaneously wonders how much of the problem occurred in her own mind.

The deeper meaning of the dream emerges only in the patient's last comment about "these idiot people" in conjunction with the sexual childhood experiences. However, the patient is making sufficiently rapid analytic progress, and enough material has already emerged for one session. Furthermore, it is the end of the session, and I therefore do not call her attention to the connection between the idiot in the manifest dream and the "idiot people" she has associated to. This deeper understanding of the dream, however, is a further confirmation of the earlier formulation that for her, manifest aggression serves in part as a defense against underlying sexual drives and fantasy.

## SESSION 12

Patient asks about paying Mrs. West for her social casework sessions before beginning analysis.

**P:** – – – – – – – – I wonder what I've been expecting from analysis? I think of myself as a failure in everything. I've been feeling so insecure and frustrated, and I'm afraid constantly. My feelings are all intensifying and I'm scared of the whole world. – – – – My life seems unmanageable and I feel just like a chicken with my head cut off. (Elaborates.)

**A:** What comes to your mind about the fact that your feelings seem to be intensifying?

**P:** I think that I'm failing with you. (Elaborates.)

**A:** What's the detail of the thought?

**P:** I've always been unconsciously able to control my parents and all of the others that I've come into contact with. But I can't do this with you. Every defense I have has to be stripped away before I can get any-where here. I've been taking all of my hostility out on Tom.

**A:** How do you mean?

**P:** We have been having all kinds of arguments and I start and finish each one of them. It's all going on in me. I feel as if you should be help-ing me, but you're so indifferent. I can't stand it.

**A:** I wonder if this isn't related to the session yesterday and you are feeling fear at the thought of expressing any hostility here. So you did it at home instead. Let's go back to your fear of expressing it here.

**P:** – – It's the same old thing. I think that you'll cut me off and you'll walk out and you'll never see me again. – – Why am I so afraid? It's ridiculous but I just can't do it. It's not what you'll do, but what I will do. My emotions will probably run away with me. It's just like it is with Tom.

**A:** What are your thoughts if it would happen here?

**P:** I'd lose my mind and it would just snap. – –

**A:** What do you picture?

**P:** I'll get up and I'll beat you and I'll grab your throat and kill you. I know that I can. I don't really feel it here, but I do feel it when I'm with Tom. Then I stop everything. I can talk about this but I don't feel it.

**A:** Well, let's start with the talk and see what comes to your mind.

**P:** – I think of killing myself or killing my children. I could do it because my children couldn't fight me. You and Tom are stronger than I am. - - -

**A:** If I'm stronger than you are, what comes to your mind about expressing and verbalizing your feelings here?

**P:** I'm afraid that I might lose my mind and try it. It's all so horrible. Why aren't you frightened? I'd be scared to death if I were you.

**A:** What are your associations?

**P:** Suppose that I were to come with a gun and shoot you? You couldn't stop me. - -

**A:** I think that you want me to be frightened of you, and yet at the same time you're reassured that I'm not. What are your associations to this?

**P:** - - I feel as if you are going to make me do it, and then it's all going to be your fault.

**A:** I think that you are not differentiating between a thought or feeling which are expressed in words on the one hand, as compared with an act on the other. It's as if you think that one is inevitably going to lead to the other.

**P:** - - - - - - -

**A:** What are your thoughts about the silence?

**P:** - - - I feel as if you expect me to be perfect and I can't be! You expect me to bring out my feelings and to know the difference between what is real and unreal! I wouldn't be here if I could do that! - -

**A:** What comes to your mind about the feeling that I expect you to be perfect?

**P:** - - - I hate this whole situation. You reduce me to nothing! I can't compete with you at all! You know so much more than I do!

**A:** On the one hand you're afraid that I'm going to react the way your parents did and that I'll get angry or kick you out or reject you and yet you know that that's not true, and at the same time you're also afraid that I'm *not* going to react and that I will be able to understand and see through your feelings and that makes you feel helpless.

**P:** How is it ever going to help me to be reduced to a child and feel that I'm in an inferior position? That's the way I've lived my whole life anyway. - -

**A:** What's the detail of the feeling?

**P:** I've always felt inferior. I felt that everyone else is smarter and bigger and has more than I do. It's a vicious circle. - -

**A:** What comes to your mind about this?

**P:** I just can't understand it. It all turns back to me and nothing has anything to do with you. It's so frustrating to have so much hostility for you and to have you not react. It's as if I'm not even worth it. You remind me of my mother and the way she used to say, "It takes two to argue and if I don't argue with you, then you can't. Ha!"

**A:** Let's look at your assumption that if I don't react to you it means that you're not worth it.

**P:** It's like the comics where the smaller one fights for all they're worth and yet they never do anything. That's me. I have no reason to be mad and so I hate myself! But I can't believe that I'm always wrong. I *do* have some brains.

**A:** On the one hand you're reassured that I'm not afraid of you or your feelings. But you're also interpreting this as meaning that I'm not taking you or your feelings seriously enough.

**P:** I *am* a person and I have real feelings and I *want* to show them. (Elaborates.) They are very *real!*

**A:** One of your fears about the analysis is that I *do* take your feelings as real and I give you a chance to show them and express them here in words.

**P:** This means that I have no escape and no excuse and I can't keep my secrets from you. I can't say that you don't know and that I'm not going to tell you. But maybe if I don't. . . . .it will make you mad, and if I give in to you, then we're going to have no relationship at all. If I accept the fact that this is a patient-therapist relationship then really there is no relationship at all. I can be satisfied if I can keep getting at you, even if it's just to make you mad or disgusted.

**A:** So this is like your feeling at the beginning of the session that you're a failure here. It's really a wish to fail and the hope that I'll feel the same way and that I'll be disappointed and that that way you can get at me.

**P:** Why do I feel that I have to control you? Why can't I be satisfied with just letting you help me? And yet I feel that I must get you to react! But the whole thing frustrates me.

**A:** We'll stop here for today.

### DISCUSSION

In this session the patient manifests an increase in her conscious resistances, partly as a result of the forward progress in the session yesterday. The reported fights with her husband represent a displacement of transference feelings away from the analytic situation, and my interpretation of this is an attempt to encourage her to face the feelings here, and tacitly to discourage the acting-out of these problems with her husband. The defense mechanism of isolation is illustrated by her statement that she can talk about her hostility but can't feel it here. My intervention regarding the differentiation between thoughts and acts is again an appeal to the developing therapeutic alliance and is an attempt to encourage her to face the thoughts and feelings directly. Her response of silence, followed by her angry criticism of me for these demands upon her, represent a shift of defenses in response to that intervention.

Throughout the remainder of the session, my interventions are still focused at the attempt to help her clarify the continuing fear of the analysis, and of the beginning regression that she is experiencing. She is caught in a continuing conflict between her wish to maintain a patient-therapist relationship and to undergo a successful analysis, as opposed to her wishes for transference gratification, or the avoidance of an analytic experience. Aside from my requests for her associations and details, most of my interventions represent clarifications of thoughts or feelings already conscious to her. It could be argued that since these issues are already conscious, there is no need for me to say anything about them. However, I want at this time to promote her partial identification with my analytic posture, and also to provide her with the reassuring experience that I can understand her feelings without reacting to them emotionally. These are tactics again designed to promote the therapeutic alliance, and to cope with the patient's needs to test me to determine whether or not it's safe for her to submit to the analytic regression and to reduce the intensity of some of her defenses.

---

## SESSION 13

**P:** I just can't figure myself out. First I get excited and then I find myself getting anxious. (Elaborates.) I've been trying to decide about you. I feel as if I could trust you and I think how wonderful that would be, and then all of a sudden I get panicked.

**A:** In that way you are able to run away from the thoughts of trusting me.

**P:** − − − It's better not to.

**A:** And yet in the moments when you feel as if you could trust me you get a pleasant feeling about it.

**P:** Yesterday I felt that it would be wonderful to trust someone who is as strong as you and not have you get mad or take advantage of me, and then the next minute I get so panicked that I can't stand it. I have the thought to cut my wrists and have an idea that I think this in order to panic myself. I get mad at myself for thinking about this and nothing else. Last night I was alone, and after Tom had gone I had my first realization that I have no reason to be afraid when I'm by myself. -- Every time I get elated I find that I get anxious. Especially if I'm feeling happy and excited. This was true when I was with Harris too. It's as if I'm saying, "It's not really me."

A: How do you mean?

P: I just don't know who I am. I always try to be someone else. (Elaborates.) It would be so wonderful to say what I think and how I feel and not worry about it. But I'm not good enough myself to *be* myself. I feel as if I'm no one and I have nothing unless I'm acting. ---

A: You mentioned that it would be wonderful to say what you think and be yourself. What's the detail there?

P: --- To me it seems impossible. Especially when I think of the thoughts that I've had, and the idea of saying them to someone else. How could they help but react to me? They'd get mad or. . . . .be shocked, or else they'd be disgusted. ---

A: What's going through your mind?

P: I'm shocked about all of this. There is something terribly wrong with me because no one else could possbly think these things and anyone else would be shocked.

A: You mention that you feel shocked yourself. What's the detail?

P: It's all of my sexual thoughts. They're thoughts about women, *and* men. No one could possibly think the same things that I do. -----
----

A: I wonder if your silence means that you're waiting for me to ask you about these thoughts?

P: --------- I wonder if I'm silent long enough if you'll eventually get mad at me. I want to get back at you somehow. --

A: What's the detail?

P: I learned that as I grew up and I found that it was a new weapon that I could use against men. I know. . . .I like for men to be very attracted to me and then I can turn my nose up at them. I want to do this to you. I want to find your weakness. I feel that this *is* a weakness in all men. -- I do it to Tom all the time. --

A: What's the detail about doing it to Tom?

P: If he puts his pajamas on, then some times I'll do it too, or else

I'll even walk around with no clothes on at all and then he goes wild. Then I can act as if I had no intention to do anything and that his ideas are ridiculous. That's why I do it. I don't have any fear of intercourse. I want it but I won't let myself do it. Because then I can feel, "Poor Tom, he must feel so insecure in his manliness." Men are supposed to be the superior sex but this is their one weakness. They can't resist a woman and this is where I can get back at them. – – – I remember when we lived in Springfield my father used to sleep downstairs in the study. I don't remember whether mother told me or whether I asked her, but I remember her saying he was so oversexed. That used to give her great pleasure. It was as if she was saying, "You don't even get me sexed up, Buddy, so take your thing and get out of here." – – – – How can you just sit there! I picture you jumping up and down.

A: What's the detail of the image?

P: I can see you having a fit. – – –

A: What's the detail?

P: I wonder if you're going to get mad at me? Or, I wonder why you don't try to seduce me in order to prove that I'm wrong and to prove that you can overpower me if you really want to? – – –

A: What else comes to your mind?

P: No matter which way you'd react, you'd still be in my power. If you got mad then I've got you in my power, and if you make love to me, then I've still got you in my power. – – This reminds me of a dream that I had last night where I wanted to make love with a man desperately, and I felt that if I didn't do it I'd die. All of a sudden I found out that he's gone! That's how I feel about you and that's what I really want from you! – –

A: What's the detail?

P: All this time that I've felt so inferior to you, I've known that I'm really not. I know. . . . .I don't know if this is a real desire or if it's a test of you, or what. I tell myself, "Dr. Dewald knows all about my sexual feelings for him and is he just waiting, or is he really strong enough to resist this?" I don't feel that I really don't or couldn't attract you.

A: So we can see that you get a certain amount of pleasure in these fantasies of seducing me and getting me in your power and so on. But we also have to see that you're hoping I won't be seduced, because only if I'm strong will I be able to help you.

P: You're right. I've spent all of this time just to see if you're just another man who will fall down. --- If I don't. . . . .when people make love, one of them gets the best of the other. It's like Tom taking advantage of me or the times that I feel that I'm holding the strings. Can I ever make love without the feeling that I'm superior? Or that Tom is superior? ---- I suddenly feel as if I've lost all of my confidence. I'm feeling like a child who could cry and feel sorry for herself. --

**A:** Let's look at the details of the change.

**P:** This whole time I've been just quaking inside. I feel just like a tiny girl in a big shell. I look like a woman but really I'm just a baby and I'm scared. I act big and mature, but really I'm scared. I'd die if you ever did try to seduce me. --- I really do think that I have feelings of love for you but I have all kinds of defenses and I talk a lot and I'm trying to control the situation. But if it actually came, I know that I couldn't resist you. It's what I want more than anything in the world. ----- I feel as if I've shown you how I feel and now I'm waiting for you to tell me how you feel. --

**A:** What's the fantasy?

**P:** - I'm waiting for you to say it and at the same time I'm hoping that you don't react. I've felt so ambiguous about everyone all of my life and that goes for you too now.

**A:** We'll stop here for today.

## DISCUSSION

At the beginning of this session, the patient indicates her spontaneous attempts to figure herself out and her beginning observations of the sequence of her thoughts followed by her symptoms. All these phenomena are indications of the growing therapeutic alliance and her increasing capacity for self-observation, developing alongside the capacity to experience and express transference fantasy. The analytic situation is being established.

Because of this progress within herself, and because up to now I have "passed" the tests that she has set up, she is now able more directly and openly to approach her sexual thoughts and conflicts. However, she immediately resorts to new testing devices, namely the prolonged silences, and the fantasied challenge to my sexual manhood expressed in the description of her behavior with her husband. My comfortable acceptance of these thoughts and feelings, and my requests for further associations represent my "passing" another series of tests. As a result the patient can then indicate that she, too, has been aware of the testing that has been going on between us, as well as her awareness of the conflict between the wishes for transference gratification and the fears of it.

Her final associations that "I've felt so ambiguous about everyone all of my life and that goes for you too, now," is an indicator of the developing transference situation. It means that an important conflict originally experienced toward earlier key figures in her life is now being re-experienced toward me in the absence of realistic provocation or stimulation by me.

---

## SESSION 14

P: I get so anxious here that I feel like crying. I can't help doing something that I don't want to do. I've been so hostile towards Tom lately.

A: What's the detail of this feeling toward Tom?

P: Everything he does irritates me. I have such a fear of letting my defenses down and I know that my hostility is covered because it's so exaggerated. But I can't stand for him to touch me. It's all just a vicious circle.

A: I think you are expressing with Tom some of the feelings that you are having from here. Everything that I do upsets you, and you have fears of this developing into some kind of a sexual relationship, and you feel helpless and like a child here, and so on.

P: Am I going to do this for the rest of my life? I can never put these feelings onto you instead of Tom. This analysis is ruining our marriage. (Elaborates.) I'm also very jealous of Jean suddenly. I've had some dreams that she and Tom were falling in love. I used to dream all the time that Tom was in love with someone else. In these dreams he'd always be calm and walk out and I'd be left having a tantrum. – –

A: What are your associations to Jean?

P: She's with Harris. I feel very jealous of her. I know that she hasn't solved her problems but she thinks that she's so perfect.

A: And what are your thoughts about Jean being with Harris?

P: She began treatment with him six or eight months before I did and I always felt that he favored her. (Elaborates.) I always thought that he and Jean were much closer than I was to him, but I would never admit that I was jealous. (Elaborates.) – –

A: I wonder if maybe you're reacting to some thoughts that you might have had about some of my other patients?

P: I saw Mrs. West when I left last time and I was jealous of her. That was on the night of the dream. I feel as if you two are on the same level with each othe . –– It was as if I had seen a face that I knew and I stopped and talkeἀ with her. And then suddenly I felt very self-conscious. I had thoughts about Jean on the way home and then I had that dream about Jean and Tom. I thought of Mrs. West as being your patient because she talks so highly of you. ––

A: What was the detail?

P: (Elaborates.) She said that you were such a wonderful therapist and her face lit up and she smiled when she said it. It's as if Mrs. West is like my mother and father, and the only way I could communicate with my father was through my mother. ––– I don't understand how you can have any interest in me, what with your other patients and things to do. I can't put my trust in you because of this. I want to but I know that I fight it.

A: So we can see that when you talk about not letting your defenses down with Tom you're really talking about your feelings here.

P: (Laughs.) I had a dream last night and it just dawned on me. We were in Maine which is where we used to go every summer. I was with a lot of girls and we were all sharing the same bathroom and I couldn't stand the thought of it after a while. I felt as if I had to get out of there. –––

A: You mentioned that something had just dawned on you. What were you referring to?

P: –– I think of my mother and my sisters and myself, and how we all really shared my father sexually. I couldn't fight for him and so I'd back out. There were times up there when I felt as if I could have my father to myself but then my mother and my sisters would always pop up and I never could, so I'd feel, "Why try." The thing that I don't understand is why you let me back out. Why don't you say, "I can love you too, even though I have others to love?" I'm testing you when I back out and you're letting me leave. –– I really never wanted my father around. (Elaborates.) I used to get so nervous when he'd be with us. He'd always raise my hopes and then he'd drop them. I wanted him to pick me up. ––

*Cry*

A: What are your associations to the bathroom in the dream?

P: I'm thinking of the two houses that we used to stay in up there.

This was one of the bathrooms. But it was so dirty in the dream. (Elaborates.) As a matter of fact it was an outhouse in the dream. (There was a loud knocking on the door and the analyst had to get up for about a minute to attend to it.) ————

A: What were your feelings about the interruption?

P: I felt something! I give up. I just got you interested and then always there's something else. ——

A: What are your associations to the outhouse?

P: There was only one up there. Oh! . . . . I've been in a few! It nauseates me to see all of that stuff in there. I used to go to the farm with my grandmother, and there was an outhouse in the back. It was like a girl's camp in the dream and it was in the woods and I was eating a salad. I didn't mind at first but then someone came and I felt as if I should mind and I wanted to get out. When my mother and my sisters and I were up there by ourselves everything was all right and there was nothing that was so dirty. But then my father would come up. Somehow that dream seems as if it was a long time ago, and I think there was something in it about school and some rooms with no doors and I couldn't get out.

A: The dream came to your mind in connection with your thoughts about me and sharing me with other patients and with Mrs. West, and your thoughts about keeping your defenses up here. I wonder whether the bathroom and the outhouse in the dream doesn't represent what you feel are your "dirty" thoughts and your fears to let them out here.

P: I wish you'd tell me that my thoughts aren't dirty. I'm tired of feeling that they are. I want to scream that I'm *not* dirty and that I don't care what you say. It's just like when I cuss when I'm around Tom. He dies when I do it. He feels that it is horrible and bad and it bothers him. He's so fragile. I have to smear my dirtiness all over.

A: I'm not the one who thinks of your thoughts as dirty. You do.

P: I can't see that. Everyone thinks this! My friends, my parents, my husband. They think it any time that I say anything that is the least bit off-color.

A: So one of your uncertainties here is the question, will I react here as these other people do? Am I fragile, or am I strong enough to take it?

P: I used to think that Jean was strong, and she's been in therapy and so she knows these things. Once I told her that I'd had some sexual feelings for my child and she acted shocked. ————

A: I wonder if you're waiting now to see if I'll react to this?

**P:** I'm sitting here and thinking how can I test you, what can I say? I wonder if *I* can accept these things even if I'm convinced that you can. – – – What will happen when I break through this fear of trusting you? That's the part that I dread.

**A:** What's the detail of the dread?

**P:** Then is when it really starts. All this other isn't looking into myself and it's not the horrible part. I can handle all this. I feel so alone and I wish someone here would say, "Yes, I've had these thoughts too." I hate all my old friends now and I feel as if they wouldn't understand me. We are not alike any more. – – –

**A:** You want someone to say that they've had these thoughts too. What comes to your mind about that?

**P:** Then I wouldn't feel as if I'm the only person in the world to do or think or feel this. I know about analysis, but I don't believe it. I really think I shouldn't say these things, and I should forget them. I feel as if I'm different from the gang and I'm going to be ostracized. It's so much easier to conform and to have friends, and I'm afraid that I'm not going to have any after I'm through. (Elaborates.) My friends wouldn't understand me now. They're all like I am.

**A:** So the main issue is a matter of trust here. You are trying not to express your feelings here and you're doing it with Tom instead, and I think you are using this as a way of postponing the analysis.

**P:** I know that if I once start, I can't stop.

**A:** Like the school without doors in the dream where you thought you couldn't get out.

**P:** If I ever do this I have to be so sure. – – – It also means that I'll attach myself to you and you will have to take the attachment whether you like it or not. But I've never done this before with anybody. – – – – –

**A:** We'll stop here for today.

## Discussion

The patient begins the session with a direct allusion to her anxiety about analysis and the developing transference, but then immediately describes the displacement of this conflict into the relationship with her husband. My wish is to interfere with this tendency toward displacement, and to focus the conflict more consciously and directly into the analysis and the transference situation. Therefore, I choose directly to interpret the displacement, which the patient subsequently confirms by indicating her fear of having such feeling toward me and her statement that the analysis is ruining her marriage. She further confirms it indirectly by expressing the recent jealousy of her friend. Although my immediate inference is that this could also be emanating from the transference, it would have by-passed the patient's material and participation for me to have interpreted directly at that point that the feelings about Jean are also connected with analysis. Therefore, I choose instead to explore further her specific associations to the friend. In this way the patient becomes more a part of the analytic process, and she is further educated in regard to the necessity for her own associations.

In previous sessions the patient's material has indicated that she transfers to me many of the feelings and conflicts she experienced with her previous therapist. I therefore understand her material regarding her friend and herself in treatment with the same therapist as a repetition in the current transference situation of this previous conflict. My interpretation of the displacement of jealousy regarding my other patients can thus be based on the patient's specific material. The interpretation is confirmed by the previously omitted associations relating to Mrs. West from the time immediately after the last session, and the associations at that time to her friend, which formed the day residue for the dream that night.

Following this transference material about the rivalry with the other patients, I want again to call her attention to the displacements, and therefore I repeat in a somewhat different form the interpretation of her displacement of conflict to her relationship with the husband. She follows with another dream and then to the oedipal association of sharing her father sexually with mother and sisters. My thought about this is that although she is crying, it is still largely intellectualized insight resulting from her previous therapy and intended either as a gift to me of something that she thinks I would like to hear, or else as an attempt to test me to see whether I will fall into the same traps as her previous therapist. However, in the midst of this material she spontaneously refers to me and the analytic situation and her further testing of me. But I feel that to refer to the transference again right now might be seen by her as a seductive overture, and I therefore listen to the material quietly without comment.

I then choose to focus on an element in the manifest dream content but before she can explore it, the interruption occurs. Since she does not mention it herself, I ask about it in order to indicate the analytic expectation that she will have reactions to such incidents. Her response is a transference repetition of the experiences with her father which she had described a few moments previously. But when she does not pursue it further, I feel we have gone as far as we can with it for now, and so I return to the dream element of the outhouse, and her subsequent associations show it to be a condensation of a good deal of other material. It also illustrates how at times a patient will fill in or elaborate upon fantasy or dream material that was previously omitted. My interpretive use of the outhouse element in the dream is an attempt to focus the material again at the patient's current conscious conflict about analysis and the analytic situation, and to tie the dream to the material at the end of last week regarding her own frightening thoughts and associations. The subsequent material confirms the effectiveness of this approach by bringing out previously unverbalized hesitation and reluctance about trusting me with her thoughts and the transference expectation of my negative reactions to them. This bit of analytic work is again focused at the level of further establishing a stable therapeutic alliance, and it brings out more clearly the distinction between her intellectual understanding of analysis and the analytic process, as compared with her continuing emotional hesitation and conflict around the issues of basic therapeutic trust.

A minor technical point is illustrated in my confrontation about her doubts whether I will accept her thoughts as she has them. By using the word "fragile" I am putting the transference response into her own idiom, since she has just previously used the word in reference to her husband.

My final intervention about the school with no exit is based on the common symbolic expression for analysis (where one learns new things about oneself) as a school.

---

## SESSION 15

P: I had a dream which was completely wild. There were so many parts to it. I can't put it all together, but it was all about my past life. I started in a department store with my parents and then I was with my mother and we left. We were in an elevator and there were a lot of people around and I was very little. Then all of a sudden we were on a rollercoaster and we were going all around and suddenly I felt it fly off and I was terribly scared but it landed all right. Then I was in Maine and I was with the darling boy that I went with. He's very big and good-looking and we were walking through the woods in the dark and he went ahead of me after my sister. Then I went through the dark to the light and I was very afraid but I finally got there. Then I was in that boy's home and everyone in my life was there. I also remember Tom's mother was there and I was doing so many things. I was with the boy and yet I was also with his parents and I was comfortable knowing that he was there but nothing was going to happen between us. And then I went upstairs to the bathroom and there was a bossy girl there who was ordering everybody around and no one would defy her. I went to the bathroom in the bathtub and all over her stockings. Oh! I suddenly remember that it was a friend of mine who used to order me around. Then I walked out and the girl was stunned because I wouldn't do anything that she told me to. All this time my daughter Sally was there. – – – I wonder why I dreamed about that boy? He was the only one in my life to give me the royal shaft. – –

**A:** What was the detail of that?

**P:** It was during my freshman year at college. I'd known him for about a year. (Elaborates.) He was darling, but then one day he suddenly said, "I don't love you any more." From then on I lost weight and I got to looking good again and I got myself another one.

**A:** What were the feelings?

**P:** I was miserable. I had all kinds of skin trouble and my face broke out. (Elaborates.) I'd cry and I'd eat a lot when I was with him. I looked much better after I broke up. I didn't even cry or react then! That's what I've done with you. I'm not going to let myself go in case you should give me the shaft. That would hurt terribly. I get ready to let myself go and then I feel that I'm in a turmoil and it's like I'm flying around. I try to make a decision that I *can* trust you but if I don't let myself go ever, I won't be hurt. It's like coming from the elevator through the dark into the light. (Elaborates.) In the dream I wasn't terribly frightened. I was afraid but I knew that nothing terrible would happen.

**A:** I wonder if on one level the dream may represent the analysis and the feeling that it was like the story of your whole life. In the dream you were going through the dark and towards the light which I think is also the analysis. And even though you were scared you finally got there.

**P:** I woke up in a very good mood this morning. (Elaborates.) That's really quite unusual for me. I had a wish to go to Tom and put my arms around him but then I had to fight against it. But then I decided that I didn't want to do that and I didn't and thought, "He's my husband." – – I had such a funny feeling in my mouth as I said that.

**A:** Try to describe it.

**P:** It was as if I had something in my mouth and I was going to chew or something. I used to lie in bed like this when I was young and my body would get all tense and I'd have that same feeling in my mouth. It was as if it was something great big. – – –

**A:** What are your associations to the specific dream details?

**P:** There were a lot of fine details. I went to the place which was light and it was the backyard. There's a well into the basement. I'm thinking about the bathroom at the girl's house, and that it played a huge part in my life. I'm thinking of Mrs. Jones and how I used to depend on her. – – Tom's mother was in the dream and she was playing golf. There was a girl with her, I'm not sure who she was although she had hair like mine. Someone said, "That girl will do anything but really she hates her." This is like when we go on vacation now to Hot Springs. I hate it, because all we do is sit around and watch the big deals, the fathers and their sons! I want no part of it. It's a slot that I *have* to fit into. "I'm the wife of their son," and that's the only reason I'm accepted there. I've been pushed around all of my life and I've had to hide my *real* feelings but no more! I want to be *me*. That's no way to live! I finally got the nerve to walk out on that girl and no one else had ever done this.

**A:** What are your associations to the fact that you haven't given me the name of this boy and this girl?

**P:** I know their names.

**A:** Yes, but you haven't mentioned them here.

**P:** – – It's so you won't know. The boy doesn't make any difference, and the girl was so involved that I would rather not go into it.

**A:** I think you are trying to keep things vague and to avoid your specific feelings, and your sense of involvement in them by not giving people's names here.

**P:** I didn't feel anything. I didn't feel anything through the whole dream. It bothers me that I don't really *feel* anything toward you. I know that I'm keeping myself from feeling anything. – – – – – – – –

**A:** What are your associations to the fact that your thoughts stopped when you said you are keeping yourself from feeling anything?

**P:** – I always cry here! I'm so tired of it! It's the only way I can feel! All I can do is just cry! – – All of my life I've been so emotional! (Elaborates.) And now suddenly I can't feel anything.

**A:** Because you still expect to get the royal shaft here.

**P:** – – Bill Sweeny was the boy's name and that was really a turning point in my life. He was the last boy I ever fell for before Tom. That was the way that I decided I'd live the rest of my life. I could really go to it before. I'd throw myself into all kinds of hostility and jealousy and feelings and suddenly it all stopped. I'd confide so easily. -- This is so hard because you *are* a man. I'd never confide in men. I think of a girl's life and how I really want a man as a buddy or to be a brother. I'd never do it because men are men and you can't confide in them or become buddy-buddy with them. And yet I have to stop because my feelings of jealousy stand in the way between any woman and myself. She'll always grind me down. It was that way with Mrs. West. We'd talk and I'd get a sudden feeling of jealousy and I'd be afraid that she would use what I'd say as a weapon against me. Men will never do this to you. ---

**A:** What are your associations to the stockings in the dream?

**P:** Uhm! -- I don't know. They were hanging in the tub. There was a girl who was very much like my sister who was waiting hand and foot on a bossy girl. I got one of the stockings but the other one fell into the tub and then I went to the bathroom on it, and I was vicious. Then I didn't want to hurt her, so I picked it up and washed it out and gave it back to her. I wonder. . . . . I think the stocking may be a symbol of a man's penis. I don't understand it.

**A:** Rather than jump to conclusions about symbols, let's look and see what your own associations are.

**P:** I'm thinking of tying it around someone's neck. --

**A:** What's the detail?

**P:** I read about it as a strangling weapon. I was trying to hide my feelings there of hating her and trying to turn it into something nice. Now everything centers on the girl who came in. I think it was my sister. --

**A:** What comes to your mind?

*Cry*   **P:** --- I was so jealous of her. I felt that she was so favored by my mother and even by my friends. And yet she felt so sorry for me! She's so meek and harmless. I feel so sorry for her now because her life is ruined. Why would I want to hurt her? Except that I used to be so *jealous* of her.

**A:** What did you mean when you said her life is ruined?

**P:** She has the same problem that I had, but she has no chance. (Elaborates sister's symptoms.) It's just the same as with me but I feel that I have Tom and the children. Carol's husband even looks like my father but I think that he's a real homosexual and that their marriage has had it. If she ever gets help she'll be on her own by herself. I feel so sorry for her. I wonder if I'm doing the right thing. Will I just go on by myself when I'm through with this? Or will I always depend on someone? How am I ever going to find out? – – Sometimes I wonder if I should kill myself or not? Do I have any kind of a chance for living? I *don't* want to kill myself!

*Cry*

A: You feel sorry for your sister, and you feel that she can't get any help and her life is ruined. What is the detail of your thoughts?

P: She's turned to religion and she wants me to do the same. (Elaborates.) I went through that myself, and I know that it's not the true answer for this. She's going through the exact same thing that I am but she's taking religion and I'm taking analysis. (Elaborates.) I know that analysis is the only answer for me, but I still wonder. If Carol ever had treatment I know that she couldn't live with the husband that she has. (Elaborates.)

A: We'll stop here for today.

### DISCUSSION

The progressive establishment of an analytic situation is indicated by the spontaneous detail and richness of her dream. But it is also my hunch that this elaborate dream is an attempt to please me and to provide me with the kind of data that she thinks I want to hear. This is a significant resistance but it would be inappropriate to interpret it at this time. To do so would indicate that I am being critical and judgmental of her spontaneous associations, and thus it would interfere with her progress in speaking freely. It would also mean to her that I am turning down the "gift" she is offering me. The patient herself associates me with the boy in the dream and thus brings up again the major current conflict over whether or not to trust me. In the manifest dream there were a number of frightening situations which she survived without harm, and in hopes of fostering her confidence in me, my initial intervention in connection with the dream is made at this level.

The patient's experience of the sensation in her mouth when describing her reactions with her husband, which by association was similar to a recurrent symptomatic experience from childhood, is an indication that significant regression in the analytic situation is taking place, and that a transference neurosis is beginning. At a descriptive level, this experience is probably related to the Isakower phenomenon and as such, it probably reflects elements of a maternal transference, with increasing trust as indicated in the manifest dream. However, at this point in the analysis, such a "deep" understanding and formulation would be inappropriate for the patient and would lead towards intellectualization and away from the significant current issues. But I want again to emphasize to her the importance of this type of sensation or experience in analysis, and this is the reason for my request to describe it in greater detail.

Subsequently, I return to the specific associations to the dream, since I do not wish to imply that my previous superficial and generalized comment about the dream is the only level at which we should be interested. However, this dream is so involved and complex that at this point, without a clearly established transference neurosis as the guide for dream interpretation, I choose instead to focus on some of the specific manifestations of her resistance. The specific and consciously minor resistance regarding people's names is not uncommon at this stage of an analysis. It may have a variety of specific meanings for the patient so that although the analyst has no particular interest in the identity of the other person per se, the tactical aim is to deal with the resistance it represents. In a patient's spontaneous thoughts, people are usually remembered initially by their names. The use of terms such as "that girl" or "the boy" represent a form of editing and change in the association as it occurred. My interpretation of her defensive wish to avoid these specific issues and feelings leads directly to the problem of her continuing reluctance and anxiety concerning an affective involvement in the analytic situation. This in turn permits my interpretation of one of the sources of her anxiety about the analysis, and I deliberately phrase it to use the expression "the royal shaft" which she had used earlier in the session. As a result of this, she is able to elaborate on the importance of the relationship with this boy, and indirectly to express the fact that at that moment she is transferring an expectation to me based on her experience with him.

My subsequent question regarding the stockings in the dream is an attempt to demonstrate to her that all the manifest dream elements are significant and worthy of specific associations. Her filling in of the manifest dream that "I went to the bathroom on it" is an expression of an anal sadistic drive, but it is still too early in the analysis to pick up on this. The same is true with regard to my discouraging her symbolic interpretation of the stocking as a penis, which permits her associations to go in a direction which she did not expect.

At the end of the session, the patient again returns to her concerns about analysis, but as represented in the dream, there is a perceptibly greater sense of confidence illustrated by her statement, "I know that analysis is the only answer for me, but I still wonder."

## SESSION 16

**P:** – – – I feel absolutely nothing. (Elaborates.) I'm not happy or angry at home. – – – – – – – – – –

**A:** What comes to your mind about the silence?

*Cry*

**P:** – Jean called me. She's marrying a social worker at Veteran's Hospital and she's not sure of it, but she may be moving. It set me in a panic because I'm really dependent on Jean.

**A:** What's the detail?

**P:** We've always been good friends and very close and I stood by her through her divorce and we both went to Harris for a while. We used to call each other "the only person I can talk to." I can't even talk to Tom about some things and she was always a mother-image for me.

**A:** I wonder if you're worried that if she leaves this will intensify your feelings about me because she won't be around any more to dilute it. As a result, you have a sense of panic and so you are blocking off every feeling because of your fear of relating to me.

**P:** – – It's like a dream that I had last night. I felt completely alone in the midst of a terrible disaster. In the dream I was at home with my two children and there were millions of tornadoes all around. I grabbed the children and we rushed to the basement, and I tried to get under something to protect us and Tom was at the office. Then an older woman came in. I've always had fears of tornadoes. (Elaborates.) The basement in the dream was a combination from the one we have now and from the one in the house where I grew up. It was like the dream of the world burning up or coming to an end. But this time I was all by myself and I had to protect my children because no one else was there. – – –

**A:** What are your thoughts about tornadoes?

**P:** I've been afraid of them ever since I was a girl. I saw a painting of one once as a girl and of how it hit. There was a mother leaning over her children and the clothes were being ripped off her back, and I know it impressed me. – – –

**A:** You were trying to get under something in the basement. What comes to your mind?

**P:** That was in case the house came down, so it wouldn't come down on us. – – I want to run back to Harris because he knows me. I feel as if I'm being forced to stand up alone by myself. No one in the world is going to give me what I want and I have to accept the fact. – – – – (Laughs.) –

**A:** What was the laughter?

**P:** I heard a noise and I feel as though I'm falling off the couch. I had a sensation of rocking.

**A:** The dream came to your mind in connection with the idea of intensifying your feelings about me. In the dream there is a lot of violence from the tornadoes and in the painting of the woman with the two children, her clothes were torn off. I think this represents you with your clothes off. You've described before how Tom gets excited and wild when you get undressed, but he wasn't in the dream. I wonder if you have a fantasy of getting undressed here, and if you have both a wish and a fear of exciting me sexually.

**P:** I have thought about that.

**A:** What was the detail?

**P:** I've thought that I wanted to stand up and take all of my clothes off but that is as far as I can think. – –

**A:** Do you mean, "can think," or do you mean, "let yourself think?"

**P:** Let myself. I'm embarrassed thinking about that. Why would I think of it? It's silly. In January I went to see my O.B. man and I know that I was sexually attracted. It was the first time that I ever allowed myself to have sexual feelings in the examining room. I hoped that he would, and I immediately ate when I got home and I wouldn't stop eating for a week, I was so shocked at myself. – – I've been thinking about being madly in love with you and it makes me excited to come every day and I feel just like a schoolgirl with a boy-friend. So I immediately say it's all silly, because I don't want to get into it, it's stupid. – – – – All of my life I've hidden my feelings of love and attraction for boys and it's the same way with you. I'd die of embarrassment if you knew. – – –

**A:** What's the detail of the feeling?

**P:** Why wouldn't you accept it? I want to have feelings and have it *not* happen. But I'm afraid that you're not strong enough to resist. I feel as if you'll think, "This idiot."

**A:** What's the detail?

**P:** It's like I'd be bothering you and that I'm not capable of getting either love or sexual feelings from you. I'd be like a love-sick little girl pestering you and it shouldn't happen.

**A:** So you feel that it would be upsetting either way, whether you get a response or whether you don't get a response, and so you are choosing to block everything.

**P:** It would be frightening if I get a response and humiliating if I wouldn't. – – – I used to dress very carefully when I'd go for my sessions with Harris. I've made a point of *not* doing it with you.

A: What comes to your mind?

P: No matter what I'd look like, your reaction would always be the same. – – – When my parents used to visit after I got married I would parade around in front of my father in nightgowns or a slip. I was conscious of wanting to attract him. (Elaborates.) It was like I was suddenly saying, "I'm a woman, Daddy, look at me and realize it." – – It never fazed him. He'd come into the room when I had the cramps and he'd talk to me and I used to feel that he was sexually attracted to me. Now I don't feel that he ever was. Somehow this makes me feel good. – – – – – How can I *really feel* sexual feeling for you and still remain a wife to my husband? I can't possibly handle both. – – –

A: What comes to your mind?

P: I can imagine myself absolutely an idiot in love with you and wanting everything and being completely involved in it. How can I go home and love my husband and be sexually responsive? I'd feel guilty, as if I was having an affair. – – – – – –

A: Your associations stopped suddenly and now there is silence. It's as if you don't want to go into something. What comes to your mind about not wanting to go further?

P: This is such a comical situation. The idea of having an affair! It's all so one-sided. It's not funny at all. But that's what I wanted. That was the way I felt before I saw Harris. It was all very exciting and yet I felt guilty. (Elaborates.) – – –

A: What comes to mind as to why you wanted to hold that back?

P: – – I can picture it really happening and that I'm not only thinking about it. – – –

A: We'll stop here for today.

### DISCUSSION

My interpretation of her continuing defenses against the emerging transference relationship represents a tacit encouragement to her to decrease the intensity of her defensive maneuvers, and it also indirectly indicates my feeling of comfort in the situation and my confidence in my own ability to deal with it. The patient's response, "It's like a dream that I had last night," indicates that the subsequent dream is associated to the transference relationship with me, which I have just interpreted. The dream element of the basement is another remote derivative of the traumatic sexual experience which will emerge later in the analysis, and could not be recognized as such at this time.

I continue to ask for her associations to several dream elements, and these are followed by her current sensations of rocking and of falling off the couch. The occurrence of these sensations in the analytic situation suggests that she is having an immediate transference experience. However, my interpretation of the dream and of its sexual transference implications may have been premature. It by-passes some of the patient's participation and personal associations, and even though it is related to her feeling as if she were falling off the couch and rocking, it would have been preferable to get her to expand on these experiences before making such an interpretation.

Although the patient's subsequent material, particularly that relating to the obstetrician, confirms the correctness of the content of the interpretation, such short cuts, if frequently repeated, would tend to interfere with her own developing ability to associate freely. On the other hand, my direct transference interpretation has the effect of "calling a spade a spade," and it helps her more openly express some of her consciously withheld awareness of sexual fantasy.

Eventually her associations lead to adult oedipal feelings toward the father which had apparently been conscious at the time. The assessment of such conscious direct sexual fantasy and acting-out in regard to the father is difficult. It may represent a significant ego defect with a failure of the usually occurring and anticipated drive controls and defenses. But it may also represent a characteristic family pattern of interaction, in which sexuality is freely bandied about with overtly seductive action and counterreaction. Or it could be that she is again trying to give me material that she thinks I want to hear as a gift and in a counterphobic fashion. In any event, the fact that such adult fantasies and behavior have already been conscious in regard to the father is probably one factor that kept her from reacting to my interpretation with anxiety or further defenses. And it is one of the factors which has permitted her to have a sexualized transference development occur this early in the analysis. It must also be kept in mind that the initial sexual interpretation may have been influenced by countertransference seductiveness, and the patient's response that she now feels the father was probably *not* truly seductive suggests that she is erecting a new line of defense against such a possibility.

## SESSION 17

**P:** – – – – – – I've had a horrible feeling that I was going to pop ever since I was here yesterday. (Elaborates.) It's been ferocious. I had a dream and I was in a panic but I don't remember it. – –

**A:** What was the detail of the feeling itself?

**P:** It was the same feeling of anxiety as if the whole world was going to crash in on me. I can't think at all and I will not let myself know anything.

**A:** You seem to be afraid of feeling anything, and of not thinking but just letting yourself feel.

**P:** I was trying to relax and was lying in the sun and my thoughts were wandering and I had a sudden sense of panic. I can hardly remember now but I caught myself plotting to destroy you. I was terribly afraid of the thoughts to follow. – –

**A:** What was the detail of the plot to destroy me?

**P:** I don't remember. – – – It's like that dream, I just don't recall. I was frustrated with my child and I had the thought that she should be dead, and I started to cry and she wouldn't go to sleep and I felt as though I would like to kill her. – – How mean you are to me. I thought about the things I would say to you but I don't remember. – – I'm thinking about yesterday and my dream. You said that I wanted to undress in front of you. That's a horrible thing to say! – – – – If I let myself go and start feeling, I just can't stand it! This way I can.

**A:** How do you mean that you can't stand it?

**P:** I can't function; I can't take care of my children, my home or anything. I'm so hostile at home and I hate it. So I'm not going to show anything. That's the only way I can survive. I've never been this way! I'm suddenly so afraid of my anger toward my children. I feel as if I'll die.

**A:** You've been having all of these feelings and fears at home. What are your associations to the feelings that you have there and the lack of feeling that you are having here in the analysis?

**P:** It's all going toward my husband and my children. The emotion should be directed toward you. I have so many feelings for you. But the only way to survive is not to feel it.

**A:** What's the detail of your thought that you wouldn't survive if you felt what you know you already feel here?

**P:** I don't know. – – You put out no feeling at all, so how can I? – – –

Sometimes I feel like . . . . . my emotions come up and I have such a fright and I just want to hold on to you and know that you're there. They overpower me and they kill me. – – – – – – – – – –

A: What are your associations to the silence?

P: – – I just don't want to talk.

A: Well, what comes to your mind?

*Cry*

P: – – You're trying to destroy me. You want to bring out feelings and you don't want to help, but you are just going to sit and watch me suffer and I'm not going to!

A: What comes to your mind about me sitting here and watching you and not helping at all?

P: I'm so frightened! I'm really frightened! I feel like a child screaming in the dark and my parents won't come. With a child you can sit and reason with it. But I can't. I know there are no boogy men or ghosts or witches, but I just can't do it.

A: You have the feeling that I'll try to destroy you. What comes to your mind about that?

P: I'm thinking about my own needs and how you're not going to satisfy them but you'll see them and you won't help me. You enjoy seeing me frightened. Why don't you ever say, "I'm sorry, I understand, I'll try to help, and there's no reason for your fear?"

A: And what would it mean to you if I did say all of that?

P: I'd collapse. I just don't know. It's like there is something wrong with me for being afraid. You think I have no reason for fear, but I am afraid and so there is something wrong. I'm thinking about the time when I was very little and I hallucinated. (Elaborates.) My mother wouldn't come. I thought that things were trying to destroy me. She finally came at the end. I was never so scared! And they knew it! – – –

A: You have the thought that I'd feel there is something wrong with you if you're afraid. What are your associations?

*Cry*

P: – – – – You don't accept my fear because you're afraid yourself. You ignore it or you'll get mad at it but you won't understand. – –

A: What's the detail of the idea that I'm afraid?

P: – – It's like . . . . . if I feel hostility it scares me and you know. It's all so horrible I just can't think.

A: If you can convince yourself that I'm afraid, then in a way you would be justified in trying to control your own feelings. I think you're using this as an excuse and as a defense against your own feelings.

*Cry*

P: – – – – – – (Sigh.) – – If I just knew what I was going to do.

A: What's the fantasy?

**P:** There is none. I picture myself lying here with my arms and legs flaying around and screaming and doing it for the rest of my life. – – – – Whenever I have this anxiety feeling, I am afraid of the physical movements and motions. I think I'd run out on the street and scream and tear my hair and I'd act like an idiot. – –

**A:** See if you can develop that fantasy further.

**P:** – – I can't stand it! – – –                                    *Cry*

**A:** We'll stop here for today.

### D ISCUSSION

Throughout this session, the patient is responding to the premature transference interpretation that I made yesterday. It has mobilized too much anxiety to be optimal, and with it there has been an intensification of the displacements away from the analysis and toward her family, as well as the use of hostility and aggression as her defense against love and sexual arousal. But this increase in her anxiety and conflict does suggest that the overtly sexual seductiveness toward the father which was brought up yesterday was probably counterphobic in nature, and that intrapsychic conflict concerning these issues does exist.

However, I also have the feeling from observing her that the patient is being somewhat dramatic in her expressions and behavior, and I feel it important not to back away from the interpretation of her anxieties and defenses against affects and drives in the analysis. To have avoided these issues, or to have indicated my awareness that the interpretation yesterday was premature, or to have actively attempted to reassure her would possibly have interfered with the developing transference situation and therapeutic alliance. She might have experienced such tactics as a sign of weakness or anxiety in me. This would have further mobilized her anxiety.

Instead, I choose to maintain an analytically neutral position with the intention of demonstrating to her that the degree of her anxiety does not worry me, and that I am confident that both of us can tolerate it. Her association that I, too, am afraid is a projection and a transference response relating to parental attitudes and expectations regarding her affects and drives. However, I choose to use it in the service of the therapeutic alliance and the working through of her anxiety and defenses against the emerging transference.

During and after the session it is necessary for me to do some self-analysis in an attempt to understand the countertransference forces which had led to the premature interpretation yesterday.

# 2

## THE SECOND MONTH

### (Summary)

In the first session of this month the patient continued in her efforts to test me in the analytic situation, and continued to verbalize her anxiety that I would eventually respond to her in some physical or sexual way. She presented a directly oedipal sexual dream, which I felt represented a resistance against verbalizing the more immediate issues of her anxiety about me and the start of her analysis. I directed her attention to these more immediate conflicts, which led to a concern about my being like her previous therapist. Subsequently she associated to the Jones family and the way in which they had been a great help to her throughout her childhood and adolescence, and had in some ways represented an ideal family as contrasted with her own. This dependency upon Mrs. Jones had continued until about three years ago, at which time Mrs. Jones had rather abruptly and unexpectedly terminated the relationship. The patient has had a mixed feeling of disappointment and relief at this, but it contributed to her suspicion that "no one is really dependable."

The implications of this for the analytic situation were obvious to me, but I chose not to confront her with their transference meanings at this time. Most of my interventions during this session were requests for detail, or interpretations of her reluctance to discuss and describe her feelings in regard to the breakup with the Jones family. Toward the end of the session she returned to the issues of her father and his ignoring of her, and her feeling of resentment at being left out of his life.

In the next session the patient presented a dream, the associations to which led to her feeling disappointed that she had to pay for her analysis on a private basis, with the implication that this shows that she and I are involved only in a doctor-patient relationship and that this is not a personal situation. She also elaborated upon her anxiety about revealing her thoughts and feelings, with a fantasy of having a bomb inside of her which would ultimately explode. My interventions were focused at her resistances against revealing what was already conscious in her mind, and ultimately she was able to talk for the first time about her experiences with masturbation as a girl and adolescent. This was accompanied by considerable shame and distress, but when I did not respond with the expected criticism or laughter, she was able to continue to describe the masturbatory behavior with less anxiety.

In the next hour the patient indicated that she had had an upsurge of anxiety and other symptoms since the previous session, but subsequently she was able to get back to the material about the masturbation and her expectations that I would laugh at her for this. After she had left the previous session, she had experienced a sense of conscious relief and acceptance about a topic which she had never before discussed with anyone, but subsequently she had become frightened by her temptation to trust me, since I had "passed the test" in regard to this material and she wanted to confide in me further. Paradoxically, this had mobilized an increase in her anxiety at the thought of trusting me, since she anticipated that I would ultimately disappoint or reject her because she confided in me, as had occurred with a number of other people in her life in the past.

She then went on to talk about having eaten a lunch consisting of carrots, pickles, and bananas, and that she and her husband had intellectually recognized the phallic symbolism involved, but this in turn led to a more affective expression of a wish "to take every man's thing and chew it up and swallow it!! I'd like to leave them all running around just like women!" This was associated to memories of her parents running around the house naked and permitting the children to observe their genitals, but at the same time the parents were embarrassed at words such as "penis," and attempted to approach the whole issue of sexuality from a "scientific" point of view. She was able to associate somewhat more freely, and there were spontaneous oscillations between past and present thoughts and experiences, and the analytic situation was progressing. I did not make any significant interpretations about the content or latent meanings of her communications, but instead maintained a focus on the individual resistances, and in so doing I was tacitly encouraging her to permit her associations to emerge more freely.

In the fourth session of the month the patient presented a dream which indicated a growing sense of confidence in me and in my ability to control myself and the analytic situation between us. There was also an appreciable improvement in her ability to associate more freely and the material led to her thoughts about sexuality in the form of rape, and also her pleasure at the thought of semen being put into her during intercourse. In connection with the semen she said, "The fact of the orgasm means that it's somehow not all cruel. Even when you are raping somebody this happens." This material is mentioned now because later in the analysis it again emerges as something highly significant, but at this particular moment its importance and relevance to a key traumatic event could not be known by me.

She went on to discuss her dependency on her mother and on other women, and from there to the idea of herself as dirty, which then led back to her sense of guilt and anticipation of rejection because of her sexuality. This in turn led to recollection of sexual experience with a boy in high school who later talked about her to his classmates.

My entire activity in this session involved repeatedly asking for the details of the material which she had presented in a condensed form, and of interpreting her anxiety about permitting her thoughts to flow freely, or confronting her with the fact that from time to time she was withholding conscious associations. In other words, my therapeutic task at this time is to help develop her ability to associate more freely and to help firmly establish the analytic situation between us. The neutrality of my comments and requests for further detail without critical or judgmental response demonstrated my continued analytic interest in her and in the material she was presenting. This, in turn, had the desired effect of permitting her to feel somewhat more comfortable, although there was considerable experience of affect when describing herself as dirty in connection with her sexuality.

In the fifth session the patient indicated her fear that I would turn against her for what she was telling me about herself, and she again expressed her guilt and shame for the adolescent sexual activity she had described previously. She was increasingly aware of a wish to unburden herself and confide in me, while at the same time she had an anticipation of rejection, criticism, or withdrawal if she did, equating this with the behavior of her parents during adolescence. With great affect this led to her recognition that much of the sexual acting-out, the drinking, and the other negativistic behavior in adolescence had been an attempt to seek love and attention from her parents, but they did not recognize the message and instead withdrew from her or else expressed their critical feelings toward her. Increasingly she recognized that she might have gotten some constructive and helpful attention from her father if she had asked him for it, but that she had never voluntarily or clearly done so. She also recalled the family difficulties during that phase of her life, and this led to an intense awareness of her anger at both parents, particularly at the mother.

The patient experienced a conversion reaction during the session, in which both hands were curled into a claw-shaped position, and from this she was able to express feelings within herself as if she were an animal about to strike and claw its victim. This led to her expression of rage at the parents, accompanied by a developing transference feeling that "I want to jump up and sink my teeth into your neck right now." She described herself as "a Jekyll and Hyde," and that she can at times feel like a vicious monster with fantasies of killing her mother with a knife. This was accompanied by a similar feeling toward me in which "I picture myself using this weapon on you and it would be one way to get something out of you."

The analysis was progressing very nicely, with the patient associating more freely and expressing her fantasies and impulses in a more direct fashion, and with affect appropriate to the content of the material she was describing. There was evidence that she was beginning to undergo a regression in the therapeutic situation in which she experienced some of the same fantasies and feelings toward me, and in which there was an oscillation between past and current experience, and an increasing willingness to express this material without the hesitation and the expectation of rejection that had occurred previously.

In the next session, after presenting a rather complex series of dreams, the patient referred back to the previous fantasy of attacking me and described how this had troubled and frightened her. However, she went on to say, "If you don't get frightened, then I have no reason to be frightened," which represents an important factor in the establishment of the analytic situation. The analyst's response to the patient's fantasies will frequently determine whether or not the patient is able to pursue further her anxiety-producing thoughts and feelings, or whether she will have to maintain her defenses against them. If the analyst indicates anxiety or discomfort at such material, or if he immediately attempts to question the patient about it, or confronts her with the reality of the situation between them, or modifies his analytic posture, the message received by the patient will include an awareness of the analyst's anxiety, and of the fact that this material is threatening or dangerous to him. As a result, she will tend to maintain her defenses and will resist the process of regression which analysis requires, in an attempt to please the analyst and obey his nonverbally expressed wishes to avoid such material. On the other hand, if the analyst can accept this material quietly and with confidence, and not experience anxiety or concern about the patient, this permits a form of tacit reassurance for the patient that the exploration of her fantasy life is appropriate here and that the analyst can accept her and her feelings without undue conflict. This in turn helps to promote the identification by the patient with the listening and analyzing function of the analyst, thereby enhancing the therapeutic alliance, and thus encouraging further regression in the analytic situation.

The patient expressed further her anxiety about the growing intensity of feeling toward me, but also verbalized an increasing capacity to trust me with such feelings. In this context she was able to describe her concern about the ambivalence she feels toward me, and then had the recovery of a memory of the house where she lived prior to age three. This led to recollections of how close she had been to her father prior to the birth of her younger sister, and to sexual fantasies about Negro men and her preoccupation with the penis. She described her fascination about this organ and began to recall some of the times she had seen her father's penis, at the same time comparing this material with her own daughter's fascination with the husband's penis.

In the seventh session there was further development of the transference relationship towards me as the mother of whom she was always afraid, and whose tickling the patient experienced as hostility on the mother's part. This oscillated with feelings towards me as the father, with a number of oedipal derivatives expressed finally in the wish to have me respond to her as a man, and with resentment that I don't and that I maintain control over the situation between us. Throughout this session there were a number of silences occurring immediately after she would bring up the transference material, and my main interventions involved the interpretation of her anxiety about the material that was occurring to her and her reluctance to express it here freely.

In the next session the patient demonstrated a further development of the transference to me as the father, displaced to her perceptions of all men. She sees them either as very strong, powerful, and so far above her that she is like a child in relationship to them, or else as weak little boys who are searching for a mother, and placing on her the responsibility of taking care of them. She was increasingly able to express this directly toward me, while at the same time voicing her anxiety about either alternative. Throughout the session there were repeated resistances to the experience and verbalization of this material, and these I interpreted in the context of her anxiety about the further development of the analytic situation and about expressing such feelings openly, as well as her fear of whether or not I would be able to tolerate them and whether she can trust me in this situation.

In the following session she again returned to the theme of her anxiety about the growing transference and the fact that she is increasingly aware of strong feelings of caring for me and wanting me to admire and approve of her, and at the same time a fear that if she expresses her feelings fully she will feel humiliated and rejected by me. This led into the issue of herself as a girl and her fantasy that I would prefer her to have been a boy, and that being a woman puts her in an inferior position. She also elaborated upon her continuing fears of the analysis and the analytic situation, and of the needs to continue testing me to see whether or not I can tolerate her feelings without either a seductive response or a rejection of her for having had them.

Once again my interventions were primarily directed at the resistances involving her fear of talking and her projection to me of her feelings of worthlessness. In response to her statement, "I'm *not* going to be what you want!" I pointed out to her that realistically this was what the analysis aimed to help her do, and I interpreted the projection that, "The feeling that I'll mold you to what *I* want comes from within yourself." An intervention such as this was another appeal to the developing therapeutic alliance and an attempt to permit the more healthy and maturing forces within her to see the analysis as an attempt to help her accomplish freedom of choice. The therapeutic alliance was also being fostered by my requests for further detailed information and associations, and by my continuing neutral acceptance of whatever material she produces. Side-by-side as the therapeutic alliance developed further, she was able to permit the increasing regression that is necessary for the development of the transference neurosis. In other words, my activity was designed to help her recognize her feelings as acceptable here, and to accept the "as-if" character of our relationship. In this context, the developing transference feelings toward me could be more readily accepted by her as a necessary part of the analytic process.

In the tenth session she was able again to elaborate on her fear of the developing transference fantasies toward me, involving feelings of love, sexual arousal and attachment, and anxiety that she might totally lose control of herself if she were to express these feelings directly. She was also able to say that she feels disloyal to her husband because of these transference fantasies and reactions toward me, and to see that she equates the analysis with having an affair. But if the analysis is to be successful, it is necessary to deal with the various specific elements of the resistances against the development of the transference, such as this issue of her feeling of disloyalty to her husband, and generalized statements about transference feelings can be only partially effective. As described earlier, a large component in helping the patient overcome such resistances is the analyst's nonverbal behavior of acceptance.

Even though I did not specifically reassure her about the issue of disloyalty, my acceptance of her equation of analysis with an affair permitted her to go on and describe frequent fantasies of having affairs long before she entered analysis. This material then permitted me to point out that the guilt about disloyalty to her husband was not so much related to analysis, but was actually a conflict over feelings that had existed long before starting the analysis. This in turn led to an increasingly regressive transference experience of me as a sexual opportunist and playboy, who would be interested in her only for sexual purposes and who was not really interested in her thoughts and feelings. Although this was clearly a reference to feelings about her father and a perception of me in his role, this connection was not specifically made at this time by me or by the patient. At this early time in the analysis when the patient is first experiencing significant transference feelings and distortions, it is best to permit them to develop more fully and with greater regressive affect before making interpretations of genetic content or meaning. To interpret them prematurely would be to dilute or intellectualize the transference experience and thereby interfere with the development of a fully regressive transference neurosis. The patient at this time in analysis needs the experience of merely verbalizing her feelings and her distortions of perception about the analyst, and needs to become accustomed to doing this, thereby decreasing the level of anxiety about further transference regression.

In the next session the patient again returned to the theme of the growing transference feelings toward me as a father, involving her increasing attachment, love, a sense of understanding and acceptance, and awareness of sexual attraction. However, a number of specific resistances against the developing transference were also manifest and eventually interpreted. She verbalized a fear of some type of overt seduction if she were to "let my guard down" in the analysis, as well as the fantasy that although she knows that in the analysis she is free to experience and express all her feelings fully, and that this is a professional situation, nevertheless other people observing the situation from the outside might think of it as a sexual relationship between a man and woman and would therefore be disapproving. She also verbalized the fear that if she were to learn to express herself fully and freely here, she would do the same outside and would hurt or insult people. This led to her expressing the wish to be able to talk to others about me and her feelings toward me, and this I interpreted as her wish to diffuse the transference and avoid the intensity of her feelings while with me.

Again it must be emphasized how the analyst must be alert to the various specific detailed manifestations of resistance and deal with each of them individually, so that they may be consciously verbalized and thereby available for the self-observing ego to assess in the context of the therapeutic alliance. The assumption is that once verbalized and looked at in the light of the therapeutic alliance and the reality of the treatment situation, the various fantasies will become less anxiety-provoking, and the patient will be able to reduce the intensity of the defenses erected against them.

In the following session the patient again returned to the theme of her multiple defenses against the emerging transference fantasies of love toward me. I was ultimately able to point out to her that consciously she knew such feelings were part of the analysis, but that I also recognized she was still afraid of experiencing them. This permitted her to elaborate on them somewhat further, and we were then able to deal with the specific resistance involved in her failure to differentiate between feeling and action. Reduction of this resistance gradually led to intensified anxiety and affective distress as she verbalized her increasing yearning and desire for me, simultaneously recognizing that such wishes would be frustrated since I would not be responding to her with similar feelings.

As part of this she was able to express resentment that such feelings were being stimulated, and that I was maliciously enjoying her suffering and was deliberately trying to make her miserable by bringing them out. I responded to these transference distortions only by asking questions about the details of the feelings and fantasies, thus allowing a fuller expression of these expectations that I was deliberately trying to hurt and humiliate her. My quiet acceptance of these transference fantasies without critical comment, defensiveness, or interpretation helped to foster the developing analytic situation through indicating by my actions that this material did not surprise or distress me, nor did I feel uncomfortable, and that I was able to accept and tolerate her various distorted feelings toward me in the interest of getting to know better the kinds of thoughts and feelings that she experiences.

In the thirteenth session, after presenting a series of dreams, the patient's associations led to her perception of her father's wish that she had been a boy, and to her own sense of inadequacy and inferiority at not being a boy and at not yet having produced a boy baby. This material led to recollections of having been a tom-boy as a child and in this way appealing to her father, as well as conflicting fantasies about physical contact with him as a girl. There was a variety of memories about vacations when she would be with her father for a longer time and when he and the mother would frequently run around the house without clothing. Apparently there had been some sexual play between the child and her father, and she had recollections of being allowed to stare at the father's penis and, on at least one occasion, to touch it. There was a further elaboration of her conscious recall of having had sexual feelings for her father as a small child, and a reference to primal scene awareness with recognition that at times as a child she had been sexually aroused. Interspersed in this material were occasional references to the growing transference to me as the father, with concern about a possible sexual seduction occurring between us. Intermittently throughout the session the patient would experience anxiety and would cry as she reported some of these distressing memories.

The analytic situation was developing nicely with the patient taking the initiative in associating more freely with accompanying affect, and with a developing freedom of oscillation between past and current relationships and experience. My role was to make a few interventions asking for details of memories and associations, and on two occasions I related some of the patient's reported anxiety about sexual arousal with her father to the current transference situation with me and the anxiety she has experienced in the analytic situation.

In the next session the patient began with two overtly sexual dreams, which were clearly oedipal in the figures and themes they represented. Her anxiety about associating to them led to her fantasy that she needed to test me and that if she were to fully express her feelings here, it would result in some type of overt sexual seduction between us. This led to her awareness that she attempts to tease and seduce men sexually, but that when they then respond to her she feels hostile and destructive toward them. She went on to talk about a number of men in the role of a father figure toward whom she manifests these kinds of behaviors, and this permitted me to make a transference interpretation that at the present moment the man she was trying to tease and test sexually was me in the analytic situation. She was able to verbalize further her awareness of this anxiety about me and her recognition that if she is to proceed in the analysis she must experience and express her feelings fully and trust me not to respond to them as other men have done in the past. She was aware that "I want to prove that every man is my father," and went on to verbalize her hostility toward such men when they respond to her.

The analytic situation was developing further, with the patient increasingly able to permit an affectively meaningful regression and experience of transference feelings to me as the father, accompanied by the further awareness of her sexual drives and of her anxiety that I may respond to her sexually. Simultaneously, she was also demonstrating a self-observing capacity, and a willingness to pursue and verbalize her associations in spite of the anxiety which they evoke. She was making rapid analytic progress, since this type of material ordinarily does not occur this early in an analysis. However, much of this material still had a defensive quality, in that she was testing me and the analytic situation to see whether I was comfortable about such material, whether I would respond to it analytically, or whether I was seducible. This type of testing behavior could be conceptualized as part of her current defenses against the emerging transference drives, and as a set of adaptive and defensive mechanisms developed to cope with the father's overt sexual seductiveness in childhood, and with the sexual responses to her of various men in her life, including her previous therapist. The genuine regressive transference neurosis will not emerge until this period of testing has occurred, and she has satisfied her uncertainty and fear about my analytic posture.

It has become clear from the material that this patient uses sexuality for a variety of nonsexual aims including: the expression of her needs to control the other person; the expression of hostility and depreciation of the man; the repetitive reinactment of her disturbed relationship to her father; and expression of her needs to reassure herself about her own value, while at the same time expressing contempt for herself as a woman. This type of sexual material might easily be mistaken for an emerging transference neurosis, but although there are transference elements involved, it is my opinion that it chiefly represents her characteristic defenses against continuing anxiety and fear in developing a transference neurosis. In my interventions, therefore, my aim was not to foster the further elaboration of this material or of the sexual drives behind it, but rather to help her recognize and consciously deal with her continuing anxiety about the analysis.

The fifteenth session was again entirely taken up with the theme of whether or not she can trust me here, and with her continuing anxiety-producing fantasy that she could seduce me sexually if she tried. She verbalized her doubt that anyone could sit in my position day after day without responding, and also her wish to elicit a response from me so that she could then feel triumphant over me and depreciate me. She elaborated on her picture of the relationship as a struggle between us, but also expressed a concern that I might not take her sexual feelings seriously and might instead laugh at her for them. Throughout the session she was involved in maintaining her multiple defenses against further development of the transference relationship to me, with perceptions of me being like every other man in her life, and at the same time experienced the fear that I would depreciate her sexuality as her father had apparently done in childhood. The fact that there was so much sexual exposure and teasing contact with him in childhood suggests that he did not take her sexual drives seriously (or that he was never aware of them), and the image of me laughing at her for such feelings probably represented a repetition of such an experience in childhood. At the same time, to take her sexuality seriously and respond to it in reality at an adult level would be to gratify the forbidden incestuous impulses and this possibility would evoke intense guilt and anxiety in her.

By my attitude of calm acceptance of her sexual references and provocations without response or depreciation, and by attempting to help her recognize the anxiety that accompanied them and the conflicts that they induced, I was endeavoring to "pass the test" that she was establishing. If I were to have ignored this material, it would have intensified her anxiety, and she might have interpreted it as a fear on my part to face such issues with her. If I were to have responded to such material seductively, it would also have intensified her anxiety and contempt, and would have made it impossible for her to continue in the analysis successfully. If I made light of the intensity or expression of such material, I would have been depreciating her sexuality in much the same way the parents did when she was a child, and this would have made it more difficult for her ultimately to distinguish between the original childhood relationship and the current relationship with me in the analysis. And if I were to have interpreted this material at a deeper level and suggested something about its genetic meanings, it would have tended to isolate and intellectualize the transference and thereby make the full development of a regressive transference neurosis more difficult. In the face of all these possibilities, the most effective tactics were the neutral acceptance of such feelings within her, the continuing requests for elaboration about them, the interpretations of her anxiety about experiencing feelings directly in the analysis, and through these interventions the tacit demonstration to her that I could tolerate such fantasies without undue discomfort.

In the next session once again the theme was her anxiety about trusting me to be her analyst, and her growing sense of confidence that I will respond differently from other men in her life. She verbalized an awareness of good and warm feelings toward me after yesterday's session, and went on as follows: "I was thinking of how nice you are and that you really want me to come here and that you really want to help me. It's all so good, the way you said it, about laughing at me about my sexual feelings. When you said: 'Why would I laugh?' it was as if you were saying: 'I'm not going to and there is no reason to.' I feel if I tell you this you'll get flustered, but I should know better than that. You're the first man that I was ever able to talk to about me and not laugh and not have you take advantage of me. It's wonderful, and I love this. I feel very close and I feel as if you really care about me." This material illustrated the emotionally significant level at which the transference relationship was beginning to develop along with the therapeutic alliance, and it illustrated the point made previously that much of her emphasis and expression of sexual fantasy and drives was chiefly a testing device to determine whether or not I could accept her comfortably enough to be her analyst. The remainder of the session involved an elaboration of these issues as to whether or not I would listen to her, be interested in her therapeutically, accept and tolerate her various feelings, and not abandon her. She verbalized the important wish to be able to trust and confide in me, along with the continuing sense of doubt that she could have found someone with whom she would feel trustful enough to do this.

It needs to be emphasized how important this material is in the establishment of a therapeutic alliance, which in turn becomes the framework within which a regressive transference neurosis can develop. At this phase of analysis, it is essential that this material be clearly worked over again and again, because until these conscious and preconscious conflicts have been resolved and the patient is able to establish a basically trusting relationship, a workable transference neurosis will not develop. Although up to this point she is not achieving any significant new insights, and although I am making no interpretations of genetic conflict or patterns of behavior, this delay in the achieving of insight is less important than the firm establishment of the therapeutic alliance and the analytic situation. Although it may appear tempting to interpret the various kinds of drives and genetic conflicts in hopes of speeding up the analysis, such a procedure would delay the analysis in the long run, and would significantly restrict the depth of awareness to which it would ultimately go.

At the end of the session I told the patient at the door that I would have to cancel her hour next Friday. When it is necessary for me to cancel a session or a series of sessions during an analysis, it is my practice to announce this to the patient one week before the session in question. I do this in order that the patient will have advanced notice of the cancellation in case she wants to make other plans for that time. The one week interval also gives us time to observe any responses or reactions that the patient may have in advance of the cancellation, and it also permits us partially to work through such reactions before the event. I also routinely use the one-week advanced notice so that if I should depart from my usual routine in this regard and forget to tell the patient about the cancellation, this serves as a signal to me of a possible counter-transference response. Of course, this cannot hold in situations where the need to cancel is an unexpected or more immediate one, and in such cases I tell the patient as soon as I myself know.

In announcing such a cancellation to the patient I deliberately do not give any indication of the reason why I am cancelling. This is done in order that the patient will not be restricted by reality knowledge about the cancellation, and she will then be free to respond to it on the basis of whatever fantasy she has, which in turn will be determined by the current state of the transference relationship and the current conflicts that are being mobilized. This procedure will tend further to mobilize conflict around such an event, and will frequently permit the patient to personalize her response to it, whereas if she knows the reality of the reason for the cancellation, her fantasy and feeling about it will not be as free or personalized. The presence or absence of discernible reactions to such a cancellation can be a helpful indicator of the state and intensity of the transference relationship at the present moment, and such reactions can be used effectively to foster the development of further regressive transference conflicts.

In this instance the entire seventeenth and last session of the month was devoted to her various reactions to the cancellation. Initially she indicated surprise, followed by a realistic perception that such cancellations would be inevitable from time to time. As the session progressed, I was gradually able to interpret her defenses against awareness and expression of a variety of reactions to the cancellation, and I was able to point out a split in her mind between realistic perception and acceptance of the cancellation, as compared with the more primitive, emotional, and (to her) irrational responses to it. This led to her recognition of demands she makes for complete loyalty from her husband and friends, of her sensitivity to being ignored or left, of feelings from childhood about the parents not caring about the effect of their actions upon her, and of the sense of personal rejection which the cancellation implied for her. As this material was emerging, she had a sudden outburst of rage at me with the wish to attack and physically hurt me, accompanied at the same time by a recognition that her hostility and aggression would probably not effectively influence me.

In this material she was demonstrating the further emergence of immediate transference reactions, and my continuing acceptance of these manifestations of her aggression tacitly showed her that the expression of such feelings is also part of analysis, and would not call forth criticism or retaliation. Once again this represented a form of testing me, in which my acceptance of her affective and immature aggressive feelings helped to strengthen our developing therapeutic alliance and her recognition that she is free here verbally to express any and all feelings, no matter how irrational they seem.

Throughout this session I was quite active in interpreting the various resistances she manifested against these emerging aggressive and hostile feelings, in order that she might have this meaningful experience and thereby further foster the development of the therapeutic alliance. For me to have silently accepted her various resistances and defenses against the hostility might have been perceived by her as my fear of her aggression, or as my expectation that she should have only positive responses to me, or as a tacit form of criticism and rejection. At the very least, such handling of this would have meant a failure to make full use of this vicissitude in the analytic situation.

# 3

# THE THIRD MONTH

## SESSION 35

P: --- I'm afraid to talk. -- I'm afraid that I'm being deserted. I have my defenses of independence and I'm afraid that they'll crumble if I talk about it.

A: What's the detail of the fear of being deserted?

P: - I'm thinking about your vacation for a whole month this summer. I feel sick to my stomach. I keep wondering if I can make it. It's like I felt on Friday. Everything is all right if I see you every day, but if there is any break then I fall apart, and I'm unsure if I'll ever see you again.

A: What are your associations to that?

P: -- I don't know. It's not logical; it's just a feeling.

A: Let's just look at the details of your associations without too much concern about the logic of them.

*Cry*

P: -- It's an emotional separation. If I'm not with you I'm never sure that you'll be there. It's just like when my parents went out. I was always afraid that they'd leave us forever.

A: What do you remember about that feeling?

P: I was so insecure. I could see them when they were there. It's just a feeling.

A: That's the very reason to look at it without so much emphasis on the logic. You're repeating with me a feeling that you once had with your parents.

*Cry, Sob*

P: --- I went through a terrible phase of fear about my parents. For a while they went out every day and I'd be sick and feel that I couldn't breathe and I thought I'd die. There was a person who stayed with us and she was up in the attic and I felt as if we were in the house by ourselves, just us three girls. I felt all alone and I thought there was nobody I could depend on and I knew that I couldn't live. I was sick once and I had a terrible headache and they just gave me some aspirin and went out and there was nobody there but my sisters. I knew that something was wrong with me. Finally they took me to a hospital. --- They never were sure whether it was polio or meningitis, but I was in the hospital about a week. That was the only time that I was ever sick, and afterwards I went to my grandmother's. My mother didn't take care of me. For instance, when I had pneumonia when I was three months old I was sent to my grandmother's. My parents never took care of me! They left me alone all the time! – – – I can't let myself depend on them or on you. You'll not always be there. I want not to be afraid when I'm not with you, and to feel that you will return and that I'm capable until you do. But I can't depend on you. No one ever knew the fear that was inside of me. *Cry*

A: What about the fear that is inside you now about me?

P: – It's obvious to me how much I depend on you! If I admit it then I'm helpless. Then I'd beg you to take care of me and love me and I'm unsure if you will and I'm mad at myself that I need you so much! – – It's so hard to admit this but my whole security lies in you. I'm afraid that you are not going to give me the security I need. I want and *need* you to take care of me. Then I try to deny it and I'll take care of myself. *Cry, Sob*

A: So we can see that the situation is different today but that the feelings are the same as when you were a little girl.

P: – It's a hopeless feeling to look to others for security and never get it. It makes me mad!

A: What comes to your mind?

P: I'm mad at you, and then at myself for needing it. And then I get mad to the point that I don't need you. I'm mad that you don't see it and do something about it.

A: So we can see how angry you are at me but you are also afraid that I'll desert you if you ever express the anger and so you turn it back against yourself. This is like the feeling Monday when you had the urge to walk out and slam the door and you were afraid that I wouldn't see you again if you did. And it's also like Sunday when you were angry at me and then had the fantasy that you were going to cut your own wrists.

P: – – – – I want to ask you like a little child, "Are you going to be back on Monday?" I really know the answer. – – –

A: Let's look at your associations to the question. *Cry!*

P: I don't like to ask it. I never had the nerve to ask my parents if they were going out, and I always sent my sister in to ask. It was silly, but I can't admit it. – – – It would be like saying, "Please stay, I'm helpless and I don't want you to go." – – I wonder why did I never cry and say it to my parents? I just couldn't. It put the reality right in front of me.

**A:** What comes to your mind?

*Cry*

**P:** I could talk myself into not needing anyone and survive. But if I ever really say, "I need you," then I have no defenses. I can at least survive if I don't admit this. But if I ever cried, then I'd be by myself. If I hold my head and my chin up then I feel stronger. But if I cried I'd just die there right on the floor. – – I get a sense of panic to be left alone to die for the rest of my life. That's my biggest fear.

**A:** And this was your feeling when Harris abruptly said he wasn't going to see you any more.

**P:** – Ha! There is no defense for this. I feel that I'll die and that's no defense. To say that I don't care would be all right if it was honest. But I keep having these spells of not being able to breathe or being afraid I'm going to die or wanting to cut my wrists, and that's just no way to live. – –

**A:** One problem comes up when you try to *fool* yourself about not caring.

**P:** I can't fool myself, and so what do I do? – – – – What if I ever allow myself to need you? I know that I do, but what will happen if I ever drop my defenses about not needing you and not loving you?

**A:** What comes to your mind about it?

**P:** I'm afraid of being left alone and emotionally not satisfied. I can't live that way. I want to be capable of taking care of myself really and not do it by fooling myself. But how do I get to this? – – – – – – – I'm waiting for doom's day.

**A:** What are your associations to the feeling?

**P:** I'm waiting for you to say that it is time to go. I have a sense of panic and I just can't stand it. I just sit and wait. – –

**A:** We'll stop here for today.

At the door the analyst hands her the bill for the previous month.

### DISCUSSION

The patient begins the session by a reference to being deserted, which is a continuation of her reaction to my cancellation which she had begun to express in the last session. At the same time, she speaks of her defense of independence and her conscious reluctance to talk about the issue lest her defenses against the anxiety weaken. My initial request for the detail of the feeling of being deserted interferes with the defense of not talking about it, and it turns out that the impact of her reaction to the separation of one cancelled session has stimulated her anticipation of the prolonged vacation separation, which I had told her about when we began the analysis, and which is still three months away. This is followed immediately by a mild conversion reaction in which she feels sick to her stomach. The symbolic meaning of this conversion reaction in all probability has to do with still-unconscious fantasies of oral incorporation as a psychological mechanism to keep me with her, and the conflicts and defenses against such fantasies, all stimulated by the separation and probably related to her presenting symptom of bulimia. However, it is far too early in the analysis to comment upon this, and the patient's associations go gack to the cancellation and to the derivative of a primary process fantasy that any separation is permanent.

After my request for her associations, she indicates her awareness that this is an illogical feeling, and attempts to depreciate it as "just a feeling." My suggestion that she follow her associations and not be concerned about their logic interferes with this resistance and leads to an immediate affective response of crying as she speaks about the uncertainty of whether or not I will be there. This is immediately associated to a reaction she had when her parents would go out when she was a child, and this immediate association of a current experience with me to a past experience with the parents is an indicator of the developing transference neurosis. It implies that she has already cathected me in the parental role and that she is responding to a current situation as if it were a past relationship.

Once again she attempts the same defense of depreciating her reaction by calling it "just a feeling," and my intervention is simultaneously aimed at the therapeutic alliance and the developing transference neurosis. To reinforce the therapeutic alliance, I point out the analytic necessity to look at the feeling without emphasis on its logic, and I then follow this with a transference interpretation that she is repeating with me an old feeling from the past. In response to these interventions the patient, with considerable affect, begins to recall experiences of separation and the symptoms that accompanied them when she was a child, again relating these past experiences to the current transference interaction between us when she says, "I can't let myself depend on them or on you. You'll not always be there." In this context she describes some of the fear that she experienced as a child, and my next intervention is an attempt again to focus the material into the current situation of the anticipated separation from me, and thereby to foster the further development of the transference response.

With this focusing into the transference, she affectively begins to describe her increasing dependence upon me and her attempts to deny this and to take care of herself instead. My next intervention that in the current situation she is repeating feelings from when she was a little girl is once again simultaneously directed toward the transference and the therapeutic alliance. By saying what I did, I am giving her a conceptual orientation within which to understand the current response and within which to accept its lack of "logic." At the same time, I am indicating my acceptance of the transference response and I am thereby tacitly telling her that such responses are not to be suppressed in the analytic situation, and that I can empathically understand and accept them without demanding that she be logical, or that she attempt to control them. In this way I am demonstrating to her that regression in feeling state and in ego capacities is appropriate here and that I do not have undue concern about its occurrence.

This intervention ultimately permits her to experience and express some of her anger, which then allows me to make the rather lengthy interpretation about her anxiety over expressing the anger directly. In this interpretation I make reference to feelings she had reported and expressed during the previous session. The patient's response of wanting to ask me whether I will be back on Monday is a simultaneous indication of the developing regressive transference feelings and also of the self-observing ego capacity, when she describes her question as being childlike and at the same time indicates that she already knows the answer to it. But her associations to the question again bring forth an intense affective response of crying, and a spontaneous return by association to experiences with the parents. With this she also indicates the defenses which she used as a girl to avoid the impact of her dependency, again referring to this as a current transference experience.

At this point my interpretation in regard to the termination of her previous therapy is an attempt again to deal with an incompletely resolved resistance of fear that I will respond in the same way as her previous therapist. My own associations are that she has always been particularly vulnerable to separation, and earlier in the analysis she had brought up but not fully resolved the identification of me with her former therapist. I want to emphasize the idea that he and I are different people, in order to strengthen the therapeutic alliance and her confidence that I will not terminate her treatment abruptly as the former therapist had done. As long as this would remain an active fear for her, it would interfere with the full development of a regressive transference neurosis.

The patient's response is not directly related to the experience with the former therapist, but is an expression of her attempted defenses against separation, while at the same time recognizing the ineffectiveness of such defenses and the occurrence of specific neurotic symptoms as a result. Her expressed feeling of "waiting for doom's day" is an indication that even the termination of each session has already become meaningful to her as a form of separation from me, and is another indication of the deepening transference reactions that are developing.

## SESSION 36

Patient pays the bill and the analyst notices that she has not endorsed the check properly.

**P:** − − −

**A:** I notice that you didn't endorse the check. What are your associations to that?

**P:** I'm terribly sorry. (Elaborates.) I worried before that I'd forget it. (Elaborates.) I wondered before if I had signed it.

**A:** So we can see from the concern and the worry and the uncertainty about it that there must be something more to this. What comes to your mind?

**P:** I don't know. I've thought about it a lot and I felt before, "There goes my life's blood." To give you that much money. I resented you for it. − − I felt . . . . . that the money kept this all realistic. But even with the money I can feel close to you and feel that you are concerned about me, even though I pay you. So why am I so nervous? I had a discussion with Tom about money and it panics him. He's doing extra work and I figure that we will borrow if necessary to pay for this. I was very upset in the talk and I have the feeling that he resents me for it. − − − −

**A:** I think you must be having some other feelings in your mind about this.

**P:** I feel settled in my mind and I can't think about it or else I'd get upset. − − −

**A:** You mentioned that you feel Tom resents the money and is worried about it and has to do extra work to get it. I wonder if this doesn't intensify some of your guilt about your positive and loving feelings about me?

**P:** Very much. − − − There again is where my parents failed me. If they'd set up a trust fund or provided for me in some way it would have been better. It is horrible to be dependent and I feel as if I'm helpless and I have nowhere to turn but to Tom. It's Tom's parents who are helping to pay for this and not mine. (Elaborates.) – – My parents talk about their great concern for me but they don't *do* anything. I can never depend on them. I should know that after twenty-seven years but it still bothers me. – – And yet I can't hate them, and I try to justify everything for them. (Elaborates.)

A: What are your further associations to this?

*Cry*     P: – I'm just worn out. I don't want to have any feeling at all for them, and I'm tired of this. All of this love and hate and this mixed-up feeling. I'd rather give in, that's better than fighting. It's all past history and I have to make a *new* life. I *can't* let my parents frustrate me. It does no good to hate them *or* to love them. I had a dream last night that I was in the Evanston house and I was by myself and I wasn't afraid and I'd gotten used to it. I was in the kitchen and my mother is the messiest person and I used to feel that I *had* to clean the kitchen up for her. (Elaborates.) I never got any thanks for it. I was always afraid that mother couldn't do it. In the dream I was sitting and waiting for my parents to come back. I wish that I'd raved and carried on like a child but it is too late now. – – – I'm thinking of a TV program about a boy whose father had gone away for the month of August. The boy kept saying, "No, I won't speak to him." I wish that I had done that. I wish I had screamed and carried on instead of just sitting there and giving in.

A: I think you are doing this with me now. The month of August is the month I told you I was going to take my vacation. I think this all comes to your mind because of tomorrow's cancellation and you have a wish to cry and scream and carry on here but instead you just give in.

P: I can't do anything else.

A: What do you think keeps you from expressing your feelings?

*Cry,*     P: – The biggest one is that I *need* you. It would be the same as
*Sob*     killing myself and I can't live without you. You have me where you want me. I'd die and so I can't. It makes me nothing.

A: If we've agreed that for the sake of the analysis you will express in words all the feelings that you have, why should I kick you out if you then do just that?

P: How do I know that you'll hold up to it? No one ever does.

A: So we can see that you still don't trust what I've said.

P: – – – I can't win for losing, can I? You'll get mad at me if I don't do all that you want. I'm sick of it. I'm nothing. I'm tired of being nothing! I want some rights of my own! I want to make you see that I *am* somebody! If I walk out without letting you know how I feel I'll just repeat history and I'll hate myself and I'll hate you and it's all just a vicious circle. – –

**A:** I think that you're the one who thinks that you're nobody and that you're not entitled to have and to express your feelings.

**P:** It's not my fault! You make me this way! You don't let me!

**A:** What are the details of the thought?

**P:** I think of all the times that my love was not accepted! – – I don't see how one person can be so unfeeling! My mother reacted and beat the hostility out of me. At least she had feelings. My father did too when I wouldn't do what he wanted, and it was just like you, and he'd also get mad at me for not being smart enough or adult enough to see a situation. That's all I got from my father and I'd get it when I wasn't an adult or manly enough. You can't force me! *Cry, Sob*

**A:** I think this is a wish that I *should* be angry and force you and make demands on you the way your father did.

**P:** What do you do? Are you going to completely ignore me? I'm so tired of you! I've been wondering how you feel and I'm hoping that I'm doing right. I want to forget about you. You'll never be what I want you to be! I never want to see you again. You make me miserable! I hope you die! I never want to see you! Life would be easier without you and I'd not have to think about you! – – – – – – That's not really how I feel. Life would not be complete without you. You are always there and the desire for you is always there. I've got to have that desire fulfilled. I've got to! Surely there is some way! – – – If I'd just run and say I never want to see you, it's just a defense. It's a defense to say that I hate you! I wouldn't be complete and something would be missing all of my life.

**A:** So we can see the conflict that is raging within you. You have feelings of love and desire and also of rage and hate towards me, both at the same time.

**P:** – – – What am I going to do? How can I go on living if I feel that my father never loved me? It panics me to death.

**A:** So we can see how you are repeating with me this same conflict that you had towards your father as a girl.

**P:** – – – – – – I hope that somehow you'll satisfy this need, not the way my father would, but that you will ease the desire somehow and make me feel it's a little satisfied anyway. – – – – –

**A:** We'll stop here for today.

## DISCUSSION

In my handling of the incident of the check, I am attempting to demonstrate to her that nonverbal behavior is another form of communication and needs to be observed and understood in the analysis. As usual I begin at the surface of the patient's awareness and move from there toward the more deeply preconscious elements of her reaction and attitudes. This material begins to illustrate why I arrange to hand the patient her bill in the first session of each month, and ask her to bring the check personally by the tenth of the month. In this way issues, feelings, and associations to money and payment are kept active between us. If I mailed the bill and she paid by mail, these reactions could be more easily evaded or rationalized. At this time the patient is only able to approach these issues superficially, and ultimately uses the resistance of fearing her upset if she were to talk about them.

My interpretation about her guilt over the developing positive transference feelings in the setting of her husband's concern about money is an attempt to deal with a potential resistance against developing a more intense transference reaction. By calling such guilt responses to her attention, my hope is to permit the patient to take more optimal distance from such guilt feelings, and the implication of my comment is that such a feeling of guilt is not realistically appropriate in an analysis. Her response to the immediate issue is a brief one, followed by associations which indicate a growing acceptance of her own dissatisfaction with the parents. She defensively attempts to take distance from these feelings, but then returns to the theme of parental frustration and of separation from them, as in the dream where she waits for the parents to return. This in turn leads to the association to the TV program and to the unexpressed hostility and anger which she had defended herself against as a child.

I have suspected from the beginning of the session that the mistake about the check might be an indirect expression of hostility and anger toward me, but the patient has not alluded to such feelings, and I have not wanted to suggest them to her. However, the associations of hating the parents and fighting with me, the expressed wish that she had raved and carried on as a child, as well as the boy's hostility in the TV program all suggested to me at this point that the patient is defending herself against expressing a similar set of angry feelings toward me. Her statement, "I wish I had screamed and carried on instead of just sitting there and giving in," represents for me the confirmation of this constellation of feelings and defenses, and suggests that they are close enough to consciousness that I can safely interpret them to her.

Initially the patient's responses are defensive ones and she illustrates the typical conflict of guilt and fear over expressing hostility toward someone upon whom she is dependent. This is accompanied by a genuine affective response, and my intervention in regard to our therapeutic agreement is an attempt to appeal to the therapeutic alliance and to her rational awareness of what analysis requires.

The next series of interactions between us involve elements of the transference reactions and also of her doubts about the strength and genuineness of the therapeutic alliance and of my role in it. Her statement, "I don't see how one person can be so unfeeling!" is a reflection of a sense of frustration she is feeling at my analytic neutrality and is followed by descriptions of the emotional responses she could elicit from both parents. My transference interpretation that she wants me to be angry and to force her as her father did serves several functions. It again indicates my neutral acceptance of her and her feelings, and although it frustrates the wish to evoke an emotional response from me, it also makes the situation safer for her, thereby permitting her more openly to experience and verbally express the anger and resentment she is feeling. However, after she has experienced and expressed the transference reaction in an affective way, she then is able to take distance from it and recognize she is defending herself against the underlying positive attachment and intensifying dependency. Her statement, "You are always there and the desire for you is always there," is an indicator of the growing intensity of the transference neurosis, and an indication that the analysis is progressing nicely.

My final two interventions regarding her ambivalence toward me, and the transference repetition of conflict with her father, are perhaps unnecessary and do not add anything new that had not already come up in the session. However, they are made with the intention of strengthening the therapeutic alliance by providing her with a more clear conceptual framework in which she can understand the transference reactions she is having to this first cancellation of an analytic session. The aim is to prevent more regression than the patient would be able reasonably to tolerate at this early point in our analytic work. Her final response, in which she partially separates me from the father, suggests that these interventions had the desired effect.

Once a transference neurosis begins to emerge, the analyst knows that any cancellation of sessions, vacation, change in schedule of hours, or other modification of the analytic situation that he introduces will inevitably produce a reaction in the patient. Usually this will involve pain or distress in the patient with a variety of responses and defenses against them, determined by the current state of the transference and the nature of the patient's personality integration. In spite of knowing this and in spite of his wish to avoid unnecessarily causing pain for his patient, the analyst must nevertheless at times respond to other demands and expecta tions beyond those of his patients. In other words, the reality principle in the analyst's life requires that at times the situations and demands other than his patient's needs must take precedence, even though such vicissitudes will inevitably have repercussions on the analysis and analytic situation. Partly because of this he tries to keep these types of interruptions to a minimum, but nevertheless when they do occur he must have resolved his own countertransference responses sufficiently that he can make a rational decision about which priority to honor, and then to deal in an analytic way with the responses of the patient. The final effect of such interruptions is not necessarily detrimental, and in fact such events will frequently be helpful in mobilizing latent conflicts, and may be effectively used to achieve the ultimate analytic goal.

---

One session cancelled by the analyst.

---

## SESSION 37

P: – – – – – – – – I don't know what to say.

A: You walked in here very slowly as if you hated to be here and as if you were scared stiff. The fear of talking probably represents the same thing.

P: – – – – – I can't decide whether I can trust you enough to break down my defenses. I can't trust anyone. I have to depend on myself solely.

A: Let's see what your associations are to the feeling of not being able to trust me.

P: – – – I'm thinking of Saturday night. I woke up in the middle of a storm and my daughter was crying. I had one of my spells and I've not had any since I left Harris. The whole world was closing in and I felt as if I had no one to turn to and I felt as if I had disappeared. – –

A: I think you were still reacting to feelings and fantasies which were stimulated by my canceling that session. Let's see what comes to your mind.

P: I was so afraid! I was so mad at you! I just want to forget it.

A: You're still afraid to express how mad you are at me.

P: You left me and you didn't care how scared I was. You have no understanding! You can't imagine what it's like. – – –

A: I think you are still trying to by-pass the fantasies about that cancelled session. – – – – –

P: – – – – – – – By not confiding and by not giving you my trust I feel as if I can hurt you. – –

A: What's the detail?

P: I don't want you to know that I care enough to be mad. I'll just pretend as if nothing happened, but you've lost out on me. You'll never get to me. – –

A: What comes to your mind?

P: – – I trusted you and you're not worthy. You turned your back on me and you don't care. So I'll sit quietly and hate you with everything I have. You'll never know. I'll not feel sorry or cry, I'll just hate you and then I'll do fine and by myself. – – – –

A: What are your associations to this pattern of reaction?

P: – – – – – – My sister comes to mind. I could always turn to her. She was like a mother to me. I felt that somehow she felt what went on within me and how I felt and how scared I was. – – – – Saturday night I turned to Tom and he helped, but he's not who I wanted.

A: So we can see how you are again repeating with me a pattern that originated with your parents. You are holding your feelings in and you are going to get along on your own and you're trying to tell me that you don't need me and you're not going to let me know what is going on, but instead you are just going to suffer.

P: It gives me a sense of satisfaction. You'll never know. I can cry like an idiot, but you'll never know!

A: So we can see the intensity of your feelings which shows up in the fact that you are willing to cut off your nose to spite your face.

P: – – I have a wish to stand up and scream and scream at you and feel better, but I just can't. If I do it I can't think of it. But you can push me just so far. – –

A: The feeling is that you can't scream at me. What comes to your mind?

P: I think too hard. I want to, but you haven't pushed me hard enough. I'm so used to reacting this way. I was thinking of the one time | *Cry* in my life when I screamed at my father. I had just broken up with a boy and I was crying, and my father was saying, "It's not so bad." He'd never know because he never cared! I screamed.

**A:** This again is like the feelings about me. You felt that I didn't understand and that I had no feeling for what it was like on Friday.

**P:** – – – – – – If I go through this analysis I'll need you more than anyone in my life. I don't know if I can stand it. I know that you'll hurt me sometimes like you did on Friday. – – Everything that hurts me gives you satisfaction. Just like my crying now. I'm mad that it reduces me to a helpless baby and that I fell into your trap.

**A:** Let's look at the detail of the fantasy that it gives me satisfaction.

**P:** It gives you complete power. You can hurt me or not hurt me as you want. I don't want you to know that you can hurt me and I'm not going to give you that satisfaction. And yet it is obvious that I need you. This is just like with my parents. It's a fact that all children need their parents. I hated to let it be known that I needed them. – –

**A:** So you see the analysis as a dangerous situation. The more that you confide and trust in me, the more vulnerable you feel and become.

**P:** – – – – – – I hate this feeling that I can't trust you. It panics me. And yet I don't feel it and it just won't come. – – – – – – – – Oh! I'm scared to death!! I want to turn around and look at you.

**A:** What's the fantasy?

**P:** I don't know. I must know that I can trust you. I've got to! You must know how much I need you and you must help me!

**A:** On the one hand you know that you can, but you also anticipate that it will be just the same as it was with your parents.

**P:** These are all old feelings and I can't handle them myself. I must know if you will help me! !

**A:** We'll stop here for today.


### DISCUSSION

From the very beginning of this session when the patient walks into the consultation room slowly with head bowed, a sad and angry look on her face, and an unusual hesitancy about approaching the couch, I sense that she is continuing to react to the cancellation of the Friday session. The response is manifest also in her difficulty and reluctance to talk, as well as in the material she brings up after the session begins. In effect there has been a temporary interference with the previously developing therapeutic alliance, and the pain of her response to the cancellation has made her withdraw from me, both as a transference reaction and also in terms of her sense of confidence and of basic trust. The priority therefore must now go toward a re-establishment of basic trust and the therapeutic alliance, as well as a further elaboration of the intrapsychic details of her response to the cancelled session.

My activity during this session is a reflection of these tactical goals, and to that extent I am considerably more active than usual, although still maintaining the position of analytic neutrality. I do not want long silences to develop, and I want to try to help her verbalize the current feelings toward me. To this end, my interventions involve confrontations focusing on the cancelled session, and various interpretations of resistance, as well as questions and requests for details, designed to help her continue with the flow of her associations. In this context there are several interpretations designed to help her recognize how she reacts to the frustration I caused her in ways that are typical of her responses in the past, along with several interventions which indicate my awareness of the intensity of her feelings and thereby my acceptance of the occurrence of reactions of this degree.

Partly as a response to my interventions, but also because of the previously established analytic situation, the patient is able gradually to verbalize some of her reactions and feelings in the current situation. She is increasingly able to recognize the intrapsychic conflict between her needs for me and the wish to trust me, as contrasted with the pain that this relationship is causing her, the expectation of hurt and further disappointment, the fear of investing herself emotionally in the analysis, and the sense of helplessness that her dependency upon me brings. All this is interspersed with an unusually long total of silences.

However, the previous analytic work which has resulted in the establishment of a therapeutic alliance is illustrated by her comment late in the session that "If I go through this analysis I'll need you more than anyone in my life. I don't know if I can stand it. I know that you will hurt me sometimes, like you did on Friday." These remarks indicate how, in spite of the transference reactions that preceded and followed them, there is still a healthy self-observing recognition of the reality of the situation between us, with the implied awareness that my hurting her was not deliberate, and that in spite of the transference distortions and defensive reactions, she is prepared to continue the analysis and the emotional involvement in it.

## SESSION 38

**P:** ----------

**A:** What comes to your mind about the silence?

**P:** I have nothing to say.

**A:** What's the detail?

**P:** I can't confide in you. It's like telling my bitterest enemy.

**A:** Let's look at the feeling about me being a bitter enemy. What are the details?

**P:** I must suppress every feeling for you but hate. It's the only way that I can survive. --

**A:** And yet you are holding back even the feelings of hate.

**P:** -----

**A:** You're still reacting to the feelings about that cancelled session. But we still don't know the details of the fantasy about *why* I cancelled.

**P:** -------- That doesn't make any difference. You cancelled! That's all that counts! -- I can rationalize it or explain it or understand it, but it doesn't make any difference, I still hate you for it.

**A:** What comes to your mind that you still don't express the hate?

**P:** I can't. I can think about it but I can't do that when I'm here.

**A:** Let's see what holds you back and what accounts for the hesitation.

**P:** I don't know. -- (There is a brief interruption of the session by a knock on the door which the analyst answers and then returns to his chair). ---------- I'm terribly afraid that you'll be mad at me if I get mad. The other day I felt that you were disgusted with me because I was mad at you. You don't accept any hostility in me.

**A:** You see me as reacting as if I were your parents who wouldn't accept this.

**P:** Where did you ever get this idea? I never got mad at them.

**A:** You never got mad at them, or you never expressed it?

**P:** I got mad but I'd take it out on a chair or on a book or on my sister. ---

**A:** I wonder if the silence may not be a way of testing to see if I'll be annoyed or impatient or demanding or if I'll force you to talk.

**P:** ------- I'm falling into the same patterns that I had as a child with you. What is there to do? I just can't seem to do it. Unless I show the hate I can't show the love or trust you and so I might as well not be here.

**A:** So this is all the more reason to analyze what keeps you from showing the hate.

**P:** This is all so stupid. Something is tying me down. I never have shown this, not to this day with my parents. I could understand this if my parents hit me every time.

**A:** The issue of what happened with your parents is hard to see because it happened a long time ago and your memory still isn't clear. Let's look at it right now, between you and me, and see what blocks you here.

**P:** I can picture myself being mad and yelling and screaming. What would you do? You wouldn't hit me. It would probably make no impression on you and make no difference to you.

**A:** What's the detail?

**P:** It would be just like talking to a wall. There is no emotion for me. It would frustrate and scare me. It would be all right if you reacted.

**A:** So we can see that you are not so much afraid that I *will* do something, but rather you are afraid that I *won't*, and the greater fear is that I won't react if you get angry.

**P:** It would make me feel secure if you did. It's just like the times I love it when Tom gets mad. It makes me feel secure. I'm frustrated and I can't stand it when he succumbs to my anger and then I don't know what to do. I would sever every connection between us if I got mad at you.

**A:** How do you mean?

**P:** I'd threaten to run away and you would probably let me and I'd die by myself. You wouldn't care enough to come and get me. – –

**A:** What are your associations to the threat to run away?

**P:** – – I don't know. My mother talked once about Carol running away in a blizzard and my mother let her. She came back and my mother was in control and had all the power. If I tried I'd have to come back or else I'd have had it and it would get me nothing.

**A:** So here we see another meaning of the silence before. It's a form of running away and it's a way of trying to see if I'll come after you or if I'll let you stay silent.

**P:** – – I want to know that if I get mad, will you let me return and will you say, "I missed you and I still love you." – – I hate the feeling that it makes no difference to you if I ran away and never saw you again. And so I don't dare run away. – – Every child threatens to run away and its parents try not to show any fright, but that's not right. They should let the child know that they'll be missed. (Elaborates.) To say to a child that, "It's all right if you want to run away," it's the same thing as saying, "I don't love you anyway." – –

*Cry*

**A:** So you feel the need to know what will happen if you get mad here. Let's look at the fantasy.

**P:** I must know that I can come back and that there will be some communication and that I'm not cut off and that you won't withdraw completely from me. It's like if I were to get mad and walk out now, would you let me return tomorrow?

**A:** So we can see you still have trouble in believing what I say about expressing your feelings here. It's as if getting mad here is off-limits to you.

**P:** – – – – – I'm insecure everywhere. I'm afraid to leave here and I'm afraid that you won't be here when I get back. It's just like Tom spending nights at the office. I always had the feeling that I'm never going to see him again.

**A:** So it's as if you equate every separation with death.

**P:** – – If I talk about this I will feel so much hostility that I'll explode like an atomic bomb.

**A:** We'll stop here for today.

### Discussion

At the beginning of the session the patient indicates that although we had discussed her reactions to the cancellation in the previous hour, she is still responding to it and still using the same defenses against relating to me in the analysis. Once again my attempt is to encourage her to verbalize these responses and I begin with a confrontation about the initial silence, followed by questions asking for details of her reactions. The tactical goal at this point is to encourage her communication, and even though my intervention may represent a transference gratification in the form of a demonstration to her of my interest in her and in her analytic progress, this is less important at this point than the necessity of firmly reestablishing the analytic situation.

My first interpretation points out to her how she is "holding back even the feelings of hate." But this intervention does not produce the expression of the hostility which I hoped for, and instead she remains rather sullenly silent. I do not want the silence to become lengthy at this point, or to permit this situation to deteriorate into a struggle between us of who will speak first, and I therefore choose to break the silence myself by pointing out her continuing response to the cancelled session. In responding to events like this in an analysis, the event itself is only one part of the total picture. More important are the intrapsychic fantasies and elaborations by the patient in her attempts to understand or explain the event to herself.

It was in order to elicit and elaborate upon such intrapsychic fantasies about the external event (viz., cancellation of the session) that I did not tell her the reality reason for my having to cancel. (In this case it was for a professional meeting.) Had I done so, it would have spared her some of the distress she felt, and it is likely that she would have responded at the level of reality, and would have felt that I did not do it deliberately or with personal intent. But her opportunity to become aware of the intrapsychic elaboration and fantasy about my motivations and feelings toward her and the opportunity to study her defensive processes would have been lost.

It is this line of reasoning that leads me to focus upon the needs to understand the details of her fantasies as to why I had cancelled. However, her response indicates that she is still too affectively involved to pick up on my suggestion that she explore her fantasy, and instead she remains focused purely on the feeling of anger about it. At this point, therefore, I change the focus to try to deal with the defenses that she is using against expressing this hostility more fully and directly toward me.

Following this she begins to work on the defenses against her anger and the fantasies of my response to it if she were to express it openly. The transference projection that "You don't accept any hostility in me" is a significant defense which must be dealt with before the hostility itself can be verbalized. My interpretation of this as a transference to me as if I were her parents is an attempt to help her recognize the reality of the situation between us, and accept my willingness to understand and tolerate her hostility. Her next line of defense is an attempt at denial when she says that she never got mad at her parents, and my question about the difference between the feeling and the expression of it is an attempt to block the utilization of this mechanism.

When she describes using the same patterns with me that she had used as a child, she is illustrating an old ego state in the emerging transference neurosis, but she then uses the defense of attempting to focus upon and recall the reactions in childhood as a means of escape from the more immediately pressing and affectively meaningful conflict with me in the current situation. My intervention that it would be more appropriate to look at the current situation between us, rather than to try to go back and recall something from the remote past, is an attempt to encourage her to give up this mechanism.

At this point she begins to express her anger toward me, along with the expectation that I would not react to it, which then permits my confronting her with her wish that I *would* respond with anger. This material leads to the fantasies about running away and the childhood experience of her mother's response when the sister attempted to do so. I now experience an empathic understanding of the meaning of the silences at the beginning of the session, which I had earlier interpreted as a form of testing me. This new understanding of the silence is in keeping with the formulation I had made to myself earlier in regard to the need for some type of derivative transference gratification at this point in order to reestablish the analytic situation between us. It could be argued that I might have remained silent and not "run after her" by breaking the initial silences, and that I might thereby have further stimulated the emergence of a more intense expression of the underlying hurt and hostility. However, it is my feeling that this is still relatively early in the analysis, that she might not have been able at this point to express these feelings overtly, and that to have subjected her to that great a frustration in the transference might have interfered with the progress in the development of the overall analytic situation.

In any event, after my further interpretation about the silence, she is able affectively to express various elements of the transference conflict as she feels it. In attempting again to foster the restoration of the therapeutic alliance, I make the intervention toward the end of the session in regard to her difficulty in believing that it is appropriate to express feelings of hostility in an analysis, and implying that I do not consider such feelings to be "off limits." This is an appeal to the self-observing and healthy ego functions, which had participated in the establishment of the therapeutic contract, and represents in essence a restatement of that agreement in hopes that it will strengthen our alliance and thus permit a deeper expression of the transference reactions.

---

## SESSION 39

**P:** I had a dream about a razor and I think I had the idea to cut my wrists. I was shaving my legs and it was an old-fashioned barber razor. Then I was in college and I was engaged to Tom. I felt unpopular and I wasn't dating and I was in the dining room. And there were the boys on one side against the girls on the other. The boys were taunting me and they felt I was idiotic and they wouldn't look at me. There was some sort of a picture going on. At the end of the dream I had a ring and I was showing it and one boy said, "All those lies are untrue." I thought that they thought I was a homosexual and that I couldn't get a man. The one boy who was taunting me was a boy I knew in the first grade who chased me on the playground and then was kissing me. I stuck up for him but he didn't care. I woke up with the horrible feeling that everybody hated me. – – – I felt that so often in college. I was unsure about being a woman. You broke that appointment and that made me feel so insecure in my womanhood.

**A:** What's the detail of the feeling?

**P:** The boy was taunting me in the dream. But then I got the ring and that was a way of saying, "She is a woman." My father never wanted me to be a female, and he took no pride in it. It was a direct insult to my femininity and not just to me. So I proved that I'm a woman to every man that I see. I wonder why?

**A:** What comes to your mind?

**P:** – – – I have a desire to seduce men, and to have all men fall head over heels in front of me, and yet it's all so hostile. I feel this towards you and I have no sexual feelings at all.

**A:** So you felt that my cancellation was a slur on your femininity, and you are trying to prove to me that you are feminine. You don't want to feel any sexual feelings for me because you are so angry at me, and so you displace all of this to the other men.

**P:** – – – – I'm realizing that to do this. . . . .I'll have to go back to childhood and feel every insecurity that I felt then. I have no security at all. I see myself so different from what I was five or six months ago. I'm so timid and I'm scared of a mouse. I'm losing any self-assurance that I ever had. Sometimes I'm even embarrassed that I'm pregnant.

**A:** What about your associations to the other dream elements?

**P:** I'm thinking about the part about the boy and I don't want to mention his name. There was a long hallway and they were showing those pictures and he was somehow related and I was standing up for him in front of everyone. I used to sit in the corner and watch the world and wish that I could be a part of it. It was Tom who brought me into it. Up until the third grade the boys used to pick me and I was the darling of the bunch. Then it all changed and I was so little and skinny. None of the boys liked me because I was so ugly and unathletic and skinny and little.

**A:** And what about your associations to the pictures?

**P:** – – – I'm thinking of some pictures of me as a girl. (Elaborates.) In one of them I was naked and I was climbing up a ladder and a friend gave it to a boy in school who was obnoxious. He put it on the bulletin board. Then one time I was swimming naked in high school and somebody took a picture and circulated it all around the school. – –

*Cry*

**A:** What comes to mind about not mentioning the boy's name?

**P:** – – – I can't understand why I think about him so much. He was idiotic and he was poor and there was one masculine girl who beat him up once. Everybody used to say, "The poor boy, he was beaten up by a girl." His name was Roger Taylor. I've always hated the name Roger.

**A:** I wonder if the boy in the dream doesn't represent me, and the wish to beat me up. In the dream you felt that you were masculine. I think this is still related to your anger at me for the cancelled session.

**P:** – – Why do you irritate me so much when you talk so gently? I can't stand it!

**A:** What comes to your mind?

**P:** That's the way my father talks to me. He's so calm. I'm raging inside and you're so calm! (Elaborates.) You're trying to cut off these emotions. You think that they are not worth thinking about.

**A:** I think this is really your own fear of expressing your feelings. It's like yesterday and your feeling that you'd explode like an atom bomb. If you can believe that I also don't want you to express them, then there is a greater reason to hold them back.

**P:** – – – – – – – – While I was driving home from here yesterday there were two boys in a truck who were acting up and it irritated me. (Elaborates.) I felt so hostile I could have killed them! I was scared to death. – – –

**A:** So the anger from here found an outlet outside?

**P:** If my feeling was so strong for those silly boys, imagine what it would be like for you.

**A:** What's the fantasy?

**P:** I just want to get my nails into you! I don't want to just yell and scream. I've got to. . . . . – –

**A:** You stopped it in the middle.

**P:** I can't hurt you or kill you. You'd stop me, so why am I so scared? I have a vision of you sitting in your chair dead. – – – –

**A:** But the feeling was that you wanted to get your nails into me. What are your associations?

**P:** It's silly! – . . . . . I want to slice you up into little bitty pieces. I want to take a razor and slice your face up.

**A:** What's the detail?

**P:** – I want to see blood run from all of the cuts and I want to see the surprised look on your face. I'd like to get a knife and cut a huge hole in your stomach. The picture of a sword inside of a penis comes to my mind.

**A:** What's the detail?

**P:** It happened before. I'd like to cut off your penis and put it on a sword and cut it all up and smash it with a stone and trample it into the grass, and see the blood all around. – – – I see myself dancing around it and being delighted. – – – –

A: You blocked your thoughts then.

P: I'd like to do this to every man I saw.

A: What's the fantasy?

P: My body tingles all over now and I feel like I'd like to jump off the couch. I'd take such a delight in it. I'm like a child in a tantrum. I'm kicking and screaming and yelling. I want to do anything I want like that. It's all so close and it's about to come out and I must *do* something.

A: We'll stop here for today.

## DISCUSSION

In contrast to the last two sessions, the flow of the patient's material from the beginning of the hour indicates that the work done in those sessions has been at least partially effective and that the analytic situation and therapeutic alliance are again reestablished. The presentation of the complex dream may well have represented a form of peace-token or gift to me, signaling the reestablishment of a more positive relationship, and at the end of the presentation of the dream, her statement, "You broke that appointment and that made me feel so insecure in my womanhood," represents the beginning of the elaboration of the fantasy as to why I had canceled the session, which I had questioned her about yesterday.

My question in regard to the details of this fantasy leads to some further exploration of her feeling in regard to the father and also feelings in regard to other men in the past, which in turn indicate how the response to the current cancellation was largely determined by the growing transference perception of me as representing these other men in her life, and it is this issue that I want to show her by my transference interpretation. She then indicates her correct self-observing perception that analysis will require that she reexperience the earlier childhood feelings, and she goes on to describe the symptoms which indicate a regression she had already begun to experience prior to starting analysis.

At this point my decision to focus on the dream is a reflection of my thought that we have perhaps exhausted for the moment the current conscious reactions to the cancellation, and my impression that the dream contains allusions to a number of other conflicts. Her associations again reflect the feeling of being rejected and, on the outside, of feeling ugly and unattractive. The specific associations to the pictures in the dream lead to the affective recall of her sense of shame about her body, which in turn is probably related to her fantasy of the reason for the cancellation and its reflection on her attractiveness as a woman.

All this material is significant, but my attention has been caught by a recurrence of the seemingly minor yet significant resistance of not wanting to mention the boy's name. As discussed in Session 15, in actual fact, the analyst has no particular interest in the names of people for their own sake, but the reluctance to mention people by name can have a variety of meanings, and can become the focus of significant resistances. It may reflect an uncertainty about confidentiality; it may be an attempt to keep the material vague and nonspecific; it may be the result of an isolation mechanism; it may be the derivative of a fantasy the analyst knows people personally in the patient's life; it may be an attempt to deemphasize the importance of the person or the specifically associated events; or it may have other implications. It is also easier for the analyst to recall the patient's material and experiences if he has a specific name to associate with them.

In any event, not mentioning the name represents a specific form of editing of conscious material, and if allowed to persist unchallenged, it may encourage the patient to withhold other material as well, and in an attempt to block these various potential resistances, I ask her about it. Her response permits a deeper insight into some of the unconscious meanings of the dream in terms of her continuing aggression toward me. Her response again involves a transference perception of me as the father, and a defensive projection that I am trying to cut these emotions off, and that I think they are not worth thinking about. My interpretation of these projections, and my reminder to her of her comment about the explosiveness of her feeling yesterday, are attempts to block this resistance, and to encourage her to face the aggression more directly.

After the silence (which in itself may be an indirect expression of hostility), the patient demonstrates another defense against the hostility and aggression in the transference by using the mechanism of displacement of these feelings toward the two boys in the truck. I interpret this resistance in my question about expressing her anger outside, and this, along with my acceptance of her feelings by the several requests for details, permits her now to go on and express the hostility in a more direct and detailed way. In this material her statement, "I want to take a razor and slash your face up," represents the latent wish expressed in the dream about the razor, but in the dream work she had turned the aggression back against herself in the thought to cut her own wrists.

Because the hostility is now emerging more directly, and is being experienced in the transference in an increasingly regressive form, there is no necessity for me to point out the connection between this material and the dream with which she began the session. Although the form of the aggressive fantasies sounds surprisingly primitive, her statement toward the end of the session that "I'm like a child in a tantrum" indicates the continuing presence of the self-observing ego in the therapeutic alliance, and therefore the primitive nature of this material does not represent any particular source of concern in regard to psychological decompensation. The fact that I have accepted these fantasies without anxiety and with the continuing request for further elaborations also serves as a form of reassurance to her and permits her verbally to express them with the tacit knowledge that they don't frighten me, nor do they cause me to reject her.

---

## SESSION 40

**P:** – – – I didn't want to come today. I locked my keys inside the house. I wonder what I'm afraid of? I don't think that it is my hostility.

**A:** I think it must relate to something that you're feeling about me.

**P:** I wonder if it is sexual? I feel as if it is, but I don't know why. It's finally been established in my mind that I must get along by myself and I can't depend on anyone so I might as well quit trying. I had a dream about two men. One was Judd and the other was the good guy from "Oklahoma." The fair-haired man was good and the black hair represented evil. But they both loved me and they were fighting over me. And yet neither one of them loved me and they were more interested in a contest than in me. The fair-haired one won, and I said to my sister, "Give up, you'll never learn, you can't depend on them and they'll never love you." If you can't depend on your parents, who can you depend on? – – –

**A:** What are your associations to Judd?

**P:** I think that's you. The other one was Tom. But there was something else and I was scared. Judd died, but I can't remember how. I don't remember whether he killed himself or whether someone else killed him. – –

**A:** What comes to your mind about him?

**P:** He was mean and no good and he was sick. I didn't really want him and the good one was too weak to take me and he ran away and so I was left by myself. – – –

A: You've left out the fact that Judd was interested in whores and in fast women.

P: – – – – I don't remember them being in my dream.

A: They don't necessarily have to be in the dream, but this was a part of the play, "Oklahoma." You associated Judd to the figure in the dream and I think this ties in with your feeling that there is something sexual going on here today.

P: – – – – – I want to tell you that I'm *not* a bad girl.

A: That suggests that you think that *I* feel that you are.

*Cry*      P: – – – – In the past one or two years I finally have outgrown my past and I'm not embarrassed to think about it any more. I not only had my own reputation to hide, but also my father's, too. This is a long time not to be embarrassed.

A: How do you mean?

*Cry*      P: – – In the seventh grade, there was a story in the newspaper about my parents' divorce. An adorable boy asked me about my father, but I felt that he knew everything that was going on. I've hated my father ever since, and wanted to be away from him. I've always had the feeling that everybody knows. (Elaborates.) I connected my father's running around with women with myself, and the things I did. It wasn't my father's fault, because he was sick. It wasn't *my* fault; it was my mother's.

A: How do you mean?

*Cry*      P: I just wished that it hadn't happened! My parents were the weakest and most neurotic people! How could they ever expect us to grow up? I must make the best of it because it's all done and I can't cry over it. But I can picture my parents and they're so weak! They had no strength at all to even raise us. They just weren't God or strong, but I still can't face it. It scares me that they are weaker than I am. That scares me and depresses me. If I talk about this I'll never get anywhere. I just can't go home and take care of my children.

A: What comes to your mind?

*Anxiety*    P: I can hardly function I'm so scared right now! I'm scared to death! I want you to give me strength.

A: And yet you see me as evil and possibly weak and possibly I'll be killed.

*Cry,*      P: I don't know what to do!! – – – – (Sobbing.) – That's why I can't
*Sob*      depend on you. What would happen to me if anything ever happened to you? I must find strength within myself.

A: What's happening here is that you are projecting on to me your own fantasy that I'm weak and evil and that something may possibly happen to me. Let's see what it means that you have this need to see me as weak.

**P:** I don't know, everybody else is weak and it will probably happen with you.

**A:** What's the detail of the thought that I'm like everybody else?

**P:** I feel like a baby who has just been born, and who in the God-damn hell else is there to depend on? There's just you, that's all. – – It's just you and me now. If you're not strong, I just don't know. I'm as strong as everybody else and so it's all up to you. – – – A minute ago I felt as if I couldn't stand it any more, I was so scared. And then I had the thought, "I wonder if you are going to be scared too."

**A:** What comes to your mind about it?

**P:** I'm begging you for help and I feel as if I could die right here and you didn't do anything about it. I hate you for it and yet somehow I'm glad. – –

**A:** I think your feeling was that if I had been scared too, that would mean that I'm weak, and the fact that I didn't get scared meant to you that I was strong.

**P:** But I hate you now. I have an urge to stand up and kill you!

**A:** That's because if I'm strong, then you'll tend to become increasingly dependent on me and that will get you even more scared.

**P:** I've never tested anyone this greatly before in my life. I guess the only way to find out if I can depend on you is to do it. – – – – – –

**A:** We'll stop here for today.


### Discussion

The patient's conflict and anxiety in the transference is indicated by her wish not to come today, and by the symptomatic act of locking her keys inside the house. However, the self-observing ego and therapeutic alliance have brought her here, and she is able to take some distance and ask herself why she is afraid, indicating that at the moment she does not feel it refers to her hostility. She is able to say this partly because of the analytic work in the previous session which permitted the more direct expression of aggression as discussed yesterday. My generalized transference interpretation that it must be related to me is an attempt to encourage her to explore this issue further and to accept in herself the existence of various kinds of transference feelings.

Her initial response is an intellectualized question of whether she might again be having sexual feelings, and this in turn leads to her description of the dream. When she mentions Judd and the play "Oklahoma," my own associations to him and to the situation of the play include the patient's father and his mistresses. This permits me a quick understanding of the major theme and conflict expressed in the dream. However, to have immediately made such an interpretation based on my own associations would have been inadvisable, since it would have meant to her that we do not need her own specific thoughts, and that I would be willing to do some of her analytic work for her. In addition, I cannot be completely sure that my understanding of the dream is correct at this point, but I do feel that Judd is the key to the dream and therefore ask for her associations to him. She immediately refers to the transference, but in her further associations to Judd she omits one of the more striking and significant aspects of his character and of the action in the play. If I had *not* been familiar with the play, her own associations would not have provided the material necessary to make the interpretation and this dream might not have been understandable at this time. My intervention, in which I point out the omission, is aimed at her repressive or suppressive defense, and her statement, "I don't remember them being in my dream," indicates that her knowledge about the women, and Judd's relationship to them, was not far from consciousness. This then permits my partial interpretation of the dream, which I then relate back to the transference conflict by referring to her earlier comment about possible sexual feeling toward me.

Subsequently, my interpretation of her projection that she is bad permits the affective expression of shame and guilt for herself and for her parents' behavior, accompanied by anxiety in the face of her feeling of helplessness experienced in the regressive transference relationship to me. Because I want to help her see in a more clear way her conflict over depending on me, I make the interpretation of her perception of me as evil and weak, and that possibly I will be killed. In this way, I am picking up on the latent dream associations, and trying to get her to see more clearly the unconscious conflict expressed in the dream.

This produces the desired effect of further mobilizing her conflict, accompanied by an intensification of the affect. Once this has been more consciously expressed, I am then in a position to interpret this perception of me as a projected transference fantasy. I am hoping to help her recognize and thereby accept more fully the difference between me in the analytic situation and the earlier figures from whom the transference is again being experienced. As a result of this appeal to the self-observing ego, there is a slight increase in her capacity to take distance from the transference feeling, and she is then able to bring up again the issue of her concern about my strength and ability to tolerate her and her feelings.

Once again she demonstrates the typical ambivalent conflict of a patient in analysis who in the transference relationship wants gratification, while at the same time in the therapeutic alliance wants the analyst to be confident and strong, and not to accede to the neurotic demands. In some ways this material represents a continuation of the issues dealt with in the previous session in regard to her fantasies of aggression and hostility. My confrontation about this conflict over my weakness or strength, as well as my interpretation that my strength tempts her to become increasingly dependent, provides her with a framework within which to understand these current reactions.

The success of these tactics is expressed in her final remarks. Although she has tested me in a variety of ways and on a number of occasions up to now in the analysis, the tests have become increasingly meaningful and intense and, as she puts it, "I've never tested anyone this greatly before in my life." This pattern of increasingly extensive and affective testing is one that will continue throughout the entire course of the analysis, but at successively more intense and regressive levels. Her final remark, "I guess the only way to find out if I can depend on you is to do it," represents the more mature elements of her personality operating within the therapeutic alliance, and preparing to make a still more significant investment in me and in the analysis.

---

## SESSION 41

P: I feel as if I'll jump out of my skin. – – – – – –

A: I wonder if you are waiting for me to comment or to intervene in some way before you go on.

P: – – – – I know that if I talk that it will come out and I don't want it to, but it's all so close. – – – It all started yesterday. I wanted to make love and I found that I wasn't afraid and then suddenly I got so nervous! (Elaborates.) I've been nervous ever since. It is somehow related to a dream that I had that I was talking with a girl and she said that her psychiatrist was blackmailing her. – – –

A: What are your associations to the dream?

P: – – I'm thinking of all of the jokes I've heard about psychiatry and psychiatrists. (Elaborates.) I'm not sure now that I'm doing the right thing. – –

A: And what about the associations to the idea of blackmail?

**P:** – It's silly. – – – – – It's do or die! – – It's you and I. . . . . – – – – –
. . . . .we're having an affair. I'd be so afraid if I let myself. . . . .we've
been over all of this before. I could have so much feeling for you but I'm
afraid that you'll take advantage of me. – –

**A:** You seem to be having trouble going on with these thoughts. What
comes to your mind?

**P:** This is all a pretense, this whole situation and all you really want
from me is sex. You want that I should fall in love with you and that we'll
have an affair but there is no love on your part and you'd just be doing it
to blackmail me.

**A:** So the fantasy about me is that I'm only interested in sex and in
screwing and in using sex and using you for my own purposes.

**P:** – – Why should I think this? I hate to think it!

**A:** I think you are identifying me with your father and you are reacting to me *as if* I were your father.

**P:** – I hate my father and I hate all men. They are all bastards and
I'll *never* love them. I feel sick because I *want* to, but it's all so unfair.

**A:** How do you mean?

**P:** It would be so wonderful to be in love without hating the man.
There must be more in life than this hatred for men. I want to love men
and have them love me, and it makes me mad that all men should be this
way. I can't believe that some man may not be and that he would love
me without sex.

**A:** In your mind you believe that I fit into this stereotyped picture
that you have of all men. But if I keep this as an analysis and if I don't
get sexually involved with you, this would mean that there is one man
who does *not* fit that stereotype. And if there is one, then there is always
the possibility that there might be others and I think it is that that makes
you so afraid.

**P:** – – I don't believe you and I still don't trust you.

**A:** So on the one hand this stereotyped idea about all men makes you
lonely and you think it's unpleasant and it makes you hate men and you
don't like to think this. And yet, at the same time we can see how you still
want to hold onto this stereotype.

**P:** I don't believe you. You're horrible and you're hateful! Why did
you use that horrible word, "screwing"? I hate you! That's all you want!
Why can't you just. . . . .just be gentle. You're so mean to me!

**A:** I was trying to express your own fantasy. You don't see sex as making love and you don't see it as part of a total relationship. In your mind
it's all pure sex and just screwing.

**P:** – I don't know what to do. I just can't trust you.

**A:** Let's look at the details of the thoughts about why you would prefer not to trust me.

**P:** Are you mad at me? Why do you keep getting mad at me for this?

**A:** What comes to your mind about the idea that I might be mad?

**P:** I've just discovered something about you and you're just mad at me. – – – I know that this is all a defense against my feelings but I've never found anyone that's not interested in that.

**A:** What's the detail?

**P:** It's true about every man that I've ever known. Even old man Stone. They all had just one thing in mind. I can see myself running to fatherly men and that's all that they want, too.

**A:** Let's see if you can be more specific.

**P:** I don't know. I'm thinking about Mr. Jones and yet he's never ever tried anything! It's true about the man next door. I had a sexual | *Cry* dream about him but I can't believe it. There's never been an older man that I've ever confided in. – – I'm thinking about Dr. Davis and I know that he was mad at me. I hate him.

**A:** What was the detail with Dr. Davis?

**P:** He just got mad. I went there to confide in him. (Elaborates.) All he could say was, "People run from such a dependency." I felt that that was mean. I needed him! And he wouldn't let me depend on him.

**A:** So the fear is whether I will get scared if you depend on me and whether I'll run from you the way you feel others have. Or else whether I'll take advantage of you and use you for my own purposes.

**P:** – – I feel right now that I. . . . .I just don't know. You'll break down every defense that I have and I'll be helpless and I'll need you. You just can't sit and say that I don't need you the way Dr. Davis did. I do! And I've depended on myself too long. Why are you doing all of this to me? What's the purpose behind it? Then you are going to sit and slap me in the face and tell me to stand on my own two feet. I'm in a turmoil! Why *should* I depend on you? Who in the hell are you that I should depend on you so much? – – Friday night my mother called, and told me that they wouldn't be able to give us any money to help with the analysis. I can't depend on them! (Elaborates.) It makes me mad! I had a dream | *Cry,* about a nursing baby that night. I could see the nipple, but I know that | *Anxiety* it was me nursing on my mother.

**A:** You're under great tension right now. Try to describe what is going | *Great* through your mind. | *Anxiety*

**P:** I can't stand it! I can't stand it! I don't know what to do.

A: Some thought or feeling must have just gone through your mind and it's terrifying you.

P: It has something to do with nursing, I know. Oh, I'm so scared!! I see a breast and I see the nipple!

A: Try to describe the details.

P: My mother is feeding me. She hates me and she hates my dependency on her. I can't do it, not even for milk and food. She hates me!! I need it and she won't give it to me.

A: You're responding to me with the same old feelings you used to have towards your mother and as if I were your mother. This is related to the idea of becoming dependent on me and the fears of how I might react. The fear is that I will repeat the same thing that happened with mother.

P: I hate her for this!! I'm so helpless. How can anyone hate me!

A: What we can see is that the feelings from the ancient past are being remobilized here with me, and you're reexperiencing the same old feelings that went on when you were very young. The problem is that you don't see me as someone different from mother and you expect the same things to happen with me as happened with her. But we'll stop here for today.


### DISCUSSION

The patient's initial comment indicates her awareness of an intense conflict which is close to consciousness, and the initial three-minute silence is a manifestation of her reluctance and resistance to pursuing it further. My initial intervention regarding her wish for me to intervene is an attempt to appeal to her participating ego and encourage her to permit her own associations to emerge more spontaneously. She then indicates further the conscious awareness of her reluctance and describes how yesterday she had experienced a brief period of relief from a symptom (her fears of sexuality), followed almost immediately by a recurrence and intensification of her anxiety.

This apparently paradoxical type of response in which a patient may take a step "forward," followed by one or two steps "backward," is a common pattern of behavior during the course of analysis. Dynamically it can be understood as a partial reduction of anxiety in a threatening situation (in this instance probably due to a partial identification with the analyst), thus permitting the patient to move slightly closer toward the threatening "danger" situation. However, since the underlying fears and fantasies about the "danger" are still present, and since no significant structural change has as yet occurred, such movement closer toward the "danger" situation is still accompanied by signal anxiety which is then controlled through regression and/or other defenses.

At this point the patient manifests her resistance in terms of the implications behind the transference dream of the psychiatrist blackmailing his patient. The dream work involves a double projection to the other girl and to the psychiatrist, and the associations that preceded her reporting it indicate the latent sexual wishes expressed in the dream. The projective defenses are further supported by references to the jokes about psychiatry, her uncertainty about the analysis, and the fantasies that I will take advantage of her. These resistances and fantasies have occurred before but are now being stimulated by the deepening transference neurosis, illustrated by her fantasy about me wanting to have an affair with her, and to blackmail her. The element of blackmail also involves a projection of her aggressive and destructive wishes, since a patient could easily blackmail a psychiatrist in such circumstances.

My intervention of clarifying this fantasy of my sexual interest in her is an attempt to show her that I can accept such distortions of me without anxiety, and without having directly to confront her with the reality. The unverbalized implications of this maneuver are that I expect her to experience these kinds of regressive distortions, and that I also assume her own capacity for reality-testing will be adequate and will permit her ultimately to recognize the transference nature of such fantasies. It is with this goal in mind that I then offer my interpretation that she is reacting to me as if I were her father. This in turn helps her partially drop the projective defense when she accepts her own wish to love and be loved by men, but she returns to it in the further elaboration of her stereotype of all men, based on transferences from the father. In several rather lengthy interpretations, I try to point out to her that she has a need to maintain such a stereotype, both with me and with other men, implying that it serves a defensive function.

In response to these challenges to her resistances (which have the effect of further mobilizing conflict and anxiety), the patient begins to express her hostility toward me. Her question about my use of the word "screwing" raises the whole issue of the vocabulary that develops and is used between the patient and the analyst during an analysis. The use of "four-letter words" can have many meanings for both participants. Such words at times are more directly representative of intense feeling than are the more elaborate or intellectual synonyms for them. However, at other times they may have a shock value, and in some situations the use of such words may be sexually stimulating either to the patient or to the analyst. If used excessively, they may after a while come to be almost meaningless, but when used judiciously and appropriately, they may at times express directly and clearly an underlying feeling or attitude. My use of the word is based on empathic awareness of the feeling she is trying to express, but it may have had too much of an impact upon her and therefore possibly have been disruptive. It is for this reason that I now explain to her my use of the word and the condensation that it involves.

Once again her defenses primarily involve a projection to me of both her anger and sexual interest, and my continuing to ask for the details of these fantasies again implies my willingness to accept them. At this point, under the impact of the anxiety mobilized in the father transference, there is a shift in her material toward the more regressive issues of dependency, and my intervention is an attempt to help her clarify these conflicts and thereby make it easier for her to see them in the light of the therapeutic alliance. This is *not* effective, and instead I am surprised that with great anxiety, she goes on to a further regression and begins to experience a set of feelings involving a deep maternal transference reaction. Having unexpectedly uncovered this level of feeling, it is essential to the therapeutic alliance that I acknowledge openly my awareness of her great anxiety and tension. This permits her to describe the image of the breast and of herself nursing.

At this point she has undergone a deeper regression than ever before in the analysis, and she is experiencing very intense anxiety and conflict. We are getting close to the end of the session and I do not want her to leave with an overwhelming level of anxiety. I also want her to know from experience that I will not permit her regression in the transference to get out of hand or to be so severe as to frighten her away from similar regressive experiences and phenomena in the future. It is for these reasons that I make the transference interpretation to her that she is responding to me as if I were the mother, and correlate this to the current transference conflict over becoming dependent upon me. The attempt here is again to appeal to the therapeutic alliance and to provide her adult and rational ego with a conceptual framework upon which to understand the current reaction. It should be noted that the interpretation is focused at the general level of her current conflict over dependency, and that the deep oral roots of this conflict are not included in the interpretation. I am thereby attempting to help her reduce the intensity of her anxiety and thus make it possible for her to leave the session under better control.

The expectation is that if she finds she can undergo such regressive and anxiety-provoking experiences safely here without having them go too far and without being unduly disabled by them, she will then be in a better position in the future to permit similar regression and expression of transference feeling and fantasy to occur. It is my impression that had I remained silent during this experience, it would have left her increasingly threatened and with a feeling that she would not be able to rely on me to help her, and therefore it might have made her more reluctant in the future to permit similar experiences to occur.

Throughout this session I have been very active and I have intervened frequently. It could be argued that this was not entirely necessary, and that I could have permitted her to maintain her resistances, or permitted her to struggle with these conflicts more on her own. However, it is my feeling that the emerging transference neurosis is evoking considerable conflict and anxiety within her, and that by the interventions I am helping her to verbalize it more directly and openly, and thereby indirectly telling her that such transference phenomena are very much a part of psychoanalysis.

---

## SESSION 42

P: I feel so depressed today. I felt fine yesterday until I went to a bridge party. (Elaborates.) It came out all of a sudden and I had the thought that no one likes me and that I'm a nothing.

A: What was the detail?

P: There were two people there and they said that they hoped I would have a boy this time. They said that life just isn't complete until you've had a boy. It made me so mad! These are girls that I used to know. They're Southern and they are so false! I used to do all of that too. (Elaborates.) But it's all not real! This is the way I used to grow up with my mother, where I'd get along fine if I'd kiss her rear end. But I didn't want to, and I would feel like hating her while I would do it. – – – Now I feel as if I haven't got a friend in the world who understands me. There's not one soul. I think that this relates mostly to women, but I had a dream about a man. It's the hardest thing for me to admit that I'm a failure, especially about men. I dreamt about the man that Joan is marrying, and I was trying to get him to like me, and I was sexually attracted to him, but he wasn't going to pay any attention to me at all. – – – – – – – –

**A:** What are your associations to the fact that your thoughts stopped just then?

**P:** – – What part do you play in all of this? I was sitting at home Friday night and I was thinking about being here, and I felt that what I want you'll never be. What if this doesn't ever help me? That idea sends me into a panic. Everyone else is against me and I feel as if I'm not strong enough all by myself.

**A:** What was the detail about the thought on Friday?

**P:** I was thinking about psychoanalysis and psychiatry and I was , ndering if it was really going to help. You're so mean! You only want sex. I really don't know anything about analysis or about you. (Elaborates.) If this turns out to be the wrong thing then I've *had* it. I've now looked too deeply ever to stop.

**A:** You mention that you had these thoughts on Friday. What comes to your mind that you had them then?

**P:** I had the feeling that you are horrible and I hated you. And I also felt that you hated me. As long as I'm nice and do what you want me to do, then you'll help me, but if I ever do anything wrong or if I ever hate you then you'll hate me.

**A:** So this is somewhat the same feeling that you had with your mother. You feel that as long as you kiss my rear end then everything is fine here.

**P:** – – – Why is it that I can't hate my parents? It's just that I do not feel it toward them. I rationalize the whole situation. – – – My mother has been running away from me lately if I ever disagree with her. (Elaborates.) It's as if they'll fall apart and kill themselves. I really don't make that much difference to them, and I get no satisfaction from it at all.

**A:** Once again I think you are talking about your feelings about me. You're wondering if I am strong enough and will tolerate your hate, or will I run from it. And also you feel that you have no effect from what you say here, so you get no satisfaction when you say it.

**P:** – – – – The minute I get mad at you I get scared that I can't depend on you any more and that you'll collapse, or else you'll withdraw yourself from me. – –

**A:** Let's look at the details of both possibilities. What comes to your mind?

**P:** I go back to Friday and the way that I felt that I hated you and I really felt it, but then my reaction was fear. And then I'd think about what happened here Monday, and then yesterday I felt all alone, and I was awake all night and I was really scared.

**A:** What was the detail?

**P:** I had lots of dreams but I can't remember them, but I know that I felt frightened and I felt as if I was all alone. – –

**A:** What was your fear about what would happen when you came here today?

**P:** – – – – – – I don't really remember thinking about what would happen today, but I wondered if you were mad. I felt that you were, but I don't remember thinking about it today. –

**A:** You were wondering if I was mad, and feeling as if I was. What comes to your mind about that?

**P:** I kept thinking that you were. It was something that I said or did. – – I think I discovered what you were really like and I told you about it. You're evil and horrible and you're just after one thing. You're not nice or kind and you really don't like me telling you about this. – – – This is where you are weak and you can't take it. – –

**A:** Let's look at the details of your feeling that I was upset and that I can't take it, and that I don't like you.

**P:** I felt as if you were nervous at first and then I thought that you got mad. – – – – As long as I do what you like, then you're an adult. But then you fall apart and become like a child and get mad and you're not strong enough to take it when I say something that you don't like. –

**A:** So it seems as if you see me and react to me in the same old image of your mother.

**P:** – I feel just like a child who is being raised by a child. Where do you ever get security? My mother was the weakest, most immature, unstable thing I can think of, and yet I can't face it when I'm with her, but if I'm honest I have to admit that I see it all the time. – – My sister was much more adult than my mother. – – I see now that I can never depend on my parents, and so now I have to depend on you. But I wonder if you want this dependency, or is it going to make you mad? Is it going to scare you? – –

**A:** I think there are other things that went on here on Monday that you haven't referred to yet.

**P:** – I can't see much of a connection. I have the feeling that when my mother fed me she'd laugh, and she'd say, "I'll either kill you or else I'll save you." I'm sure that you are going to take sexual advantage of me. That's all you really wanted from me. – – –

A: I think there may be more to all of this than we ve seen up to now. For example, I think that you may be confusing what happened here Monday with what happened last Friday. It's as if you have a need to take greater distance from it. Let's see what comes to your mind.

P: − − I feel as if I have to *hate* you. (Elaborates.) Now I'm thinking about Friday and I'm not sure any more what happened. I wonder what it was? − − − −

A: What comes to your mind about it?

P: I felt as if I had to make one of two decisions. Am I able completely to trust you? Or do I have to find some reason to hate you? I think I decided to hate you, because really you're not worthy of my trust. − −

A: We'll stop here for today.

### DISCUSSION

The patient's initial comments that she had "felt fine yesterday" and had gone to a bridge party are indicators that she had been able successfully to tolerate and reverse the intense regressive experience in the maternal transference, and in the image of being nursed by her mother, which occurred in the previous session. And as part of this reversal, she begins this session by expressing a set of conflicts reflecting derivatives of a later stage of psychosexual development. Her friends' hoping that she would have a boy, and the dream about wanting to attract her girl-friend's fiancé, at this point represent a defense against the maternal transference by movement forward in psychosexual level toward derivatives of her conflicts over phallic strivings and her sense of phallic inadequacy and inferiority. The silence is an indication of her hesitation in approaching these issues at either level, and my question about her associations stopping short is an indirect attempt to encourage her to face them.

Her response is spontaneously to focus the conflict back toward the transference and her fear of depending on me, expressed by the fantasy that I will not be able to take care of her. My own thoughts at this time are that she is still attempting to defend herself against further exploration of the mother-transference conflicts stimulated here on Monday, and for this reason she had experienced a confusion of times and had referred the entire experience backwards to the session of last Friday. In hoping to begin to unravel her anxiety and conflict about this, I begin by asking the questions regarding her thoughts on Friday.

Her associations are again to the elements of resistance and to her fear of trust in me at the oedipal level ("you only want sex") and so I repeat my question about the misidentification of dates. This time she brings up associations which are similar to what she had said earlier in this session in regard to her mother, and I try to clarify this maternal transference response by quoting what she had said previously. The further associations to her mother strike me as an attempt to avoid full impact of the idea that such conflicts are being stimulated in the current analytic experience, and thus I make my interpretation again of her continuing fear of trust in the transference. I feel it necessary to deal with this issue of basic trust before we can make further progress, and because her material indicates that she had been anxious and afraid of the analytic situation last night, I suggest that she must have had some type of frightening fantasy about coming here today, and I suspect that it was related to the regressive transference experience.

Although initially she denies any such fantasy, she does then express the fear that I was angry at her and that I was responding defensively to her transference criticisms of me. In asking her to elaborate about this, I am attempting to demonstrate that I am not anxious or defensive, and that I can tolerate such criticism without retaliation. She again reverts to the transference image of me in words and feelings similar to those she had earlier used to describe the relationship to the mother, which permits me again to make the transference interpretation that she is responding to me in the image of her mother. Following this interpretation there is a further elaboration of uncertainty in regard to mother and the inability to depend on her, with a spontaneous return to a similar set of conflicts in the current experience and relationship to me.

Up to this point in the session I have the feeling that she is avoiding the full impact of the transference experience that had emerged on Monday, and that this is evoking the current feelings of depression and conflict. I therefore begin by pointing out the omission from her associations of some of the other things that occurred, to which her response is an association to the situation of being fed by the mother. However, this is almost immediately replaced by associations to the fantasies of my taking sexual advantage of her, which I at that moment feel is a defense against the anxiety in the maternal and dependent transference. Once again I try to help her elaborate on this conflict by pointing out the confusion between Monday and Friday, but this maneuver is not particularly successful, and results only in some generalizations about the question whether she should trust me or hate me. It is now apparent that the resistances against a return to the regressive experience of Monday are still intense, that the experience itself has been partially repressed, and that in spite of my effort on Monday the experience has mobilized too much anxiety.

---

## SESSION 43

**P:** I dreamed that I killed myself. At least I guess it was me. There was a friend in the dream but she was pregnant and her baby was due at the same time mine is. I was in a cafeteria and someone said that she'd taken five bottles of aspirin. We were sitting at a table and I asked about the baby. She said that she'd lost the baby on June 8. Actually she's had several miscarriages.        I wonder why that date showed up in the dream. It just comes to mind that my daughter is going to be operated on on June 10, and I'm upset about it.

**A:** This is the first time that you've mentioned it.

**P:** I don't like to think about it.

**A:** What are your thoughts?

**P:** She has a duct in her neck and they have to put her to sleep and that worries me. I've put it off for three months ever since March. I just didn't call the doctor because I'm afraid of doctors. It just doesn't make sense, but I picture the doctor as mean and cruel. He knows my father and I was scared to call him. – –

**A:** What about your associations to some of the other dream elements?

**P:** I wasn't frightened. I was thinking about this girl but yet I'm sure that it was me. I put on clothes but they weren't maternity clothes but regular clothes and I thought to myself that I looked nice and slim. I also had a dream about school and I was in class and we were having lunch but we were watching a movie and then we were in an auditorium. I felt toward the teachers just the same as I feel towards you. This teacher was a woman but I felt that she was so stupid and I was above her and then I was doing the whole thing because I have to. – – – I have had a terrible urge to eat lately. I sometimes think I'm going to die if I do, and yet I feel as if I have to, but I hate myself for eating. It's somehow related to feelings of hostility. Harris used to say that it was sexual but I feel that it is hostility. – – –

**A:** What are your associations to this other girl?

**P:** – I wonder if it could be my sister? Not really. – – She has a lot of problems and yet it's not really her. – –

**A:** And what about the five bottles of aspirin?

**P:** That was to throw me for a loop. I had the thought that I would experiment with them and first I took three, but then I took all five. I think I was going to kill myself but it was going to be less vicious than slitting my wrists. – – – And there was someone with us all the time too. I think the table represents a picnic table. – – – It was all so dark, as if it was in the past, and it all took place in the woods. – – – – That makes me think of rain and the days that mother used to pick us up at school in the rain. I've never been afraid of the rain until lately. (Elaborates.) It was raining the night of my shaking spell. (Elaborates.) It was also raining last night. – – – – –

**A:** What about the other dream of the teacher? What are your associations?

**P:** – – – I think my mother is the teacher, and yet it didn't really look like her. She had black hair and she had her back to me and she was very domineering. – – – – She wasn't really teaching and she didn't really want us to learn. She was doing it for her own self atisfaction. That's the way I feel about this and also about my mother. It's all for your satisfaction. You're not going to help me but you must do it.

**A:** What's the detail of feeling that way about me and the analysis?

**P:** How will it possibly help? – – I was raised all wrong but I'm an adult now and I can't go back, so how can it possibly help to bring it up? It's like that girl in the dream who was just sitting there but really she was dead. – – –

**A:** I think you are still trying to give yourself excuses in order to avoid trusting me and trusting the analysis and going ahead with it.

**P:** – – I just want to argue with everything that you say. – – This is just like walking up to a stranger and asking him to raise you for the rest of your life and give you all that you need. – – – – – I feel that you'll be mad at me if I depend on you. I'm throwing myself at your feet and yet I feel that I'm an idiot. I feel that I can't even stand on my own two feet. – – –

**A:** The feeling is that I'm doing all of this for my own satisfaction. What's the detail?

**P:** You're never with me when I need you and I feel as if you're withdrawing.

**A:** What comes to mind?

**P:** You don't say anything and you just sit there. That's what you do for this helpless person on the couch. – – – – You just sit there. Just like now. I might as well be in a room by myself.

**A:** Let's look at the fantasy of what you would like for me to say or do.

**P**: I want you to be kind so that I can trust you.

**A**: But what's the detail?

**P**: I want you to encourage me. I don't know what I want. – – I just babble on and on and I get the feeling that you wish I'd shut up but you'll have to take it and you're just not yelling back at me. – – I don't understand what I'm supposed to do here. – – –

**A**: I think you *do* understand, but you don't want to believe it.

**P**: I feel as if I'm lying here all by myself. How can I possibly go through this unless I feel that you care about me and that you're strong? And do I know that if you don't say anything?

**A**: We'll stop here for today.


### DISCUSSION

Throughout this session the patient's resistances against the emerging transference neurosis are maintained and probably this is still part of her continuing response to the intense anxiety mobilized by the regressive experience in the Monday session. Although the first dream was not analyzed, the theme is of a mother-child relationship with danger for the baby. This leads to the daughter's operation, and my pointing out that this is the first time she has mentioned it is an attempt to block the mechanism of isolation in which she separates from the analysis some of the important real external events in her current life situation. This leads to the recurrence of associations about her mistrust of doctors, which has obvious transference implications at this point.

I am no longer clear as to why I did not explore further the mistrust of doctors, and instead chose to focus upon her associations to the dream. In her associations she reports the second dream involving her contempt for a woman teacher whom she associates with me, and toward whom she feels superior and feels as if she is not being helped. This in turn leads to her mentioning the recurrence of the symptom of eating, but it all remains rather superficial.

I feel that we are not significantly dealing with the current conflicts, and hope that perhaps the particular girl in the dream might provide a further clue. However, it does not and so I next attempt to do the same thing with the five bottles of aspirin. When the analyst is having difficulty in precisely understanding the current situation, or in situations where the patient's associations tend to be superficial and generalized and therefore to represent resistances, it is sometimes possible to use associations to specific dream elements as a means of by-passing the defenses. However, in this case, neither of these attempts is successful and instead of associating to the dream elements, she merely continues to elaborate on the manifest dream content. This is another indication that her resistances are too intense to be dealt with at the moment, and so I choose to return to the theme of the transference and fears of basic trust by asking for her associations to the teacher whom she had already indicated was a representation of me.

At this point she is able more directly to approach the transference conflict and give verbal expression to her intensified sense of mistrust and uncertainty about analysis. This theme occupies the rest of the session, and although in fact I am being very active, it becomes increasingly clear that in the maternal transference she perceives me as a nonsupportive and frustrating mother who does not meet her needs, and toward whom she then feels a sense of hostility, alienation, and a reluctance to establish basic trust.

However, another element in this material is a form of testing me to determine whether or not I will be comfortable if she is hostile, critical, and demanding, and to find out whether or not I am comfortable in my role, confident of what I am doing, and that I will not be unduly influenced or manipulated by her negativistic comments. The unspoken issue here is to separate me as analyst from the real mother who she had felt would respond either with hostility or withdrawal if the patient "did not kiss her rear end," as had been mentioned in yesterday's session.

---

## SESSION 44

**P:** This thing is driving me nuts. I'm so depressed and I can't sleep and I've had all kinds of dreams but I don't know what they are. I've had anxiety and I'm tense and sometimes I don't even know what I'm doing. I've been thinking about Sally's operation and I've got myself in a twit about it. I have so many physical symptoms. It's just like when I was a child and the feelings I used to have in bed. It's hard and it's something black and solid and square and I suddenly have a picture of a horrible woman. It's all solid and yet it's all in my mind. The woman is trying to devour me and kill me. I have that funny feeling in my mouth right now.

**A:** Try to describe it.

**P:** It's as if there's something in my mouth. It's weird and it's almost physical. I had it so much when I was younger.

**A:** You mean that your mouth feels filled?

**P:** There's a feeling in my mouth of something hard and square and black. It's square and it means a woman to me but I don't see it and I have the feeling that it is going to devour me. (Elaborates.) I had a dream that Tom and my daughter and I were in Maine by ourselves. My parents were there too and I was in a house with lots of rooms and we were going through them. My parents didn't care whether we were there or not and I was hurt that they didn't ask us to go with them. There were a lot of rooms, but I can't remember whose house it was. Tom wanted to leave, but I didn't want to. --- I hate everyone and I've been directing a lot of my hostility towards the baby and yet I'm so sorry for her.

**A:** What comes to your mind about where this hostility really belongs?

**P:** -- Yesterday I was so hostile towards you! I could have screamed and hit and kicked.

**A:** Let's look at what kept you from expressing it while you were here.

**P:** I was about to yesterday, but I stopped. I had the thought that it can't be me saying all of this. I don't know what it is. I don't want to yell and scream at you. --- I can't put love and hate together. If I hate you then I can't love you, and I want to love you. If I ever hate you, that's it, boy. All I want is love.

**A:** What's the detail of the feeling that if you ever hate me that's it?

**P:** It's just like with Tom and hating him. How can you possibly hate, and yet love someone at the same time. If I hate you then I haven't got anything.

**A:** I wonder if you aren't frightened by a fantasy that if you ever hate me and let yourself express the feeling that you'll destroy me?

**P:** I know that something will be destroyed. --- Hate is something that I'm always afraid of. I'm afraid that it's going to overpower me and you and that there will be nothing left.

**A:** What do you picture?

**P:** -- I can't picture anything. There is no communication between us. --

**A:** And yet you have the feeling that it will overpower you or me. What comes to mind?

**P:** -- I'd overpower you and you wouldn't fight back and you'd be nothing. --- It would be much easier to live with my hatred suppressed than with nothing at all.

**A:** You mentioned the idea that you might overpower me, and so on. This is all rather general and vague and it's as if you are afraid to see the details of what you're thinking.

**P:** - (Sigh.) -- When my little girl whimpers I sometimes think to myself that I hate her and I would like to take a knife and kill her! At the same time I know that that wouldn't help. – –

**A:** I think the fantasy is of an attack on me. You've mentioned before your thoughts of wanting to claw and bite and tear at me.

**P:** – In hating you, it's as if I'll kill you and be alone and have no one to love *or* hate, or have any feeling for. – – And yet I can't picture myself attacking or killing you. – – – – – – – –

**A:** Let's look and see why it's necessary to blot out the thoughts that are coming to your mind now.

**P:** – I don't know what hate is. It would be such a much better world without it and if emotion wasn't there. And yet there is so much of it inside me. I'm sick and tired of putting it into my children.

**A:** Let's look at why you feel the need to keep it inside you while you're here.

**P:** It's ruining me! It's ruining my life! It's ruining my family! I haven't tried any hostility on you. What would you do if I did? It probably wouldn't destroy you and yet what if you stood up and screamed at me?

**A:** If, for analysis, I asked you to tell me all that comes to your mind and not hold anything back, then what right would I have to scream at you?

**P:** I don't know what I'd say.

**A:** But regardless of that?

**P:** It's not a matter of what right you'd have. You don't like me and you wouldn't help me and you sit here day after day but something would be ended. If any hostility would be expressed it would be the end of our relationship and it would never be the same. You couldn't accept it and it would be there forever. – – – This is just like with my friends, the way I feel about you. I always have the feeling that they don't like me. I've done that to everyone I've depended on. There will be one time when I say something that they don't like and that's it. That happened with my sisters and now it's happened with my parents.

**A:** So you still expect me to react, not the way I've said, but rather as you feel others have reacted.

**P:** – – – There are things that I'd say to you that if someone said them to me I'd swear it would make me mad.

**A:** And this is another element in your fear. You are projecting onto me the way you'd feel if the situation were reversed.

**P:** – – – (Laughs.) – If you weren't so much like my father this would be much easier.

**A:** In what way?

**P:** You sit and talk just like my father did and it's all so calm, as if he's saying, "What's the big deal?" And yet there was nothing there. I don't think that you could believe what you're saying. It's all so reasonable and it's all part of a plan and there's no emotion in it. But with my father, underneath he'd be jumping up and down.

**A:** I wonder if you have the fantasy that I'm jumping up and down underneath?

**P:** Only that one time on Monday. I felt that I'd scared you and got you upset. I can't believe that you can sit so quiet and be so reasonable and not have this upset you.

**A:** If you *do* believe it, and accept the idea of this analysis, then there would be a greater temptation to express your feelings. The reason that you *don't* believe it is your fear of expressing these feelings.

**P:** ------

**A:** But there's a part of your mind that wants to believe that it is safe for you to express yourself even though the other part is afraid to. We'll stop here for today.

### DISCUSSION

The patient begins by elaborating upon the multiple symptoms she is now experiencing as conflicts over the emerging transference neurosis are being mobilized. Her statement that "It's just like when I was a child, and the feelings I used to have in bed" is an indicator of the extent to which she is undergoing a transference regression to relationships and feelings from childhood. The same is true of the somatic sensation in her mouth, which has some of the characteristics of an Isakower phenomenon, although it is not completely typical. The transference neurosis is indicated by the fact that this sensation in the analytic situation represents the return of an early childhood symptom. My questions about it are an attempt to show my interest in her various somatic sensations, as well as the other psychic experiences she is undergoing during analysis. This type of sensation represents a derivative of deeply repressed psychic experience and conflict, but it is still far too early in the analysis to explore this at any depth. I therefore am satisfied merely to encourage her elaboration of the sensation itself at a descriptive level, since to go further at this time would intellectualize and isolate the process.

After she reports the dream and the expression of her hostility toward her child, I feel that this is a displacement of aggression mobilized in the transference, but acted out upon the child. Because I want to discourage this type of displacement and acting-out, and because I hope to focus the emerging hostility more directly into the transference relationship, I ask where the hostility really belongs, thus indirectly implying that a displacement has occurred. The patient is then able directly to indicate that the hostility had been experienced here toward me yesterday, and my intervention regarding her failure to express it while here is an attempt to get her to explore the resistance against expressing the transference reaction directly.

The next series of interactions represent my active attempts to help her cope with her conflict and anxiety over the ambivalence she is feeling toward me, and to help her verbalize some of the preconscious fantasies which block her from full expression of the already conscious and preconscious transference reactions. In this series of exchanges I interpret the possibility that she might have the fantasy of destroying me if she were ever to express her aggression directly. This is based partly on the material from the current session ("If I ever hate you, that's it, boy"; "If I hate you, then I haven't got anything") and partly on the fantasies of attacking me which had emerged earlier in the analysis. Her responses may represent a confirmation of the correctness of my interpretations, but it must also be kept in mind that they might represent a response to the suggestions involved in my interpretations.

After the period of silence, I confront her with her resistances to the expression of currently conscious transference reactions, and at this point she is able to express more superficial, but probably more pertinent, transference fantasies regarding my disapproval, retaliation, or withdrawal if she were to express the hostility toward me. This suggests that the previous material and fantasies about physical attack or destruction were "too deep," and although possibly valid in terms of the underlying primary process fantasies, at this point they represent a defense against the more superficial but immediately and emotionally conscious anticipations in the transference. In other words, what is needed now is work toward further strengthening of the therapeutic alliance and further conscious acceptance by her that feelings of hostility and aggression are also part of analysis.

It is this reasoning which leads me to remind her of our basic agreement regarding her expression of all feelings, and of my responsibility not to retaliate or respond with counteraggression. This intervention is apparently successful in that she is now able to elaborate the fantasy of expressing the aggression, and then reflect her awareness of this as a transference response similar to expectations of reactions that she has experienced with friends and with her family. After I interpret her projective defense, she is able to take increasing distance from the situation, as evidenced by tne brief laugh, followed by the perception of me as being like her father. The next series of associations involves both a transference response to me as the father, and a self-observing development in the therapeutic alliance when she says, "It's all so reasonable, and it's all part of a plan and there's no emotion in it."

The patient's reference to having scared me on Monday requires some self-analysis. Although I had not consciously felt anxious and had been aware only of surprise at the depth of the regression, it is possible that I projected my anxiety to her in my concern about controlling the depth of the regression. In that case my interpretations at the time would have been motivated by my own anxiety, as well as by hers, and she might have perceived it. In such an event, the transference fantasy would be supported by a reality perception and thus be intensified, leading to the increased resistances during the rest of the week.

My final two interventions are again focused at strengthening the therapeutic alliance, and helping her see and accept more clearly the fact that analysis involves expression of the full range of emotional reactions, impulses, and fantasies.

During this week's work, the sequence of events involved the intensely regressive maternal transference experience on Monday, with the mobilization of anxiety which was of greater intensity than optimal at this stage of an analysis. Although I attempted to offset this with the interventions I made at the end of that session, the remainder of the week can be understood as reflecting the effects of a heightened resistance and defensiveness against reexperiencing a similar reaction, and a partial disruption of the therapeutic alliance in the face of the acute discomfort and conflict that the analysis is producing. The problem for me during the remainder of the week was to attempt to reduce the intensity of the conflict and anxiety she was experiencing, and to strengthen the therapeutic alliance in order that she would be better able to tolerate similar regressive transference experiences in the future.

---

## SESSION 45

**P:** I've been doing all kinds of crazy things. It's as if I've been walking down a road that has been planned for me. I was a nervous wreck on Saturday. (Elaborates.) But then on Sunday I was in a good mood. I had a dream about an older man who lives across the street who can't work and just sits. I dreamed that my daughter overslept and that she couldn't go to nursery school. I was doing it at the neighbors and I was dependent on them but I was breaking glasses and making a mess and carrying on and they hated me. (Elaborates.) There was a question whether they would keep Carol or whether they would take her for me. The man was mad and he didn't want me to depend on them. Then I was going downtown and I saw a man but I didn't speak. I was mad at him and I said that I was sorry that I was so dependent on him. (Elaborates.) – – I've been in a twit about money again this morning. I wonder why this man was in the dream? He's an idiot and he's really not doing anything.

A: You mentioned that he just sits and I think that that represents me and your feelings about me.

P: – – – – – – I feel that you are bringing out all of the hostility in me that I've suppressed for twenty-five years. I feel just the way I used to when I was growing up. I'm mad and I take it out on everything but the right thing. I know why I suppressed it then and it's no fun to live that way.

A: There may well have been good reasons why you felt you had to suppress it when you were growing up. But the question would be why you need to take it out on others now, and what the fear is of expressing it here?

P: I'm thinking about Saturday and my determination not to take it out on the children and Tom. (Elaborates.) Right after I thought that I got terribly nervous.

A: In the dream you were smashing the glasses. What comes to your mind about it?

P: There were four of them on a stick and they were full and I was breaking them and making a mess and spilling everything around. I feel it here too. I feel that you are mad at me and that you just must put up with it. In the dream he never said anything, and he never would. (Elaborates.) I wanted to depend on him but I couldn't. And also I didn't really have to. (Elaborates.) I'm thinking about the neighbors and the baby-sitting arrangement for coming here. I have to start paying my way. (Elaborates.) It makes me mad.

A: So again we can see how you get mad at me but you're nervous about expressing it here and so you take it out on the others.

P: It's like I was nursing at my mother and I was mad and I had the urge to bite her. But then she'd never feed me again and so why do it. I can't win for losing.

A: Again we can understand the situation from when you were very little and the possibility that this might have happened with your mother. But what about here and now in the analysis with me?

**P:** I can't convince myself. And, I'd have nothing to fall back on. It's not safe yet. How would I live without being able to have the analysis now? I know I can yell and scream at you but I get so scared! I have to feel it and I can't force it. (Elaborates.)

**A:** Let's go back to Saturday morning and the thoughts that you were not going to take it out on your family. What comes to your mind?

**P:** I thought that I could do it for a while and then I got scared. Then I was in a horrible mood and I screamed and I took it out on the house and the cleaning and the chasing around. In the dream I finally got mad at the man, and somehow that's like a hopeful sign. (Elaborates.) I feel as if I'm on that elevator again. – – – – – – – –

**A:** What are your associations to the silence?

**P:** If I say anything then I'm putting you in that upper position again.

**A:** How do you mean, that upper position?

**P:** There are things that I can do to avoid hostility. I can show you my weaknesses, or I can fight you, or I can make you my therapist and my teacher and make myself inferior to you. – – I'm so tired of that picture and those curtains!

**A:** What's the detail?

**P:** This is such a degrading experience! You know that I'm hostile and that I'm afraid and you just sit and gloat in it. And I hate it. I'll *not* shed a tear in here! I'll be God-damned! Why do you get satisfaction from seeing me cower in front of you! Now I have that tingling feeling all over me. What is it? – – – – – I can't stand this!

**A:** What's the detail of the feeling that I'm sitting here and gloating?

*Anxiety*

**P:** I can't stand being put in this position. I don't like it at all! (Elaborates.) I'm *not* this weak! If I have to get up and look at you, I'll collapse. It would scare me to death. Why? It's all right as long as I don't have to look at you. – – I can't stand it! This is all so ridiculous! I must get out of here! (Patient gets up and starts to leave the room.)

**A:** Why do you want to leave early? (The analyst points out his awareness of her anxiety but suggests that she try to express and analyze her feelings rather than run from them.)

**P:** (Returns to the couch, and for the rest of the session remains sitting on the side looking at the analyst intermittently.) (During the rest of the session the patient elaborates her anxiety and the feeling that she is tiny with the analyst being big. There was also a fantasy that she was big and equal to the size of the analyst and a fantasy that she'd destroy him. She described her needs to look at him and her anxiety and fear in the total situation.)

**A:** (The analyst remains calm throughout, looks directly at the patient and permits her to look at him a few times before asking for her associations to looking at him. The analyst interprets to the patient that her feelings towards the mother are being transferred here and the fantasy is of either killing or being killed and of feeling helpless. He points out how she has evaded this feeling ever since she grew up. He also interprets the looking at him as a reassurance to her that he is really *not* mother.)

**P:** (Patient gradually became calmer and less anxious as these interchanges went on.)

**A:** We'll stop here for today.

### Discussion

The patient begins by describing the recurrence of anxiety symptoms over the weekend, and then presents the dream. In the setting of what has been going on recently in the analysis, it has obvious transference implications in terms of her conflict over dependency upon me and the fantasies that I will not be able to tolerate it and that I will not do anything to help her. When she says, "He's an idiot and he's really not doing anything," the shift in tense from the dream to the present indicates further how close these transference feelings are to her current conscious awareness. I might have waited or asked for her associations to this man before making the transference interpretation, but I feel that the material is close enough to her conscious awareness that I can immediately focus it upon the transference. Her response indicates that she had been aware of the transference conflict and when she says, "I feel the way I used to when I was growing up," she is demonstrating how the transference neurosis is emerging more clearly. She also indicates her own awareness of the defense of displacement which she is using in trying to cope with these conflicts.

My next intervention acknowledges that there were reasons for these defenses in childhood, but emphasizes the difference between the childhood situation and the current analytic relationship, as well as the need to understand the utilization of these old mechanisms in the current scene. This is an attempt to appeal to the healthy ego functions and to the therapeutic alliance, and to help her more clearly differentiate the past situation from the current one with me. My hope is that a more firm differentiation of the present analytic situation as compared with the transference expectations will then permit her more freely to express the currently conflictual transference feelings and fantasies. Apparently the attempt at home to give up this defense of displacement had shifted her dynamic equilibrium, and the unverbalized fantasy of expressing her transference affects directly had again mobilized acute anxiety. My explanation that the anxiety is related to her progressive wish to give up the displacement mechanism and to express the transference feelings directly is an attempt to strengthen and reinforce these analytically appropriate motivations. However, she remains silent and there is no immediate confirmation about the effectiveness of this intervention.

For the moment we have gone as far as we can with this material but I want to help her deal more consciously with the hostility she is experiencing, and I therefore select the dream element of smashing the glasses as a starting point for her associations. Her response that there were four of them is probably another reference to the analytic situation and the four sessions per week. But it is not necessary to point this out directly since spontaneously she says, "I feel it here too," and then goes on to elaborate upon some of her hostility and disappointment, both in connection with the man in the dream and the realistic sacrifices she must make for the analysis. However, these references are again directed away from the conscious transference feeling toward me, and I choose to interpret this defensive displacement, also acknowledging that the anxiety at expressing the transference directly is motivating the defense.

I feel at that time that her association to the infantile relationship with her mother represents the defense of returning intellectually to the remote past in an attempt to avoid the more important and immediate current conflict with me. It is this reasoning that leads me to indicate tactfully my acceptance of her associations that such a sequence of events might have occurred as a child, but I also want her to elaborate on the conflict in the current analytic situation. This is an attempt again to help her differentiate the current situation with me from the past situation with her parents, thereby strengthening the therapeutic alliance. She is able to verbalize her need to continue testing the current situation with me, at the same time indicating a growing recognition that she increasingly knows it would be safe and appropriate to express her feelings here directly, even though accompanied by anxiety.

Because I feel it important to help her control the acting-out with her family, and help her focus the conflict into the transference, and following her increasing recognition of the realities of the analytic situation, I now return to the anxiety she had experienced at home when she made the conscious attempt not to go on displacing the transference reaction. She elaborates on the displacement itself but then, with a bit of self-observation and appropriate perception, describes how "in the dream I finally got mad at the man and somehow that's like a hopeful sign." However, having taken this short step forward, she then uses another more extensive defense of suppression and silence.

My focusing on the defense of silence results in a resumption of her more direct expression of hostility toward me and toward the analytic situation, which now involves the more regressive projection to me that I am gloating and experiencing satisfaction in her feeling of being degraded. This in turn mobilizes an increase in her conflict and anxiety, so that she now uses the more disruptive and extensive resistance of getting up from the couch and preparing to leave the session.

Although I have been aware that she is anxious and under stress, her getting up to leave the session takes me by surprise. I want to block this form of acting-out if possible, but if she had carried it through, I would not have made any active attempts to stop her and would have had to wait until the next session to analyze the conflict and the anxiety which made her leave. At this point I stop taking notes, but try otherwise to maintain the analytic atmosphere and situation and to remain analytically neutral in my attitude and comments. My initial request for her associations as to why she wants to leave the session early leads to her further description of the intense anxiety she is experiencing. I acknowledge my awareness of the intensity of her anxiety and discomfort, but also indicate that it would be better for the analysis if she could deal with these feelings verbally so that we could understand them better. Throughout this I remain seated in my chair looking at her quietly and directly, and although I had been surprised by her getting up, I am not particularly personally distressed by it and can therefore remain calm, composed, and analytically objective.

My activity has its desired effect in that the patient does not leave, but instead continues the session, although sitting up and looking at me as described. The material deals with her intense anxiety, the regressive images of herself and her fear of something overt occurring between us, and her sense of helplessness in relationship to me. This material evolves through several active interchanges between us, and I am able to continue the analysis even though we are now sitting face-to-face, and I am able to interpret the maternal transference and its implications for her current regressive feelings. As this is going on, the patient's anxiety subsides appreciably and I terminate the interview at the usual time and in the usual way.

This experience was an extremely important one for the patient. I had perhaps been too persistent and vigorous in interpreting her defenses against the emerging transference neurosis, and as a result mobilized greater conflict and anxiety than was appropriate. In retrospect, a pattern of increasingly intense and broader defenses against this conflict can be seen as one follows the material of this session. However, once the conflict reached the levels it did, with the major defense of attempting to leave the session, it was crucial that I maintain my position in the neutral participant-observer-analyst role. I could feel calm and comfortable within myself while continuing to interact with her and continuing my analytic responsibility of interpreting her behavior in a way that she could grasp and understand. As a result of this, and of looking at each other while it went on, I helped her reverse the regression she was undergoing, and thereby reestablish the therapeutic alliance. In a sense, this episode may also have represented a form of additional testing of me and my strength before she would be able further to invest herself in the analytic situation and in the experience and expression of the transference neurosis.

---

## SESSION 46

**P:** I had two sexual dreams Monday night. In one of them Tom and I were in bed and the kids were playing around on the floor in the room with us. We couldn't make love because the kids were there but I wanted to, although Tom didn't. – – Then I dreamt that I was a bad girl, I mean that I was a prostitute and I was with a man. My sister and I were in a house in Springfield and there were two boys with us. We were all having intercourse and there was an emotionally soft part of me but I wasn't going to let myself feel it. He ridiculed me all through it and I hated him. The boy who was having intercourse with Carol didn't care either and so she couldn't care for him. – – – I was in a very good mood yesterday until I thought about my mother coming. Then I was suddenly in a bad mood and I felt awful. (Elaborates.) Then I had a dream last night that Tom and I were at a dinner party. Tom got up to leave and suddenly we were in the house in Evanston and I was sitting next to an attractive boy. I scooted my hand across his lap and I could feel his penis and I could feel it change size. Then suddenly Tom turned into my mother and we were in the bathroom together and she had a long penis and it was like a snake. (Elaborates.) I've been in a panic ever since. I feel like crying or killing someone. I am emotionally so wild this morning. We were at a party last night and I felt as if I were looking and acting just like my mother does at parties.

**A:** What about your associations to the dream elements?

**P:** The first two are obvious. I felt I was in love with you on Monday, and that you were so sexually attractive to me. Then I got very afraid because you weren't going to love me back. Being a bad girl lets me have an orgasm and the only way I can do it is to fantasy that.

**A:** What's the detail?

**P:** I always think of myself as a prostitute and I can never think of myself as loving Tom. He can't hurt me if I don't love him.

**A:** What's the detail of the prostitute fantasy?

**P:** I'm always being paid. I don't dare think that we're ever married.

**A:** What was the detail in the dream?

**P:** I was looking and acting very sexy, and I was enjoying the idea that I was a bad girl. I hated the man and I knew that that was all he wanted from me. That was the only way that I could enjoy it. I got pleasure from the fantasy that someone was watching and they were taking pictures.

**A:** What are your associations?

**P:** This is all so embarrassing for me. We were making love and the other men were watching and they were getting sexual pleasure from it. – – – I feel so sorry for myself these days and I keep feeling that I'm like a little girl who didn't have anything in life. I keep trying to bring myself back to reality but I feel as if I never had anything in my whole life. I'm always feeling sorry for myself. (There is a brief interruption of the session by a knock on the door and the analyst answers it and then returns to his seat.) – –

**A:** Let's go back and look at some of the further details of the prostitution fantasy.

**P:** It's sickening to me now. As a prostitute I'd think that it didn't make any difference who the man was and he could be anybody. He could even be my father and it wouldn't make any difference. Just as long as it was a man, and he was paying me. In the fantasy I always get pleasure from feeling that I wanted to give him pleasure and the dirtier that I could be the better it was.

*Cry, Sob*

**A:** How do you mean?

**P:** – The more I responded. It makes me sick to think about it now, and I keep trying to tell myself that there is nothing to this. But I have a great desire for sexual love and not to have to think, and so I always have to say that I don't love this person.

A: You mentioned that the dirtier you could be the more you enjoyed it. What's the detail there?

P: – – I just can't talk about it. – – – When I think about the man. . . . . that's all that any man wants, the dirtier she is the more he enjoys her. Men just can't enjoy their wives.

A: You still seem to be afraid to express the details of this fantasy about being dirty and enjoying it that way, and of what a man wants. What comes to your mind about the hestitation?

P: – – You're a man and I hate you. It will probably give you pleasure to have me talk about it. I no more want to give a man pleasure than I'd fly to the moon! – –

A: I wonder if this doesn't tie in somehow with the panic you felt here on Monday in connection with the feelings you were having towards me?

P: There's not a nice man in the whole world! They're all just sons-of-bitches! I'm not about to leave myself open for you to stomp all over me. I'm so much like my mother in this. These are all her ideas! It's not true! I just don't know what's true any more. My mother's idea was that men are all horrible and dirty and disgusting. I know that's not true! It's not true about my father! I hate them all, all men *and women*. There's no one that I want to be like. My father was so horrible and my mother was so mistreated! God-damn it, it's just not true! My mother beat the hell out of him all the time. I can't stand to be their daughter!

A: Let's look at the details of the conflict you have in these feelings about me. On the one hand you feel that I'm a man just like all the others, and that all I want is dirty sex with prostitutes. And on the other hand you're trying to tell yourself that it's not true and that these are all your mother's wrong ideas.

P: – – –

A: I think this may tie in with the panic reaction you had here when you wanted to walk out on Monday. Let's see what comes to your mind.

P: I felt so relieved as I walked out. I felt as if you were the most wonderful person in the world. I felt as if you counted and as if I was somebody. I know that I was having sexual feelings for you but I can't stand it because it's such a tug-of-war. If I believe in you, then it goes against all the things that my mother told me and I'll fall apart. She wants me to hate all men and to be masculine and have intercourse with women. I don't want this but I'm scared to death not to be like this.

A: What was the feeling of relief when you walked out Monday?

P: I don't feel it now! I feel all pent up! I hate you guts! This is all your fault. I'm tired of crying and being like a child  d being nothing I want to know who you are and what you are and what you think! Thi all makes me so mad! – – I feel as if I'm a child and I'm fighting against my parents' authority and I want to kick and scream but I know that it is going to do no good. I feel as if you are telling me that I'm bad and wrong. – – –

A: Let's look at Monday again and the relief you felt when you walked out and the positive feelings that you had after you left. What was the detail?

P: I felt that it was all very unusual for me. You didn't get upset and you didn't cry or fall apart and you didn't hit me and you didn't get involved with me. And I had a slight glimmer or feeling that maybe you're for real! I never realized before how much I *need* my parents' ideas and thoughts, but I'm also fighting it like mad. Somehow this seems like it's a turning point and I'm scared to go back *or* go forward.

A: Let's try to look at what it is that scares you from going forward.

P: If I do, then I'm on my own and this is all new and I don't even know you. I'm breaking the strings of what I've lived with for twenty-six years. – – – Isn't it time to go yet?

A: I wonder if that means that you're trying to avoid something?

P: No. I feel as if I just have to go. Suddenly I'm very scared again.

A: Which suggests that you are avoiding something.

P: – – – I don't know what it is. –

A: We'll stop here for today.


### D ISCUSSION

The patient's material in this hour probably represents a continuation of the conflict she experienced in the transference during the previous session, indicated by her statement at the very beginning that the dreams had occurred that same night. At that time my interpretation had been at the level of the maternal transference, and so initially today I am somewhat surprised when she presents two dreams with predominantly heterosexual and primal scene themes. But after presenting the dreams, she attributes her "bad mood" yesterday to the thought about her mother coming for a visit. At this point it is not yet clear whether the more significant conflict concerns the mother and the maternal transference, with the heterosexual material as a progressive defense, or whether the major level of conflict is at the heterosexual oedipal transference level with the conflict about the mother and maternal transference as a manifestation of a regressive defense. Almost immediately she goes on to another dream in which her husband turns into the phallic mother, with the bathroom as a reference to prephallic levels of conflict. This again adds to my uncertainty as to which conflict is currently activated and which represents the defense.

In trying to unravel this uncertainty, I therefore begin by asking for her associations to the dream elements. Her initial associations of having felt sexually attracted to me on Monday, and the fantasies of being a prostitute are references to an oedipal father transference with an identification of herself with his mistresses. In response to my requests for the details of these fantasies, she includes a reference to a derivative of the primal scene and the taking of pictures, which had been part of the manifest dream where the children were playing in the room while she and her husband were in bed.

I want to pursue this material further, and after attempting to deal with her reluctance at expressing it openly, the patient eventually brings it back to the transference when she says, "You're a man and I hate you. It will probably give you pleasure to have me talk about it." This gives me an opening to make the generalized and nonspecific transference interpretation of the possible connection between these feelings and the panic reaction during the previous session. This leads to her expression of hostility toward me as a man in the father transference and her defensive statement, "I'm not about to leave myself open for you to stomp all over me." From here her associations again lead backward in time toward the recollection of feelings and attitudes toward both parents, and although this is significant material, it is my feeling that for the moment it again represents an attempt to avoid further exploration of the more immediate conflict about me. I therefore attempt to focus her back toward the emerging transference neurosis by clarifying and restating the conflict she is experiencing toward me at the moment. She is able then to begin to explore her reaction Monday, first by describing the sense of relief and positive feeling toward me, and then to go on and elaborate that "I know that I was having sexual feelings for you but I can't stand it because it's such a tug-of-war." She describes being in conflict between the wish to believe in me (the father figure) and the fantasied expectations of the mother's demands upon her in regard to men.

Once again she is avoiding the more immediate transference implications, and therefore I again attempt to focus her back to the feeling of relief and the positive reaction she had from the Monday incident. Her initial response is a defensive one, using hostility and aggression to defend herself against the expression of what had been a positive and reassuring experience for her and projecting her sense of guilt to me. I cut through these defenses by again asking for her associations to the sense of relief and the positive feelings.

At this point she is finally able to elaborate on the important positive meaning that the experience had held for her, and to demonstrate that the most important element had been my nonverbal behavior and attitude. The material of this session suggests that the content of my interpretation on Monday, in which I had seen her reaction at the level primarily of a maternal transference, was probably incorrect in that it focused on the regressive defense rather than at the level of conflict over heterosexual oedipal drives which had evoked the anxiety from which the regression had occurred. However, the fact that I had maintained the analytic situation and did not experience or manifest anxiety or other counter-transference emotional involvement with her, and that instead I could maintain my role as an analyst, was crucial and more important than the content of the interpretation itself. Her statements that "I had a slight glimmer or feeling that maybe you were for real!" and that "Somehow this seems like it's a turning point. . ." are further confirmation of the importance of my handling of that regressive experience.

At this point, however, her anxiety and resistances again emerge in her fear of going forward, her awareness that she would have to change her basic attitudes, her desire to end the session, and the recurrence of her anxiety. But the intensity of the conflict is tolerable for her and she is able to maintain the analytic situation.

Whether or not this experience will prove to be "a turning point" is not yet clear and can only be determined in the light of subsequent events. However, even if it is not of that magnitude, individual experiences of this type and the analyst's response to them and his ability to manage them comfortably tend to have a cumulative effect in fostering the therapeutic alliance and thus help to promote the further unfolding of a full-blown regressive transference neurosis. Contrariwise, if the analyst fails to manage such incidents effectively, or if he manifests significant countertransference responses or significant departures from his usual analytic posture and role, this can interfere with the developing analytic situation, disrupt the therapeutic alliance, and thereby delay or prevent the unfolding of a manageable transference neurosis.

## SESSION 47

**P:** – – I don't know what's happening, but I have a reaction every time I leave here. Is it hostility? Is it fear? Yesterday I felt convinced as if I was going to die after I left. (Elaborates.)

**A:** What comes to your mind about it?

**P:** I can't decide why I feel this. But I have the feeling as if I'll die. I have a decision to make and I can't do it. I keep dreaming of being in regular clothes and having a good figure again. I was feeling sick and I dreamed that I was in college and I was getting dressed. I hated everyone and especially one particular girl who was very masculine. Suddenly she turned into this guy at the grocery store and then my ex-boss was there and I was telling them all to go to hell. I woke up petrified. – – – I hate everyone. I hate my mother and my father and I'm not going to be like either one. And so I'm drowning because I have nothing to hold on to. – – And I try to tell myself that I'm feeling hostile towards you but I don't feel it. – – – My mother called me on the phone and every time she does it throws me for a loop. (Elaborates.) They pull me down all the time. She had spent $70.00 for maternity clothes for me and yet she keeps telling me that they're broke. (Elaborates.) I wonder if maybe my father is having another affair. (Elaborates.) She buys extravagantly to get back at him. (Elaborates.) He doles out the money to his broads. (Elaborates the conflict between the mother and father.) I've got to stop fighting it because I know that I can't change them. – – – – – – – I've been fighting all my life just to prop my parents up. I know that's not true but they're so weak and they don't give me strength and really they're nothing. And yet I feel as if they'll always be there. It hurts me! If they'd tried, then I could hate them. But they're just too weak, and I can't hate them for that. But I do want to run away from them and I know that I can't.

**A:** This is related, but it is somehow off-center a bit from this main issue of the reaction that you are having towards me here every day.

**P:** I just haven't got the strength to hate you. Or, to hate my parents. I wish that I could. I wonder if my hate would shatter you? And yet I know that that's not true.

**A:** I don't think it's your hate that you are so much afraid of. If we go back to the situation here on Monday, and the feelings that you were having when you had that panic reaction, it was the warm, close sexual feelings of love that you had for me that terrified you.

**P:** I can't feel that toward you. Yesterday I had a sudden feeling that you're *not* trying to hurt me or to destroy me, and I could believe it for a moment. – –

**A:** So yesterday there was a brief movement in the direction of warmth and love and feeling close and having generally positive feelings here.

**P:** It was wonderful to feel that way. Then I began to wonder if there had been a change in Tom or maybe there had been a change in me. But I felt as if he was hostile and I began to wonder if he hates me. I felt it was all connected to the analysis. For instance, before we went to that party on Tuesday, I had the feeling that I just can't go out. – – – In that dream Tom went into the kitchen, and I was being sexually aroused with that boy's lap but I went on in to Tom and then he turned into my mother.

**A:** You haven't associated to that part of the dream in detail yet.

**P:** – – It's obvious to me. – – –

**A:** The meaning may be obvious to you but you seem to be blocked in trying to put it into words.

**P:** – – I feel as if I'd be disloyal to Tom and I can only love one person.

**A:** This is another reason for saying that you feel hostile toward me, because you are afraid to feel any sexual or warm or positive reactions here.

**P:** I think Tom will get mad if I have any of those feelings. (Elaborates.) It's like it was with Harris. I used to talk much more to him about Harris than I do about you. It would be so obvious to everyone. . . . . I'm not being realistic about this. I keep picturing it as a two-way deal and I know it's not.

**A:** What's the detail?

**P:** I picture. . . . . It's not really. . . . . but. . . . . this is what I've been looking for all of my life. I've been looking for a man to love with all that I have, who will also love me. That's all I want. And you enter in on this. – – –

**A:** In these ideas that it would be disloyal to Tom to have any feelings here, I think you are not distinguishing between a thought or a feeling on one hand, and acting on these thoughts and feelings on the other.

**P:** – – I feel as if it will overwhelm me and I won't be able to function at home. – – – Why am I so afraid for you to know about it? – – – I suddenly have a wish to crawl into a hole and not have you see me.

**A:** What are you trying to hide?

P: I'm feeling so incompetent. – – –

A: I think you're trying to beat around the bush here.

P: – – – – – – What do you mean?

A: You're having a lot of very direct and conscious feelings about me but you're trying to hold them back. And then you use a word like incompetent to try to express something. See if you can be more direct about this whole thing.

P: – – – – –

A: I think you are trying to exclude a whole group of feelings that you are having from the analysis. It's as if you are saying that you'll talk about everything except these and you are trying to blot out this whole part of yourself.

P: But this is the absolute core of me.

A: So all the more reason to ask why you should keep it out of the analysis.

P: I don't know how to put it in.

A: I think you do know how. We've agreed that you'll try to express all the feelings and thoughts that come to your mind without editing them. But you are afraid to do this and you still don't want to.

P: – – I keep telling myself that I'm not realistic in thinking that you are perfect. What's going to happen when I find out that you're not? If I ever put you on a pedestal then you won't dare to fall down.

A: We'll stop here for today.


## Discussion

The theme of this session is the patient's continuing conflict and anxiety about the emerging transference neurosis, and her defensive reaction to the regressive transference experience that had occurred in the Monday session. She begins by describing her anxiety and her sense of an affective reaction at the close of each session, and when I ask for her associations about this, her response indicates a conscious awareness that "I have a decision to make, and I can't do it." In previous sessions this issue of making a decision had come up several times and was related to the question of whether or not she could trust me enough in the analysis to make a significant and sustained emotional investment, and permit herself to experience the regressive transference phenomena. Because of these previous transference associations to "the decision," the material that follows it in this session can safely be assumed to relate to the transference, and her subsequent associations are to the wish to appear attractively feminine (not pregnant) and younger (in college) to two different men toward whom she in the past had experienced sexual arousal. My assumption therefore is that in her manifest hostility she is reacting defensively to the heterosexual oedipal transference feelings that are being mobilized. Furthermore, there is an almost limitless number of subjects from which the patient can choose to begin each session, and therefore the one she finally picks is usually of particular psychic significance. Not infrequently the patient's initial comments reflect what will be the theme and understanding of the rest of the session.

As a result of this reasoning, I choose to try to focus her attention to the active conflict occurring in the transference relationship by confronting her with the reaction she is having toward me each day, and her response to my intervention is to concentrate on her hostility toward me, with the fantasy that I will not be able to tolerate it. But I had seen in past sessions how she tends to use hostility as a defense against love, dependency, or positive attachment, and it is on the basis of this past awareness of this defensive pattern that I now choose to interpret the hate as a defense and to confront her again with her reaction on Monday to the occurrence of positive loving and sexual feelings.

This interpretation permits her to recall the previously unexpressed fact that yesterday she had again experienced a brief feeling of security and positive expectation with me. My intervention of essentially rephrasing what she had just said is probably unnecessary, but my intention is further to prepare the groundwork for a more specific and detailed interpretation of the defenses she uses against this type of positive involvement. After acknowledging that it had been "wonderful," she goes on to displace and project the conflict to her husband, while at the same time indicating an awareness that it is related to the analysis.

Her next associations are to the dream she had mentioned yesterday which I had understood as an oedipal transference dream, although this had not been explicitly interpreted to the patient. However, before it would be possible to elaborate on the latent dream thoughts and ultimately bring out the unconscious dream meanings, it is necessary to reduce the intensity of her resistance and defenses, and my first intervention in this regard is to point out the omission of her associations to that dream element. Her response that it is obvious without putting her associations into verbal form represents another line of defense which I again attempt to block by my intervention. She then is able to express her concern about disloyalty to her husband, and after I again interpret her hostility as serving a defensive function, she is able to express in somewhat fuller form her anxiety about the positive transference and her wish for transference gratification.

My interpretation in regard to the distinction between thoughts and feelings as compared with action is another attempt to strengthen the therapeutic alliance by implying that although she might experience such feelings in the transference relationship, and although the feelings are acceptable here, there will be no overt and realistic seduction or love relationship between us. My aim is to help her adult ego functions more clearly recognize the necessity for verbalization of feelings in the analytic situation and relationship, and this permits her to express a little of her fear of being overwhelmed by her drives. This is followed by my subsequent interpretations of her conscious resistances against expressing the emerging transference neurosis. Toward the end of the session I follow this up with a reminder to her of our original therapeutic agreement, which again carries with it the tacit implication that the expression of such feelings in analysis is not only appropriate but expected, and represents an encouragement and appeal to her to try to reduce the intensity of her conscious resistances.

Although I am applying pressure upon her to reduce the intensity of her conscious defenses, this is being done with acknowledgment of her anxiety, and my nonverbal attitude is one of acceptance of her difficulty in doing what the analysis requires and expectation that she will have trouble relinquishing her defenses. In other words, I am able to make these interventions in an analytically neutral fashion because I can accept the occurrence of resistance as acceptable, and because I am just as interested in analyzing the defensive ego functions as I am in bringing out the drives which they defend against. This equal interest in the various conscious and unconscious functions of the ego permits the analyst to interpret these functions to the patient without impatience, annoyance, or hostility.

---

## SESSION 48

P:  – – – – – I was so afraid that you'd not be here today.

A: What was the detail?

P: I can hardly stand to talk about it. It was connected to something that happened in a dream. I had the idea. . . . . that I was in love with somebody who didn't love me back. There were so many things that went

on in the dream that I don't remember. I can't express my feelings very
well. – – – – – –

A: What comes to your mind about having feelings for me, and that
I don't respond in the same way to you?

P: – – – I feel it now and I felt it earlier this morning, and it was in the
dream also, that I'm feminine and soft and cuddly and warm and loving.
I was never accepted by my father this way as a child, but now I feel as
if you might accept me. In the dream we were in the playpen and it was in
Evanston and all of us girls were there. We were dressed up kind of frilly
and there were people looking in on us and the men were in tuxedos. I
was lying on the floor and I had no pants on and I kept wondering what
the men would think. Before this, when I used to dream that I'm naked,
I'd feel embarrassed because I was missing a penis and I would want to
run and hide away. I wasn't last night, although I was unsure, but I
thought I wanted to take the chance.

A: What comes to mind about this feeling that I might accept you as
feminine and soft and loving?

P: That's just the way you are. You are capable of loving me and of
not caring what I look like, and for you it wouldn't make any difference
about the. . . . . . – –

A: You cut something short there.

P: The surface things.

A: I think you mean the presence or absence of a penis.

P: I'm suddenly getting very nervous and hostile. I had a wonderful
feeling until I came but now you are making me feel that I had a penis. I
don't want one.

A: Let's try to see what it means that what I said changed your feelings so drastically and so suddenly.

P: I don't know, but it was a very sudden feeling. – –

A: What are your associations to what I said?

P: – – Something in my mind snapped just as you said it. I knew that
you would and I wasn't ready for it.

A: You had talked about the dream and being feminine and that you
used to feel embarrassed when you'd dream about being naked because
you were missing a penis. Then you tried to avoid this by talking about
"the surface things" and I said that you were referring to the penis. Now
let's see what it means that you felt that this is something that you're not
ready for and also that you see it as *my* wanting you to be masculine.

P: You brought my attention to it. I guess . . . . . it's obvious that I don't have one, and you will either accept or reject me because of this. But even if you accept it, it's like saying it's alright or it doesn't matter. You'll never say, "I'm so glad that you don't have one and it's wonderful just the way you are." – – –

A: What about the men in the tuxedos in this dream? What are your associations?

*Cry*

P: My parents used to entertain a lot and have a lot of formal dinner parties in the house and I used to love them. – – – It makes me sick to think about all of this. I feel so mad and yet I'm so frustrated. I can't do anything about this. – –

A: In that dream you were ready to take a slight chance. But you're still afraid to take a chance here.

P: – – – It makes me mad that I have all of these feelings. I'd love to feel this way but it would make me mad if you didn't accept me. I can't see why you wouldn't. – – – – – – You or someone else keeps telling me this. I *don't* want to be a boy. I don't want a God-damn penis! You can have them all! I never did. I just want to be accepted as I am and as a girl! I think *you're* missing out, not me. I feel that I have very much to offer you. – –

A: What's the detail?

P: I feel that I was made to make you happy because I *am* a female. I'm not hard and I'm not. . . . . . – – I feel that I have a place. I *love* children and I *love* my body and I feel that I'm pretty. I can sit on your knee and I can flirt with you and I can make you happy. A little boy couldn't do this! I know what I want, but it has to be a two-way deal and I want to love you and give you everything, but I want you to love me and to appreciate this. – – – I feel as if I'm in a world of women-haters and they all laugh at a woman because she *is* a woman. – – I wonder if you are a woman-hater too. – –

A: What do you think?

P: Every man in the world has a problem about this. They all hate women. I think they are all trying to fight for their superiority and I think you have this problem too.

A: Let's look at the details of the thoughts about me, in connection with this.

P: I don't really know. I know you are supposed to be able to sit there and not react to my emotions. – . . . . .

A: What did you stop at?

P: I feel that if I talk about this you'll get mad and that maybe this is your problem, and then you will degrade me. A man is a man and he is born with a penis, and he doesn't have to fight that, so why can't he love women? – – A man is so insecure sexually he *has* to degrade all women.

A: I think you are talking about all men and generalizing here in order to avoid some specific feelings about me.

P: But I don't know about you.

A: That's true, but you have fantasies about me.

P: I'll build castles up in the sky and they'll crash; I won't do it! I'll not build you up! I'm not going to think that you're something you're not! I want you to be this way so badly that I couldn't stand it if you weren't. – – I feel as if I've been an idiot all through this hour. | *Fury*

A: What's the detail?

P: I just feel it. As if I were a dunce. As if I were stupid and like you think I'm stupid. – – – I can't pretend to be masculine any more. I *am* what I *am.* – – – What will happen if you *do* accept me this way? – –

A: What comes to your mind?

P: – – I feel as if you are forcing yourself not to get mad. – – – –

A: We'll stop here for today.


## DISCUSSION

This session represents a continuation of the work from yesterday in which the discussion and interpretation of the patient's various resistances against the emerging oedipal father transference has been effective to the extent that she can now permit a little greater expression of the underlying feminine wishes to be sexually attractive to me in the feminine role.

However, initially she begins in a vague and nonspecific way by referring to the dream in which "I was in love with somebody who didn't love me back." At this point the defenses are intensified, she does not recall the details of the dream, and she then lapses into another period of silence. Based on my interpretations of defenses against the transference that occurred yesterday, and on the manifest dream fragment that she has just presented, I decide to interpret this directly into the transference in a matter-of-fact way, recognizing that there are many transference feelings that are already fully conscious to her. My matter-of-fact acceptance of the occurrence of these feelings encourages her then to explore and elaborate upon the feminine loving feelings she had experienced, their connection to her father, and then she is able to recall the manifest dream previously omitted. In other words, in this instance her associations to the dream precede reporting the dream itself, and having verbalized them there is less defensive need to go on repressing the manifest dream content.

Her feeling that I might accept her as she is represents a forward movement into the therapeutic alliance as well as the transference neurosis, and in order to foster this I choose to focus upon it in my first intervention. She then goes on to elaborate her growing feeling of confidence and trust that I will not reject her, but her associations are interrupted as her anxiety mounts and she substitutes the euphemism of "surface things." Once again I want to be direct and matter of fact and thereby provide her with an analytic model to identify with in presenting her associations, and so I verbalize directly the obvious association to the penis.

This turns out to be a poor intervention since I did not anticipate that the transference reaction would cause her to experience my remark as depreciating and would thus cause her to withdraw. Once the withdrawal reaction occurs, it becomes necessary to shift the focus away from the content of the dream and its associations, and instead to attempt to analyze and help her recognize the defensive ego functions involved in her reaction to the feeling of depreciation. This culminates in my clarification to her of the sequence of events ending with my interpretation of the transference projection. In response she begins to express further some of her feelings of phallic inferiority, which she had previously projected to me as part of the withdrawal and anger at my earlier remark.

I feel we have probably gone as far as we can for the moment, and therefore choose to return to one of the more obscure dream elements which is then associated to the father, and the original oedipal reactions. After I point out her conscious reluctance "to take a chance," she resumes the expression of the transference distortion that I want her to be a boy, accompanied by multiple examples of negation in regard to her phallic strivings, her sense of inferiority in being a girl, and her projections of this in the transference and in her general feelings about men. I want to focus this more directly into the transference perception of me, but she rather quickly again generalizes the issue to all men. I therefore interpret this defensive generalization in an attempt more directly to help her develop these specific conflicts in the transference neurosis, and toward the end of the session she is able to experience her anxiety over possible rejection as a woman in the specific relationship to me.

## SESSION 49

**P:** – – – – I can't talk about all of this because I feel embarrassed and self-conscious. – – – I feel as if I have suppressed all of my feelings for men. (Elaborates.) I can't do that when I'm here.

**A:** Let's analyze what it means that you want to do it here.

**P:** It's much easier not to get involved with you. I had a dream about you on Saturday night. It didn't look like you, but you were the most self-centered and egotistical person. It all took place at my house and I was waiting to go and see you. You were putting me off and you were standing in front of a mirror and combing your hair. Then you said to me, "I'm not able to see you today, so go and see my assistant, the engineer, instead." You meant I was supposed to go see the janitor and I was in a panic and I felt, "I can't do that." – – – I've been thinking about what you're really like.

**A:** What's the detail of the fantasy?

**P:** You're probably just like this man. You have no character or morals or strength and you don't stand for anything. You are just a little boy with so many problems you can't get through life. – I know that's not true. But I wonder. . . . . I see you suddenly collapsing. – –

**A:** What's the detail of the thought?

**P:** You just put on a front of being strong and a feeling that you can handle yourself and take care of me. But if I don't watch out you'll crumble and I'll have to go back to mother and then where will I be? I *can't* go back to my mother. – – I've been holding myself off from everyone lately. (Elaborates.) Tom worked all weekend and I was home alone with the kids. I wasn't nervous or depressed the way I usually am, but I just sat. (Elaborates.) I had a fantasy of killing myself and I also thought I was disconnected from the world. (Elaborates.) I felt as if I just could not attach myself to anyone.

**A:** You said earlier that it's easier not to be involved here with me. But what we have to see is that it's *not* so easy and that actually you pay quite a price.

**P:** – – – I just don't want to be hurt. I get hurt so easily. (Elaborates.) – – – My sexual feelings are all coming out lately but it's all so screwed up. – –

**A:** How do you mean?

**P:** I have a fantasy of somehow killing myself and I have all of these sexual feelings and I have a sensation in my clitoris. And then when that happens I also have a fear that there is someone in the house. I turn them all around even though I know that I have them, but I suppress them or else I'm hostile. I can't just relax and let them exist. I'm so afraid that I'll be hurt by men or that I'll want to be hurt by them and so I won't take a chance on them.

**A:** Just like in the dream where you see me as selfish, egotistical and vain, and you have me walking out on you. You do all of this so that you won't take a chance on me.

**P:** – – – – – – I'm getting it again! I'm having a tremendous sexual feeling right now and I feel as if I must kill myself because I'll do something about it otherwise. – –

**A:** What's the detail of the feeling itself?

**P:** I have a funny tingling in my wrists and it's in my clitoris and it will go to my mouth and then I'll have it all over. – – I shouldn't have it at all and I feel that I must stop it. If I can't suppress it then I feel that I have to kill myself.

**A:** Let's look at the detail of the thought that you shouldn't have it at all, and that if you do, then you have to kill yourself.

**P:** It's all right to have sexual feelings in one sense, but not in the way that I want.

**A:** What comes to your mind?

**P:** If I'm a *bad* girl then I can have them. Then I'm bad and you're bad. But with a feeling of love and where I want to give myself fully I can't. (Elaborates.) I know that this is the opposite of what I should believe.

**A:** What are your associations to these feelings?

**P:** – – – I want to scream that I love you. – – – Now I'm bracing myself because I don't know what will happen if I ever do.

**A:** When you say that you don't know what will happen if you do, it suggests that you're having fantasies of various possible alternatives. Let's look at the details.

**P:** If I were to ever do it with my father when I was a girl he'd laugh and he'd be embarrassed but he could never say, "I love you too," and come and pick me up. And if I ever did it I would certainly want it to happen. So I must accept the fact and not do it. – – – It's not as if you hate me or I hate you. I have to accept the fact that you are too weak to take my love and it would embarrass you and that you wouldn't know what to do with it. And so I just don't say anything and I just dream on.

A: You feel that I'm weak and that I'll collapse and that I can't tolerate your feelings and so on. These are all ways in which you described your
father today and also last week. So it means that you are seeing me as if
I were your father.

**Cry**

P: I can't stand to think about it. It hurts so God-damned much! I
can't stand it! I don't want to look at it or you or to face you! – – – I can't
make you into anything else and so it's useless to try. I want it so much
but it's just like beating my head against a wall. – – – You're *all* that matters to me in this life and I really don't care about anyone else. You're
*all*. If you disappoint me then no one can ever take your place. It would
be something that I *have* to live with. – – – – – I feel like the fight and
hostility is gone out of me. I realize what you are and I know that you
can't be anything else and that's all there is, there is no use fighting and
screaming and crying about it. – – – If I didn't need you, I'd tell you to
go to hell, you bastard!! That's ridiculous. It's not true, not any of it, but
I do hate you. Why don't you try harder! Why should I suffer? I'm just
like a mouse in a corner.

A: What's the detail of wanting me to try harder?

P: I *am* someone, so why can't you try! This is all your weakness, you
should think of me a little. I have problems too. Why should I sacrifice
myself for you? I don't want to be a martyr. I want to live. All of my life
I've felt that I am just a poor thing and that I've been mistreated and
that no one has thought of me. It's all just a bunch of bull! – – I could
get mad if I don't stop to think about where the love comes from.

A: What are your associations to it?

P: I hate you and yet I love you. And if you can't take all of this, then
I just can't stand it. I *do* need you. I can't stand the idea of never getting
this love from you. I need it! – – – – – –

A: We'll stop here for today.

### DISCUSSION

Once again the patient begins this session on a resistive note, indicating her wish to avoid experiencing the developing transference relationship.
My first intervention is an attempt to help her specifically focus on the
defense of suppression, and after saying she does not want to get involved
with me, she presents a dream in which I appear as a negative unpleasant
person. Later in the manifest dream she projects to me the wish to send
her away, which is also a defense against her growing attachment and
relationship to me.

After describing the transference fantasy of me in unpleasant and negative terms (in the midst of which her statement, "I know that's not true," indicates the continuing presence of self-observing ego functions) the patient goes on to describe her symptomatic exacerbation over the weekend. This associational sequence and temporal continuity of the two ideas suggests that they are causally related, and it is this line of reasoning that suggests to me the interpretation that her symptoms are the result of an attempt to withdraw from facing the transference conflicts.

She then goes on to describe her growing awareness of sexual arousal and the stimulation of sexual drives which is occurring as a result of the increasing regression in the developing transference neurosis. Drives which had been formerly repressed or otherwise defended against because of their attachment to the unacceptable infantile and childhood object are now being again stimulated by my presence and availability to her as a substitute infantile and childhood object. The various features in the analytic situation which promote regression and the lack of reality feedback from me, along with the reduction of the previously used defenses against feeling and fantasy, all combine to stimulate the return of these drives in the current treatment situation.

Another defense is the generalization about her fears of being hurt by men, and my referring this back to the dream and the defensive function of the negative image of me is an attempt to block the generalization and again focus the conflict more directly into the transference. This has the desired effect in that she now begins to experience actual sexual arousal in the analytic situation, accompanied by anxiety, a fantasy of loss of control, and the defensive fantasy of needing to kill herself. Once again I want in an analytic way to get across to her the idea that the occurrence of such sensations and feelings during analytic sessions is not unusual, that I can tolerate them, and therefore she can permit their expression and better learn to tolerate them herself. To this end I ask her to elaborate on the detail of the feeling itself. After briefly describing the feelings, she goes on to elaborate upon her sense of guilt and shame for having such feelings. My request for associations to the sense of guilt represents an attempt to block the automatic superego judgments involved, and is an attempt to encourage her to suspend preconceived moral judgments in order that we can gain access to the feelings and then analyze the conflicts which accompany them.

After I interpret the probable existence of fantasies connected with her wish to scream that she loves me, the patient associates to her experiences with her father, and then begins to experience me as at this moment having the same characteristics and attitudes that the father did. After the transference interpretation of her seeing me as if I were the father, she is now free to experience the transference reaction to me more openly, directly, and with greater affect, and she is also able to express how centrally important the relationship to me has now become. During this last part of the session she is directly involved in the actual experiencing of transference feelings, and is more freely capable of expressing them openly in a direct and immediate form. This quality of immediacy, along with the central importance which I now have in her life and experience, are two of the important hallmarks of the developing transference neurosis.

---

## SESSION 50

**P:** I felt so glad that I can come here today and then the minute I see you I lose this feeling.

**A:** So you are still afraid to trust me.

**P:** – My parents are here for a visit and I've been watching them. I *am* deserting a sinking ship. All the time they have been here I've had the thought, "Dr. Dewald is so strong and he's like a whole new set of parents and it's wonderful." But then I get here and I have so many emotions at once that I don't know what to do. I had a dream about the man who lives behind us. He's very good looking and he has four children. He was interested in me as a friend. I was married and I was relieved to find out that he wasn't married but just living with this woman. She was a sister and they weren't his children. Nothing was going to happen in the dream but I was so relieved to find out he wasn't married. – – – I also dreamed that there were a lot of people chasing after me. They were from outer space. And then they turned into Germans of World War II, and then suddenly they were women and I was running and trying to hide but then I'd be found. Then they'd let me go and I'd run again. – – – – – – –

**A:** What comes to your mind that you haven't gone on to associate to the dreams?

**P:** I was wondering why you won't talk to me? I felt it when I was here on Monday too.

**A:** What's the detail?

**P:** I feel so much like a nervous little girl. I feel just like my own daughter. When she is insecure, she talks to be sure that we are tied together. It makes no sense and it's all garbled. Instead of just saying, "I'm so scared I need you so much," I have to go on and talk.

**A:** What's the feeling of being so scared?

**P:** It's all a very guarded emotion. I talk and talk to try to cover it up. But if I am ever honest with you then I'm laying myself open. – – It was like when I was little. If I'd feel insecure I'd just want to get home and I'd feel very secure there. That's the way it is while my parents are here. I feel as if I have to come here just like I used to run home as a child, but I'm always afraid that I'm not going to get what I want here.

**A:** I think that your feeling that I won't talk to you really represents another defense against trusting me more than you think you're safe to do.

*Cry*

**P:** – – – I know that I'll never have you all to myself. Every time I leave here I think, "Is someone else waiting and seeing you?" I also think about your family a lot.

**A:** What's the detail?

**P:** – – – – I think about your wife. . . . . I don't want it any other way and yet I keep thinking about it.

**A:** Let's see what your associations are.

**P:** I keep wondering what it would be like to be your wife. I'm sure it would be fun. You're so strong. I think about having children and making love and fixing dinner and keeping house for you. That's all that I would want. – – – It seems so useless to keep thinking about this! It does nothing but frustrate me. I think of all that I missed as a child and it's like crying over spilled milk.

**A:** What comes to your mind?

**P:** I want something and I can't have it. I want to get away from my parents. I hate them, because it was all so frustrating and was such an abnormal home. There was nothing there to guide me, and now I feel as if I had nothing. I wish that my parents would love each other. When my father used to be home we'd all do things together, and I used to help set the table. – – – I feel as if escape is the only answer for this. (Sigh.) – – – Something keeps bothering me. I can't accept the fact that that's the way this is. I want to *do* something about it. – – I feel as if I'll. . . . . I don't know what.

**A:** What did you stop at?

*Cry!!*

**P:** I can't stand it! I'm going to scream and scream and just break loose. I can't just sit by and yet I know that I can't do anything. I don't know how I feel. – – – I've *got* to do something. My parents used to go on trips and then they would frequently go out at night and it seemed to me they were never home and that we were always ignored. I could go through that house and wreck it! Or I could beat my head against a wall! I want to scream! −− I can think of my parents! I want to claw them both. I hate them! I want to kill them!

**A:** These are feelings from the time when you were a little girl and they are coming back now. They have really been with you all of these years but you have tried to ignore them and to repress them and to pretend they didn't exist and to avoid facing them.

**P:** −− I feel as if I'll die. I feel so frustrated! If I could just *do* something. I'm thinking about my parents. I hate you! I would never say it. I will just grin and bear it until they leave. −−−− Why am I so nervous and frustrated and upset with them? I'm twenty-seven years old and I have a husband and two children. Why do I need them? They give me nothing! I *don't* need them. And yet I go on thinking of all of the ways to get them to do something for me. I know it is all ridiculous. −−− I'm thinking about the time when I'll be through with my analysis. If I let myself get involved with you can I ever break away? And I know that you'll make me do it. But can I go through my whole life without a parent? Can anyone? My parents gave me nothing! I can't depend on them. I know that I've got to break away from them but I'll have to break away from you too and then where will I be? Then I won't be able to go back to my parents either. −−

*Sob,*
*Quiet*

*Cry*

**A:** So what we have to see is how on the one hand you have a realization that they gave you nothing, and yet at the same time you have the persistent hope that maybe the next time you can get something from them.

**P:** I really know that I can't. −−−− I've got to *know* that I've got someone that I can lean on. I can go from people to people as long as I *know* that I can *really* depend on this other person. When I depend on you, it's not going to be a neurotic dependency because you are strong, but with everyone else, they need me as much as I need them. And so with everyone else we sink together or else we prop each other up. But I *need* this game somehow. I'm taking inventory now. The only person I ever really had was my sister and I can't even depend on her. But if I depend on you I'm going to throw myself at you. I'm going to love you but I also know that it's not going to be *real* love and it will just be my horrible needs. (Elaborates.) −−− I'm beginning to realize that you are the one that I've got to depend on, and the only one that can really help me. But I can't just call you if I feel frustrated during the day and I want to talk about it. −−− I'm wanting you to say something now!

**A:** What would you like for me to say?

**P:** I want you to say, "You poor thing, it's all right, I'll take care of you and I'll build you up." That's what I wanted my parents to say and Jean to say too. I want you to say, "You'll make it."

**A:** We'll stop here for today.


## DISCUSSION

The patient begins by indicating her pleasurable anticipation of coming to the analytic session followed by the awareness of conflict that the relationship to me is stimulating. My initial interpretation is aimed at the therapeutic alliance and at the conscious and preconscious fears of basic trust in me, and this leads to her description of how she is beginning to invest me with the thoughts and fantasies from childhood and as a substitute for her unsatisfying parents. In her statement, "Dr. Dewald is so strong and he's like a whole new set of parents and it's wonderful," she is indirectly expressing the fantasy that the infantile wishes toward the parents will be ultimately gratified in the relationship to me. This leads to the dream, and my own associations are that the man who ". . . . . lives behind us," represents me in the analytic situation sitting behind her. I think the four children refers to the four analytic sessions per week and my understanding is that the first dream represents a defensive denial of her thoughts that I am married and possibly have children of my own. My own associations to the second dream are that it is a reference to the previously discussed regression from a sadomasochistic fantasy of sexuality to the more secure oral ties and attachments to the mother.

However, after presenting the dreams the patient lapses into a relatively lengthy silence and so my first intervention is aimed at her resistances against spontaneously analyzing the dreams. The implication of my confrontation is that by now she understands and consciously knows about the process of dream analysis, and therefore if she spontaneously avoids it there must be some resistive reason for doing so.

Her immediate response suggests that the resistance is connected to the transference relationship, and as she continues to associate she describes her conflict and defense over the increasing dependence upon me. In this she indicates that the transference neurosis has developed to the point that she now equates coming here with being at home as a child, but simultaneously she indicates her awareness that the various transference fantasies will not be realistically gratified by me.

In describing her thoughts about my wife and her fantasies of herself as my wife, she is continuing her associations to the dream. But in

the transference reaction to me (which at the present moment is a derivative of the oedipal tie to the father), she anticipates ultimate frustration of
her wishes, which by association leads to her further elaborating on the
frustrations originally experienced as a child. My recapitulation of this in
pointing out to her that these feelings and conflicts have been defended
against since childhood represents another attempt to foster the therapeutic alliance. I am providing her with a framework within which to understand the emergence of these feelings and reactions in the transference,
while at the same time tacitly indicating that it would be reasonable to
try to relinquish the various defenses she has used for so long.

Her response is initially in the transference, but after the silence the
rational adult ego functions take over as she consciously recognizes the unreality of her persistent needs and wishes. In this context she goes on to
describe her realization that the analysis will also ultimately involve separation from me as a parent figure. My comment is an attempt to help her
clarify the conflict between the adult rational awareness and perceptions of
the situation, as contrasted with the persistent infantile and childhood
wish for continuing gratification. The aim here is to acknowledge the presence of her reality-testing functions, but simultaneously to encourage verbalization of the transference demands by acknowledging my acceptance
of their expression here in the analysis. This permits her to express her
awareness of what some of her needs are and of what the transference relationship will entail, accompanied by her perception in the therapeutic alliance of the realities of the situation between us. Her acknowledgment that
"I'm beginning to realize that you are the one I've got to depend on and
the only one that can really help me" is an important reflection of the
therapeutic alliance, but is followed by a return to the derivative transference wish of wanting me to reassure her as she wanted her parents to do.

This material demonstrates that she is simultaneously developing an
effective and reasonable therapeutic alliance, side by side with a deepening
regressive transference neurosis. Her awareness of the realities of the relationship between us in analysis and her increasing recognition that this
will remain at a verbal and fantasy level permits her to undergo the regression involved in the analytic situation and to experience the transference
reactions directly. It is this therapeutic alliance which helps her recognize
the analytic significance of the transference and the analytic necessity of
experiencing and expressing it as directly as possible. If she were to develop such transference reactions without simultaneously developing the
therapeutic alliance, the net result would be an unmanageable transference
psychosis in which the demands for realistic gratification would be so in-

tense that she would be unable to tolerate their frustration. Contrariwise, if she were to remain purely bound by the realities of the therapeutic relationship between us and not permit herself to undergo the regression which results in the developing transference neurosis, the development and progress of analysis would be inhibited or prevented.

---

## SESSION 51

**P:** – – – I have had a horrible time suppressing my sexual feelings. The other night I had a dream about sexual feelings and I woke up so frightened. I've been trying to separate you and my father. My father has been here for the last three days and I see that there can never be anything there. I can never be myself with him. If I think of you the way I do about him then I'll never get anywhere. I want to be able to love a man. I have feelings of love and of sex for you and I don't think that that's bad. You're not sick and you won't be weak or get mad or upset about it.

**A:** Let's look at the details of the need that you feel to suppress them.

**P:** I just can't understand it. They are trying to come out but they make me so nervous! I dreamed that I was in high school, only I was the way I am now. I was really very shy when I was in high school, but in the dream I wasn't shy or afraid of boys. There was one boy in the dream and I was sexually attracted to his brother. There was an adorable boy sitting behind us and I had the feeling "He's so darling and he's the cutest boy that I've ever seen." In the dream the boy behind me was so shy. I wonder why I was so scared? I also dreamed that there were cockroaches in my bed. I used to be very afraid of them but this time in the dream I felt, "It won't hurt me, I just don't like them being there." – –

**A:** What are your associations to the boys in the dream?

**P:** One was a fellow by the name of Pete, who was really sort of an idiot. He was much older and he went out with a friend of mine. The other is a baseball player but he is so shy, but he is really so darling. All of the sexual feelings that I've ever had in my life are suddenly there right in front of me and there are so many of them to suppress.

**A:** What's the detail?

**P:** I spent my life this way. I know I'll explode if I ever let it go. I can just look at a man and have sexual feelings for him. I just can't go around like that.

**A:** What are your associations to the boy sitting behind you?

P: It just hit me! It's obvious. You're sitting behind me. If I say what I feel, what is going to happen? I just don't know.

A: But what do you picture?

P: I don't. When I think about it it doesn't really frighten me. It only frightens me at times.

A: If it frightens you, then there must be some kind of a fantasy attached even though it may not be completely conscious.

P: I wish it would come out. When I left here Wednesday and I was at the door I had the impulse to put my arms around you. I want to grab and to hug you. – – –

A: That's just the start of a fantasy. What would happen next?

P: (laughs) – I see myself as a bug and I'd crawl on your leg and you would kick at me and I'll irritate you and you won't want me. You'll get so excited about this that you can't stand it. – –

A: What's the detail?

P: I'll come over and I'll hug you and I'll love you. You'll get upset and you'll be frightened and you don't know what to do and you'll crumble between my fingers and there'll just be nothing there. – – – | *Cry*

A: Let's go back to the image of yourself as a bug and crawling on my leg. What comes to your mind?

P: You were absolutely nothing! I don't understand you! You can't accept the fact that I'm human and that I'm a woman. You always see me just like a piece of furniture, as if I'm nothing. – – – – . . . . . It's horrible for me to look at my father the way he really is! There's nothing there. He has nothing! – – I want a man to be strong and mature and warm and to be loving and I'll never have this! Sometimes I think of you that way, but if I tell you and show you how I feel, you'll kick me in the face.

A: What's the fantasy?

P: You'll say, "Don't touch me, you're just dirty." You'll treat me just like I'm a bug.

A: I think this ties in with the cockroach in your dream. This is part of your own image of yourself, that you see yourself as a bug, and I think that is part of the fear that you always had about cockroaches, because part of you identifies yourself with them.

P: Oh!! That makes me sick. I can't stand it – – – I don't care what *you* think, I'm *not* a cockroach. | *Shrill*

A: This is not an issue about what I think. The image of the cockroach was in your mind and you project it now to me. But the idea originally comes from somewhere in your own mind.

**P:** ----- (Sigh.) -- I start to relax and I want to tell you that I love you and that I *am* a woman, and that I just do love you. And then I think why I don't and I get mad and I think you're overpowering me again. ---- Why does hostility always have to follow love for me? With every warm thought it happens and then I get so mad. I'm so mad now! I hate you!

**A:** Let's spread out that sequence of feeling love and then feeling hostility into slow motion and see what comes to your mind.

**P:** Just then I felt like taking a chance and I wanted to tell you and I was willing to leave myself wide open. And then I'd think about my father. I guess I'm really afraid that you will accept me and accept this feeling. All of the feelings that I have about you are feelings I have for every man, and I know that I must have gotten them from my father. But I know how *he* feels and so I project that onto you and that could be the way you feel about me. I *hate* my father. At least that is familiar to me, and I can live in a world like this.

**A:** So what we can see is that the hate is really a defense against love. Your fear is that I'll accept your feelings and not be upset by them. That again is the start of the fantasy. Let's see what comes next.

*Cry!!*
*Anxiety*

**P:** (Sigh.) – I'm feeling so nervous! I don't know. I get this feeling now! It's sexual and then I feel that I can't breathe. If only I knew! I can't stand this not knowing. What will happen? --- What's the matter with me? I don't understand what is happening. What will happen? -- That damned idiot in the grocery store! ---- I wish I knew what is happening to me.

**A:** What's your own fantasy?

*Very*
*Panicky*

**P:** I felt as if you were forcing me into something. I'm feeling so embarrassed! I don't know. I can't stand it. It's as if I'm lying in my bed at home and thinking of my father coming into the room. --- There were so many times that I must have thought of this! ---

**A:** We'll stop here for today.


## Discussion

The patient begins the session with a reference to her conflicts over the sexual feelings which are being mobilized in the transference, and indirectly indicates her awareness of this in the comment that she is trying to separate me from her father. She goes on to indicate a greater degree of acceptance of her loving and sexual transference feelings, and also a firmer perception of me in reality as part of the developing therapeutic alliance when she says, "You're not sick and you won't be weak or get mad or upset about it."

Since she has emphasized the strengthened perception of the reality of the analytic situation, I now want to help her further decrease the intensity of her defenses and therefore I focus on the issue of her need to suppress the sexuality. After briefly describing the intensity of her conflict, she reports the two dreams, in association to which she elaborates on her conflict and anxiety over the intensity of her sexual fantasies in the transference and alludes to the existence of unverbalized fantasies of what might happen between us if she were to express them directly and openly.

I want to help her verbalize these as-yet-omitted fantasies of what would happen between us, and it is to this end that I make the nonspecific inference that her fear is a sign of the presence of such a fantasy. Her response is now to report the impulse to grab and hug me which she had experienced in the previous session. By focusing on these fantasies and pointing out that she has not completed them, I am tacitly encouraging her to permit herself the full range of freedom in her fantasy life, and I am again indicating my willingness and capacity to accept and tolerate such phenomena. By doing this in a matter-of-fact way, I am also encouraging her to identify with me in this analytic attitude toward her own thoughts and thereby reduce the intensity of the defenses against verbalizing them.

Partly in response to this, the patient now permits herself a further ego regression in which the image of herself as a bug emerges, and in which she increasingly experiences me in the transference as not accepting her and thinking of her as a piece of furniture. After the silence this is directly associated to the father and then again re-experienced as a transference reaction to me with the expectation that I will withdraw from her as if she were dirty and just a bug.

When she first mentioned the image of herself as a bug I had associated this in my own mind to the manifest dream of the cockroaches in her bed, and as the further associations to the bug image were expressed, I had increasingly felt that in some way this represented the latent thoughts behind the dream. When she says that I will treat her like she is a bug, I respond with the interpretation of the dream in hopes of helping her more clearly see the projection involved and the fact that her self-image includes the element of the dirty bug. Her response is an immediate shrill angry reaction in which she projects the bug image as my idea of her and then reacts against it and against me. Although I thought she would herself recognize the existence of the projective mechanism, her response indicates that she has not done so, and so I follow this up with a more specific and detailed explanation of the projective mechanism. I might have remained silent and permitted her to go on using the mechanism of projection in this instance, but my thought is that to do this might again interfere with the developing therapeutic alliance and I prefer not to take that risk unnecessarily in this still early phase of the analysis.

My intervention is apparently successful, because after the silence she again resumes the experience of positive transference feeling, accompanied by anxiety and multiple defenses against the growing attachment. My intervention is an attempt to help her recognize that there must be a series of intermediate unverbalized fantasies that take place between the affect changes and that these would help to explain the sudden shift from feelings of love to those of hate. Although she does not specifically elaborate on the fantasies themselves, she associates to the father and to the role of the transference expectations about me in understanding the sudden change. My intervention is an attempt to clarify the existence of the central issue that I will accept her feelings and not be upset by them, and an attempt to encourage her to become aware of the missing specific fantasies associated with this idea.

In response to my comment she now undergoes a further transference regression with the simultaneous experience of sexual arousal as well as anxiety accompanying it, and she is finally able to associate this to the childhood experience of lying in her bed and thinking about her father coming into the room. The specific oedipal fantasies growing out of the expectation of the father coming into the room have not yet become conscious, but their existence can be inferred from the setting in which this material emerges and the implicit sexual wishes existing at the moment in the transference relationship to me. These last associations have been accompanied by significantly increased affective response and anxiety, but the patient's last remark, "There were so many times that I must have thought of this!" is highly significant. It indicates a spontaneous recovery from the regressive transference experience that has just occurred and the ascendency of the self-observing and more mature ego functions. In this remark she is standing somewhat aside and observing her experience from the vantage point of her current adult self and of her therapeutic ego functions.

As can be seen from the material of this session as well as the flow of material over the past several weeks, the analytic situation is now well established. The patient has developed a reasonably firm therapeutic alliance and simultaneously has developed the capacity to permit herself to undergo psychic regression in the treatment situation. This capacity for regression which is increasingly focused into the analytic situation, and the pressures of the infantile drives and fantasies, lead the patient into an emerging regressive transference neurosis in which she repeats toward me in an immediate, direct, and affective way the unconscious relationships, fantasies, drives, conflicts, and expectations that existed when she was a child. The transference neurosis will from now on become the central theme of the analytic work and it will be the tool by which repressed conflicts can return to consciousness and ultimately be resolved through the analytic process.

In other words, the opening phase of analysis has now been completed and we are now embarking on the middle phase of the treatment process.

# The
# Middle
# Phase

# 4

## THE FOURTH THROUGH
## TENTH MONTHS (Summary)

During this time the patient manifested an increasing capacity for effective free association and regression in the service of the ego, with the result that the psychoanalytic situation developed steadily and rapidly. Both the therapeutic alliance and the transference neurosis emerged more solidly. In the transference relationship I was perceived chiefly as the father with a gradual elaboration of the historical events of her childhood and latency. There was a continuation of the transference wish to seduce me sexually, along with hopes in the therapeutic alliance that I was strong enough not to be influenced by her transference demands.

Following a month's summer vacation she entered the last phase of her pregnancy. The analytic material reflected her preoccupation with the pregnancy, her sexual identity conflicts, and the elaboration of memories relating to the birth of her younger sibling. Anticipation of delivery stimulated the emergence of conflicts in regard to nursing and her own oral experiences, as well as recall of a significantly positive relationship to her father prior to the birth of the younger sister.

At the end of the seventh month of analysis, she was delivered of a boy by Caesarean section, and returned after an absence of fourteen days. In the transference neurosis she oscillated between an oedipal father relationship and regressive mother reactions dominated by primitive oral yearnings. In this oscillation between mother and father transferences, the psychic equation penis = breast, semen = milk, and fantasies of fellatio emerged clearly as transference phenomena.

The affectively intense, ambivalent transference relationship was increasingly focused at the oedipal father level, with emergence of castrating fantasies in response to frustration of the sexual wishes. This was followed by a phase in which the major wish was to acquire the father's penis for herself and to identify with him in the negative oedipal relationship. There were repeated regressions from these fantasies to a maternal transference,

197

experiencing the analysis as a nursing situation in which for one hour per day she was allowed to gratify her oral needs with me.

The oedipal phase father-transference wishes were accompanied by phallic drives and aggressive fantasies of castrating the male, with emergence of the childhood idea that the penis in erection, which becomes small and limp following ejaculation, represents a destruction of this organ. In this context there was an initial recall of possible directly sexual experiences with an uncle, but these memories were immediately repressed and replaced by phallic identification and wishes to use the penis in a sadistic and aggressive act against the mother and other women. These fantasies were related to the recovery of primal scene experiences with a typical sadistic interpretation of that event.

Following this there emerged feelings about the uncle with an increasing sense of conviction that something overtly sexual had occurred between them in early childhood. Initially this was experienced as a hypothetical possibility, but in response to manifest transference fantasies, wishes, fears, and guilt feelings, she began to recall her relationship to the uncle, including an intensely positive and erotized attachment to him. At the same time she expressed intense anger and contempt that he would gratify such wishes and behave in an overtly sexual way toward her, and there were continuing attempts at denial and repression of any sexual experience between them.

Early in the tenth month there occurred, as an intensely affective transference experience, fantasies and memories of an exciting yet guilty and anxiety-provoking initial version of an overtly sexual incident with her uncle. In the ensuing sessions there was a further elaboration of her conflict between the phallic wishes to castrate and keep the penis for herself, and her feminine oedipal wishes to be the wife and mother. She continued the defensive repetitive attempts again to repress and deny that any type of overt sexual activity had occurred between herself and her uncle. All these issues were repeatedly experienced as transference reactions accompanied by intense affects and conflict. Subsequently there emerged, first in the transference and then as a recollection, her childhood fantasies that she had killed her uncle by taking his penis away, accompanied by the thought that it had come out of her at the time of the birth of her first child. She saw herself as a vicious black monster of whom I should be afraid, and expressed fears that she would kill me.

Following this she regressed again to a maternal transference, reexperiencing her nursing expectations and demands, and recalling information that she had been nursed for six months and then suddenly weaned. She felt she never was allowed again to experience the gratifications she had lost, expressing intense rage about this in the transference and in recall of childhood memories. She again reexperienced the feelings of helplessness and sudden rejection which had accompanied the weaning experience, with further elaboration of recollections of her relationship to her mother and rage at the frustrations of her wishes to be loved. At the same time, however, in the transference she equated being loved with death and the loss of herself and of her awareness, with feelings of being suffocated.

Following the emergence of this material she returned again to the oedipal phase experiences and relived in the transference her anxiety, con-, flict, and wish to get away from me as the uncle, with further exposure oι her guilt and fear over the sexual relationship. At the same time in the therapeutic alliance there was a realization that the return of this memory was close to consciousness, but that she still could not grasp it or its details.

# 5

## THE ELEVENTH MONTH

SESSION 143

**P:** I feel so excited about coming here today. I felt as if I was going crazy when I left yesterday, and I had the thought that I should give up or quit, or something like that. Then I felt OK, but I was so nervous just before I came back. (Elaborates.) It all has so much to do with my children and with my uncle. I feel as if I am about to relive the whole thing about my uncle here with you. I feel as if I love you and I trust you and I can feel that I am letting my guard down. I feel just like I did in Springfield. I feel as if I'm pregnant.

**A:** You mentioned a sense of excitement before you came today, and also that there was a nervous fear. What comes to your mind about that?

**P:** At first I felt excited and then I was depressed. I know the excitement was about you, and I have the feeling that it's love.

**A:** What's the detail of that?

**P:** Why should I feel this way about you? It's something that I should never let myself do. There's no use to it. Something always happens to it. I've never been fulfilled before and I know that I never will be. I know that I am going to be thrown down. – – I think of all the men that I've given my love to, and I realize that Tom is the only one to really accept it. But he wants to have intercourse with me. – – – Now I feel as if my uncle was really the first man in my life and I realize that he weakened, and I know that my father would have weakened too. It's the same with all boys and that's what they all wanted. It's true of Tom and it is also true of Harris, and now I know that it's true of you.

**A:** What comes to your mind?

**P:** I know that you are trying to build me up for a fall. It's either that or else you are going to be strong. It's all a laugh. Just give me enough time. I can't believe it! – –

**A:** What did you stop at?

**P:** I just don't know what I want. If I show any love I feel it's as if I have to go back in my shell whenever I'm around men and boys. Ever since I began analysis I find I am able to begin to peep out. But every time I do let myself go! . . . . . – I could screw them all. I want to prove that I can do it in order to show you that I'm right, and yet if I did screw you I couldn't stand it. – – I always wondered is it something in me? I ask myself can you function with a male and still not screw him. I feel as if I either have to hide myself completely or else flaunt myself and I know that all the other women hate me for it. – – When I do this I prove that I can castrate any man in the world and I know that that's what I want to do. I wonder could any woman in the world get Tom? Is he as weak as any of the other men that I have known? – –

**A:** I think that the question that you are asking really belongs here with me. I think you are still wondering if you really flaunt yourself and try to get me and show me that you want to, would you be able to screw me?

**P:** I almost die thinking about it each time. – –

**A:** What's the detail?

**P:** I can only think of it in terms of rejection, and it always kills me. It feels as if it is the end of the world each time. I see you as being so strong, but I know that it is always there in the back of my mind. I wonder about it. – – I wonder what it would be like if you didn't do it, but I am sure that you'll be just like my father. I can't believe it. –

**A:** I'm not clear what you mean.

**P:** There's not a man on earth. . . . . . – – If I didn't seduce you when I really tried it would be because there is something wrong with you. I know that you'd want me and that I'd be capable of taking you. It's just like it was with my father. – – – But it panics me to think that I couldn't get a penis any time I wanted it. That's all that kept me going while I was in Springfield.

**A:** What comes to mind about that?

**P:** – I always had a boy interested in me when I was in Springfield. It's what kept me going while I was there. I think how the penis goes inside and becomes a baby. It's just like with my father. If I were my father's penis then I could go up inside of my mother and be part of both of them. And yet I take all of my hostility out on my own children. – – | *Cry*

**A:** You mentioned the idea that if you were your father's penis then you could go up inside of your mother and become a baby. What comes to your mind about that?

**P:** – Then I could be born again and I could nurse. I could go back and just stay there. And I know that's what I always wanted. That's the only way that my mother would ever have me. All she wanted from me was as a tiny baby. She *hated* me as I started weaning. – – And that's why I hated my sister so much. Instead of me nursing it was her.

A: This is like the hostility that you feel towards your children now. It's as if you identify them with your sister and you feel that they are getting the thing that you want for yourself.

P: God! I feel so depressed. And I know that it will never be! I'll never be my father's penis and I'll never nurse my mother again. I'll never have either one of them again even though I want them. – – Why do I keep on having more children? I wonder if I think that *I* will be born again? – –

A: It's as if in the mother-baby relationship, emotionally, you are both parts. You're the mother who loves and takes care of the baby, but you also identify with the baby as the one who is being loved and nursed.

P: This all depresses me so because I *know* that I'm *not* that baby. – – It's all so odd! I think about New Year's Eve, and I went in to see the baby and he was lying on his back. I had to turn him over. It's so funny! A baby can't even turn over! It's all so odd! – –

A: What's going through your mind?

P: I feel that I want to dig my teeth in! It's like I'm. . . . . It's me. It's as if I'm the baby. All he can do is smile and he was so happy! I just can't imagine ever being that helpless. Now I can see my mother's hands come down and turn me over. She has such gentle hands. I feel and see myself *Cry* as a baby and I see my mother pick me up and change me, but I don't have a "thing." – – I feel completely helpless. He survives out of my love and yet he doesn't know it. He takes it all for granted. It would scare the hell out of me if he knew. But he doesn't know! He doesn't have that fear like I did! I always wonder why he can smile so much. (Elaborates.) I think about the whole time when I was a baby. I often wonder if I ever slept. I feel as if I was never sure that my mother would come back. I knew! But I felt that she would not come and that she's not going to feed me and I felt it to the point that I'd wonder if she would ever come! It would be so horrible for a baby to have to scream and scream. – – – Now I feel as if I'm in a panic, but I say to myself that I can always go to the ice-box. I can hardly believe all of this. It's just like turning the baby over. What did my mother expect? There I was about two months. – – That's the feeling of panic that I have so often. To just lie in bed and scream and still not know if my mother is going to come! It's such a fright! I could kill her! It's the most horrible feeling in my whole life! – – – I don't know why it is that I'm so relaxed here. I feel as if I could go to sleep. I know that you're there and that you're not going to go anywhere. But I have such anxiety when I leave here. I ask myself will I ever get back here? And then

I feel nervous the whole time that I'm gone, and also for the first five or ten minutes when I get back here. – – Why do I do this to my two children? I just let them cry! (Elaborates.) It makes me sick to think about it. But I don't let Thomas cry at all. It's as if I'm the one who will die from all of this and not them. – – – – – Suddenly I wonder if I can seduce you.

A: I think that you retreated just now to the feeling of being a helpless infant, because then you know that you definitely can't seduce me.

P: – – I don't want ever to be that helpless. – – – – –

A: We'll stop here for today.

At the door the analyst hands her the bill for the previous month.

### DISCUSSION

She begins this session with a description of the excitement she felt at the thought of seeing me, and immediately associates this to the preconscious awareness that she is about to relive the experience with the uncle in the transference relationship. Her statement, ". . . . . I feel that I am letting my guard down," indicates that even though she has now been in analysis for more than ten months and even though this issue of trusting me has been repetitively brought up in the transference relationship, she is still maintaining her defenses against fully relating to me, stimulated by the fantasy that in my behavior I will repeat with her the childhood traumatic relationships.

The patient mentions that she feels the way she did in her adolescence (". . . just like I did in Springfield") and goes on to say, "I feel as if I'm pregnant." At this point I have several choices. I can remain silent, or I can focus her attention to the feeling of being pregnant, or to the adolescent experience. However, I feel that no matter what these issues represent they will be most effectively experienced as part of the transference neurosis, and I therefore ask her to associate to the excitement and fear at the thought of seeing me. This leads to her description of the continuing hesitation about fully experiencing the transference relationship to me and the expectation of disappointment, but also to the fantasy that I will eventually weaken as her uncle did and as she fantasies her father would.

Following my requests for further elaboration, the patient goes on to describe her ambivalent conflict between the wish to be able to seduce me and thus repeat her childhood history and prove to herself that I am like all other men, as contrasted with her awareness that if this were actually to happen ". . . I couldn't stand it." She then goes on to generalize the issue and to displace it to her husband, and my interpretation of the displacement is an attempt to bring the conflict back into the immediate transference perceptions and conflicts.

Once again she elaborates upon this ambivalent conflict in connection with me, and she goes on to defend herself against the impact of the possibility that I will not respond to her in overt sexual ways by depreciating me when she says, "If I didn't seduce you when I really tried, it would be because there is something wrong with you."

My acceptance of her fantasies about getting the penis permits her now to undergo a further regression with the emergence of the primary process fantasy of identifying herself with the father's penis, and being inside of her mother and thus part of both parents. Although this is accompanied by the affective response of crying, the patient has now gone far enough in the analysis that she can permit the emergence of such primary process fantasies without disruptive anxiety, and she can accept the occurrence of them in the stream of her conscious thought which now immediately reverts to the current situation of expressing hostility toward her own children.

My attention is drawn to this fantasy of identifying with the father's penis and I ask her to elaborate upon it in the hopes that we can begin to expose some of her early childhood fantasies about intercourse, conception, and the processes of pregnancy, since it is my hunch that these issues are crucial in the understanding of her manifest symptoms. She then goes on to elaborate upon the fantasy of fusion and reunion with the mother in the oral dependent relationship, projecting to her mother the anger and hostility over the process of weaning and the "loss" of the breast. And in this context she is able to recognize the source of some of her hostility toward the younger sister. My immediate association is to the derivative expression and displacement of this conflict in the material she has mentioned about her hostility toward her own children, which she has apparently been acting-out in her behavior with them. My interpretation of the derivative of this old conflict is an attempt to point out to her the displacement that is occurring in the present situation with her children, and hopefully thereby to help her reduce her tendency toward acting-out this conflict with them.

Following this interpretation, the patient's more mature reality testing and synthetic ego functions take precedence as she recognizes the realistic impossibility of ever gratifying these infantile wishes. Spontaneously, she goes on to describe another derivative of them in the current behavior of wanting to have more children. My interpretation about her psychologically playing both roles in the mother-infant relationship is another attempt to help her control the tendency to act out these archaic conflicts in derivative forms in her current adult life. This permits her increasingly to become aware and to express recognition of her identification with her baby, while simultaneously attempting to reconstruct some of the conflictual feelings and experiences from her own infancy. In the midst of this she indicates that she is repeating some of these experiences in the mother transference relationship when she feels relaxed and comfortable while actually with me, but anxious and unsure of herself when away from me between sessions.

The patient had begun the session at the level of a heterosexual oedipal transference to me as uncle (father) and from there had gone to her fantasy of participating in the primal scene by identification with the father's penis. This subsequently led to the fantasies of reunion with the mother at the oral level, accompanied by a repetition of this oral maternal tie in the transference to me. Following this, however, she spontaneously expresses the sudden thought, "I wonder if I can seduce you." At this moment my own response is that the material regarding the maternal transference and the oral ties to the mother have served as a regressive defense against the conflict over oedipal heterosexual drives toward the uncle and father, so that when she suddenly reverts to the question of seducing me sexually I point out in my interpretation the function of the regressive defense. Her response, "I don't want ever to be that helpless," neither confirms nor negates the correctness of my intervention, but her silence at the end of the session suggests that conflict, anxiety, and the defense of suppression have been mobilized by my intervention.

---

## SESSION 144

Patient gives the analyst the check for the previous month.

**P:** I feel as if I'm up against a huge wall. And it's not worth my fears to let my defenses down. I'm sick and tired of being scared shitless! It just doesn't pay.

**A:** I think that's true, but I think we can see it two ways. One way is to keep up the defenses, and although you try to avoid the fears, it costs you a lot in effort and in symptoms and in being scared. The other way would be to understand all of this and ultimately to do away with these fears once and for all.

**P:** I'll bet you were never this scared! I'm telling you that it's pure hell. (Elaborates.) I felt it yesterday and all last night! I was so mad! −− I hate anyone ever being kind to me, and I felt that you were kind to me yesterday. Then I got scared. (Elaborates.)

**A:** You had the feeling that I was kind to you yesterday. What was the detail?

**P:** I had such a feeling of love for you when I left. I can't remember it all, but I really trusted you yesterday, and I felt that you were being honest and I felt that you were behind me. Now I feel as if I should know better and that no one is ever behind me. −− I dreamed that I'd killed my kids. −− I don't mind hurting myself but not my children! Analysis is just not worth hurting my children. In my sleep I feel as if I'm a girl, and I felt very jealous. There were all mother and father figures around in the dream and it was like there was a world of jealousy. I hated everybody and I felt lost in an ocean in the dream. I was freezing and I had to make my way home. And then I found that no one had missed me. Tom didn't even care and I felt lost in the shuffle. There was one beautiful girl in the dream but she was very standoffish and I wondered if she represented me? I liked her. Then I was trying to go to the bathroom and I found that I couldn't go. −− And then there was something about food and then Tom gave a girl a pink hairdryer. I need one and my father gave my mother one for Christmas. I wonder if I was jealous about him giving it to her? I didn't feel it at the time. But I'm mad! It was the first time that my father didn't get mother a present by telephone. He was so proud of himself. And yet my mother complained! There was only one person who ever really cared about me and that was Mrs. Jones, and even there Helen came first because Helen was her daughter. −−− I feel as if I'm two years old now. −−

**A:** Now let's go back to yesterday, and the feeling you had that you loved me and could trust me and felt that I was behind you. What comes to your mind about that?

**P:** I want to scream! I can't, damn. . . . . . It's a feeling that's never been fulfilled in me. Now I'm scared. It never amounted to anything and something would always happen. And yet I know that that's not true and that it's really all in me and its the way I feel. You'll turn it all around. . . . . −

**A:** What did you stop at?

**P:** I know that you'll hurt me somehow. I just can't believe this feeling. I've never had a relationship where the other person didn't want me to give and where they didn't want more from me and didn't get mad at me. Do I want more? −− I know that I'll be very disappointed. −− I let

*Cry!*

myself think that you like me and that you want to help me and that I can trust you and that you're honest, and I think that that's it and that nothing else is being demanded. But I can't stop there. I think that you are going to pull away from me and tell me that you can't take this.

**A:** What's the detail?

**P:** I think of it as an ideal relationship and then something always happens. Are you going to demand too much of me? Am I going to demand too much from you? It's just like with my mother. She always demanded so much! – – It's as if she always said you can get just so close but no closer. It's all so frustrating. – – – I can't admit how much I really want it, but I know that I'm never going to get it. I know that I'll die without it if I ever admit it. – – – And yet gentleness is so important to me. For instance, when I love my children. That's the way that I want to be handled. I can see myself so gentle with my own children, and I feel so warm towards them. (Elaborates.) – – – I think over and over again that my mother didn't love me. She was so hostile! She would just grab! She'd jerk me! I'd nurse! And then she'd throw me into bed! – – – I know my mother hated me! (Elaborates.) I know that she was jealous of Mrs. Jones' love for me. – – – It was really a devouring hostility. My mother was going to devour me. I've fought against it all of my life. She was going to eat me up! I could see it in the look in her eye. She'd have her tongue between her teeth and I knew that she hated me and that she was going to eat me up and get rid of me. – – Suddenly it dawns on me that I've always looked toward my mother for the mother image and now I know that it's not there. It never will be. I keep hoping to find it but I know now that she never will be it. Now I feel as if I can't breathe. I have the urge to stick my whole hand into my mouth and chew on it. – – Now I think about you. – Am I going to find it in you? And yet I don't really want it because it makes me so helpless. For me the idea of love is the same thing as helplessness, and if I show hostility and if I fight then I know that I'll live. – – I know that if I had ever gone to sleep at my mother's breast, she'd have killed me, and so I had to keep awake the whole time or else I'd have died! – – – – I feel as if I must keep running and as if I have to run and run and keep moving. (Elaborates.) – – Now I have such a sexual feeling. I feel as if I'll be gobbled up. But it's all so sexual! –

*Cry, Sob*

**A:** What are you feeling?

**P:** I feel it in my clitoris. I lie here and I feel as if I can't do anything and as if I will die, and it's just like being in a big ocean last night, but yet I love it, and yet I'll die and it's all so sexual. It must stop. I just can't relax. But I feel as if I am relaxed right now. I feel that I must stay awake.

*Cry! Anxiety*

**A:** So your fear is of going to sleep because for you to go to sleep means to be devoured.

**P:** I don't want to be. – – – But I do. I do want to go to sleep but I don't want to be devoured. I want to relax! I'm so tired of all this running. – – This is the most frightening thing. You think that you will die! And there's nothing to do about it.

*Quiet*

**A:** So what we have to see is how you equate sleeping with death.

*Anger*

**P:** – – – I think about one time when I went to sleep. My mother forgot me. Now I feel as if I can't breathe. I must stay awake and I have to wiggle and squirm so that my mother will know that I'm there! – – A baby is really so helpless and you must take the nipple out occasionally so that they can breathe! – – – A baby sucks so hard and after a while he can't stop and then he also can't breathe. (Laughs.) – Why is that

*Anxiety*

funny? It's really pitiful and it's not funny. And yet I want to laugh and scream and laugh and it all seems so funny!! Now I suddenly feel that if I'd ever gone to sleep nursing with my mother I'd have died! She'd have let that nipple completely engulf me! I'd have died and I couldn't

*Quiet*

breathe. – – – – – This all scares the hell out of me. – – – – (Laughs.) When this happened I went to the bathroom in my pants. I know that I did. – –

**A:** What was the detail?

*Anxiety*

**P:** It's like in the dream. This is the way I feel. As I relive all of it at home I go to the bathroom. I go over and over again and it's a physical act. I felt as if I almost died. I know that I went to the bathroom in my pants.

**A:** So it's as if you were scared shitless, and as if there is no shit left

*Quiet*

inside of you because you've been there so often.

**P:** (Laughs.) You can have too much of a good thing. – – How am I supposed to get control of the situation? How am I supposed to stop this? – – Now I want to get up and leave! – –

**A:** What's the feeling?

**P:** I can control it and I can stop nursing when I want to and it's not going to devour me if I can just get up and leave. – – – –

**A:** We'll stop here for today.

### DISCUSSION

The patient begins the session on a note of heightened resistance based on the intense anxiety she is experiencing in the transference neurosis. My initial intervention is an appeal to the self-observing ego and the therapeutic alliance, and is a tacit encouragement that if she can tolerate the anxiety enough to deal with the emerging conflicts she can then overcome her neurotic suffering. I am no longer clear as to why I felt this type of encouragement was necessary at that moment, and in retrospect it could be argued that this intervention was unnecessary and that the material which emerged subsequently might have come up anyway. In any event, the patient goes on to indicate that the anxiety is a response to the perception after yesterday's session that I had been kind to her. My asking for the detail of the feeling of kindness is the first step in analyzing the experience as a transference phenomenon. At this point, however, I am not yet clear whether the current transference conflict and the anxiety that accompanies it is at the level of a heterosexual oedipal transference to me as the uncle and father, or a more primitive and regressive oral transference to me as the mother.

The subsequent dream and her associations to it suggest that similar to yesterday's material, there is conflict at both levels with an oscillation between them and that the mother and father transferences are being used as defenses against each other. In the first part of the dream she is alone and cold and then is trying to go to the bathroom. In the second part of the dream there is the typical oedipal constellation condensed around the element of the hairdryer. Because I want to focus this material into the transference where it can be more easily and specifically observed, I now go back to focus upon the feelings of love and trust toward me yesterday, which had triggered the upsurge of conflict and anxiety and which in all likelihood represent part of the day residue contributing to the dream formation.

Her response is to elaborate on the issue of trust versus mistrust toward me, which is then associated to the relationship with her mother. After describing her wish for an ideal mother-child relationship as occurs intermittently in the relationship to her children, she returns to her contrasting perceptions of the mother's behavior and attitudes toward herself. As she talks about the mother and her perception of mother's "devouring hostility," the patient increasingly undergoes a further regression with the emergence of the primary process fantasy of being eaten by the mother and the breast. As this regression occurs, it is accompanied by an intensification of affect as well as the conversion symptom that she can't breathe and the wish to put her hand into her mouth. This is accompanied by her own perception of how much she still wants this type of gratification with the mother, and she repeats this conflict of whether or not she will be gratified in this way with me. She also illustrates how in her fantasy the needs to run and keep awake represent defenses against the primitive fantasy of being eaten by the mother.

This material represents the beginning emergence of the so-called "oral triad," described by Lewin in his book, *The Psychoanalysis of Elation*. This triad consists of the wish to eat, the fantasy (wish) to be eaten, and the wish to sleep, which is a recapitulation of the infant's experience at the breast. The infant aroused from sleep by hunger actively suckles and nurses, thereby reducing the drive tension which had awakened him. As the infant becomes satiated there is a general relaxation of tension accompanied by drowsiness, which is presumably perceived as being engulfed by (eaten by) the mother and her breasts. This is followed by a return to sleep with its loss of awareness. In the healthy and gratifying mother-child relationship this entire sequence is primarily a pleasurable one, but in relationships involving frustration, disruption, lack of fulfillment, fears of loss or separation, etc., the entire experience can become a source of conflict and fear of being destroyed or devoured by the mother.

It is this line of reasoning that leads me to make the interpretations equating sleep with being devoured and with death. The patient continues to experience this as an immediate transference reaction when she feels that she can't breathe and has to wiggle and squirm so that I (the mother) will know that she is there. At the same time, the more adult self-observing functions are present as she describes the needs for a mother to take the nipple out of the baby's mouth. The sudden inappropriate laughter can be understood as a dynamic shift in which the psychic energy previously used to repress this entire sequence of fantasy and experience is now momentarily excessive to the degree that the fantasies and conflicts have emerged into consciousness. The laughter itself represents a partial discharge of this psychic energy.

The patient continues to oscillate between regressive reexperiencing of the nursing situation and more progressive self-observation and recognition of the events as having occurred long ago. She herself equates the memory (fantasy?) of soiling herself with the incident in her dream and also describes how in a symptomatic act at home she apparently relives this experience again and again. This material now permits us to understand the first part of her dream in which she killed her children as a re-creation of the mother-infant relationship with a reversal of roles in the dream work.

In retrospect my comment, "You were scared shitless . . ." seems inappropriate and tangential to the central issue at the moment, and I have no recollection of the line of reasoning that led me to say what I did.

At the end of the session, her wish to get up and leave as a means of controlling the situation with me represents an attempt in a derivative form in the transference to relive the conflict-producing situation and to achieve a derivative form of belated mastery over it.

---

## SESSION 145

P: ---- When I lie down here I picture my house in Evanston and I feel as if I'm right there. (Elaborates.) -- I feel as if I'm a baby in a crib and yet I'm trying to live like I'm twenty-seven. I feel like someone has a stick in my throat and my stomach is gnawing as if I hadn't eaten. It's all so real! And yet I just ate breakfast a little while ago. I feel huge. I get bigger with every bite of food that I take. --- Now I'm back to reliving the time when I was a baby. What's the advantage of all of this? It's really hell! -- I feel such hostility! I get so mad! I feel as if I could go crazy! (Elaborates.) Now I have an urge to scream and yell right here on the floor. --- I have a terrible feeling in my stomach and it's all sour and hot and it gnaws at me. I feel sick and I can't talk.

A: What are your associations to this sick feeling?

*Cry*

P: - It reminds me of what happened on Saturday. I caught myself saying, "Mother, where are you?" I felt so scared! I'm twenty-seven and I know where my mother is. I feel like a baby and as if I'm lying in a bed and I'm all cried out and I'm sick and I've done all that I can and there is no use to cry and I'm so tired! I want to go to sleep and I can't. -- My head hurts. I feel like I'm dead inside and it feels like it's rotten and hot and burning and sour and dry. -- I'm not a fat pink plump baby. I'm a dry wrinkled shriveled up mess. That's me. --- I eat things in order to make me *big!* It's just like when I'm pregnant. I eat all kinds of meat, fish, and vegetables in order to get big.

A: Although chronologically you're now twenty-seven, you still have the feelings about yourself and your mother and the relationship between you which was so painful. These feelings were buried at the time and so they've never been changed, and now in the analysis you are reexperiencing them with me.

P: I feel as if I could eat you up and make you disappear because I hate you so much! ---

A: What's the detail?

P: I see a baby in a crib and the mother is leaning over her finally! There is such hate in the baby's mind! I could eat the Goddamn woman up! – – She leans over the crib and I see two huge breasts which are just hanging there. – –

A: What's the detail of those breasts?

P: Suddenly I feel so sick! My mouth is so dry. There's something crammed in my throat and it's dry. It makes me sick and I feel sour. – – – – – – Those two huge things hang down over the crib and it scares me to think about my mother picking me up. – – – Usually a baby is so sweet but I am *not* a sweet bouncing lovable baby. – – – I think about those breasts and nursing and how wonderful it is. And then I think about my mother and hate! I can't think that it is wonderful. My mother's face is so cruel and mean, and yet her breasts are so loving. It's all cruel. It's hate. But it's all so mixed up and it's horrible. – – –

A: You have the feeling that the breasts are so loving. What comes to your mind about that?

P: – They're what I want! I see the nipple and I want to suck and I feel the milk and that's what I need. It's all so comfortable. I'd like to. . . –

A: What did you stop at?

P: – That's all there is. They're two big pillows, and you put your body up to them and they're nice and warm. Now I'm sucking. This is what I want. It must be love because it is so wonderful to me and I love it.

A: So what we can see is that you love the warm, good feeding breast. But we also have to see that you have a fantasy of a poisoned and hating breast. So because of that fantasy, when you take it in you feel sick and sour and poisoned.

*Cry*   P: – – – Suddenly I don't want to have anything to do with you. I want to work this out by myself. I'm sick and I feel as if I could throw up. I want to sit in a corner by myself and I don't want anyone to touch me.

A: So it's as if you equate my interpretations with milk. If the interpretation is good or pleasant, it represents loving and nourishing you and you feel strong. But if the interpretation is an unpleasant one, then it's as if for you it represents poison and it makes you feel sick and afraid.

P: – – (Laughs.) – Now I feel that I want to go home to bed and just curl up and be sick and stay there. That's the only relief that I could get. – – – I wonder why do I think some of this is poisoned milk? – – – – I feel as if it's killing me, both physically and mentally. Now I really feel like hell. – –

A: You're repeating all of this with me and in the analysis. At times I'm the good loving breast and I make you feel wonderful, but at other times I'm the poisoned breast and you feel that I make you sick and I make you upset and make you feel like hell.

P: You just can't help me. I feel as if I'll lose my mind and I just can't stand it. – –     *Cry*

A: And at the times when you see me as the poisoned breast you feel as if you must withdraw from me, and you can't let yourself get close because you're afraid that I'll kill you.

P: – – – Now I want my sister to come and put her arms around me and tell me that I'll be all right. – – – – I want the loving you to come through! But I know that it won't. I feel like hell and I feel as if I'll die. I don't want anything to do with you. – – – I don't even feel mad at you anymore. I feel as if you destroy me and yet I don't feel mad! – – – – – – –

A: We'll stop here for today.

### DISCUSSION

The patient begins the session by illustrating how during a transference neurosis in analysis the process of regression occurs chiefly in the analytic session itself and begins with the start of the session. "When I lie down here I picture my house in Evanston and I feel as if I'm right there," illustrates how the process begins with a self-observing perception of the immediate situation followed by associations which in turn lead to the reexperiencing of earlier feelings. But she also illustrates the continuing perception of herself in the current scene as she describes herself trying to live like someone who is twenty-seven or having had breakfast just a little while ago, or of wondering what are the advantages in reliving these experiences.

The content of her material and conflict represents a continuation of the regressive maternal transference conflicts from the previous session. The incident in which "I caught myself saying, 'Mother, where are you?'" indicates that the regression is not totally limited to the analytic session and that occasionally it still occurs in her life outside the analysis. She goes on to elaborate the regressive infantile experience, putting it in the present tense and describing the conversion reactions it is causing her.

My generalized explanation to her about the recurrence of symptoms is a response to the unpleasant distress and suffering that the analysis is causing her, and is an attempt to try to make this suffering understandable and therefore more tolerable to her. It represents a counterreaction

in me to the fact that even though my motives are therapeutic and helpful, I am still inflicting pain upon her. Without acknowledging my comments directly, she continues in the regressive transference experience, in
association to which there is a further filling in of the ambivalent
memories, fantasies, and feelings in the nursing situation. With this
comes an increasing awareness that in spite of her chronological age
there is a strong persistent yearning for and conflict about the mother's
breast.

After these descriptions, my initial intervention is on the positive
loving attachments to the breast and she elaborates upon the pleasure
involved. Remembering her earlier description of the painful sick feeling,
I remind her that the attachment to the breast is an ambivalent one. It
could be argued that this intervention was premature and that I might
have permitted her to enjoy further the pleasurable associations to the
breast, and that perhaps my intervention was motivated by an unconscious
countertransference wish to frustrate such a pleasurable experience. In any
event, the patient's response is one of negativistic withdrawal from me
with a recurrence of the sick feeling.

Throughout the remainder of the session we are dealing with her
response to my intervention. In this response she is repeating in the
transference the reactions to the mother's frustration that occurred as an
infant and child. These responses include withdrawal, the feelings of
hopelessness, the turning to the sister as substitute maternal object, and
the repression of the hostility toward me. In other words, although my
initial intervention about the ambivalence towards the breast may have
been premature, the patient responds to it on the basis of the transference neurosis and we continue to work at her response from an
analytic point of view.

---

## SESSION 146

**P:** I feel like running out of here! I'm so scared! (Elaborates.) – – –
I've had so many emotions for you that I can't handle them all. (Elaborates.) – – – I've been feeling so much love and I think you're wonderful
and you're helping me. But I also feel like destroying you. I feel like
kicking you right in the rear. – – – I must decide if this love is real. Are
you a fine adult analyst or are you a weak spineless idiot? I could chew
you up! I have such a funny feeling in my mouth! I'd start at your foot
and chew until I'd swallowed you all!

**A:** You can't be sure whether I'm a fine adult analyst or whether I'm a weak spineless idiot. What comes to your mind about this?

**P:** As you say that I get dizzy. There is something in my mouth and I could chew and chew and suck. I know what you are. I love you, but you're also a bastard and you're no help when you're trying to destroy me. (Elaborates.) I'm thinking about what you said yesterday about the poisoned breast. It makes me so nervous and insecure! I think you're stupid. I feel as if I'll die and you're trying to destroy me with all these words! I don't believe you! -- I had a dream in which there were two huge houses. They were mansions. One was in Evanston and the other in Springfield. We moved from Evanston to Springfield. In neither one was I ever accepted and especially in Springfield. It's like two breasts and that's the way I feel. I'm thinking of Harris and how I could kill him! He was like the bad breast. I nursed and nursed and suddenly he destroyed me. -- I wonder if you are going to do this to me. -- In the dream I was having a miscarriage around 4½ months. J. M. rushed in and I was bleeding and my legs were up in the air and my arms waving around and the blood was spurting and they were going to have to do a section on me. Tom told me about it and I didn't know what was going to come off. He said, "They're not going to be able to save the baby." I thought that I would not be able to go through another section, I thought that I was dying or that I was going to be killed. It was just like I feel right now. I feel as if I'm dying and I have a funny nasty taste in my mouth. I can't stand the idea of having a baby through the vagina and have the baby come through me, I just can't stand it! -- Somehow I think this is all related to killing Harris and to getting my period and to my thoughts about dying. --

**A:** You mentioned that in the dream you were having a miscarriage at 4½ months. What comes to your mind about that?

**P:** I'm thinking of something! It's half-way to term. Oh! I feel as if I'm about half-way through my analysis. All I wanted was a chance for this baby to live. If I can just hold out and keep it in, then it might live. ---

**A:** You have the thought that I'll destroy you like you feel Harris did. What comes to your mind about that?

**P:** It always happens to me. It's just like with my mother. No, it's really not. I saw through Harris the whole time! (Elaborates.) They would always say, "Trust me!" and yet, they always used me. (Elaborates.) Both he and my mother, they were such idiots. I want to let myself go with you! -- That whole deal with Harris was like reliving

*Cry,*
*Anger,*
*Anxiety*

the whole thing with my mother. He was trying to destroy me with the breast! It was like he was saying, "Come and suck," and then, damn! He threw me away as if he were destroying me. I can't trust anyone! And yet I know that I *can* with you. But mother and Harris keep coming to mind and it shakes me up! Dr. Davis was the one who saved me. How can Harris be so unadjusted? He's been through analysis. And yet it's like he wasn't. I have such an urge to cut my wrists whenever I think of him. I think of the blood! It's like he was a nail and he was driving it into me. I bled and bled! He was trying to bring me out and I held back and I couldn't trust him. It was just like with my mother. He wasn't capable of handling my feelings! And yet he wanted them! But he just wasn't capable. – – I wonder if this is all reality? He helped me but he got involved and he tried to do an analysis and take me further than he could and he fell into a trap because he was no stronger than I was! We

**Cry!**  just floundered and it scared the shit out of me! It makes me sick to my stomach! Suddenly my hand feels numb! Oh, you can't do this to me! I want to trust you and put myself into you and say, "Here I am, the raw horrible me," but I hate you and I can't stand you. I know that I'm weak, but I've managed somehow up to now.

**A:** So the issue seems to be, am I strong enough to tolerate and accept you and all of your feelings, or am I like Harris and mother, and in that sense weak and unable to do this?

**P:** I know that I've got to decide. – – The child in me wants to cry and flail around. I know that I'm on the right track! This is right for me and you're not using me, you're here to help me. But then this thing comes in and says, "Watch out." I can see what you are. You're here to help me but not to get emotionally involved. You're a good analyst and that *is* the right track for me! – – I can survive my mother and Harris! I did it! But for six months afterwards every day I thought that I'd kill myself! (Elaborates.) I had to combat them because they couldn't destroy me! – – Oh! I feel as if you are mad now! It scares the hell out of me, because if I thought you got emotional about one little thing I said I just couldn't stand it! – – My hand!! – –

**A:** What's the detail of the feeling that I'm mad right now?

**P:** I'm picking on your hostility against Harris. If it's so, then you're weak. But he is an idiot! He ruined my friend and he said that he'd do my analysis but Dr. Davis said no! Maybe it's *my* hostility that I'm picking up on! – – Oh my hands, they feel so funny!

**A:** What's the detail of the feeling?

**P:** It scares me. I feel as if they are deformed and they're cramped and I can't move them! I feel so tense! I feel as if I could grab your penis and pull it off and ram it down my throat and choke it. My hands feel helpless. I used to get this way in Harris' office. But it's also as if my hands are on the breast. I'm losing my mind! – – *Cry!!*

**A:** You feel as if your hands are on the breast. What are your associations?

**P:** I see the curve of the breasts and I see a pair of baby hands. I'm so mad I could kill someone. I'll die, I'm so mad and so helpless!! — *Fury* I feel as if I'm nursing. I could chew and I'm so mad and helpless and I can't do anything! God damn it! I could kill someone! – – I feel so mad right now I could die! I want to grab someone and pull that God-damned nipple off and eat it! ! – – I hope to God that you don't hurt me, please, please, please! – – Now I suddenly feel an urge to love! I want to hold you and love you! – –

**A:** What's the detail of the feeling?

**P:** I love you. I see the nipple and I'm holding it, and I'm mad because the milk isn't coming, but suddenly it does and I love it and I love you. I've kicked and screamed and now I want to love. The whole damned time I'm nursing, my mother is so hostile and angry. I felt it until the milk came and then it was a wonderful feeling. I loved it. Then the nipple was gone and I went back to my hostility. It was always back and forth! I feel beat! But I trusted you though! That milk did come! Jesus, I feel I'll go crazy with joy! That milk came! I wish it would go on forever. I want to hold you so tight and gobble you up because I love you. Because you gave me milk. – – – For the first time I feel the love and I feel as if I have been nursing with a sexual feeling and I love it and I can have it! I can have it for about five minutes, and then I have to leave for twenty-four hours but then I can come back and get it again. I love it. I'm feeling so nervous. I know that it will be here. – But after I love I'll kill myself, I'll die because I can't live without it. – – – I feel so nervous and I feel scared to death right now! – – I think that I swallowed that damned nipple! – –

**A:** What's the detail of the feeling?

**P:** I'm enjoying this feeling with you. But then we have to separate and I'm destroying the breast and it destroys me and the whole thing ends up in death. I want to take your breast with me and eat it, but it will destroy me if I do. So I can't enjoy it. These are all of my feelings for you. I even enjoy it so much that I want to take it into myself but then I'll die, so I had better not enjoy it. – – – I feel so great! But it makes me so nervous! ! – – – (Laughs.) – – When I leave here I'm going to love you so much! I want to put you inside of myself. I love you! And yet it's all so destructive! – – – – I really do believe that I swallowed that whole big thing! – – – –

A: We'll stop here for today.

## DISCUSSION

The patient begins by describing the ambivalence toward me in the maternal transference as a continuation of the theme from the end of the last session. She is simultaneously experiencing these issues as regressive transference phenomena, and also to some extent observing herself as she does so. Starting at the level closest to conscious awareness, I pick up on her doubts and uncertainties about me as an analyst, to which her response initially is the conversion reactions of dizziness and the sensation of something in her mouth. She refers to my interpretation last time about the poisoned breast, which also represents an association to the dream which follows. The first part of the dream and associations to it represent a continuation of the maternal transference conflict, and while the second part of the dream also deals with the themes of birth and mother-child relationships, it is also suggestive of conflicts at a later psychosexual level of development.

Something unusual about the way in which she mentioned the precise time of 4½ months drew my attention when she reported the dream, so when she finishes her spontaneous associations to it with a resistive generalization, I decide to ask for her associations to that particular element. After her thought about being half-way through her analysis, the association of keeping the baby inside until it is ready to be born is a reference to herself, displaced to the baby in the dream.

This material reminds me that in talking about Harris in presenting the dream she had said, "I wonder if you are going to do this to me?" Because this and the earlier material suggests that her fantasy of rejection and destruction in the maternal transference is prominent, I now focus her back into that aspect of the transference conflict. As a result she now begins to experience more intense affect as she describes the relationship with Harris and mother, and tries to separate her perception of me from them. But she is again overwhelmed by the transference expectation that I will respond as they did.

Once again I focus the issue into the therapeutic alliance by pointing out the transference expectation that I will react as they did, but at the same time, indirectly asking her to check this expectation against what her experience with me has actually been up to now. She again fluctuates between the realistic perception of me in the therapeutic alliance and the transference expectation of me as mother, and progressively she develops the conversion reaction of cramping in her hands.

Since the conversion reaction is a means of expressing symbolically (through a physical symptom) a set of feelings and fantasies that should be verbalized in connection with the current transference experience, I now question her about it and thus focus her attention toward the mental contents that are being omitted. After further describing the symptom, she becomes consciously aware of the wish to grab my penis. This represents the fantasy and impulse which had been defended against through the conversion response, and then with great affect she begins to expose the fantasied equation of the penis with the breast.

At this point her anxiety is intense as she says, "I'm losing my mind!" and in order simultaneously to reassure her about this while at the same time encourage her to explore the fantasies further, I ask in a matter-of-fact way for her associations to her hands being on the breast. Once again my attitude of calm acceptance of such material permits her partially to identify with me in my analytic attitude, and this promotes a further regression accompanied by an affect of fury in which she expresses the aggressive cannibalistic fantasy. It is as if for the moment she is re-experiencing toward me the aggression that she once experienced toward the breast, and in the brief silence I suspect that she is waiting for me to have an angry or rejecting response. Her statement, "I hope to God that you don't hurt me . . ." reflects what she has been thinking during the silence and it's as if in the ensuing silence she is still waiting for my reaction. When I do not react as she had expected and instead continue to accept her feelings calmly, she has the sudden rush of feelings of love followed by the fantasy experience of the pleasure in being fed by me as the good and loving mother. At this point she again verbalizes fantasies of incorporating me, but now motivated by positive loving feelings rather than the hostile and destructive drive described earlier.

Her statement, "I can have it for about five minutes and then I have to leave for twenty-four hours, but then I can come back and get it again . . . I know that it will be here," is a repetition in the transference neurosis of the development of the sense of object-constancy in the infant's relationship to the mother. This first step of remembering the positive and gratifying experience, accompanied by the expectation that it will happen again and that she can count on my being here, represents a significant step forward since it now permits the infant to experience separation more comfortably and with less fear, knowing that the object is not permanently gone and that it will return.

As part of the primary process fantasy of incorporation of the loving breast, the patient illustrates the typical conflict that gratification and pleasurable incorporation may also result in the loss of the object "out there." In other words, the childhood fantasy of oral incorporation, whether motivated by aggression or by positive attachment and love, results in the fantasied disappearance of the external object. And it is this fantasy which must be dissolved and replaced by the awareness of object-constancy which then protects the child against his own involuntary destructiveness. Her final statement, "I really do believe that I swallowed that whole big thing!" reflects simultaneously the regressive, primitive fantasy and the corrective effects of the secondary process and mature thinking of the self-observing ego as she reflects upon the experience that has just transpired.

This fantasy of destructive oral incorporation of the breast serves as an important organizing factor in her subsequent experience and development. The effects of a later traumatic sexual experience, which will emerge from repression shortly in the analysis, will be understandable in terms of the persistence of this fantasy. But at this time in the analytic situation I did not yet know of its existence.

---

## SESSION 147

**P:** I've done nothing but eat! I've been so mad at you! You take away all of my happiness! I'd be a beautiful woman if I lost 10 pounds, and so I eat. This is all your trap and I have to fight against you and hate the world.

**A:** The thought is that you would be a beautiful woman if you lost 10 pounds. What's the detail?

**P:** I'd have a gorgeous figure and a pretty face. I know I would! (Elaborates.) I'd be wonderful. I'd be loving and strong and I'd be just about perfection. But I can't reach it because of you.

**A:** How do you mean?

**P:** You make me eat and you pull me into this trap and I have to fight to get out. – – I picture myself falling and just being broken apart. I feel as if I'm so vulnerable. – – – I'm ready for you to destroy me and I can't fight, so go ahead. It scares me, it's like the end of the world. I feel as if I'm a tiny baby and I'm helpless and scared to death and I have no defenses without my hostility. I'm lying here waiting for you to destroy me and kill me. – –

A: What's the detail of the image of me killing you?

P: I don't know, but I know that you can. – – – If I ever let myself go then you'll let me nurse on you and I'll eat you up and then I'll destroy you, it's not you destroying me. – – –

A: How do you see all of this happening?

P: I feel as if it did yesterday. I felt as if I had to look at you as I left, just to be sure that you were still there. If I trust you completely then you won't be there. I felt as if I'd really eaten you up and that you were all gone. – – You want me to say that I'm weak and that I'll die without you and that's why I eat you. – – – I had a dream that I really trust you and in the dream you were a policeman and you saved me and I got into your car and you took me home. There was a huge balloon in the back. There was a girl there who wasn't afraid and she blew on it and was having fun. I was afraid. I felt, "This thing will kill you." Both girls really represent me. – – –

A: And what about your associations to the balloon?

P: It's a breast and it's so symbolic. It fits all that I feel. Then in the dream we were on the ice skating rink, and then we were zooming around in a car in the park and I had the feeling that "I'm going to make it," and I was not going to fall into the man's trap. He was a nice policeman and I could trust him because he took his job so seriously. There was a $1.00 bill there and I picked it up. Then the shy girl said that it was her's and I gave it to her. The policeman wasn't mad but then there was another car that was full of bad men. We were in a swamp and I kept wondering how we were ever going to get through. – – –

A: And what are your associations to the $1.00 bill?

P: That's the only part that I don't understand. I wanted it, but I didn't care if the other girl took it. She was really me and I think that we were really one. I was so afraid that you'd be mad about it. – – Why am I never afraid that you're going to be hostile? – – – I feel just like a child, as if I have to take a chance and I don't know how my parents are going to react, and they really don't react at all because they're not mad or approving. I wonder how am I doing that here? – – There was a boy in the car and he was so nice. He was quite young. I think, these are all three parts of you. One part is trying to destroy me and one is the stern analyst who is trying to do a job, and has no heart, and one is the young boy who understands and is so nice. – – I'm thinking about love and about you and about how much I feel and then I think that I'll never make it. – – – – – I'm feeling such love and I want to cry because I'll never have it. But I know that it's I who will prevent it. I could have it, but I just won't let myself. I've got to learn to stop crying. – – – – That deal with my uncle proves it to me. I know that I'm right. I get a headache every time that I think of him.

**A:** There are still details of that situation with your uncle that you don't want to look at.

**P:** I just can't imagine! – – It's all symbolic. I gave in once on that love bit and it destroyed me.

**A:** You mentioned at the beginning of the session that you thought you would be a beautiful woman with a gorgeous figure and a pretty face if you just lost weight, but you were worried as to what would happen here if you did. What's the detail of your fantasy?

**P:** Lately I feel as if every man thinks that I'm great and beautiful and seductive. I really believe it! I know that I could seduce any man in the world, especially if I looked my best.

**A:** I think that you are generalizing about all the men in the world in order to avoid the issue of what's going on between you and me.

**P:** – I can't imagine. I know that I hide the woman in me by looking dowdy every day. I wish I knew *you* and what you were like. I'm thinking about those three men in the dream. I wonder if one was a sex maniac? And what about that policeman? I think that you really can hold onto yourself! . . . . .

**A:** What did you stop at?

**P:** I don't really think that you are like my father or my uncle. I'm thinking about all of their terrible sexual problems. – – – – What keeps . . . . . I don't want you to see me as a woman! I couldn't stand it.

**A:** How do you mean?

**P:** I'm conceited. I know that it takes more than a face and a figure! I'm thinking of all of my own sexual feelings that I've had for you! They're OK and I don't mind that. – – But I have a feeling within myself that I can walk in safely only if I look like hell. You will change if I look well.

**A:** What's your fantasy?

**P:** I'd try to seduce you in some naive disguised way. But I'd just be castrating you if I did.

**A:** And suppose you were *not* successful?

**P:** Then I'd have to stay a little girl for the rest of my life. That's the only reason my father didn't give in to me. If I'd been a woman he'd have screwed the hell out of me, I know it. – –

A: What's the detail of your image?

P: As a girl my father was just one big sexual organ. All he wanted to do was screw, he didn't love anybody. He would use his thing on any good-looking woman, and if I'd been one, he'd have done it to me. All he reacted to was pure looks. Fortunately I was just a little girl.

A: I wonder if this could be one of the reasons for wearing bobby-sox today?

P: I feel as if I'm so ugly right now, otherwise you would take advantage. But I'm *not* a beautiful young woman.

A: What comes to mind about the fact that you've been chewing gum all the hour?

P: I want to eat, I want to chew! I want to get something in my mouth. It drives me nuts! I'm a baby and I want to be sure that you know it. And yet I could kill you for it. – – –

A: So the feeling seems to be that if you choose you can seduce me just as you feel you could have seduced your father. You feel that if you were to think of yourself as a beautiful young woman that I'd react to you just the same way that you think your father would have.

P: Why don't I try? I wish I could prove it one way or the other. But I couldn't take the result whatever it is. – – –

A: I think that at times you use this feeling of being a helpless baby as a defense against being an attractive young woman.

P: – – Women can destroy any man they see and they can even destroy babies. I don't want to be one of those destroying people. – – – – –

A: We'll stop here for today.


### DISCUSSION

The patient begins by describing the displacement of the conflict from yesterday into the symptom of excessive eating and by projecting the source of her difficulties into the transference and on to me. Her emphasis on being a potentially beautiful young woman with a sexually attractive body suggests that she is responding in the transference today at a more advanced level of psychosexual development than she was yesterday. On the other hand, the references to herself as a tiny helpless baby and the fantasy of herself nursing on me and eating me up indicate that the conflicts which emerged in the transference yesterday are still active. At this point I am not yet sure whether the advance in the level of activated conflict serves as a defense against the maternal transference, or whether the experience in the transference yesterday has sufficiently reassured her in regard to her conflicts over the oral attachment to the mother that she can now move ahead psychologically into the oedipal phase conflict.

Because I am still uncertain about the current dynamic configurations, my interventions are merely attempts to encourage her associations in hopes that the pertinent material will emerge. The patient herself refers to yesterday's experience and the intensity of her transference regression expressed in the fantasy that she had actually eaten and destroyed me. She then reports the dream in which she can really trust me and in which she sees herself simultaneously in two different images. Her reference to the other girl who "blew" on the balloon is an allusion to an incident of oral sexuality which occurred with her uncle when she was a child, although at this time that incident has not yet fully emerged in the patient's material and I am therefore unable to make use of it. Her subsequent material about the nice policeman who takes his job seriously is a further reference to an increase in basic trust and confidence as a result of my handling her reaction yesterday. After describing the further elements in the dream and the three parts of me, the patient goes on to associate to "that deal with my uncle," which suggests that today there has been movement in the level of activated conflict toward the oedipal phase.

Because the traumatic incident with the uncle has not yet fully emerged from repression, I use this opportunity to ask her about it further. However her response is a defensive one and not particularly promising as far as further recall of this material is concerned. But having decided that the current level of conflict is significant at the oedipal phase, I now remind her of the material she brought up at the beginning of the session, in regard to herself as a beautiful woman and her fantasies of seduction. I am thereby trying to focus the material further into the oedipal transference conflict.

Initially she uses the defense of generalization of this conflict, which has occurred frequently in the past. Once again I interpret this mechanism to her, with the response that she begins to describe another defense of looking dowdy in the transference. She also illustrates the mechanism of negation when she says, "I don't really think that you are like my father or my uncle." And she goes on to refer to the fantasy that her father would have had sex with her if she had been an attractive woman at the time. Her statement, "Fortunately I was just a little girl," offers me the opening to point out to her that in her nonverbal transference behavior (the way she dresses to come here) she is reenacting that same defense, and I am also in a position to help her see that other nonverbal behavior (chewing gum today) reflects the same regressive pattern.

She emphasizes that she is a baby and wants to be sure that I know it as a defense against the heterosexual transference conflict, and so in my next intervention I focus at the level of the heterosexual oedipal transference conflict from which the regression to being a baby has occurred. And I subsequently follow this up with an explicit interpretation of this regressive defense.

Her final response illustrates another aspect of the oedipal fixation in her reluctance to use her mother as the model for identification as a woman, and this may well represent a continuation of the conflict with mother from yesterday.

---

## SESSION 148

**P:** – – – – I fall apart the minute I see you. It takes me twenty minutes here just to get myself together. I think and I feel such love for you and I think how much fun it is to love you and to be close to you. But then I get so depressed! (Elaborates.) Now I'm so nervous! I feel like I want to run. – – – It all depresses me. . . . . but I know it's all a defense. I love you and I can't have you. And yet I can have Tom and I do it with him too. (Elaborates.) – – Now I'm thinking about my father. I never had anything from him. – – But that really doesn't bother me too much. – – – It's the same feeling as I have with you. I ran away from my father. If I tried and got close to him and let him know what I wanted, could he have. . . . . I think I could have won him if I'd wanted to. I was just a child but all it takes is flattery and I think I could have done it. It's all related to not having a penis. Now I think about you and I think about my body. I don't want you to see me. I want to cover myself up. If I say that I'm a woman and you reject me then it's because I don't have a penis. I know that that's why my father rejected me. I didn't have a penis. As a girl I could have won him and I could have done it as a bitch. All I had to do was sit on his lap and coo. Instead, I withdrew from him and I said it's because I don't have a penis. – – It's all so depressing to be a woman. – – – – – There are so many reasons for my problems and I'm trying to analyze them.

**A:** Are you saying that you did all of this to yourself?

**P:** I try to analyze it but so what. It's all of no help. Yes, I guess it does help. I apologize for what I said. – – – Now I feel as if you could just tear me apart.

**A:** What do you picture?

**P:** – . . . . . – I just can't say it! I'm trying to fool you. You know about me because you have eyes and you can see me! Now I think about my daughter when she is wearing her nightgown and sitting on the couch and she has no pants on. She'll put her legs up in the air and show that she has the cutest bottom and she just doesn't care.

**A:** What comes to mind that you talk about your daughter rather than say it about yourself?

**P:** I can see myself with big eyes and I have no clothes on and I'm about two feet tall. – – Now I wonder about you. – – Are you going to accept me without a penis?

**A:** You mentioned the big eyes. What's the detail?

**P:** I see myself with big eyes and I'm just looking and I'm waiting.

**A:** I think when you speak of yourself with me right now it represents the situation as a little girl with your father. You're wondering if you can seduce me and it's as if you're wide-eyed at the size of my penis. You think about your own bottom being so cute, but it's also small, and I think you have a fantasy that you'd be torn apart by my penis. On the one hand you want to be, but at the same time you're terrified of it.

**P:** – – – – – This makes me so nervous! I feel so flustered that I just can't think! Why is that? – – – Now I feel as if I have snakes and bugs crawling on me and I can't stand it. – –

**A:** What's the detail of the feeling?

**P:** I want to throw it away and get rid of it all but it just keeps pestering me. It's like I'm a bug and my father is a snake. This is all too much! – –

**A:** You feel as if you're a bug and your father is a snake. What comes to your mind?

**P:** It's all vicious. The snake eats the bug. It's horrible!! – – It's so hard to believe that little girls can have thoughts like this. – –

**A:** How do you mean?

**P:** That they can think about penises. – . . . . . Now I think about my father's penis inside of me, but it's all too adult. It makes me so nervous and it's so ugly. I feel so depressed and like it's the end of the world.

**A:** Let's try to follow the thought about your father's penis being inside of you. Then what happens?

**P:** – Now I can picture myself growing bigger. The penis is inside of me. It gets bigger and bigger and now I'm it! – – It's the same old thing. Ugh! I become the penis and I go inside of my mother.

**A:** Let's go on. You're the penis and you're inside of mother. Now what comes to mind?

**P:** – – It's all so dark! – – . . . . . Now I go into mother. . . . . . I'll destroy her and I'll destroy that baby up in there. – – I'm going to tear everything up! – – Who is that baby? Is it me or is it my sister? – – – Now I feel so mad! Good God! – – I want to go in there and I want to be born again and this time be born with a penis! It makes me so mad! I hate you! I could scream! Now I'm so mad at myself. If I just come out as a boy I could stand up and say, "Look at me." But I hate this person. I hate this. – – God damn it, I'm a girl! I'd be destroying myself and I'd be a completely different person. – – I'm so mad! It's all so childish to think that I could kill myself and then come back as a man and then all would be fine. – – I could tear someone apart!! – –

**A:** What do you picture?

**P:** I want to tear into you and pull your God damn penis off and. . . . .

**A:** What did you stop at?

**P:** I want to eat it or put it on myself and then I'd cram it into my mother and tear her up! Why is this all so great? It makes me so mad!

**A:** You wondered why this would be so great. What comes to your mind?

**P:** I just don't understand it. Why would I kill myself over such a stupid God-damn thing as a penis! Why should that cause me so much trouble? I'd like to destroy them all! They are all competition!! – – This has made me so mad all of my life! Why is it so superior? I hate all men and I don't want one and I don't really think it's so great to be a man.

**A:** I think we ought to go back to that image of yourself as a wide-eyed little girl. I think you must have seen your father's penis in various different stages. There must have been times when it was erect or when it wasn't, and times when it was big or small or hard or soft. And I would guess that you must have been fascinated by it.

**P:** This is all so frustrating. I just can't stand it. It's just what I want but I can't take it!

**A:** When you say that you can't take it, that has a double meaning.

**P:** I can't take the thought! Oh shit! I'm too little for these God-damn problems. I'm just a little girl. – – I'll never have it and I'll never have you and I'll never have anything. I'm just a little girl.

**A:** But we saw before that as a little girl you had the fantasy of yourself as a charmer and that you'd be able to use your wiles and sit on your father's lap and coo, and that way you can get to your father's penis. And I think you feel the same way about mine. And the fantasy is that *then* you'd have it.

**P:** – That idea scares the hell out of me! – – – But now I can see myself let go and open up. I can see myself being warm and womanly and completely naked.

**A:** We'll stop here for today.


## Discussion

The patient begins with the non-specific expression of anxiety relating to the transference conflicts but then associates to her father and the fantasy of winning him. This represents a continuation from yesterday's session in which I had interpreted her wish to be the infant and little girl as a defense against the oedipal wishes. As part of this she mentions her phallic stage conflict and the feeling that she is being rejected for lacking a penis.

My first intervention is a response to an impression I had gotten while she was talking that she has a fantasy of having total control of the situation and that everything that happened as a child is attributable to herself. Such a fantasy would represent a defense against helplessness and passivity by reversing roles from passive to active and controlling. However, this intervention is ignored by the patient as she expresses her feeling that analysis is of no help. But then in response to the feeling that she has depreciated (castrated) me, she apologizes and then feels that I will tear her apart. Her statement that I can see her reminds me of what she said earlier in the session about wanting to cover herself up and not have me see her, so that when she then talks about her daughter showing off her genitals I assume that she is referring to a fantasy about herself displaced to the daughter. I want to block this displacement and therefore call her attention to it, and in her response the mention of her own big eyes strikes me.

As this material is unfolding I am reminded of the many times that she saw her father's penis in childhood and the exposures she had to the primal scene. I am also reacting to her earlier phrase, "Tear me apart," as well as the reference to her small daughter's genitals. All these elements are synthesized intuitively and empathically by me, and I offer them to her as an interpretation of the current oedipal father transference conflict.

Initially the patient responds with anxiety and with the conversion sensation of the snakes and bugs, but she then undergoes a further regression and the fantasy of the snake and bug emerges, followed successively by the fantasies of her father's penis inside of herself and of her identification with it. My responses to this material are to encourage her emerging fantasy and eventually she expresses directly the wish to use the penis as a weapon to destroy her mother and/or the baby. Several times she uses the phrases, "tear everything up," "tear someone apart," "tear her up," etc., all of which confirm the existence of the mechanism of projection which she had used early in the session when she had the expectation that I was about to tear her apart.

Her next line of defense is an attempt at denial of the significance of her own fantasies about the penis through depreciating it and men generally, as well as an attempt to deny the existence of her own wish to be a man. In attempting to reduce these resistances, I make the reconstruction of her having seen the father's penis in various stages of erection and of having been fascinated by it. Here the attempt is to show her that such reactions and fantasies are expectable in a child, and to show her through my acceptance and verbalizing of such thoughts that they would be understandable and appropriate at the time. The attempt is thereby to reduce the intensity of her guilt and shame over having been fascinated by the father's penis and of having had multiple and varying fantasies about it in relationship to herself.

The remainder of the session represents an elaboration upon this theme, with a regressive image of herself as a little girl serving as a defense against the oedipal fantasies. My last intervention is an attempt to block the utilization of this defense by pointing out to her from the material earlier in the session that even the fantasies of being the little girl on her father's lap would bring her in contact with and close to his penis. Her last associations of herself as a sexual woman suggest that the previous work has been effective, that there is a temporary reduction in the level of conflict and anxiety about the fantasies regarding the father's penis, and that therefore she can now experience the thoughts of adult sexuality with slightly less conflict. The increment and permanence of such a shift is likely to be relatively small, but its significance is in the fact that subsequent return to this material is likely to be easier and to be elaborated at greater intensity, and thus ultimately lead to more significant and lasting structural change.

---

## SESSION 149

There is a snow storm with significant delays in traffic and the patient arrives twenty-five minutes late.

**P:** I wonder why did I come? I felt as if I can't go until Wednesday. I thought about the idea of going from Friday to Wednesday.

**A:** What was the detail?

**P:** It put me in a panic. – – It's silly I guess, and I had a real conflict about it. (Elaborates.) But I finally said to myself that I must go and get my bottle. I ate all day on Saturday and also again yesterday. I had such anxiety and I was restless and I couldn't be still. It was like the ideas about going to sleep. I just couldn't stand it. I had the fantasy that I'd lost my mind and that this was all too much for me. – – I want to blame you and to say that you pushed me back to being a helpless child again, and I'm not going to bother to fight you or to cover it all up. I have such a wish to be in bed and just have someone wait on me. Yesterday I was able to get Tom to do it but I was so nervous while he did. Then I had a dream about my mother and it was something about my grandmother and about a breakfast. – – – I feel just like a helpless baby. (Elaborates.)

**A:** I wonder if this feeling of being a helpless baby doesn't represent a retreat and a defense against the sexual feelings and the ideas of being a woman.

**P:** I'm not a woman and I have absolutely no sexual feelings. I'm just a tiny little baby.

**A:** Yes, that is the feeling. And that's the meaning of the defense.

**P:** This all scares me to death, and yet it can't be that frightening. I was fine on Saturday until Tom called to say that he was coming home early. Then I started to eat. I had the thought that he'll probably want to make love. We had a date Saturday night with some friends and there was an unattached boy there. I felt as if I was going to go nuts if I had to be exposed to men or to you or even to my husband. I know that I have sexual feelings for all men and I'm constantly thinking about the penis. I think about it even with the janitor in this building. I have the picture that they're all going to invade me.

**A:** So we can see how what happened Saturday represents the kind of retreat I was just talking about. You were fine until Tom called and then you had the thought about making love and then you began to eat.

**P:** I just wish that he were a son-of-a-bitch. I can handle them just fine, but Tom and you are both so nice! I just can't take it. I know that he loves me and that's what bothers me.

**A:** So on the surface it looks like a paradox but let's see what comes to your mind.

**P:** He brings sexual feelings out in me. Really he's wonderful. (Elaborates.) He does so many things *for* me, but when he does I *die* inside. (Elaborates.) And the kids were so cute and yet the better they are the more I hate them. The more I love, the more I must kill and hate.

A: I think the wish that Tom were a son-of-a-bitch is because if he were then you could screw him without such conflict.

P: I know that I can't have sexual feelings unless the man is a son-of-a-bitch. It's just like Saturday night. It was like with my father. I could seduce those men and that way I could cut off their penis. But I love Tom and I'm afraid that I'm going to do it to him anyhow. I'm afraid that I'm going to destroy him.

A: So we can see how sex and love are separated for you.

P: But why is that? It doesn't make sense! Love *is* sex. I have sexual feelings because I love, and the urge to castrate a man is not sexual or love. It's just a way of doing it. – – Suddenly I feel very weak and it's got something to do with sex and there is something pushing in my mind. I feel so nervous right now.

A: You're feeling it here with me this morning. What comes to your mind?

P: I feel so nervous. I know that I love you and I want to be with you and that's shown by the fact that I came today. (Elaborates.) I could have called and not come and it really would have been so easy because I had such a perfect excuse. By coming I show you how I really feel and that I really need you. Are these feelings of love going to leave me helpless and unable to move? I realize. . . . . that I love you and so I know that I'm helpless. – – – Now I feel my forces rally and I'll *not* be helpless. – – But it's all such a vicious circle. Can you love without being dragged under and without having to drown? I want to try to get there and yet I feel that it will kill me. It's just like a dream I had about water.

A: Your feeling is that to love me means to be dragged under. What's the detail?

P: I've never before loved in this way. But I know that I'll have nothing and that I'll have no defenses and just be an idiot. I'll be unable to get up and I associate the whole thing with letting myself go. If I don't fight you then I know that I'm going to be dragged under and you're not going to help. You're just going to sit there and watch me drown.

A: We'll stop here for today.

## DISCUSSION

The patient begins the session by using the same regressive defenses against the sexual transference which had occurred last time. Initially, she describes her conflict over coming to the session as related to the feeling, "I must go and get my bottle." The same regressive defense of the oral maternal ties is demonstrated in her description of eating over the weekend, her wish to sleep, the dream about the mother and grandmother, and the feelings of being a helpless baby. This type of defensive retreat and regression from the conflictual feelings about being a woman which had emerged at the end of the previous session is characteristic of patients in analysis and is part of the working-through process. I therefore interpret it as a defense, and thus try to help her recognize the conflict from which the regression has occurred, but her initial response is to maintain the defensive position of being a tiny baby without sexual feelings.

My intervention of accepting this as her present feeling and explaining it as a defense encourages her to face the conflict more openly and also encourages the perception in the therapeutic alliance that "It can't be that frightening." She then is able to confirm the interpretation by filling in the sequence of thoughts at home in regard to making love with her husband, which had led to the regressive behavior of eating. And she then goes on to describe the intensity of her sexual fantasy and preoccupation.

My pointing out to her a second time about the sequence of events on Saturday is an attempt to confirm the previous generalized interpretation I had made, but now based on the specific associations which she has recovered. It could be argued that this was an unnecessary intervention since it did nothing to further the analytic process and the patient essentially ignores it as she goes on to describe her separation of sexuality from love. This separation represents a reenactment of some of her oedipal fantasies (the father and his mistresses having sex outside of marriage), but at the same time it also serves as a defense against sexual arousal toward the oedipal object (in spite of everything, the patient had many feelings of love for her father). The fantasy of castrating the man through sexual contact ("I could seduce those men and that way I could cut off their penis.") is a derivative reference to the sexual traumatic event which has not yet emerged from repression, and which I therefore do not yet fully appreciate at the time. Her feeling that ". . . there is something pushing in my mind," in retrospect suggests that the repressive defenses against recall of this event are beginning to weaken.

These conflicts are being re-experienced in the transference neurosis to me as the father, and she goes on to describe the feelings of love and need for me which are increasing in their intensity and thereby are mobilizing the fantasies that she will be overwhelmed by her own drives and wishes.

## SESSION 150

P: I haven't slept for the past two nights. I've had all kinds of dreams and my nerves have been all upset and I've been tense and everything is terrible. And I can't stand it. I hate the nights and I hate going to bed because I'm so scared and my heart pounds and I shake all over. I had a dream that I was here and you were trying to poke me with a pencil. And in the dream you said to me, "Slow down." I was so scared! And then last night it was the same situation again. You were very blasé and you were going to bring a date to our next session. You couldn't care less. Some of it took place in my bedroom in Evanston. – – – After you poked me with the pencil I had another dream about a boy who was built very much like my father. He was very nice and we were going to lie down on the couch and make love. He said to me, "Are you going to use something or should I?" I didn't want to. And then I was in my grandmother's house. – – – I just had a fantasy of you going crazy and sometimes I wonder if Tom is crazy. I guess it's really all me and my fears about myself.

A: What's the detail of the picture of me if I were to go crazy?

P: I feel as if I must identify with somebody who is normal after I have finished with the analysis. Is it going to be you? Is it going to be Mrs. West? You all lean up against each other and you can't stand up alone. I want to be able to stand up alone. Now I think that I can see Tom crack up.

A: I think the thought still is of me being crazy. What's the image of what I would do?

P: I know what it is now. I know it's something sexual. You'll probably take out your penis and show it to me. It's just like a nut! I feel as if I am going to go crazy now!

A: The fantasy is of me being just like your father and your uncle, which means that I represent a sexual danger for you. It seems you think that either you are going to seduce me or I'm going to seduce you just as you did with your father and your uncle.

P: But my father was never around and we really had no contact! (Elaborates.)

A: But we both know that you wanted to.

P: – – Why would it scare me!? Especially if it never happened. My father was never there and I could wish all I want, so why would it scare me?

A: Let's look at the details of the present fear that you feel with me.

**P:** It's such a tremendous wish on my part so I think it's all possible. – –

**A:** And what about the image of this tremendous wish?

**P:** – – Now I see myself and I'm all naked. I'm like a nymph and this is something like a fairy tale. I'm with you but it's all not real. – – Now I think about your penis. But if you didn't have one then we could dance together naked.

**A:** And yet your fantasy was that I'll take my penis out and show it to you, just like a nut. What comes to your mind about that?

**P:** This is all too crude. It feels just like an awakening. To dream about it is all right, but to actually see it! Now there's nothing to dream about. There it is, it's right there! You put your penis in me and you have an orgasm and the whole thing is ugly and horrible to me. It's just not right! Something is so wrong! I'm just a little girl. It's not right! It's not right for a little girl. Now I think about Maine and my mother and father and them being naked. (Elaborates.) I just can't believe it!

**A:** What's the detail about your father's penis in this memory?

**P:** It looks so big and long and it has hair around it. – – It's just too much! I'm so near it. It's my father's! I look and look! I just can't act as if I don't know! I know there is something there. Suddenly I think about a teapot!

**A:** So you must have seen him urinating too.

**P:** I never have!! – God-damn it! – –

**A:** If we think about the image of the teapot, it involves water coming out of a spout which I think represents a picture of a man urinating.

**P:** I just don't remember. I was standing by a big chest! I can see that I was watching! What was he doing?

**A:** What do you see?

**P:** He is standing there for my benefit! Shit on him! God-damn him! He didn't just pass through.

**A:** I think the thing that frightens you the most was your thought that he enjoyed you looking at him.

**P:** I had such shitty parents. Them and their whims! I have so God-damn many sexual feelings I want to die and he loves it. That is frightening. If I'm enjoying it and he's enjoying it! He has a hold of himself.

**A:** What's the detail?

**P:** Why should I give him a thrill? There is something sexual going on. He'd like me to feel it and I'd like to feel it. Is it as a woman? Or is it just because it's there? Would it make any difference if I was a boy? – – If I'd touched him he wouldn't have cared. I know I could give him pleasure. God-damn it! It's all up to me to control *my* self. And I'm twenty years younger. I'm supposed to control myself! My fear is my only control.

**A:** So we can see that your fear serves the function of helping you to try and control yourself.

**P:** I feel as if that's what saved me then.

**A:** But what about here with me now?

**P:** I feel such a tremendous sense of desire. – –

**A:** I think you are doing the same thing and using the fear now. We see that in the dreams, in the difficulties that you have been having at night, and in the feelings that you have while you are here. And these are all attempts to control yourself and the question we have to ask is, whether it's necessary and whether it's the only way?

**P:** Today what else could I do? I suppose I could tell him to get his God-damn clothes on and go in the bathroom and pee! I could act as an adult and tell him to get your clothes on. But I know and it's all too much! It was too much when I was a child. I was all feelings and I wanted to touch that! I'd never seen one before. It was my father's and all I had to do was to reach out and I could have played with it!! – – I know that I can seduce any man to the point of bringing his penis out and showing it to me. But I've never done it. It's all just a fantasy, but if I am alone with him this is what would happen.

**A:** So it's as if when you were a girl you had a chance to do it and you didn't take it, but there still is a wish to do it and a sense of regret that you didn't. So it's as if you repeat that situation over and over again.

**P:** I run when I get a chance to do it with any man and I always blame them for being so weak. – – I think I really want a man who would put his penis inside of me and react normally, but I haven't ever run into one. – –

**A:** Let's go back to the dream. In the dream the boy says, "Are you going to use something or should I," and then it all stops. What comes to your mind that you didn't want to use something?

**P:** – I feel as if my whole drive in life is to get pregnant! I wonder why? It really scares the hell out of me. It's just like when I was sixteen and even though I was having sex I didn't use anything. I was really smarter than that. I used to have such cramps with my periods. – – I used to think that it was smart of me not to want to do it, but I wonder why? I feel as if I missed a connection here. I feel as if I'm using my head and I do know that it would be smart to use something. –

**A:** So we can see that one wish is to get yourself pregnant. But we have to understand what the situation represents.

**P:** – It's just like. . . . . taking his whole being inside of me. – – – Maybe

I want to be ugly or maybe I want to be a man, or maybe I want to castrate the man or maybe to relive my birth. There are 10,000 reasons why I want to get pregnant. Now I think about the time on my parents' bed when my sister was conceived.

A: What comes to your mind about it?

P: I see that big penis go in and then my mother's stomach is big and my sister is born.

A: But you mentioned your parents' bed.

P: I'm watching my father put on a rubber and then I see him have intercourse with my mother. – – –

A: But you seem to be omitting the details of the scene.

P: I feel so nervous! This is all so sickening! I see my mother's legs spread apart and my father's huge thing go into her. This is all so sexy! There's a wild storm and then damn! The storm is over. – – – It's all like it's me! – – – Now I have a sudden desire to try to seduce you. I know that I'm a woman and I want you to put your big thing into me. – – – Through this union I feel like I want to be born again. This just doesn't make sense to me. – – – – –

A: We'll stop here for today.


### Discussion

In the previous session I had interpreted the patient's defensive regression from the oedipal transference feelings and fantasies, and thereby focused her back toward the sexual conflict involved in the relationship to her father and to me in the oedipal transference. The patient begins this session by indicating that my intervention had mobilized further conflict and anxiety, and as a result she has had a number of neurotic symptoms presumably stemming from the conflict being mobilized in the transference. This leads into her reporting of the dreams, all of which involve clear references to the sexual conflict in the oedipal relationship, repeated in the transference with multiple allusions to the childhood situations.

The fantasy of me going crazy is a complex one in that it simultaneously represents a transference image of me as the father who loses control of himself, but it also represents a projective defense against her own fantasies and fears that she may lose control of her impulses. And in the context of the current conflict and the material she is discussing, there is a strong suggestion that behind this is a fantasy of some type of sexual activity between us. It is with this idea in mind that I begin at the level of her conscious awareness by asking her to elaborate on the fantasy of me going crazy. Initially, her response is a defensive and evasive one, and after I encourage her to give up these defenses by again focusing on the immediate transference fantasy, she describes the image of me taking my penis out and showing it to her. In all likelihood this is an association to the dream component of me trying to poke her with a pencil.

At this point in the analysis I am still not clear whether there has been some type of overt traumatic sexual activity in childhood or whether the entire conflict is a function of her own sexual wishes and fantasies about them. Therefore I make a rather generalized transference interpretation, indicating that the current fantasies in the situation with me are a repetition of a childhood situation with the father and uncle, in hopes that this will ultimately lead to a further exploration of the childhood situation through an elaboration in the current transference material. Her initial response is a defensive one in which she seeks to deny the possibility of any overt incident with the father, and therefore in an exploratory way I attempt again to encourage her to elaborate on the current transference fears with me. Eventually this approach leads to a further elaboration of the voyeuristic-exhibitionistic transference fantasies, followed by her own awareness that real gratification for a little girl is a threatening experience, whereas to fantasy about such a relationship provokes less anxiety or guilt.

This material leads by association to a reliving of some of the childhood experiences with the father, culminating in the elaboration of her memories of seeing him naked and the sudden symbolic association to the teapot. My interpretation regarding the teapot is based on an empathic awareness of her in that situation, as well as the obvious symbolism of the teapot. After her initial denial, my explanation of the symbolism encourages her to continue in her recall of these memories with the father. Her statement, "He is standing there for my benefit!" indicates the existence of a fantasy that he is deriving sexual pleasure from exposing himself to her and reminds me of the transference fantasy earlier in the session that I will go crazy, lose control of myself, and expose my penis to her.

It is this line of reasoning that leads to my reconstruction that she must have thought he too was enjoying this situation, and this reconstruction then leads to her elaboration of the fantasy that this was a mutually exciting and stimulating experience. This in turn leads to her unverbalized sense of guilt in the situation and her perception that control of the situation to prevent overt acting-out of the sexual fantasies with the father was up to her, and to the fact that she used fear and anxiety to motivate her defensive controls. I then point out to her how she uses the same mechanisms with me and how the anticipation that I will respond with an overt sexual seduction serves the same function of motivating her controls and defenses as occurred originally in the relationship to the father. At the end of my interpretation, by asking the question of whether such defenses are still necessary today in the relationship with me, I am indirectly appealing to the therapeutic alliance and attempting to encourage her to recognize the realistic differences between the current situation in the analytic relationship and the childhood experiences with the father. I do this in hopes that by strengthening her realistic perceptions of me, she will simultaneously be more free to expose and express the unconscious transference wishes and thereby fill in on the recall of the details of the original oedipal situation.

This intervention is partially successful in that she is now able to elaborate further on the childhood conflict between the recognition of her needs to control the situation, as compared with her wishes and curiosity about touching and playing with the father's penis. Spontaneously she goes on to describe how this conflict of forces has been displaced into her relationships with other men and how the same wishes and inhibitions have continued into her present life. And this material permits me to interpret to her how she reenacts that traumatic situation again and again under the impact of the repetition compulsion.

Having taken this material as far as seems feasible at the moment, I now return to one of the unanalyzed elements in a dream with which she had begun this session. My choice of this specific element is based partly on the generalized wish to return to the dream and to indicate that there are other latent meanings which have not yet been discussed. But it is also determined by the preconscious memory that material around the issues of pregnancy has come up earlier in the analysis but not yet been fully understood, and also by the preconscious recollection that the onset of her acute neurotic decompensation had occurred during the latter part of her first pregnancy.

This is successful in that she begins to fill in some of the previously unmentioned details about her adolescent attitudes in regard to contraception and ultimately to the recognition of her wish to become pregnant. She defensively depreciates the situation by indicating, "There are 10,000 reasons why I want to get pregnant," but she is then able to resume her associations which lead to the primal scene experiences, accompanied by her recognition that she would like to participate in it, as well as the wish to identify with the baby inside of the mother. And finally at the end of the session this is experienced immediately as a transference wish toward me.

From the material of this session it is still not clear how much of the patient's perceptions and recollections about the father and his attitudes represents a realistic awareness of him and his conscious motivations and, therefore, represents an actual and overt sexual seduction, and how much of this is a projection to the father of the fantasies stimulated by the oedipal conflict raging within her at the time when she was a child. In either case, the psychic reality for her, repeated in the transference with me, is of a father who was overtly sexually seductive. Whether it will turn out that this is based on a realistic seduction, or whether this is purely a projection of the patient's fantasy, will require further work to determine.

## SESSION 151

**P:** I have no words to tell you how I feel today. – – I'm just scared. – – – I feel like I want you to be my mother. I want you to pick me up and let me cry on your shoulder. I've begun to realize how much I hold myself off from you.

*Anxiety!*

**A:** How do you mean?

**P:** – – There are so many things that I want to pour out to you and I don't. I know that I haven't been telling you the things that I should and it's because I don't trust you. – –

*Cry*

**A:** Let's try to look at the details of both sides. You want to pour things out to me and at the same time you don't trust me. What comes to your mind?

**P:** I feel just as if I've lost a battle. I want to lie down and die, but I really don't want to die, but I want to give up everything and just relax.

**A:** I think you are saying that you want to let down all these defenses.

**P:** I want to be able to tell you how scared I am and tell you everything and how horrible it all has been. And yet it's all so childish because you're not going to be my mother, and yet that's what I want.

**A:** Are you saying that to tell me everything is the same thing as being childish?

**P:** I'd have to admit that I'm incapable of handling my problems and hurts by myself, and I'd have to ask you to do it for me. And I have such a fear that you won't. I don't like the wish to ask you to kiss my stubbed toe. It's all so childish and yet I need to. – – How am I supposed to do this *and* still take care of three children and a husband and a house and all the other things I have to do? It has to be one or the other, and I know that I want you to completely take care of me.

**A:** I think the problem is that you are not going to be able to do it effectively until you have resolved this wish and the problems that it causes you.

**P:** I feel so scared as I get closer to telling you everything. (Elaborates.) It's like losing a battle! I feel as if I give up!

**A:** I wonder if you might be afraid that if you let down the defenses and express it all here, that you are going to do the same thing when you're not here, and not have any control over yourself?

**P:** I know what I am and what you say I am. And I also know what I should do. – – – I think about that thing with my uncle and I know that I'm using it, but if I talk then I've broken down the barrier. – – – But I know that I want to talk and talk and talk! – – – – I tell myself that you'll *not* help me. (Elaborates.)

**A:** I think this is a defensive attempt to justify not talking about it.

*Anxiety, Cry*

**P:** But I'm so scared! I feel like the whole world is closing in on me! – – – I don't want to give in to you! Because once I do I've had it! And you just sit there and wait for me to! – – I have all kinds of visions of myself falling apart. – – – I think about my children and my husband! I just can't give up! What is going to happen to them? The whole world rests on my shoulders! – – – There's something that I am so afraid of and I know that it's more than just falling down and hurting myself, but I don't know what it is. – –

*Quiet*

**A:** I wonder if you may be afraid of the fantasy of merging with me and of losing yourself *in* me?

**P:** – – I know that that's how I feel about my mother. I want to get inside of her and just be safe. – – I want to find a nice warm dark place and go to sleep and have my stomach be full and not feel any pain, and have no responsibilities and just be nothing. – – But I can't do that. I want

*Cry!*

to scream! I can't take any more! I've had it! – – That's what I mean by going crazy, just to scream and cry as I feel like doing, but then they'll take me off and put me in a mental hospital. Is that what I want? Then at least you'd have to take care of me. But I can't stand it about the children if that happens. Oh shit! This is such a conflict! Where am I supposed to go!! – – Now I think about my happy childhood. We felt free and there were acres of ground around us and we ran and ran, but I had no communication with my parents, but I guess I was happy that way. But now I have three children, also a husband. I'm me and they want *me* to take care of them. Their *lives* depend on *me!*

*Quiet*

**A:** I think at the moment that you are also identifying with your children in that you feel that your whole life depends on me and on my strength and ability to help you.

**P:** – – I feel like the whole world is closing in. – – It makes me mad to have you think that you can do this. You just don't know! I want to scream and cry and yell. I want to kick your teeth and yet at the same time I love you. I dare you. You can't possibly do it. – – – I feel as if I get more con- *Cry* flicts every time I come here. – – Now I feel as if I'm lying here completely helpless. – – – I want so badly to trust you! I know I have no alternative! That's the only way out! And you're the only person who can help me! – – – But I'm so scared. I remember my childhood and I think about the Evanston house. It's no good. – – I'm so scared! – – I feel as if you are just *Cry!!* a man and I know that you can't help me! I just can't stand it. I'm so scared. I'm scared. I don't want to fall apart. – – This is all so blank and I feel as if it's all just closing in on me.

**A:** I think here you're not distinguishing a wish from a real act. It's as if you see the two as the same and you have the idea that you'll be able to do it to me or else I'll do it to you. The problem is that you're not seeing it as a wish and you react to it as if it was real.

**P:** I can't stand to hear you talk so reasonably! I feel as if I'm long *Anxiety* past reason! I'm scared to death! – – I just can't! – – – – It seems to me as if nothing matters. I don't care if I please you or if you please me or if I'm going to be strong or an adult. Nothing matters any more. It's all just a pretense and a front. I'm scared to death. Now I see you picking me up and I'm so helpless. I don't like to think that I'd owe you so much for getting me out of this black well. – –

**A:** What's the detail of the thought that you'd owe me so much?

**P:** You'd always have me under your thumb and I'd never be able to break away. You'd get me under your thumb and I'd need you and I'd think about it and that would be the end of everything. I'd be your slave and I'd be a nothing and I wouldn't be able to do anything for myself. And I feel as if you are a monster. – – – I wonder if I could just trust you and just ask you to help me. – – – I feel as if I'm completely in your hands and you've stripped away every defense that I have. The only thing that is left is you. – – – – I've faced as much as I can on my own and I know that I must have you with me in order to be able to finish this. I can't go any farther unless I *completely* trust you in here. – – I don't *really* want to suck at a breast, and I have such a fear that if I do that you will keep me there and you won't let me grow. But it takes once to let me grow. But then you've got to let me go. You've got to be able to let me stand on my own two feet. I know that I may fall, but please don't use me. (Elaborates.) Everyone else that I've ever gone to has used me. That was true with Harris and I know that he *loved* having me so dependent on him.

A: We'll stop here for today.

## DISCUSSION

In the previous sessions, conflicts mobilized in the transference neurosis have led her to the verge of a fuller and more detailed exploration and recall of the original oedipal situation and the conflicts which it entailed. In the current session, her resistances against these conflicts and their elaboration have been further mobilized, along with her anxiety regarding the issues of basic trust of me. This has led to a regression to a maternal transference relationship, and the issues of helplessness, her needs for help, dependency on me, and conflict over basic trust are in the forefront. Although this is material which has come up repetitively throughout the analysis, beginning with the very first sessions, at this point she is dealing with it at a deeper, less defensive, and more involved level.

I might have interpreted this material as a regressive defense from the oedipal conflicts being mobilized in the transference neurosis. However, she is acutely anxious and severely discomforted, and is experiencing genuine and disabling distress, and in addition my attention is drawn to her statements that she holds herself off from me and that she still has difficulty in trusting me. I therefore decide that further exploration of the oedipal level conflicts is likely to be limited and unsuccessful until these issues of basic trust and freedom to express herself to me are further resolved. Therefore in this session my focus is at that level, and it represents an attempt to foster her capacity for basic trust, and to encourage her to face her conflicts by reducing the intensity of the suppressive and withholding defenses.

In the first part of the session, most of my interventions are either aimed at her specific conscious resistances or else are attempts to encourage her to accept my offer of help in the therapeutic relationship. My first real interpretation occurs when I point out her fantasy cf merging and losing herself in me. This intervention is based on the fact that the transference has shifted from the oedipal father to the pre-oedipal mother, on her statement that the whole world is closing in, that she feels she would be giving in to me, and on the recall of previous material that had emerged several sessions ago when we had been working more extensively at the level of the maternal transference. In addition, it is based on the general theoretical formulation that issues of basic trust usually relate to the mother-child interaction.

Her response to this interpretation is to elaborate in an affective way on the regressive wishes and the feelings of being helplessly dependent upon me. Accompanying this is a recognition in the therapeutic alliance of her realistic needs to trust me and of the fact that potentially I can help her. However, this is offset by the intensity of the fantasy of fusion with me and loss of herself, and my intervention in regard to the difference between a fantasy and reality is again an attempt to appeal to the self-observing ego and to strengthen the reality-testing functions in order that she can more effectively control the anxiety mobilized by the primitive fantasy. In this context she is able to mention the fantasies of owing me so much if she gets the help.

This last reference to owing me something if she is helped is a specific new conflict involved in this defensive struggle, and because I want to bring it out more clearly, I ask her about it. This leads to the elaboration of her fears of dependency upon me, as well as the more adult recognition that she does need my help in order successfully to complete her analysis and this does require a basic trust in me. In an appropriate fashion she describes my analytic task of permitting her to experience a sense of full and complete dependency, but also of not prolonging this beyond an optimal duration and of being able to tolerate growth within her when it occurs. And in this connection she once again elaborates on the possibility that I might react as her previous therapist had, and at the same time expresses a hope that I won't.

As mentioned previously, the continuing exploration of the oedipal conflict had to be suspended temporarily in this session in order that analytic work could be done at the level of the therapeutic alliance and the working-through again of the conflicts over basic trust. Although on the one hand this may appear to be a digression from the oedipal theme of conflict at the present time, it is nevertheless a necessary one since without further working-through of conflict over basic trust any attempt to force or push in the direction of further oedipal exploration would be ineffective and unsuccessful. Once this analytic work has been accomplished, we can then anticipate that there will be a return to the oedipal material and that it can then be explored with greater effectiveness.

## SESSION 152

**P:** – – – I get so excited when I think of what I could do if I just trusted you. It's so great but the idea of happiness just scares the hell out of me. – – – If I trusted you I could show any part of myself to you and not be afraid. There would be no part of me that you wouldn't accept. It's really not all that bad. – – I had an argument with a friend yesterday and I don't want to tell you about it. She said to me, "The sooner you grow up, the better it is going to be for you." Do I act just like a suckling baby? Do other people really see that? And yet I felt that I was the adult one. – – I feel as if I have to avoid all of this talk about love and happiness by talking about all my fears and problems and all the bad things. It seems to me that you will take the problems much better than you can take my love.

**A:** What comes to your mind about that?

**P:** It's such a corn-ball thing, with all this talk about you as being so wonderful. – –

**A:** But what's the detail of the thought?

**P:** I feel as if you'll laugh and you'll think I'm an idiot and a child to think that I could love you. This is all a defense. But when I think about being able to care I couldn't stand to have you laugh at it or to take advantage of it. – – – Now I feel like I want to unzip the zipper on my stomach and let you see everything, but it's wonderful and it's like being in the sun and having flowers all around. – – It's the greatest thing in the world to trust someone and show your complete self without worry. It's the best thing in life that anyone could ever give me. And especially without clamping iron bars around my neck. – – – I can fantasy about it and think that it would be wonderful but I just can't do it. I always have to keep it to myself. It's fun to think of, though.

**A:** You mentioned that talking about happiness and love and pleasant things frightens you. What are your associations to that?

**P:** It always has been that way. If I ever get happy and excited about anything, then I immediately get depressed and scared. It's like letting a feeling out and I know that I must keep it inside. It's all wonderful but I know that I can't show or feel it, and I know that I wouldn't ever want anyone to know.

**A:** But let's look at how that works out here with me.

P: – I know that you are going to take advantage of me.

A: What's the detail of that fantasy?

P: . . . . .I can see myself with my uncle. I'm happy and I'm feeling love and I'm not trying to hide it. I love him and I want to kiss him and I want to hug someone. – – I want to laugh and be cute, and have the person love me back but I know that it doesn't work.

A: Let's look at the details of that fantasy here with me. You're feeling gay and happy and loving and you don't want to hide anything. Now what happens?

P: . . . . . I see us having intercourse. I would say, "I love you," and I would feel as if I didn't have a care in the world.

A: So the fantasy would be of me taking advantage of that feeling. What comes to your mind about it?

P: You'd turn into an old monster. You'd say to yourself, "I've got this girl where I want her. I know that she loves me and so I'll be able to take advantage of her." – – – I wonder if I want you to or if I don't? It gets me all so excited just thinking about it. It's like a girl with her daddy. But really I'm a woman. (Elaborates.) I want you to put your arms around me and love me as a woman. – – But I also don't want you to do it. – – Now I feel as if I'm stripped to being a baby and I have no defenses. You're my parents and you're the only one that I can depend on to help me. I'll sit on your lap and I'll love you and I'm a girl but now I am going to turn into a woman. I am a woman. So I can't sit on your lap without having sexual feelings and wanting to make love with you. But I know that I must be a trusting girl in order to get through this analysis, but this evolves into my being a woman. I'm afraid to be a woman with you. Now I feel sick to my stomach! That happens as soon as I begin to feel like a woman. If I feel like a woman then I immediately think of you as a man and I want to try to seduce you. And if I succeed . . . . . – I know that I've been trying to seduce every man that I run into. And I know that I've been successful but it just doesn't help me. All men like to be flattered and they like me when I'm cute and when I flirt with them. And I like men who flirt with me. That's the bitchey part of it all. I turn something wonderful into something black and horrible and it all takes place in about ten minutes.

A: I think in the last few minutes you have, in a sense, relived what it was that went on with your uncle. But we have never as yet fully reconstructed what happened between you.

P: – I think a lot about it. There's all that stuff about a basement.

But then I get so scared! Now I see a pink chair and it's in the living room, but it's another house and I think that I am about seven years old. I'm sitting on his lap and I feel as if I'm cute. I can feel his hands on my waist. It's just like a little girl with her father. She wants to love and be loved and she wants to open herself up and she is loving. Now I feel his hand. Suddenly I think that I am a woman and I think of him thinking that I am. That lets out the basement bit. – – Now I just want to go to sleep. I *can't* believe that anything could have happened in that basement.

**A:** But you still don't want to find out for sure.

**P:** Did I make all of this up? And if I did, why? – – Now I have such a desire to feel a penis! I want to reach out and feel it. It's just like eating and it's such a sexual pleasure! I want to reach out and. . . . . this is such happiness! I feel so excited. It's like it's the most wonderful thing in the world. The penis is so soft! It's the greatest thing. I'm feeling such happiness and I love it and it's so much fun! – – – – – I wonder what happened next? – –

**A:** What do you see?

**P:** My uncle is so excited that he can't control himself and his thing has gotten hard. It's all so natural. I only feel it as soft. – – And yet I know that it would not have stopped there. – – This is where the wonderful love feeling goes away. It was so wonderful and I don't want it to go away. – – Now I feel so. . . . . – I had to stop this thing and it's as if I'm 100 years old. I realize that it has gone too far, but not my stupid fucking uncle! I don't trust him any more and I never will! I feel so discouraged! There was such happiness and then, bang! Someone knocks you across the face! – – If I could just try it again and have it not happen that way. I would like to be innocent and warm and loving instead of being jolted so suddenly. – – – Could I ever find a man and want to masturbate him and have his thing stay soft? I doubt it. This is all so ridiculous. – – – I don't like this feeling at all. – – – – – – – – Oh! – – I feel as if all men are after me and they are just ogres. You just can't even talk nice to a man! – –

**A:** How does that apply here?

**P:** I feel so mad and now I'm scared. It happens any time that I go up to a man and want to be friendly with him. His penis will get hard and then he'll get *lovely* ideas. – – I've turned you into my uncle now and it makes me sick. But it's inevitable. Love will always turn into hatred and that makes me so mad. It was *so wonderful.* – – – –

**A:** We'll stop here for today.

## Discussion

Although the patient begins the session by verbally indicating that she still is unable to trust me, the nonverbal and affective tone of her communication, as well as the elaboration of the fantasies of trusting me (verbally she indicates these as hypothetical), indicate that the work done in yesterday's session was effective and that there has been a significant movement toward a positive and basic trusting relationship to me. Her statement that I can accept her problems better than her love feelings involves a projection of her anxiety about positive feelings of love and trust, but in one sense such a defense is perhaps a step forward in that it acknowledges that such feelings do exist, whereas previously there had been attempts at denial of the very existence of such wishes.

My questions asking for the details of her associations to this issue initially lead her to continue projecting the rejection in the transference, accompanied however by a recognition that "This is all a defense. . . ." She then goes on to describe in positive and rather glowing terms the hypothetical fantasy of what it would be like to trust me, ending with her statement, "It would be wonderful but I just can't do it." In actual fact, however, she has just done it in an attenuated way. Her nonverbal behavior, the words and images that she chooses, and the way in which she perceives this hypothetical experience all indicate that she is partially permitting it to occur right now. This is a type of transitional experience which is still partly defensive and isolated in its full impact upon her, but which simultaneously permits a kind of experience that she has not allowed herself before, and as such represents a progressive movement. It is analogous to the concept of fantasy as trial action, and by permitting the patient greater confidence in these types of transitional experiences, it will ultimately allow her to move further toward their full impact at some future time.

At this point I want to pick up on the anxiety she experiences when considering things that are pleasurable or happy. My intention is to help her more clearly see the projection of this to me when she feels that I prefer her to talk of her problems rather than of pleasurable feelings or experiences. And when she responds with an elaboration of her anxiety over happiness or excitement, I encourage her to deal with this at the level of an immediate transference response by focusing it toward her relationship with me. This leads to the fantasy of my taking sexual advantage of her, and subsequently to the associations about the uncle and the traumatic experience with him. This sequence of material further confirms the hypothesis that the work done in the analytic session yesterday was a necessary precursor to enable her to begin to reach this material today.

Initially the patient fills in some details of this experience with the uncle in the present tense, thus indicating that it is at least partially a current emotional experience. I might have merely encouraged further expression of the memories and fantasies toward the uncle, but I prefer to use the immediate experience in the transference as a more accurate, direct, and detailed repetition of the earlier relationship and experience. Therefore I again focus this into the fantasy of the immediate relationship with me. She describes the fantasy of herself, "It's like a girl with her daddy," who then experiences sexual feeling and fantasy, begins to feel like a woman, expects to succeed in seducing the man, and then feels sickened and "black and horrible." As she reports this sequence of associations, there is a concomitant change in her nonverbal behavior with a shift in mood from positive spontaneity to a depressive negativism and disappointment.

It is my observation of this change in her verbalization, as well as her mood and behavior, which has taken place before my eyes in the transference relationship to me as the uncle, accompanied by my recollection that the incident with the uncle has come up previously and that it must have been significant, which lead to my interpretation that in her behavior in the analytic session she is repeating some element of the traumatic experience. This is accompanied by my pointing out that the full elaboration of that incident is still missing.

Having "remembered" through her transference behavior and having been accepted by me without a change in my attitude or behavior towards her, she thereby gains a little further ego-mastery of the affects relating to the experience involved. And accompanied by my implicit encouragement that she further recall the details of the experience, she is now able further to approach the recovery of this important memory. She says, "I think a lot about it," and initially refers to the element of the basement, but this is immediately accompanied by anxiety and a shift in the scene to the living room, another house, and a later age. She now expresses an associated but derivative memory in the relationship to the uncle, followed by the defensive statement, "That lets out the basement bit." This in turn is followed by the wish to sleep and then by the mechanism of negation when she says, "I *can't* believe that anything could have happened in that basement."

This use of the mechanism of negation implies that the material being defended against is very close to consciousness, and in this entire sequence the patient has indicated her wish to avoid her associations to the basement. Because this is so close to consciousness, I feel that I can appropriately encourage her to face whatever it is, and therefore I point out her resistance of still not wanting to find out.

At this point, in an emotionally regressive experience, she describes her pleasure connected with fondling the penis in positive terms and with appropriately positive affects. After the prolonged silence, her self-observing nonregressive ego causes her to raise the question about what happened next. My response is merely to encourage her to pursue her own recollection, and this leads to the further development of the sexual situation, the uncle's sexual response, and then the sudden shift from a positive loving pleasurable experience to an unpleasant depressing negative one. The images and affects toward the uncle have shifted from positive love to a hostile depreciating anger and resentment at having been taken advantage of. This is further elaborated in derivative forms toward other men, and when I focus her attention back into the transference, she indicates that the same shift has occurred in relationship to me and that she again sees me as the uncle which now makes her sick and makes her hate me.

In these last experiences in the session, the patient has again reexperienced as a current phenomenon the sequence of changes that she had described earlier in verbal form at the beginning of the session, when she said, "It's so great but the idea of happiness just scares the hell out of me." Initially by transference experience and subsequently by memory, in this session she is beginning more directly to recall and regressively reexperience the original traumatic event. As yet it has not fully emerged, but this session represents an important step towards its ultimate recovery.

---

## SESSION 153

**P:** I seem to have just two sets of defenses. Either I'm feeling hostile or else I am eating. I can watch myself do it. If I'm not hostile then I eat. Today I feel as if I'll never get anywhere in here, so I might just as well forget it. – – – I feel so hostile right now. It's as if I'm ten feet tall and I want to tell the world to go to hell. I compare this with my helpless feelings and they make me so mad right now. I say to myself, "You little shit." Suddenly I can feel myself shrink right now and now I'm scared again. – – – You sap all of my strength. Now I'm thinking about my children and that I have to go home to them right now! – – – I always feel as if I have to fight for something. I wonder if I ought to quit analysis and just go back to my old ways, or should I trust you and try to get well. I just don't know. – –

A: What comes to your mind?

P: If I . . . . . if I let go, I know that I'm just going to collapse. I'll probably be a baby and never get up again, and yet that's what you want me to do. – – Am I afraid that my baby mind is going to win out? I'm so afraid. (Elaborates.) – – If I ever let myself go here with you, how can I then leave and go home and function at home? I'd feel completely helpless. I'd want you to pick me up and never let me go and take care of me. – – – I can see myself at the breast and I'd lie here and suck and I'd feel my stomach get full and warm. This scares the shit out of me. And yet I love it. But I'm so helpless if that happens. – – I used to be so afraid that you'd hate me, but I don't feel that anymore. Now I feel as if you're nice and you *would* take care of me. But I don't *want* that! – – –

A: So the fantasy seems to be that I *want* to keep you as the infant sucking at my breast. What comes to your mind about it?

P: Everyone does this to me. I appear like a child and I look as if I'm needing help and you'll just gobble me up if I ask for just one minute of help. – – – That makes me so mad! – – – Now I think about hating my parents. I feel as if my mother slapped me down just like a fly. I was her burden and she was going to make sure that I stayed her burden. – – Sunday I realized for the first time what a horrible thing it was that my father did to have intercourse with another woman. –

A: What was the detail?

P: That should be the most sacred thing that a couple has between them. – – I just can't stand it. They knocked the legs out from under me. I'd like to shake them from the shoulders. They weigh me down so. Because of that we had to move to Springfield and it was so horrible. – –

*Cry*

A: I think you're holding back some of your feelings right now.

P: I have nothing and I feel as though I'm completely lost. I don't know why I was born and I feel as if I have nothing!! My whole world has suddenly been shattered. (Elaborates.) This makes me feel just like a fish out of water and as if I'm dying and I can't stand up. That reminds me I had a dream about water. I was never going to get in and I was standing on the edge of the pool but I would never go in even though I wanted to. If my parents had been killed it would have been much easier and at least I would have had some memories of strength. But they pulled out all of the plugs. It made me so angry. (Elaborates.) It's as if they were kids, both of them. I have nothing inside of me, so what is it that is holding me up?

**A:** You mentioned the dream about the pool where you wanted to go in but you're not going to. I wonder if that isn't like the idea of trusting me completely here, but being afraid and feeling that you don't want to.

**P:** I just couldn't go through the business about Springfield! – – If you can't trust your parents then there is no one in the world to trust. I did trust them once, but they showed me that I just can't. There is no one that you can ever trust. You can only rely on yourself. – –

**A:** And yet the wish is to trust me.

**P:** I have a picture of handing myself over to you and saying, "Please, put me back together." But that takes an awful lot. What if you don't, or what if you can't? I feel as if I've passed the line. – – On Friday I was thinking that if I ever trust you there are so many horrible things inside and I'm so afraid that they'll scare you. I'm afraid that you'll fall apart if I show you one thing. – –

**A:** What's the detailed fantasy that this would scare me and that I'll fall apart?

**P:** – It's like . . . . . – I really have nothing to compare it with. You're saying to me that "I can take anything." And so I bring out all of my monster and then you are going to die. You just can't stand it. – – – Now I think about Jean asking about Harris and his anxieties and his uncertainties. – – These are my fears too. You show no emotion no matter what I do and it's as if you're like a wall. Have you ever seen anyone fall apart? Have you ever seen anyone die? Please help me! You are the only one in the world who can! But you are going to get into a panic and then you are going to run! (Elaborates.) I've felt all of that before.

**A:** I think right now that you're using Harris's weakness and anxiety and uncertainty as a justification for not trusting me and for not going ahead here and jumping into that pool like you wanted to do in the dream.

**P:** – – – (Laughs.) – I'm going to run out of excuses and defenses pretty soon. It is happening slowly but surely, but it's such a conflict. I love you so much for being solid and not being involved with me and being an analyst and keeping this on a business-like basis. It's really the greatest thing in the world and I love you for it, but then all of my fears of love come up. – – But it makes me so happy. I could laugh and sing because of this. – – – Now I associate happiness with the feeling I had when I wanted to put my uncle's penis in my mouth. It was the greatest thing. I'd love it. – – – –

A: We'll stop here for today.

## DISCUSSION

The patient begins this session after the weekend separation with a note of heightened resistance and defenses against continuing the transference regression. She again refers to the conflict over basic trust, with the fantasy that if she were to permit herself to experience the full range of transference feelings, the oral dependency would be so intense that she would give in to it completely and undergo a total and irreversible regression. My intervention attempting to clarify this conflict involves interpreting the projection that I would want to keep her attached to me, which is the material alluded to in her statement, "But I don't want that!" but which also refers to similar previous transference fantasies expressed in earlier sessions.

She elaborates briefly on the perception of me in the maternal transference, in which she feels the mother wanted to keep her as a burden, but then the level of transference conflict shifts to the father transference at the oedipal level, expressed in terms of her reactions to his extramarital affairs. As she expresses these latter thoughts, the patient begins to cry and my assumption is that the crying stems from something as yet unexpressed, and therefore I make my interpretation of her defense of holding feelings back. This leads first to her sense of helplessness in the situation, and then to the feeling of being unable to gain any strength or support from the parents.

My own association is that she is expressing in terms of past experience a current transference attitude and response, and I therefore choose to focus this issue back into the more immediate transference experience. Once again her response is defensive, in that she rationalizes the basis for not trusting me. And to counteract this, my intervention is aimed at strengthening her own more appropriate and therapeutically useful wish to be able to trust me completely. This is an attempt to encourage the further development of a growing force arising spontaneously within herself as a result of the repetitive experiences she has had up to this time in the analytic situation.

This intervention helps her clarify the immediate conflict between the wish to depend on and expect help from me and thus to express the previously withheld aspects and images of herself, as compared with the fantasies and expectations of rejection and of a destructive effect on me if she were to do so. She attempts to support the defensive side of this conflict by referring to Harris and his inability to tolerate her regression, with the recurrent transference of me repeating her experience with him, and through him with the parents. My intervention seeks to block this defensive transference expectation, and again emphasizes her own spontaneous wish to move ahead and trust me as someone different from these previous figures.

The patient's laugh and her own perception that she will soon run out of excuses are evidences that in spite of the anxiety mobilized by the transference expectations, there is still operating a significant self-observing and more mature ego which recognizes on the basis of her own experience that I am different from these earlier figures. She goes on to elaborate further upon the security offered her by my maintaining the role of neutral analyst who is not affectively involved with her, again indicating that in spite of the transference distortions the therapeutic alliance is solid. It is this factor which permits her to experience the transference distortions as a necessary part of the analytic situation.

Her final comment, "Now I associate happiness with the feeling I had when I wanted to put my uncle's penis in my mouth," is made possible by the growing confidence she is able to experience in the therapeutic relationship with me. This represents a sudden return from repression of one element of the situation with the uncle which has not been mentioned before. It illustrates how traumatic memories emerge piecemeal, often one element at a time, and frequently unexpectedly either to the patient or the analyst. In this setting, the material emerges in an almost casual aside and in a form in which it almost seems as if the patient had "known" about it all this time. However, the awareness of this element had been unconscious in the past, and the "knowing" had likewise occurred at an unconscious level. This material about the oral wish towards the uncle's penis is extremely important, but we are close to the end of the session and further significant exploration will be impossible today. Furthermore, since it is the initial emergence of such material, I do not want to focus upon it too vigorously and thereby evoke unnecessary anxiety about revealing it too soon. For these reasons I choose to remain silent on the assumption that this will return at another time.

The issues of the therapeutic alliance and basic trust, and the transference fantasies of rejection, etc., have all come up repetitively since the beginning of the analysis. In spite of the analytic work that has been focused upon these issues in the past and in spite of the progress which the patient has made in these areas, this session illustrates that such material must be worked over again and again throughout the course of analysis. Although the transference neurosis is well established, the analyst must still maintain his observation and interest concerning the maintenance of the therapeutic alliance. This type of transient interference with the therapeutic alliance not infrequently may occur as some new and previously unexpressed or unexplored conflict or early trauma is about to be uncovered. In such a situation, the patient has an unconscious awareness that new or deeper material is close to expression and with this goes the transference expectation that the emergence of this new material may alter the previously established therapeutic situation and may provoke the previously avoided transference rejection or attack.

---

## SESSION 154

**P:** – – – – – – – – – – – – Suddenly I felt so calm last night, and this morning I'm free from all of those anxiety symptoms. But I'm afraid of this. If I'm *not* scared, then it means to me that I've lost my mind and I'm completely cracked up. If I talk to you here I'll go back to that horrible black well. – – – We talked about Springfield on Monday. I had the worst dream about it, it was horrible. I've never been able to face it. I felt absolutely alone and helpless and as if I had absolutely no security. I feel just the same talking to you now. I feel alone with nothing to keep me alive.

**A:** Let's start with the further thoughts about Springfield. What was the detail?

**P:** I get that black feeling just talking about it. I feel as if I have nothing and as if I'm cut up in pieces. I used to get sick to my stomach every single morning and I had such anxiety. It all went on for years. I went wild. That dream was so scary. Am I going to fall apart? My parents were so scared and sick during that time, and I feel that I *was* alone and that I had no one to depend upon except maybe my sister. – – I felt as if I was going to go crazy! – – – Now I'm thinking about my daughter and how she has been acting lately. She seems so regressed. I wonder if something happened to her that she can't tell me about? – – – – During my *real* eating spells I eat Pablum. Now I'm thinking about the dream. It had worms in it and I'd eaten it and I was upset to think that I'd fed it to the baby. – – – Somehow this has something to do with my uncle. – – –

**A:** It seems as if you're not able to pursue any one theme this morning and as if you're not able to let the doors of your mind open up. You talked about how calm you felt yesterday and Springfield and the dream and your daughter, but it's as if you're afraid to go deeply into any one of these.

**P:** Now I feel as if I could scream and I feel scared again. (Elaborates.) In that Springfield dream I was at a party. Tom was working and I was alone last night. I had the wish that someone would be there with me. I was at this party and I was with Helen and with both of my sisters and these are the people that I was most secure with. There was a damn boy there and I was trying to get to him but I found that I couldn't. And yet really he is nothing and he's not worth it. Then I was in an apartment in Atlanta and my sister was in the bed. I was in the bathroom and Tom was gone, and then Sally got out of the bed as if she was going to do something terrible. She was so embarrassed in the dream. – – I am thinking of the feelings I had right after Sally was born. I was so scared. All this is reliving one thing. It's all so black and scary and horrible, but I don't know what it is! But every day I go through it again!! – – They thought that I had worms.

**A:** I'm not clear what you mean.

**P:** They were all in my bottom. I was a little girl and I remember I got hysterical. They were all there and I couldn't get away from them. It was the worst feeling and I felt helpless, and I had to go on and live with these worms. They were inside and I couldn't get rid of them. I felt all alone.

**A:** What was the further detail about having these worms as a girl?

**P:** I used to have to take violet pills. (Elaborates.) But I can remember that I couldn't swallow them. I also used to sit on the john and my mother would squirt that stuff into my bottom. I remember that I saw the worms and I was so frightened. They're inside and I can't do anything about them. (Elaborates.) Mother is going to get them out of me. She was fascinated by them.

**A:** That's only part of the picture. What's the further detail of your own thoughts about it?

**P:** It used to bother me so. I'd sit there. It was in my mother's and father's bathroom and my mother was trying to get the worms out of me. My mother was doing something for me but it was her own pleasure. But she helped me. I can see the toilet paper and she used it to rub me and then she'd show me and they were small white things. – – Now I think about those pills. Was it that I didn't want to get rid of the worms? Is

*Cry!!* | that why I couldn't take the pills? – – – Suddenly I want to scream and yell and go crazy because I'm so happy! What's going on!! I'm associating happiness with craziness.

**A:** In the last part of the session on Monday you associated it with taking your uncle's penis in your mouth.

**P:** This is all so crazy. The feeling of excited happiness always means to me the same thing as the worms, penises, and kissing them and things like that. This is all so abnormal. I know that I'm nuts. There is something wrong with me. Can't I ever have a normal nice happy association? – – – Now I picture myself and I'm just a tiny girl with my uncle's penis right there. – – I'm crazy!! (Elaborates.) This means such happiness and love. I love this thing. I loved playing with it and I wanted to kiss it. – – It's what I wanted to do all of my life and I finally had a chance to do it. It's there and I did it. (Elaborates.)

**A:** What comes to your mind that you're using this experience as a proof that you're crazy?

**P:** Because I don't understand why I love it so much. I love you and I feel the same way and it's crazy. It's just not right. Love doesn't originate with a man's penis. You're supposed to hide it and suppress it and it's all wrong. (Elaborates.) That was the first and last time I ever felt love. I know that it's crazy. I feel the same way here but I know.

**A:** You feel as if this is all nutty and crazy and it has to be wrong and you're supposed to suppress it all. What are your associations?

*Cry* | **P:** I enjoy it so much! These feelings are so wonderful. But what if anyone knew? I know it's wrong. It's just not right. – – – Now I have a sudden picture come to my mind. I'm relaxed and my grandmother is calling me at the stairs. I'm going up and she is shaking me and I'm horrible. I want to scream and I can't stand it. – – She's yelling at me, "What are you doing?" – – I got caught with his stuff on my hands and she took me to the bathroom and washed my hands. – – This was her son. – – I'm

*Anxiety,* | so afraid that you're mad at me. I know that you'll hit me! – . . . . .
*Cry*

**A:** What's going through your mind?

**P:** I know you are going to hit me over the head, and I'm so scared. I want to tell you that I didn't mean to do anything wrong, and I didn't know. I'm afraid that you're never going to talk to me again and I'm scared. It's as if I'm horrible. (Elaborates.) – – I know you are going to beat me over the head as if it was my fault and I'm the one who is so horrible. I want my mother. I'm being blamed for something that wasn't my fault. I want my mother to help me. I'm alone and there is no one to help me. – – My mother never knew about it. She never came and never helped me. She didn't care. I hate her for it! I can never trust her again. I hate my grandmother! She's a bitch. I hate her.

A: We'll stop here for today.

At the door the analyst tells the patient that he will have to cancel her session tomorrow.

### DISCUSSION

After the lengthy initial silence, the patient begins by describing the partial remission of her anxiety symptoms and her paradoxical thought that to be free of anxiety is pathological. She then goes on to refer to our discussion about Springfield in the previous session, indicating that she has had an unpleasant dream associated with it, and then goes on in a general way to describe feelings of helplessness and loneliness. My own immediate associations to the silence and to the material are to the mention of the fellatio experience with the uncle at the end of the last session. I assume that verbalizing it was partly responsible for the relief from anxiety, but that the patient has again repressed it and is mentioning other material from the previous session instead. This is analogous to the mechanism in the structure of a screen memory.

Respecting these defenses, and because the thoughts about Springfield are currently conscious and refer to specific rather than generalized feelings, I choose to begin the inquiry at the level of those thoughts and experiences. I might alternately have focused on the current transference feeling of being "just the same talking to you now."

In describing her feelings during those years, the patient associates to her daughter's recent behavior and raises the question, "I wonder if something happened to her that she can't tell me about?" In this way she is identifying the daughter with herself and thereby is projecting to the daughter the unconscious or preconscious awareness of some type of traumatic event that had occurred to herself. After the silence, her association that she herself eats Pablum is a further expression of her identification with the baby, and in an apparently off-hand way she mentions that the dream had worms in it and subsequently indicates the feeling that this has something to do with her uncle.

Although in retrospect these allusions and references to her own experience are understandable, at this time in the session I am unclear as to the theme or understanding of her material and so I merely make a nonspecific confrontation and interpretation regarding her generalized resistances. This leads her to elaborate in somewhat greater detail about the dream, and also about the symptoms she had after the onset of her neurosis which occurred with the birth of her first child. Again she indicates a preconscious awareness that, "All of this is reliving one thing", and yet at the same time indicates that whatever this refers to is still repressed and unconscious to her, although there is again a preconscious awareness that is "black and scary and horrible."

At this point, after a brief silence, she mentions the apparently unconnected association, "They thought that I had worms." This is a clear illustration of the value and effectiveness of the method of free association and of how important it is that the patient report her associations as they occur without regard for their logical connections. This association proves to be the beginning of further recall of a traumatic event in the patient's life, but neither she nor I recognize this consciously at the moment.

My response, "I'm not clear what you mean," is not ideal, in that it implies that the last association seems to be out of context and therefore suggests that I expect some type of logical meaning, but at the same time it is sufficiently general that it does not significantly interfere with her continuing to recall the important childhood screen experience with the worms. In the course of describing this, the patient suddenly undergoes a further regression to an immediate experiential level, accompanied by intense crying and by the sudden feeling of happiness which she subsequently associates with being crazy. I have been waiting to see whether or not she will return to the material from the previous session about her feelings of happiness when she wanted to put her uncle's penis in her mouth. Although I have not consciously been aware of this specific material at this point in the session, it now returns to me as an involuntary preconscious association of my own, and without any particular hesitation or debate I make this connection as an interpretation to the patient.

At this point, encouraged by my interpretation and by the reduction of her own resistances, the patient elaborates on her associations to the worms and penises. Transiently she attempts the defense of denial of the significance of these associations by considering them to be evidences that she is crazy, but very quickly the pleasurable elements of the sexual experience with the uncle again come to the fore and are expressed.

I want to help her keep her resistances as low as possible and therefore return to the defenses implied in her thoughts that this is crazy, and I phrase it indirectly to indicate that I do not agree with her that this is crazy and thereby I also show my acceptance of the primary process symbolism involved. This permits her to go on expressing her positive and pleasurable reactions to the penis, and she simultaneously refers to it in the transference as well as in the recall of the original experience. Once again I want to help her diminish her resistances against further recall, and therefore I focus on her reaction that this material is inappropriate and that she should suppress it. This leads to the affective response of crying, and to the conflict between pleasure in her feelings and simultaneous guilt. And the fantasy of being discovered merges into the recollection and recall of the subsequently traumatic elements of the experience through the grandmother's discovery and her reactions.

At this point the transference shifts from the uncle to the grandmother, with the expectation that I am reacting as she did and that I will punish and withdraw from her because of this event. Her subsequent associations indicate that the trauma in this situation was not merely the sexual seduction itself, but was also in large measure the reaction of the grandmother and the fact that apparently she received no help from the adults in her environment in understanding, integrating, and accepting the occurrence of the event. In all likelihood it was soon repressed, along with her various responses to it, and thus they remained inaccessible to change in the intervening time.

Although there will be need repeatedly to explore and work through the details and reactions to this event, we have now recovered the fullest version of it yet to emerge in the analysis up to this time. The patient has already indicated in random and brief associations throughout the last few sessions that this event has had many derivative symptomatic repercussions in her development and in her current life, and the specific understanding of these will be an important task as the analysis proceeds.

Between the last session and today there has been a sudden and unexpected death in my family and I must plan to be out of town tomorrow to attend the funeral. This comes at a particularly difficult time for the patient, inasmuch as this traumatic event has just been recalled along with the angry, punitive, and critical response of the grandmother, which likewise has been experienced in the transference. It is therefore probable that she will interpret my cancellation as a rejection of herself because of what she has just told me, and this is all the more likely since ordinarily when I cancel a session I do so one week in advance. I might avoid this by telling her today the reason for my cancellation, thereby disassociating it from the material of the session, but my thinking is that although this would protect her somewhat from an unpleasant and distressing reaction, it would also prevent her from having what may turn out to be a meaningful transference experience. Therefore I decide to say nothing about the reason for the cancellation, and to wait and observe what her reactions will be.

---

## SESSION 155

**P:** – – – – – – – – – – – –

**A:** What comes to your mind about the silence?

**P:** I just can't talk. I came here for help and yet I feel, "I'll be Goddamned if I'll ask him for any help." – –

**A:** What's the detail of the feeling?

**P:** The girl and the woman inside of me are having a battle. I feel as if it is best if I don't talk because no one ever wins. I had a dream on Wednesday in which I finally dove in and everything was very serious. There were a lot of people around and they were all watching me. I dove in like a clown and everyone laughed at me. That's just the way I feel here. I could get mad and scream and act wild and upset, but why should I bother? –

**A:** I think you are having a reaction to what went on here in the session on Wednesday and then to my having cancelled the session for yesterday.

**P:** – – I just can't stand to think that you have so much control over me. That episode threw me for a loop and I'm still spinning from it.

**A:** What's the detail?

**P:** I felt dazed and then I got so mad! I could have killed you. I said to myself, "See, you're right, you just can't trust him." But I really can't believe that. I just don't know.

**A:** Let's see what comes to your mind about both sides of this problem, where on one hand you feel that it's a proof that you're right, and you can't trust me, whereas at the same time you feel that you can't believe it.

**P:** I know that you're really not like Harris or else I wouldn't be here. But it's such a battle. I just don't know. Did you do it on purpose?

**A:** What do you think?

**P:** Was it supposed to be therapeutic? If you did, then I'm going to quit. A manipulation like that would just be ridiculous. I feel that you rejected me and you rejected what's really me.

**A:** Like your grandmother did.

**P:** – – I feel dirty and ugly. I feel as if I'll never get clean again. Inside

I know that I'm dirty. I think about myself and my house and my kids and my car and I know that none of it is ever going to be clean again. I'm just a dirty fat slob and it's all *your* fault.

A: What's the detail?

P: – – I had a dream of myself as pretty and thin and happy and motherly and wifely and it was wonderful. The real me represents none of that, but I feel as if I could be. I hate the people who are. If I was ever allowed to let go of all of the stuff that is inside of me, I could be that way.

A: I think the feeling is that I rejected you as dirty and ugly and because you have dirty stuff inside of you. What comes to your mind about that?

P: – Why did I never tell my mother about what happened? Why didn't my grandmother? Actually she was my great-grandmother.

A: What we have to see is that you told me something about this incident with your uncle which you felt was bad and dirty, and then I cancelled the next session. It was as if this was a repetition with me of the sequence of events that happened with your grandmother, and your feeling was one of a personal rejection. Actually this was a distortion based on these old guilt feelings which have been inside of you for so long. The reality about the cancellation was that there was a death in my family and I had to be away for the funeral.

P: – – I guess that I really thought that you were punishing me. After you told me about the cancellation I felt that you'd beat me! (Elaborates.) Maybe I wish that you would beat me because that might ease my guilt. – – – – – Now I feel like a child who pulls on its mother no matter how much stress she's under, and I'm so embarrassed.

A: How do you mean?

P: Instead of being a woman and saying that I'm sorry, I feel like I'm a child and I'm saying, "No matter what, you're supposed to help me and be here." I'm so selfish and I can't see anything but myself and my own problems. – – – – I feel relieved to know why you cancelled and yet it throws me for a loop.

A: What's the detail?

P: I can't go on and be a child. You are treating me as a normal human and as an adult, and I want to run away from it. I look at you as a human being, and I love you and feel womanly and motherly toward you. – –

A: You're feeling anxious and like you want to run. What comes to your mind?

P: It's like I'm losing the child in me. It's always been such a father relationship here! But I feel like I'm losing it. I could scream! I want to remain a baby here! I just want to come in here and suck for a while. – – It scares me to think of being on the same level with you.

**A:** You have this wish to come in here and just suck and be a baby. The question we have to ask ourselves is whether this is the primary wish or whether it represents a defense against your fears of being a woman here with me.

**P:** – – – There are just two possible things that can happen here. I can be the baby and have you as my mother or father, or else I'm the mother and you're the baby. This is like with my father. He is nothing but a baby and I feel so motherly with him. The in-between is the one that I don't know about but that's the real one. – – – Now I think about the time when I terminate my analysis. I guess I'm going to be on your level and feel it, but that scares me. If I'm ever on your level I'm going to be alone. – – I can't *stand* not to have any defenses against you. But I know that's what's happening.

**A:** What comes to your mind about it?

**P:** Really you are so nice and kind to me. You're *not* an evil monster and you're not going to try to eat me up or seduce me or take advantage of me or do other things to me. But I just can't stand it. It makes me want to leave you alone and get up and never see you again. – – If that's the way you are, I'll have to watch it! I might crush you!

**A:** What's the detail of that fantasy?

**P:** That way you'd be so vulnerable. I might say something to hurt you, and if you're not this strong monster that I've been thinking about, then you're just weak. – – But I know that this too is just a defense. – – Suddenly I can picture you as a kind loving father who is watching me grow up. I can't stand it. That makes me sick to my stomach. – – – Now I want to tear you apart! I've never loved anybody! I never will! I'll use these defenses until I die!!

**A:** Let's look at your associations to this fear of love.

**P:** It's as if I have known you before and I don't like you. You scare me! I'm so used to fighting and hating! That's the way I grew up. And yet I feel as if I've known you before. You sit so quiet and you're so defenseless and I'm going to eat you up!! – – I feel scared to ever stop fighting! I'm scared to relax in here and I can't stand it! – – – You're just like my mother and she's letting me suck on her breast. – – – – –

**A:** We'll stop here for today.

## DISCUSSION

The patient's nonverbal behavior as she comes into the session, as well as the initial lengthy silence, are indicators to me from the beginning that she is having a reaction to the coincidence of having remembered and expressed some of the details of the sexual incident with her uncle and of my having to cancel the next session. However, rather than interpret this to her directly and thus bypass her associations, I prefer to encourage her participation in the analytic process and therefore begin at the level of the conscious resistance of prolonged silence. Her initial response is the negativistic withdrawal, followed by the dream in which she finally "dove in," only to be laughed at by the people watching. Her statement, "That's just the way I feel here," in association to this dream indicates that she is consciously aware of the reaction to the cancellation, and therefore I can feel confident in making the transference interpretation connecting the Wednesday session with the cancellation. Her response about, "that episode," indicates that all of this has been conscious for her, and she follows up with the verbalization of her conflict between suspicious mistrust in the transference and a more confident sense of trust in the therapeutic alliance.

I am planning to tell her of the reality of the cancellation because the timing of it is a significant departure from my usual analytic routine, but before doing so I am hoping to develop the full transference potential which the incident offers, and therefore I ask her to continue associating to the two sides of the conflict. Had I told her immediately of the reality situation, the fantasies that I did it on purpose, or that it was a rejection of her on the basis of herself as dirty and ugly (a transference from the grandmother), might never have emerged. Once these fantasies are expressed, I then give her the reality information in order that she may correct the transference experience and thereby reestablish the therapeutic alliance. However, I choose to do this by combining an interpretation of her response based on transference with the reality of the cancellation.

Her response to this indicates the projection of the sense of guilt to me in the transference situation, but also the wish for punishment as a neurotic mechanism for offsetting the immediate effects of the unconscious guilt feelings. After the silence, the patient's self-observing ego functions again assume dominance as she perceives herself responding in a narcissistic, childlike way, where her own wishes and demands are central without regard for the reality of my situation. But at the same time, this conflicts with her ego-ideal of a mature personality, thus resulting in a sense of shame and embarrassment. The elaboration on this conflict, between being the adult who can accept reality and the child who wants to ignore it, ultimately leads to the expression of her regressive wish for infantile oral gratification with me as the mother on whom she suckles.

By my intervention, in which I accept the existence of this wish but then raise the question of whether it is primary or a regressive defense, I am encouraging her to experience it further in the transference, as well as simultaneously to observe herself and her responses in the light of the therapeutic alliance. This leads her to anticipate her ultimate growth and maturity, but at the same time it mobilizes anxiety that in her current psychological equilibrium it would mean that I am as immature and weak as was her father. This is followed by a perception of me as a loving father who will permit her to grow up, which then evokes further feelings of love toward me, accompanied by the still unresolved childhood fantasies. The idea of growing up thus stimulates anxiety and conflict over the possibilities of loving me or of allowing her defenses to be diminished.

Her statement, "And yet I feel as if I've known you before," sounds somewhat reminiscent of a déjà vu experience, but may be merely a way of expressing her awareness of the relationship to me as a transference phenomenon. In any event, at the end of the session there is a recurrence of the regression to the maternal transference, with the experience perceived in oral terms. My understanding is that as a result of the analytic work in this session and of having been given the reality information about the cancellation, the previously strained therapeutic alliance has again been reestablished and strengthened, and with this she can now experience the sense of basic trust in its original infantile form.

As the patient described in the session, if my cancellation had been a deliberate and conscious manipulation, even if for therapeutic goals, it would have been disruptive to the therapeutic alliance and sense of trust, and it would have meant that I was actively repeating some of the manipulative childhood experiences with the parents. Although her threat that she would have quit analysis in such a case is probably unlikely, it would nevertheless have been a contraindicated type of therapeutic maneuver. However, once the vicissitude in the analytic situation has occurred beyond my conscious control, the handling of it in an analytically exploratory fashion permitted us to make effective therapeutic use of the occurrence and actually, in the long run, it represents a positive therapeutic experience for her.

## SESSION 156

**P:** – – – – – – I think what it's like not to be here for two days. I always feel so scared about it. It happens every Sunday. (Elaborates.) The only picture I ever get is one of you falling apart.

**A:** What's the detail of that picture?

**P:** I saw you the way I feel so often. I just can't think and all I do is lie down and feel as if I'm going to die.

**A:** But you mentioned the idea of me falling apart. What is the actual image that you get when you think about this?

**P:** I can see you cower in a chair and you're all hunched over and you shake like mad. – – I wonder if this has anything to do with my uncle? Every time when I come in, I wonder what will you be like? I'm always so scared every time. – – – The first thing that I remember about the house was my grandmother telling my uncle that he could never use her car again and he was crying. – – – I know that my parents eventually found out. They all whispered together and I had the feeling that they were saying that it was horrible and awful and something very bad. But they never talked to me about it. I know that that's the reason my grandmother took the car away from my uncle. It's like they were saying to me, "We hate you and you are dirty and you're too horrible to talk about, and we are never going to love you again for the rest of your life." – – – I've had the feeling all of my life that everywhere I've gone people already know about me. People would ask me why my father would move. – – It's as if I'm so dirty and filthy. . . . . .

**A:** What did you stop at?

**P:** – – I always feel as if I'll never be accepted or even liked. But I'm used to it by now, and it's as if something is wrong with me and everyone knows about it. Wherever I've gone no one really *likes* me. People may say that they forget about it and they may not talk about it, but I know that it's always there. – – – And I guess that that's what you'll do to me too, and so I prepare myself in advance.

**A:** How do you mean?

**P:** I draw into myself and I cry inside and I just feel that I have to take it. You know about me now, and so I know how it's going to be. I'm used to it by now. I just don't want any more.

**A:** So what we can see is that you internalized your grandmother's and your parents' reactions to that incident, so that now you also feel that you deserve this. Then you projected that criticism and judgment on to me and feel that I'm reacting the same way you are.

**P:** If I don't act that way, I feel as if I'll fall apart. I could only live by taking whatever they wanted to give me. – – Now I see myself telling my mother and Carol that I enjoyed what I did. They'd think that I was crazy, so we all *act* as if it was something horrible! That's the only way that we can live with it. But if I ever tell you that I loved it and that I enjoyed having it and that I still love my uncle and that I don't think that it is bad, then you'll say that I'm crazy and that I need to go to a mental hospital. – –

**A:** See if you can elaborate the details of that thought.

**P:** I don't know what it's all about. I'm not strong enough to stand up against the whole world about this thing. – – It really wasn't so bad, especially for me, because I was so little. I think and compare it to my daughters and their fascination with Tom's penis. It would only be *bad* if Tom let her do it. But I'm all by myself with this thought and I feel as if I'm the only one in the world who thinks it. I expect that my parents would tell me that I'm crazy and all mixed up and all wrong. I feel as if I depend on them and as if I'd die without them, but still I'm not convinced about their feeling about this. I believe that my parents are wrong about this. As a matter of fact, I *know* it. And that's the only thing to keep me sane. But I know that they think, "She's a monster." And so I take it all in, so that the monster won't show and I feel as if I'm caught. I really feel like killing them but I know that I need them, but I also know that they're wrong and they are really vicious about this and that it's all horrible the way they are reacting to it. But it all makes me feel so scared. I'm doing this for you too, now. I'm acting as if it was something horrible and bad and wrong that I did so that you won't kick me out the door for having done it. I want to be able to tell you to go to hell and tell you that I don't care what you think and that I can live without you. But I can't. Instead I keep myself a scared little child! I can't say that I'm twenty-seven years old and that I'm a woman and that I'm right. And so instead I sit and suck my thumb and I cower and I'm scared and it's all for your benefit so that at least you will let me stay here. – – I can either stay a scared little girl, or else become a woman. I'm *tired* of being a child. I want to be a woman and a mother and a wife! But I'm so scared of it. – – Now I have the feeling that you're falling apart and I can smell alcohol and I wonder if you had to drink in order to face this? It's a matter of either you or me. If I'm an adult then you are going to completely fall apart.

**A:** How do you mean?

P: All of my life I have had to be a child so that my parents don't fall apart! If I ever tell them that I'm right and that I'm not bad and that they're wrong, then my parents just can't take it.

A: What's the detail of that?

P: You make me feel helpless but I know that I'm *not*. I know it. But this other is the only relationship in which we can both survive.

A: You have the feeling that if you tell me that you're a woman and that you're right and you didn't do anything wrong, then I'll fall apart. What comes to your mind about that?

P: You'll think, "That girl is a sex maniac and so I can do anything I want to her." You're just like all men that way. And you're just like my father. But with a woman and not a baby and with someone who expects to have intercourse he gets so shook! I know that I'm bad and evil and I'm the type of woman you love. I've been here a long time and you didn't even know! But you know it now! And my uncle made me this way! Am I really so horrible? But it's still you and your problem and I know that you are going to fall apart and you'll never help me. – –

*Cry*

A: The fantasy is that I'm saying, "This girl is a sex maniac and so I can do anything I want to her." What do you picture me doing?

P: I see you pulling out your penis, just like my uncle did. Everyone is scared.

A: Which of us is scared, you or I?

P: You are. I wasn't scared then. I'll do it because that's what I am and that's what you expect of me. – –

A: The fantasy is that I'll pull out my penis and also that I'm scared as I do it. What are your associations to that?

P: You want me to . . . . . play with you. You want me to masturbate you. I know that you love it. You're such a child, but that's as far as it goes. This is all so childish and weak on your part. – – This wonderful thing turns into something horrible and then I'm branded with it. But I know that all men like me, because I'll do it to them, but when I do all my love is buried. I know that I'm not a child and I'm a woman. But I know that that's what all men want me to do. – – It doesn't scare me and I'll do it, but I also know that it's the end. – – It's so hard for me to believe that I can make a man helpless this way. And I know that I can have an orgasm just watching him.

A: This is like the situation you described in the past about the vacations in Maine when your father would be naked around you. You had the thought then that, "He wants me to do it to him too and he's just like my uncle."

**P:** He is! And you are! Who do you think you are fooling? I hate you. I'll be a child for the rest of my life just so that my mother won't think of me as horrible, but my father and I know what it's all about. – – –

**A:** We'll stop here for today.

At the door the analyst asks if she can change the time of her sessions to 9:00 a.m. The patient agrees to do so.

### DISCUSSION

After the initial silence, the patient begins by describing her reactions to the weekend separation, projecting to me in the transference the fantasy that I am "falling apart." Initially I am unsure as to the origin of this transference response, and therefore I encourage her to associate to it and eventually she indicates that it is being transferred from the uncle and that it occurs each time she comes for her session. My own association is that this must be a repetition of uncertainty with me as to how each of us will react, based on repeated experiences she must have had with her uncle each time she saw him after the traumatic incident. She is experiencing this as a transference phenomenon in the present scene, and her associations lead to the further elaboration about the uncle and his punishment and guilt, as well as the further elaboration about the parents' reactions.

In her initial description of the incident two sessions ago, she indicated that her mother had never known about it, but she now recalls further details to the effect that the parents did find out, although she now says that they never talked with her about it. The continuing reaction of guilt and condemnation since that time represents her own projected fantasy on to the parents (although it is realistically possible that the parents did hold her responsible for the incident), which is then reinternalized as if it originated from the parents. This internalized superego reaction results in the chronic sense of intense guilt, which is then displaced and projected, as in her statement, "Wherever I've gone, no one really *likes* me. People may say that they forget about it and they may not talk about it, but I know that it's always there."

She then projects the same sense of guilt to me in the transference, which gives me the opportunity to make the interpretation about the origin and development of this unconscious superego reaction. This in turn leads to her expression of the pleasure and gratification involved in the sexual incident, with the further elaboration of the superego response indicating that the sense of guilt is really not genuine and personalized. In the further elaboration of this reaction, she expresses it from the standpoint of the healthy self-observing ego and the recognition as an adult of the existence of childhood sexual curiosity and impulses. But her dependency upon the parental objects (and in the transference relationship) reinforces the need to accept the parental moral standards and views of reality. As this response continues, she goes on to experience the same pseudo-superego reaction in the transference, when she says, "I'm acting as if it were something horrible and bad and wrong that I did so that you won't kick me out the door for having done it." Once again she elaborates on the transference response to me, as if she were a child expecting my criticism and condemnation, while at the same time recognizing herself as an adult who no longer has to feel guilty about the incident.

The recovery of this incident and the various intrapsychic reactions which accompanied it is suggestive evidence that the sexual trauma itself was not the crucial aspect of this event, but rather that the major traumatic effect was the way in which the event was handled by the adults involved. Material like this suggests the importance of the adults' helping the child effectively to integrate the event and deal with the inevitable fantasied reactions to it, and that these issues are more important in determining whether or not such an event will have lasting traumatic psychological effects. It is possible that if the parents, instead of maintaining silence about the incident, had discussed it with her openly and directly and had permitted her to verbalize her anxiety and fear before reassuring her about their continuing interest and love, this event might not have resulted in permanent psychic fixation.

At this point she undergoes a further regression in the transference, with the fantasy that I am falling apart and with an olfactory hallucination of smelling alcohol. This leads to the transference experience of me as the father who has sexual fantasies about her as the child, which complement her own sexual fantasies about me. This material indicates that the incident with the uncle was a displaced form of acting-out of her oedipal fantasies about the father, and this is again repeated with me in the fantasy that I am about to seduce her by pulling out my penis as her uncle did. In this context she goes on to elaborate upon her willingness to participate in this kind of sexual experience and her excitement and pleasure at the thought of doing so. This offers me the opportunity to present her with a reconstruction of the fantasy that she must have had in the situations where her father was exposing himself to her sexually, and in which the perception of the father and uncle were fused. This interpretation leads to the further transference experience that, like the father, I am interested in this type of sexual contact with her and that she and I share this sexual secret yearning which we must hide from her mother.

At this point it is difficult to know how much of her perceptions of the father are accurate, and how much they represent a projection of her own oedipal fantasies to him. The most likely possibility is that it represents a combination of both, but in the transference situation this remains pure fantasy. The therapeutic expectation is that as this material is further worked through in the transference relationship and as I show her (through my verbal and nonverbal behavior) that I intend to remain her analyst and will not participate in overt sexual seduction, she will be better able to separate intrapsychic fantasy from external reality in the current scene. And as a result she will ultimately be able finally to resolve this now-current conflict through the renunciation of the fantasies and wishes toward the infantile object in the transference.

Once again this material indicates how important it is in analysis that the analyst not participate overtly in physical or other seductive interactions with the patient, since to do so would be to confirm that the current object in the transference is acting very much like the original oedipal object, and therefore that the current situation is the same as it was in childhood. If this should occur, there would be less opportunity to correct and modify the intrapsychic elaborations of the childhood situation.

---

### SESSION 157

**P:** I've been so anxious since I left here. Suddenly I feel so excited and I want to let go! I want to love you and love the world, but I wonder if this is a sign that I've cracked? -- I've been so scared for the past two days. (Elaborates.) Why am I so scared of you? (Elaborates.) I still think of you as a monster who is going to try to destroy me.

**A:** You mentioned that you are feeling excited and you want to let go and you want to love me. What are your associations to that?

**P:** I want to let you know how I feel and I want to be able to feel my love. I had the thought that nothing is going to hurt me and that really nothing will happen. (Elaborates.) But I'm so scared of it all. I've been so afraid all of my life to show that I really *like* someone. --- Now I suddenly feel that I really like you. (Elaborates.) It's all so sexual but I think that you are the nicest and kindest person in all of the world. I don't want to be anxious about it or to think about my uncle or my father when

I feel this. But I think about all of the anxiety I have gone through! It's really been hell! –– But now I'm able to get a glimpse of reality and to realize that you are not my uncle or my father and that we're not going to get all involved. I can see myself as a woman and still realize that this is not going to happen between us. But then I feel, "It's coming," and I think that you will crack. I'm tired of running and I want to relax and let go and let myself love. That's the reality that I want. –– And yet at the same time I could cut my wrists! (Elaborates.) I don't feel womanly at all and I feel that I must think about killing myself or my kids and that my life is horrible and that everything is a mess and all kinds of thoughts like that. –– I use these things as a defense. (Elaborates.) –––

A: So we can see that you are afraid of your own wish to let go of your feelings. What's the detail of the fear?

P: I can see myself as a woman. (Elaborates.) And I know that you're a man and I know that that is the reality between us but I am scared to reach it. It's just like the idea of death, or it's like the thought of cutting my wrists. It's all a part of me that I don't want, but I keep asking myself what happens to the child in me? I need it! If I could just get over this I'd be such a different person. The woman in me is so real, but if I ever let her out then the child in me dies and then I feel like I die. The child is such a big part of me and I'm so used to living as a nervous wreck and feeling insecure and beating my kids and having all kinds of symptoms and other kinds of trouble. It's as if that is the only way I can live. –––
Last night I was out with Tom at a show. I had a feeling of panic as we were driving in the car and passing the State Hospital. –– It makes me think about a TV play I saw about the subway and lots of people on the subway that were helpless. It felt just like me. I'm helpless to fight and I'm afraid that if I stand up for what I want I'm going to get killed. –– So instead I feel that I must kow-tow to you and to the world and I have to act helpless because that's the only way that I can survive and I can live. (There is a knock on the door and an interruption to the session. The analyst goes to the door, talks briefly to someone there and returns to his chair.) ––– That threw me for a loop. I got scared.

A: What was the detail?

P: When I'm on the couch and when I can't see you, then I lose myself. But if you stand up then I can't stand it.

A: How do you mean?

P: Then it's you! Then you're real! It's not the same as when I'm on the couch. When you stand up I don't want you to see me. ––– I know that I must face something here that I haven't been able to face as yet. It all revolves around me being a woman and my fighting against it all of the time. -- When I come in here, I lose myself after about five minutes in here and I feel like I become a child and I don't even know who you are anymore. But if you get up, then I'm a woman and I know that I have a woman's body and I want you. --

**A:** And then?

**P:** – I ask myself what will happen? I see myself as a child and I see you as my uncle and I want to play with your penis, and at the same time I know that it will not happen. But I also know that I still want to be this child. Now I suddenly realize *I'm a woman* and I have a woman's body and I have so many feelings, but I don't want you to know about it. This is just like the time my father walked in and I hid under the bed because I was so embarrassed and scared. -- I can picture you as being kind and nice and understanding and strong. But then I think of myself as a mature woman and then the whole world explodes!! It's like dynamite. --

**A:** What's the detail of the explosion?

**P:** We'd be two equals and there'd be something between us and suddenly it explodes because it's just too much. -- I know that it must be me. -- But my feelings are so strong that I'm sure that I'll throw myself on you and put my arms around you and love you. I know that I've wanted to do that in the past. It's like the idea that my feelings are just so much that I can't handle them. -- You are going to sit there and take my feelings and so I must let them out here. But they are so strong. Do you know how strong they are? My feelings are so big and huge and strong and they seem so real! -- Now I want to run or else go out and eat. ---

*Anxiety, Cry*

**A:** You have the fantasy that your feelings are too strong and that they're too big for me and that I don't really understand how intense they are. What comes to your mind about it?

**P:** I've never before let them out. I think of all of the feelings of love and sex and it's all the *woman* in me. I sometimes have this fantasy of myself as a woman and I'm feeling love and sex and all kinds of closeness. But I also know that you can't possibly. . . . .I know you must get mad at me or else I think I'll swallow you and destroy you. I feel as if you must change and you've got to be angry and throw me out or kick me or do something to push me away! You can't just be nice and sit there! -- And yet I don't think that you'll be weak and let me seduce you, so what is it that I'm afraid of? Except that maybe my feelings will scare you. I don't really see how you can stand up to them. I'm sure you are going to be scared or else you're going to succumb to them and I can see you get very nervous. Now I think about my body. I'll look like a million dollars and

I want to work on myself as a woman. And yet here I have the feeling, "I've got to eat and get so fat that Dr. Dewald wouldn't even look at me cross-eyed." – – Now I suddenly feel weak and shakey. – – – And now I get a vision of me standing up and taking off all of my clothes. – –

**A:** And what's the rest of the fantasy?

**P:** It's the ultimate. There are so many things to do to arouse a man. I could masturbate you. A man has his limitations and there is a line beyond which you can't go and I know where it is. I know I can get you over it if I really let myself go. – – – I know there are so many hidden ways to seduce you and these are ways that I've never had the nerve to use on anybody. – –

**A:** What's the detail of those ways?

**P:** I could strip and show you my body or else I could play around. Or else I could work as if I were a child and tell you that "You are so much of a man." I can either be a bitch or else a child and I know that you'll succumb to one of those. My father does and my uncle did and I know there are so many men who do. – – – It's the in-between that scares the hell out of me and I don't know what it is. – – – – This love feeling makes me so nervous! I feel like I'm going to jump! – – – Now I imagine myself lying in bed and I'm waiting for Tom to make love to me and I'm feeling so embarrassed.

**A:** We'll stop here for today.

After the patient has gone the analyst finds that she has left her glove behind.


### Discussion

Partly as a result of the work done in the last analytic session which has permitted her further to differentiate me from the oedipal father and uncle, the patient is now able to permit herself somewhat more fully to experience positive feelings of love and arousal, knowing in the more mature part of her mind that this will not deteriorate into an overt sexual relationship between us. As a result, she is able to begin the session by describing that she has felt excited and wants to let go and permit herself to love me, but this is almost immediately followed by the recurrence of the transference image, now being used defensively, of me as a destructive monster. My intervention is therefore at the level of the excitement and wish for love, which had mobilized the anxiety against which the regressive defense was instituted. With this indirect encouragement to observe herself and her conflict more directly and openly, she is then able to express further the underlying positive oedipal feelings toward me, while at the same time to perceive this situation with me as different from the one from her uncle and father.

This material illustrates an important step toward the beginning of structural change. In the previous transference situation, her responses toward me on the basis of her projected expectations that I will react in the same way as her father and uncle did have occurred repetitively, automatically, and without significant regard for the specific realities of the analytic situation and therapeutic relationship between us. The repeated experiences, interpretations, and confrontations regarding this repetitive transference behavior toward me have now resulted in a blocking of the automatic nature of these responses, and a feeble beginning recognition of the difference in the current situation from past similar relationships, and therefore a beginning dissolution of the previously existing "structured" responses. This new mode of response, recognition of reality, and awareness of the potential for a new type of reaction and relationship is transitory however, and it gives way to the old, repetitive, automatic, and anxiety-provoking associated fantasies. And thus the old expectations recur that "it's coming," with the perception that I would be unable to tolerate her feelings and with the expression of the regressive symptomatic disturbances. However, at this point she is spontaneously able to recognize her use of these patterns as a defense, and to this extent the old "structures" are less automatic and preformed.

Once again my intervention is focused at the level of conflict over potential new patterns of response, from which the regression occurred. Appropriately, she is able to recognize that to become more mature and womanly is to renounce the continuing childhood wishes and fantasies, with their associated fears, and that this would mean development of a new self-image and associated capacity for functioning as a woman. But she has still not fully recognized that it is the continuing wish for infantile and childhood gratification of these drives that maintains her psychological fixation at the level of childhood. In this material she is also indicating another important source of resistance to change in analysis, by reacting to the idea that the old neurotic patterns are familiar, and that to establish new patterns of functioning (structures) means to move into unfamiliar and therefore frightening levels of integration.

The patient's response to the unexpected interruption of the session illustrates how the structuring of the analytic situation fosters the type of psychic regression necessary for the conduct of an analysis. She describes very nicely the difference between me as a real object when she is able to see me visually (as when I got up to answer the door), as contrasted with the perception of me as a fantasied transference object when the visual cues are removed. As she says, "When I come in here I lose myself after about five minutes in here and I feel like I become a child and I don't even know who you are anymore." She then goes on spontaneously to elaborate upon her recognition of her own wish to be the child, while simultaneously recognizing herself physically to be a woman who would be capable of an adult sexual seduction. In this latter image of herself she is beset by anxiety that the childhood oedipal transference wishes and fantasies will lead her to act out in an adult form and will cause her to lose control of her impulses. With this is a conflict as to whether or not I am going to be able to accept and tolerate the full impact of her feelings, which is then followed by another symptomatic regressive expression of the wish to run or else to eat.

Once again my intervention is aimed at the level of conflict from which she regressed, as I focus on the uncertainty she experiences regarding my capacities for control. In response to this, she begins to express her defensive wish that I reject her and thereby protect both of us from the conflict situation she fears. A similar line of defense is the fantasy of eating so much that she becomes fat and unattractive to me. It should be noted that in this fantasy of becoming fat as a means of avoiding possible sexual seduction, the patient is now expressing a wish for the very condition which was one of her symptoms and which led her to seek analysis. In other words, this illustrates how the symptom for which the patient presents himself for therapy represents an attempt at the compromised resolution of an unconscious intrapsychic conflict, and that painful or distressing as the symptom may be, it represents an attempt to cope with an even more anxiety-producing or potentially disruptive unconscious psychological disturbance.

The patient then goes on to elaborate further on the transference fantasy of me being seducible, as was her father and her uncle, and of the various fantasies she has entertained over the years as to the way in which such a seduction might be accomplished. At the end of the session she experiences sexual arousal and expectation in a somewhat more womanly fashion, displacing it in the transference from me to her husband. The motivating drive behind this remains the infantile and childhood oedipal wish in the father transference, but its form of expression is somewhat changed, which again represents a minor tentative step in the direction of a more mature orientation toward sexuality and ultimately toward conscious ego mastery of her own sexual desires.

The final interaction involves a form of acting-out, in that she leaves the glove behind her. At this point, however, it is not completely clear what the leaving of the glove represents. There are a number of alternative specific fantasies that may accompany it, and the elucidation of this piece of acting-out will have to await further analytic work in the next session.

---

## SESSION 158

As the patient comes in she sees the glove on the analyst's desk and retrieves it before lying down on the couch.

**P:** I feel so embarrassed about leaving my glove. I realized I'd left it just after I went out but I wouldn't come back and get it.

**A:** Why not?

**P:** I wondered did I do it on purpose? I thought about my gloves before I came in and worried if I might leave one, but the whole thing makes no sense.

**A:** If leaving a glove was a pure accident, then there's no realistic reason for the embarrassment. The fact that there is embarrassment is related to what is behind it all. What are your thoughts about this?

**P:** I suspect it has a sexual meaning. It's like leaving a part of yourself or trying to get personal with you. – – – I still can't believe that I did that or that I was trying for a personal contact with you.

**A:** What are your thoughts about it?

**P:** – I guess I wondered how you'd react. It would be like I dropped my handkerchief and it would be a way to test you.

**A:** What's the detail?

**P:** . . . . .It would give you a chance to get personal with me. – – I was so anxious all day yesterday and I had wild dreams. I know I was testing you. I had a dream about my boss from last year. It was you and my boss and my father all rolled into one man and I dreamed that I seduced you. It was all wild. My mother and I were lying on twin beds and both of us were in love with one man and he had an affair with both of us. But I felt that he would really prefer me. He made love to me but after a while I stopped him and I said, "I don't want to do this to Tom." But mother was egging me on and telling me to go ahead. She was trying to get him to do it to her but he didn't want to. My daughter Sally was there and then I said, "I can't do this in front of her." Tom was in school while all of this was going on. Then the dream switched to my boss and I was trying to call Tom. I was working the switchboard when a man came in and said he wanted me to work for him and that it was a chance for me to learn a new job. I seduced him and he acted just like my boss. – – – I feel like I'm not doing well in here. Does anyone else have the same kind of problems I have? I had another dream that I killed Jean's ex-husband. He started to chase me and I tried to call the police and then I had thoughts to shoot myself. –

**A:** You asked if anyone else has the same kind of problems you have. What are your associations to that?

**P:** When you asked me about changing the time of our appointments, I felt that probably someone else had quit treatment and I wondered why. Did they also have a problem in trusting you? I feel as if I can't break through. Now I'm thinking about Harris and what he used to say about things being on a higher level. I think about myself and about how poor my function is at home.

**A:** You mentioned the fantasy about someone else having quit and not being able to trust me. What's the detail?

**P:** – I think you probably made a pass at someone. I have such a conflict about trusting you and I wait to have you make a pass at me every time I come in. I just don't give up. –

**A:** I think this is connected to the idea about testing me about the glove. Leaving the glove behind gave you a chance to come back and possibly to see me with some other patient and to compare that situation with your own.

**P:** – – – I wish I knew what makes me so anxious. (Elaborates.) All of this scares me.

**A:** I think you have a wish to trust me and to feel secure here and then to let your defenses down. But at the same time you see it as a danger and you think I am going to take advantage of you and make a sexual pass at you, and so there is also a fear of trusting me.

**P:** Now I think about playing bridge with my girl friends. It causes me such anxiety because I'm so different from what they are. What would they ever think if they knew about me? I feel so different! (Elaborates.) I think about my horrible wishes and how they're so full of sexual desire and it's like that dream I told you about. I want it so badly. It feels like there is a monster inside of me that wants to have affairs and wants to seduce men and I'm trying to do it in here. I'm so afraid that it will come out.

**A:** You mentioned earlier the thoughts about seducing me and using the incident of leaving the glove as a chance to get personal with me. What else comes to your mind about it?

**P:** I think about all kinds of other men. I think about my boss and there's also a man at church. Now I get a sudden red light. I'm afraid that you're going to catch on because I gave you the go-ahead signal. I know that I *do* this to other men and they do go ahead.

**A:** Let's look at how that works out between you and me. You gave me a go-ahead signal. Now what happens?

**P:** I want you to make love to me. I'm telling you that it would be all right, but I'm also so anxious. Even though I talked about it, I would hold off before this. (Elaborates.) But leaving the glove is a way of letting you know that I'd now let you do it. – –

**A:** Let's go back to the fantasy that I made a pass at another patient. What are your associations?

**P:** It's what I'd do. If you ever went ahead I'd leave and I'd never return. But I've proved my point.

**A:** What we have to see is that you choose to think that I made a pass at another patient who then quit. There are many other possible explanations about why I might suggest that we change the time of the hour to 9 o'clock, so we would have to wonder what it means that you would choose to believe what you did.

**P:** – – I feel as if I can't stand this any more. There's such anxiety. I know I'd fall apart if you really were this way, but I also know that I'd manage. It's the not knowing that's so hard. If you were this way, then I could quit analysis without any trouble. (Elaborates.) It's the not knowing but also feeling that it's probably true.

**A:** So if I *am* like your father, then it confirms your belief about all men and then you could go on as you were before. But if I'm *not* like your father, then it means that your old belief about all men is not true and that means possibly changing that old stereotyped idea about all men.

**P:** I know how to act and feel and behave in the old pattern. But to give it up means a complete loss of all that and means living in a world that I've never known and being totally unfamiliar in the other situation. It would all be so easy if you would make a pass at me.

**A:** What's the detail?

**P:** I feel as if I'm still stronger than you are. I'd be shook. I know I hope to find the other but I don't really believe it. – – Then I could say, "There *is* no such man." But if you *don't* make a pass at me, my hope to find him would still be there, but I still can't believe it and I'll never be convinced. – – Then I can hate and I can feed on the hate! But what do I do with love? It would totally envelop me and I'd melt into a puddle of nothing. – – Now my mind is going blank. – – –

**A:** So we can see that there's a part of you that wants to find a man whom you *can't* seduce and who remains strong and trustworthy. But the rest of you sees that belief that there could be such a man and that you could hope to find him as a dangerous situation. Now let's look at both sides of that conflict.

**P:** If I can't seduce you. . . . . now I think of myself as a teen-aged girl who's about to fall for an older man. – – Maybe it's not a matter of strength at all, but maybe you are a homosexual. Maybe you'll still fall apart with all of this. I want to transfer *everything* onto you and I want to put my whole self into your hands. But by not trusting you I keep some strength for myself. Now I'm so scared! I know that you can't help me because you're not really strong.

**A:** I think this idea that I'm not really strong is a defense, just like the thought that maybe I'm a homosexual.

**P:** Can I place my whole self in front of you? How are you going to react if I do? I can only think of you as a monster and an ogre and I can't stand to think of you as being nice and kind. Now I want to throw myself all over you and to keep *nothing* to myself. – – But now it feels like that's like death. You scare me so. Why is it that I don't know who you are? How do I know what you are? Now I want to turn around and look at you but I'm scared to death if I do it. – – – Now I compare you with all the other men I've ever known I want to have someone say that what we are doing here is all right, including all of the anxiety that I feel. But I feel that something is wrong with the whole thing and maybe with you, and that you're not going to give me what I need. I think that anyone I talked to would be scared to death! They'd say, "The poor girl is ready to crack." (Elaborates.) – – The closer I get to trusting you the more anxious I get. (Elaborates.) If I trusted you I'd give up all of my strength and all of my defenses and I'd be wide open and then I'd be dead if you were not strong and trustworthy. I feel that I must reserve some strength for myself and I must *keep* things to myself. – – When will you hold my hand or pat me on the back? I know it is bound to come! Is it going to come when I completely trust you? (Elaborates.)

**A:** We'll stop here for today.

### DISCUSSION

The patient begins with the incident of leaving her glove. In her comment, "I thought about my gloves before I came in and wondered if I might leave one. . . ," she demonstrates that the idea of leaving a glove had been present and was being offset by the mechanism of negation, and therefore that the entire experience probably had a number of psychic determinants. Rather than be satisfied merely with her generalization that she might have left it on purpose, I want to analyze the incident and the fantasies behind it in greater detail, and therefore begin at the surface of her conscious awareness that there must be specific associations to the incident.

Her initial statements that she suspects it had a sexual meaning, and that it was like leaving herself or trying to get personal with me, are essentially intellectualizations and generalizations aimed defensively at concealing the full impact of the experience. This is indicated by her subsequent statement that she really doesn't believe she could have done it or that she was trying for such a type of personal contact. My interventions are attempts to indicate to her that there must be other more specific associations and fantasies connected with the incident, which begin to emerge whén she associates to her anxiety yesterday and her awareness that she was testing me. This is followed by the dream with its obvious oedipal triangular relationships, as well as a reference to primal scene associations expressed in the element of not wanting to make love in front of her daughter.

At the moment it appears as if we have lost track of the incident with the glove since her associations have led to the dreams and to the issue of how other patients respond in analysis. However, if we accept the concept of psychic determinism we must assume that there is some type of hidden connection between the incident of the glove and the dreams which were associated to it, as well as the subsequent associations to the dream, even though for the moment such a connection may be obscure. To have suggested that she was avoiding the issue of the gloves would have been to do violence to the pattern of her free associations, and would have meant to her that she was expected to come up with a logical answer. So instead of pursuing this issue right now, I postpone it in my own mind for the moment, and instead continue to work with the material at the level of the associations she is spontaneously presenting.

In this context, my attention has been drawn to her statement that she is not doing well in here (a sharp contrast to the reality that she is actually making very rapid analytic progress) and to her question and curiosity about how other patients react. I may have also associated this question to the dream elements of watching or being watched during sexual activity, and therefore I focus my initial intervention on this point. Her response that someone had quit therapy takes me by surprise, since I had merely been trying to arrange my schedule for greater convenience when I asked her two days ago about possibly changing the time of the sessions. She had agreed to it readily at the time, and I was not aware that the request had had any particular intrapsychic repercussions. But the fantasy of someone else having quit treatment suggests that there must be more going on in her mind about it, and therefore I ask for the further details.

Her statement that I had probably made a pass at someone is an obvious transference reference to the father, and in this context I have an immediate empathic association to her curiosity about his mistresses, buttressed by the voyeuristic elements in the manifest dream, and therefore I present this to her as one of the possible motivations in leaving the glove. Her response neither confirms nor denies this, but emphasizes the intensity of her anxiety, and so I attempt to clarify for her the continuing conflict between her wish and her fear of trusting me.

This leads to a further elaboration of her own awareness that the fears of sexual seduction originate within herself, and that the "monster" that she has so often accused me of being is really a projection based upon an image of herself. This material now permits me again to try to analyze the incident with the glove by relating the just-expressed wishes regarding seduction to the previous associations between seduction and the glove episode, and this leads to her elaboration of the idea that the episode was a way of giving me the go-ahead signal.

Because she is still experiencing me in the transference as the father who makes passes at other women and who therefore is susceptible to the same thing with herself, and because the voyeuristic fantasies have still not been fully explored, and because earlier in the session the glove incident had led by association to the fantasy of someone quitting, I therefore now return to this issue with my request for her associations to it. She indicates again the partial conviction that it really happened, which leads me to confront her with the reality of other possible explanations for the time change and thus to interpret her wish to continue seeing me as sexually weak and unreliable. This leads to her expression of the continuing conflict and doubts about me, which I then interpret directly into the father transference, adding the element of resistance on the basis that to recognize me as different from her father would involve changing the old structured images and expectations. She confirms this element of the resistance by indicating how frightened she is of ". . . living in a world that I've never known. . . ," and that in many ways she would prefer that I be like the father, although simultaneously there is the active hope and wish that I am different. At the same time she elaborates further on the "dangers" involved in this type of new orientation toward men.

At this point she makes use of another line of defense by thinking of me as a possible homosexual and therefore using this to buttress the arguments for not reducing her defenses against the full impact of the relationship to me, while simultaneously indicating the growing wish to do just that and to permit herself fully to trust me with all of her feelings. From here she goes on to elaborate further this continuing conflict over recognizing me as someone different from her father, and therefore someone with whom she can experience and express her feelings freely and fully. This is the type of ideal experience a young girl should have with her father, without fear of overt seduction, in order to become a sexually mature and free adult.

Once again it should be noted that this issue of trust is still an active one, and that the working-through process regarding it continues. It is a particularly difficult and specific issue for patients who have experienced real sexual gratification or seduction by the oedipal object. This is because once there has been an overt gratification, the expectation that it might occur again tends to be stronger than in cases where the original oedipal relationship was entirely a fantasy without real gratification, and where the model is one of abstinence by the oedipal object. In the latter situation, the transference expectation is that even if the oedipal fantasies are intense and are fully experienced, the transference object will react as the original one did and *not* provide overt gratification. At the end of the session, her question about my holding her hand or patting her on the back is a reference to the experience with her former therapist, who was a specific derivative oedipal figure who also gratified her demands in his overt behavior.

---

## SESSION 159

P: I completely surround myself with my defenses. I'm determined to be hostile and I feel that everyone is full of shit. I had a dream that I was swimming at a pool and everyone felt that I was horrible. I did it all wrong but I still loved it. There were a lot of bitches who were sitting around.

There was a boy that I was looking for but I couldn't find him. He was alcoholic and I think he was homosexual but I still liked him. – – Then I was cleaning my house and I'd left the vacuum cleaner up on a hill. It was all taking place in Maine. It wore me out to go up and get it. Then I was walking on some comic books and each of them was worth 25 cents but I thought to myself, "What does it matter?" – – – When I woke up I felt especially hostile towards Jean. – – If I ever decide to trust you it would be wonderful but what's the use? I hate you and I think you are horrible, and I feel that you can't help me. (Elaborates.) So what's the use of it all? – – – I fully realize what I'm doing but I want to. Now I think about the weekend coming up. I can be so nervous or have all of my symptoms or else I can be hostile and depressed and just not care about anything. – – –

**A:** What comes to your mind about the swimming pool in the dream?

**P:** I was with my sisters and they were much younger than they are now. It was like the times in Springfield when I loved the boys who used to hang around at the pool. We used to play around there. The pool was shallow. I dove into the deep part. I used to get such criticism. I'd jump off the high dive. I *love* to swim. (Elaborates.) Now I think about the boys I used to know and the times I used to be in Maine but it makes me so depressed. In the dream they all thought that I was nuts. I went to Tom's aunt's house for lunch and the rooms were all blue and they seemed emotionally very cold. His aunt is a psychology major but she's got such problems. She ruined all of her children. It's just like Jean. I hate her. I think about all of these people who are so concerned with emotions and I think it really ruins them.

**A:** What else comes to mind about that?

**P:** I think about all of these people and they try so hard. (Elaborates.) They just can't see the forest for the trees.

**A:** What is the forest that you think I am not seeing?

**P:** I don't know! – – We go into all of these things and you're so sure that you're strong and that you can handle this. But you're stupid and you can't possibly be that strong or sure! I just can't trust anyone completely. Everyone is human. – – I know this is your professional responsibility and you should be able to take every emotion that I have. But then I'm going to get drowned by them! (Elaborates.) I know the analysis is supposed to help get the shit out of me and there should be no problem. But how is this possibly going to work out? I think of all the people in my past and I compare you with every one of them and I know that you are going to fall too.

**A:** What's the detail of my fall?

*Cry*

**P:** Now I'm having a horrible time breathing. It's just as if someone was sitting on my chest. My mother did try to give me nose drops when I was a girl. She was supposed to give me the treatment but she took her hostility out on me. I was so little and I was in a panic and I remember *Cry* her sitting on me. I couldn't do one God-damn thing. Who could I yell to for help? My mother was cramming love down my throat. She was suffocating me literally. She'd grab me! It was her duty to see that I got love. I know that you'll do this to me and get me vulnerable and then you'll sit on me! –

**A:** What else comes to mind about that?

**P:** I see myself as weak and helpless, and you're going to sap life out of me. You'll shake me like a wet noodle. I'm helpless.

**A:** I think there's a reversal of this idea in the dream. In the dream there were those 25-cent comic books and you were walking on them. I think they represent these $25.00 sessions where you feel I'm walking on you.

**P:** (Nods agreement.) I feel like I'd like to try it, but I don't do it. I want to open up and receive your help and I know it's just one breath away. It's right here and I know it could be so easy. It makes me feel happy. (Elaborates.) But it would be the *end* of me! I've *had* it. – – Now I feel like a child again. I have a swelling in my chest. I'm feeling *so* happy but it never comes out. – – Now I see myself nursing and I'm anticipating it all and I'm thinking that I'm going to be full and I'm so happy. But then I think, "Why should you get so excited because it won't last, so don't get your hopes up. It's better to fight it and hate it instead." I guess I want it to last forever and I can't stand it if it's ever taken away, and it always is. – – You may be here now but you're going to be gone for two days over the weekend, and I don't even know if I'm going to be able to survive. So I fight it all and I hate it! – – – – And yet I feel so comfortable here. I love it and I know I always will. I think about this warm feeling that I have. – – I've loved so hard! It would always last about a year and then bang! *I'd* turn it off. It would kill me and I'd feel crushed and I would feel like it was the end! But I'd forget it all so fast. Now I want to yell at you about my father. How can you expect me to love you? My father never gave me anything. So how am I supposed to love someone who is nice or mature or fine and warm and comfortable?! Now I feel frantic. – – – All I can do is remember my father's affairs and realize that that's always the end result. There's love and warmth and then that. – – I feel like I could go crazy! I'm convinced that you're my father right now! I feel you sitting on my head and I can't stand the weight. Now I want to run back to the breast because that is the only safe place. I just can't allow myself to feel happy! It's all going on right now. I feel good and then suddenly I'm so anxious.

A: I think the fantasy is that if you will let yourself love me that I'll have sex with you, which would mean incest, and that would mean the end for you.

P: – I feel as if I must change my father's personality. I'm convinced that you *are* my father right now. I'm trying to tell myself that you are Dr. Dewald and that you're not my father but I can't do it.

A: You can't do it because you don't want to. Part of you feels the horror and the anxiety and the pain and the guilt, but there's also a part of you that still has a wish for this incest. This is a part of you that still has a *wish* to have your father and a wish to have me.

P: – – – What's going to happen if this desire should ever come out in full force? Then it would all be up to you. If you're my father, then I don't stand a chance. – –

A: If I'm your father, then it would mean that you *could* have me and satisfy this wish for incest.

P: That's what I'm scared of and that's why I'm so anxious.

A: The problem is that you want it and you also *don't* want it at the same time.

P: I know that I suppress this desire. If I trust you, then it's out in the open, and then I feel myself drawing closer and closer. Then I feel that you'll seduce me or else I'll succeed in seducing you. – – – –

A: We'll stop here for today.

### Discussion

In the session yesterday after I "passed the test" in regard to the incident with the glove, she was able to go somewhat further than previously into the wish and yearning to trust me and thus be able to reduce her defenses against the oedipal drives. Having taken this step forward, she comes in today with a mobilization of resistances and defenses against her own desires to move ahead. After presenting the dreams, both of which relates to the current transference conflicts, she returns to the defenses against her positive and trusting attachments in the father transference.

As she reports the first dream with the homosexual boy for whom she was looking, I am immediately reminded of her defensive association yesterday that I might be a homosexual. In the second dream my attention is caught by the figure of 25 cents, which I immediately associate to the fee she pays for each analytic session. The 25-cent comic books therefore suggest to me her continuing defensive needs to depreciate me and the analysis, while the dream taking place in Maine suggests to me an association to the various sexual scenes and experiences with her father which have come up previously in the analysis. However, these are my own associations at the moment and rather than use them immediately as the basis of an interpretation, or immediately focus upon them by asking for her associations (which might be seen by her as a strong suggestion that these are the focal elements in the dream) I choose to ask her about the less specific element of the swimming. In addition to the above reasoning, I have seen in the past that diving into swimming pools has been associated for her with the analysis and with the concept of going ahead in it, and considering the manifestations of the defensive wish to avoid the analytic relationship that she has just described, I am also thinking that this may prove to be an avenue of approach to the reduction of these resistances.

In her response she elaborates chiefly on the manifest dream content, which suggests that my intervention is not particularly effective and does not produce the hoped-for result, but at the same time it apparently does no harm either. The dream element of the husband's aunt whose rooms are "emotionally very cold," is understandable only when she goes on to associate to the aunt being a psychologist who has ruined her children, and subsequently to her thoughts about ". . . people who are so concerned with emotions. . . ." This material clearly has transference implications in terms of her immediate perception of me, and by my question I am hoping that she will spontaneously focus this issue into the transference. This does not occur, but I am quite sure that she is aware of the mistrust of me and her doubts about committing herself to me emotionally, and therefore I decide to interpret this directly to her by indicating my awareness that these conflicts refer to me.

This does produce the desired effect in that it evokes the affective response of crying, accompanied by the elaboration of her conscious doubts and fears about me and my capacity to maintain a professional relationship. This in turn leads to a conversion reaction, followed by the perception of me as the mother through the recall of an incident where mother was providing "treatment," and the patient felt helpless to cope with what she had perceived at the time as the mother's hostility. My aim is to help bring out this fear of helplessness more clearly, in order that the more mature self-observing ego functions can assess the danger with me more realistically, and I therefore offer her the partial interpretation of the defensive reversal that occurred in her dream.

Although it is not elaborated upon verbally, the interpretation is successful since its effect is to permit her to begin to express the positive wish for basic trust, along with her recognition that she is increasingly closer to the point of making this kind of emotional investment in the transference. This in turn stimulates a further regressive maternal transference experience of the nursing situation, accompanied by the hostility and anger at its anticipated interruption, and therefore activating her defenses against accepting the positive experiences. Immediately after reexperiencing the positive gratifications and their interruption in the relationship with the mother, the transference shifts and she moves into the conflict about the father and her frustration about his affairs. In the face of the anxiety mobilized by the father transference, there is activation of the regressive wish to ". . . run back to the breast. . . ."

Having observed the sequence of events of the session and recognizing that the associations involving the nursing situation and the maternal transference are regressive defenses against the oedipal conflict, I therefore interpret the source of her anxiety at the oedipal level from which the regression occurred. This results in her recognition of the intensity of the transference identification of me with the father, and in her description of how the transference distortion at the moment is stronger than her capacity to experience me as her analyst in the therapeutic alliance. And at this point, for the first time in the analysis, I interpret to her directly that this identification of me with the father is based upon her own wish for gratification in the original oedipal situation, as well as in the current transference relationship. The timing of this direct oedipal interpretation is based upon all the work previously done in the analysis, the clearly oedipal recent dreams, and the acting-out of this fantasy in the glove incident yesterday.

Her response after the brief silence, indicating the conscious acceptance of the existence of this wish, is a confirmation that the interpretation is appropriately timed and that she is capable of tolerating it without undue anxiety. My final intervention acknowledging that although there is an intense wish, there is simultaneously a part of her which wants to avoid and prevent its gratification, is an attempt to help her integrate this material more easily. Patients can more readily accept interpretations of anxiety- and guilt-provoking wishes if the analyst, in making the interpretation, acknowledges and indicates his recognition that the patient is simultaneously opposed to the gratification of such wishes, and that the existence of the wish does not mean that the patient is totally accepting of it. The knowledge that the analyst recognizes that the patient is struggling against the demands of such unacceptable impulses frequently permits the patient to accept their existence without undue anxiety, shame, or guilt, and without perceiving the analyst as judgmental or critical. This type of approach also helps the patient more clearly distinguish between a wish or impulse and an act, and it also helps to promote an acceptance of a less harsh superego by partial identification with the noncritical analyst. If such an interpretation is made in a way which implies to the patient that this is his entire attitude, this makes it more difficult for the patient to accept the interpretation since he is aware on his own of the various defenses, evasions, and avoidances that he has used in the past in coping with these types of impulses.

As a result of this series of interventions, the patient is able to say, "I know that I suppress this desire." The conscious acceptance of the existence of the oedipal drives represents a significant step toward ultimate resolution of the oedipal relationship.

# 6

## THE TWELFTH MONTH

### (Summary)

In the first session of this month, the patient experienced sexual arousal and excitement in the transference to me as the uncle, accompanied by conflict between herself as a sexually mature and capable woman, contrasted with the image of herself as the asexual little girl. She was excited at the thought of playing with my penis, but felt guilty because she also felt she is a little girl who is "a horrible monster to have such big feelings." She went on to verbalize in a regressive way the fantasy of a huge penis tearing her up and killing her as if it were a knife, along with the little girl's uncertainty about ". . . which hole does it go in?" This led to an anal penetration fantasy, and then to the equation of the penis with a huge bowel movement. With this she experienced a tingling sexual feeling, and verbalized a fantasy of taking off the uncle's penis, and ". . . sticking it up inside of myself so that he just shrivels up to nothing, and then I'd have it. I'd be ten feet tall and I'd be a monster and I'll kill everyone in sight with it."

Throughout the session, my role was merely to ask for details of associations, or else to confront her with the material she had already presented during the hour. I made no interpretations and merely listened quietly as this material emerged with intense affect, accompanied by spontaneous recognition of the intense conflict associated with these wishes.

In the second session the patient presented a directly oedipal dream with multiple transference elements, in which she was consciously aware of sexual arousal and desire for her father who came into the bathroom, but in the dream the father refused any overt sexual contact between them. The dream had followed an experience of feeling very close and womanly toward her husband and children, and a conscious desire to make love with her husband. In associating to the dream she avoided the element of the bathroom, and I asked her about this several times. It finally resulted in the memory of an experience with her father while on a vacation in which she was sitting on the toilet when he came in with his penis exposed, but although there was a memory of mutual looking at one another, there was no overt sexual activity. The patient spontaneously contrasted this with her uncle, with whom the incest barrier was less and with whom a similar situation had resulted in overt sexual experience. Both the relationship to the father and to the uncle were experienced actively toward me in the transference, followed by a further elaboration of the bathroom incident with the father. "What am I supposed to do? I'm just a little girl and these men throw their penises at me. What am I to do? I'm supposed to eat the God-damn penis and never see it again!"

In response to this, I offered the reconstruction of a fantasy that she may have felt she was to eat the penis and then, "shit it out the other end." This was followed by a feeling of being inside of a black hole, which she associated to the male and female genitalia, as well as to the toilet itself. In response to this I interpreted the idea that she has identified herself with feces, with a fantasy that because of her sense of being dirty and disgusting, she is to be flushed into the toilet. She elaborated on the fantasy of being flushed down the toilet as the final result of her sexual fantasies and impulses, experiencing this fear in the transference as well as in the recall of "the fear that I live in all of the time about this." Throughout the session she oscillated between heterosexual feeling and sensation in her genitals, and the regressive fantasies of being dirty and "inside that black hole."

In the third session the patient began with intensified resistances which, after interpretation, gave way to a further elaboration and description of the situation in which her acute neurosis had first begun. This had been during the latter part of her first pregnancy, in which she had gained thirty-five pounds and had felt that she must have worms. In association to the thought about the worms, she described her needs to eat, as well as her feelings of being dirty. After I had interpreted her reluctance to permit her associations to occur freely, the following material emerged in the session.

**P:** What comes to my mind is shit! But I don't understand why? I think about eating. . . . . and I feel that it means to eat my uncle's penis. I feel as if I put it in my mouth, and I do it again whenever I eat and then I feel dirty and filthy and I want to get rid of it. I want to clean myself up after I pass the dirt out. – – I want you to help me! But how?

**A:** Your thoughts are inside of you and I think you see them as dirty and that they smell and that they are filthy and so on. So I think that for you the idea of letting them out is the same as having a bowel movement. This is similar to what we were talking about yesterday, and I think you associate all of this with the smell, and the fantasy that I'll be disgusted. You expect that I'll walk out of the bathroom because of the smell, the way you mentioned that your father did yesterday.

**P:** – – – Somehow it's like I sat on Tom's lap, and then I gained thirty-five pounds. I asked him, "Do you think that I look fat?" And he said very nicely, "Yes." It was just like. . . . . like he said, "I know now why you eat." (Elaborates.) – – – Now I want to turn around and scream something shocking to you but I don't know what it is.

*Anxiety, Cry*

**A:** What occurs to you?

**P:** I know it's something about the penis.

**A:** What's the thought?

**P:** – It's like I. . . . . I want to yell. . . . . I love your penis and I want to put it in my mouth and suck it and kiss it and let it get hard. – – – I love my uncle's penis and I don't care. You can all go to hell.

**A:** I think you're holding back your thoughts and feelings right now as if to let them out would be like having a bowel movement, and shitting all over the couch. What comes to your mind about it?

**P:** I think of having an orgasm. I want to have one just as my uncle did. His finger is up my vagina and I love it. – – Now I feel as if I'm going crazy. I have a feeling in my mouth and its also in my vagina and I love it.

**A:** I think right now you are equating going crazy with having an orgasm, and the whole thing is connected with thoughts of letting go, which means letting everything out.

**P:** – – I'm really scared! – – – I want to put the penis in my mouth. – – I want to let it have an orgasm in my mouth. – – It's wonderful! – I love it! I experienced an orgasm at the time. It was complete. It was the whole thing. – – Now I have a feeling as if I'm straining and it's like an orgasm and I'm straining to get it.

**A:** What do you feel?

**P:** I want something in my mouth and in my vagina. It feels wonderful and I want to let go with my whole body. – – Now the penis is in my mouth and it's so sexual and the feeling comes to a head. Oh! ! If I ever reach it, I will. I'll go to the bathroom all over everything.

*Anxiety*

**A:** What's the detail?

**P:** It's all so good. Everything will come out! It will build up and suddenly, zoom! ! – –

**A:** You have the image that everything is going to come out. What's the detail?

**P:** – (Laughs.) – The semen is in my mouth and it came out as me. I have a feeling of letting go! I want to let go of everything! I want to go to the bathroom and I have an urge to pee all over, just squirt it out. It's the greatest sexual feeling, because it comes out of him and then it comes out of me. – – I feel as if I'm ready to climb a post, and I can't stand it because I want the orgasm so badly. Now it's all over, and all I see is a tiny penis and there's nothing and it all ends. It was so big and huge and was so explosive, and then it's gone!

*Cry,*
*Anger,*
*Anxiety,*
*Tremble*

A: Where did it go to?

P: I probably swallowed it! Oh shit! You can go to hell! I don't care ! ! I don't care! That's what I'm covering and I've been covering it the whole time. I cover the penis up and I'm surrounding it to cover it up. That's what makes me sick! I do care! I'm trying to cover it up with my body. (Elaborates.)

A: We'll stop here for today.

In this session an important new dimension of the sexually traumatic experience with the uncle began to emerge. This was the result of the previous associations in the past two sessions to the bathroom, and the equation of the penis with feces. In this material, which emerged in an intensively affective way, the patient for the first time mentioned the existence of a fantasy that she had swallowed the uncle's penis. The penis which had been so big in erection was suddenly tiny after ejaculation, and the fantasy was that it had gone and that she had destroyed it. In elaborating upon this issue, my question, "Where did it go to?" was a way of participating with her at the moment in the regressive psychic reality that this fantasy had actually occurred. The question implied that I accept this version of reality for the moment, along with the intense affects that accompany it. By encouraging her to describe the fantasy and experience the feelings, I was offering her an opportunity, for the first time since the incident occurred, to express the details of her reactions to it and to bring this previously repressed unconscious fantasy into conscious awareness where we can both discuss it. Once this fantasy and its various repercussions has become conscious to her, and as she then elaborates upon it and works it over in future sessions, the painful and distressing accompaniments can begin to subside, and ultimately the entire fantasy can be subjected to secondary process rational thought in the therapeutic alliance. Then the psychic reality of the fantasy can be corrected and the fantasy itself thus dissolved. Once dissolved, the various defenses against it, as well as the multiple derivatives and the sexual fixation accompanying it, can likewise be modified and the psychic structures established to deal with the conflicts surrounding this fantasy can then be changed.

In the next session the patient continued to elaborate on the fantasy of having eaten the uncle's penis, with the accompanying guilt and fear about it and the feeling that she had done a horrible thing. And at the same time, the experience had been exciting and stimulating for her. She elaborated on the fantasy as a child that with every bowel movement she had felt that the penis was coming out, and how with the worm infection she had felt that the penis turned into the worms.

**P:** I had a dream about my sister's twins, and it was horrible. They were like pieces of hamburger with white heads and it was all disgusting. I couldn't understand why she was so proud. I feel as if I must run. I want to get out. I'm scared! (Elaborates.) It's as if my children suddenly are nothing but monsters. *Cry*

**A:** I wonder if this might explain your fears of the Caesarean section. Could you have had a fantasy that they were going to cut you open and find a penis in there?

**P:** – I've thought about it all of my life. I always felt that if I can go to the bathroom enough, then I can get rid of this thing. I have an urge to throw up now. But there's nothing I can do. – – I hate myself. Every morning as I grew up I woke up as a bear and I'd have to face another day. It was another day of hating myself. Now I feel as if you're so innocent. If I were to love you, I'd want to. . . . . it would be so wonderful, but then I'll take your little white penis and I'll destroy it.

**A:** So it's as if all of your life you've accused yourself and felt guilty for a crime that you didn't commit. You've had the feeling that you swallowed your uncle's penis, and you can't get rid of it because it's not in there. And that's why this whole thing has persisted so long. *Cry*

**P:** I picture the thing as huge explosions, with intense sex, just like the Fourth of July. I can see his penis and I'm playing with it and it's huge and now it's in my mouth and I swallow the stuff. But the next time I looked it was gone and it was so little! It was so big and explosive. . . . .

**A:** What did you stop at?

**P:** — If I could. . . . . relive this and when it was all through have it still be hard. – – It was horrible. It was the worst thing in my life. I'm so destructive. It's the end of the world, and so sex and love and everything that is connected with it is the end of the world. – – Where in hell did that thing go? ! ! I can't figure it out! ! I'm looking and looking! (Elaborates.) – – Do all women have them? I get so depressed! – – – I wish you'd talk to me! I want you to explain this thing to me. This is why I hate my children and why they scare me. It's why I get so depressed! It's the end of the world. If I were just not married, and if I didn't have any children, then I could do it all differently.

A: It's as if you're still looking and wondering where that thing went. What comes to your mind?

P: I can't believe it, but I am. I know that it gets hard and big and that it has a skin that stretches and that this all connects with blood and then it goes away. But it's two different things. It's so hard and muscular. How can blood do that? Now I can see it again. Did he just keep it in his pocket? This is all ridiculous.

A: How do you mean?

*Cry*

P: If it's hard, then I didn't swallow it. But it's a different organ! It's not the same thing! I don't understand it. I'm convinced that it's inside of me! But it's impossible! But it's a matter of my feelings against my adult mind. Tom has explained it to me over and over, but I can't get rid of the feeling. I'm scared to death. My uncle laughed at the time and told me that I ate it, and that he gave that horrible thing to me. He wasn't upset about it, or maybe that's why everyone *was* so upset. I know my uncle was a joker but he saw my wonder and he laughed and he said, "You swallowed it." Or else he panicked, and it was like he died and I felt that it was because I had eaten his thing. – – I'm crazy. Why am I so scared? Now I hear bells in my head!

A: So it was horrifying and you felt guilty and as if you had been destructive and it was the end of the world for you. But it was also the most exciting sex that you've ever had, and I wonder if you don't have a wish to feel it again?

P: I do with you. I can hear you say, "Trust me and then I'll let you do this." Now I feel as if I'll lose my mind and regress and I'm going to do the whole thing again. But it *was* wonderful! It's just like yesterday here. I got that feeling as if it burst in me, and I can explode because I'm so happy. I can't take it! – – Now I'm convinced that this is the whole reason for my analysis, and that this is what you want me to do. And yet it means throwing every sane idea in my mind away.

A: I think this may be part of the fright. It's as if you want that pleasure so badly that you'd be willing to throw everything away in order to get it.

P: This fear is the only thing that's stopping me. (Elaborates.) – – – – Suddenly I want to talk about how exciting it was and I want absolutely to relive it. – – But the culmination of it all was the destruction of it. (Elaborates.) It was all so exciting and then, bam! It was destroyed. – – I had such a wide open feeling, and my whole body was wide open and I was so excited. – – I feel it all with you and this is what I want. I want to go through the whole thing again (Elaborates.)

**A:** We'll stop here for today.

This session is being quoted in detail because it was a crucial one in the understanding of the patient's psychopathology and in the recognition of the meaning behind many of her symptoms. Because the patient was not helped to express and explore the feelings and thoughts connected with the incident, and because of the nature of the fantasy, it was apparently repressed and therefore not accessible to reality testing and modification with growing experience and understanding. Although rationally as an adult she now knows the factual information about erection, ejaculation and detumescence, this does not influence the existence, content, or affects associated with this important unconscious fantasy.

The fantasy itself became a central organizing element in her psychic life, with multiple derivative manifestations. But these various manifestations could be tolerably controlled and managed until the specific precipitating situation of being told that her first delivery would occur by Caesarean section. This vicissitude in her life had specific associations and connections to the unconscious fantasy, with the result that the conflict previously contained now threatened to emerge from repression. In the face of this anxiety and threatened return of the repressed, the acute neurosis began.

The existence of the fantasy was also maintained by the unconscious awareness of the intensely exciting, pleasurable, and fulfilling sexual experience that was associated with it so that in spite of the unpleasure, guilt, fear, and shame that accompanied it, the fantasy was supported by the drive seeking a repetition of the gratification that had occurred with the uncle. And the maintenance of the structured defenses against the drive and its accompanying fantasy was necessary because of the conflict and unpleasurable affects associated with it.

In the fifth session of this month the patient described how, "Each time I come here I feel as if it might be a chance for me to relive that experience with my uncle. I always get excited at the thought of coming, but then I feel depressed and I know that it can't happen." The theme of the remainder of the session was her positive and sexual transference feelings, wishes, and fantasies toward me as representing the uncle, with anxiety over her wish to repeat the oral sexual experience with me. She verbalized her intense excitement and pleasure at the thought of this form of sexuality, which for her is "the ultimate," and "the greatest feeling in the world," and how surprised she is to have this feeling in her mouth also occur in her vagina.

After describing the intense pleasure that this produces for her, she indicated that "afterwards it is absolute hell," and went on to mention how reluctant she is to engage in fellatio with her husband. She spoke of the image of herself with, "that huge thing in my mouth, but then suddenly it's tiny and it will never come back." She went on to describe the guilt she continues to experience over the fantasy of having orally castrated her uncle, and of being able to do the same thing to any man. She verbalized the feeling that her father's rejection of her was based on his awareness that she might castrate him in the same way. And then she elaborated on the automatic sequence of thoughts that love for a man leads to fantasies of this type of sexual experience, which in turn means castration and destruction of the man, and therefore his hostility and rejection toward her, along with guilt and depression.

In the sixth session the patient described her recurrence of excessive eating, with the wish to become obese and unattractive as a defense against the sexual fantasies. Analysis of this defense revealed again the fear that her sexual drives and fantasies toward me in the father transference would destroy me. This led to my interpretation that she was equating her mouth and her vagina in connection with the fantasy of having eaten the uncle's penis. In response to this the patient elaborated upon the intense and active feeling of guilt for having destroyed the uncle, and eventually I was able to offer her a reconstruction of a fantasy that getting fat was equated with being pregnant, and that as a girl she must have had the fantasy that pregnancy is achieved by the woman eating and swallowing the man's penis which then becomes a baby. She confirmed this reconstruction with subsequent associations, elaborating on the feeling of pleasure at being pregnant, ". . . but when it comes out it's not mine any more, and I feel as if I've lost it." This in turn led to fantasies of her wish to acquire the penis this way, and the depressing realization that the fantasies of eating or of becoming pregnant will not result in her acquiring a penis for herself.

Ultimately her associations permitted me to point out that one of the reasons why her fantasy of having eaten the uncle's penis had persisted is that this fantasy represents her wish to acquire a penis for herself in that way. This interpretation resulted in an affective response in which she said, "That's the only reason that I've come here! It's finally dawned on me!" This was followed by a further awareness of the same wish and by her feeling, "For twenty-seven years I've been thinking that somehow I'll get a penis! And now I know that I'm not going to! I feel like hell and like the world is against me and that I got a raw deal. I hate them all!" This material was accompanied by depression and crying, and was followed by associations indicating she experienced rejection as resulting from the fact she doesn't have a penis, and that she has been "hiding" this fact from me throughout the analysis. This was followed by transference fears that now that I know about this, I too will reject her completely.

The patient experienced this material as an affective transference reaction to me, interspersed with reality-oriented perceptions of herself from the standpoint of her rational adult ego. The final effect was a meaningful step forward into the area of her phallic conflicts and feelings of phallic inferiority, along with the various derivative attempts to conceal or in other ways defend herself against these fantasies.

In the seventh session the patient continued to work on the theme of her phallic level conflict, elaborating upon past fantasies as to how she might acquire various men's penises. She went on to indicate a greater sense of openness with me, based on feelings that I now knew that she does not have a penis and that I was still accepting her in spite of it. She reported a dream in which an old house was being redecorated, and in which she felt happy because with the redecoration the house would now be beautiful and attractive. She went on to describe how she no longer had the feeling that she needed to hide things from me or needed to pretend to be anything other than what she is, and expressed positive loving feminine sexual feelings toward me.

However, this forward step was immediately followed by a return of the fantasies that to love me in a sexual way would be destructive toward me, elaborating on the fantasy that my penis going inside of her would be huge and masculine, but that following a wonderful wild orgasm, I would be nothing and my penis would have disappeared. "I can't find it! It's not in my vagina and you don't have it anymore either. Where is it? I can't see it. It must be inside of me. Something beautiful has suddenly been turned into something shitty!!" She went on to associate this to similar feelings she has experienced during sexual relations with her husband, and ended the session by indicating she was experiencing feelings toward me that she had never felt before.

In the eighth session, accompanied by intense anxiety and crying, the patient presented a series of associations indicating her childhood confusion about masturbation and sexual thoughts relating not only to her uncle but also to other older men and also to her mother. She thought of herself as having been "a sex maniac" as a child, elaborating on the confused questions she had been unable to answer for herself as a girl, and asking for reassurance that her actions and thoughts do not actually destroy men's penises. Toward the end of the session, with great affect, she shrieked at me that she had an intense desire to grab my penis and eat it. Then in a quieter and more reflective fashion she indicated that similar thoughts occurred to her with all men, and that even with her son when she changes his diaper she sometimes has the thought of putting his penis in her mouth and swallowing it. Throughout this session I said very little except for occasional questions regarding details of her associations, and occasional comments indicating her fear of pursuing her own thoughts and fantasies.

In the ninth session she described a remission of symptoms over the weekend, accompanied by significantly improved functioning and the capacity to experience pleasure during sexual relations with her husband. She went on to pick up the material from the previous week relating to her childhood sexual fantasies, including a wish to have been masturbated by her mother. This led to further expressions of her loneliness and sense of rejection as a child, with the attempt to compensate for this through attaching herself to the Jones family, and followed by a transference fantasy of attaching herself to me and becoming a part of me. Subsequently she returned to the theme of childhood masturbation, and began to recall for the first time that she had actually enjoyed masturbating as a girl. In an angry outburst she accused me of keeping her from a pleasurable and wonderful life because I don't love her without a penis, but she also began to indicate an acceptance of herself the way she is (without a penis) and to express the feeling that she could be lovable without one. Although still projecting her sense of phallic inferiority to me, her ability to oppose what she felt was my attitude toward her and to indicate her beginning acceptance of herself as a girl in the transference conflict represented a small step toward the resolution of these conflicts over her phallic wishes.

In the tenth session she continued with the theme of increasing pleasure in the thought of herself as a sexual woman pleased with her own genitals and enjoying the woman's sexual role. This led to her childhood uncertainty as to where the penis would go, and was followed by her recollection of primal scene experiences in which the mother sounded as though she were in pain, and a comparison between her mother's large vagina and her own tight "little bottom." She expressed the wish to have been involved in the primal scene, but simultaneously the fearful fantasy that the father's penis ". . . would have killed me or torn me up, and I couldn't have stood it. It's so depressing that I'm not a woman yet, and that I'm missing something."

After describing her sense of inferiority at her delayed feminine development during puberty, she went back to the fantasies of sexuality as an aggressive act in which she would destroy the man and thereby prove that he, like herself, was nothing, Eventually her associations returned to the primal scene experiences with the accompanying excitement and sexual stimulation, as well as angry resentment at having been excluded from the act. Ultimately this led to a fantasy that she could have been a better woman sexually for her father than was her mother, and this was then experienced in the transference in a similar competitive relationship to my wife. In this context she began pleasurably to experience a fantasy of herself as a warm and loving sexual woman who could be gratifying to me and also receive gratification herself in this role.

These fantasies and images of herself as pleasurably gratified and gratifying in the mature feminine role represent the new emergence within her of previously repressed fantasies from the oedipal phase of development, in which a healthier identification with the woman was beginning to occur, and in which the previous phallic fantasies were being replaced. In expressing this material she oscillated between the immediate transference feelings and fantasies toward me, and the recovery and reconstruction of the childhood oedipal relationships and fantasies.

In the eleventh session the patient continued with the theme of her anxiety over the oedipal sexual relationship. If she were to be thin and attractive she saw herself as "evil inside" with the power to seduce all men, including me. In the associated sexual fantasies she saw it as a wild, explosive, violent experience, and this was associated to a conversion reaction yesterday at home of a pain in her ear. Associations to this conversion reaction led again to the primal scene and herself lying in bed as a child listening to the noises of the parents during their sexual activity. She recalled fantasies of going into the parents' bedroom, taking the father away from the mother, and offering him all of the love, affection, and support that he would need. This was then associated to the current transference experience toward me as a father and led ultimately to fantasies of my impregnating her, at which point she would become "huge and ugly," and then she fantasied that I would leave her.

This fantasy was accompanied by intense anger toward me and represented a repetition of the experience when the father left home during the time of the mother's pregnancy with her younger sister. This fantasy was also accompanied by acute anxiety in regard to her childhood question of where the penis would go, with the fantasy that it went into the rectum, and the association of this to her experience with the worms. She elaborated on this and saw the penis as a destructive ". . . huge snake that will lie in my stomach forever and I'll never get it out," and this fantasy resulted in an acute anxiety experience. Following this there was a wish that I could be her mother, with a fantasy of regression to a loving relationship with the comforting and protective mother who would never hurt her as the father would, and with the thought to give up men, boys, and sexuality forever.

In this material she was again reliving the oedipal fantasies stimulated by the primal scene and the oedipal attachment. It involved the typical oedipal fantasies of a young girl's misinterpretation that the father was in some way harming and damaging the mother and inflicting pain upon her. Throughout this session there was relatively little self-observation, and most of the material was experienced as an immediate affectively charged series of thoughts and fantasies in the father transference relationship to me. We were uncovering some of the oedipal phase fantasies which had been repressed at the time of the childhood experience. Because they are still accompanied by intense anxiety and "dangerous" primary process implications, these fantasies have been significant in evoking and then maintaining the various defenses she has used against awareness of her sexuality and against enjoyment of it. This, in turn, has precluded her enjoyment of sexuality in the marital situation, even though consciously and rationally she "knows" the realities of adult sexual relationships.

In the twelfth session she again resumed the working-through of the oedipal conflicts, recovering more of the details of her childhood experience and fantasies. With interpretative help from me, she was able to elaborate more fully on the conscious awareness of having wanted her father sexually as a girl. Partly because she succeeded in having the uncle, she maintained the feeling that she might also be able to get the father. But at the same time, she experienced intense anxiety and guilt at the prospect of possible oedipal success.

This conflict was repeated again in the transference relationship with the experience of simultaneous desire and anxiety in regard to her sexual fantasies and drives toward me. She again brought up the separation of sexuality from love, and her identification with the father's mistresses rather than with the mother. But this time she also elaborated on the anger she felt that the father and mother would have sex even though they did not love one another or have a satisfying nonsexual relationship. She was able to recognize her hostility toward the mother for getting the father's sexual attention, as well as her hostility toward the father for giving it to the mother rather than to herself. "It would all have been all right if they had loved each other, but they had such hatred and they really were not a family. There was no affection at all between them except in the God-damned bedroom!"

This material led into a series of fantasies that the father had left the mother and the home because of the presence of the patient and her sisters, and the mother had made a decision that the children and her relationship to them came ahead of the father. At the same time she recalled childhood games of an oedipal family constellation, which she used to play with her teddy bear and dolls while in bed. This led to a further recognition of the intense dependency toward the mother, with the fantasy that if the mother were to decide that the father was more important than the children, she and her sisters would have been abandoned. She then felt as a current experience that she must make a decision between the father and the mother, voicing the question, "Will my father's penis do for me what my mother's nipples do? That's a decision which I know I have to make."

In the thirteenth session the patient continued the theme of the oedipal desires, both in the memory of her relationship to the father and in the immediate transference situation with me. At home and during the session she was consciously aware of sexual desire and arousal, which was intensely pleasurable and exciting, with increasing fantasy of herself in the role of an adult woman rather than as a nonsexual little girl. Once again she returned to the primal scene experiences, when she would lie in bed and fantasy her father leaving the mother and coming into her room for sexual activity, with the awareness that she wanted to "go wild" with him and indulge in all types of sexuality. She recognized that to experience and enjoy these types of adult sexual gratification meant to lose her mother and not be able to revert to the childlike maternal attachment. She saw this in the current scene, "If I let Tom make love to me, it's just the same thing as me committing suicide as a child."

In this context, the repetitive wish and fantasy of cutting her wrist occurred, with several meanings becoming increasingly clear. To cut her wrists with blood flowing meant on the one hand to become a woman who menstruates, but at the same time to cut her wrists would mean the death of the child within her and the loss of the attachment to the mother. Increasingly she came to recognize that she cannot have both the attachment to the mother and the sexual relationship with the father, and it became increasingly clear that she identifies her husband with the father, and that if she were to enjoy the husband (father) and relate to him in a sexual way, the mother would be angry and would get rid of her.

She felt that she must assume responsibility for control of the situation with the father and in the transference, and that if she were to "let myself go with my body" she would seduce both of us, and the transference identification of me with the father was again clear to her. Once again she became aware of how exciting and satisfying it would be to experience and enjoy this type of sexual relationship, and she elaborated in detail on the intensity of her sexual desire and the fantasy of how gratifying she thought a sexual relationship with me would be. This led to a series of associations in which "I'm thinking of myself as a bad girl and it just came to my mind why that is. I knew that I couldn't replace my mother with my father as a mother, but that I *could* do it as a mistress. There were many women who did that and so I had to identify with them." This material led again to her image of herself as "a whore" and to the needs to separate sexuality from love as a result of these conflicts. "If there had been no mistresses, then I know that I could have had all of these sexual desires and I'd know that they would not be fulfilled, so why would it be necessary to be afraid of them?" She then went on to elaborate her recognition that the wish to be a prostitute was within her, but at the same time that she could never permit herself to do this, and that what she wanted was a full, loving relationship with a man which included herself in the role of a mother with children whom she loves.

In the fourteenth session the patient described how in her symptoms and behavior at home she was converting the present family relationships into a repetition of her own childhood situation. Ultimately this material led to fantasies of stabbing her husband with a knife, which was followed by a further elaboration of the primal scene, accompanied by conscious sexual arousal in the session. This led to a set of fantasies in which she was identified with the mother and was enjoying the father sexually in the mother's place. Concurrently there were also fantasies of having a penis herself, being identified with the father, and making love to the mother as a male. I pointed out that the image of stabbing her husband with a knife had been a disguised expression of this fantasy, and this led to a further elaboration of both the positive and the negative oedipal wishes. She elaborated on the wish to love, which automatically becomes a source of anxiety because it quickly shifts to fantasies of violence and destruction, and she experienced this in the transference relationship through the continuing fantasy that her love would destroy me.

In elaborating on the fantasies of loving the mother, she regressed to the oral phase images of mother's breasts and herself nursing, and ultimately this material led to verbalization of an anxiety-producing fantasy that the mother wanted to eat her. I interpreted this material as a derivative expression of the oral triad, in which the urge to nurse and eat from mother's breasts was subsequently experienced as being eaten by the mother, with the ensuing sleep equated with death, and hence the intense anxiety and fantasies of destruction. The patient elaborated upon her awareness that there exists in her simultaneously the adult wife and mother, and also the baby who is nursing. She verbalized the fear that she would again completely revert to being the baby. In response to this I pointed out that "the adult in you wants love, knows what the reality situation is, and wants to enjoy it and participate in it. But the baby that has continued to live inside of you still thinks that to love means the same thing as to eat or be eaten by the person you love, as we just saw in the fantasies about nursing. And so this part of you that still feels like a baby and has all of the terror and destructive fantasy about it keeps the adult part from enjoying the love that you could be having."

Earlier in the session, while describing her reaction to the primal scene in an intensely affective way, the patient had said, "Now I see that door! I'm glued to it. I'm fascinated with my ears and my eyes. I want to walk in." My response was to ask what she was seeing, hearing and feeling, to which she said, "I have a sexual feeling in my vagina. It's all so wild! Now I can hear screaming and bells and all kinds of violent action going on and it's all like dying." In light of the subsequent material about the oral triad and fantasy of being eaten, her statement regarding the primal scene, "It's like dying," seemed to reflect the influence of the oral phase fantasies and conflict in the organization of the oedipal phase experiences. Sexuality was perceived as an oral-destructive experience with the consequence of death. This organization of the oedipal phase fantasies in oral terms was reinforced by the sexual experience with the uncle and the fantasy of having orally incorporated his penis, and this lends further support to the previously exposed equation of mouth with vagina. None of the material in this session was new, but in bringing it up again the patient was illustrating the process of working-through, with repetitive elaboration and reexperience of the conflict situations as an important step toward ultimate conscious ego-mastery over them.

In the fifteenth session, the patient began by expressing a greater intensity of sexual transference feelings than she had previously experienced, and went on to describe several transference dreams in which she felt herself to be a mature sexual woman who was enjoying her role. She related this shift to the material in yesterday's session in which she had to make the decision about being a woman or a baby, and then went on to elaborate on her fantasy of seducing her father if she felt herself to be a woman around him. She then went back to yesterday and the oral triad and fantasy of the devouring breast, in which she now perceived herself as an adult woman with the breast which offers love, both to men and to children, but then ends up destroying the one who loves her.

I pointed out how she still equates sleep after the nursing experience with death and destruction, and simultaneously that she equates sleep after orgasm in the same way, which she excitedly confirmed as a thought she had experienced at home yesterday. This led to further fantasies of herself as an adult who takes people she loves and puts them to her breasts, but then inadvertently ends up destroying them, and this was followed by further fantasies of herself and her husband being interrupted in their love-making by her children. She went on to elaborate upon the oedipal triangle between herself, her husband and her daughters, identifying herself both as the hostile parent and the child. In this relationship she felt herself to be both the mother who can easily attract her husband's attention through her sexuality, and also the child who is thus excluded from this experience by the sexually more capable mother. "I should accept the fact that that's the way life is and that fathers shouldn't seduce their daughters. And yet I resent it so much! I'm still trying to get it and I shouldn't be!"

This material led to a further elaboration of the childhood feelings of competition with her mother for the interest and affections of the father, and an elaboration of the fantasy that the mother was afraid of the patient and her attachment to the father, and therefore the mother encouraged the girls to criticize, hate, and depreciate the father. "That's just the same way that I feel with you. I can never have you as a nice gentle loving woman, and so I must either fix myself up as a prostitute or else I have to forget it. That makes me *hate* so much!"

Once again none of the material in this session was particularly new, but it was affectively charged and its expression reflected the repetition of the traumatic and conflict-laden material as part of the working-through process.

In the last session of the month, the patient returned to the conflict within herself between being a woman and being a child, and then went on to say that she had experienced an intensely gratifying and free orgasm with her husband during intercourse last night, which for her was a new type of experience. As the act had begun, she again had the feeling of being a little girl standing in the hall outside of her parents' door, "but suddenly I'm doing what I want to do so badly, and yet at the same time

I'm saying to myself, 'No, you shouldn't do this because you're just a girl so you can't do that.'" In response to a question, the patient went on to describe new vaginal sensations that she had never before been aware of, and a definite feeling of wanting to have the penis inside herself with the thought that "I'm not going to take it and so it's all right to let go." She described the sensation in her vagina of clamping down on the penis, and how this was something she had wanted to do in the past but, "Before this, I've always been afraid to open myself up and to let him in." "I was always afraid before that I'd take his penis off, but last night I felt so open, so I could enjoy it and I didn't have to worry about this thing any more."

However, following the orgasm she had experienced a recurrence of anxiety, and associations to this led again to the oedipal situation with a recurrence of fantasies of chewing her father's penis, since hostility and hate "always comes with love." This led to the transference situation and her feelings about my wife, who is in her way since the love and gentleness that I can offer go to my wife and not to her. She elaborated further that since I was married, the only role she could have was to be my mistress, expressing intense anger that she could never experience this part of me. Ultimately this led back to the often-asked question of whether she might actually successfully seduce me if she tried hard enough, with the continuing fantasy that she could do so. "I lose track of who you are, and I actually think that you're my father sitting there in that chair."

This material illustrates that in the working-through process and in the father transference she was beginning simultaneously to experience sexual desire, love, and the wish for a warm, gentle, kind relationship. In other words, there was a beginning fusion of love and sexuality toward the same object, a step in psychological development that she was unable to make in the original oedipal situation because of the conflicts, anxiety, and fantasies of oedipal victory. In the safety of the analytic situation, where the therapeutic alliance reassured her that there would be no overt sexual seduction between us, she was now able to reexperience this oedipal phase conflict in consciousness, so that love and sexuality may ultimately be fused. As part of the working-through process and the elaboration of these conflicts in the analytic situation, she was somewhat freer at home with her husband, and therefore was able for the first time last night to experience a real sexual gratification with him. This behavioral step forward was an important one, but the occurrence of anxiety immediately afterward indicated that the conflicts which had prevented this step in the past had still not been resolved.

# 7

## THE THIRTEENTH MONTH

P: When I'm away from you I feel just as though you *are* my father. It's always such a shock to see you and to realize that you *aren't*. I was hating you all of this weekend. I kept thinking about my father and his mistresses, and I did nothing but eat this weekend. (Elaborates.) – – If I could just lose weight and be beautiful the way I know I can, and be an attractive woman, then I know it would all be possible. And yet I just go ahead and eat! I'm so mad at you! It's all your fault that I have to eat! You just don't understand anything!

A: How do you mean?

P: – I hadn't really thought about that, but there is so much going on. There is such a hurricane of feelings for you, and you just sit there and you don't know about it.

A: I think what you are saying is that what you feel I don't understand is that if you were to lose weight and become a beautiful and attractive woman, then I'll be automatically seduced by you and a whole hurricane of feelings will be loosed and we will both be destroyed.

P: I don't see how you can say that you understand this.

A: I think you may be wondering how I can possibly stay calm and why it is that I'm not as scared of these feelings as you are.

P: – – I have the feeling that you're pushing me to be a woman and to let myself be attractive and be free with my feelings and that you're not going to even look at me until I am. You just don't realize that I can't! You want perfection from me and yet it's just *because* of you that I can't be perfect. My father and I used to meet so often about this business of dieting.

A: What was the detail of that?

P: He's so conscious about my weight. (Elaborates.) He used to talk to me and try to reason with me and try to encourage me to go on a diet and want me to lose weight. – – My father is so *many* people for me. I love him for this side of the way he is but I could *hate* him about all the mistresses. But when we used to talk I always felt that he was such a

306

different person and that he really understood me. --- I don't want anything to do with you! --- I had a dream on Thursday. It took place in a
basement and there was a mirror there. I had no clothes on and I was
dancing around and admiring my body. Then there was some noise behind
a bunch of boxes and I went upstairs. Bill, our old yardman, was there and
he was looking up at me. He had tears in his eyes. --- I don't understand
all of this! Now I'm thinking about my uncle and the time that my grandmother talked with him. He had tears in his eyes.

*Cry*

**A:** What do you remember about your grandmother talking with him?

**P:** She was bawling him out and she was telling him that he could
never use the car again, and all I can think of now are his tears! I want to
talk about something else!

**A:** I think you are trying to hold something back here.

**P:** --- Why am I so afraid to be an attractive woman? (Elaborates.)

**A:** Let's look at the details of the fear of what would happen with me
if you were?

**P:** I feel as if you are completely helpless. You just can't understand.
(Elaborates.) You're fine and strong and mature just as long as you're not
tested. But I know that you couldn't stand up to my test and that you'd
be a man and you'd give in and be helpless in front of a woman. I've
watched my father with all of the other women. He's very tough with me
but he's a complete child with women. He tries to get their attention and
to flatter them and to get them to notice him and be attracted to him.
Men are such fools! They're all so weak! That's true about my uncle and
my father and every man I ever knew. I have such a fear that you will be that
way! You may not be now but I know that you'll change! --- You're so
ignorant not to realize all of this, and so I have to hide behind being fat
and ugly and I have to be miserable just because you're so weak. But also
I just can't give in and be a big fat mother. It's like I'm two people and
there's a push and pull going on inside of me and I feel as if I am going to
rip apart. This is such a thing with me! Why do I worry about it? If I do
give in and if I start dieting I know that I'll try to seduce you. But I can't
stand to be it.

**A:** Which way do you mean?

**P:** I can't stand to be the bitch. To me it's the same thing as death,
and it would be like killing myself.

**A:** You saw yourself dancing and looking in the mirror and admiring
your body in the dream. What comes to your mind about that?

**P:** It's just like the situation here. I know that I want to have you look
at me with my clothes off. I have the feeling that the reason Bill had the

tears in his eyes is because I don't have a penis. And yet that's so silly! In the mirror I had just discovered how beautiful my body was without a penis. –– And yet I felt that I took my uncle's penis away. That's what I'm going to do to Bill by looking beautiful. It's as if I took his penis. If only I could say that *all* men are weak, then I could be a bitch and I could castrate every one of them! Then I wouldn't care. Why am I trying to protect you? What difference does it all make? ––– A man is the most important thing in my life and yet I feel that I can't be a whore. But I *need* a man and I think about you. I think about marriage and having children and that's why I can't go ahead and just not care about it. –– You can understand me just as long as I keep this relationship of a child who is needing help. But if I ever become a woman who doesn't need help . . . . . –

**A:** You stopped in the middle of a sentence. What were you thinking?

**P:** Then you've *had* it. Then you would not be the strong and understanding father. ––– Now I think about all of the men that I've seduced. They were all weak. There were others who would also admire me, but I wonder if I *could* seduce them and take them away from their wives. I can't see how *you* could be just one man in the world and could be the only one who is different. (Elaborates.) I want you to tell me, "Yes, you're attractive but I'm not going to make love to you because I have a wife of my own and I love her." ––– This has not been a question about you so far. But it's a matter of how much of the woman inside of me will I let out in order to be able to seduce you.

**A:** You mentioned earlier that I'm fine and mature and all right up to now, but that you've really not put me to the test yet.

**P:** I'd like to! You don't know how much I'd like to. I'd like to see how far I could go! I wonder if I should do it to my friends first? This is all so ridiculous! ––– I always feel that if a man looks at me I can seduce him. Now I'm beginning to wonder if that's true. –––– Feeling that I'm able to seduce men is a need that I have to have also, so it's not only a fear. I keep throwing my uncle at myself! That's because my father ignored me!

**A:** And I think that's part of the wish you have here. The wish is that you and I would talk about your weight and your diet and whether or not you are attractive and so on, and that I would be as concerned about all of this as your father was, and that you could repeat with me some of those interactions that you had with your father.

**P:** That's the only time that I could remember that he showed any interest in me and showed that he was concerned about me and my welfare. (Elaborates.)

**A:** We'll stop here for today.

At the door the analyst presents the patient with the bill for the previous month's sessions.

## DISCUSSION

The patient's initial comments show the intensity of regression in the father transference, and she goes on to indicate a connection between her thoughts about the father and her symptom of excessive eating. She describes the overeating, which interferes with her sexual attractiveness and thus makes acting on the oedipal seductive wishes less possible, and at the same time she projects the responsibility for this behavior to me. After she alludes to the intensity of these transference drives and conflicts, I interpret the defensive implications of her weight gain and the anxiety mobilized by her fantasy of seducing me in the transference if she were to lose weight and become more attractive.

My interpretation that she cannot accept my lack of anxiety about her sexual transference feelings represents an empathic response to her statement that I do not understand the intensity of her conflict, but it also serves to reemphasize my role in the therapeutic alliance. This is followed by the recurrent transference projection that I am responsible for her fear of permitting herself a free range of feeling, and then by a specific reference to a type of interaction that had occurred between her father and herself. I ask for the detail of her contacts with father around the issues of dieting in order to encourage her to elaborate upon that element of their relationship and the feelings she had in response to his interest in her. These positive feelings are immediately replaced by a defensive transference response to me, but then are followed by the dream of the yardman with its associations to the sexual seduction of and by the uncle, and his punishment by the grandmother.

There is still a need for further recall and elaboration of that experience, and my question regarding the grandmother is an attempt to foster the recovery of this memory. The uncle's response about the use of the car may have a symbolic connection to the patient's fantasy of having castrated him, inasmuch as a car frequently represents a phallic symbol in the primary process. However, she immediately indicates her anxiety and reluctance to pursue it further, and my attempt to encourage her to overcome the resistance is ineffective.

This last interchange is an indication that at present the resistances against further exploration of the traumatic incident with the uncle are very intense, and therefore it is probably pointless at this time to try to pursue it directly any further. After she reverts to her question about being an attractive woman, I therefore choose to explore this by again focusing her associations into the immediate transference experience which had been alluded to earlier in the session, and which in all likelihood will provide us with a more emotionally meaningful exploration of this issue.

Once again she responds to me as if I were the father and the uncle, indicating how this response has been the prototype of subsequent experience and fantasies with other men as well. And she further indicates that the fantasy of testing me sexually has still not been resolved, in spite of the many times it has come up throughout the course of the analysis. She also indicates that her fantasy of me as sexually weak and seducible stimulates her use of her symptom of excessive eating ". . . to hide behind being fat and ugly. . . ." She goes on to elaborate indirectly upon her conflict over identification with the mother or with "the bitch."

My aim is to help her begin to accept her womanly attractiveness as a more ego-syntonic characteristic and to try to help her disassociate physical attractiveness from an identification with the father's mistresses and being the bitch. It is for this reason that I return to the element in the dream in which she is admiring her body. Her immediate association is again to the transference, and a reference to the continuing conflict over phallic inferiority. However she once again then attempts the significant step toward maturity when she says, "In the mirror I had just discovered how beautiful my body was without a penis." But this progress is short-lived and there is a recurrence of conflict over phallic strivings, with fantasies of seducing and castrating all men if she permits herself the identity of an attractive sexual woman.

However, there is a beginning differentiation of me from other men, expressed in the fantasy of my telling her that she is attractive but that I will not seduce her because of my love for my wife. This is the type of real experience which would have been helpful as a child, had her father directly or indirectly behaved in this way at the time of the original oedipal conflict. To provide her with this type of reassurance in the analysis might make her significantly less anxious and more comfortable with me for the moment, but such overt reassurance in the transference would tend to reduce the intensity of the conflict that is being mobilized, and therefore in

the long run would interfere with its further emergence and ultimate resolution. The most effective and complete resolution of this conflict will
occur when the patient analyzes and resolves it on her own without active
reassurance from me.

Therefore, rather than offer the kind of reassurance she is seeking, I
attempt to stimulate the clearer emergence of the oedipal conflict by focusing her attention on the issue that she feels has not yet fully tested me in
this sexual role. Following her elaboration on the desire to test me sexually,
she takes another brief step forward by beginning to recognize the unreality
of her fantasies of being infinitely attractive to all men, as she says, "I
always feel that if a man looks at me I can seduce him. Now I'm beginning to wonder if that's true." And following the silence, she goes a step
further by recognizing that the fantasy of being able to seduce all men
comes from within herself, and by reducing the intensity of the projective
mechanisms she has used in the past to blame the men for this conflict.
This leads to a growing recognition that her father actually did not seduce
her and that therefore she displaced the oedipal wish into the acting-out
with the uncle.

My aim at this point is to help her recognize further that she has used
fantasies of sexual seduction, projected to the father and to other men,
partly as a defense against other positive elements and experiences in her
relationships to them, and that her image of the father as totally committed to sexual seduction reflects a projection to him of her own oedipal
fantasies. It is for this reason that I emphasize the current transference
wish to repeat with me some of the nonsexual components of the relationship to the father, expressed also in her eating symptom over the weekend.
This results in a confirmation of the father's interest, at least to some extent, in her and in her welfare.

This last interchange about the father, the positive feelings toward
him, and his functioning in a fatherly way is similar to some of the other
small steps forward she has taken during this session. These are still highly
tentative, transient, and uncertain, but they reflect a beginning change as
a result of the repetitive working-through that has been occurring in the
analysis. These small steps forward are indicators that the previous "structured" responses to the father and to the fantasies about him are beginning
to become less automatic and stereotyped, and they are being subjected to
greater reality-testing and secondary-process reasoning. She is slowly increasing her conscious mastery over the various oedipal fantasies, both in
terms of the recalled relationship to the father (uncle) and the immediate
transference experiences with me, and as a result the old structured and

automatic responses are beginning to be dissolved. This process of dissolution of these old fantasies and "structures" will have to continue much more extensively, but the anticipation is that ultimately out of the elements of these old reactions and out of the further recall of the realities of the childhood situation, new and more realistically appropriate "structures" will be synthesized.

---

### SESSION 176

Patient hands the analyst the check for the previous month's bill as she enters the room.

**P:** Every night that Tom works I have all kinds of thoughts about killing myself. I know that I don't want to do it and yet I'm afraid that I'll do it. I always have the feeling that no one cares. I felt that you were mad and disgusted with me on Monday. A lot of my friends are leaving and my Mother hasn't written to me and Jean hasn't called. All kinds of things are piling up. I have the feeling that it has to do with my father's affairs.

**A:** You felt that I was mad and disgusted with you on Monday. What was the detail of that?

**P:** I felt that you were giving up on me and that you were saying, "Ugh. To hell with her." It was nothing that you or I said, it was just a feeling I had. I felt as if everyone is pushing me off and as if I'm dirty and no good. I'm also afraid that Tom is going to be tired about spending the money on the analysis. (Elaborates.) I feel as if I'm completely *alone* and that I have no one and that I must stand up all by myself and I can't do it. I have three kids and I have a life that could be full of happiness and I really can't stand the idea about killing myself, but I feel desperate.

*Cry*

**A:** What are your associations to the thought about killing yourself?

**P:** Why is it that I never did it before? I know it has to do with my father and my mother and my father's affairs. I'm very little and I just sit here and I have to be the brunt of all of that stuff. And I feel like I'll explode because I feel so violent.

**A:** What's the detail?

**P:** I'm mad!! It seems as though I must sit by and just watch everything. I'd like to kill my parents and to stab both of them but that makes me so scared because I know that if I did it I'd die, and so I am going to kill myself instead. And yet I am so afraid of death. I plunge into it but

I'm so scared of it. I'm so scared that everyone will leave me. I feel all *Anger*
pent up inside and that I must break loose but I know there's such fear
and hate in me and I'm scared to let it out.

**A:** You say you feel that you have to just sit and watch everything that
is going on and that you're so mad about it. What are your associations?

**P:** I'm so mad at you but I know that you can't take it.

**A:** What's the detail of the thought?

**P:** You just don't understand any of this, and you don't give me anything and you don't help me. I want to break loose but I can't because I'm
so afraid. – – And yet all last night I felt that I wanted to put my arms out
and love you but I can't. – – I can't. I'm so afraid that you. . . . . that you
won't help me. I know there's something that I want to get out. Is it love?
Is it hate?

**A:** I think it's probably both.

**P:** – I feel that I need you and I'm so desperate but I'm so afraid that
I won't get it.

**A:** You have the feeling that you love me and need me and that you
want to put your arms out to me. But then there's a feeling of rage and
hate that I don't love you in the same way or don't respond to you the way
you want me to. But then there is a fear of expressing this rage because
the fantasy is that if you ever do you'll kill any chance of me ever loving
you.

**P:** Now I feel so mad!!! I just start to feel it but what's the use. *Rage*

**A:** How do you mean?

**P:** My father has left me and my mother won't have me. She hates me
and so I have to go to Mrs. Jones or my grandmother. – – I'd like to tell
my parents that I hate them. – –

**A:** I think you want to tell me how much you hate me too. What
comes to your mind about that?

**P:** – I don't know how you will react if I do! But it would be just like
stabbing you. What good would it really do? Because I need you so much
it means that I would also be killing myself. I hate you and yet I know
that I need you so desperately.

**A:** What's the detail of your picture of what I would do and how I
would react if you expressed this?

**P:** You'd be just like Harris and you'd sit there with that terribly surprised look! You'd be just like my mother and be so afraid of me! – –
You'd get mad at me and then you'd say, "No, I never loved you and I
never will. I don't care if you do die and I wish you would." – – I can't
imagine you ever saying something like. . . . saying, "There's really nothing

to be afraid of and I do love you and I'm willing to help you and I'm strong and I know that everything will be all right."

**A:** So I think we can see that you're repeating with me the same rage that you felt toward your father when you were a little girl. Let's try to analyze your fear of expressing it here in words and feelings.

**P:** I can get as far as the image of standing up and screaming and screaming at you. I really can't convince myself that you'll get mad.

**A:** What's the detail of that?

**P:** I'm thinking about all of my father's affairs and I'm wondering if I'd let him know how I felt and how I hated it and how I hated him for it, would it have made any difference? I see my father as a person who is seeking love and that my mother was not able to give it to him. But it was such a desire with me and it makes my mouth water to even think about it. I think that I could have. . . . . taken him away from my mother and I could have had him devote his whole life to me because I loved him so much. Under all of his brusqueness and everything else he was really just a little boy. – – I feel as if I need your help so desperately but it's all so

*Cry* confusing to me. – – This is such a touchy subject. You're incapable of handling any of this just like my father was. In my childhood when I felt all of this I ran away and my father just left me. If I ever dove in and showed all of this emotion. . . . . I know that you can't stand up and that you'll fall apart.

**A:** How do you feel that I'll fall apart?

**P:** I know that you'll just *eat* me and you'll suck me up! I want a little bit but I don't want to be eaten up. You'll say to me, "You poor thing, I love you and I want to give you anything that you want. It will just be us two forever and we'll die together and so we might as well kill ourselves." That's what would happen. I know you are so weak! *I* have to be the strong one and I'm *not*.

**A:** So the fantasy is that I'm just like your father and that I'll be helpless both about your love and your hate. And the final result is that I'll be destroyed and you'll be destroyed, either way.

**P:** – – I had a dream that I was swimming and I was having my period. There was a lot of blood on my hair and I felt something on my hand. First I thought it was a shark but then it turned out that there was a penis in that water and that was why I felt that I can't dive in. – – –

**A:** I think the fantasy was that you can take your father away from your mother and that way you can have his penis for yourself. And so you have the same fantasy about me with the idea of taking me away from my wife and having *my* penis for yourself.

**P:** – – If I could just separate you and my father. I keep telling my-self, "It's not that way with Dr. Dewald." But then I always think about my father and I lose it. If I can convince myself that my father would never give in to me, then I know I'll be all right. – – – Now I have an im-pulse to cut my wrists. I've got such a feeling in my vagina and clitoris right now and it's as if I have a penis in it and I feel as if I'll have an orgasm. – – Now I'm so mad at you.

**A:** Let's look at the details of both sets of feelings. Both the sexual feelings and also the feeling of being mad.

**P:** It's a feeling in my vagina and then I think of you as a God-damned bastard! *Cry, Fury*

**A:** That sequence of thoughts from having the feeling in your vagina to thinking of me as a bastard means that the connecting thoughts have been left out. What comes to your mind about them?

**P:** That's what I'd think if you *did* make love to me. I know that I'd hate you forever. Just like with my father. He's so weak and he'll do any-thing for a hole to put his God-damned fucking penis in. This makes me so mad! I want to explode! I want to take the God-damned penis and tear it up! I want to do it to yours! Weak God-damned penises is all that you both are. – – – That's the way I feel about Tom when he works at the office and has conferences with his women clients. I think to myself, "You'll do anything to get your God-damned hands in a vagina. It's just like a baby sucking. That's all that you can think about." – – – – You're going to cut me off now just like my mother would. I want to cut my wrists so that you can't come and slobber over here. *Fury*

**A:** How do you mean?

**P:** I know that you are going to say, "Get out." I'd rather have you do that than have you say, "You sweet thing, I really love you so let's have intercourse." – – – It's all a devious way of getting it done anyway. – –

**A:** What's the detail of the thought?

**P:** If instead of my telling you that I love you, I were to go home and cut my wrists then I'll get your sympathy and love that way. I have one huge sense of anger and it's either that I have to cut my wrists or else to direct it at you. – –

**A:** And what's the fear of directing it at me?

**P:** Because you're so weak that you can't take it and you'll cry. Or else you'll love me and pamper me and then I'll take you away from my mother. –

**A:** We'll stop here for today.

### DISCUSSION

The patient begins by referring to a sense of loneliness and depression she has experienced since the previous session, and refers to a feeling that I was "mad and disgusted" with her then. I don't understand the origins of this transference fantasy (I was actually rather pleased with her progress last session), and therefore I focus her attention upon it.

This leads to an elaboration of her sense of depression, which may have been a response to the fact that in the previous session she was beginning to decrease her use of projection as a defense mechanism. As the result of a slightly greater acceptance that the sexual fantasies and drives originate within herself, her sense of guilt over them is less well defended against, and therefore becomes more conscious. As this material is emerging, the affective response begins to intensify and eventually this leads to the expression of her own sense of outrage at both parents. It is this resentment that she has projected to me in the transference following the last session and again today.

She goes on to a further elaboration of the hostile fantasies toward both parents, but accompanied by fear of being abandoned by the love objects if she were to express it, and therefore she defensively turns the aggression inward in the fantasy of killing herself.

As she continues to experience the anger towards the parents, it shifts into the transference, which I finally attempt to summarize for her as a response to the frustration of the oedipal wishes, adding the element of her defense against expressing the hostility directly. This leads to a further intensification of the hostility, which now is expressed directly as hate toward me and then again toward the parents.

I want to bring this back into the immediate transference situation and therefore interpret her wish to tell me that she hates me. This leads to her intense fear that to do so would be destructive toward me, as she feels it was toward others in the past, and would ultimately result in my rejection of her. However, the self-observing ego and the therapeutic alliance make it possible for her to take slight distance from this immediate fear as she says, "I really can't convince myself that you'll get mad."

Having thus been somewhat reassured by her own observations in the current situation, she then is able to return to the oedipal attachments and to elaborate on how she withheld any expression of her anger and resentment toward the father. With mounting affect she continues in the expression of the positive oedipal wish to love the father, and then immediately re-experiences this conflict in the transference as she sees me incapable of tolerating her feelings, and the psychic reality for her is that she herself must maintain control of the oedipal relationship lest something disastrous happen. This is indirectly expressed in the reporting of the dream of the shark and the penis.

After I summarize this material by interpreting the current transference oedipal conflict and the various fears of it, the patient attempts to apply her adult secondary process reasoning to the issue of separating me from the father, and then retroactively she is able to say, "If I can convince myself that my father would never give in to me, then I know I'll be all right." This represents a more realistic perception of the father in the actual oedipal relationship, since even though the father may have been sexually provocative and even though he had a number of sexual affairs with other women, it is highly unlikely that he would ever have actually participated in an overt sexual seduction of the patient. Likewise, the reality is that the patient, despite her wishes to do so, was not equipped to provide the father with the kind of love that he needed and therefore it is unlikely that he would have turned to her for this.

At this point she experiences sexual arousal and excitement in the analytic situation, followed immediately by the intense hostility which she feels toward me. With intense fury, she expresses the rage and wish to castrate both father and me, and goes on to indicate a similar displacement of affect toward her husband. Ultimately this material leads to the awareness that whether I (father) reject her or succumb to her wishes, she is in an intolerable conflict either way. In the course of this she also indicates how her aggression is directed either toward herself, by cutting her wrists, or outwardly toward me in the transference.

This is an active session in which the process of working-through the oedipal ties, and the responses to the various conflicts involved in them, is going on in an effective and progressive way. The conscious awareness of the intensity of both her sexual and aggressive drives is increasing, and these drives are being experienced and expressed to a greater extent than previously in the analysis. This awareness is a necessary stage toward ultimate resolution and mastery over the effects of these conflicts.

---

## SESSION 177

P: – – – The minute I saw you this morning I felt as if I adore you, and as if you're really all masculine. But then I felt, "That's all wrong and you really don't feel this." Now I'm thinking about your chair and I'm comparing it to my father's chair at home. I think about you sitting in it and I think about my love for you and then suddenly I realize that I'll never have you and you don't care two cents about me and so I *hate* you. Whenever I love like this I begin to hate because it's just not worth it. – – Now I have the urge to cut my wrists again, and I know that I must work it through. I'm thinking about the razor blades at home.

**A:** The feeling is that you love me and I don't respond the way you want me to and so it all turns to hate and then you want to hurt yourself. What are your associations to all of this?

**P:** Yesterday I felt very good as I left here. I had a real feeling of love for Tom and for the children, and I felt excited. I felt it this morning too but then I realized that I was afraid of it. In my dreams last night it seemed like just the opposite. Carol and Thomas were sleeping in the same room. They kept waking each other up and so I felt such anger at both of them. Then there was someone out there who was going to take Sally away. – – It was a man and he seemed very tall. He wanted me to be feminine. I was wearing a pink robe and he said, "I love you in it." I had some sexual feelings and I also felt as if I loved the baby and the other children. It was all a wonderful feeling and yet I got so scared. – – – I really saw you when I came in just now and I love your coat and the shirt you are wearing. I also love your chair and that desk over there. This is all so silly! And yet I feel so hampered with all this hate. I feel as if I looked at my father from a great distance every day. I loved him and I thought he was so tall. I loved his pajamas and his chair and his pipes. But I was never able to communicate this feeling and it's all stayed locked up inside of me. I wonder what would have happened if I'd sat on my father's lap and loved him? He'd have loved me back! He got *nothing* at home. My mother always used to want to turn us against him and she would always say what a monster he was. If he'd gotten *any* love, would he maybe have stayed at home? Either from my mother or from me? He would have given all of his love to me. My mother gave him nothing. I know we'd have had an affair! And so instead I let my father go off to those other women *Cry* and I hated him for it. – – I realize that suddenly I'm blaming myself for my father's affairs. – – I wonder if you're the type of man who would go around having affairs. That idea makes me sick to my stomach. – – How does a woman love? How does a girl ever learn to love without being overwhelmed? I feel as if it's impossible to be a woman and to love a man in a good right way. – – I'm just a child and my mother and father have these children and that's what drove my father away. So it's all *my* fault. Now I feel a terrific hostility towards my mother and I feel as if it's all her fault! -- And now I just feel sorry for myself. I was never able to run to my father and grab him and to feel any sense of love. I never got anything from my father. I just sat back and felt bad and sorry for myself. And I felt such hate, but I had reason to. I have so much reason to feel that. (Elaborates.) But I never expressed *any* hostility towards my father. I always directed it towards my mother and my sister. Why was it that I never got mad at my father? It's just like when I'm here, and when I get mad at you I just swallow it.

A: This is like what you were saying here yesterday. You had the feeling that if you ever got mad at me that I couldn't take it. What are your associations to this?

P: I'm thinking about yesterday. . . . . and you don't know how mad I could get. (Elaborates.) I feel as if everything would break loose and my body is racing and my muscles are all tense and I'm all tight. - - -

A: You stopped the fantasy right there, and you seem afraid to pursue it and see what comes to your mind.

P: – It all seems so oral. I know that I eat it and that makes me think about my mother's breasts and the thought of eating them, but that also gives me a sexual feeling. But it all means death. -- Any thoughts about my anger always ends in death.

A: Those ideas are rather general and vague and I think they're a defense against a specific fantasy about what would happen between you and me if you were to express these feelings. What are your associations?

P: It always ends in intercourse! --

A: How do you mean?

P: I always destroy you by becoming a whore. -- I feel as if I'll get so mad that I don't care if I destroy you. I *want* to. But then I think about the after-effects! And then I know that I'm not going to survive. It's just like my daughter and the fantasy that I had once about the shotgun. -- I'm afraid that I'll be so mad that I won't care, but then I'll *die* afterwards. (Elaborates.) It's just the same thing as with a baby. I get so mad at you! That you'd *let* me destroy you and that you are not going to be strong enough to take it. -- I know that I'd be just like a small child and that I'd yell and scream and explode with my thoughts. --

*Cry*

A: And then what?

P: – Oh! Then you'd die because of my horrible thoughts. That's why I can't let it out. But I want to.

A: And what would you let out if you could?

P: I have a hopeless feeling that you don't care and that it all would make no difference. And I want a result.

A: So we can see that your thought that I'd be weak and destroyed and unable to tolerate your anger really represents a defense against your own sense of helplessness and your own feelings of being weak.

P: When you say that it makes me want to kill you! You reduce me to just being a baby! I'm nothing but a mouth! I want to eat you! I want to eat you up! I hate you for making me *feel* so weak and helpless! – – I'm *not* and I know I can destroy you.

A: What's the fantasy?

*Cry*

P: I know that as a woman I can destroy you. You turn my every love feeling into hate! (Elaborates.) I'm in a terrible fix. You're both my mother and my father! If I wish that my father would die. . . . . it keeps alternating. First I want my mother out of the picture, and then I want my father out. I could kill you and I wish that you would die right now! I hate you! – – And then I'd die because I know that I'm helpless. And the more helpless I feel, the madder I feel. I want to stand here and just give you hell!

A: What's the detail?

P: I feel as if I'd die and that scares me. I can't imagine ever being mad here and then just walking out and being able to function and being able to return. It's like the end of the world and everyone dies. I know that these are all just excuses for me not to be mad. I am mad! But I'm afraid and I know that I can't live without you. – – Now I'm feeling how helpless I am and I feel as if you're going to push me out of the nest. But I can't do it. I'm not capable. You're just like my father and you're telling me, "Be a big girl." (Elaborates.) He'd always get disgusted if I'd ever act like a baby. It makes me so mad! Now the idea of wanting to cut my wrists comes to my mind! – – But then I get that sexual feeling every time! Now I want to be a tough woman and I want to tell you, "Come on over here and I'll screw you and I'll destroy you that way." I know I could.

A: I wonder if your thought about cutting your wrists may represent a way of telling me that you are a woman and the blood from your wrists would represent your menstrual period.

P: I know that I could be so destructive as a woman and that I could destroy you! These ideas always come to my mind whenever I feel like a woman.

A: We'll stop here for today.

### Discussion

The patient begins with a reference to the on-going oedipal transference, both in terms of the underlying positive attachment as well as the feelings of anger at its frustration. After the brief silence her associations lead to the fantasies of cutting her wrists, and because I feel it necessary to develop both sides of this transference conflict more extensively, I choose to rephrase her feelings and thereby confront her with both elements of the current conflict. Initially she indicates the awareness of a transient shift in her feelings, with an intensification of positive and loving responses both toward me and toward her family after yesterday's session, but she also demonstrates how, in an apparently paradoxical fashion, these positive, warm, and loving feelings also evoke fear and anxiety.

Her statement, "I really saw you when I came in just now. . .," is a reflection of both the therapeutic alliance in which she is beginning more appropriately to differentiate me from the father, and a decrease in her transference inhibition about looking at me with an increased conscious awareness. Associations from the transference lead to similar perceptions and inhibitions in regard to the father in the original oedipal situation, as well as a description of the repression of feeling and fantasy that had occurred during the oedipal phase, when she says ". . . it's all stayed locked up inside of me."

From there she goes on to elaborate about the oedipal wishes and the competitive situation with her mother, as well as her fantasies of magical omnipotence as a child (repressed ever since) that she did have the necessary qualities to change her father and make him happy. The guilt expressed when she says, "I'm blaming myself for my father's affairs," is actually a defense against perception and acceptance of the reality as a child that she was only a small girl who was helpless to influence significantly the events in regard to her parents. The implication of this is that there has been a denial through fantasy, in which the feeling is that she is attractive and capable enough as a sexual object for the father. This fantasy represents the defense against the full recognition of her feminine and sexual immaturity in that situation. Once again there is a return to the perception of me as the father, and the expression of similar defenses against hostility toward me as occurred in the relationship with him.

Because the issue of expression of aggression had come up yesterday and been incompletely analyzed, and because her associations again lead to this same conflict today, my immediate aim is to explore both the aggression and the various defenses against it further. It is for this reason that I focus her attention to her defenses against expressing aggression in the transference, and this leads to the resistances of breaking her fantasy off without completing it, and then of using vague and general concepts to avoid more specific imagery. After expressing the fantasies of the destructive potential of her aggression, and dealing with several of her resistances after my specific questions and requests for associations, the patient finally expresses the feeling that this situation seems hopeless for her, ". . . and that it all would make no difference. And I want a result."

In this material the patient is indicating her use of the same defense of denial through fantasy that was described earlier in regard to the positive oedipal attachment and wishes. The fantasy that her rage and hostility are so powerful that they will destroy me and make me fall apart actually serves as a defense against the recognition that even if she were to become verbally hostile and aggressive toward me, she would not significantly influence my behavior and that she would therefore have to face the awareness of a sense of helplessness. It is this understanding that I try to convey to her in my interpretation regarding her fantasies of the effects of her aggression. When this defense against awareness of the helplessness is challenged, and the patient begins to confront her own image of herself as helpless, the response is an intensification of the aggression as well as anger and resentment at me for having forced her to face this unpleasant reality of herself as no longer omnipotent. She attempts to protest that she is not helpless, and returns to the fantasy either of destroying me through her aggression or through her role as a woman sexually, but ultimately she is able to begin to recognize the transference feeling of helplessness and to see how the helplessness evokes further feelings of aggression.

However, this recognition gives way shortly to a recurrence of the oedipal fantasy accompanied by a sexual feeling that she wants to be a "tough woman" and destroy me sexually. My interpretation that cutting her wrists represents menstruation is a response to the immediate juxtaposition of cutting her wrists and the sexual fantasy, and this in turn is a repetition of a similar sequence of associations which had occurred at the very beginning of the session. It is an intuitive response to the patient's material which was not sufficiently considered prior to making the interpretation. Although it may have been ultimately correct in terms of the associations regarding the blood, it is somewhat apart from the main theme of the session and therefore out of context from the current material. Her response ignores the intervention I have just made, and suggests that it was not correct but also it has apparently done no particular harm. This is not infrequently the case with incorrect interpretations when an analysis is going well, and often patients merely continue to associate on their own as if the intervention had not occurred.

---

## SESSION 178

**P:** I had a dream last night that I was at a party which was going on in Atlanta and that I was trying to get Tom to go home. I wanted to go to sleep but he wouldn't come with me and then I was running around with a huge butcher knife. Then I was being chased by someone and I was in a car and so I locked the doors and suddenly Tom wanted to get in with me. Then I was with a woman and she wanted the knife and she was saying to me that she wanted to cut herself. I didn't want to let her have the knife. There was a woman with a baby on some steps and I slit the baby's head with the knife without meaning to. I was in a panic and then I woke up. – – – I know that I've had some thoughts about killing Thomas. – – I think I was more trying to protect myself and to get away from the people who were after me. I couldn't tell reality and unreality in the dream. (Elaborates.) I feel as if it's really happening.

**A:** What are your associations to the party?

**P:** I walked in and I was wearing a green dress. It reminded me of the dress I used to have when I gained 10 pounds when we first got married and that was such an awful time. (Elaborates.) I was so fat then. I came into the room and everyone seemed wild and drunk and there was a girl who was lying on the bed and she had passed out. I liked Denise, but her husband scared me because he's very attractive. He was telling Tom about some nurses he had once had in a hotel. –

*Embarrassed*

**A:** What was the detail?

**P:** – He didn't. . . . . the detail. . . . . I said "the detail" because I like the thought about how he screwed them.

**A:** So I think you are imagining it in detail. What are your associations?

**P:** – I'm thinking about his penis. It gives me such strong desires. I want to be a girl with him and I want to *kill* him.

**A:** How do you mean?

**P:** It would be so exciting to be the girl that he seduces and I think I'd love it. But then I'd want to kill him and I think about his penis and I'd want to take a knife and chop it up! That's what the baby was in the dream. The baby's bald head was like the end of a penis. – – I hate a man like that and I hate myself for wanting him to seduce me. I could kill myself. This is all so sickening. I know I'm a *nothing* to him. (Elaborates.)

I wish that my parents had given me some place to light! I feel like I'm going back and forth. What do I want to be? I want to be my father's mistress and I know it excites me but that's not real! I'd get him physically but not emotionally and I know that I wouldn't get his love. And yet I can't be my mother! I can't stand her! How could my father have liked her?! All he wanted was a mamma in her and I'm not going to be that. My father didn't want a wife who's a woman. I want it but I can't have it, so it makes me so mad at my father! – –

**A:** And what are your associations to the woman in the dream?

**P:** I'm not sure now whether it was a man or a woman. But I know she was old and ugly and I think she wanted to destroy me! Somehow it reminds me of myself. I *am* a woman but that scares me, and every woman that I know is out to destroy her husband. I got my period yesterday and I felt so excited to be a woman. But then I got cramps in order to punish myself. And then I had an urge to eat but instead I fixed myself up. I tried to fix may hair and make myself attractive for Tom. We were out in the car and there were some men around and I got sick to my stomach! I felt that they were looking at me and I was going to fall apart. To be a woman is wonderful until I go outside. But every man wants to seduce me and I know that I want him to. I just can't function with men. Then last night I had tremendous sexual feeling for Tom but the baby began to scream and I fell apart and I started in to eat. And then I had that dream! – – I guess I had to reduce myself to being a child and not let myself be a woman. Now I'm thinking about the light plug. (Laughs.) –

**A:** What are your associations to it?

**P:** It plugs in. –

**A:** But what's the detail?

**P:** I was thinking about that plug over there. It's as if I'm the plug and I'm thinking about a penis. It's all a huge explosion. But I know that it's really so normal, but with me it's always an explosion. I'm thinking about yesterday when I was here and I was feeling sexual and thinking about you and other men and about my ideas of being a woman and how worried I was about it. But the depression never came. It was all so exciting! I feel as if it's a possibility! I loved getting my period and feeling like a woman and having a man love me. But I know that the hostility *is* there and that I still want to destroy the man. It all scares the shit out of me! But it's also exciting and it seems possible. – – Now I'm having a sexual feeling for you. I know that I'm a woman and you're a man and I love it. I feel I can trust you. And now I think that I'm going to go home and go into a thing because I let myself trust you. (Laughs.) This is all so silly. I think that you're a light and a lamp that's shining, and I think you're wonderful and I love you. – – But I still have thoughts to destroy and I know that I must figure them out. (Elaborates.) – – Now I'm getting so nervous and excited! I feel just like a girl who is so excited by her father and as if I just discovered him and he's wonderful and I want him to look at me and love me. Now I have a sensation in my mouth and I feel as if I can't open it. One time my father was playing with us on the couch. I felt that he was adorable and that I was adorable. And he was a man and I was wiggling all over and thinking how a man is so cute. – – And then the destructive feelings come. I know it's an excuse. I feel love and sex for you and my father and for Tom. But then I think, "But I hate him because he left me and so I hate him."

A: So it seems that you have to keep reminding yourself that you hate me.

P: Yes, I know it. – – I hate the feeling that you're strong and that if I reached around and said that I love you that you wouldn't fall apart or attack me. I honestly don't think that my father would have done it either. – – – I can picture myself as I'm feeling now and there's love but it's so explosive and then it turns to hate! And then back to love! And then hate! It's all wild. I want to do it and I wish I could relax afterwards. I feel so spastic and nervous right now and I want to talk and talk. I feel as if everything is all swimming around me and there are all kinds of noises and firecrackers and it's all wild. I'm all emotion inside and I want to let it out by talking and to get your attention and to have you understand that I'm so nervous. – – Suddenly I'm frightened and I want to cut my wrists.

A: I think there was a connecting thought or fantasy left out there between the feeling of being excited and having me understand and being frightened and wanting to cut your wrists.

P: I felt that you really don't care and that you don't want to listen and understand me. You're not going to give me any attention and love and I hate you. You're a bastard. God damn it! This is all your fault. I'm going to get back at you by killing myself. (Elaborates.) I have all of these wonderful feelings for you but I hate you because I can't trust you with them. You're just trying to ruin my world! And it's worse because you let me have a little bit of that wonderful feeling first. If I'd not had *any* of it then I wouldn't know what I was missing. – Now I feel so depressed! Why should I ever be a woman? Why should I have these wonderful feelings? – – You won't let me *keep* my wonderful feelings and that's why I get so depressed about it. – – – I'm so mad at you! I have a sexual feeling in my vagina! I feel like I'm going to die! I want to take your God-damned penis and snap it off! That's the only kind of woman I can be! – – – I feel completely helpless. I want you and your attention so badly but I know I'll never get it and I don't know what to do. – – – I want to yell and scream and go wild and I want to see you fall apart and say, "God, what have I done?" – –

A: And what else comes to mind about that?

P: Then you'd pick me up and love me and tell me that you're so sorry. Then I get a sexual feeling and I feel like cutting my wrists. It's like I destroyed you. – – All I'm trying to do now is to think of a good way to destroy you and to get out my hostility toward you and get you to pay some attention to me. I want to have a temper-tantrum and get it out of you that way. I feel desperate. I *must* get your attention. What's the matter with you that you don't give it to me? Now you're trying to bring out the worst in me. I feel wonderful feelings like a woman does, and then you reduce me to being a child with temper-tantrums just in order to get your attention. Thanks a lot (sarcasm). – – – If I say that I want to kill and destroy you a thousand times maybe it might work. – – – I hate *you* and it's not my father. It's *you!* I hate your *guts!* I feel like walking out of here! But I'm scared to death. And you just sit there and give me absolutely nothing! –

A: We'll stop here for today.


### DISCUSSION

While the patient initially presents the dream I am unclear as to its meaning or its place in the continuity of her psychic life and experience. But as the session progresses, the meaning becomes somewhat clearer, particularly when she spontaneously associates the baby in the dream with the penis she wants to cut up with a knife, and when she describes the day-residue of having been out in the car with her husband, and having experienced sexual feelings for him but being interrupted by the baby crying. However, initially none of this is apparent to me and therefore I start the analysis of the dream by requests for her associations to some of the component elements. Ultimately her associations to the party lead to the experience with the friend and the fantasies about sexual orgies, which are derivatives of the positive oedipal attachments as well as aggression against the father for his sexual behavior and for his rejection of her love.

The patient's remark, "I got my period yesterday and I felt so excited to be a woman," is particularly interesting in view of the final interpretation that I had made yesterday regarding the blood from cutting her wrists as equated with the blood of menstruation. It raises an interesting theoretical question whether preconsciously or unconsciously the patient was aware that she was about to menstruate and whether this may have influenced the associations to the idea of bleeding yesterday, although in a disguised form. Or if her period was not due yesterday, it might illustrate the concept of somatic compliance to my interpretation. However, from the data available none of this can be confirmed at present.

The acceptance of the period and the excitement at the thought of being a woman, accompanied by various attempts to "make myself attractive," ultimately lead to a new expression of pleasurable fantasy and gratification at the thought of being a mature sexual woman who is loved by a man, and a new sense of anticipation that such experience and feeling about herself may be possible. This fantasy then shifts into the transference, with a feeling that she can and does trust me, and although this is still accompanied verbally by destructive fantasies, it represents a significant step toward a more synthesized and complete image of herself as an adult woman. Experiencing this in the transference, she says, "I feel just like a girl who is so excited by her father and as if I just discovered him and he's wonderful. . . ." The implication is that in the safety of the therapeutic alliance she is able to experience a genuinely positive, warm, and loving feeling toward me in my transference role as the father, and to experience it as if for the first time, although in actuality it represents the return from repression of a childhood feeling. This in turn leads to the recovery of a positive memory regarding the father and an incident (undoubtedly representative of many similar such incidents) in which she actually had experienced such feelings toward him.

The positive and progressive experience is rapidly replaced by hostility, and my comment implies that this hostility serves a defensive function against the underlying positive feelings. This is followed by the increased recognition that I will not fall apart or attack her, and then by the further elaboration of a new percept regarding the father when she says, "I honestly don't think that my father would have done it either." Subsequently she goes on to elaborate the wild fantasies of being overwhelmed by her sexual drives, which are probably distorted derivative perceptions of sexual arousal resulting from the primal scene experiences she had as a child.

At this point (as probably happened with the father following the episode of playing on the couch), there is a sudden angry response to the anticipation of transference frustration by me, accompanied by the fantasy of getting more of my attention through regressive temper-tantrums. Throughout this outburst, there is a projection to me of blame for the loss of her positive feelings and experience, and in this she is probably repeating the sequence of responses toward the father. Toward the end of the session she illustrates the intensity of this transference experience when she says, "I hate *you* and it's not my father. It's *you!*" For the moment the therapeutic alliance has been suspended, the self-observing ego functions are decreased, and she is again experiencing the relationship to me as if it were really the childhood situation with the father.

---

### SESSION 179

P: – – – – I took one look at you when I came in and I felt I could kill you. It just hit me. I feel like a little girl who is striving for her father's affection and she can't get it. But if I get fat then you'll be mad. (Elaborates.) And if I go out and seduce every man, then I can say, "Ha! Ha!" When I eat I know that I suppress my hostility. I think about all of my murdering thoughts! They scare me! But the funny thing is that they're not about you. They're always about Tom or the children and myself. It makes me so mad for you to sit so safe in that seat and you're the cause of all of this hostility! After I'm done eating I always feel as if I must murder someone. – – – – I want to burst loose with all of this hostility and yell and scream!

A: And what comes to your mind that you hold it back here?

P: – I don't know why I do that. I think about it so often. I don't know what would happen afterwards. (Elaborates.) It makes me afraid to hate so much and I feel as if I'd get out of control and I'd go into a black hole if I ever let it go. I've held it in so long that it has gotten to be enormous in size. Friday I felt so depressed and I could feel myself dropping into that dark well. I thought of my parents and I realized that it was all hopeless and I'm never going to get what I want. – – I feel just like a baby and I could sit here and scream, but I'll be helpless if my parents don't pick me up. Could I ever destroy someone with this hostility? – – I felt it with Sally yesterday and I had thoughts to kill her. I'm so sick of these feelings and I'm mad that you bring out this hostility towards some-one whom I love so much. I could go on and on about how much I hate you.

A: You mentioned before that I sit safe in my chair and that I'm the cause of all of this hate. And yet you don't feel it towards me but you feel it towards Tom and the kids instead. What comes to your mind about that?

**P:** For some reason I'm afraid to show it or feel it here.

**A:** What's the detail?

**P:** – I can see myself blow up. Is this just a fear? I'm not *really* afraid that you'll kick me out but it's all so frightening! – Saturday night I was getting dressed to go out and I was standing in front of the mirror and I thought how fat I looked and I looked just like my mother. Tom was mad at the kids for something and I thought to myself, "This is just like my mother and father." – – My father used to get mad at us occasionally. (Elaborates.) He'd line us up in the morning and he'd whack us, sometimes he'd do it in bed. Now I'm thinking about my mother and father being in bed. This all makes me so mad! I *do not* want to talk to you. I could throw up all over you! I hate you! – – –

**A:** And yet there must still be some reason why you choose to edit out this hate. You feel it towards me but you still are afraid to express it.

**P:** I just don't know! – –

**A:** But you must have some associations.

**P:** I have to keep them inside. You are bigger than I am and you have the power and you have control over me. – – I'm thinking about the violent tempers that my parents had and how they'd get so mad at me that they'd stop and shake.

**A:** What do you remember about it?

**P:** I wonder did they scare me? Was this all my reaction? I know he couldn't control it and it would build up inside him and then suddenly he'd explode and it would come out all over me. – – I feel like hell! – – – It's better to sit back and just take it and just accept whatever my parents give me.

**A:** You mentioned that your father couldn't control it and it would build up inside of him and then come out all over you. What was the detail?

**P:** – I have a sudden. . . . . shit! I've got his penis in my mouth! This is lovely (sarcasm)! – – – What does all of this have to do with you? It scares me! Now he's pushing his God-damned penis in my mouth and it is killing me. It's like he is going to stab me with a knife and I can't breathe. It's a weapon and all men use it. – – My father is going to bring his huge thing out and destroy me with it.

**A:** So you can *get* his penis if you can get him mad at you.

**P:** You make me so mad! Why do you say things like that?! Jesus

*Anger,*

Christ! You must sit up at night and think up things to scare me! – –

**A:** I think this is the fear that you have with me. If you express all of this anger at me, the fantasy is that I'll get mad at you and use my penis as a weapon against you.

**P:** But I'm such a frail, thin, skinny thing! This makes me so mad that I could. . . . . –

**A:** What did you stop at?

**P:** I *am* so helpless and I know that the penis could destroy me. There's such anger I can't even tell you.

**A:** I think there would also be a sense of pleasure in getting an emotional reaction from me even if it were to destroy you in this fantasy.

**P:** Oh, that depresses the hell out of me. – – I have a helpless feeling. I feel completely hopeless.

**A:** What comes to your mind?

**P:** The end is always destruction, either way. If I suppress it, then I destroy myself, and if I don't, then you are going to destroy me. So to get any pleasure at all I have to destroy myself. – – – I'm thinking about the time that my father was teaching me how to drive. I didn't put on the brakes when he told me to and he screamed! He was so loud and so angry. (Elaborates.) He yelled at me, "Get out of my car." – – I'd like to destroy you right now. You're going to tell me to get out just like my father did because you can't take it. I feel like I won.

**A:** How do you mean?

**P:** You've got to run away from me because you're scared that I'll take your penis, just like my father. You're weak and you can't take it and I've got you. If I really made you mad, you'd run like shit and you'd get me out of here and then I'd know that I'd won. I'd love it!

**A:** We'll stop here for today.

### Discussion

The patient begins where she left off in the previous session, involved in the hostile angry reaction to me in the transference as the result of the frustration of her positive oedipal wishes. She then indicates how one function of being fat is an indirect way of provoking or getting back at the father, and that the same is true of the fantasies of sexual promiscuity. She then demonstrates her self-observation by recognizing that she has displaced the hostility and aggression from the transference to her family, and this leads me to focus on the conflict in the transference over whether or not to experience and express her aggression directly. My attempts are to deal with her various resistances against expressing the aggression directly in the transference, and eventually there emerges a fantasy of the father losing control of his aggression toward her, with the implication that a similar fantasy exists in regard to me.

As she describes the thoughts about her father losing control of himself, there is a sudden eruption and return from repression of a primary process fantasy and image of the father using his penis as a weapon to attack the patient and force it into her mouth. This fantasy probably represents a condensation of the images of father and uncle, indicating the displacement of oedipal wishes to the uncle that had occurred as a child. However this image has emerged in the context of a transference reaction in which she has been experiencing but defending herself against anger and rage at me (and at the father) for frustrating the oedipal fantasies, and in the past she has expressed a variety of aggressive and destructive fantasies of castrating all men.

With this as a background, and also associating to the bulimia and its multiple determinants, I have an empathic and intuitive hunch that the latent meaning behind the image of the father's penis in her mouth is the attempt orally to incorporate it, thereby castrating him and also acquiring his phallus for herself, and I make this as a direct and immediate interpretation to her. Her reaction is angry resentment over the interpretation, which I then follow up by indicating that she may have similar fantasies in the transference. Her response, "But I'm such a frail, thin, skinny thing!" indicates the extent of the regression, and the perception of herself as a small girl in the face of her fantasies in regard to the father's penis.

My assumption has been that the image of the father forcing his penis into her mouth, and the fantasy of being destroyed by it, must represent some type of disguised and distorted gratification of a drive. Although the fantasy of the father's penis being destructive is frightening, nevertheless to be destroyed by it would also represent fulfillment of an exciting oedipal fantasy. And therefore I interpret this to her in the form of pleasure in the fantasy of eliciting this type of emotional response from me, even though at the same time in her fantasy it would destroy her.

Ultimately this material leads to her elaboration of the wish to evoke an angry response from me as a signal of her triumph and control over me in the father transference. Her final statement, "I'd love it!" indicates again that the fantasies and fears about my hostility and anger toward her actually represent a form of transference gratification she is seeking.

## SESSION 180

**P:** ---- I have a driving desire to completely overpower you but I don't know how to do it except to keep my mouth shut.

**A:** How would that overpower me?

**P:** Don't worry, it will. I'll be able to say, "Ha! Ha! Ha!" I feel like I'm belittled by confiding in you, so why should I tell you anything? -- This is like the battle of the sexes. -- For the last two days I've wanted to castrate every man that I saw. --- I start getting excited and I have the fantasy that I'm going to get your penis. It's just like when I look pretty at a party. I get excited but then I get depressed and then I get excited and then depressed again. It makes me sick to think that that's the only reason that I like men. To think that all I want to do is to cut off their penis and eat it. But I know that this is also a defense because I also have strong love feelings for you. -- But it makes me so depressed to say it. You just sit in that chair and I'll never have you! I'll never get anything from you. I'm thinking about Tom and I had a huge desire to make love with him but afterwards I realized that I *can't* ever get his penis and I hated his guts this morning. -- Being a woman is my strongest weapon against men and yet I fight against it. I've spent my whole life trying to figure out how to get a man's penis almost from the day I was born. ---

**A:** Let's take that fantasy a step further. Suppose that you do get the man's penis, then what?

**P:** I'd use it to destroy my mother.

**A:** What's the detail?

**P:** Like my father does. -- I'd run around and I'd have affairs and I'd have intercourse with lots of women. That would destroy my mother. But I'm a woman too and it destroys me and I could *kill* my father. --- It's such an act of violence. It seems like the woman is going to destroy the man or the man is going to destroy the woman and they both succeed. It's like a sword or a knife and I'd jab my mother and myself and I'd kill us. And yet we always destroy the man because we reduce it to nothing. -- Now I have a surge of feeling like I'm going to explode and I'm going to yell and scream. I hate you! *All* of this is your fault! --- I'm thinking of ways to get my hostility out without saying anything. I'd like to get up and walk out and just turn my back on you! ----- I know I'd give you satisfaction if I got mad at you, so I'll make you mad if I say nothing. It's just like with the kids.

If they're quiet and just sitting I get furious. I want them to yell. (Elaborates.)

A: You have a fantasy about how I'd feel if you stayed silent. What's the detail?

P: I can see you being furious. Just like I am. You'll feel as if you'll well up and let loose like I do. That would give me the greatest satisfaction. I know my yelling at you would prove nothing. I'm still not getting anything out of you. I want to get something, anything at all, so badly!! – –

A: You have an image of me welling up and letting loose. What are your associations to that?

P: – Suddenly I feel so scared! I feel as if the world is closing in on me! I can see myself fall apart in front of you. It's like I'm saying I can't stand it any longer! – – Shit! I'm running away again. – – I've got to *get* something from you. I'll have to reduce myself but I'll get you if I do and get something from you. – – I can't stand up here and. . . . . if I got mad at you I'd be on my own and I can't do that. So I must be a child and go on and be dependent on you. I can't say to you, "I'm an individual and I have feelings, and you can go to hell." Because that makes a woman out of me and I can't do it. – – I don't trust you. I almost did but it scared me shitless. So I'm going back to floundering around like a baby.

A: This came up at the point of the fantasy where you felt you were going to be able to make me well up and let loose and attack you. Let's see what comes to mind if you go back to that fantasy.

P: – – I don't know!! I think about my father and the car and he's yelling and screaming at me and it is horrible. And I'm feeling satisfaction! What in shit am I doing? God-damn it! – – – Why is all of this? What would happen if you would yell at me and if you were mad? I'd fall apart and be scared. But I feel that I can get to you. Why? I know of all times I really can't then. –

A: How do you mean?

P: You'd be *mad* at me. – – It would be just like violence. That shows how weak you'd be if you were losing control of yourself and you wouldn't know what you were doing. That's the only way my father took out his hostility. – – Where do I ever get these ideas?!! You'd get so mad that you'd lose control and take out your penis and jab it inside of me. You'd do it just like you do it to all the other women. That way I'd be satisfying my sexual pleasure and my hostility and I'd destroy you and I'd love you. I'd get all the things I ever wanted and yet it would destroy

*Marginal annotations:*

*Cry*

*Cry, Fury*

*Anger*

*Cry*

me and the whole world. I can't stand it! -- I was almost convinced just now that if I got mad at you, you *would* get mad at me. It will build up in you and then it *has* to explode. -- It's such a *desire* in me! God-damn it! I'd *love* it. --- That's what would happen if I let this desire go! I think about it with every man I look at. And it's true with you!

*Shrill* | That's all I want! And I know it will happen! I know it will sometime! (Elaborates.) I'll let all of my defenses down some day and then I know it is going to happen! -- I can't stand you sitting behind me. I feel like any minute you will reach over and grab me! It's going to happen any minute! -- But I'd love it! I wish you would do it. I can't stand the

*Cry* | fighting and bickering any more. I'm running all the time and I hate it. -- I want to give in and be a woman to you. -- And I know it would absolutely destroy you and tear you up but I'd also be loving you. I can satisfy so many things this way, so it's no wonder I want it so badly.

A: We'll stop here for today.

### DISCUSSION

The patient begins with a continuation of the conflict from the previous session in which the negative, provocative, and angry transference feelings toward me predominate in her conscious thoughts. However, in this session the previously used mechanism of displacement to her family is reduced, and she is experiencing the feelings directly toward me. The defensive wish is to be able to frustrate me and demonstrate her capacity for control of the situation through silence. The fantasy is that by silence she will manifest her superiority in what she perceives as a struggle between us, so that even though this results in an interference in her analytic progress, she is willing to sacrifice herself for the sake of the supposed negative transference satisfaction.

Analysis requires the active cooperation of the patient, and if a patient consistently chooses to do so, he can defeat the efforts of the analyst, make the analyst ineffectual, and easily succeed in "proving" analysis to be unsuccessful in his case. Without the patient's cooperation and continuing active participation in the analytic process (through the presentation of associations, and through his own attempts to understand the material as well as the analyst's interpretations and other interventions) the analyst cannot conduct an analysis by himself. The analyst must therefore recognize and accept his own "weakness" in this regard so that if, in a phase of negative transference, the patient elects to block therapeutic progress, the analyst is not unduly threatened by it nor does he actively attempt to do the patient's work for him. By resolving this potential countertransference difficulty, the analyst can then more readily accept the patient's defiance without being personally threatened in his professional role, and he then can ultimately help the patient recognize the self-deceiving implications of such reactions. It is this line of reasoning that is behind my question as to how she thinks her silence would overpower me.

The patient responds by elaborating the feeling of our being in some kind of struggle and competition, with the fantasy that by not telling me anything she is robbing me of my power and thereby in a symbolic way is castrating me. In this material she is demonstrating the theoretical concept of layering of conflict and defense. In this instance, she describes her conflict over the wish to castrate men, and at the same time demonstrates that beneath the wish to castrate the male is a positive transference feeling of love for me, against which the fantasy of a struggle between us is a defense.

She goes on to describe the experience of transference frustration and to express again the fantasy of acquiring a man's penis. My wish is to help her recognize that the fantasy of castrating the male must represent the fulfillment of a still "deeper" fantasy, for which the idea of castration would be the fulfillment. It is with this in mind that I now ask her actively to fantasy about what she would do with the penis if she were to have it.

In response she begins to express again her mixed sexual identification, in which she wants to be like the father, while at the same time identifying with both the mother and the father's mistresses in a woman's role. In passing, she demonstrates the symbolism of the sword and/or knife as a phallic equivalent, and as this material continues she undergoes an intense transference experience toward me as the father in which she feels these conflicts to be all my fault. In this context she elaborates upon the various indirect ways in which she expresses her hostility towards me, which are presumably repetitions of the way in which hostility was directed toward the father as a child. But she expresses the growing recognition that expression of her hostility directly is not likely to have a significant impact upon me, and therefore her fantasy is of doing it in an indirect fashion with the hopes thereby of frustrating me.

Once again this is dealt with from my standpoint through recognition that if she chooses to frustrate me in my therapeutic endeavors, I would be unable to force her cooperation. If I can accept this within myself, I then will not be manipulated by the patient's provocative transference efforts. And by not responding to the provocation I make such a line of defense less gratifying for her, and therefore it is less likely she will use it for any extended period. In my question about the image of me welling up and letting loose I am indirectly trying to point out that the transference gratification she seeks through frustrating me is not likely to occur.

Expressing her fury in an affective way in response to this transference abstinence, she goes on to elaborate on the intense resentment and hostility she feels toward my analytic posture and elaborates on the gratification she experienced when the father yelled at her in the car, implying the wish for similar gratification with me if she can provoke my hostility and aggression. Experiencing this in the transference, she again reverts to her perceptions of the father, and this leads to the association between sexuality and aggression and the expression of the overdetermined oedipal fantasy in which my sexual attack on her is seen as a gratification simultaneously of a number of different but related wishes toward me.

Once again it becomes clear that the fear of my hostility, which she has expressed so often in the analysis, is actually a wished-for form of transference gratification and a type of behavior she is seeking to provoke in me. The fact that I do not respond in terms of her transference wish adds to the sense of frustration, but in the therapeutic alliance it helps her more clearly differentiate the present from the past relationship, and it also makes it possible for her to express these wishes in an increasingly direct and overt way. If I were to respond with counteraggression as she wants me to, it might momentarily make her feel satisfied, but it would confirm for her the reality of the perception of me as similar to the father. This would interfere with her ability to resolve the problems with the father, through their repetition with me, while simultaneously recognizing the differences between the present and the past objects and her relationship to them.

---

## SESSION 181

**P:** I wouldn't have come here today if I was not going to throw $25.00 down the drain by staying away. I've set up my defense again of I don't care. It's just like it's been all of my life. I just sit and hate you with all that I've got. I get satisfaction from smugly hating you. I felt it yesterday when I was so *mad!* I was so mad at you and still I don't know why. But then I got so nervous! And then I wasn't mad at you any more. – – – – The thing that bothers me most is that I take it all out on my children.

I hate them, especially Thomas, and I have the wish that I didn't have him. – – – I've had the same dream so often. I'm in Springfield with the girls that I ran around with. In the dream they don't like me and we're at a swimming pool and there are lots of men around. I'm trying to get their attention by hitting golf balls and baseballs. I always have this dream. There were two girls in the room and I came in with a new hat. One of the girls left and I said, "What's troubling you?" I woke up in a panic. (Elaborates.) I'm sitting here trying to get your attention and you don't give it. I'm embarrassed and I'm so mad I could kill you. But I'm not going to admit that I want your attention in case I fail. – – – Now I get the same feeling that I had with my parents. Why? Why is it that you don't love me and fall all over me? What's the matter with me that no one likes me? – – – I can't get mad at you. It takes all of my defenses not to, but I just can't do it.

**A:** How do you mean?

**P:** I just can't! I have 10,000 excuses not to, but it means the end of the world to me. – – I'm so mad at you that I can't get mad. It's your fault that I can't and that makes me hate you even more!

**A:** What's the detail?

**P:** – – I don't want to talk about it! – – Tom said that Sally has started to wet her pants ever since she walked in on us making love one day. Does she think that Tom should do it to her? Maybe that's the way I feel. I know that my father hated my mother and he jammed his penis into her to take it out on her and I'm afraid that he is going to do this to me! – – Now I'm getting mad at you and the time I was in the car with my father comes to mind.

**A:** What else do you remember?

**P:** He was really *mad* at me. He acted as if he was hysterical and I was in shock! (Elaborates.) What did I think my father was going to do?

**A:** What do you think that *I* will do?

**P:** I'm so afraid that you will get hysterical like my father and you'll be so mad that you won't know what you are doing. – –

**A:** And then?

**P:** – I think this but I don't really believe it. But I think that you'll get so mad! And then you'll pull out your penis and stick it into me. – – I get excited just to think about it. I'm so afraid and yet I want it so much. – –

**A:** I think you cut up that fantasy into pieces and then you stopped. Let's go back. I'm so mad and hysterical just like your father and I pull out my penis. Then what happens?

**P:** All I can think is that I'll end up with a baby. – – – Now I feel that suddenly I've ended up with something I don't want. – – I feel hysterical! This is too much for me to take. I end up with your penis inside of me and I never thought it would happen. Here's the baby that I want to love and yet I hate it and I want nothing to do with it. – – How can anything that's supposed to be so wonderful be so horrible?! – Now I've got a sexual feeling in my vagina and yet it makes me sick to my stomach! I can't stand all of these emotions that you are bringing out in me. I want to kill you. I can't stand it! – – It would all be so violent if you ever got mad! It would be wild! (Elaborates.) And all of this just because of your God-damned penis.

**A:** So we can see how you hold back your rage and hate and excitement here and instead you take it out on the kids and Tom at home. Why is it necessary to take it out on them? What keeps you from expressing it here?

**P:** My mind goes completely blank. Suddenly I feel as if I've just walked into Carol's room and I see her lamp. Oh! I don't feel safe with you. – – I feel as if you are completely incapable of handling anything. You have only one thing and that is your penis and I know what you use it for. It's so wild! And you don't care who you use it on. I feel like I have to handle you with kid gloves because you are just a wild emotional thing and I wish you didn't have a penis. You are not going to get me! You can get anyone else you like but not me! But if I get wild, then you'll get wild so I must stay calm and quiet. But I feel wild. . . . .

**A:** What did you stop at?

**P:** I want to tear into you and I want so much to yell and scream but I can't. I'd try to get to the door but you'd stop me.

**A:** What's the detail?

**P:** You are just one huge emotion and you'll throw me down and jab your penis into me! And there's a huge explosion! And it's all hate! And sexual desire and shit! I get so mad every time I think about it. That's when I feel like I'm your equal and like I'm a woman. – – And I know I'd *love* it and I'd end up being one of your mistresses.

**A:** We'll stop here for today.

### Discussion

The patient's initial comment that she would not have come here today if she were not going to waste $25.00 is an illustration of the general practice in analysis of charging patients for all appointments, whether they attend the session or not. The reasoning behind this practice is to encourage the patient to attend all sessions in order that the resistances which might have led her to avoid the session can be brought to light and ultimately dealt with. Furthermore, if the patient is not held financially accountable for missed sessions, then she has a tool by which to deprive me of something in reality (my fee for time which would otherwise not be usable), and thereby could achieve realistic transference gratification in this phase of negative transference. In order to frustrate this type of transference gratification, if I charge her for the missed session she is unable to deprive me in this way. Also, if I would suffer a financial loss each time the patient missed an analytic session, it might evoke in me either a countertransference feeling of annoyance and anger at the patient, or else a countertransference manipulation in such a way that I might not fully bring out conflicts which could lead the patient to avoid the sessions, in order thereby to avoid this type of financial loss.

She then goes on to the sources of her resistance, which at the moment is the frustration of the transference demands toward me and the wish to defend herself against this by withdrawal and by not expressing her feelings. This is the same mechanism she apparently used with the parents as a girl. She also interprets the transference frustration in a personal way as a reflection upon herself and her attractiveness, when she says, "What's the matter with me that no one likes me?" This is the reasoning of an oedipal-age girl who feels that the father's failure to fulfill her fantasies is a reflection upon herself and her femininity, and who was unable to recognize the reality behind the rejection as a child, or to feel the difference between herself as a child and as the woman whose growth and maturation have occurred in the interim.

In the context of this negativistic and hostile transference conflict, the patient associates to her daughter's primal scene experience and reaction to it, and then to herself and her sado-masochistic perception of the primal scene in terms of a hostile attack by the man upon the woman. With my focusing this into the immediate transference relationship, she is able to recognize the fantasy that I will use sexuality as an aggression against her, and that although this frightens her it also excites her. Both of these reactions again represent childhood fantasies and feelings, experienced in the current relationship to me. Her attempt, however, is to avoid some of the details of these fantasies, and my interpretation of this resistance results in her elaboration of the childhood fantasy about pregnancy resulting from the woman incorporating the man's penis, which then becomes the baby.

She elaborates further upon this primal scene derivative in the transference fantasy of a wild and violent type of reaction between us, which then permits me again to point out the displacement of this reaction toward her family, which she mentioned at the start of the session. Once again, as part of the working-through process, she sees me as potentially wild and emotionally interacting with her and sees herself as the one who must maintain control over the situation since she cannot trust me. In this transference relationship she is again working-through the childhood fantasies and defenses that she used in the unsuccessful solution of her original oedipal attachment. And in this material she again illustrates the ambivalence between the wish and fear regarding her violent primal scene fantasy.

None of the material in this session is new and almost all of it has come up in one form or another earlier in the analysis. The session illustrates the working-through process, in which important wishes, fantasies, conflicts, and defenses must all be brought up again and again during the course of analysis. This repetition is necessary in order that ultimately the patient can separate the past from the present, gain mastery over the transference drives and wishes, adopt new defenses toward them, and finally in the resolution of the transference neurosis, modify the original oedipal wishes in such a way that they can be appropriately and realistically expressed and gratified through adult relationships and behavior.

---

## SESSION 182

**P:** – – – – – – – ⁀ – – – I don't feel like I can talk to you. It's easy when I'm scared but I don't feel like a child now and I feel I'd put you on an equal level. – – – I have love and sexual and hostile feelings all mixed up into one thing. – – –

**A:** You mentioned that you picture talking to me on an equal level.

**P:** If I show you my hostility and my sex and my love, then I'd feel like a woman and not like a child. But I don't know if I want to. I like being a child and having you being the mamma. This morning when I came in I had the feeling, "Why am I so afraid here? I *am* a woman." – – – I know if I'd ever get this hostility out the love must come too. – – – – And if I show you my love and I'm not satisfied, then I'll be so hostile. Love can turn into such rage and violence. – – I couldn't stand letting my love out and having you reject me. And I guess there's not much you can do because I'll feel rejection no matter what. – – – The main thing I can't face is rejection! But I feel it all the time and it makes me feel like such a nothing. – –

A: How does that work out here?

P: It's a wild thing to think of! Now I get a sudden attack of butter-flies. Can I move you at all? Can I rile you up? Can I get you wild? Some-times when you talk I get the feeling that you force yourself to talk and that you're not the least bit interested and it's just your job and you're doing it for money and you really don't care. Maybe if I tried hard enough I could get you so mad that you wouldn't know what you are doing. I know I could.

A: I think the fantasies that you *can* seduce me or else you can make me wildly angry serve as your defense against the rejection that you'd feel if you let yourself go and you tried and I didn't respond emotionally to you.

P: That makes me mad for you to talk so calmly! I feel as if you couldn't possibly understand rejection! You can sit there so calmly! – –   *Cry*

A: What's going through your mind?

P: You're a stupid idiot and you can't understand how I feel. You talk about how I feel rejected, but it's just like the business about the penis. You *have* one and so you've never been rejected. I've been re-jected my whole life! You're so condescending! It's like you say, "Tough shit," and you don't do anything about it! I can't stand it! It makes me so God-damned mad! I want to stand up and say, "Look at me! God-damn it, I'm around here, you know!" I feel that you are so condescending towards me that it's as if I *am* a little child. Once in a while you take pity on me if you're in a good mood. I wish I could tell you to go to hell and walk out! Why don't I! It would be such a satisfaction to say that I don't need you! I've been a quiet mouse all of my life with such a fear that I'll explode and do something horrible.

A: What's the detail of that fantasy?

P: I used to make up stories. My parents were always violent and they seemed wild and I'd sit and watch and never demand any attention from them. But I used to think that when I'd grow up then I'd kill someone   *Cry,* or do some violent sex act and shock the hell out of them. And it was   *Anger* all because I was so quiet. I'm so sick and tired of it!

A: You used to make up stories that you'd kill someone or else do some violent sex act. What was the detail?

P: I'd kill my parents or else maybe my sister. I'd go up to my father and bite his God-damned penis! I'd terrorize my parents and *make* them look at me and *make* them scared to death of me! They've taken advantage of me for so long. I could kill them! God-damn them anyway! (Elaborates.) They're so sure of me! I'm such a quiet mouse and I never do anything wrong! I'll kill myself and my children and Tom. I'll make the world sit up and look at me!

A: And this is the feeling that you were repeating with me a few minutes ago when you said that I should look at you because you're around here.

*Anger*  P: I want someone to look because I'm tired of sitting in a corner and saying, "You're wonderful." I don't understand why you won't do it. It makes me so mad! I'm sick of it! – – The only time I ever rebelled against my parents was when we moved to Springfield and I messed around with a lot of boys and was drinking and cussing. That was the first time I got something from my mother and father. But my mother's looks used to say, "You're so shitty I hate your guts." – – It's all so hopeless! I got negative attention if I'd say, "You're wonderful." Shit! How do you relive your

*Fury*  life. My parents were flops and there is nothing you can do about it. Why do I feel like I want to kill myself? I want to do something violent!! I want to turn on you and claw your eyes out!! I just want to do something violent!! – – I want special attention from you and I get so mad when you say

*Anger*  that it's time to go. You give me nothing! I really don't want to do something violent or kill myself or someone else but I feel like you force me to do this! – – In my daydreams you always say, "To hell with the world, let's go off together." I want you to say it but I'm never going to let you know and I'm never going to tell you and so I hate you. You should fall head over heels for me! What's the matter with you? You act like I'm a nobody and yet I want to look you in the face and say that I hate your guts. But I'm so scared! And I never will! But I want to so badly! – – I want to run to your lap and love you but if I ever get that close I'd tear you apart and my hostility would come out. – – And yet I want to love you because those feelings are so nice and it's fun and I love them. But I can't ever get that close. – – The woman in me loves you and the child in me hates your guts. And I feel both of them so plainly and so I stay away from you. – – – I still don't understand! Why don't you fall in love with me? What's the matter with me? I think that you should! I have love feelings for you and you won't accept them or give me anything in return! I don't understand it! – – – If I completely let myself go will you reject me completely? – –.– How do you stand up to someone who couldn't care less about you and say, "I won't let you reject me." – – – – I can't stand it!

What are you doing? I feel as if you slapped me across the face. – – I feel hysterical and panicked! –

A: We'll stop here for today.

## DISCUSSION

Once again the patient returns to the theme of the oedipal father transference with its ambivalence between the positive and erotized wish for a response from me and the negative angry resentment when the positive wishes are frustrated. Although she experiences this in a reasonably composed and controlled way early in the session, and although the self-observing functions are still active, as when she says, "And I guess there's not much you can do, because I'll feel rejection no matter what," as the session continues the regression becomes more pronounced and with it comes an intensification of the accompanying affects.

She again reverts to the fantasy that if she really tries harder she will be able to elicit the transference gratification she is seeking. My interpretation that these fantasies of successful seduction or provocation serve as a defense against the recognition that this will not occur in reality, and therefore that she will experience it as a rejection, is in essence one I have made earlier in the analysis. But on this occasion it seems to have been more effective, in that she begins to cry and then to undergo a more intense transference regression in which she experiences the full impact of her sense of rejection in the father transference. This regression leads to the emergence and recovery from repression of some of her childhood fantasies of violence or sexuality by which she hoped to achieve the oedipal gratification. After I focus this material back into the transference, she elaborates with accompanying affect of intense hostility the various wishes for revenge because of her frustration in the past and in the current relationship to me. After expressing this fury, she spontaneously expresses the underlying positive wishes and yearnings against which the rage had served partially as a defense, and she again repeats in the transference the feelings of being unable to understand why the father does not accept her love and sexual feeling in the form that she wants.

In the latter part of this session the patient is primarily experiencing transference affects and drives in their full intensity. For the moment, self-observation, integrative judgmental capacities, and reality testing are suspended as the transference is being experienced. This is part of the working-through process in which the full impact of the infantile and childhood wishes and demands for gratification must be mobilized in order that ultimate mastery of them can be achieved. In this working-through process she is learning by experience that she can permit herself the full range of affective and drive awareness, and still maintain an analytic situation and relationship without recourse to overt action toward me and without response of overt reaction from me. These repetitive experiences of feeling the intensity of her drives, and yet being able to withstand their pressures toward overt activity, will in the long run enhance her adult capacity to accept the drives and their derivatives into consciousness without fears of loss of control, and ultimately to adopt a more tolerant and confident attitude toward herself in regard to these drives.

As a child faced with drives of this intensity, her capacities to test reality and to control herself and avoid overt action would have been limited or distorted, and therefore these forces were repressed with resulting inhibition, conflict, and disturbance in her subsequent development. The work of the analysis has now succeeded in undoing this repression and in permitting these drives and the conflicts associated with them again to emerge into conscious awareness. Over a period of time she can now apply rational secondary process adult ego perceptions and integrative and controlling mechanisms to deal with these issues in a less conflicted and more effective, fulfilling fashion.

## SESSION 183

**P:** – – – My parents came for a visit. I hate them. I could go on and on! They don't care about me or my children! I feel totally rejected. (Elaborates.) My mother and I fight and we're always in competition and my father doesn't care about either one of us. I've got such weak parents! And it makes me so insecure! (Elaborates.) I've let them know how I feel about them but they just cut me off. We have no relationship at all (Elaborates.) My father bothers me the most! I can't understand it! He acts as if I'm not even in the room with him! The least that he could do is to talk to me! And it makes me so mad that I care about it! (Elaborates.) Even if I try to seduce every man it doesn't work! We all went out to a big party on Saturday night. (Elaborates.) And with all those other men around my father didn't even look at me. (Elaborates.) I'm so angry at my father. I was so jealous! He just kept asking Mrs. Jones to dance. It's so damned hard to have a father like that! He's so inconsiderate! He kicks over his wife and daughters for a pretty woman. How did I ever get a father like that? I wanted him to ask me to dance! I know it was so stupid

*Cry*

of me that I was so jealous! And then Mrs. Jones said, "Your father is
such a wonderful dancer." My father won't accept me as a woman or as
an adult or as anything! But why does it keep bothering me? He's such a
baby and such a bastard! (Elaborates.) I feel that until my father accepts
me as a woman that no one ever will. I want to say to him, "Look at me,
I'm a beautiful woman." And I feel that I am but I miss something because my father won't admit it. (Elaborates.)

A: What else comes to your mind about that?

P: . . . . . He's always so attracted by beautiful women! So why isn't     *Cry*
he proud of me?! I'm missing something! If I'd been a boy he couldn't
have stood it. (Elaborates.) I know I'm *not* ugly or a disgrace to him, but
he just sat and sulked! I had a dream that my father and I had an affair.
It was a stupid man who is in our church and who is just like my father. –

A: What was the detail of the dream?

P: He physically made love to me and I knew it was my father but I
didn't care. (Elaborates.) It was the same thing in my dream last night
when that boy in Springfield and I were sitting on the bed and I was
showing them the blood from my period and I was saying, "I am a
woman." My father would just sit on the side of the bed. – – – I know
that I will never get what I want from him. I've been waiting for twenty-
five years. What is there to do? I *know* that I'm attractive and I really
don't *need* every single man, but I do need that one extra thing. Look at
my hands! (Both hands are spastic in a claw position.) The hostility is
unbelievable in me! I *have* to accept the idea of complete rejection from
them but it's so hard without hating their God-damned guts. It always
makes *me* feel inadequate as if I'm not whole. It's like I'm missing something and I'm walking on one leg and it always hurts. I could kill them!
But I know that I'm scared to feel it.

A: What's the detail of that fear?

P: Am I afraid that I'll die without them? (Elaborates.) It's just like
the times that they used to go out when I was a child and I'd fall apart
and feel that I'd die without them. I was so hostile towards them but I'd
always turn it to myself. I can't stand up by myself. It's just like it is with
you. I need you so desperately and so it's better to swallow my hostility.
It has come true with my parents as I know they *are* cutting me off. And
so you're all that I have left. And if they do it, why isn't it the same with
you? You're not even my mother or father and so you don't need to take
anything from me. You're asking me why I'm afraid to be mad? It's
reality! If I am, my parents will cut me off!

A: We can understand about your fears as a child, but what about today? You react today as if the situation is the same as it was then.

**P:** I know it's a matter of pure emotion and that I *don't* really need them. And yet I go into a panic because they give me nothing. I'm still a complete child. – – It's a matter of logic against emotion. (Elaborates.) It's a matter of knowing that I'm a bigger woman than they are, and at the same time thinking, "You will die without them." – – – I'm an emotional wreck. How could I possibly be mature with them as parents? How can I ever rise above them?

**A:** What comes to your mind?

**P:** I'm a product of my parents. They're so neurotic and immature and unstable that it scares me. And I know that I'm still attached to them.

**A:** If you feel like an adult and you feel mature and you understand the reality of the situation, then you know that you can't get it from them any more. But the problem seems to be that you're still seeking what you missed from them as if you didn't understand the reality.

**P:** I know that's true. (Elaborates.) And I know that I stay a baby in order to get it. I really don't want to.

**A:** And that's the conflict that you're facing. A part of you does want to and another part of you doesn't. The question is, which one is going to win?

**P:** The most important thing is that you will accept me as an adult. Then I can be all one person. (Elaborates.) – – – Whenever you talk to me I feel that I *adore* you but then I am so scared because I think that *you* are my father. – – – I really have the feeling that my father is scared of his own feelings for me and that I *am* so beautiful for him.

**A:** What's the detail of the feeling?

**P:** I'm thinking about Saturday night when all of the men there were flattering and attracted to me. My father wouldn't even *look* at me. Maybe he had sexual feelings of his own and it scared the hell out of him. How do you react to this?

**A:** How do you think?

**P:** You probably go ga-ga over young girls just like Mr. Jones. These men are all so sick! It's true about every single man. Maybe you're not! But all other men are!

**A:** What's the detail of the thought about me?

**P:** You're just like Mr. Jones and you're going to lean over me and tell me that I'm beautiful. (Elaborates.) I'd love it if you did. But I also pray to God that you're not like that! But I still picture it.

**A:** What comes to mind about that fantasy?

**P:** I think of what would happen if we met outside of this treatment.

You'd probably be like all men! You'd give in if a girl ever let you know that she wants you. (Elaborates.) This all makes me so scared but I also want it so much. – – If I ever let you know how I feel I know you'd do it! It's all so strong in me. I think I could wear you down and make you forget any logic. There's such a great need in me to do this.

**A:** Let's see what it would mean to you if you *can* do this, or if you can't?

**P:** I want them both. It's the childish part of me that wants it. I really want you to say, "You're very beautiful, but I'm not going to make love to you because I have a wife and you have a husband." I need men to be attracted to me in order to be sure that I'm still a woman. But I know I'd fall apart if you ever gave in to me. (Elaborates.)

**A:** We'll stop here for today.


### DISCUSSION

In her report about the parents' visit and the experiences at the dance, the patient is demonstrating that the oedipal drives and fantasies are still partially directed toward the parents themselves, as well as into the analytic transference relationship. She demonstrates by her angry frustration how she is still striving to achieve gratification from the father, which she missed as a child, and even though her own reality perceptions of herself and of the situation tell her that she no longer needs this, the affective and drive components dominate her feeling and her attitudes toward herself and him.

The overtly incestuous dreams are an indication that as a result of the analytic work which has thus far been done, she is now able to accept into consciousness the previously repressed and warded-off incestuous fantasies and impulses toward the father, and is able to do so without the previously automatic superego guilt responses or the fantasies of sexuality as a sadistic and destructive act. In other words, ego mastery is being achieved to the point that she can now permit these images and wishes to be conscious and rely upon her own conscious integrative ego mechanisms to control them, rather than use the automatic distorting unconscious ego defense mechanisms, as had occurred in the past.

However, the occurrence of a conversion reaction in which her hands and fingers are spastic and in a claw-position indicates that she is not fully facing this conflict in conscious thought. And as the session progresses, she experiences again the fear of loss of the parents, the fantasies that she will die without them, and the feeling that ". . . you're all that I have left." The likelihood is that the conversion reaction is related to conflicts toward me in the transference, which she cannot fully experience in her thought processes at the moment. This conflict leads her to the expectation that she will lose me, as she apparently feels she once lost her parents.

As mentioned in the previous session, the transference and affective components of her reaction have been dominant for the past few days, and self-observing reality-testing and adult integrative functions have been more in the background. Because I now want to help her reflect upon both the transference reactions and the real life experiences with the parents and thereby stimulate the self-observing functions in the therapeutic alliance, I ask her to focus upon the difference between the childhood and current adult situations. This is successful as she now begins to reflect upon the conflict of ". . . logic against emotion," and I ultimately follow this up by pointing out how she is still seeking to achieve what she missed as a child, and the existence of the conflict between the childhood and adult parts of her personality.

"The most important thing is that you will accept me as an adult. Then I can be all one person." This response illustrates one of the important therapeutic factors in the working-through of the transference neurosis. By accepting the patient's infantile and childhood transference feelings and thereby permitting her to experience, express, and explore them, the analyst helps to undo the childhood amnesia and the neurosis which it conceals. The analyst and the situation of transference abstinence help the patient develop tolerance of these neurotic conflicts in consciousness and ultimately help her recognize the advantages of accepting the frustration of infantile and childhood wishes in favor of more realistic and gratifying age-appropriate adult relationships and satisfactions. And by then accepting the patient in the adult role, the analyst is providing a setting in which the patient can now accomplish the psychological maturation that was interrupted and blocked by the childhood objects and the childhood neurosis.

The patient is able to follow this up by a more adult and probably realistic and psychologically astute perception of her father and the possibility that he may today recognize her as a sexually attractive woman, but be threatened by his own sexual fantasy and attraction toward her and therefore manifest only the defense against such feelings within himself.

For the moment the adult and rational ego is operative. But this promptly gives way to a transference reaction in which she sees me as similar to her father and the other men, and in which the ambivalent conflict between the wish for gratification and the adult hope for maintenance of an appropriate professional relationship is again experienced and expressed. In her final associations the patient indicates how secondary-process rational ego functions are gradually being strengthened as she describes (not for the first time) the wish to have me accept her as a beautiful woman and yet *not* gratify the neurotic wishes and fantasies.

---

## SESSION 184

P: – – – I feel absolutely horrible and like hell. I feel as if I'm dirty and full of black shit and all kinds of hate. I'm the worst mother and the worst wife in the world and I'm worth nothing. I blew my stack at the children last night. I completely exploded. I had that horrible feeling in my mouth as if I'd eaten a big hard penis. I even tasted it and I had to remind myself that I hadn't eaten one.

A: What was the detail of the explosion?

P: It was at Sally. And I know it scared her. And I really shook the baby and it was all because Tom called and said that he was going to come home late. I *have* to eat my hostility, but I felt as if I could have killed him! – –

A: What was your feeling about the call?

P: – . . . . . I know that Tom is *not* like my father and is not having affairs, and yet that thought came to my mind. I thought that he was lying and he was calling up at the last minute and was really seeing a woman. – – – – I feel all confused. I'm all mixed up with my father and Tom and you.

A: Let's look at the mixup.

P: I think about all of my father's affairs and how they affected me and yet I never struck out at him. But I'm reliving the whole damn thing with Tom and I know it is unrealistic but I just can't control it. I want to tear into somebody.

A: I think you're really reliving it in your feelings here with me, but you are afraid to express them here and so you displace them onto Tom. So it ends up that you take out on Tom the feelings that you have here towards me.

P: – – · I wish that I *could* let my hostility out here. – – – I think of how my parents are acting towards me now and I'm so scared! It's as if I'm hanging from a string and I'm just waiting for something horrible to happen. (Elaborates.) For the first time in my life I realize that I'm on

my *own* about my parents and it scares me. And yet I know that I can't.
. . . .

**A:** I think you still feel that if you express this anger towards me that I'll cut that string.

**P:** – I feel so desperate! – – I feel like I must explode and I know that I should do it here, but I'm so afraid that I will at home. (Elaborates.)

**A:** Let's look at the details of the fear of exploding here.

**P:** I feel as if I'd never see you again. – –

**A:** What else comes to mind about the fantasy?

**P:** I am thinking about all of the times with my mother and with Tom's mother and how they both have cut me off completely! And I picture it like it would be with my father and he'd just stand there. Ugh! He'd say, "This girl is crazy and I want nothing to do with her because she's nuts."

**A:** I think there are two things going on here at the same time. On the one hand you are afraid that I will react like your father and think that you are crazy or nuts or something like that. But I think you are also afraid that I won't. With Tom and the kids you can upset them and churn them up and get them to react to you and be scared of you, but here the fear is that you're not going to get an emotional reaction from me either way. It's the same thing with your feelings of love.

**P:** – – I feel as if my mind will snap and I can't stand it. – – – I know I *do* have a desire to bring out some kind of emotional reaction in you, but it's all so negative.

**A:** What's the detail?

**P:** I think that maybe I could please you by doing well in therapy and that it would be just the same as it was with Harris. (Elaborates.) But I also know that that's not going to work with you and so I flip and think about going the other way and maybe going crazy or doing something crazy. – –

**A:** And then what?

**P:** That would make you mad and maybe it would even hurt you or make you feel like you've failed.

**A:** Let's look at the details of each of those.

**P:** If I were to cut my wrists then you'd feel that you've failed. But that scares *me* so much more than it does you. It's ridiculous and it would just hurt me and my family, so I'm between the devil and the deep blue sea. I'm completely frustrated. I'm not going to get anything out of you and I *need* it. I've got to have something from you. If I were ever to tell you to go to hell, I'm afraid that I'd kill myself and that I'd die. And yet

I hate you so much! You bring out all of these emotions in me and then I take it out on my children. It's all so horrible that I feel like I could die and I feel that I've hurt myself and you've *made* me hurt myself. – –

**A:** So the feeling is that if you explode here and express this hate for me, that you'll kill me and that way you feel as if you'll kill yourself because you think that I'm your lifeline.

**P:** I think that you like that idea. You're my whole life and I can't function without you and you just sit and gloat about it.

**A:** I think the problem here is that you confuse your thoughts with actions. It's as if you think that your words are like magic, and as if you *could literally* kill me.

**P:** – – I feel that I could kill you! It happens every time you talk to me! – – I feel just like you are a condescending parent and I feel like screaming! – – – I can't believe that anyone can be so emotionless. No matter what I do! I can't get anything out of you!

**A:** I think this may be another device that you use. You feel that I *want* you to explode here and so you won't do it. Your hope is that I'll get impatient if you don't. And if you make life too hard for the kids and Tom, your hope is that I'll step in and stop it.

**P:** Suddenly I feel that I couldn't care less! You're nothing to me. I'll just go home and be a wife and a mother and you can go to hell! It gives you satisfaction to see me being so childish! – – If I could just be *positive* that I could *not* get you emotionally upset, then I could do anything in the world. I could do anything I want.

**A:** What's the detail of the thought?

**P:** I could rant and rave and scream! Suddenly I don't care any more! Why is that? – – – – – I feel like you are my *enemy* and that *you* are out to *get* me. That scares the hell out of me because I feel that I *need* you so much! –

**A:** We'll stop here for today.


## DISCUSSION

The patient begins by expressing self-directed hostility and aggression, manifested by her sense of guilt and worthlessness. After passing quickly over the incident with her children, she goes on to talk about the feeling as if she had eaten a penis. My thought at the moment is that this latter material was expressed for my benefit, with the fantasy that she would be pleasing me by producing that type of primitive material, and that it is equally important for me to keep track of her real life behavior to see the repercussions of the analytic process in her outside relationships. It is with this in mind that I focus on the explosion with the children, which leads to her reaction to the husband's call. And it becomes clear from the nature of the call and the patient's reaction to it that she has displaced the oedipal conflict from the transference into the relationship to her husband. Rather than make this as a direct interpretation, I choose instead to get her to elaborate upon it, and she herself indicates through her negation that my supposition is correct, and she then goes on further to indicate how the father, the husband, and I are all equated in her mind.

Once again she describes the displacement of the oedipal conflict to her husband, and at this point I interpret again the existence of this defense mechanism and of the anxiety which leads her to use the husband as the object of feelings that belong in the transference. This leads to her awareness of the changes in the relationship to her parents, as well as the anxiety over experiencing and expressing her hostility toward me. In a series of interventions I focus upon this issue which finally leads to the anticipation that she would be rejected as crazy if she were to express herself in the relationship with her father.

At this point I interpret the two sides of her conflict over aggression toward me, and add that the utilization of displacement toward her family permits her to evoke the kind of emotional counterreaction which is frustrated in the transference situation. This leads to increased awareness of her wish to elicit a positive response from me by doing well in therapy, and if that fails, to elicit an affective reaction in a negative way. And this in turn brings a further elaboration of the mechanism by which she turns her aggression inward in self-defeating or self-destructive ways, in the attempt to achieve transference gratification. In this context she maintains the fantasy that if she were to express the aggression toward me, it would mean the end of our relationship and therefore of her dependency upon me.

After my clarifying intervention, she projects to me the idea that I am experiencing pleasure in this type of relationship between us. In one sense the patient may be correct about this, inasmuch as my therapeutic ambition includes the necessity that she experience and elaborate upon this sense of total dependency, with the goal of ultimately resolving this dependency through analysis. It is therefore a sign of analytic progress that this type of relationship has developed, but the perception of me as personally gloating about it represents the transference projection.

My response of pointing out the fantasy of magic omnipotence of thought is an appeal to the therapeutic alliance, in that it provides her with a base for understanding the anxiety about experiencing and expressing the aggression. However, at the same time it represents a further transference frustration of the wish to evoke the affective response, in that it indicates that her aggression is not a source of anxiety for me. Her response is to the transference frustration that "I can't get anything out of you!" and I follow this up with further evidence of my capacity to remain the analyst in spite of her provocations. This last intervention may have been more than optimal, and in a sense was "rubbing it in."

Initially her response is to withdraw from me, to fantasy giving up the infantile and childhood transference demands, and to recognize that when she finally accepts the transference frustration she will then be psychologically more mature. But after the silence toward the end of the session, she returns again to the perception of me as the hostile enemy upon whom she is none-the-less dependent, with a reversion to the transference experience.

---

## SESSION 185

The patient came in and sat up on the edge of the couch facing me while she talked, and in that situation I did not take verbatim notes. The essence of what she said was that she felt pressured and pushed as if she couldn't take it any more, and felt me to be her enemy and that I was trying to destroy her and that she couldn't trust me. In my response I pointed out that her hatred of me stemmed from the fact that I didn't love her as she wanted me to, and from the fact that in her fantasy if she were to kill me she could not depend on me any more. I pointed out that she was experiencing this conflict between us as if she were two or three years old and not twenty-seven, and that she was reexperiencing and reliving old problems with me. I also pointed out that it was inevitable that she would feel awful until she got through with these conflicts. At that point the patient lay down on the couch and continued talking.

P: I felt completely wild yesterday. I ate enormous amounts. (Elaborates.) I know that I eat my hostility and I turn it against myself.
A: What makes that necessary?
P: My clitoris was tingling all day long yesterday. (Elaborates.)
A: What was the detail?
P: I know it has to do with. . . . . with eating a penis and with turning

into a penis. That's just the way I feel. It's like I'm a huge penis and I can destroy my mother after I destroy my father.

**A:** In this situation here you feel towards me as if I'm both your mother and your father and there's this same wish to destroy me. But then you project that onto me and you think of me as your enemy who is trying to destroy you.

**P:** – – – – I can see myself standing up and I stab you and then you lie there dead. – –

**A:** I think the question you have is about expressing these aggressive feelings and you're wondering is it really safe to express them here. I think you are still wondering if I'm strong enough to tolerate them and you're still unsure that I will *not* retaliate and attack you for them just the way your parents would.

**P:** All of this hostility followed my sexual and love feelings yesterday. I know it's all still sexual and I'm thinking about your penis. That's your most vulnerable point. I've had all kinds of sexual dreams. – – –

**A:** What's the detail about my penis being vulnerable?

**P:** I could kill you and then I'd take your penis and do anything I want to with it.

**A:** What do you see yourself doing?

**P:** I'd put it in my mouth and I'd suck on it. You'd be dead and you can't give me anything. Then I'd destroy all of the women who have hurt me. Mostly my mother. That scares me to death. I can picture my mother and father and they are dead and they're helpless and it all scares me.

**A:** So the fantasy seems to be that you'd kill your father and put his penis on yourself and use it to kill your mother. But then they'd be dead and you'd be scared because you would be wondering who would take care of you.

**P:** – – – . . . . . To think that you'd sit there full of life and strong and then I'd kill you. You'd lie helpless on the floor. I don't like it at all because you're all gone and then there's nothing there. – – – Now I get that feeling in my clitoris and also in my mouth. It's sexual and I feel so weak and yet it's all so violent. – –

**A.** What's the feeling in your clitoris?

**P:** I feel as if I could have an orgasm and it's wonderful and I love it. I want to take a penis inside of me. It's all so wild! Now I see myself taking off my clothes and *absolutely*. . . . . destroying you! I'd be so vicious.

**A:** What do you picture?

**P:** – I see us making love and your penis is inside of me. I'm a child and I'm vicious and I yank your penis and grab it off and stuff it in your mouth and then I put it in mine and I chew it up. My mother and father are making love and I go in their room. . . . . I hate them! I want to destroy them for all the. . . . . I'll stop that noise.

**A:** I think what's happening is that you are reexperiencing a feeling from when you were a little girl and it's a feeling that scared you but that you never were able to express then. You're hearing the noise and you're going into their room where they are making love. What are you doing?

**P:** I'm going in there. But first I am going to go down to the kitchen and get a knife. I'm in my parent's room and I stab my father in the back. Now I yank his penis off and I'm stabbing my mother with it. I can't stand that noise!! I feel as if I'm standing over their bed and my parents are dead and I've done it and I'm delighted. Now I'm going to take that God-damned penis and do a million things with it. – – I feel so vicious and I'm going to do vicious horrible sexual things. – –

*Cry*

**A:** You stopped that fantasy abruptly.

**P:** . . . . . I'll put it in my vagina and then in my mouth. I'll put it in their mouth and in their ears. – – It's that noise that they make that causes all of these feelings in me. I hate them and I'm going to destroy them! I'm going to do wild things! I'll do anything at all that I want! This is such a weird feeling! I'm going to grab your penis and pull it off and destroy you. (Elaborates.) Now I'm going to scream. I'm so tired of being hurt with it! You'll never hurt me with it again. I'll kill you for giving your penis to those other women! (Elaborates.) You don't care how you hurt me. You destroyed me with it, but you don't care. I'll see to it that you never do it again! You can't ever put it into another woman again. I'll kill you and I'll kill them. I'll eat it. Then it will be inside of me forever and you'll never get it. I'll show you! This is such a pleasure! – Now I've got such a pain in my hip! It's like with intercourse. I can't stand it. I'm just a big sucking mass and that penis is in my mouth and my vagina and in my hands. Those are all the ways to get it. (Elaborates.) I love to think that I could do that! I'd really fix my father so that he could never ever do that again. – – – I feel like I've gone wild.

*Cry, Scream, Fury*

**A:** What's the detail of the thought?

**P:** I'm scared and I feel just as if I've done all of this.

**A:** This is like what we were talking about yesterday, that for you thinking is the same as doing. It's as if you still think that your thoughts and wishes are like magic and they can make things happen and that's why you are so afraid of them.

**P:** But it would all give me such a pleasure. It would be the greatest. It would be just like having an orgasm.

A: I think this helps us understand some of the fear of expressing your thoughts and feelings here completely. If you did, you'd find out that I'm not killed or castrated or terrified of you. On the one hand that would be reassuring, but it would also be frustrating because it would mean that you'd have to face the fact that your thoughts are *not* as powerful as you'd like them to be.

P: – – – Now I feel trapped and I don't know what to do. – –

A: We'll stop here for today.


### DISCUSSION

In her behavior when she first comes in and sits on the couch, the patient is indicating the intensity of the conflict currently experienced in the transference, and is confirming the idea that in yesterday's session the transference frustration had been more than optimal and had produced a transient interference with the therapeutic alliance. In spite of this I maintain the analytic situation between us, responding in an analytically appropriate way even though she is looking at me at the time, and appealing chiefly to the therapeutic alliance through my explanation of the transference responses. I also offer some indirect reassurance when I point out the inevitability of the painful experiences she is having. Both through what I say and also through my nonverbal behavior of composure and control, I am able to help her reestablish the temporarily disrupted therapeutic alliance and thus resume the analysis in its usual form.

After describing her symptoms yesterday, she goes on to express a primary process fantasy in which she destroys both parents through her identification with the father's phallus. I want to be sure that the therapeutic alliance is again consolidated, and because earlier in the session she had seen me as wanting to destroy her, I choose to point out the origin of this projection of me as her enemy. This interpretation has two functions. First, it explains one of her psychic mechanisms, and thereby is an appeal to the self-observing ego designed to help offset the transference perception of me as the enemy, and thus to strengthen our working together. Second, by interpreting this defense I am also preparing to bring out the conflict against which it was used. Following her perception of herself stabbing me to death, I again appeal to the therapeutic alliance in my intervention about her fear of expressing the hostility, and this ultimately leads to the regressive fantasy of castrating me and the using my penis as an aggressive instrument.

By rephrasing her fantasy, I am again indicating my acceptance of its content and my lack of anxiety that she feels this way, and I am thereby indirectly encouraging her to explore the fantasy further. This intervention has the desired effect of reducing the intensity of her anxiety, and permits her to experience the rest of the feeling more directly as a sexual experience. With my encouragement by asking her for details, she elaborates on the experience in the transference, with its elements of sexual excitement and of violent aggression. Without transition this transference experience leads immediately to the primal scene, which is then described in the present tense.

The first part of my intervention is an explanation of the current transference phenomena, addressed to the self-observing ego and designed to assist her in the mastery of the conflict being mobilized. The second part is an attempt to encourage her to continue to reexperience the primal scene directly by expressing the intervention in the present tense.

Her response indicates that this is successful, in that she now verbalizes a detailed immediate expression of the feelings and fantasies which had accompanied the primal scene experiences as a child. As she goes on, her affect mounts in intensity and the experience is shifted from the memory of witnessing the parental intercourse to the immediate father-transference response to me, with fantasies of revenge on me for the infidelity. As this continues, she has a sudden conversion reaction of pain in her hip, the immediate transference experience subsides, and she begins to take greater distance from it and gradually to resume her composure and her secondary-process thinking.

In this context she brings up the fantasy, ". . . I feel just as if I've done all of this," which indicates the intensity and psychic reality of the experience just completed, and at the same time is a reflection of the interference in present-day reality-testing by the previously unconscious fantasy. This permits me in several lengthy interventions to help her again recognize how thought and action still tend to be equated in her mind, and also to help her recognize that the fantasy of magic omnipotence of thought is actually a rather subtle defense against feelings of weakness or helplessness.

This has been a meaningful session. Although we have considered and discussed the primal scene experiences many times in the past, on this occasion she did so with greater regression and more intense affect and elaboration of fantasy than ever before. This is one of the hallmarks of the working-through process, where material must be gone over in a repetitive manner. But with each successive approach to the same material, the qualitative and/or quantitative factors involved in the experience or the thought process are intensified. When this working-through has occurred sufficiently so that the patient is capable of full experience and recall of the memories, fantasies, and accompanying affects without needing unconscious defenses against them, mastery over this material can then be achieved. The material can then be admitted to consciousness more readily, the affects associated with it can be discharged, and the fantasies which accompany it can then be subjected to the correction of learning and of the adult ego functions.

## SESSION 186

**P:** – – I felt so much better when I left here yesterday. I had such love for you but then I got so nervous! And then I felt hostile. It was a wild love and not the relaxed kind. (Elaborates.) I dread this coming weekend because Tom is going to be working.

**A:** Let's look at the sequence of those events. You felt better and then you felt love and then you were nervous and then you felt the hostility and then you felt wild and so on. What comes to your mind about the connections between all of those?

**P:** If I let go and just felt the love, I know I'd destroy you because there is also so much hate there. It's the same thing as it was with my father and that's why I am this way. I had such love for him but it was completely rejected and so it all turned into hostility. And that's why I do it now. I get so excited and then I start to expect love and then you slap me in the face and I don't know what I'm doing. Now I've got feelings in my bottom and in my mouth and it's just like I felt yesterday. – – I felt fine after I left here yesterday and I had lots of fun with the children and I was happy and was a good mother. We went out to get an ice-cream cone. – . . . . . I was all family-oriented and content and so happy with everything. . . . . . I still think that every man I look at I can seduce and destroy and I know I want to. That's just like I want to do with you. But I wish I didn't have all of this hostility.

**A:** I think the primary wish is here toward me, and then you shift it secondarily onto the other men you see. It's like the fact that your primary problem was with your father and then got shifted to other people. Let's look at the wish to seduce and destroy me and see what comes to your mind.

*Anxiety,*
*Cry*

**P:** It all starts with my love feelings. – – I think about my uncle. – – If I ever let my love feelings. . . . . men are all suckers. – –

**A:** You broke that thought off in the middle.

**P:** If I ever let them go I know you'll act on them. I see my father in Maine and I can see his penis and I could reach out and get it. This makes me sick because that's all that I would have to do. Men are all huge sexual things. All they are is just a penis. (Elaborates.) That's all they ever think about, no matter who they are. It can even be a two-year-old child. I just have to say, "I love you and let's play," and then I know I can get it.

**A:** So the fantasy is that if you let yourself go here that I'll respond and let you play with my penis. But if I don't respond to that, then you'll feel rejection and feel that I've slapped you in the face and that I don't care about you. So what we can see is that you've set the situation up to be impossible for you either way.

**P:** Either one of them brings such hostility! – – I feel wild! I want to destroy you sexually! I'm going to prove that you're *not* God!

**A:** What's the feeling?

**P:** I feel that you're rejecting me and so I tell myself that I'll show you. I'm going to go wild and have a tantrum and destroy you! I'm going to get a knife from the kitchen and stab you. I hate you and hate your guts. I am going to take your penis and destroy anyone that I want to with it. I'll stab them with my penis. Especially when you reject me I know that you are vulnerable.

**A:** How do you mean?

**P:** It's as a child that you reject me, so I'll be a woman and a bitch and that way I'll destroy you. (Elaborates.) I'll become a great big woman and absolutely destroy you. It makes me mad at myself that I can have any feelings of love for you. It makes me such a patsy and such an idiot! – – I feel so completely frustrated! God-damn it! Now I'm remembering a time when the whole family was around the Christmas tree and I was feeling love for my father and happy that the family was together. Suddenly he turns on me and says, "I can't stand you," and he just leaves the house and goes off to his mistress. I hate him! I could kill him! It's just like he wants to take every wonderful feeling in the world and cram it up my rear just like a bunch of shit. I don't feel like giving you the same chance! – – I'm eating my hostility. What else is there to do with it?

**A:** So we can see how these old conflicts from the time when you were a little girl with your father have been buried all this time. Now you're repeating them with me and that leads you to feel that I'm just like him and that I'm going to react as he did. And so you don't see me as your analyst but rather as your father.

**P:** I can't believe it. I feel as if I hate you so much! And I know that you hate my love feelings and so I hate you worse. And that makes me hate them too.

**A:** Your thought is that I hate your love feelings. What comes to your mind about that?

**P:** If I ever let them out, you'll throw them back in my face because you don't want them. – –

**A:** What's the detail?

**P:** You just don't want them. Anything *outside* of the family is all that you want. (Elaborates.) I feel like I'm two years old and you're reject-ing me and now you'll run off to your mistress and I'm supposed to sit and swallow my hostility when all the time I could kill you! You just want to bring out my love feelings so that you can kick them around the room because you get such joy out of it!

**A:** I think that this is the same sequence of events that happened last night. You were feeling warm and you were having fun and you were focused towards the family and the kids and you had gone out to get some ice cream, and then you reacted to Tom working just the same as you would to me. It was just like your father and the Christmas tree. You expected that the same thing would happen, so you became angry and resentful in advance and everything was all spoiled.

**P:** I know that I'm reliving my childhood here and I feel very little and I see you as a big horrible bastard. It would be like a dream to think that you are anything else.

**A:** What comes to your mind?

**P:** It would be a fairy tale to have a father who will stay at home and who will love the family and it's just not true! I can love you but then I always say to myself, "Watch out because you are going to be hurt. He's a bastard and you can't trust him." I'll climb too high and then I'll fall flat on my butt. – – Oh hell, now I'm so depressed. It would be such fun to love you and feel free and be able to express myself without fear. But that makes me ten times more mad than I was. I get so depressed and hostile. I had a small chance to love you this morning and to have you respond in a positive way.

**A:** What was the detail of that chance?

**P:** That you'd take my feelings and be warm and fatherly and that you wouldn't kick me or run around with other women. I occasionally do feel that I *can* love you and that you're warm and nice and strong and that you're not going to let me down. But it's as if I *want* to hate you and get back at you and get back at my father that way and think of ways to destroy you. *I've* decided to hate you and to go on thinking that you're just like my father. – – If I ever had feelings of love and let them out and if you didn't reject me for them, then I'd feel that I'd seduced you and that I'd destroyed my mother. I know that I can take rejection better and then I can hate and hate and it's almost fun. – – – Now suddenly I'm scared! I'm getting that feeling in my clitoris. – – – I feel just as if I'm alone and I'm scared. It's just like I've gone in there and killed my parents! – – I guess that I again am thinking that the thoughts will actually happen! – – – – This idea to kill you comes to my mind and I'm so afraid of you. I'm afraid that you'll hurt me and I'm afraid of being alone. – –

A: We'll stop here for today.


### Discussion

In the first part of the session the patient's material indicates that the analytic work done here yesterday has resulted in a somewhat greater capacity for ego mastery over the conflicts accompanying the primal scene experiences. This illustrates the theoretical concept that when previously unconscious fantasies become conscious in a meaningful way, the intensity of the accompanying anxiety is reduced. In this early portion of the session she is capable of standing off, taking distance, and commenting upon this material from the vantage point of her adult integrative capacities, and she goes on to describe the brief symptomatic remission when she was able to be happy and content in her role as a mother.

However, as her associations continue the transference elements again come to the fore, with the fantasy of seducing and destroying me followed by a return to the conflict with the father and the fantasy of successful seduction of him. At this point I want to focus the conflict back into the transference by pointing out the double-bind type of psychology she has established for herself here. This confrontation results in the resumption of the experience of conflict in the transference, which then leads to the recall of another traumatic experience at Christmas with the father. This experience might not have been particularly traumatic by itself, but the likelihood is that for her it represents a number of similar types of experience that must have occurred throughout her childhood, condensed and now symbolically represented by the specific memory that has just emerged.

My generalized transference interpretation is probably unnecessary, since it does not represent anything new and does very little beyond re-

iterating to her the fact (which she really already knows) of her transference response to me. However she does add a new element when she
projects to me the idea that I hate her feelings of love, and when this is
explored she again experiences the father's desertion of her as a transference reaction. This permits me to point out to her how the sequence of
events which had occurred in childhood is being repeated not only in the
analytic transference situation, but also that the same sequence of events
occurred in her external life with her family in response to what she felt
was a mild rejection by her husband.

In her response to this interpretation she indicates an important step
toward modification of these archaic, automatic, and unconscious mental
processes when she says, "It would be like a dream to think that you are
anything else." The elaboration upon this leads to the fantasy of how
things might have been in the original situation with the father, and in
the current transference situation with me. She goes on to recognize that
the current perception of me as the father is actually the result of a wish
to see me that way. But this type of progressive movement is short-lived,
and is followed almost immediately by a regression to the transference feelings, accompanied by the fantasy that she has actually killed her parents.
However, this is followed by the capacity for increased self-observation and
mastery as she says, "I guess that I again am thinking that the thoughts
will actually happen!" The analytic work yesterday and my pointing out
that she equates thought with action has produced within her a greater
capacity for recognition and awareness of her own mental mechanisms,
thereby enhancing her chances for ultimate successful mastery of the conflict.

This session is a continuation from yesterday, in that it deals with the
same conflicts but with significantly less transference distortion and with
a greater capacity for reflection and understanding of those experiences. In
this way it is again part of the working-through process, and in this she is
making a small bit of progress toward ultimate resolution of the archaic
conflicts. This movement is as yet tentative and transient, but nevertheless
the beginning of structural change is occurring. There is somewhat greater
mastery than previously, the transference responses are somewhat less
automatic and are accompanied by greater self-observation, there are beginning attempts at integration of the traumatic experiences, and the regressive affective components are significantly less today than yesterday. It is
out of small increments of progress, as illustrated by this material, that
ultimately successful resolution of unconscious conflict and mastery of the
traumata can be achieved.

## SESSION 187

P: I feel so wild! I could kill or else I could seduce every man! All except Tom. I feel that I could. . . I want to be a woman and be attratcive to men and love it. Then with every man I'd take his penis and shove it down his throat. I hate them! I know this is all a defense and it's really like an egg-shell, but I'm sick and tired of being left alone! (Elaborates.) And I'm also tired of being scared to death. Occasionally I get a real good feeling and I love you and Tom and the children, but then I always tell myself, "Watch out," and I run like hell and turn into a real bitch! (Elaborates.) Sometimes I get such strong feelings of love for Tom, but then I die and I could kill him for being so nice. I had a dream where I was running. It was in Springfield and I was with that boy and also some other friends. It was typical of how I feel about you. Jean was there. One time in high school we went swimming in the nude and somebody took a picture of me and passed it all around the school. I was taking a sunbath and I got caught and they said all kinds of sexual things about me. Now I think it was you in the dream and I'm thinking about all of the stuff that I've told you. He was trying to make love to me and I expected him to slap me. He had an umbrella and it was all taking place on a hill. There were a lot of eggs. I kept trying to find one that was hard, but they were all soft. Then suddenly *I* had the umbrella and I beat that guy over the head with it. I woke up with wonderful strong sexual feelings and they were the first I've had in so long. – – Then it all turned to feeling like a bitch and I wanted to destroy any man that I want. – – The dream started with Tom kissing me and it gave me such sexual feelings. I *want* so much and I can't have it! I want a normal life and love and a husband and children and I feel I could die! – – It all boils down to my father and how the son-of-a-bitch rejected me. So my defense is to seduce and destroy and be playful and it's all a defense against complete rejection. But there's no way I can compensate and really the whole thing makes no difference. (Elaborates.) He was so sick and weak and he was nothing and I wanted him to be. What good does it do to feel that I can seduce and destroy men or even do it to my father? That's not the things that I want. I was so scared in that dream until I got the umbrella! And then I had a surge of feeling that was mostly anger. – – I really have no defenses and I know that I *know* that I do care so much! But I hate to admit it. Because then I leave myself wide open and I'm hurt and hurt. It's like with Dr. Smith

*Cry*

and I sometimes wish that he'd left me wide open. Sometimes I wish that people would stomp all over me and stab me in the mouth because I don't give a shit. – – And yet I know that's not true. I want to take you and cut you open from head to foot so that you're just one big open sore and then I'll pour salt in it, but I know that I'd just be hurting myself. – – – – I'm beating my head against a wall. I can feel what I want but I can't carry through. I want to love Tom and have sex for him and love the children because they are Tom's but I can't. But why can't I? Tom is a wonderful person and he deserves love. – – And I also feel it about you and you won't let me carry it through. – –

**A:** How do you mean?

**P:** Well, you're not my husband and my children are not yours and you have a wife and family of your own.

**A:** And what comes to mind?

**P:** You're just not very nice.

**A:** But what's the detail about my having a wife and family?

*Cry*

**P:** You do and I'm no part of it. And I want to be! And yet that scares the hell out of me. Do you run around and have affairs? You're a son-of-a-bitch but *this* is the one way I could ever get you! Now I feel frustrated by your wife and family! That's just fine! That's what I want! I can see you running around and having affairs and I know I want it! But if it's true I'll kill you! And yet it's the only way. It's sick and horrible but it's the only way I have. That excites me and I feel that maybe I have a chance! And yet it goes against everything that is inside of me.

**A:** So we can see that one of the things keeping you from loving Tom and the children is your own wish to have your father sexually, and that's being repeated today here with me. It's as if you've never given up the little girl's wish to have her father.

**P:** But that's the only way I can ever be satisfied. It's the only way that I can get out my hostility. – – – There's something else that I forgot! – – – Now I think about my father and of all the different phases of our relationship. It all comes down on me! – – – Now I have that feeling in my mouth and vagina! It's the ultimate in life. It's all I want! I'm mad that you constantly point it up to me! You trap me into it, and no matter how I dodge, you drag me into that thought! – – I feel that you want something from me and that you're keeping me from my happiness and you're constantly gouging at me. – – – – – I hate you and I wish you'd let go of me. You're destroying me and my family. I wish I could let go and make you let go, but I can't. It's as if you're *not* my father and you never were and I'll never see you again and I'll never be satisfied! – – – – – – – – – Now

I'm scared and I feel like this is it. I don't like you and I don't trust you and you can't help me.

**A:** What's the detail?

**P:** You're a horrible person and you're not nice at all. I feel like walking out because you'll never give me what I want and it's all so depressing! – – The thing I want most is to love you and I know I'll never!

**A:** To love me or to have me love you?

**P:** (Sigh.) To have you love me. That's for sure. – – It's *all* that I want in life and it would make *me* so happy. – – I've been dreaming that you'll sweep me off my feet and take me, and that this psychoanalytic situation will disappear. But it never does! It makes me so mad that I could kill you or I could die! – –

**A:** And yet the healthy part of you knows that this is the only way for you to get what you want in life. For me to give in and love you and respond to you sexually and so on would be to doom you to a life of chronic neurosis.

**P:** That's what scares me. Why do I want it so badly?

**A:** That's a good question. What comes to your mind?

**P:** – It would be like everything else.

**A:** How do you mean?

**P:** It would be like all of the other men. I always go from one to the other and I tell myself that I'm madly in love and that he's all I want. But then I get it and I lose interest and it's not what I want after all. But it drives me nuts wanting it. – –

**A:** We'll stop here for today.


### Discussion

The patient begins with a description of the generalized conflict relating to men, in which the wish is to seduce them sexually as the first step toward castrating and destroying them. This is experienced toward her husband, as well as other nonspecific men, and is also a continuation of the transference wish and conflict relating to me. It leads to the dream, with its references to adolescent exhibitionistic conflict and its symbolic reference (the umbrella) to her phallic strivings and fantasies of castrating the man. Accompanying the dream, however, are feelings of sexual arousal, reflecting the reduced defenses against such drives as the result of the analytic work being done, and the mobilization of such feelings in the transference relationship. This, in turn, leads to her expectations of rejection in the transference, as had occurred in her childhood with the father, with subsequent elaboration of her aggressive fantasies as the defense against the passively experienced rejection.

After describing the more mature and adult feminine wishes in relationship to her husband and children, she focuses them spontaneously into the transference, but then in a regressive fashion projects to me the defense ". . . you won't let me carry it through." My questions are an attempt to block this projective defense. and lead to the elaboration of the derivative oedipal triangular relationship concerning my wife and family, with herself excluded. She goes on to the fantasy of herself identified with the father's mistresses and thus achieving oedipal gratification, while at the same time expressing her hostility and resentment against being forced into that role in her attempt to achieve satisfaction with the father. All this is experienced in an immediate way in the transference reactions toward me, as she goes on to elaborate the ambivalent conflict over wanting the father sexually, compared with wanting him in a more complete relationship.

My oedipal transference interpretation is an attempt to appeal to the more rational and mature ego functions, and thus reduce the intensity of the defensive projection of her conflict by pointing out that the source of her current difficulty is her continuing wish for sexual gratification by the father. This results in further elaboration of the oedipal wish, but also a recurrence of the projective defense that it is my fault for pointing these issues out to her and that I am keeping her from potential happiness. This is partially true in that the continuing transference fantasies, wishes, and demands (which are a repetition of the continuing oedipal attachments to the father) keep her from relating in a more mature and gratifying way to her husband and family. However, the idea that this is my fault represents a continuing use of projection and unwillingness as yet to face fully the fact that it is her own persistent wishes for infantile and childhood gratification that create and sustain the transference and the incestuous fixation upon the father.

Following a further elaboration of the oedipal wish and the anticipation of its ultimate frustration in the transference, my intervention is an attempt to highlight the conflict between the regressive wishes seeking full and direct gratification, and the more mature reality-oriented self-perception which recognizes the needs for frustration of these oedipal wishes and the ultimate long-term advantages in renunciation of the childhood objects and fantasies. At the end of the session, the patient elaborates upon this issue by describing her acting-out of this conflict with other men. The search for the oedipal object leads her to experience love for a particular man until the relationship is gratified, at which point there is a recognition that the man is *not* the father and therefore that the oedipal wish is not being satisfied. At this point she breaks off the relationship and again seeks the gratification of the oedipal object in another man, with a repetition of the same cycle of disappointment.

This session has not produced any new material, but is part of the working-through process in which the now-conscious oedipal wishes and expectations of frustration are again experienced and expressed as part of the ultimate movement toward mastery of the conflict. This type of repetitive reexperiencing of the childhood conflict is a necessary precursor to its ultimate resolution through voluntary renunciation.

## SESSION 188

**P:** ––––––––––––––––– I felt on Monday that you kicked me out of here. –– I don't know how I feel except that I'm mad. I felt that you said it's senseless for me to have these dreams about you and these wishes that you love me, because you never will. ––

**A:** You felt that I kicked you out of here?

**P:** I don't know. I felt like. . . . . you drew a line and you said no. It was like a little girl going to her father and she says, "I love you and will you marry me?" And the father says, "No." ––

**A:** And you felt mad?

**P:** I want to completely withdraw and tell myself that I don't trust you, and that would be my way of hurting you. Monday I was in a bad mood and I had the urge to slash myself and to bleed and bleed. I felt as if I've been deserted.

**A:** What was the detail of that feeling?

**P:** I feel hopeless. I guess I must have the fantasy that I'll actually get you and so you were telling me that I'm not going to. It's killing me. I can't stand it and I feel deserted. It's just like when my parents would go out and it's just like Springfield. It's all so black and I feel stunned.

**A:** What are your associations to that?

**P:** It's as if I must hang on even more. I can't cut you up and I feel as if I *really* need you now. –––

**A:** You mentioned before that you wouldn't trust me and that you were going to withdraw from me, which would be a way of getting even and of trying to hurt me. What comes to your mind about that?

**P:** I can't figure it but that's the way I feel. It's like the girl saying,

"He's just a mean old man." That's always my defense. You probably can't care less, but I feel that it hurts you. You say, "Trust me," and I hurt you by not doing it. And then you desert me. This just doesn't make sense. – –

**A:** I think you are repeating with me the feelings that you had about your father and also all the defenses that you used against those feelings.

**P:** I just don't know where I stand.

**A:** And that was your thought as a little girl too.

**P:** – – I have to have my defenses. Nothing is ever carried through. You say, "Come over to me and trust me and I'm your father." But then I start to do that and then you push me away. – – I can't just fall apart. – – This is what keeps me from really getting mad, the idea that there's a chance.

*Shout,*
*Cry*

**A:** I think it keeps you from *expressing* the feeling of being mad. You already *are* mad.

**P:** I don't know what you are going to do! Are you going to fall apart or hit me or what? (Elaborates.) I hate you. I could kill you! It's all your fault! – – – Now I think of the time that I found out about my father's first affair. He took all three of us girls to a baseball game and while we were sitting there he said to us, "Please forgive me because I love you." I wanted to kill him! It should be one or the other! I wish you'd beat me up and tell me to get out. I know I'll never have your love! You just want to dangle that lollipop. I don't need you! I could kill you. I want to slice you up and make you bleed as you do to me! (Elaborates.) Can I stand up to a weak person and tell you to go to hell and say that I hate you? I can't do it. – –

**A:** What would happen to me if you do?

**P:** I've destroyed you. But I've got such a desire to do it. I don't know. I couldn't stand it. I'd *like* to see you shatter in front of me but it's all too much. I wanted it but I couldn't take it. – – This is all a ridiculous game. I'm the child but I must also be the woman and you're a child and I must protect you. What am I afraid of? – – What am I so protective about? You've destroyed me and you've taken me apart so why should I care about you?

**A:** What comes to mind about the feeling that you have to protect me?

**P:** For God's sake! I know you're so weak! And my hostility is so strong! I'd destroy the thing I love the most and want the most. That's all that matters. – – I don't know what I'm afraid of. Am I afraid that you'll shatter or maybe that you'll completely withdraw?

**A:** I think you are even *more* afraid that I won't do either one.

P: – – – – It makes me *mad* to think that you could sit there and just take it and that you would *not* react in one of those two ways. I know that you would.

A: What's the thought?

P: I *know* that you wouldn't just say that it's all right. I could kill you if you did!

A: What's going through your mind?

P: I'm so mad! I get mad at you and you just sit there! I *want* to hurt you and to ha∠e you react somehow! Or else I'll explode! And you're so calm! I'd like to stick a pin under you. I know that you must have some feelings. – – – You'd like me to get into a rage just so that you can sit and watch me. I guess I'd throw you by saying that I couldn't care less and just walking out the door. – – – It makes me so mad that you just *sit* there! You don't *do* anything! I feel so wild and you just sit there! I'm going to sit you out!

A: What's the fantasy?

P: I'll be God-damned to jump up and down for no reason! I can sit here just as long as you can! I want you to get wild too! I want you to get mad at me!

A: And what's your goal?

P: At least you'd be showing some feeling! I'm a human being! I wonder if maybe you're raging inside just like I am and you just won't admit it? I think you're trying to overpower me.

A: We'll stop here for today.

### DISCUSSION

The initial lengthy silence is an indicator of the intensity of the resistances operative at the moment, and suggests an angry withdrawal from me as a continuation of the transference conflict from the last session. Her first association that I had kicked her out of here on Monday is the confirmation that this is her reaction to the felt rejection of the oedipal wishes. Her elaboration of this response to the oedipal frustration leads to the description of the frustration of a girl whose father says he can not marry her. At the present moment she experiences this as a rejection, with the accompanying negative affects. However, it must be remembered that several sessions ago she expressed the other side of her conflict in the hope that I would be capable of accepting and tolerating her wishes and fantasy about me, but at the same time *not* react to them with an overt seductive response.

With the help of my suggestions that she associate in greater detail, the patient is able further to elaborate upon her reactions to the frustration of the oedipal transference fantasy. However she is also able to recognize that she still has a fantasy of real gratification of the oedipal transference wishes. Simultaneously, this is perceived by the self-observing adult ego and also experienced as a transference frustration, accompanied by the wish for revenge. In the fantasy of feigned indifference and frustrating me by not showing that she cares, the patient is again repeating a pattern of defenses used against the father in her overt behavior toward him during latency and adolescence.

My first interpretation is a generalized one involving not only the transference of the wishes but also of the defenses used against them in childhood. When she indicates that the fantasy of hope keeps her from "really getting mad," I point out the defensive nature of this in terms of her failure to differentiate the existence of the feeling from its conscious verbalization and expression in the transference. This leads to a further elaboration of the hostility and aggression, followed by the recovery of another fragment of childhood memory in regard to the baseball game and the father's asking forgiveness of the children. There is a transference repetition of the conflict between her feelings of sympathy and wish to protect and comfort the father, as contrasted with her contempt for his apparent weakness, and anger that he expected of her an adult response he was incapable of achieving within himself.

The recall of the incident at the baseball game is another illustration that the working-through process is proceeding. As working-through occurs, the recall of the traumatic relationships, experiences, feelings, and fantasies becomes increasingly detailed with filling in of new elements. This indicates that the defensive repression of these memories is gradually lifting, and that there is greater confidence that the ego will be capable of conscious mastery of these repressed memories as they emerge.

Subsequently this material leads to a recapitulation of the hostility, the defensive withdrawal, and the wish to provoke an emotional response from me, and thereby to achieve at least some derivative transference gratification. My remaining quietly calm and analytically neutral in spite of the provocative wishes serves as a reassurance that it is safe to experience her feelings fully, but also as a further transference frustration, thereby intensifying some of the negative transference experiences. Her elaboration of the wish that I become angry and attack her, as well as the fantasy that I want to overpower her, are manifestations of a masochistic component in her relationship to me in the transference, and as such reflect a similar orientation in her other relationships and attitudes.

The provocation and wish for the attack in the masochistic individual can be clearly seen as a result of the wish for a meaningful affective response from the object as an indirect sign of attachment and love. In this particular patient, these masochistic elements, while present, are not the predominating mode of interaction, but the structure of her response in this instance is in some ways similar to that seen in more classically masochistic people.

---

## SESSION 189

The patient is ten minutes late.

**P:** – – I'm sick and tired of everything. I feel that you've ruined my life and you couldn't care less. You turn me into a mess and I feel like hell and you're blasé and just sit in that God-damned chair and you don't care about the anguish inside of me. I'm torn apart. I'm so depressed. And to you I'm supposed not to have any feelings.

**A:** How do you mean?

**P:** I can't believe that you know.

**A:** What's the detail?

**P:** It's hell. I think of all of the fears! (Elaborates.) I'm hurting myself and Tom and the children and there's also the question of all of the money. And you're telling me that I should just take it. You can't see me as a woman. (Elaborates.) I've been depressed and eating and I'm anxious and I'm just a mess. I expect more from you and I expect you to help me. But you think I'm tougher than I am. Well I'm not! You're keeping me from a wonderful family life.

**A:** What comes to your mind?

**P:** I can either love Tom or else my children but not both at once. I can't believe that you don't feel anything for me, but I guess I *am* believing it.

**A:** What comes to your mind about both sides of that conflict?

**P:** Somehow I'm going to get your attention. I feel that you've shunned me and I can't believe that you can sit there and not know what I'm going through. When I leave, you don't even think about me. It's worst when I leave. It's hell every minute. I want more from you than you'll ever give me. I want you to love me and I want you to care and not to push me. I feel as if you're pushing me to be strong. – – I know that you listen but then you go off and go your own way. I feel so hurt by you. How can you

*Cry!* | see me go downhill and not care? If I came uphill then you'd praise me. – – I *need* you. Please don't reject me like this! You're turning the knife in me. It hurts! You son-of-a-bitch, I could kill you.

**A:** So we can see what's happening is that you are reactivating with me the old feelings about your father.

**P:** I just hope that you'll see how horrible I feel.

**A:** And then?

**P:** Then you'll *do* something.

**A:** What's the detail of the thought?

*Cry* | **P:** Then you'll love me. I feel just like a little girl and I'm getting kicked in the pants constantly.

**A:** So apparently your father didn't see how unhappy and miserable you were feeling. And he didn't love you or give you the attention or the concern that you wanted.

**P:** It's those other women! That's what hurts the most! (Elaborates.)

**A:** So if your father had loved your mother, then perhaps you could have accepted it. But he didn't, and so you thought that instead he should love you. But then if he screws around with other women you can't forgive him, and that's where all these intense feelings were stirred up.

**P:** I want you to see me and to know that I'm full of feelings. I'm a warm soft woman and there's so much to me, but you don't see it. All you would have to do is snap your fingers and I'd be. . . . –

**A:** Again it's like with your father. It's as if you said as a girl, why can't he see my love and see how much I could give him. Why can't he be satisfied with me and why does he have to go off to those other women?

**P:** – – I feel like such a nothing. How can I possibly be a mother and a wife? I need recognition. –

**A:** It's as if because I'm not responding as you want me to, *therefore* you're a nothing.

**P:** My father just didn't care! We three girls tried! But it made no

*Cry* | difference. Those women were all that he cared about! The *only* way that I can get my father's attention is to be a sexy siren. And that goes against everything that is in me and so I have nothing. I *want* something so badly and I can't get it!

**A:** What comes to your mind?

**P:** I don't know why it is. My children and my husband could be the happiness that I need but something is keeping me from it.

A: What are your thoughts?

P: I fight with my children for Tom and his attention, and Tom represents my father and then I always have the feeling that Tom is off with some other woman and it just goes on and on.

A: So we can see that you are kept from it by your own wish still to have your father. And that's what you repeat with me today in the feelings of needing my love and recognition.

P: Why can't I be loved just for being a woman and a mother? Why is it all sex?

A: But it's *you* who feels, "I've *got* to be that sexy bitch in order to get my father."

P: – But that doesn't solve my problem with you.

A: What's the detail?

P: I see you as a block that is keeping me from my family. I have all kinds of sexual feelings and dreams and yet I hate you. But you don't care and I'll just go beating my head against the wall and yet I'll never. . . . . –

A: What did you stop at?

P: Why can't you love me? Why do you force me to be this adult? What if I got myself to being a sexy siren and if I were to walk in and try to seduce you? Now I hate you for that! You won't accept me in any other way.

A: Let's look at your question. What if you *were* a sexy siren and walked in trying to seduce me?

P: I swear I *could* seduce you and I could do it as a woman.

A: And if you couldn't?

P: I don't know. Then I could. . . . .I don't *want* to be your little girl any more. I can't function that way and it's not fun. Now I'm just a fat housewife. I love my children but I can't have any sex with my husband. And I want that so God-damned much! I don't know if Tom really loves me or if he just wants sex. (Elaborates.) I can't believe that he loves me and the children both.

A: So you are also confusing Tom with your father.

P: You're all alike! The only reason that I'm safe here now with you is because I look so horrible!

A: If you became a sexy siren and you tried to seduce me and you didn't succeed, then it would mean that you would have to change your ideas that all men are just like your father.

P: – – – I don't know what to think of you. I wouldn't know what to do with you if you were *not* like my father. I've handled him for twenty-seven years and I know him. I don't *want* you to be nice to me. I hate you. | *Cry, Scream*

I don't know how to react to you. That's why I can't stand Tom. He's so God-damned nice and he loves me. And I hate it. I wish I could get to your ego and make you so God-damned mad at me that you couldn't stand it. – – –

A: We'll stop here for today.


## DISCUSSION

In a mild way the patient continues the masochistic theme from yesterday, emphasizing her symptomatology and suffering and attempting to elicit my sympathy and love, or else to make me feel guilty for the pain and distress she is feeling as part of the transference neurosis. Analogous to the surgeon who, in the course of his professional responsibility, must inflict a certain amount of pain upon his patient, the analyst must inevitably also cause his patient pain and distress. Although I am aware of the intensity of her distress and although I regret the necessity of inflicting pain upon her, I nevertheless also know that the analytic process demands that she experience and master these painful states in order that ultimately, through a renunciation of the oedipal object in the transference neurosis, the conflict can be definitively resolved.

Knowing this, I am able to tolerate her painful experiences without feeling guilt for them and without feeling called upon specifically to alleviate them or to respond to her masochistic provocations. To respond with sympathy, to gratify some of her transference wishes in this state, or to respond in ways that minimize her conflicts would be to reinforce neurotic suffering as a mode of adaptation in achieving childhood gratification, and would ultimately foster the masochistic elements and orientation in her object relationships. Instead, my responses initially are an attempt to encourage her to elaborate upon these issues and then to interpret them as transference repetitions of earlier ego states, and to offer on the basis of her transference perceptions of me several reconstructions of what her thought processes might have been as a child. In these reconstructions I am attempting to help her recognize that the necessary conditions for the normal resolution of the oedipal relationship (the father's love and attachment to the mother) were not present, and to try to help her recognize again the specific impact of the father's extramarital affairs upon her oedipal organization.

This leads to the feeling of herself as "a nothing." My intervention is an attempt to help her begin to recognize that this perception of herself as inadequate because she was unable to attract and hold her father, with its subsequent impact upon her self-image, is based upon an unrealistic expectation of herself as being qualified to fulfill his many needs. This is presented to her in the transference, and results in an immediate association to the father and to the fact that as a girl she had tried to do just that, but had been unsuccessful because of his sexual interests in the other women.

She goes on to describe how she reacts to her husband in the same way and with the same fantasies. My intervention that it is her own wish still to have the father which sustains the neurotic suffering is an attempt to help her more clearly recognize the impact and effect of the childhood fixation. In other words, I am preparing the groundwork for her ultimately to recognize that although the distorted relationships in childhood may have produced and accentuated the childhood neurosis with its distorting effects upon her subsequent psychological development, it is nevertheless her own persistent wish for this gratification of childhood fantasies that sustains and maintains the neurosis today. When this awareness is ultimately fully appreciated and recognized by the patient, it will represent an important step towards final resolution of the neurosis, inasmuch as it then indicates to the patient that she carries within herself the potential for renunciation of the childhood demands and thus for resolution and cure of the neurotic suffering.

The patient is not yet ready fully to explore and accept this facet of the conflict, and instead she returns to her complaint of being unloved and to the projection of the feeling that a relationship with a man is "all sex." My confrontation that it is she who wants to be the "sexy bitch" is an attempt to block this projection, but she maintains it in the perception of me as keeping her from her family. This projection is also continued in the complaint that I don't love her and in the fantasy that if she were to be the "sexy siren" she could seduce me. My question as to what would occur if she could not seduce me is an attempt to block this transference projection and ultimately leads to her perception of her own sexual desires for her husband but also the identification of her husband with the father in terms of the same derivative fantasy that "he just wants sex."

In spite of my pointing out the displacement from the father to the husband, the patient maintains its validity, elaborating that it is only the result of her symptoms (that she is less attractive than she might be) which keeps me from seducing her. At this point I again attempt to block the use of this defense by pointing out that if she were to try to seduce me and fail, it would have significant repercussions on her perceptions of other men. This intervention has the desired effect of mobilizing conflict and intense affect and of helping her to recognize and express the idea that the perception of me (and of the husband) as being identical with the father represents a continuing childhood wish. This causes her to distort the real loving qualities in her husband and to reject them in favor of the neurotic perception of the husband as similar to the father.

In other words, in spite of the conscious anxiety evoked by her suspicions and doubts that the husband might be having extramarital affairs, this material demonstrates that this particular symptom represents a disguised unconscious wish-fulfillment that the husband be like the father and thereby provide her with the oedipal gratifications which were frustrated in childhood. Her statement, "I've handled him for twenty-seven years and I know him," also reflects another source of resistance to change, in that the neurotic patterns are automatic, structured, and therefore familiar; whereas to give them up would mean facing the uncertainty of establishing new patterns of perception and response which would be unfamiliar and therefore would require a new form of psychic integration and the development of new structured patterns of behavior and adaptation. It is a combination of these forces, along with the reluctance to accept ultimate oedipal frustration, which leads to the apparently paradoxical response of anger and resentment if the man is nice to her or, as in the case of her husband, if he loves her.

---

## SESSION 190

**P:** – – – – – – – – – – I wonder why it is that when I feel so much going on inside I just can't talk. I feel like I'm going wild and yesterday I felt completely helpless! I felt like I needed Tom and that I'd die without a man. This morning I feel fat and ugly and completely unattractive. I know it's just an escape and I hate it.

**A:** This is something of a contrast from what you were feeling yesterday of being a sexy siren, and I think it's your attempt to try to feel safe here with me.

**P:** – – – This morning I feel lost in the world of my mother and father and I identify with my mother and I hate it.

**A:** You mentioned that you feel you're going wild inside this morning. What's the detail?

**P:** – I've got so many opposite feelings! Tom worked at the office all

last night and he didn't come home until this morning. I feel like I love *Cry,*
him! And I also feel like I hate him! I don't know who he is or who *Anxiety*
you are or who I am. I just orbit around. – – – I wonder why I can't see
you for what you are, but I know that I can see no reality. I hate
you and I feel that you rejected me and that you're mean and horrible.
I feel ugly and fat.

**A:** You mentioned that you can see no reality. What are you referring
to?

**P:** The reality of myself as a woman who is pretty and happy, and
the fact that you are nice and you're my analyst and that I shouldn't
try to get something from you all the time. I should want to go home
to my children and my husband because they're everything. I know that
I miss something the way that I'm living. – – But I hate feeling rejected
by the little girl and it always makes me feel like a nothing. And so I
eat in order to feel like a big woman and to try to be attractive. (Elaborates.) But more men are attracted to me and I feel I look uglier than
ever.

**A:** So it's as if you are repeatedly asking yourself the question whether
there is some way you could seduce me. It's like you've tried to do it
by being a good patient or a poor patient or being pretty or a child or a
woman or being fat or being thin, or any of the other things you have
thought about yourself.

**P:** I'm so scared to accept the thought that I can't do it. It would be
just like losing my father completely. It would be like he'd leave and
never come back!

**A:** What comes to your mind about it?

**P:** It's as if seduction can be our only tie. I can't stand the feeling
that I can never have you! That's just the way I felt yesterday. I felt
lost! (Elaborates.) I feel so helpless that way and so I hung onto Tom. *Cry!!*
I was having all kinds of realistic problems yesterday. (Elaborates.) But
I was so mad! I don't want to talk about it! – – Now I'm thinking about
the times that my father left home. I felt so relieved when he did. One
time my parents were planning a divorce and he went to live with my
grandmother. Right now I feel like crying, "Are you coming back?" I
want him to get out or forget it. He's going to drive me nuts! Get the
hell out! Just let me know where I stand. – – – – I'm so confused. I
have a wish to feel superior to men and not to need them and to be
able to do without them. If my father had left the first time he went
off I'd be able to be like that, but as it is I'm a mouse and I need a
man and sometimes he comes back and sometimes he doesn't. I want to

say that I don't care and that I don't need him and that's what I'd like to do with you. I just don't know where I stand. I keep wondering where is your vulnerable point? –

A: What's your fantasy about it?

P: I still think that somehow I can get you. –– Now I feel hysterical. –– I feel like I'm back in the hall in the house in Evanston. How did mother get my father back?

A: Apparently you have some fantasy about it. What's the detail?

P: Did she do it by getting pregnant? She probably let him make love to her. –– If I could just understand it! My father is in an affair and then all of a sudden he's at home making love to mother and I don't know how it all happened and I ask myself what's going on? –– If my father had left and he'd never returned then I could tell you to go to hell or else I could seduce you and cut off your penis and not give two shits about it. –– But when my father came back is the time when I hated him the most. –––

A: So it's as if each time that you come here it's equated with your father coming back and each time you leave it's like your father going away again.

P: It makes me so mad!! ––– My father would look at me and seem so innocent with his big brown eyes and act like he doesn't know. Those

*Cry, Scream*

are the times I could kill him. ––––– I feel so wild inside I can't get it out. My father took all of his guilt and he put it on me! He's not a man! I want to kill him! –

A: You mentioned that your father put his guilt on you. What are your associations to that?

P: He's done wrong! Why does he come back and just say, "I'm sorry!" It's not right! We have to take it every time. I hate him!! I'll *not* take it any more. God-damn it, I hate him! –– It scares me the most to hate him, but I have an urge to yell, "I don't want anything to do with you, so take your God-damned penis and get out." (Elaborates.) –– Why did I never say it to him? I just kept my mouth shut and accepted him back every time. –––– I want to say, "Get off my back forever. You're squashing the hell out of me." But that idea scares me. –––

A: We'll stop here for today.

## DISCUSSION

The patient's initial silence, followed by her description of the agitation and anxiety she is experiencing and coupled with the defense of feeling ugly and unattractive, suggests to me that she is defending herself against conflict mobilized in the transference yesterday in connection with the oedipal sexual fantasies. In actual fact, her appearance does not change very much from session to session, and I have seen previously how her insistence that she is ugly and unattractive is part of her defensive system against fantasies of seduction of me and of other men. Therefore, instead of waiting further I confront her with the contrast to her feeling and behavior yesterday and interpret immediately her defense against the anxiety mobilized by the transference conflict.

After the brief silence, she responds with an intellectualized generalization and, in an attempt to deal with this resistance, I inquire about the detail of the inner turmoil she is feeling. This intervention has the desired effect of further mobilizing the suppressed affect, and leads to her description of her regressive transference perceptions of her husband, herself and me, which are part of the reexperiencing of the childhood relationship to the father. Simultaneously, however, her question about seeing me as I really am indicates that there is no actual loss of reality perception. But this is immediately followed by the regressive transference experience, and in order to help her conceptualize the situation between us and to support the more mature ego functions, I refer her back to the question of reality. This leads to the expressed recognition of the realistic situation between herself and me, but is then followed by a further elaboration of the transference perception of having been rejected.

At this point I switch from a focus upon the therapeutic alliance to the interpretation of the various disguised ways in which she has attempted to seduce me in the transference, and this leads to her valid perception that to accept the idea that seduction cannot occur between us is ultimately to renounce the transference and thus to give up the childhood attachment to the father. There follows an intensification of the affective reaction of sadness and grief at the thought of renunciation of the father, and then a further elaboration of a component in the relationship to him by reexperiencing the specific thoughts and feelings connected with his separation from the mother. At this point she spontaneously reverts to the transference experience of confusion as to where she stands with me, with the experience again of the fantasy that she can have me.

Her question, "How did mother ever get my father back?" is an indication that she has wondered about this in the past, and my pointing out that she must have had a fantasy about it brings out the thought of the father impregnating the mother. This leads to the simultaneous recall and experience in the transference of her hostility at the repetitiveness of the separations. My own immediate association and intuitive response is to the daily reunions and separations from me in the analytic situation, which I feel was part of her reaction at the beginning of the session.

My intervention has the desired effect of helping her recall the further feelings and thoughts about the father's return, and with an increased mobilization of affect it leads to her description of feeling "so wild inside," which is the phrase she had used at the beginning of the session. Her comment about feeling guilty at the times of his return is an allusion to a new element in the situation which has not yet fully emerged, and my wish to explore this further leads to my question regarding the guilt. She responds with a further elaboration of her ambivalence as a child over the father's return, with the wish and simultaneous fear to tell him to leave forever. The issue of why she felt guilty is not yet clarified, but since it is the end of the session I can only make a mental note to myself to explore the matter further on some subsequent occasion.

Although no significantly new material has emerged today, the general theme of this session involves the continuing working-through in the transference neurosis of the ambivalent attachment to the father in the oedipal phase.

---

## SESSION 191

P: −− I want to get well and yet I hate you! I feel trapped. −−

A: What's the detail of the feeling?

P: I know that this is the only answer and I've gone so far so I must keep going. And yet I don't trust you. But I guess I do or else I wouldn't be here. I had a dream that I was in a prison and I was in the executive offices and couldn't get out. I was running from room to room. There was one man there that I was sexually attracted to and he seemed so nice. I was sure that it was you, but he was so nice to me. And still I felt trapped and I couldn't get away. − − − I have all of my real fears at home so that you really don't know me. I only show you one part of me.

A: What's the detail of the part that you don't show me?

P: It's the hostility that I feel. I never let any of it out. (Elaborates.)

A: And yet getting well also involves analyzing the hate and the resentment and other negative feelings about me. What comes to mind as to why you should keep from showing this?

**P:** I felt that you were very *mad* at me on Friday as I walked out. (Elaborates.) – – Yesterday I was out with Tom and we were driving when he suddenly stopped. I felt my terror that Tom was mad at me for yelling at him and I was scared to death. But it turned out that he wasn't mad at me at all. I'm so afraid that you'll get mad at me. I had my feeling at home on Saturday. It seems just like an earthquake to me. I have feelings of the earth ending and a big explosion and it always scares me so. – – – I wish that I could shake you off me. If I really got mad at you then I'd be cutting the string and you'd be off my back forever.

**A:** How do you mean?

**P:** Then I'd be a person and I'd be able to stand up and live on my own and not be so dependent. But I just can't. It scares me and I don't know why. – – This way I'm still hanging on to you. – – – My biggest fear somehow has to do with death and I guess it's that I'll kill someone else or else I'll die. – – – I used to get so mad as a child and I wonder what my thoughts were? Did I really want to kill my father? I would think about stabbing him with a knife. I wonder if sex comes in here too?

**A:** I think right now you are going back to remembering these thoughts about your father as a defense against the more immediate feelings you are having about me.

**P:** When I walked in I saw that letter opener on your desk and it scares me to death! | *Cry*

**A:** What's the detail of the fantasy?

**P:** I can see myself pick it up and put it into you and kill you. – – Now I have thoughts of actually killing you. And then I'd do more. It's something sexual. . . . . . I'd cut off your penis. – – – Why doesn't that make you mad?

**A:** Why should it?

**P:** This is the one vulnerable point. It was my father's and it's the same for all men. Without it they are lost. I'd like to do that to you and to make you a woman and make you feel helpless and like a nothing. I hate you. I know that doesn't bother you and it doesn't scare you. But I *want* to scare you. But you don't scare, do you? – – But if I get you mad enough then you'll pull your penis out and say, "I'll show you, and I'll destroy you with it." – – Why don't you get mad? Why don't you ever get scared? Is this some kind of a game? Are you trying to goad me? Are you trying to see how long you can sit there? That's just like my mother all over again. – – What bothers me most is that you just sit and don't say anything. That makes me mad! It scares me because I have a fear that I'll explode and do something terrible. If you'd just react to me then I wouldn't. – – – But by you not reacting at all I can't do anything and so I just sit here! – –

**A:** And what comes to your mind that I don't get mad or scared?

**P:** It means that you're not my father! You're my mother! My father would be scared, but my mother can outsit me! I know my mother wants to cut loose. You throw me! What's the matter with you?!

**A:** So you felt that your mother really *was* mad but she was just not going to show it.

**P:** It was a constant battle! One time I stuck my tongue out at mother and she made me sit in a chair. That's what you're making me do.

**A:** With your mother you felt that she *was* mad but was trying not to show it. With me you feel that I'm *not* mad. What comes to your mind about the difference?

*Anxiety, Anger*

**P:** – I want to cut you up in tiny pieces! I am going to get a rise out of you! I want to make you react. But if I let loose would it be worse if you *do* react or if you don't? I'll bet it would scare you if I grabbed that letter opener, but I bet I'd scare myself more. – –

**A:** So we can see that your thought that I was mad at you as you left here on Friday was really a *wish* and was an attempt to fulfill the fantasy that you had gotten an emotional reaction out of me.

**P:** I hate you! Don't you realize and believe what I want to do to you? (Elaborates.) I need controlling! (Elaborates.) Do something! Control me! Don't let me do it! – – I sit here and think about how I want to cut your penis off and put it inside of me and do vicious things with it. (Elaborates.) I get real pleasure thinking about it but it scares me. – – I

*Scream*

feel like a child and then as a big woman I have such sexual feelings. That should scare you!

**A:** How do you mean?

**P:** Doesn't it scare you? (Elaborates.) It should! I'll destroy you! – – My every thought will destroy you. All of my thoughts are about love and sex and hate. – – I've got a thousand knives inside of me and if I ever show my thoughts to you they'll destroy you. They're all right here! They're right here in my bust!

**A:** What's the detail of that fantasy?

*Anxiety*

**P:** Here's where the love is. And the hate. Mother's breasts could destroy me, so if you ever put your head here I have such a fear that I'll destroy you. I'm a woman and I have everything that a woman has. What

*Anger*

will happen?

**A:** Let's go back to the fantasy that you have knives in your bust. What's the detail?

**P:** If I turn my bust to you then my thoughts will come out like knives and they'll be able to destroy you just like penises. So I can't love or hate or do anything. And yet I do so much! It all evolves into my being a woman. I feel like a woman and like a mother and I remember how as a child I wanted to be a woman in order to love and also destroy my father. But now I *am* a woman and I want you to know this.

**A:** We'll stop here for today.

### Discussion

At the beginning of the session after the weekend separation, the patient verbalizes some of the elements of the therapeutic alliance, followed by the dream with obvious transference implications relating to her perception of being committed and trapped in the analysis. Her statement that she only shows one part of herself indicates that a number of already conscious resistances are operating, and it is against these that I ask the question about the part she doesn't show me. This leads to the intellectualized and defensive expression of the hostility, and my comment about analyzing the negative transference is an appeal to the therapeutic alliance and simultaneously an interpretation of the resistances against expressing the aggression.

Initially she deals with this by projection, describing the feeling that it was I who was angry at her in the previous session, but this is immediately followed by her account of a similar projection toward her husband over the weekend which had been apparently corrected by the reality of the husband's behavior or explanation to her. Once again she returns to the anxiety about expressing the aggression toward me, and in this is repeating the behavior pattern described in the previous session where she had intense wishes to verbalize the hostility and rage against the father, but instead kept her mouth shut and accepted him back every time.

She goes on to elaborate her recognition that to deal with the negative transference is another step toward renunciation of the oedipal ties. Then in a somewhat removed and isolated fashion she begins to wonder about the nature and extent of her aggressive childhood fantasies and adds the intellectualized question as to whether there may not also be a sexual component to this. I am struck by the patient's remoteness and intellectualized distancing of herself from the material as she describes this, and interpret it as a resistance against the immediate transference reactions. This intervention has the desired effect, encouraging her to express the previously withheld thought about seeing the letter opener as she came into the office. At this point, with genuine affect, she does begin to express the regressive transference fantasies of stabbing me with it.

Her question, "Why doesn't that make you mad?" presents a complex problem for me. In actual fact, rather than being mad I am pleased that elements of the negative transference are emerging more directly. However, to show this would be to give her "permission" to verbalize this hostility and would therefore interfere with the emotional transference experience of expressing the aggression and taking the chance that I might react, but ultimately finding that I don't. It would also be a depreciation of her hostility and its effects, and might be seen by her as my treating her like an impudent child. On the other hand, to indicate or express anxiety or concern about the emergence of these hostile feelings would mobilize further defensiveness in her and would interfere with the expression of the aggression. My responsive question, "Why should it?" is an attempt on the one hand to maintain her awareness of the therapeutic alliance, and at the same time is a request for further associations to the conflict she is experiencing over her aggression.

This leads to the fantasy of castrating me, accompanied by the recognition that I am not scared but also by increasing conscious awareness that she wants to frighten me, and this is followed by the transference perception of me being "just like my mother all over again." Accompanying this is the expression of anxiety over loss of control of the hostile and aggressive impulses, followed by the simultaneous transference experience and recollection regarding the mother's counteraggression. My intervention pointing out that within her own perception there is a significant difference between the mother's feelings and my own is again an appeal to the therapeutic alliance but it is also an indirect interpretation that at the moment she is using the maternal transference defensively as a justification not to express the aggression completely.

This has the desired effect of mobilizing further aggression and conflict about it, along with her determination to make me react in an emotional way, which then permits me to make the interpretation of the projection of anger to me in the previous session, which had been by-passed earlier. At this point the aggression and her anxiety and guilt over it emerge even more clearly, along with the feeling that she needs me to help her control her impulses and that I should be scared of her.

This sequence of material illustrates the theoretical concept of the importance of transference abstinence. Had I responded to her previously with anger or less direct expressions of counteraggression, the wish to evoke a reaction from me would have been unconsciously satisfied in a derivative form, and it would have subsided. By not gratifying the provocative wish, its frustration leads to its further intensification and eventual eruption into consciousness in her determination "... to get a rise out of you!"

With the elaboration of this material, her fantasy of the magic omnipotence of thought begins to emerge more clearly than ever before in the analysis, accompanied by intense affect as she elaborates upon her fear of the effects of her aggressive thoughts. Unverbalized by either of us at this point is the rational self-observing ego, which will ultimately be able to recognize and thus eventually master the anxiety evoked by these unrealistic fantasies of her omnipotence. Mastery of this conflict, and thereby achieving relief from the danger which such thoughts produce, can only be achieved after the fantasy emerges into consciousness accompanied by the affect appropriate to it. This material represents a significant step towards such ultimate resolution of the conflict.

In the meantime, however, she expresses the archaic fantasy of having knives in her breast and of using her breasts in a womanly sexual way as a means of expressing her ambivalence toward the father. Earlier in the analysis the oedipal fantasies connected with the father and with the seduction by the uncle were understood as having been organized in a regressive fashion around the unconscious fantasy of having castrated the uncle orally. In this current material, the reverse pattern is also demonstrated, in that the oral fantasies and ambivalence toward the mother's breasts and the fantasies of the oral triad are now organized in accordance with a later-stage phallic-level fantasy involving the equation of the phallus with a knife, and fantasies of phallic destructiveness. In this context she is now simultaneously identified with the mother who carries the destroying breasts and also with the father whose phallus can be used as a destructive weapon.

This fantasy emerges as a complete surprise to me at the time, and demonstrates once again how the analyst can provide the situation in which such fantasies can become conscious and can interpret the defenses against their recovery, but he has no way of knowing in advance what their content will be. Once these primitive fantasies have been experienced and expressed verbally by the patient, they can then be subjected to reality testing and secondary-process thinking. The final result is that what was previously an unconsciously experienced situation which once evoked intense anxiety is no longer perceived as dangerous, and hence it is no longer threatening.

As a result, anxiety is no longer experienced and the structured automatic response to the fantasy is eliminated, with subsequent more mature means of coping with the conflict established, resulting in a reorganization of the psychic structures involved.

# 8

## THE FOURTEENTH MONTH
### (Summary)

In the first session of this month the patient continued the theme of transference wishes for gratification from me in the role of the father, with increasing expression of anger and rage that I do not satisfy her infantile and childhood wishes. She followed this with an elaboration of how differently some of her friends are being treated by Harris, in that he is personally concerned and much more actively positive in his behavior toward them. Once again I pointed out her ambivalent conflict about the analysis, where on the one hand she knows that it can provide her with the opportunity for development and maturity which this other form of treatment will not do, but at the same time this induces in her a frustration of the infantile and childhood oedipal fantasies.

Her response was a positive one, recognizing the potential that analysis provides for her, but accompanied by a renewed perception of herself as a child in a temper-tantrum who is willing to defeat and destroy herself as a means of getting back at me for what she perceives is my rejection of her. This led to further working-through in the transference of the realization that her overt hostility and aggression serve as a defense against underlying feelings of love, and to elaboration of the fantasies that love is destructive toward the object. As part of this process she expressed again the fantasies that her vagina is like a mouth and that sexual activity will lead her to engulf me in a destructive fashion, and that to love in a sexual way involves swallowing and eating the object.

In the second session, the patient began by elaborating upon the conflict between her wish to be a warm, mature, and loving mother for her children, and her feelings of rivalry and envy of them for receiving the kind of love that she felt she had never gotten. This led to her fantasies that she would be anything that I wanted her to be, and that with Harris she had been able to please him by figuring out what he wanted, whereas with me she gets fewer cues as to what I want her to be. Both Harris and her father had wanted her to be a strong, masculine kind of woman who suppresses her femininity, and that she had tried to do this in an attempt to gain their approval. With this came the projected fantasy that I do not want her to be soft, warm, or feminine. With my attempts to help her recognize her reluctance to decide these issues for herself, she increasingly indicated her own desire to be a soft and feminine woman, with an increasing hope and acceptance of the possibility that this might be appropriate and that I would not reject or laugh at her for such feelings.

In the working-through process she is beginning to accept the possibility that she has a choice and that she need not continue the old pattern of trying to please the transference object in terms of the kind of person she becomes. In this process the automatic stereotyped patterns of behavior and response, based upon the patient's fantasy of ultimate transference gratification, come under increasing scrutiny and ultimate frustration. If I were directly or indirectly to indicate what I wanted her to become, the likelihood is that she would try to develop and maintain such patterns of behavior in the hope that this would ultimately achieve the gratification of my loving her. This kind of unconsciously fantasied transference response is utilized in the various "behavior-modification" forms of therapy in which the therapist directly tries to change, influence, or mold the patient's manifest behavior.

In analysis, however, where the goal is to help the patient free herself from childhood dependency upon a parental object for guidance and direction, this form of influence upon the patient is contra-indicated. Instead, the strategic goal is for the analyst to frustrate such expectations and demands for control and direction, and to foster her own independence and conscious free choice of behavior and adaptive patterns by which she wants to live.

In the third session, the theme was the transference conflict, with an increasing awareness of loving and trusting feelings toward me, accompanied by anxiety, headache, and a sensation of nausea. The desire to be a warm and loving woman was increasing, again leading to fantasies that she might successfully seduce me in that role. This led to the childhood oedipal fantasies that she could be a better wife to her father than her mother had been, and that she could have kept her father at home and made it unnecessary for him to seek other women. There was further recall of details of the father's affairs. One woman had been a feminine and loyal person, and apparently the patient had been subjected to gossip regarding her father and mother, and had been told repeatedly that the father's affairs occurred because the mother had been so difficult for him as a wife.

In this context the patient returned to the current transference fantasy that she might successfully seduce me, with growing awareness of the richness of the many feelings she was experiencing toward me as a repetition of the childhood oedipal situation. Once again she recognized her own wishes to be a feminine, soft, warm, and loving woman in a total sense, with intense transference anxiety that I would reject her for such feelings, and therefore accompanied by defensive withdrawal.

In the next hour the theme was the father's repeatedly leaving the family to go off to his various women. There has been a gradual reduction of the preexisting repression, with recovery in this hour of details of times when the father would leave or would not show up when he was expected at home. This was accompanied by a good deal of fantasy and recall of the distress and unhappiness that she experienced at those times. There was also an identification with the mother in her frantic feelings of helplessness when faced with the possibility of living alone without a man. The mother turned for help at those times to her own mother, leaving the patient to flounder and ultimately to turn to Mrs. Jones for encouragement and support. This entire sequence was being reenacted in the relationship to the husband, with similar fantasies when he is away from home, and simultaneously in the continuing transference feeling that I was repeatedly abandoning her and that the entire current difficulty was my fault.

But there was a growing perception of herself as a mature and responsible mother who does not want to go out and have affairs of her own as a form of retaliation, yet still feels anxious and threatened that if she permits herself to love her husband fully, he may some day walk out on her as the father did. This material led to another determinant of her fantasy of cutting her wrists which involved the idea that if she was hurt or in danger of serious illness, then her father showed a greater sense of concern and attention than at times when she was well. She then was able to recall the details surrounding her tonsillectomy as a small child, at which time the father spent a great deal of time sitting at her bedside and actively reassuring her. However, the image of being the type of woman who uses illness to manipulate and gain the attention she misses when she is strong was likewise upsetting and distressing to her, and she felt it would produce severe and irreversible damage to her children.

In the fifth session the theme again was the transference frustration, with the expectation and demand that I love her as an ideal father should love his daughter. The recognition of frustration of these wishes in childhood, both by the father and the mother, was accompanied by fantasies in the transference of going too far and being gratified in the sexual desires.

Accompanying this were thoughts that she is entitled to feel that she has missed an important part of her life, and that the world and the various people with whom she interacts owe it to her to make up these deficits before she can be expected to mature. With this came a recovery of the childhood fantasies of such experiences and the use of television programs and fairy tales as a means of achieving these gratifications in her imagination as a girl. There was a conscious refusal to accept the fact that it is now too late for these types of satisfactions and that she must mature in spite of never achieving them, accompanied by an angry screeching demand that someone make up for the fact that her parents had never adequately fulfilled her needs.

She demanded that I fulfill her needs first, and that only if I give her the love she is seeking will she be able then to feel fulfilled and thus return such feelings of love to her husband and children. Her insistence was that she receive some type of foundation for maturity before she is in a position to move ahead in her life. Accompanying this was a feeling of rage at the recognition that I will not provide her with this type of transference gratification, and in expressing this she screamed at me with greater feeling than ever before, "I hope you die!"

The patient reacted to the intensity of her fury with considerable anxiety, a concern regarding the magic omnipotence of her thought with the fantasy that it might cause me to die or have an accident, and with great uncertainty as to whether or not I would still tolerate her in spite of the intensity of her negative feeling toward me. As she reflected upon this, she expressed her ambivalence by apologizing for having said it, indicating that she had never before experienced this much associated feeling. But at the same time she felt a sense of accomplishment that she had finally been able to say it, although still concerned as to what effects her words would have on me. She indicated that she would have to wait until the next session to be sure that I would be all right.

In the sixth session the patient announced that she would be cancelling three sessions next month because she was planning a trip with her husband. I responded by telling her that I would also be cancelling her sessions for one week at the end of this month. This was a departure from my usual procedure, which is to announce any cancellations at the door one week prior the time. At the time I had rationalized my telling her on the basis that since she had brought up the matter of missing sessions, I could deal with the whole situation all at once. But the fact that this was a departure from my usual procedure is a sign that it was a countertransference response to her announced cancellations.

The remainder of the session was taken up with her correct perception of my countertransference reaction, although distorted in that she believed that I was cancelling the sessions as a means of controlling and getting even with her for her having put a trip with her husband ahead of the analysis. Actually, the countertransference was manifest in the timing of my announcement, rather than in the cancellations themselves (I was attending a scientific meeting). The patient then went on to elaborate on her anxiety about manifesting any significant independence from me, along with pleasure in the feeling that doing so had evoked an emotional reaction from me which represented for her a partial transference gratification. Although I did not overtly confirm the countertransference response to her, we were able to elaborate upon the gratification provided her by the incident, and by the supporting fantasies of her ability to evoke hostility and anger in me.

In a situation where the analyst recognizes the existence of a countertransference response immediately after he has made it, there are various opinions as to how this can best be managed. Some therapists believe it appropriate to discuss their countertransference reactions with the patient immediately as part of the on-going analytic process, claiming that this fosters open and direct communication and honesty between patient and therapist. My own attitude is that such a response requires the analyst to work at personal introspection and understanding, but that his chief responsibility at the moment is to the patient and her material and that it is not his prerogative to burden her with his own countertransference reactions. Although I accepted the existence of the countertransference response and in no way attempted to be defensive or evasive with her about it, I felt it more appropriate to make use of her reaction to it in a therapeutic way, rather than to interrupt the analytic process between us by focusing with her upon my own intrapsychic reactions. However, after the session was over I pondered introspectively about my reaction and its implications.

In the next session the patient continued her associations and responses to my countertransference intervention from last time. Initially there was a defensive withdrawal, but ultimately she was able to verbalize the feeling, "Yesterday I actually felt you were being mean to me on purpose." This material ultimately led to the feeling that I was retaliating for her having demonstrated her independence from me, and eventually to the further elaboration of the persistent fantasy that sooner or later she would be able to seduce me sexually.

My own associations at the time were that since she had been able to provoke me in terms of expressing a negative countertransference reaction, she therefore felt it equally possible eventually to elicit a positive sexualized response. This material eventually led to a transference experience as if she were with her father in his study and then to the same fantasies of magic omnipotence of thought she had expressed several sessions ago in her outburst of wishing I would die. In the analytic situation, however, she developed an acute panic reaction over the possibility of seducing me, feeling that I should be as frightened as she, that she needed to be controlled, and that it was about to happen.

After the acute anxiety subsided, she reflected upon my apparent continued composure and freedom from anxiety or seduction, but expressed continuing uncertainty as to whether or not the fantasies of which she was so afraid would ultimately be gratified.

In the eighth session she described an intense recurrence of depression and bulimia over the weekend. This quickly gave way to an elaboration on the theme of seduction, against which the bulimia and depression had been defensive manifestations, and she then verbalized fantasies of being the prostitute and mistress and of ultimately seducing me. These alternated with fantasies that I find her unattractive and would find her friend Jean appealing and more experienced, and therefore would be seduced by her.

These transference fantasies ultimately led to the further elaboration of her image of intercourse as a destructive act in which the woman incorporates and keeps the penis for herself, thus castrating and destroying the man, while at the same time the penis grows bigger and bigger inside the woman and ultimately she becomes a penis which is then a vicious object that destroys the world.

In my understanding of this material she was reacting at various levels simultaneously. In the first place, she was still responding to the countertransference reaction, and her conflict and anxiety over the possibility of eventually eliciting other kinds of countertransference responses had been intensified. In other words, my response had shaken the security of the therapeutic alliance. Part of this perception, however, was also based on her continuing transference to me as the father, and to the extent that she perceived an emotional response in me, she equated me that much more intensely with the father and hence the transference conflicts were likewise intensified. At another level she was responding to my anticipated cancellations as a form of rejection, which repeated some of the experiences of her father being away for various lengths of time. This stimulated further the old fantasies and conflicts over how she might keep him from leaving, as well as what forms of hostility and revenge she would like to express because of his departures.

In the ninth session she began by overtly expressing her anger and resentment over my cancellations and over the feeling that this meant I was abandoning her. She felt that her only defense against me in such a circumstance was to repress her positive and loving feelings in favor of neutrality or an angry withdrawal. This led to subsequent material regarding her fears of love and its implications for her of swallowing or being swallowed by the object, whereas hate meant to disconnect herself from the object and therefore to preserve her identity.

When I pointed out her fantasies of fusion in response to any loving or sexual feeling, she was able to report an overtly sexual oedipal dream and to follow this with further elaboration of her sexual arousal, both in the transference and also by filling in memories regarding the various incidents with her father. She recalled her excitement and sexual arousal during the various childhood situations in which the father would permit her to see him naked, and elaborated further upon the depth and variety of her loving feelings about him. She expressed distress at recognizing some of the father's healthy and loving aspects, while at the same time elaborating further on his overt and covert seductiveness toward her. With great distress she cried, "My father is starting to emerge! I see that I have so many different feelings about my father!"

Accompanying this further emergence of the image of her father she once again returned to her fantasies that she could not count on him for control of the situation between them (another reference to the countertransference incident), and to a further elaboration of her expectations that he might respond to her overtures and that therefore the control of the situation was her own responsibility. This was simultaneously experienced in the transference as an intensification of her sexual arousal and fantasies about me, accompanied by curiosity about my penis and an overtly expressed wish to fondle and play with it. The fantasy was of ultimately stimulating me and taking my penis for herself, as she once fantasied she had done in the incident with her uncle.

In this session her response to the anticipated separation led to a further elaboration of the oedipal attachment to the father via the transference feelings and fantasies. The reenactment of these oedipal drives was followed by a further decrease in the infantile amnesia and an emergence from repression of a fuller and more complex image and relationship to her father.

In the next session the general theme was the patient's continuing reaction and response to my having cancelled the week's sessions. This involved feelings of depression, loss, and desertion, and she reacted with angry feelings of helplessness and fantasies of suicide. The cancellation had evoked memories and reactions to the father's frequent separations from the family, with similar transference fantasies that I would be off on a vacation with a mistress, and these stimulated the intense murderous fantasies of rather having me dead than behaving the way the father did.

Accompanying the fantasies of murdering me were feelings that this would mean death for herself as well, in the sense that there would be nothing left to live for, and she experienced intense anxiety and guilt over them. There was a series of fantasies that I should give up everything in my own life and never leave her, but also that I should be anxious and threatened by her hostile fantasies as she herself felt frightened by them. The feelings that I should die evoked memories of similar fantasies about her father, with intense anxiety as he left for work each day that her death wishes might actually be powerful enough to cause him to be killed.

At this point the patient was reacting chiefly to the conflicts evoked by my cancellation, and responding to the anticipation of the week's absence as a transference experience. This permitted the reaction to this frustration to become part of the ongoing process of working-through of the oedipal phase conflict in the transference neurosis. It must be emphasized that although the analyst does not deliberately attempt to manipulate the situation artificially to provoke these kinds of responses, once they occur in connection with the inevitable vicissitudes of the analytic relationship they can serve a useful function in the elaboration and ultimate resolution of the transference conflict. The issue was not merely the fact that she would miss four analytic sessions. The more important elements were the transference fantasies which accompany the actual cancellation, and which are determined by the nature of the experiences and reactions to them that occurred in childhood.

In the eleventh session she continued with the theme of her complex reactions to the cancellations. She had been aware of a conscious sexual fantasy about me since the last session, but then had a dream in which there was a sexual depreciation of me as a means of coping defensively with the disappointment about my approaching absence. After this defense was interpreted, the recollection emerged of similar defensive reactions to the father's daily leaving for work, accompanied by a recognition of her ultimate need to separate me from the father. There was also a series of fantasies that if she had shown her love and sexual arousal for the father openly, he might not have gone off and left her as he did. These were accompanied by the feeling that since he did go off and leave her, her love must be worthless.

This material led to a recall of childhood feelings that she would have been a better wife to her father than was her mother, and that she would have been willing and able to satisfy him completely as the mother never did. This group of recollections was interspersed with immediate transference experiences of a similar nature toward me, expressing both sides of her conflict over wanting me sexually and feeling she could gratify me and prevent me from going, as contrasted with her hostility, anger, and fear over expressing and being gratified in such feelings.

With this material came an elaboration of the complexities in the ambivalent feelings toward the father, accompanied by a further recovery of the intensity and depth of her love for him and her feelings of competition with and from the mother. Toward the end of the session she felt I was demanding that she say her parents had never truly loved her and that her father had rejected her, experiencing this with intense sadness and active crying.

Once again the working-through process was going on in this material. One of the signs of effective working-through was the more extensive and affective elaboration of details from the childhood relationships, experienced first in the transference and then by association recalled as memories of the childhood situation.

In the following session the theme again was her reactions to the forthcoming cancellation. These were primarily connected with feelings of being unloved, by me and in the original situation by both parents, with feelings of total involvement and dependency so that she felt helpless and totally frustrated by the separation. Accompanying this were feelings of intense hostility, and she felt that my leaving was equated to death and that I might just as well be dead and thus "get it over with." At the same time, however, there was still anxiety about the magic omnipotence of her own thoughts, with the fantasy that if she experienced and expressed these ideas fully, her wish that I die might come true. Several times I confronted her with this magic omnipotence of thought in the transference, and I also pointed out her use of the same mechanisms in connection with separation from me as she had used as a child in relationship to the father.

In the thirteenth session the patient again returned to the theme of oedipal rejection and frustration, experiencing this in the transference as my having rejected her. This was related to the fact that her mother had been visiting and had left that morning. In the feeling of frustration by

the father there was an identification with the mother, with further elaboration of the earlier fantasy that she had a gun or knife in her breast and
would use this to kill me. In the further expression of her hostility there
emerged a regressive anal fantasy of her "pooh-pooh" being dangerous to
me, accompanied by the transference wish to leave her feces here on the
floor and in that way get back at me. In this context, she remembered an
anal dream which had occurred shortly after the termination of her treatment with Harris, and in association to this there emerged the feces-penis
equation, with the fantasy that "If I left it here, it would get bigger and
bigger and it would destroy you. It might be dirty as hell! But it's all mine!
I can destroy you with it and I know that I can make you so upset by it!
It's *not* something that I hate. I want to pick it up and shove it in your
face!" This was followed by further elaboration of the mother's ambivalent
excitement and disgust in regard to feces, and of her experiences during
the anal phase of development.

This material is quoted in some detail because it represents the emergence into consciousness of conflictual material which previously had been
minimal in her associations. The anal-phase equation of the stick of feces
with the penis is important in understanding the pathogenic significance
of the fantasies of oral incorporation associated with the sexual seduction
by the uncle. In the hostile and aggressively castrating response to frustration and impending separation from me, the childhood wish to acquire
the father's phallus as means of revenge and also as a way of coping with
the separation had been reactivated, and was currently experienced in the
transference by use of the feces-penis equation as a means of expressing
the underlying wish.

At the same time, this regressive anal-phase fantasy supports the patient's unconscious identification with the father in the negative oedipus
complex (she can manufacture and have a phallus of her own), and
thereby permits fulfillment in fantasy of her wish to love the mother as a
male, acquiring the mother's love as a means of coping with the situation
of loss of the father. This dynamic shift was manifest in the transference
experience of me as the father changing to me as mother during the session.

In the fourteenth session the theme once again was the forthcoming
separation and its association to the loss of the father to his mistresses.
She felt I was going off on vacation with a woman other than my wife, and
she pictured me romantically involved in a far more meaningful and deeply
varied relationship than merely a physical, sexual one. At least one of the
father's mistresses had not been particularly attractive physically, but had

been a warm and giving person with whom he shared housekeeping and other kinds of marital activities beyond sexual love.

Her associations led to the primal scene, to fantasies of pleading with me to remain with her, and to feeling helplessly overwhelmed by her intense love for me in the transference. As she recognized the reality of the situation and experienced the frustration that her wishes would not prevent me from leaving, she reverted to the hostile and castrating fantasies about me, and then to a fantasy of eating me as a means of preventing the separation. With self-conscious laughter and self-observation she became increasingly aware of the psychic reality of this fantasy, accompanied at the same time by the realization "... I can't eat you! It's all ridiculous!"

Once again there was nothing particularly new or unusual in this session, but the working-through process was continuing and the connection between the loss of the father and the symptoms of eating became somewhat more clear than previously. As the psychic reality of this fantasy was exposed, the adult self-observing and reality-testing ego processes recognized the irrational unreality of the fantasied connections she had been so afraid of in the past. Simultaneously throughout the session, there was intense fear of total disruption and helplessness in anticipation of the separation, accompanied by more mature and rational self-perception and awareness which recognized that I would be gone only for a week and that she would be able to function and get along as an adult without me.

The fifteenth and final session of the month was the last one before the week's absence, and once again the separation and her reactions to it were the predominant theme. The issues were her feeling of abandonment and desertion; her sense of helplessness at being left; her feeling of anger and resentment that her love was not returned; and her various fantasies of how to cope with the impending separation. These included fantasies of holding on to me; of castrating me and keeping my penis if she couldn't keep all of me; of her anger and resentment destroying the world; of sitting in my lap at my breast and being incorporated so that she is inside and therefore not separated from me. This last image represented death, in keeping with her thoughts of the oral triad, and as a defense against this anxiety she expressed the fantasy that she would eat me instead.

The fantasy of eating me was accompanied by rage and a hostile destructive incorporating urge, and I was able to help her see how this reaction was a repetition of a recurrent experience in response to separation from the mother and the father as an infant and young child. "But I can't nurse at my mother's breast until I'm 100 year old! – – – But I know I'm still waiting! I'm twenty-seven years old and here I am still waiting for something that will never come. I know that I'll not die, but I'm not sure of it." This material was accompanied by the symptomatic urge to eat as soon as she got home from her session.

In this material the psychic reality of desperation and intense anxiety about separation from me was once again experienced by the patient. Having become conscious, it could then be subjected to more mature reality-testing and self-observing ego functions. When repeated sufficiently in the working-through process this will result in the elimination of her fantasy equating separation with death and destruction. The final outcome of this working-through process should be a conscious state in which separation may be experienced as painful and may be accompanied by a yearning for the lost object, but in which the patient's integrity as an individual would be maintained. In such a state the experience of grief, mourning, and the pain involved can be consciously tolerated, and more effective, nonregressive, nonneurotic adaptation should be possible. This latter type of core structural change will be completed only in the termination phase of the analysis, as the transference neurosis is finally resolved. However, experiences such as the present one are necessary precursors and stages in movement toward final elimination of this particular aspect of her conflicts.

# 9

# THE FIFTEENTH MONTH

---

## SESSION 207

**P:** I feel so nervous! -- I'm so glad to see you. -- I started out that week hating you and I ended up by loving you. It's because of you that I did so much better than I thought I would. I had a fantasy of you having an operation and that you were maybe in a hospital.

**A:** What was the detail of your doing better than you expected?

**P:** I expected too much. It was Hell at first. (Elaborates.) I figured out for myself what I was doing and suddenly it all changed and I realized all of the good that you have done for me. I felt that you'd be there today and that I could trust you. (Elaborates how she analyzed her feelings, even though she was scared.) I'd expected perfection of myself. But for the first time I could begin to accept my own fears even when Tom was away. (Elaborates her awareness of how Tom represents her father.) I found out that I really don't want to cut my wrists and I was so happy to realize it. I was thinking things out by myself without you because I had to. I accepted my dependency on you and this was a tremendous thing for me. I don't like that feeling of dependency at all. Why am I so nervous now? --

**A:** You mentioned the feeling that you could accept your dependency on me. What are your associations to that?

**P:** When you first told me about taking this week off, I immediately thought about terminating, and I felt such anxiety. I felt that I'm not ready, that it's too soon, and that it wasn't right. But I realized this week that when we do *terminate*, it will be hard but I will be able to do it. You helped me so much. I feel that I love you and that you have done me so much good. I don't feel that I'll drown anymore. I can stand on my own without you and so it is all right to let myself depend on you. I felt that *you* were all *real* and that you were helping me to get well and that you were doing the best thing for me. I trusted you. But I had a dream of eating spaghetti, and then I was going fishing with some worms. There were some bugs crawling in my vagina. What does all this mean? --- I saw a little girl on the street Saturday, and she looked so thin and unhappy and pitiful. I wanted to kill her. I think about all the unloved children in the world and it reminds me of how at times I want to kill myself.

**A:** What's the detail of that feeling?

**P:** As a child I would see a baby and I would want to hurt it. (Elaborates.) Once I locked a child in a garage. (Elaborates.) I liked watching her cry for her mother. I felt very sadistic and I sometimes feel that about myself. Sometimes I have the urge to cut someone, but then I turn it against me. I have thoughts of wanting to hurt myself, or to cut myself up, and it gives me great pleasure when I do. (Elaborates the urge to make the girl cry.) – – I had such strong fantasies of Tom having affairs this weekend. That was the only thing that I could shake off. I know that it's not true and yet I always feel that it is. – – – For the first time I talked about my analysis this week. I kept going back and forth from being a woman to being a child this week, but I was able to reason it all out.

**A:** You mentioned talking about your analysis this week. What was the detail?

**P:** I never talked about my analysis before even when people asked me questions. But this week I told one girl about it. There were three other people who came to me for help this week with their problems. I identified myself with you, and suddenly I began to love you! I got such a good feeling from helping them. (Elaborates.) I never had any feelings like this before. I talked with them about life and love and marriage. – – I had an image in which I saw some cuts on an arm or on a penis Friday night after

*Cry* | making love with Tom and falling asleep. – – – Suddenly I feel like crying because I thought he had all of those affairs.

**A:** What's the detail of the feeling?

**P:** I think of how much it hurt! And how scared I was! I just don't like to be left. It scares me and that's the way I feel about you. I hated it and I was so scared. But you didn't try to hurt me as my father did. He did! It was like he stabbed me with a knife. You didn't. And I'm so grateful. I suddenly realized how upset and scared I was when I was a child. (Elaborates.) I used to have all kinds of fantasies of killing him while he was gone. I'd think of cutting off his penis and I see him making love to some woman or to his wife. I want his penis for myself and no one else is going to have it. It's just not fair for me to have to go through all of this

*Anxiety* | anxiety and fear. – – – I could tear you up! I'm getting so mad at you! I wish you'd die! I could dig my nails into you! I have a terrific fear that if I ever discovered that I don't *need you*, I'll *kill* you. I just can't stand the love and hate all coming together, it's rushing in on me all at once and I feel as if I'm going crazy.

**A:** You feel it rushing in on you all at once. What are your associations to that?

**P:** If I don't depend on you, then I'll kill you. But I also love you. I hate you. It's as if you are two people and if I love you, I can't hate you, and if I hate you, I can't love you. I have such fears that my hate will destroy you. (Elaborates.) I suddenly remember feeling all of this about my father. Each time when he'd come home. My hate thoughts are so destructive. – – When I think about my hate, I feel my love and when I think about my love, I feel my hate. I have been having so many thoughts about you. I love you and I'd like to be your wife and I'd like to be your child and I hate you, and yet you came back to me. I have such sexual feelings for you and yet I want to cut off your penis and destroy you. – – I suddenly feel the wish to be a baby and nurse on you.

**A:** That way you can try to avoid these other problems of your feelings about me.

**P:** But they rush in on me so. There are so many of them at once. There are so many feelings. I think of how much I love you and how much I hate you and I want you to die. – – They keep coming on and on! You helped me, and I'm sexually attracted to you and yet I hate you and I want to cut off your penis and yet I also want to nurse on you. It's the wish to be a woman with you that brings this all on.

**A:** What's the detail?

**P:** I feel like a woman. I think about your mind and your body and your personality and I want to be a woman with you. You helped me so much and you came back! I want to be your wife and I want to have you love me and have you all to myself. But I can have this with Tom! When I think that, then I get mad. I can't have these things with you really, and it would be so wonderful to be able to think about them without the hurt. I feel so destructive and yet I love you so much. I can't understand that I'd love you and yet want to destroy you. – – I talked with one of my girl friends whose boy friend doesn't love her any more. Love is so wonderful if you are loved in return. But if not, I could kill you. – – – I'm building up my defense of hating you again! – – I want to be a bitch and seduce all men! And yet I can't do that.

**A:** We'll stop here for today.

At the door the analyst hands her the bill for the previous month.

### Discussion

In the first part of this hour, the patient reports her conscious experiences during the week's absence from me. Initially, she emphasizes the positive gains and experiences, but knowing the nature of the transference involvement and of her sensitivity to separations, I am questioning in my own mind how much her positive assessment of her own behavior represents the operation of the mechanism of denial. It is this thinking that leads me to ask her to elaborate about having done better during the absence. This question tends to lead her away from the immediate transference fantasy of me being in a hospital, but the tactical goal at the moment is to explore and evaluate her defensive response to the separation. She goes on to describe her improvements and some abilities to carry on the analytic work on her own, but then describes her subjective feeling of anxiety. Again, the denial is maintained, but the mechanism begins to break down with her reporting of the dream about eating spaghetti and the worms, and of the experience of feelings with the little girl on the street.

The experience with the little girl (occurring in the setting of separation from me) leads to the recall of a childhood experience in which she had reversed the roles of passive victim to become the active persecutor of another child. This is the mechanism of identification with the aggressor, and it has implications for the transference in which I am the one who has hurt her by actively leaving. But at this moment in the session, the attempt at denial continues with her emphasis on being able to reason things out and to talk with others. Another mechanism of defense against separation from me is manifested in the further identification with me in which she played the role of therapist to the friends who came to talk with her. I might more forcefully have challenged the operation of these various defenses, either by pointing out their presence, or by interpreting that underneath such defensive operations there must have been a sense of intense loss regarding me and a yearning for my return. However, to have done this would have meant my taking an active, interpretive role prior to the time that these drives and transference feelings were close to her consciousness, and I therefore elect to wait and see what happens spontaneously.

The patient's denial, passive-to-active reversal, identification, and repression of the transference conflict suddenly begins to break down as she reports the dream of cuts on the penis and the feeling of crying because of the father's affairs. The presence of the affective experience of crying signals that this is the beginning of the opportunity I have been waiting for, and I therefore need to exploit this by encouraging her to develop the details of the experiences. Initially, the patient responds by differentiating me from the father, in terms of our motivation to hurt her. However, as she goes on the regressive transference experience becomes increasingly intense, and she begins to feel and express toward me the rage and urge to kill me as a result of having left her. Her statement, "Suddenly I'm remembering feeling this way about my father. I'd feel it whenever he'd come home," indicates the repetition of feelings in the transference separation from me and my return and in the experiences of repeated separations from the father. At this point she is reexperiencing the original oedipal frustrations in the transference neurosis, accompanied by the intense anxiety over that conflict. She then attempts the further defense of regression to an oral wish to be the nursing baby. This regressive shift is partially blocked by my interpretation of its defensive function, and she then resumes her experience and expression in the transference of the typically ambivalent oedipal wishes. Toward the end of the session, she is almost entirely involved in reexperiencing in the transference neurosis the conflictual feelings that occurred when her father would return home following one of his absences. The stimulus for the further recall of the childhood separations was the reunion with me after my return from the week's absence. This results in an increment of working through of previously repressed affects and drives, with resulting increase of conscious ego mastery over them.

The two dream fragments are not specifically referred to or interpreted by me, but the spontaneous associations to the wish to attack and destroy the penis make such specific interpretation unnecessary.

The continuing presence of the self-observing ego and of the controls that keep the entire experience an intrapsychic one is indicated by her last comment, when after expressing her hostility and fantasy of revenge she says, "And yet, I know I can't."

---

## SESSION 208

The patient hands the analyst the check for the previous month.

**P:** I'm so afraid to feel good. I get thrown into a terrible funk! It's just not worth it! I'm reliving the times when my father had his affairs, and I feel just like a discarded housewife. I hated it!

A: You seem here to be identifying with your mother, and to feel that your father has just returned to you.

P: There are just two possibilities for me, either to feel that way or to be a whore. I'd rather be my mother.

A: Why do you have to be either one?

P: I have no idea what the other is like! It is scaring me to death. I feel such a sense of loss of reality to feel that my husband is having sexual affairs. It's ridiculous and yet, I can't get out of it. It scares me! The only safe thing is for me to withdraw from everyone.

A: Let's go back to the idea that there are only two possibilities for you, either to be like your mother or else to be a whore. What are your associations to that?

P: I just can't stand it! I have to be a housewife. I can't be the other. I feel stubborn! There just is no out! I had a dream that we were all in Maine. There was my father and my mother and Tom and Mrs. Jones, and my sisters. My sister was killed and there was something to do with orange juice. Then we were in an apartment and my sister was dead in the freezer. We stayed in Maine but Tom went to Florida with Mrs. Jones and my sisters. He didn't ask me to go. I was sweeping under the bed, and I found some bits of paper. There were several beds and there
*Cry!!* | was also a closet. Someone said the Logans are in Florida, and maybe they . . . . . I have such fears that Tom has a suppressed wish to have sexual affairs and that this will all burst loose. I'm so jealous but there is nothing I can do about it. Tom's black hair looked like a woman's and it was long and it hung in his face and then I thought, "That's really not Tom." My father and Mrs. Jones were sitting on the bed and my mother was there and my father was flirting and I was trying to be in on it. --- I can figure it all out except the idea that my sister was dead. It was an upstairs apartment and it reminds me of a couple that I know. The boy is just like a baby. There was a half can of orange juice. I am losing my mind! The Logans and my own parents were so against me getting married, and they were right!

A: What are your associations to the orange juice?

P: It makes me think of babies. It's a new way of feeding them and you can fix half a can of the orange juice and leave the rest frozen. But
*Cry* | the trouble is that Thomas can't get it through the nipple. It reminds me of my own metrecal which I use. In the dream I showed it to Tom and it was like saying, "See, I know how to do it." I get a sexual feeling in my clitoris right now about that orange juice. Last week when you took

off, it meant that I was thrown back into the times when my father would leave. But I put it all over on to Tom.

**A:** Instead of feeling it with me.

**P:** I can't stand it! It scares me.

**A:** Before I left your fantasy was that I was having an affair and that I was going off with another woman.

**P:** I just can't stand to think of it. I trust you, and I just hope that you're not that type of a person. (Elaborates.) I'm reliving it all right now. I didn't have any fantasies that you'd do this, but now I am convincing myself that you are! There's no hope! – – I *know* that you're having affairs and that that's the type of man you are. You're my father. My father wouldn't do it with me, but he'd go off and do it with others. You are capable as an analyst, but in your private life! I couldn't stand it and it's so possible! You're capable of being my father, and of helping me, but you are also capable of having affairs.

*Cry!!*

**A:** Try to follow the fantasy through and see what comes to your mind.

**P:** Nothing! I'm dead! There's nothing left! Nothing! There's just no hope! I might as well be dead!

**A:** What's the detail of the feeling that there is no hope?

**P:** There's just no hope of. . . . . There's just the hate and the whores. It's my whole life all over again. I hoped that I'd get a different feeling about you and then I could transfer that different feeling to Tom. (Elaborates.) But if you are this way, then every man is. Then I'm either a discarded housewife or I'm a whore. I'm thrown right back into all of this. I'd hoped for something in between, and for happiness and stability and a good life.

**A:** What's the detail of the feeling of being thrown back into everything?

**P:** It's the same situation that I grew up with. It proves it to me, but I can't break through it! I just can't! (Elaborates.) I want you to give me an answer as to whether or not this is true. There must be some way to live happily.

**A:** You have no way of really knowing whether I was having an affair or whether I wasn't, since you don't know anything about my personal life. And yet, your feeling is that I was having one. Let's try to analyze the wish to believe that I was.

**P:** I know that that's right. But I want to push myself, and that's the only way that I can have you. And yet, it's misery. The children suffer, and Tom does, and I do too. But if I just sit and wait, you'll come back to me. Because you can't break away from me either. It's just like in the dream. I feel mad and hurt and jealous and yet divorce is not the answer.

A: Let's go back to the feeling that this is the only way that you can have me. What comes to your mind?

P: I think that maybe I could have you as your mistress. Not forever, but there is always the possibility of being a housewife, isn't it. If you are that type then I can get to you, even though it's not with love. I just don't know. I think of daddy and that woman in her apartment. She was a housewife and she lived upstairs and she had a child.

A: Which is like the upstairs apartment and the child in the dream.

P: If he'd do it with her, why wouldn't he do it with me?!! Why wouldn't he do it with my mother! I could take and understand bitches and whores, and could see that they were physically attractive. But the other means, "You're not good enough for me and I want the good things in life, but not you." I just feel discarded and kicked out on my butt. That's my role and no one wants to lead it with me.

A: What are your associations to sweeping the paper off the bed in the dream?

P: I think of the beds in Maine. My hands are getting stiff! My daughter, Sally, when she takes her nap will frequently tear up paper. *Cry!!* It's her hostility and she throws the paper on the other side of the bed *Sob!!* and thinks that I don't see it. That way she cuts me up to bits. – – It's just like the times when my father and mother would make love. I want to cut her all up and sweep it off. It was no good, and he then just goes off to his other women. It's just like here. I feel that I could have a good *Rage* relationship with you and then bam! You throw me out! All the good feelings can go to hell and I just don't have them because he'll just throw them out again. I want to kill you! I wish you were dead! I'd like to take a knife and just cut you to pieces! You can't do this to me! – – I've had it! I don't care. I'll not let you come back to me! I wish you were dead. I can't let myself take your smiles and your help and your love, because you'll just leave again! I want more! What can I do to you? I'll have to go up to the attic and think.

A: The feeling is that you are not going to let me come back to you. What are your associations there?

P: I've had it! I'll be happy for one or two months, and then damn! You're off again. You're either going to stay with me or I'm not going *Cry* to take it back. (Laughs.) Oh shit! – – – I wonder what happened in my parents' room when they were making love so that my father would leave. I remember their noises at home making love and how frequent it was. I wonder if my mother tried to get his penis and keep it? I don't blame her! I'd like to take it off! -- It turns into a baby, and then it drives my father off. It's just like when my sister was born. That is when it started! I don't want anything to do with it!

A: You feel that your sister drove your father off. What's the detail?

P: When my sister came my father left. Up until then my father would play with me and we would get on the couch and he would give me a nickel. But then my sister was born and we lived in the big house and that was when my father left. My father just couldn't take any responsibility. My sister was blond and she was the baby and she was the penis and I could kill them both.

A: So part of your feeling is that it was your sister's fault that your father left. What comes to your mind?

P: I remember my mother putting her down in the middle of the bed. That's it! I felt that she didn't want me any more. I remember my sister squirting my mother with urine. She was just like boys doing it, but my sister had no penis! But she was blond and she was beautiful and my mother loves her more than me. I can take that. But it's my father being gone! No, I can't take it. They don't want me any more. (Elaborates.) I'm nothing and it's as if I'm not even there, and mother just wants the baby. All of this comes from this wonderful intercourse and it just brings the baby! Except with me. I was a mistake! My mother didn't want me at all! I do *care*. It hurts like hell! It hurt.

A: We'll stop here for today.

### DISCUSSION

The patient begins immediately by indicating that the transference feelings from the previous session in regard to the week's absence have continued, and that she is reexperiencing in the present situation with me the childhood feelings in regard to the father. Her feelings about the role of discarded housewife or whore are signs of a childhood wish to identify either with mother or with the father's mistresses in the oedipal wish to have the father for herself. My interventions regarding these as the only two possibilities are premature attempts to encourage self-observation and ultimate recognition that other alternatives exist. However, the underlying transference fantasies and drives have not yet been explored fully, and the interventions have no effect.

After expressing some of these feelings and reporting the dream with its clearly oedipal wishes, the patient shows her self-observing functions by the spontaneous recognition that this material relates to the week's separation and that there has been a displacement of the jealousy onto her husband. The previous material in regard to the father, and the re-experiencing of this with me in the transference, indicates that the specific fantasy about me is close to conscious awareness at this time, and the tactical goal is to deepen these transference experiences. These are indicators of her readiness for my direct interpretation of the transference fantasy that I was off having an affair during my absence.

Initially, the patient attempts to maintain the feeling of difference between me and her father, but as a result of my interpretation the transference experience is intensified, so that with increasing conviction she regressively experiences the feelings associated to the thought that I (father) have a mistress whom I prefer over her. Her comments about "every man" and about her husband indicate how this displacement from father has been generalized. Because I want to deepen this transference experience and ultimately uncover the further fantasies that accompanied it in the original relationship with the father, I deliberately do not reassure her about the reality of my absence. In fact, by my comment that she doesn't know whether I was or was not having an affair, I am indicating that I can accept her transference fantasies and feelings about me without discomfort, and I am actually providing her with a stimulus toward further fantasy and transference distortion. This, in turn, leads to the further uncovering of her identification with the whore or the mistress as a means of getting to her father, and to the further regressive experience of feeling inadequate, discarded, and left out of the father's life.

I am no longer clear as to the specific thinking that led me to ask her about the bits of paper in the dream, but I suspect that there may have been an intuitive awareness in me that this dream element might lead to the further repressed rage regarding the father. Her immediate response is a conversion reaction involving a sense of stiffness in her hands, which symbolically represents the wish to attack and destroy me (father) as well as the defense against such a wish. Initially, the wish is verbally expressed in a derivative form through a displacement to her daughter's behavior and an identification with the feelings expressed by the daughter. This attenuated expression of the drive and accompanying fantasy leads her to a more direct and immediate experience of her own fury and rage as a child, again repeated toward me in the transference.

Although there is an ongoing regressive transference experience occurring at this time, the healthy, self-observing ego is still functioning as indicated by her sudden laughter and her explosive, "Oh, shit!" After a short silence, she again begins a self-observing introspection about the primal scene, which is another one of the father's relationships from which she was excluded. As she talks about this, one of the primary-process distorted fantasies about the primal scene increasingly emerges. It seems that this fantasy was used by her in childhood in the attempt to explain the reality of her father having left the home shortly after the sister's birth. The common childhood sexual theory that the woman keeps the penis, which then becomes the baby, is alluded to here, but closer to consciousness are the feelings of resentment and blame toward the sister for the father's departure. My intervention requesting elaboration about the sister is focused at this element of the conflict, since it is closer to conscious awareness. This elaboration leads to the recovery from repression of the feelings of sibling rivalry, accompanied by the painful affect of hurt and total rejection which occurred at that time.

The further exploration of the deeper meanings regarding the primal scene and the distorted childhood sexual theories are issues which at this point must be postponed for a later time.

---

## SESSION 209

P: – – – There's just not *one* thing in the world that can make me happy. I feel like hell and I have all kinds of fantasies to kill myself and my kids or kill Tom. – – – I feel that no one cares about me, and no one pampers me. I had the thought that I would kill myself and then you will see that I wasn't kidding. – – – – I think about all of the things that everybody said to me against analysis, and why I shouldn't go into it. I stood up against the whole world about this and I put all my trust into one human being but how do I know? – –

A: How do you know what?

P: How do I know that I'll make it or that this is right. These feelings may be dangerous. My fear is that I'll go so far and then you'll get scared and you'll drop me like a hot potato. I've never heard anyone say that they feel like this, the way I do. Is it possible that I'll get dangerous?

A: The fear is that I'll get scared and drop you. What's the detail of the fantasy?

P: I have some awfully bad thoughts, mostly about my hostility. What if I scare you? How will you be able to get me out? Maybe you don't know how bad it is. I had a terrible argument with Tom the night that you left and I got so mad that I had the urge to kill him. What keeps me from doing it? And I never thought about things like that with my anger before. I wanted to get a knife and maybe even stab myself in the stomach! These feelings and thoughts come with my hostility now. They used to just pop out of the blue before. — — I'm on the verge of not thinking at times when I'm mad. That happens here and sometimes at home and I just can't afford to.

A: What's the detail of when it happens here?

P: I don't quite burst loose! I feel as if there were all kinds of rockets and they might explode, and that I just wouldn't be aware. I feel driven there. I feel like running now. — —

A: Your fear is that you are going to burst through here and just let go completely. What's the detail of the fantasy?

*Cry!!*

P: — — I feel wild, and I can picture myself standing in the hall and listening to my parents.

A: What are you hearing?

P: It's so wild! — — — How can I picture it when I never saw them? It's as if I did, and yet I know that I didn't! — —

A: How do you *know* that you didn't?

P: — I couldn't! They wouldn't do that to me! And yet I can see . . . . . my father mainly.

A: What's he doing?

*Anxiety,*
*Cry,*
*Restless-*
*ness*

P: It just makes me sick to talk about it. I almost feel it myself. I can see him with no clothes on, and his black hair, and he's on his hands on top of my mother and he's moving up and down and I see his penis going in and out. I want to hide! And I'm so afraid that you're looking at me!

A: What are you afraid that I'm seeing?

P: I feel that I'm getting pleasure out of this. I'm getting lost. I want to ask you, is it really so bad? I'm acting so stupid that I hate myself.

A: What's the feeling of asking me is it so bad?

P: I look at him and I'm aware of the love feelings that I get seeing his penis go in and out. It's terribly sexual for me. I think I watched him having an orgasm. It's wild, but it's great. It's like it's me! It's like I'm having these feelings! I love to watch his orgasm. This is all so sexual for me. Is this really Tom, or am I seeing this? It gets wilder and wilder and I get more and more excited, my father goes faster and suddenly it's all over and he lies there and I see his penis all flat. I feel like screaming! — — — —

**A:** Let's go back to the feeling that you were having just now. You were restless and you felt that I was watching you. What comes to your mind?

**P:** – – You know what my feelings are. I'm embarrassed. I still feel them. I have a funny feeling in my hands and I want to grasp something and I feel nervous and I'm embarrassed for you to see me act this way. It's all so childish. I'm a woman and I should be able to take this. – – I think this is all a defense against the fact that I know that I am a woman. But I want to cut my wrists and get mad at you, and I want to enjoy this and to enjoy thinking about it, but it makes me sick and depressed and embarrassed instead. I want to run and I want to act like a child. – –

**A:** What's the detail of the embarrassment?

**P:** For you to catch me feeling this way. To catch me having sexual feelings about this. It's like I shouldn't be, because I'm just a child, especially about my father! Ye Gods! – – Never again will I be able to have any sexual feelings at all. They are so wrong. I must hide them and I can't ever have them again. – – Now I have the opposite feeling! I want to take off all my clothes and show you my body. I'm so embarrassed! I could die! – – I want to burst loose and let myself go with all of my sexual feelings. – –

**A:** What's the detail of your fantasy?

**P:** I have the feeling that I'm a woman and that I'm proud of my body. You're a God-damn stupid man so I can never do it, and I hate you! I will always hate you! – – I wouldn't be safe if I let out all of my sexual feelings that I have for everybody that I see. – – – I have a feeling that I'm being like my mother. It's as if she says, "This is my power over men because they are so weak and so sexual. I can keep my own sexual feelings in and then I have him and he's nothing." (Elaborates.)

*Cry!*
*Rage*

**A:** We'll stop here for today.

## DISCUSSION

The patient continues to feel the transference rejection from the previous week's absence, and these transference fantasies reproduce the feelings of rejection and exclusion from the primal scene which began to emerge in yesterday's session. The aggression mobilized by this was displaced to her husband and children at home, while in the analytic situation the threat of suicide, as a means of showing me that she isn't kidding, is an example of the expression of aggression by turning it against the self. When I do not respond to this threat, a new line of defense is the depreciation of analysis and the recurrent defensive resistance against trust in me and in the analytic situation.

Her question, "Do you think that it's possible I might get dangerous?" is a complex one with many implications. If I answer the question in the negative and reassure her that she will not act on her fantasies, I would be depreciating her and the intensity of her drives and I would, in effect, indicate that I do not take them too seriously. This might, in turn, indirectly challenge her to prove to me how strong they are by some type of impulsive acting-out. On the other hand, to answer such a question in the affirmative would mobilize further anxiety and fear regarding the adequacy of her ego controls, and would seriously interfere with her capacity to permit the regressive experience of such fantasies and drives. I, therefore, choose to reassure her indirectly by ignoring the direct question itself and instead continuing to focus on her transference concern about my responses to the expression of her drives. In essence, this represents an appeal to the healthy ego functions supporting the therapeutic alliance, and a tacit indication to her that I am not afraid of her drives and that I am not going to "drop" her. This leads to a somewhat reflective self-observation regarding the nature of these aggressive feelings, and such statements as "I never thought about it with anger before this," or "These feelings come with my hostility now; they used to just pop out of the blue," are evidences that the previously used mechanism of isolation of affect is gradually being reduced. My interventions which focus the aggressive drives and conflict back into the transference are a further reassurance to her that I am not afraid to face her aggression, that I believe she can control it and use verbal means of expression, and they offer her an object for healthy identification in the therapeutic alliance.

As a result of these preparatory interventions, and under the pressures of the transference drives, the patient again moves away from the self-observing position and begins to experience the regressive fantasies and feelings. The immediate association to the primal scene is something of a surprise to me, but by phrasing my question in the present tense, I am encouraging her to pursue the experience and memory as if it were occurring right now. This is a further attempt to heighten the affective component and to avoid the mechanism of isolation. Her immediate response is one of anxiety, followed by a defensive use of the mechanism of denial when she says she knows she never saw them. At this point my question of how she could know that she never saw them serves to block this use of denial, and this, in turn, is followed by an affective reexperiencing of some of the elements of her childhood responses to the primal scene. The most important new element in this is her conscious awareness of vicarious participation and of direct sexual arousal from the primal scene. At this time the material does not yet allow a definite conclusion as to whether this was a real or a fantasied childhood experience, but for the purposes of the analysis now it does not make a significant difference since the psychic experience is the important issue. However, my hunch at this time is that there has been an actual traumatic experience.

My inference is that her embarrassment about my watching her represents a reexperiencing in the transference of an as-yet-unverbalized fantasy that the father would be aware of her observing the situation, would recognize her sexual arousal, and would then invite her to participate in it. It is this reasoning that leads me to return to that experience in the transference, and her subsequent associations to my questions bring into conscious awareness an immediate transference reaction to both sides of this conflict. On the one hand, there is her feeling of being a child who must run away from such a sexual scene, but on the other hand, there are the wishes experienced in the transference to participate actively in it as a woman. The latter are once more defended against through the use of the opposite affect of hatred and through the identification with the controlling and depreciating mother.

This session again illustrates some of the elements of the working-through process. The stimulation of transference drives leads to the recall of childhood experience and a further elaboration and deepening of awareness regarding a set of conflicts that had already been partly conscious as the result of the analytic process. New and significant affective elements of the childhood trauma are freed from repression, and the experiencing of them in the transference neurosis permits her to establish a further increment of ego mastery over the conflict.

---

## SESSION 210

P: I've been arguing with Tom all week. (Elaborates.)

A: I think that you have been displacing onto Tom a lot of the feelings that you have about me for my absence last week.

P: -- I feel rejected and I feel dejected. You just can't understand how hurt I am or how mad I am, or anything. I have just three choices.

I can hurt you, or I can hurt myself, or I can withdraw and say that I don't care.

**A:** You are repeating with me the feelings that you had in the situation with your father, after he'd gone off with a woman and then returned home. It's as if you feel yourself still to be the little girl with these three choices. In your fantasy about me you saw me screwing around for a week and now you feel that I've returned to you.

**P:** — — I wish I could get you off of my back. My life should be so full and happy! Why do I keep taking it? I guess this is something I need and I still want to get, or else I'd walk out. It's all so silly.

**A:** Your wish is to withdraw here and pretend that you don't care and not feel anything, but then you displace all of the feelings to Tom and you argue with him instead.

**P:** You're so logical and you're just like my father that way. (Elaborates.) I guess you think I'm supposed to be an Amazon and to jump over the moon. I hate logic.

**A:** What's the feeling?

**P:** You're so logical and you just show no emotion, as if I'm a pupil and there's no love and there's no hate. It's like I'm supposed to be a robot, and I'm supposed to have no feelings in me. I have none.

**A:** On the contrary, you have a great many feelings. What I'm suggesting is that you try to express them here where they belong, and *not* stamp them out or hold them back or pretend that they don't exist.

**P:** I *know* that I displace my hostility. (Elaborates her awareness.) But I still go right ahead and do it.

**A:** *That's* what we ought to analyze.

**P:** I'm so afraid that if I really *get mad in here*. . . . . what is my need? What can you really *give me?* It's as if I'll die and I just couldn't survive.

**A:** You left out some of your intermediate associations between the thoughts of really getting mad in here and the idea that you would die. What comes to your mind?

**P:** — — I wonder what life would be like if you were dead. Really *dead.* — — I think of wanting you dead and of wanting to kill you. My thoughts are not right! They are weird! — — When you hurt me I think that it would be better if you were dead. But if you love me then it is better if you're *not dead.* If you hurt me or if you stay away . . . . . — I'm so afraid that you'll get me so mad that I just won't care.

**A:** And then?

**P:** You're pushing me! I have to work this out or else quit. It's right there and it will burst out if I get mad enough. – – – Either I'll die or you'll die. I'm so mad that I don't care. But then I get so depressed.

**A:** You seem to think that I ought to be as afraid of your anger as you are.

**P:** I don't understand it. I feel that *I* can't take it. – – – I'll explode! Why am I keeping this in! It's silly! This is not a game any more! It's *real*. It's *me!* You can't help me. This is for *real!* – – – – – – I just can't stand it I'm so scared! I want to yell and scream that I hate you, and that I wish you were dead! I hate you. (Elaborates.) I'll give you all of this hate and I'll not have to take it home with me. I hate you. You couldn't care less about me! I can't stand it! – – – This is *your* hate, not mine. . . . . . –

*Anxiety, Rage, Scream*

**A:** You're afraid to express something that is on your mind right now.

**P:** I want to turn around and fire you. I don't know what will happen.

**A:** What's the fantasy?

**P:** I've never done this. What are *you* going to do? I don't know.

**A:** What do you picture that I'll do?

**P:** You might hit me. Oh! You probably find this is all sexually exciting. (Elaborates.) You'll probably grab me and seduce me. . . . . You'll seduce me! I can't trust you, because you'll probably let loose your emotions if I do. It's so sexual to you. I watched you and this wild, exciting love-making is all part of this hostility. – – I picture you doing to me what my father did to my mother. They hated each other. I'll be mad and then you'll seduce me and then everything will be all wild. – – – – I can't stand it! I actually *want* this to happen. I want to test you. – – – Is it hostility or is it sexual feelings? – – – – I'd be mad if you did it, but I'd also be mad if you don't. I know that you won't, but I think maybe that you'll grab me as you walk me to the door, and I'm so scared. – – –

**A:** We'll stop here for today.

## DISCUSSION

In the first half of this session I have the impression that the patient is actively retreating from the conflicts that had been partially mobilized in the previous few sessions. I am more active than usual in interpreting the resistances and defenses, and in my appeals to the healthy ego and to the therapeutic alliance. In retrospect, I would raise the question of whether I was too active and whether it might have been more appropriate to have allowed these resistances to be maintained for a while. However,

I do not believe that these doubts occurred to me during the session itself. Midway through the session, the patient's response that "You're pushing me" indicates her awareness of these pressures from me.

However, my maintenance of the analytic position and my continuing to interpret the resistances as they are manifested results in a slight increase in her confidence in my ability to tolerate her feelings and, therefore, in her own ability to express them. The most significant intervention seems to have been my interpretation of her thought that I should be as afraid of her aggression as she herself is. These interventions produce a further transference experience of me as sexually aroused by her expressions of hostility and aggression. However, this is immediately followed by evidence of simultaneous self-observation in regard to the testing of me and in her expression of awareness that she will be frustrated no matter what my response is to her.

The dominant theme of this entire week is the responses in the transference neurosis to my having been absent from the analysis for the previous week. This illustrates the importance of making analytic use of the inevitable vicissitudes in the therapeutic situation. The reality of my absence is that I was attending the meetings of the American Psychoanalytic Association. But if I had told her this either in advance or after my return, it would have precluded the emergence of these important transference reactions. Had she known where I was or why I was gone, she would have responded to the separation at a reality level and in keeping with secondary-process logic. As a result, the transference elements would have been less likely to emerge. By not knowing the reason for my absence, the patient is free to experience the separation in accordance with whatever transference drives and fantasies are associated to it, and the occurrence of the separation, in turn, serves further to stimulate the emergence of these forces. My neutrality and acceptance, my interpretation of the various resistances against the emergence of these transference fantasies, the interpretation of the content of some of the fantasies, and my not confronting her with reality all help the patient to project these fantasies and drives to me. She can thus reexperience in an immediate affective way one of the recurrent traumatic situations of her early life.

Had this separation not occurred at this time, the material might have emerged in some other form or it might have been delayed to some later occasion. Had such a separation occurred much earlier in the analysis, prior to the beginning mobilization of these particular conflicts, it is also unlikely that this specific material would have been the result. An analyst would not artificially manipulate the analytic situation to create or stimulate such transference responses, but when such vicissitudes in the analytic situation do occur, the analyst can then make appropriate use of them in accordance with the underlying transference existing at that time.

---

## SESSION 211

P: Could you tell me when you are taking your vacation this year?

A: I'll be away for the month of August.

P: --

A: What comes to mind about the question?

P: Nothing. I just want to make my own plans. I want no more separations. I had it with the last one. -- I had a dream of climbing up a flight of stairs to a man at the top. The theme of the dream seemed to be men against women, and there were ten or twelve of us. There was a man at the very top and he had a baby with him, and we wanted to get it without the other men getting us. The man wanted to give us the baby because we had saved his life. --- I finally got the baby and I had the urge to tear into it and cut it up. It had black hair. --- I felt sick to my stomach this morning. -- *You* are the one that I'm having feelings for and this is not about my parents. It's about you. It makes me so frightened to be this involved with someone that I don't even know. ---- I've done nothing but eat since I left here, and it's all your fault. I must hold all of my feelings away from you. That week that you were gone I lost five pounds, then you come back and I start to eat again. But it was a relief. ------- It makes me so mad for you to know what I'm thinking. -- I feel so guarded. I can't feel anything for you. And yet I know that I do. All that I want is love. I've eaten it for three days and it hasn't satisfied me. I'd like to feel like a baby, all warm and sleepy and it all involves so much. I picture my parents making love and somehow I see a baby with black hair. ----

A: You say that you have a guarded feeling with me. What's the detail?

P: Friday I felt such a strong feeling about you, and so much love, but then I was so mad that day. I was mad at you, because you had been gone that week. I felt like I was a person, and that you are *not* God. You are someone here on this earth. -- I did all right until my father came for a visit and he was there alone for about four hours and I had all kinds of feelings. I tried to analyze him and then my mother came.

*Cry* | I wish that they had come together, but I do like my father so much more than I do my mother. But I realized on Friday how little I really mean to my parents. My father was so wrapped up in himself and he acts like a baby. My parents have simply left me out of their lives. – – There just was no love in my mother for me. (Elaborates.) I could make my father love me if I tried, but really it would just be a need in him and it wouldn't really be love. – – – – – I feel somehow as if I have grown up past them and that I'm not going to stay under their thumb. Somehow it is my decision and it is somehow related to you, but I just can't go back because my parents can't give me what I want. I guess I expect to get it from you. I wonder if you are going to do the same thing to me? It's

*Cry* | like you're taking a vacation. My first thought was, does he want me to be all upset? – – You just don't realize how much I need love! I *need* someone to love me! – – – – – Why can't I get mad? I am so mad that I could die, and yet I just can't get mad.

**A:** Your feeling is that it's really *me* that you're involved with. What's the detail of that?

**P:** It is you. –

**A:** But what is the details?

**P:** I'm very sorry, but it *is*. I love you. But you'll never love me and I hate you for it. It's the circumstances now and it's not anything in the past. Maybe this is crazy, but this is the way I feel. All this business about displaced aggression. I only *feel it* toward *you*. *You* caused my troubles and my problems.

**A:** What's the hesitation in expressing it?

**P:** I'm putting my whole life in you and nothing else matters. You are all that there is and you could destroy me if you want to. I can't transplant my happiness to anyone else. It's all dependent on you. This is horrible! This is like a baby with a mother. Give me food or else I'll die! I feel so mad! I want to destroy you! I can't! You are all that I have! – – I wonder sometimes if you are going to destroy me. Are you going to sit on me and squash me? Are you going to take away all that I have? – –

**A:** What's the image of this?

*Anxiety* | **P:** I think of the statistics about children committing suicide. It scares me. I can't even breathe right now. I'm thinking of a balloon that I blew up when they took my tonsils out. I had a terrible fear that it was going to suffocate me. I must get out of here! – –

**A:** We'll stop here for today.

## DISCUSSION

The patient begins the session by indicating that she is still reacting to the week's absence and to the intensity of her feelings in the transference neurosis, and in association, by anticipating a known future vacation separation. The reporting of the dream at this point seems to me to be a resistance against awareness of the transference conflict, and her return to the immediate transference awareness may support this idea.

In spite of the immediacy of her feelings, however, the self-observing ego is still manifest in the comment that "I'm so frightened to be so involved with someone that I don't even know." She then goes on to describe some of her symptoms in the transference neurosis, but also the defense of isolation in her statement "I can't feel for you, and yet I know that I do." Although her spontaneous associations lead to the image of the primal scene which had occurred last week, and was already associated to the fantasies of my activities during my absence, and although the baby with black hair probably represented the younger sister (also present in the dream), I feel that the defensive isolation of affect in the transference is the most important issue at this moment. This is the reasoning behind my intervention suggesting that she associate to the "guarded feeling."

The patient begins to describe ambivalent transference feelings of an immediate nature, and from there her associations lead to the weekend visit from her parents. This material illustrates a characteristic of patients who are currently involved in a transference neurosis. As the analyst I have now become the chief object of her libidinal and aggressive drives and drive derivatives, as well as of the conflicting fantasies and defenses against them. Because there has now been a dynamic shift of psychic energy away from the original infantile objects (parents) and on to me in the transference (even though I now represent the parents), she is now no longer making such intense use of mother and father as the chief objects of her drives. Although the self-observing ego functions are clearly maintained and she recognizes the reality that she actually doesn't know me, the *experiencing* of the transference occurs in an immediate, direct, and forceful way. As a result the experiencing of past and present is intermingled, and the neurotic conflicts are increasingly associated to the analytic situation itself. She therefore can experience the current relationship to the parents with less neurotic distortion and can begin more realistically to see their problems and limitations, and her own progress in relationship to them. This is illustrated in her statement of feeling she has grown past them and that "My parents can't give me what I want. I guess I expect to get it from you."

The continuing effect of my focus on the defenses against affective experience is that the patient goes on to describe the immediacy of the transference reactions and at the present time the experiencing ego functions take precedence over self-observing functions. In this context she illustrates a typical transference conflict of increasing attachment, affective involvement, drive investment, and dependency leading to fantasies of danger lest the hostile and aggressive drives destroy or turn away the object of these wishes.

In the context of past and future separations, increasing dependency, and the fantasy early in the session of wanting to feel warm and sleepy, and considering the final association to the balloon and fears of suffocation, it appears descriptively that the predominant transference at the moment is a maternal one, with the accompanying, still unconscious, fantasies leading to anxiety and danger in the primitive mother-child relationship. The symbolism of the balloon and the sense of suffocation are suggestive of a fantasy about the breast and a return to the oral triad in the transference, but to remind her of such a meaning at this point would tend to intellectualize the material.

However, from this material alone it is not yet possible to decide whether these maternal transference conflicts are the major source of her anxiety at present, or whether they represent a defensive regression from the conflicts in the father transference which were mobilized last week. Judgments of this sort during the analysis must often await the uncovering of further clarifying material.

The decision not to try to analyze the dream which she reported early in the session is based on my judgment that to focus on the dream would be to promote further intellectualized distance from the immediate transference experience, and that work on some of the defenses against the full impact of the transference needs to take precedence in the analysis at this time.

---

## SESSION 212

P: _____

A: What are your feelings about the silence?

P: – I can't trust you. (Elaborates.) –

A: What comes to your mind about not trusting me?

P: You're my enemy. I hate you. You've not been one bit of help. – – It's a fight for survival against you. If I trust you, you'll devour me. You force my emotions to come out and I feel so many I can't do anything about them.

A: What's the image of me forcing them out of you?

P: You get me to the point where I can relax and not suppress my feelings and they start to come out, and then you *do* something and I have to run. You're not my friend at all. What if I tell you that I'm scared that I'm going to Florida? That I'm scared that I have to leave you. I feel scared to death.

A: What's your fantasy of what would happen if you told me about Florida?

P: I'm terrified that I'll never get back. I had a dream about it with my daughter. I had let her go with some neighbors to visit my mother-in-law and she wouldn't send her back. – – I can't stand it! – – Now I can see why people quit analysis. (Elaborates.)

A: The fantasy is that if you trust me I'll devour you. What's the detail?

P: It's all got to do with my stupid mother! I think she hates me. I just can't trust you! I don't know what you'll do to me. If I ever let go of myself! I want to. I'm tired of holding it in. But if I ever let it go, I'm hanging onto you for my life and then you could manipulate me any way you want to and I have no life of my own. Monday night I had a dream that I was nursing. I had my mouth on that thing, and it was in front of my face. I feel a sudden switch! You've done it again! I almost told you. You get me into your confidence and then. . . . . *Cry*

A: What did you stop at?

P: You just sit there and I relax and I start to tell you something.

A: And then?

P: I don't know, I just don't want to tell you. . . . . . – –

A: What did you start to say?

P: – – I have a picture of my mother masturbating me and she puts her fingers in my vagina. That's what my thought was. I went from nursing to thinking that I had to have Tom's penis in my vagina. – –

A: What was the fear of telling me about it?

P: My mother comes to mind. I wonder if she ever put her fingers in my vagina? I know she didn't. But I feel I've *had it* with people taking advantage of me. It's just like my uncle. I just can't trust any-one. – – – When you're gone it's just the same thing as when my father was gone and I really managed better! I didn't have to go into things like I have to do now. –

**A:** I think you are repeating with me the feelings you had with your mother. On the one hand there is the wish to nurse on me, and yet you're terrified that I'll swallow you up and destroy you.

**P:** I'd much rather have my mother than my father. But my mother was just one big bunch of hostility and if I don't give anything to her then I can live. – –

**A:** Just like with me and the silence at the start of the session. You didn't want to give me your thoughts and your feelings. What's the detail of the fear of giving them to me?

**P:** My thoughts are all about you. – – I feel like I'm sinking under water. There's all these sexual feelings and the hostility and the love and I can't imagine talking about them to you. They are all about you, and you'll get mad and maybe you'll get excited. – –

**A:** What's the detail of the fantasy?

**P:** These feelings aren't about my parents. They are about you! (Elaborates.) I can tell easily about my parents! But what if I told you all the things that I thought about you? There are none of your reactions that I would want! You'd either be scared, or you'd be mad or you'd be indifferent. Or else you would be very sympathetic and devour me. I feel just like a big bug! I feel that I *am* talking about my mother. Just the way Sally does to me. – – I can't tell her about my sexual thoughts because I can't tell anyone about them. I feel horrible and depressed and dirty about them. – – Suddenly I have a feeling that I would love to. . . . . I think of a baby that is so happy nursing, and has all kinds of sexual and love feelings. I'd love to talk about them. – – I really enjoy it but then I feel that there is something wrong with me for doing it.

**A:** We'll stop here for today.

### Discussion

The patient begins the session with a flurry of defensive maneuvers stimulated by the fantasy of a devouring maternal transference relationship which had begun to emerge again in the last session. However, before the fantasy can be verbalized it is necessary to deal with the more superficial resistances expressed in the silence, in the lack of trust, and in the feeling that I am forcing her emotions. I therefore choose to deal with these resistances first.

This is followed by the expression of her anxiety about separation, the analysis, and the fantasy of being lost, as illustrated in the brief dream. The associations to this dream are the transference feelings that had been expressed just previously.

At this point, having consciously verbalized her reluctance and resentment about the analysis, I feel she is ready to go back to the underlying fantasy of being devoured, and in response to my question the primitive maternal transference image begins to emerge more clearly, and in her analytic behavior she "acts-in" regarding the underlying fantasy. That is, she begins to relax her resistances and to tell me of her dream as a form of psychic surrender in the transference. At this point her anxiety about surrendering is acutely mobilized, and her defenses against such a surrender are alerted. By my questions regarding her fears of talking I am indirectly encouraging her to try to face the fantasy and feelings consciously. An important factor here is the wish to please me as a patient, as well as the continuing though unverbalized working alliance.

It is here that the erotized fantasy of the mother breaks through into consciousness and is displaced into the transference. My thought is that at this particular moment the reference to the father's leaving her is a defensive attempt to avoid the danger situation regarding her wishes toward the mother. This understanding leads to my interpretation of the maternal transference, which helps her to express the feeling she is directly experiencing toward me as the seductive yet devouring mother. The transference experience is intense but her passing comment about her daughter indicates the presence of simultaneous self-observation. Because I am able to maintain the analytic situation and am neither rejecting nor aroused or seductive in regard to her material, she is able to end the session with a growing sense of trust in me as an analyst and is thus able to experience the positive wish for the gratifying oral maternal attachment.

Although in this session the anxiety has been consciously perceived as a fear of me and of my wishing to devour her, what has been clarified is the powerful source of danger and anxiety in her own wish regressively to experience the gratifications with the mother. At present it is still not possible to determine clearly whether these represent a continuing, unresolved primary attachment, or whether they represent a regressive retreat to mother as a defense against the stimulation and frustration in the relationship with the father and the uncle. Earlier in the session when she says, "It's just like my uncle. You can't trust anyone," she is again alluding to the traumatic sexual seduction, the memory of which is now conscious and easily accessible, but the derivative effects of which are still not completely resolved.

## SESSION 213

This session was conducted in a different office than usual because of workmen repairing my office window.

**P:** I had a dream. I was in bed sleeping with a girl who was a friend that I grew up with. Then I wanted to go for a swim. And then I was making some candy for the girls before I left. – – – I've been making some cookies before I leave on the trip.

**A:** Up to now you've said very little about the trip.

**P:** I have so many fears I just want to throw them away. I'm scared to fly with Tom on the same plane, so we are going to take separate flights. My mother is staying with the kids, and I'm so afraid that she is not going to treat them right. I also have such fear about leaving you, so I feel I just have to do it and there is no sense in being scared. Tom's parents seem to dominate the whole thing. There just is no love in my mother at all so how could she possibly make the kids feel secure? (Elaborates.) In the dream I was visiting my mother in Springfield. There was a man there and it was all in a huge house. I asked for an audience with my mother because my sister was having intercourse with some boys. I was going to tell my mother. Mother was mad that my sister hadn't told her. I said that she wouldn't understand, and mother said, "You don't know, you've never tried me." – – – – I feel such an urge to talk; I think of myself as a child. I want to tell you things, and tell you all of the things that I didn't tell my parents. The sexual things and all about my hostility and the things that I've done, and so on. I think about the time when I was in Springfield when I had such an urge to talk but I couldn't and yet I was so wild. I was afraid that my parents would either be mad or be scared and that they wouldn't be capable of understanding. (Elaborates.)

**A:** This is the same feeling that you are repeating with me now when you wonder what would happen if you tell me about your feelings. This is what's behind the questions of whether I will be mad or excited, or not understand and so on.

**P:** I just start to have feelings of warmth for you and then I run. It is just the same as with Tom or with the children. I just can't reason with myself. – – – Now I'm leaving again. I have such a fear that you'll change your mind about me. – – I'm thinking about you. . . . . I don't like this room and I don't like the chair you're in and I don't like anything about it.

**A:** What's the detail?

**P:** It's not you. You're too human here. You're just like a person so how can I possibly talk to you? We are just two people in this room. You're a man just like every other man. – – – Yesterday at home I had a sudden image of two men fighting and one of them was in a white shirt. It was like a story I had seen on TV and then I had a sudden flash come to my mind of a huge penis. –

**A:** What was the detail?

**P:** It was hard and it was standing up. It was as huge as a man. I thought about my cousin's pictures from World War II, which showed some Japs all cut up. Their heads and arms were cut off. – . . . . .

**A:** What are you trying to say?

**P:** I feel hysterical. I think of cutting people up, murders, and things like that. Gangs of boys. I just can't stand it.

**A:** What was the detail about your cousin's pictures?

**P:** I can't remember. They were taken on a beach and there was water there and a sword and some rocks and there was some grass on a hill. Whenever I have the thoughts of cutting a penis up, I think of this picture. There were two of them and they were horrible. They made me sick to my stomach. But it gives me such a funny feeling in my mouth right now. – – – He stayed with my uncle and he had the pictures in his room and I'd go in there all the time and I'd look at them. They fascinated me, but they also scared me. I feel like such a little girl and I feel so helpless. I think of the time that I was in a T-shirt and shorts and I was looking at my father's penis in Maine. I had the thought then that it is too much and I can't stand it.

**A:** What do you remember thinking as you were looking at his penis?

**P:** It was hard and it was standing up and I wanted to touch it. It was so sensual. It's just like I'm the penis myself. I feel so open and so raw! I think of the skin. I never felt this way before!

**A:** What did you stop at?

**P:** I feel that I want to cut my wrists now. I want to cut it off. I don't want to say that. What is this thing? I used to think so hard about it. I know that it goes inside of a woman, but I want to cut it off and I want to know the women that it goes inside of. – – What would happen if I cut it all off? – – Doesn't this make you nervous? It makes me so nervous. If I cut it off, then I can take it with me and then I don't have to worry again about my father leaving me, or raping me or anything like that. Now I'm starting to get mad! I *don't want* to do this! Why do I keep thinking about it!? Because if I ever do it he'll never be able to make love to me.

*Cry*

-- I wish you'd tell me that I'm crazy. I torture myself with how evil I am. Really I want to feel that I'm wonderful. Right now I want to put your penis in my mouth and nurse on you and have you make love to me. I feel that I have to beat myself with these awful thoughts. Why doesn't it bother you? It's you!.....

**A:** What's the trouble with saying what's on your mind?

**P:** I'm picturing *your* penis as you sit in that chair.

**A:** What's the detail?

**P:** This *must* bother you. -- I think how fascinating your penis is and I want to touch it and feel it and taste it and know what it is, because I don't have one. I want one of my own to experiment with. I liked looking at those pictures. I used to think the guy is dead and maybe I can take his penis. You make no attempt to control my thoughts and you don't condemn me and you don't reassure me. You make me have them. So I have to do with them whatever I can.

**A:** You used to look at those pictures and think of the guy that was dead and maybe you could have his penis and so on. What was the detail of your thoughts?

**P:** Then I'd be a big tough man. I'd be huge and I'd be a great big penis. I could bore a hole in anyone that I don't like. I think of that picture. Then I'd have it and I'd be a man and I'd be big and strong and my parents couldn't do anything to me. I feel that I'm larger and larger and the whole world disappears and only the big penis is left and then I get so scared. I wonder what it would be like to put myself inside my mother. I can feel this sexual feeling. -- My poor mother. I could destroy her by doing this. I feel sorry for her. These are the thoughts that make me sick because they are so weird and they are not happy at all. -- Sometimes I wonder if my mother ever gave me any love? Was there anything soft and warm in her? -- It's horrible to feel that you want to destroy anyone that you love. It's like an evil monster that comes out and wants to destroy them. If you would just leave me alone I'd be all right. -- I feel like I'm back in a black hole and its horrible. I feel as though I'm going to burst out! I want to stand up and give you hell and that would be the end of the world and there would be a violent explosion.

**A:** We'll stop here for today.

## Discussion

My initial intervention in this session in regard to her trip to Florida is an attempt to offset a tendency she has shown of leaving out of her analysis events from her everyday life. By indicating my interest in the trip, I am trying to block this resistance of isolation and separation of her daily experience from the analysis.

In talking about the mother staying with her children, the patient is identified with the children and projecting her own insecurity upon them. However, the later dream in which the mother says, "You don't know, you've never tried me," seems to reflect a beginning shift in her attitude toward the mother in the transference neurosis, resulting from the interactions between us yesterday. This is followed by her conscious awareness of wanting to trust me and to confide her more troublesome thoughts to me which I attempt to foster by my interpretations of the defensive transference.

The patient then demonstrates the oscillation described yesterday between her oral maternal yearnings and her phallic masculine strivings. Her associations shift from the transference fantasies and experiences in the relationship to the mother, and move toward the phallic castration fantasies exemplified in the childhood fascination with the cousin's pictures. This material also illustrates the body-phallus equation, as well as her identification with the penis, and the fantasied wish of acquiring a penis for herself as part of her masculine identification. My question and requests for further associations in regard to the cousin's pictures are an attempt to encourage her to relive this important childhood experience and to recapture some of the fantasies of that time in an experiential way.

The result of her spontaneous associations is a regressive reliving of the little girl's fascination with her father's penis, stimulated by the continuing transference experiences of the previous separation from me, and of the upcoming trip she is planning. At this point she turns her aggression against herself with the fantasy of cutting her own wrists as the defense against the subsequently expressed fantasies of castrating the father. The stimulus for this material is the current transference experience and fantasy, expressed in her question whether this material makes me nervous, and in the rapid oscillations between remembered experience with the father and current fantasy and experience toward me. The fact that I do not respond with anxiety, judgmental criticism, seduction, or arousal is an important factor in permitting her to pursue and experience this material openly.

She also illustrates the oscillation between phallic and oral drives and conflicts and the reciprocal influence of each stage on the organization of the other by the fantasy of nursing on my penis. She briefly verbalizes the

reassurance received from my attitude when she speaks of my not attempting to control her thoughts or to condemn or reassure her, but then uses
the mechanism of projection again when she says, "You make me have
them."

After the patient has verbalized this reassurance, I ask her to go back
again to the cousin's pictures in an attempt further to explore the childhood phallic fantasies. She again returns to the body-phallus image and
the image arising from her masculine identification, but again experiences
anxiety in regard to the phallic wishes and retreats to the passive, oral
position in relationship to the mother with her question, "I wonder if my
mother ever gave me any love?" At the very end of the session, with the
fantasy of being in the black hole and of the horrible explosion, she is
again returning to the phallic masculine wishes, one aim of which is the
wish for dependent gratification from the mother.

Some of the material emerging in this session is relatively new to the
analysis and represents the expression of drives, fantasies, and conflicts
stimulated by the transference neurosis. This entire complex is being activated by the transference wish to keep my "penis-breast" with her during
our forthcoming separation. However, to interpret this now would tend to
generalize this experience, to promote premature closure, and to permit the
avoidance of detailed elaboration of these childhood fantasies.

In response to this material, my activity has involved the interpretation
of several resistances and the requests for further elaboration of detailed
associations. No interpretations of content are made since the material is
flowing freely and none are needed at the moment. Furthermore, in response to this type of initial uncovering of new material, an interpretation
of content going significantly beyond the point of the patient's own awareness might mobilize more anxiety than would be optimal at this time. By
quiet listening and requests for further detailed associations, I am merely
setting the stage in which the patient can permit herself to experience the
force of the underlying drives and become aware of the fantasies which
these drives have helped to produce.

---

### SESSION 214

**P:** I can't stand to be alone. (Elaborates.) I'm thinking about the trip
to Florida and I don't want you to forget me.

**A:** What's the detail of the thought that I might forget you?

**P:** When I see you every day you can't forget me. I'm tied to you and

I'm dependent on you. But what happens if I don't see you? If I close my eyes I have a feeling that you'll disappear. I think of the phrase, "Out of sight, out of mind." We may never see each other again. You may disappear off the face of the earth.

A: What's the detail of the thought that if you close your eyes I'll disappear?

P: It's just like a baby nursing. I want to go on this trip and have fun, but I also want to be sure that I'll see you again and that I'll return. I don't dare relax and enjoy myself and know that you will be here. I feel that I *have* to love you. Before I leave I want everything to be all wonderful. I'm leaving and yet I'm mad at *you* for it, and I feel that *you're* the one who is leaving. – – You'd show me that you cared if you'd only ask me not to go. Then I wouldn't worry about anything. I want to take your penis with me. Regardless of how much I love you, I'm going to miss you while I'm away. I feel that I want to grab your penis before I go. I should apologize for talking like this.

A: Why should you apologize?

P: I'm afraid that I'm going to make you mad. I shouldn't talk like this because it's a mean thought, and I should feel love. This is hate. I want to take your God-damn penis with me!

A: I think that you are repeating with me the feeling that you once had in the nursing experience. If you close your eyes and go to sleep after nursing, then it's as if your mother disappears and your fear is that she won't return the next time. The wish is that you want to keep the breast with you always so that you don't have to worry about her coming back. With me, my penis is like mother's breast, and the wish to suck on it is the wish to nurse.

P: – – I suddenly feel as though I've never been able to relax and enjoy anything in my life. This all makes me so nervous! It would be so wonderful just to open my arms and to love and to feel loved. And yet I draw inside myself and I don't give to anyone. – – – I love to think about my son taking the bottle. He'll be so nervous and jumpy and restless and then he relaxes. (Elaborates.) I love to watch him, but it makes me so nervous. It's just like me with my eating. I feel so mad when I stop, and I can't stop. It makes me so mad! That feeling of love and hate is coming back again. I feel so good in here and I love you and I relax and I trust you and then, damn! I get so mad! I feel as if you are a monster and I hate you! There is just no explanation for this.

A: There's a transitional step that you left out in your associations between the feeling of loving me and relaxing and suddenly hating me.

**P:** I experience such a good feeling and it's just like an orgasm. I wish that it would go on forever. I'm twenty-seven years old and here I am enjoying nursing! I picture myself lying in your arms and I get that feeling in my mouth and my vagina and I wish it would go on and on and never stop. Why should it? I'm twenty-seven, I have three children and a husband. And yet I want it to go on and on and never stop! That makes me sick. It's better not to enjoy it and not to love you and have good feelings. I feel as though I have to be nervous and always have hostility. I have a terrible fear of what will happen if I ever do relax. I start to and then I get nervous and then mad! I feel afraid and then I want to come out of it. I have a huge desire to give up everything in life and just be a baby and nurse for ever and ever. I just can't believe that I actually want this, and that is why I can't have intercourse or sexual feelings or love. It would mean carrying out my desire. To have an orgasm is to relax and let it carry you away. It's the most wonderful feeling in the world, so why should I get mad, and why should it depress me just thinking about this? I just can't have it. I feel wild and I have such a wish to flail around in all directions. If I were really a baby I'd scream so loud. It's just like Thomas when he screams and gets blue in the face. -- I wonder what would happen if I completely let go and accepted the fact that I'm mad about this. I *know* that this is it, and yet I feel so mad I could die. I just can't accept it. It all starts with having love feelings and then this shit comes after it. Now I want to yell and scream. I want to nurse forever. Why can't you take care of me forever and let me lie on this couch forever? I have such a headache now! (Elaborates.) When I'm through screaming I think about all of the things that I can do to get revenge. I'm just like an animal and I feel so mean and evil.

**A:** What's the detail of wanting to get revenge?

**P:** It's just like being an animal in a jungle. They have no inhibitions and they kill and then they eat what they kill. That's me. It's like I'm another person. It's normal for babies to feel like this because they're born with it and then they learn not to do it. I just can't convince myself that it would be all right and so I can't let the evil monster out. I want to kill you and eat you. -- I feel so afraid. It's like the feeling of relaxing, because if I eat you then you'd disappear and I'd be all by myself. I feel like these thoughts are horrible. Relaxing is like being a baby inside of you. I know that it's not true and yet I have such a wish that it would be true. When I'm pregnant I feel as if I'd eaten someone that I hate, and that became the baby and the baby then is harmless. At times I feel as if I'm such a wonderful person and so I just can't believe all of this. -- I feel

*Cry*

like the times when I'd sit in my room and think these horrible thoughts. The more I'd think the more scared I'd get. Even stamping around mad is an escape for these thoughts. -- The problem is that I really do *enjoy* these thoughts. But the fear is that if I ever do enjoy them, then they'll happen. Then I get hysterical and have a temper-tantrum and I say that I hate you and then the thoughts go away. -- I'm so mad! I feel like hitting someone! I get this feeling in my vagina and I don't want to tell you about it, and I just want to walk out of here. You won't stop my thoughts and you won't control this and it makes me mad that you don't. You let me go into this fantasy of myself as an animal and I'll destroy and I'll eat you! I feel so nervous! Why don't you do something about it!! I've lost track of reality! When I go into this thought I have a feeling that I just want to hang onto you and have you tell me that I'm all right! It scares me! I want *Cry!!* you to love me and I feel like I'm a helpless child who has done something terrible. -- I wonder if it's good to let children have thoughts like this and express them? (Laughs.) This must be a defense This fear is really a defense! (Elaborates.) It's a horrible fear.

A: What's the thought that the fear is really a defense?

P: It brings me back from thinking these horrible thoughts! I sat *Anxiety.* there and enjoyed thinking about it. It makes me want to kill myself, so I *Cry!!!* have to stop thinking. I have to have a tantrum or cut my wrists or bang my head or do anything to stop me from thinking this. The eating helps for a while but then I feel worse when I stop.

A: We'll stop here for today.

### DISCUSSION

The patient begins by continuing the theme of the previous day's session, stimulated again by the upcoming transference separation. She begins with her symptoms and then goes on to talk about the immediate conflict stimulus of the trip to Florida which, in turn, is followed by the intrapsychic danger situation that I might forget her. This in turn is a projection of her own difficulty in the maintenance of object constancy, as illustrated by her response after my question which serves to point out the defense.

Immediately after she expresses the thought that if she closed her eyes I would disappear, I have the personal association to the nursing situation partly from the material of this session, but also as a continuation of yesterday's material. I could have interpreted the content of this fantasy to her directly at that point, but had I done so, it might have seemed external to herself, intellectualized, or like a magical inductive leap. Instead, I choose to try to get her to express the fantasy herself through my request for further associations, and at this point, in an affective way she herself provides the direct connection to the fantasy of nursing. She also provides the link between the breast and the penis and the transference fantasy of grabbing my penis. This is immediately followed by the resistance that she should apologize, which is dealt with by my question as to why she thinks so. At this point, in a still more affective way, she expresses the direct wish to take my penis with her.

Now that the patient has provided the raw materials, in terms of her fantasies, it is possible for me to make the interpretation regarding the penis-breast equation and its manifestations in the conflict over leaving me. By the interpretation and the linking of the transference experience to a genetic reconstruction several things are accomplished. I indicate my understanding and acceptance of her primary-process fantasies and drives, I demonstrate that I am not threatened by them, I promote her identification with my analytic attitude, and I provide her with a formulation of their content which promotes secondary-process integration and mastery. As a result, her anxiety about the transference experience is reduced, thus permitting further elaboration of the experience.

This interpretation proves to be crucial for the rest of the session, in that it is followed by an outpouring of material directly related to these early regressive experiences. The interpretation has made it possible for her to crystallize her own feeling and fantasies, and regressively to experience these in the transference relationship. But interspersed with the transference experience are comments and questions which indicate that self-observing functions are occurring simultaneously. The observations of herself and her symptoms, the comparisons to her infant son, the analogy to the animal in the jungle, and the recognition of her fantasies as distortions, are all evidences for this. Probably the most telling of these comments is her statement, "The problem is that I really enjoy these thoughts," and her own recognition of the fallacy that thinking these things will lead to actual occurrences.

However, she becomes more anxious as she experiences the vaginal sensations (which are another derivative of the penis-breast equation) and then expresses her defensive wish that I control her thoughts and that I not let her go into these fantasies. Anxiety mounts further in the regressive transference experience and she actively seeks reassurance. The reassurance is offered silently through my acceptance of her associations without comment, and it is then followed by a spontaneous reversal of the regression expressed by her question as to whether it is appropriate to let children have such thoughts and express them. This, in turn, is followed by the recognition that she has enjoyed her fantasies, but that simultaneously they have aroused intense guilt and anxiety.

In this session she has affectively begun to experience in consciousness some of the fantasies which previously had evoked the signal of anxiety with resulting automatic defenses, so that the fantasies had been maintained at an unconscious level, and the drives expressed through these fantasies kept under control. In the relatively safe situation of the analysis, reassured tacitly by my neutral acceptance of her fantasy productions and accompanied by her own capacities for self-observation while regressively experiencing these transference drives, she is now able to permit some access to consciousness of the previously warded-off material. Her conscious awareness and recognition of these issues now permits her to apply other conscious integrative mechanisms toward their understanding and control. The use of these other conscious mechanisms, along with the unconscious identification with me in the analytic attitude and posture, will now permit her to experience these drives as somewhat less threatening and dangerous, and she will feel a gradually increasing sense of confidence in her ability to control them consciously, along with a decreasing sense of guilt in regard to their occurrence. This process will have to be repeated again and again as the analysis proceeds, but it illustrates the role of repeated experience of regressive early childhood drives and fantasy followed by mastery of conflicts, as they are mobilized by the transference relationship to the analyst.

---

## SESSION 215

The patient comes in wearing high heels, and she has a sophisticated new type of hair-do.

**P:** I've felt more nervous than I ever have been about coming here. – – I feel as if I'm going off to the big world all by myself and I feel like a baby. I'm scared to fly all the way to Florida by myself. I feel like a baby in a woman's world.

**A:** What's the detail of the anxiety about coming here today?

**P:** – – I don't know. I'm scared to death of something. I'm afraid of myself and of my own thoughts and when I get all dolled up like this, I'm afraid that I'll seduce men. This is a defense for me and it's just like nursing. I wear a sloppy dress and I don't really fix my hair when I come here every day. But in Florida I have to have my hair fixed and I'll be wearing dresses and I feel so scared. These are all *my* thoughts, but I want to take you with me. I have a feeling that I'm evil and I want to escape back to being a child.

A: You're dressed up here today and you have a new hair-do. You must have had some fantasies about this.

P: I'm so embarrassed. I had the thought that I'll destroy them and seduce the hell out of them.

A: What effect did you think the dressing up would have on me?

P: It all sounds so stupid. But I got myself all worked up coming here.

A: It's as if this is a test situation here with me today. You got yourself all dressed up and you fixed your hair and for a little while you gave up the defense of sloppiness.

P: I'm dividing myself all up again. I'm much more afraid of the way that *I* am. For me to look nice is the same as being a bitch and it means that I want to destroy everyone. I *do not* want this. But I feel as if it is uncontrollable in me. So to be a baby again is like a defense against these thoughts. (Elaborates.) I want men to think that I am a baby. This is all so silly! Men do look at me. And then I fall apart and get scared to death. I feel as if I can't handle it and I can't handle myself and I have a sense of panic.

A: All of these thoughts and feelings about men are condensed into this relationship with me and the fantasies about coming here today dressed up, and the thoughts about what effects it will have on me. What comes to your mind?

P: If I really let myself go I'll seduce you and then I can take you with me.

A: What's the detail?

P: I want to feed on you and take the breast with me. So I'll take your penis with me, but then I destroy you. I'm a monster and so I just can't love you. I can only be either a baby or a bitch. And yet I can't run away from the fact that I'm a woman and that I *am* attractive to men. I just can't take a situation like this.

A: Why not?

P: We're by ourselves. I have to run away from what it is that I want. If I let you know how I feel, will you act out on my feelings? Will you take advantage of me? I was so scared about having had my hair done. -- Somehow this is related to Friday night. Tom and I made love and I was so embarrassed and it had never happened before. It was about a thought of mine and I had a fear that you'd find out. -- I'm thinking now. - I had my hair done and I'm really beautiful. Are you attracted to me? – –

**A:** I wonder if you are waiting for me to ask you about Friday night?

**P:** – I was in such a panic Friday. (Elaborates.) At the time I felt I'm going to fall apart and I'm so scared and this is all related to Dr. Dewald. I'm so scared to relax and let go of my feelings and just feel this complete relaxation. I'm scared to make love and then go to sleep and feel loving and feel that I'm being a woman and a mother. –

**A:** I think you are still censoring and editing the fantasies you had Friday night.

**P:** I don't know! Friday night I had the thought, "I'm afraid to feel like a woman tonight." I don't want to talk about it! (Elaborates.) My love feelings are just like evil monsters. – – They are destroying. I'm so afraid that I will. – – – All my thoughts rush in on me! I'm so scared. I just can't think. I love you and you've helped me so much and I want to take you with me, and I know that I'll be so hostile toward you when I leave. I want something from you. – – – When I feel love for you then I have such sexual feelings and then I'm a woman. I think then maybe I can be able to take you. I just can't be separated from you when I love you so much. I had another dream about the house in Evanston, and my mother and father going on trips. – – This is all related to a need and it's like I can't function without you. I really need *you*. I started having my period this morning and I shouldn't! I'm on Enovid and it's not the time for me to have my period. I feel as if I am losing my mind.

*Anxiety, Cry!!!*

**A:** What's the detail about getting your period this morning?

**P:** I've gone and done it and I've destroyed you. That's you! I think about my uncle!

**A:** What are you referring to?

**P:** A penis. I've eaten it and it's inside me and it's bleeding! I'm a woman and there is something inside me that is going to get bigger and bigger. What have I done? I've done something horrible. – – I'm so worried about why my period would have started this morning.

*Cry, Anxiety*

**A:** You have a fantasy that you have a penis inside of you and that it's bleeding. It seems as if you think that it is either your uncle's or mine. What comes to your mind about it?

**P:** I'm a monster and I'm just wild! I'm a woman! Shit! I think of eating a penis and how it would be mean and hostile to do this and I want to!! It's all this love and hate and nursing and orgasm. It's all one thing. I've *got* to take your penis with me. God-damn it, I must do it! I sometimes feel as if I have already done it.

*Scream*

**A:** The fantasy seems to be that you are going to use your vagina as though it were a mouth and you are going to bite the penis off. You're reacting to the blood this morning as if it was from my penis or your uncle's penis and as if you feel that it's still in there.

**P:** I feel as if I've done this. Why do I feel I've done it? I had a dream about the Evanston basement where all of this business went on and I meant to tell you about it, and I forgot.

**A:** What's the detail?

**P:** I was a woman in the dream and I felt so good about it and the basement seemed so clean. – – Our yardman was there and also my uncle. I feel as though I have actually done this and I do have a penis inside of me.

**A:** This is the fantasy that keeps you from letting go with Tom. It's as if you think that if you don't control your sexual feelings that you actually will do this.

**P:** (Laughs.) My vagina has teeth in it and I'll bite him off. Why do I believe this? I feel just like a child. – –

**A:** What comes to your mind about the yardman in the dream?

**P:** We had one who was an alcoholic. Most of the time our yardmen were bums, but his name was Frank. He had no teeth. He was so interested in me. There was another one called Bill who was like my uncle. He would put his arms around me. I've had dreams of his bathroom and he used to babysit for me. I wonder if I used to have fantasies about him? I know that I was scared of him, but in the dream he put his arms around my waist and he was drunk and he wouldn't let me go. He was very nice to me actually. I had an evil eye for any man who was nice to me and I used to have wild thoughts like they are nice to me and maybe I can get their penises. I used to think this about Bill and Frank and my uncle and Mr. Jones and all of the other men. I used to wish that I could just know their thoughts. But I *feel* as if something really happened and as if I am a monster. – – –

**A:** We'll stop here for today.

### DISCUSSION

This is the last session before the patient leaves for her trip and the happenstance that she is dressed up and ready to leave shortly after the session now puts her into a more intense situation of conflict in regard to the previously mobilized transference wishes. She has avoided this conflict situation in past sessions by not dressing as attractively as she might have. Because this has represented an unverbalized defensive acting-out, I call her attention to this issue, encourage her to verbalize some of the fantasies, and then interpret the conflict and transference test situation previously defended against. The patient responds defensively by generalizing the issue to involve all men, and I deal with this resistance by focusing her attention more specifically and precisely into the transference fantasies about me.

After some oscillation between the phallic-oedipal and the oral-maternal fixations, the patient begins to approach the issue of the current oedipal transference wish and fear that I will be sexually attracted and interested in her. During the course of this, she mentions that it is connected to an incident with her husband after her previous session. At this point my choice is either to continue the current elaboration of the transference wishes directly, or to explore and expand upon the incident that occurred during her sexual relations with her husband. Her direct question, "Are you attracted to me," poses a problem. In actual fact, she does look prettier and more attractive than usual. But to answer affirmatively would represent a seductive transference gratification, while to answer negatively would be an unnecessary and painful (as well as untrue) rejection. From her nonverbal attitude and from an intuitive hunch, I also have the impression that significant transference elements had erupted during the sexual act with her husband and that she is intent on withholding this information at this moment. I also feel that because her associations have spontaneously returned to the immediate transference fantasies of dressing to come here this morning, possibly the conflict is greater in regard to the areas that she has omitted. For these reasons, after the silence, I point out her reluctance to describe the events further.

Her response to my intervention is that of vague generalizations and after I point out the occurrence of these resistances, she begins to experience a rapidly mounting affective response, indicating the mobilization of a significant conflict. At this point, in a somewhat chaotic way, the material oscillates rapidly (but typically) between the experience with the husband, the transference feelings, a dream about a childhood location, and the onset of her menses.

The breakthrough of menstrual bleeding while on contraceptive pills is a suggestive illustration of the concept of somatic compliance. Because of this, because it is unusual for her, and because she seems to be experiencing so much anxiety about it, I choose to focus my question upon it, but her associations to it take me completely by surprise. At this point the previously explored fantasy of having swallowed the uncle's penis begins to emerge into conscious awareness again, accompanied by intense affect.

My initial response is one of clarification, the aim of which is to indicate my acceptance of this fantasy as something important and worth exploring further, and thus to maintain our therapeutic alliance in the face of her intense affect. The patient is regressively beginning to relive the old experience under the pressure of drives stimulated by the impending separation from me and the transference wish to take my penis-breast with her and thus symbolically avoid the separation.

My interpretation of the content of this fantasy is an attempt to make it more clearly conscious for her and thereby permit a sharper differentiation of fantasy from reality and permit the use of secondary-process ego-integrative mechanisms to cope with the fantasied danger situation she is now experiencing. It is also an attempt to provide her with a model for conceptualizing the experiences she is now having, and through identification with me in the analytic function to feel less threatened by them. Although the incident with the uncle and its accompanying fantasies had been uncovered months ago, this material and the affects connected to it indicate that repression has again occurred and that much working-through must still be done. My interpretation of the dentate vagina fantasy takes account of the psychic development that has occurred in her since this material last came up, but the most important function is that it offers her a reasonable and internally consistent conceptualization as to the meaning of her current experience.

The interpretation produces several immediate effects. There is a reduction in the intensity of the affective storm with a greater sense of control experienced by the patient. The self-observing ego functions are almost immediately stimulated, as indicated by her question, "Why do I feel that I've done it?" She immediately goes on to report a fragment of a dream and describes her intention to have told me about it but having forgotten to do so. In essence, the interpretation has controlled the depth of regression in the analytic situation and has shifted the patient's psychic forces away from the regressive experience in the transference neurosis, and instead toward the self-observing awareness and curiosity in the therapeutic alliance.

After the patient again indicates her feeling that she has actually incorporated the penis, my interpretation of her fear of letting go with her husband is an attempt again to strengthen the therapeutic alliance by explaining the meaning of the specific symptom mentioned by her earlier in the session. Her response of laughter, confirmation of the fantasy of the dentate vagina, and appropriate curiosity and distance indicate that the therapeutic alliance has been effectively reinforced.

Ordinarily, just before a significant separation in analysis, patients tend to be increasingly resistive and defensive in order that affectively painful or frightening material not come up just as they are about to leave the analyst. A number of speculations might be entertained about why in this case such affectively distressing material emerged just prior to such a separation. One likelihood is that the separation itself served as a mobilizing force to stimulate the emergence of the wishes described above. Other possibilities include the fact that she is ambivalent about leaving and has a wish that I would encourage her not to go, possibly on the basis that she is too sick; or the fear that I will forget her while she is away or not want to accept her when she returns may be stimulating her to give me "something really good and exciting" to make sure that my interest in her stays active. But since there is no way at this time of verification or confirmation from the patient, these must remain only interesting speculations.

---

## SESSION 216

Patient returns after a one-week absence.

**P:** –– I feel as if I was testing myself this week and as if I failed. I just floundered around. The evil monster inside me just completely came out. ––– I'm scared to death that I'll be able to seduce you. It's all in *me*.

**A:** You mentioned that the monster came out. What was it all about?

**P:** I had a chance to go out in the world and I realized that men are attracted to me and I had thought, now is my chance. I actually *wanted* to seduce men. It scares me and it never did before. We were at a party when it happened and I had the feeling that something is *wrong* with me! I feel like a bitch! That's all that I am. I'd never do anything but I know that it's there. It drives me nuts. Yesterday I ate all day and I was worse than I ever was. I can see what I am doing and yet I can't do anything about it. There's a certain type of man who just scares the hell out of me.

**A:** What's the type?

**P:** The sick type. There was a thirty-two-year-old bachelor there who paid a lot of attention to me but I could handle him easily. But it's the type that's quiet and just looks, and that wants to destroy women. I'm scared with them to have these thoughts come to mind.

**A:** Let's look at the type that scares you. What comes to mind?

**P:** All I can do is think of my father! This is the type that is so stoic and quiet, but they are *looking!* The open type doesn't scare me at all. It's the quiet ones, because I know their thoughts and nothing is ever said. But it's the old men who bug me the most! There was one man there who was sixty-five and he really got to me! – – And there was no one to protect me. I couldn't get away from these feelings. That old man was so like my uncle. (Elaborates.) It all starts out so honest and then suddenly it is all so horrible and I turn into a bitch. I just can't sit here and tell you about it! – –

*Cry*

A: Why not?

P: Why should I tell you? You're one of them.

A: You mentioned before that you are scared that you'll actually seduce me.

P: In my mind you're one of these men. You are one of this type. There is something in *me* that feels it. It is just like my father. There is something inside of him that I can get to. It's just like me. I'm so soft and I'm such a woman that it scares me. A man can look at me and he can know that there is a woman inside me who's warm and whom they can get into, and it's not the same as in other women. I can be used for dirty purposes but I can't have it as a wife or as a mother but only as a lover, and yet it's such a wonderful feeling. I've never let this feeling out in here.

A: What do you picture would happen if you did?

P: You will look at me and you will say, "This is a woman and not a child." You'll wake up one day and so I feel that I have to hide it from you every day.

A: I'll say that this is a woman and not a child and then what?

P: I'm so afraid that you have that feeling inside you that attracts you to me. I'm a woman and you'll want to crawl into my arms and I'll protect you and love you and give you the things that you want and I know that I can give it to you. This is basic in all men, even if they have all kinds of defenses against it. (Elaborates.) All men are boys looking for their mother, and if you ever see your mother in me, that's it. You've *got* to be like them. You're a man! I have no defense against this.

A: What's the thought?

P: I used to feel like a child or I'd feel ugly, or I'd feel that I'm really not a woman or I'd run to Tom and ask him to be my mother. I can't do any of those any more. You've opened me up! There's a big mamma there, a big woman! Shit on you!

A: You seem to be making an automatic equation that because *I'm a man, therefore,* if you are a woman and you show me, you'll seduce me. What comes to mind about this?

**P:** I've got what you're looking for. Your wife can't give it to you and I know that I can. And so I'll put myself in the role of a bad girl. All wives are cold and I'm not. As a wife I am.

**A:** The thought is that my wife is cold and can't give it to me. What are your associations to that?

**P:** A wife takes care of children so she can't give romance and sexual love. That's what a man wants and it must be outside of marriage. If we were married I couldn't either. I have such a desire to give you this, and I feel that you are not getting it at home.

**A:** What's the detail of the fantasy?

**P:** There are all kinds of other things to think about in marriage. Things like finances and the house, children, and worries. There is just no time for love. Your wife probably gets caught up in these things. It's not her fault, but she does. – – I suddenly feel just like a child and I'm *mad* at you. Because regardless of anything you shouldn't leave home! I don't care what! – – I'm on the other side of the fence now and it's much better on this side.

**A:** What's the detail?

**P:** The other is just black and sexual and getting inside of people and I'm all by myself and I don't have my mother there and I'm losing my mind. I'm just a child here. But over there I'm a woman and having intercourse with a man.

**A:** So for you, the idea for you to be a woman is the same as getting your father and giving him what you feel your mother didn't. You want this and it excites you and tempts you but you also feel terrified and guilty and so you feel it is safer to be a child.

**P:** I've been able to get this all of my life.

**A:** How do you mean?

**P:** Other men always see me as a woman and so here we go! That is unless I eat and I get ugly. Then it's safe.

**A:** You seem to have a feeling of helplessness if another man is attracted to you. What's the detail of your thought?

**P:** There's my chance! And it's always with the quiet type.

**A:** What's the feeling about "there is my chance?"

**P:** To get my father and to get his penis and to get everything. I picture myself in bed with him. – – – I want to have my father say, "You're attractive to me and let's go to bed." It's such a temptation! Everything I ever wished for and feared has come true.

**A:** We'll stop here for today.

## DISCUSSION

The patient begins the hour by a brief reference to her trip, followed immediately by a return to the expression of direct transference feelings. Since the transference neurosis is well established and I know that transference wishes will soon emerge again, and since she has a tendency to isolate and briefly slide over the events of her external life, and since I want to interfere with this tendency toward isolation of reality, I therefore elect to focus her attention onto the events of the trip. The correctness of this maneuver is verified by the spontaneous flow of material regarding some of the men she had met on her trip who, in turn, were associated to the father and uncle, and then the focus of her conflict is again returned into the transference neurosis with the feeling that I am one of these men. At this point I remind her that at the beginning of the session she had felt able to seduce me and we then return to the current version and edition of the oedipal conflict in the transference neurosis with me.

However, her statement, "I've never let this feeling out in here," indicates a continuing resistance and fantasy of danger in the fully affective experience of transference wishes. The defenses involved include suppression, isolation, projection, displacement, and continuing repression. My interventions are an attempt to challenge these defenses by encouraging the expression of the underlying transference fantasy. By reporting that the various behavioral defense mechanisms which she has previously used are no longer effective for her in dealing with this conflict, the patient indicates that there has been a beginning structural change, as well as a beginning shift in her image of herself. Although these shifts and changes in structure and self-image are by no means permanent or even well established, the patient's reference to them indicates that analytic change is taking place. These types of tangential references to modified functions that are mentioned only in passing are often more reliable indicators of structural change as a result of analysis than are the patient's consciously planned or elaborately expressed descriptions of change.

At this point, the patient begins to elaborate on typically triadic transference feelings and fantasies and begins, for the first time, extensively to include my wife as a transference object (her mother). At this point, through the description of her feelings in the transference experience, the patient illustrates the characteristic oscillation between the feminine oedipal self-image and wishes, and the defensively regressive position of the pre-oedipal child. My intervention in regard to this is more of a clarification than an interpretation to her, but it serves the function of blocking this regressive defense and of encouraging her to face the oedipal conflict from which she had retreated.

The patient has returned from the trip with her husband and has resumed the analysis without delay or apparent interference with the analytic process. This can occur because the transference neurosis had long since been established, and therefore the brief trip does not serve as a distancing maneuver from me, or as a resistance against developing a transference neurosis. However, if the patient had mentioned the wish to make such a trip early in the analysis at a time prior to the full development of a transference neurosis, I would have attempted to prevent it by interpreting its defensive and distancing function and effects, and by indicating that it might interfere with her analytic progress. Once the transference neurosis is well established, however, this type of reality interruption does not have the same resistance effects and therefore it can be accepted with less concern (although the patient was charged for the missed sessions). In fact, at this point in the analysis, her decision to make the trip represented a small move toward greater independence and maturity of decision. She had been conflicted about announcing it, had expected (and probably wished) that I would oppose it, but had elected nevertheless to do what she and her husband felt was appropriate and best for them in spite of the possibility of my opposition. My not opposing the trip was therefore a tacit recognition and acceptance of these psychic changes within her.

---

## SESSION 217

**P:** I've been having such wild nightmares of my grandmother's house. It was dark and it was night and I had to go to the bathroom so I got out of bed. I went down on the street and there was someone at the door. My children were with me and there was someone old there in a granny nightgown who shook her finger at me and said, "You haven't learned anything." It was as if I was yelling and I was mentally sick and the words wouldn't come out and everything was just horrible. And then there was a rubber penis which turned into a nipple for a bottle. I felt completely disconnected, as if there was just me and there's no one else here. The people that I used to depend on are dropping by the wayside. It's really good and I see that I can't depend on them anymore but it's frightening. I think of Mrs. Jones and Helen's problems. I'm disconnecting myself from every-

*Cry*

one. I just heard that Tom's brother is in a mental hospital! It's just like my own parents and me. I'm all confused and scared and I feel as if I'm going a different way from everybody else.

A: What's the detail about Tom's brother in the hospital?

P: He has so many emotional problems. (Elaborates.) I think of Tom's parents and I realize that I can't depend on them either. I then wonder if maybe Tom is sick. And also I think about Helen.

A: What's the detail?

P: I think about her problems and how bad they are. These are all the people that I was so close to and so dependent on. I find out now that they are actually sicker than I am. And I think of my own life and these outside circumstances hit me and then I wonder, am I doing right? Analysis is supposed to help me. I've been finding that people are starting to confide in me and I'm scared. I just can't hold back and I can't escape from my own problems any more and it scares me to death.

A: What is it that scares you?

*Cry!*

P: Just life itself, and facing it. No one can give me what I need! I need an emotional dependency and these people just can't give it to me. I think about my dependency on people! They cannot give it to me any more. I think of Tom. He has his own problems and I don't even know Tom any more. I have such a tremendous dependence on you! Can I do it? I feel so hostile toward you! I wish I didn't need anyone! But I know it's not true and I know that you are the only one who is left. But I don't know if I can depend on you. I *am!* There is something so wrong about me as compared with the rest of the world!

A: What do you think this is?

P: I don't have a penis. I'm looking at the titles of your books and they are all about females and their sexual problems. There are none there about males with sexual problems.

A: The feeling is that you don't have a penis, but then what?

*Cry*

P: It's just a feeling that I'm lost and have no hope. I feel like hell. I'm helpless and little and worthless. I get so mad to cry in front of you! I wish I could hide it. All women are fighting for supremacy. They have to adjust or else destroy men but there's just no place for us. Why did God ever make *a woman?* There must be a reason. Even Tom feels this. Some women seem to overcome being a housewife and a mother but I just can't compensate.

A: Your feeling is that you don't have a penis and therefore you are helpless and inferior and worthless. What are your associations to that?

P: I just can't become a male. And to eat a penis doesn't work either! So I either have to be my mother or else be a mistress. That is the only role that women can have. Why can't you just accept me as I am? What's the matter with me?

A: What do *you* feel is the matter with you?

P: I'm so mad! I just want to strike out! What else can I do? You're not going to force me but you are saying, "Be a stupid nothing like your mother." – – I'm not! I'll try to be whatever you want me to, but I'm so unsure of what you want. I feel so confused. You just don't care what I am unless I'm a whore, and then you'll look at me. I want to be but I just can't. I *demand your* attention! I've got to have it! I think of my father telling me to go to college and face my problems, and of him saying, "You're just like your mother." I'm just beating my head against the wall and there's just nothing I can do.  *Cry*

A: Let's go back to the feeling that you want to demand my attention by being whatever I want you to be. What do you think I want?

P: I hate you! You just sit there! All I want is one simple thing from you! Love! And I never get it. You just ignore me! Or you are going to try to make me into something else. I only want it one time. . . . . . I can feel it about my own children. I want to hear you say that "I love you anyway in spite of your failures." But I can't. My father did it once in Maine. We were out on the water in a boat and I got terribly scared. He accepted the fact that I was a little girl. One time! He said, "We'll go back in" and I was so happy. – – I just can't talk to you. It all goes too deep and I get too involved. – – – (Laughs.) – – I want a big bottle in my mouth and I want to live like that forever. I have such a sense of panic when I feel that I'm all by myself and it scares me to death.  *Rage*

A: The feeling is that you want a big bottle in your mouth and to live like that forever. What's the detail of the fantasy?

P: It's the only safe thing in life that there is. It's inanimate so I can control it. I just can't face this, whatever it is. I can't trust you.

A: What's the detail?

P: You're a man. You scare me! I just want to get under the bed and hide.

A: What's the feeling that I scare you?

P: You want something from me. You're not a nice, comfortable, big woman. You're a man and you've all kinds of designs on me for something. You don't accept me as a child. You're a huge thing and I know that you'll destroy me.

*Cry*

**A:** What's the detail of the image of me as a huge man who is going to destroy you?

**P:** – I'm in bed and you come in and you kill me.

**A:** Your fantasy seems to be that I have a huge penis and that it would rip you and tear you and destroy you. What comes to your mind about the fantasy?

**P:** I see my father in the door and his penis gets larger and larger and it takes up the whole room and it squashes me. I can't breathe and it stabs me in the middle and leaves a big hole in me. I just can't depend on you! I need help and you're a man and you are going to do this to me. I want to yell and scream! I need to run! I'm so scared! It's such a dilemma! I have no choice. This huge penis suddenly turns into a breast and it destroys me. – – –

**A:** In the fantasy the penis turns into a breast and destroys you. What are your associations?

*Anxiety,*
*Cry*

**P:** I think of my father in his swimming trunks and his thing gets huge and then he disappears and it all becomes a huge, big, soft, pushy thing! You don't understand how scared I am! It's my only security and I have to have it. It's you, but you'll destroy me.

**A:** When you go from feeling like a woman to feeling like a baby as a defense, then my penis turns into a breast and destroys you. But then at other times you go from being an infant to being a woman and my breast becomes a penis that you love but you are also terrified of.

**P:** I feel as if I'm losing my mind. – – – All of my fears go back to the thought of death. – – I suddenly have a feeling that that picture (points to picture on wall) was in Harris's office.

**A:** So you're still expecting me to react the way Harris did.

**P:** – –

**A:** We'll stop here for today.

### DISCUSSION

The patient begins this session with a continuation of the conflict that had been mobilized by the separation from me. After mentioning the dream, she begins to experience sadness and crying while describing to me the successive losses of the various people that she has depended upon in the past. There is still some self-observation going on, as when she says that it's really good for her to give up her dependency, but the affective response suggests to me that it would be more important to explore these feelings than to try to work with the dream at this time. In response to my requests for her associations, she becomes increasingly emotionally involved in the material, returning spontaneously to the immediate transference dependency and attachment.

Parenthetically, it is precisely *because* she has increasingly cathected me as the chief object of the infantile neurotic drives and wishes that she decreases her use of the various other external objects for these neurotic purposes. As a result, she can partially free herself from some of the neurotic interactions with them, and can begin to see these various people in a more objective and reality-oriented way, and since they no longer provide important sources of neurotic gratification, she no longer idealizes them and can begin to see their weaknesses and flaws.

Her association to the lack of a penis represents a somewhat deeper and more immediate level of experience of the conflicts mobilized by the separation, and the sadness and crying that she experiences while describing this represents the little girl reliving her feeling of disappointment and rejection over her lack of the phallus. My intervention about her sense of inferiority represents merely a clarification and rephrasing of the material that she has already described and results in a further deepening of the immediate transference experience.

The immediacy of her transference experience of me as psychically identified with the father is illustrated by her question as to why I can't accept her as she is, and then her further projected perception of me as rejecting her because of the absence of the penis. In keeping with the technical concept of maintaining transference abstinence, I neither reassure her nor try to correct the transference distortion. As a result her conflict is intensified, which permits this transference experience of rejection to reach its height in the expressed rage toward me, followed by the defensive regression from the penis to the breast, and the transference shift away from the father to an attempt to see me as the mother. My intervention asking for associations to the feeling that I scare her is aimed at bringing her back to the phallic conflict from which she has defensively regressed, rather than allow the regressive defense of elaborating the oral-breast fantasy at this time. Her statement, "You're a huge thing," is a direct reference to the penis which in the past she frequently has called "a thing," and it is this recollection of my own that permits my subsequent direct interpretation of her fantasy of the destructive penis.

This interpretation of the fear of the phallus permits her to elaborate on the childhood fantasies of the oedipal father's penis, but to reexperience these and the anxiety over this conflict in the immediate transference situation. In response to this transference fantasy and the anxiety that accompanies it, she again undergoes the defensive regression from drives toward the penis to drives for the breast. The session is almost over so, in an attempt somewhat to allay her anxiety, I make the rather lengthy interpretation of the defensive oscillations in the wishes and fantasies towards the penis-breast. This is partially successful, and she becomes more reflective. But the immediate transference fantasy returns in the misperception of the picture, thereby identifying me with another important man in her recent life who was seduced by her and whose drive controls she could not trust. My final transference interpretation is actually an appeal to the therapeutic alliance by indirectly helping her further clarify through her own experience that Harris and I are different. Unverbalized in this intervention is also the fact that I am different from the seductive father who had responded to her oedipal wishes.

The dream from the beginning of the session was not directly interpreted, but the subsequent material of the session represents the associations to some of the dream elements. The elements of the grandmother's house, and of the old person in the nightgown are references to the traumatic incident with the uncle, which was so important in organizing her feelings and attitudes toward men.

---

### SESSION 218

**P:** I feel just like I'm a failure. I'm a failure to my children and I'm a failure in here. (Elaborates.) That's really just an easy out. There's just one thing in life that will make me happy and I know that I'll never get it, so I'm always going to be unhappy.

**A:** What you are looking for is a penis. Try to fantasy that you've gotten it. Then what would you do with it?

**P:** It scares me. I have a vision of a penis on me and it grows huge and suddenly everything disappears. I just can't control it.

**A:** What's the detail?

**P:** – – I think of you and of my mother. It would do something to you and my mother. – – – I feel all disconnected from things. – – Suddenly I feel so depressed. – – I feel just like a child and I'm embarrassed. This is all so laughable. I think of my whole body and I'm just one big thing.

**A:** What's the detail of this being laughable?

**P:** It's all so ridiculous. It's stupid. No one has ever thought about this

before. I'm a girl, but I want to be so big and I have a fear that you are
going to laugh at me.

A: I think that your wish is to *be your father's penis*. Let's look and
see what's behind the wish.

P: – (Sigh.) – I have the God-damn picture of my parents. . . . . .
I'd go inside of my mother. – – I have such a conflict about my mother.
It's all so dirty and so sexual and I could destroy my mother. – . . . . . –
. . . . . – . . . . . – I suddenly have all kinds of love feelings. I never felt | *Cry*
this way about my mother before. But suddenly I feel that she is *love* and
she is capable of love and she'll not hurt me. – – I think about her body
and it's so big and soft. Suddenly I want to talk about love and to relax
and just give love and I can't do it and it depresses me. I just want to
relax with the whole thought and it would make me so happy.

A: What do you think would happen if you did *relax* and feel happy?

P: I'd be so close to my mother and connected to her and I'd be with | *Cry*
her and inside of her and have her hold onto me. I get this feeling sometimes with my daughter when I lie in bed with her. I started to feel it last
night and suddenly I got so depressed I felt like a complete failure. – –
It all starts out so clean and I want to put my head on her bare chest. But
then I turn into my father and I put my penis inside of her and it all gets
horrible.

A: You say that you want to put your head on mother's chest. I wonder if you aren't avoiding the idea that mother has *breasts* and that it is
these that attract you.

P: – Ugh! They frighten me. If they were flat then I wouldn't have
any fear.

A: I think that this is what you were referring to yesterday. You were
talking about the big soft squashy and folding quality of a full breast and
it scared you.

P: – (Sigh.) – Why am I so afraid of it? It would be so wonderful and
so comforting and secure. I feel as if *you* are building the fear of them in
me. I'm *not* afraid of them. I really love them. *You* make me afraid of
them. There is really nothing greater than them. My children love it and
I know that. But I think of my mother and I get scared. I can see my
mother with no clothes on. I wonder if these are her feelings too? Will she
destroy me, or will she let me put my head there? She goes over the line.

A: The feeling is that I have made you afraid of the breast. What's
the detail?

P: I see myself with my own children and they love to have their head
on my breasts. They love it, and I do too, and I have no fear. But now I | *Cry*

get scared! I *did* love it. *You* made me afraid of it. Everything bad in me is your fault! The first feelings I ever had were so good and you made them so bad.

**A:** How do you feel I did it?

**P:** I have such a fear that you'll get mad at me! I divide myself all up. I see myself as sexual and so full of love with my head on mother's breast. But then you made me afraid because you think they're terrible. – – – I get so frightened by this. I'm in that black hole again.

**A:** You said that I think they are terrible and then your associations stopped. What comes to your mind?

*Cry*

**P:** I'm so scared. And it makes me so mad. I must think the same way that you think, and I don't want to. I feel so helpless and so mad! This is all so frightening! And yet it is something so good! Why? It's so good and so wonderful and I *want* it, but you don't let me have it and so it makes me mad.

**A:** Right now am I your mother or your father?

**P:** You're my mother! – –

**A:** In what way don't I let you?

*Cry!*

**P:** I'm so scared! My whole body feels cold! I'm much too little to get mad. I have no chance at all and I can't. I'm completely helpless. Suddenly I have such a funny sensation that I'm being jerked around and being hit and I'm so scared! It's like I've done something terrible just now.

**A:** We'll stop here for today.

### DISCUSSION

The patient begins this session with the continuation of the theme from yesterday. My direct interpretation of her wish for a penis is an indirect encouragement for her to face the issue openly and directly, and my suggestion that she try to fantasy having the penis is an attempt to begin to expose the drives and fantasies behind the wish to acquire the penis for herself. The fantasy about the mother begins to emerge, but is abruptly replaced by a defensive shift away from the transference experience in her comments about things being laughable and being disconnected. This reaction is dynamically similar to experiences of depersonalization and/or derealization, and serves the function of defense against intense anxiety occurring when an unconscious fantasy suddenly returns from repression.

In order to deal with this resistance against regression in the transference, I focus on the feeling of things being laughable, but she goes on to express more of her self-observations and distancing maneuvers. As in yesterday's session, her phrase, "I think of my whole body and I'm just one big thing," permits me to make the direct interpretation of the body-phallus equation. This indicates to her that I take these fantasies seriously, do not consider them laughable, nor am I disturbed or frightened by them.

Thus reassured in the therapeutic alliance and unconsciously identifying with my analytic attitude, she now can permit herself again to regress in the analytic process. This regression now carries her into a new level of feelings, fantasy and experience in regard to the wishes for love and physical union with the mother. This further deepening of awareness of drives and fantasies toward the mother is a further link in the understanding of the penis-breast oscillation which we had been working on in the previous sessions. Since at this moment I cannot be sure whether this new material about the mother represents a regressive defense from the oedipal phase conflict, or whether it represents the emergence of a more basic maternal dyadic conflict, I decide to suspend such judgment and follow the patient's spontaneous associations. Her comments about feeling depressed with her daughter last night now clarify her remarks at the beginning of the session.

But the resistance against full awareness of these drives and the anxiety that accompanies them is manifest and condensed in her use of the word "chest" and my interpretation of this defense has the desired effect of reducing the resistances against the immediacy of these feelings. Once these resistances are reduced, I can hook this material up to the experience in the previous session, and the patient follows up with a continuation of the regressive maternal transference experience. I have become the mother for her, and as part of this she projects on to me the blame for her anxiety and discomfort concerning these impulses.

By accepting the transference distortion that I am to blame, and that I have caused her fears, and by not attempting to get her to see the reality of the situation, I encourage her continued regression and immediate experience of the maternal transference. This leads at the end of the session to the recall, through transference experience, of some type of traumatic incident that probably occurred during early infancy. It is not yet possible to know whether this was a true event, or only a fantasy, but nevertheless it represents a new and deeper level of regressive experience for the patient. My own association at the time is of a nursing infant who suddenly hurts the mother by biting the breast, and the mother reacts with a startled pushing away of the baby.

This material regarding the maternal transference and the attachment to the mother's breasts has been brought up months ago, but has not yet been resolved. It has major significance in understanding the overeating which is one of her important presenting symptoms. Such a symptom would represent a displaced and disguised acting-out of these unconscious underlying impulses in relationship to the mother. Thus, it is clear that in terms of her psychosexual development there is a significant oral fixation. Simultaneously, these regressive maternal drives are being used defensively against the conflicts of the later oedipal phase of development. These kinds of speculations are appropriate at this phase of the analytic work, but they will require a good deal of further elaboration, exploration, and working-through before they can be significantly verified or confirmed.

---

## SESSION 219

**P:** – – I ate so much yesterday! I looked as though I were about five months pregnant. I had a sudden desire that I *must* get pregnant. Why did I do all of that talking about nursing? I've had such sexual dreams. I dreamed that I was with a man and I was in a huge house. I don't know who the man was, but he was bad, and yet I still loved him. I reached under a sink and there was a huge silverfish which kind of skipped off my arm. I went to tell Tom but then I couldn't find him. Then I was trying to get the babysitter to take Sally to a birthday party. – – – I was eating everything in sight yesterday. And afterwards I just felt hysterical. It was horrible and I feel as if I'll never live again. I just don't care about men and I feel absolutely nothing. But I'd be so sexed up for every man around if I was only thin!

**A:** What about the dream? What are your associations?

**P:** It reminded me of a TV program and a man that I saw there. I was so sexually attracted to him that I could almost have an orgasm just watching him. (Elaborates about the program.) On the program the man killed a woman in order to get a ring that she had. She loved him but it didn't matter. He used a knife. (Elaborates about the program.) She was hiding him. In the dream I was hiding the man in the house. I'm thinking about that silverfish. Ugh! In the dream I gave in and I loved him and I wanted to be a woman and a mother and a wife. And then that awful fish was there and it scared me. Somehow it makes me think of a penis.

**A:** But this was specifically a silverfish. What are your associations there?

**P:** We had them in our bathrooms at home. They are harmless and I'd look at them. – – There's just so much coming up in my mind that I can't handle it all. – – I see myself in Springfield and in that huge house. – –

**A:** What are you seeing?

**P:** I see my parents having intercourse and I'm standing in the bathroom and I'm looking at them. –

**A:** And what's the further detail about what you are seeing?

**P:** I'm wondering what is going on here? I see my mother and my father, and I can also see my father when he is with other women. It just makes me go to pieces. . . . I'd like to just grab my father's penis and throw him and his penis out of the window! I feel so protective towards my mother! He has no right to do what he does. – – It gives me such a sexual feeling to be thinking about my father and his mistresses. And then when I think about my mother and father I feel mad!

*Cry*

**A:** The feeling of being protective toward your mother suggests that there is also a wish to have your mother for yourself and that maybe you feel jealous because your father has her.

**P:** That's the way I felt yesterday. It's the only time I ever saw my mother in a soft, warm, and loving position. She was so hostile toward me usually. I always felt she would either eat me or kill me.

**A:** You were inside of your mother once, and we know that at times you think of your whole body as being a penis. I think yesterday that while you were eating, the fantasy was that you would get big, which to you is the same as being a penis in erection. The wish is to be your father's penis and then you'd be able to get inside of mother which I think is represented in the big house that you were inside of in the dream.

**P:** – – – Lately I have been having some love feelings for my mother. They have all come on rather suddenly. – – The love feelings are not so much for her as a mother but it's as if she is a poor little child. In a sense I see everyone that way. They all seem to need something, and they all need to be accepted just as they are. I feel as if I am saying that I'm a big mother and you can come to me and I'll give you love just as you are and then you don't have to worry about anything. I see an image of my mother's naked body and myself nursing on her breast. And then all of a sudden I turn into a man.

**A:** There's a gap in your associations between seeing yourself nursing on your mother and then suddenly turning into a man. What's the detail of how you would fill it?

**P:** – – I see myself as a baby nursing and I wonder, why can't I relax and enjoy it! It reminds me of my son and how at times I could be him.

*Cry!*

He's a boy and his whole little body is a penis. – – But instead of staying as a baby I turn into something else. I feel as if I turn into something big and dangerous and mother is suddenly frightened of it. I feel just like a boy! I wonder why that is?

**A:** Let's go back to yesterday and the end of the session when you had the feeling that you were being jerked around and hit, and felt as if you had just done something bad. What comes to your mind about it?

**P:** I think of a penis being hit and slapped because it is big and hard. I feel as if mother is suddenly mad at me. – – I feel myself letting go as if I'm enjoying this just too much. And it is making mother mad. – – I feel frantic all of a sudden. I see that look on my mother's face when she has her tongue between her teeth and it looks as if she is about to eat someone up and I've a feeling that I'm letting go. It is as if I'm suddenly having an orgasm! I feel that there is something inside my mouth and it is the only thing that is connecting me to anything. I feel as if I'm going wild! I feel that I'm smacking my lips like wild. – – I'm so afraid to tell you all of this! Somehow this is just like what must have happened. I'll sit there and enjoy it and then you'll hate me.

**A:** Again you've left something out in your associations on this transition from enjoying it. What is it that you've done and why will I hate you?

**P:** I feel as if I'm biting! I'm not relaxing, but instead I'm about to go wild and I have this funny sensation in my mouth as if that thing is in it!

**A:** What's the detail of biting it?

*Anxiety!!*
*Cry!*

**P:** I don't know!! I feel as if I'm trying to eat it, the whole thing! Mother is spanking and spanking me! She is hating and shaking me and I'm so scared! I feel as though I'm going to die! I'm suffocating and I just feel so frantic! What have I done?! I'm so scared! I feel as if I've got this thing in my mouth! What's the matter! I'm so scared! Something is going on and I'm wild. I feel as if she is going to cram it down my throat! I see that great big red thing right here! I feel I'm going wild! I'm going to die! I know that if I relax I'll just die!! I'd feel better if I could just get up off of this couch! What's happening? Someone help me! Get me out of here. I feel as if I'm being suffocated and I'm getting too much! And yet, I'm also not getting enough and I feel as if everything is being withheld and I'm going to die and I'm frantic! I'm chewing and chewing and I'm sucking and sucking and nothing is happening! – – I'm so mad! God-damn it! – – This is where I get so nervous. I start to feel relaxed, and calm and sleepy, and then bam! All of this starts and I'm frantic and I feel as if I'm going to die! I'm so helpless that I can't do anything. I feel like I'd like to bite that nipple off and get blood. I'm so mad at my mother! I hate

her! I'm trying so hard! This all gives me a sexual feeling because I'm
trying so hard! – –

A: We'll stop here for today.


### DISCUSSION

The patient begins by describing the exacerbation of her symptom of
eating after the session yesterday, which I assume to be a direct result of
the mobilization of drives and conflicts in the maternal transference, related to the yearning for mother's breasts. This conflict evokes more anxiety than she can comfortably tolerate, and therefore she intensifies the
use of the mechanism of displacement to food (a symbolic object which
stands for the mother and her breasts), resulting in the symptom exacerbation. At this point in the analysis, the major source of anxiety and conflict
is in the maternal fixation, and I believe she is using the heterosexual
fantasies about men as a progressive defense against the more threatening
oral impulses. This is illustrated by her intellectualized association of the
silverfish to a penis, which I attempt to block by asking for her specific
associations.

This intervention results in a series of more personalized and specific
associations which lead into the primal scene. However, the primal scene
is now experienced from the shifted perspective of a positive maternal
transference accompanied by hostility toward the father, as illustrated by
her statement, "I feel so protective towards my mother. He has no right
to do this." It is the recognition of this shift (which is a continuation of
yesterday's session) which leads to my interpretation to her of the wish to
have her mother for herself. This, in turn, is confirmed by her response,
and because this material is so close to consciousness, it permits my rather
lengthy interpretation of the fantasy of being inside of the mother. In
retrospect this lengthy interpretation was probably unnecessary, and it was
an intellectualized attempt at a reconstruction which was premature and
possibly inaccurate.

Initially, the patient's response to my suggestion about this fantasy is
experienced and expressed defensively with a reversal, so that the patient
is the big one and the mother is the helpless child. This same defensive
reversal probably explains her wish to become pregnant which she reported
at the start of the session, in which case she would be the mother and
would unconsciously also identify herself with the fetus. However, this
defensive fantasy is given up spontaneously and the more appropriate
image of herself as the nursing baby takes its place. Again this image

evokes anxiety and the defensive fantasy occurs of turning into a man or of getting big and dangerous.

In my own thinking at this time, I am aware that she is defending herself against the reexperiencing of the oral yearnings, and I am reminded of her acute anxiety and sense of helplessness at the end of the session yesterday. I feel that the fantasies of being big, of being a man, and of having the mother afraid of her all represent a reversal, and thus, a defense against the experience of helplessness that had begun to emerge in yesterday's session. It is this reasoning which leads me to remind her of yesterday's experience and to ask for her further associations. The experience is now an immediate one combining images of the mother from the past, current and past somatic sensations, and immediate transference distortions of me, as the mother, hating her. In asking for and accepting her associations to the hatred, I am encouraging her to permit herself to experience these conflicted memories, feelings, and desires. With this there is a reexperiencing in the immediate situation of an early nursing experience and of the mother's response to it as if it were a current event, accompanied by the appropriate affects. The oral rage is expressed in the wish to bite the nipple off and get blood. This represents the confirmation from the patient of the speculations I made regarding the material at the end of yesterday's session.

This reexperiencing in the treatment situation of a set of primitive drives, possible memories, fantasies, and affects represents the emergence of this complex once again from repression, and thus it gives us another therapeutic opportunity to resolve these issues. Having become conscious, they will still require repeated working-through and elaboration in the future. Although this transference recall and experience is felt by the patient with much of its original impact and accompanying affect, the fact that she can continue to report the experience as it occurs, and that she can make occasional comments indicating observation of herself, all indicate that the therapeutic alliance is strong enough and effective enough to permit the regression which allows her to function in this way.

Although no direct or inclusive interpretation of the dream is made, it serves as the take-off point for the unfolding of the session. Initially, the dream associations represent the defensive movement toward the heterosexual oedipal conflicts, and it was the request for specific associations to the silverfish which ultimately led to the associations to the bathroom and from it to the primal scene. It might be emphasized again that the patient is capable of permitting this degree of regression because she has established a strong and effective therapeutic alliance; because my role in that therapeutic alliance is one of acceptance without anxiety of her associations, fantasies, drives, and transference distortions of me; and because of my interventions which alternately focus on the resistances to, and the content of, these conflicts. As a result of repeated past experience, she has developed a sufficient sense of confidence in me that I will not permit her anxiety to reach intolerable levels, nor will I permit the situation between us to become uncontrolled.

Given these conditions, she can permit herself to regress in the service of the therapeutic task, permit the expression of otherwise unacceptable and intensely anxiety-provoking fantasy and thought, and in this way begin to permit the deeply repressed conflicts to emerge into conscious awareness. This form of reexperiencing a conflict in the transference neurosis results eventually in the recall of genetically significant experiences or fantasies which in turn had in derivative form produced the immediate transference experience. In other words, the various transference distortions represent a form of remembering, initially without conscious recognition, of repressed conflict or experience. This session illustrates how genetic material from preverbal phases of development can return to consciousness in the forms of visual imagery, somatic sensations, and affective experiences in the transference neurosis. At the same time as the patient undergoes these regressive experiences, the therapeutic alliance, self-observing ego functions, and adult verbal capacities make it possible for her to describe these phenomena verbally. Such verbalization represents the first step in a process that ultimately will result in conscious ego mastery of these conflicts as the result of repeated working-through.

In the first four sessions of this month the patient continued on the major theme of the maternal transference and her regressive oral yearnings for attachment and gratification from the mother. There was a good deal of talk about women's breasts and of her wish to suckle, as well as her fantasy of identification with the penis as a means of getting inside of the mother. Her reactions to the weekend separation in the maternal transference were feelings of loss, fears of death, and the wish orally to incorporate me as a means of maintaining the tie during the separation.

This theme of her sense of emptiness and her wish to be filled-up orally was accompanied by consciously experienced fantasies of suffocation or of destruction of herself or of me. In the second and third sessions there were brief moments in which she could permit a pleasurable state of relaxation in the transference situation, each time followed by a defensive retreat to hostility and fantasies of warding me off. In the fourth session, however, she was able to permit a more extended regressive transference experience of positive pleasure in fantasies of nursing on my breasts and fusing with me, and she could accept it as an enjoyable experience. She consciously equated the whole issue with sleep and with orgasm, and she also equated milk with semen.

Late in the fourth session, and throughout the fifth session, there was a progressive reinvestment in the father transference at the oedipal level, with further working through of the typical oscillating conflict between the wish and fantasy of seducing me, accompanied by the fear and guilt that this would produce, as compared with the safety and security in the transference situation if she *cannot* seduce me, the latter accompanied by angry frustration. In this material there were images of the father as a baby and there were intermittent regressions to her wish to be the baby with her mother. In the transference she experienced oscillations toward me between her wish to be a naked nursing baby, and her fantasies of being a heterosexual woman. She was aware of an increasing need to permit herself the full range of her feelings with complete trust in the analytic situation, but this was accompanied by fantasies of being abandoned by me, and she related both sides of this transference conflict to maternal and paternal childhood relationships.

All of this was illustrated at one point in this session when she said, "Now I feel so sexual and I have such a desire to make love and I really want to be a woman. It's just like the feeling I get with Tom which I have in my mouth when we make love, and I can't get enough and I want to do more and more with my mouth!" She went on to elaborate a fantasy of sexual intercourse organized in an oral form, with destructive incorporation as its result.

In the next few sessions there was continuing working through of her conflict over trust of me in the analytic situation and of her fantasies about seduction. The simultaneous wish and fear regarding seduction were worked over again and again, and as her seductive efforts were unsuccessful in eliciting this response from me they were replaced by a growing angry frustration and rage at me in the transference. This was increasingly manifest and ultimately expressed in her fantasies of frustrating me in return by not getting well and by remaining a child, and thereby thwarting my therapeutic ambitions for her. She was determined to be attached to me forever and willing to ruin herself and her life to do so.

In the ninth session of this month, the theme of her determination not to get well as a way of frustrating me reached its peak. Finally she indicated that she was already responding to her anticipation of the summer vacation, which was still two months away, and that she was expecting me to terminate her abruptly at that time just as her previous therapist had done.

During this session the patient illustrated her conflict over the establishment of object constancy as she described her sense of detachment from me between sessions, with the recurrent fantasy that she might never see me again each time she leaves. She expressed her difficulty in "taking it home with me" referring here to her relationship with me. In speaking about love and security in the transference situation, she said,

When I walk out it means that it's gone until I come back. I get filled up but it never lasts and it never stays with me. I want it to stay. I want to know that I'm all right disconnected from you, and that I still have a part of you in me. That's why I'm so frantic all the time. I can see myself just relaxing but I have such a fear that you'll leave me and I'll never see you after I walk out!! If I only knew that I would see you, it would be all right and I would have something inside of me.

Later in the session she indicated that she was experiencing love and sexual feelings for me and said, "I want to let you into my mouth and into my body and everything. – – – Now I can see myself go home and be a mother and a wife and a person because I have this love feeling for you."

In the next session she indicated that yesterday she had let go of her feelings and trusted me completely, and she had been relaxed and felt that I would accept her feelings without question. This had produced for her a significant rush of positive loving feelings toward me, although with continued oscillation between the fantasy of being a woman and of being a child. Increasingly she gave up the conscious control of her own feeling and fantasy with the expectation that I would control the situation for us. This material was accompanied by references to the primal scene experiences, and to her sense of positive stimulation and pleasure from it, with fantasies of how wonderful it would be for her if she could participate.

In the eleventh session she continued the theme of the oedipal father transference with the fantasies of seducing me as a way of finally achieving the childhood wish of having this type of experience with the father, but with continuing frustration and anger at the increasing realization that she was not going to be able to seduce me.

In the following session there was further working through of the need to recognize and accept the frustration of the oedipal transference wish, and the realization that only such frustration can allow her safely to experience her feelings here. All this was accompanied by intermittent expressions of intense deep positive attachment and love, as well as a return toward the efforts at seduction and angry resentment at its frustration.

In the thirteenth session the patient indicated an awareness of new and deeper sexual and love feelings with her husband than she had ever experienced before. This was accompanied by a direct oedipal dream in which she was in bed with her father, who had an erection, and she was rubbing up against it but she was sure they were not going to make love. Following this there was an increase in her experience of the sexual, loving, oedipal father-transference yearning towards me, accompanied by a great sense of pleasure, warmth, and comfortable security. At the same time there were fantasies of her mother at the level of the oedipal conflict, with the image of mother as hostile, angry, jealous, and resentful of the patient's sexuality. She also had images of the mother as resentful of her wish to give up the breast and the infantile gratifications in favor of the heterosexual oedipal fantasies. All this was experienced directly in the transference as illustrated in her crying, anxiety, and distress as she said, "I want to be a woman! But you're not going to accept me that way. If you were my father, then it means that you are going to grab me as a baby. I want to get out of here. I hate you. I'm open and I'm falling apart now." This working through of the conflict in the oedipal triangle, as well as conflict over giving up of the dyadic relationship to the mother, continued throughout the session, with a continuing ebb and flow between past memory and current transference experience with me.

In the following session she continued to work over the same material with the fear that she could successfully take the father away from the mother, as well as a fear of the mother's hostile and jealous reaction to her fantasies. Toward the end of the session, in reference to the fantasy of seducing me, she said, "Suddenly I want to tell you something. I don't think that it really was my uncle. I think that it was my cousin that I had the sexual thing with. It was his son. – –" I asked for her associations and she responded, "All the time that I talked about it I saw Charles in his white shorts with his penis sticking out, but I never told you. It's just like the dream. Does it really matter? But I think it means that I'll seduce you. – –"

The next day she continued to express her uncertainty as to whether it had been the uncle or the cousin with whom the sexual trauma had occurred, and to experience me in the transference as both of them. The fantasy was increasingly vivid for her that she would successfully seduce me as she could seduce most of the men with whom she came in contact. Increasingly this conflict was focused into the transference.

It's all your fault because you're so weak. And yet I know the reality of the situation. It would be so wonderful to tell you, and have you be a doctor and just sit, and then I would be able to get it out. I have to let go! I *have* to completely trust you! I have to become a tiny girl and have the same feelings and enjoy it but have it not happen! But I'm so afraid that you will become him! I know that I *have* to *feel* like this little girl but it scares me. I'm helpless. – – I think that you're so nice and then I get such sexual feelings. My heart is going so fast right now. – – – This guilt is more than I can take. – – I've never been so scared! Nothing could be this bad! Now I've got feelings that I've got to get something inside of me. It's as if all of my life I have been trying to get it out. – – I keep picturing him putting his penis in me. – – – I feel as if I swallowed it. – – (She now begins to whisper quietly.) I swear that I can feel a penis inside of me right now and it is wonderful and I love it and it makes my mouth water. I just want to relax and have that wonderful feeling. It's just like when Tom and I make love. It's wonderful! I can have an orgasm right here! I know that I will if I don't stop. But I want it inside of me so badly! I feel faint. There is such a feeling of love! I think about this man!

This experience in the transference situation represents the regressive reexperiencing of the original pleasure in the sexual seduction and is probably the most direct and affective experience of sexual arousal that she has undergone thus far in the analysis. It is now apparent that in the actual childhood sexual situation itself, she was very much an active participant and for her it was a very pleasurable and fulfilling gratification of her displaced oedipal fantasies. The guilt, fear, and traumatic effect occurred subsequently as the result of her own fantasies of having eaten and swallowed the penis, and also of the reactions of the adults in her environment through their criticism of her and their punishment of the uncle-cousin.

In the next session she indicated her awareness of progressive changes and improvement within herself, accompanied by intense anger and resentment at me for such changes since they implied the ultimate frustration of the transference fantasies and the necessity to give up the search for childhood gratifications. This transference resistance was worked over, with increasingly conscious recognition of how she prefers to sacrifice her own well-being today in order to gratify the continuing infantile and childhood transference wishes.

In the seventeenth and last session of the month she again worked over the transference resistance and the awareness of the changes occurring within her. There was a greater positive wish to become and be a woman, and to give up her old masculine protest with its fantasies of acquiring or growing a penis. This was interspersed with doubts and wishes to maintain her old attachments and object relationships and anger at me because of the continuing transference frustrations. However, there was also considerable self-observation, with expression of her recognition of the ultimate positive gains involved in renunciation of the infantile demands. There was also a great deal of expressed hostility and rage at me in her anticipation that to get well means termination of her analysis and of her relationship to me.

# 11

# THE SEVENTEENTH THROUGH
# TWENTY-SECOND MONTHS (Summary)

During the first part of this phase of the analysis, she continued the working-through of previously mobilized conflicts, both in the transference neurosis and in the further recall and elaboration of the childhood relationships. Issues that were repetitively dealt with included her conflict over accepting the necessity for frustration of her positive oedipal wishes, as well as repeated elaborations of her conflicts over her sense of phallic inferiority and the feminine castration complex. As part of this she repetitively worked over the primal scene experiences and her sado-masochistic perceptions of it, as well as her mixed identification with both participants in it.

The summer vacation was perceived by her as a rejection, and was experienced as a repetition of the infantile weaning process, accompanied by varied fantasies of oral aggression and incorporation as an expression of frustration and rage, and also as an attempt at fusion and maintenence of her ties to me in the maternal transference.

Following the vacation there was a return to the theme of the oedipal transference and its frustration, and a further elaboration of the childhood sexual conflicts. Gradually there occurred a further working-through of the displaced oedipal seduction by the uncle, experienced both in the transference and in the filling in of details and recall of the original sexual situation. This included her multiple responses of excitement, pleasure, guilt, and shame, as well as anger at the uncle for his weakness in permitting the incident to occur and in his fear and rejection of her afterwards. As a result she developed an adult realization that what she had felt as a child to have been love from the uncle was in actuality a manifestation of his immaturity and sickness. With this realization there occurred a sense of depression and rage at me for having by analysis destroyed her fantasy of a positive, loving experience with the uncle.

Throughout this time, as the working-through process continued, the patient was undergoing a significant and steady change in her current level of adaptation. She began to participate more maturely in her overall relationship with her husband, and as she was able increasingly to differentiate him from her father she began to enjoy increasingly mature sexual intercourse with full and gratifying orgasm. She established a greater sense of independent identity as a woman, with pleasure in the feminine role as a wife and mother, and her relationship toward her children improved significantly. There was a marked reduction in her symptoms of anxiety, phobic reactions, bulimia, and depression, and she found herself increasingly mature and fulfilled in her relationships with friends and in her daily activities.

Beginning in the twentieth month, the patient suddenly became aware of her fear that further improvement and solidification of her adult identity and resolution of her infantile and childhood conflicts would mean approaching the termination of her analysis. With this anticipation of termination came a typical exacerbation of her neurotic symptomatology. Over the course of the next three months we again worked over the various conflicts at all different levels of psychosexual fixation, experienced as intensely affective and repetitive father- and mother-transference responses and reactions. In the mother transference she experienced intense rejection as the anticipated termination was equated with weaning and loss of oral gratification. This was accompanied by a return of the regressive fantasies of primitive fusion as defense against such separation.

As she repetitively worked this material through, there was an increasing recognition of the transference resistance, and an acceptance of the reality of her childhood relationships and frustrations. She came to a realistic acceptance of her parents as relatively neurotic and ineffectual people who, however, did not deliberately and consciously seek to disturb or upset her life. Accompanying this was a greater sense of fulfillment in her identity as a woman, with increasing pleasure in sexual relations and in her role as a mother. There occurred a growing sense of confidence in herself and in her own capacities to control her life and relationships. As part of this there was also a more realistic appraisal of me in the therapeutic relationship, and a recognition of the extent of her transference distortions of me in the past. She developed an increasing realization that although she wanted neurotically to cling to me and to the analytic situation, in reality it had relatively little to offer her any more and that her future life lay with her family outside of the analysis.

This phase of the analysis was also marked by her sense of psychic truth and personal conviction about the manifestations of her various infantile and childhood neurotic conflicts. Relatively little new material was uncovered, but there was an increasing capacity for ego mastery of the conflicts involved and for self-analytic awareness of her associations, including the capacity to understand and analyze her own dreams effectively.

Throughout this period I did not at any time suggest that termination of the analysis was imminent or appropriate at present, but rather continued to permit her to experience the conflicts based on her own anticipation of termination at some indefinite future date. My other main functions were to continue the focus of analytic work into the transference neurosis, and to continue to allow her to use me as the transference object toward whom voluntary renunciation would be necessary in the final resolution of the neurosis.

# The
# Termination
# Phase

# 12

## THE TWENTY-THIRD MONTH

### SESSION 321

**P:** ––––––––– Why have I suddenly changed my mind? I don't *Sadness* feel like fighting it any more, but I can't stand to talk about it because all I can do is cry. –––– All weekend I've gone in and out. I'd feel so happy with everything being so wonderful and then I'd get so depressed and scared and go back into that hole again. And then I'd get out of it. –– Last night I was having some murderous thoughts to kill Tom and the children, and then I thought, what if I get them after I leave here? I was trying to figure out why I should have them. And I thought that when someone dies I feel guilty as if I'd killed them with my hostile thoughts. *Cry* It's like with my grandmother. I killed her by rejecting her. I just grew up but she never forgave me for it. I can think it all I want and I'll still leave here. I'm through here. I'm through. There's nothing more to do here. Every time I feel happy I'm so sad and I feel like crying. –– I just nurse my wounds. With my depression I think of all of the times in my life that I've been rejected. I *try* to think about it but it does no good, because I *know* that it's not true. It's either pick myself up or lie down and die. –– It all came to a head last night. Tom was talking about our finances. He never talks about the analysis, but he blurted it out, "When are you going to be through?" I got upset and I jumped all over him. (Elaborates.) I felt that I was going to take Tom over you. I've kept you separate from Tom and I haven't let him in. I don't want to do that, but then I realized that I've made my decision. –– I walked in here this morning and then I think about some other person who is going to walk in here at this time, and I'm so jealous of them. I'm so scared that I'll need you and fall back. But if I do then I must work it out for myself. You *can't* help me any more. You just can't. ––

**A:** You mentioned that your grandmother never forgave you for growing up. I wonder if you have any thoughts that I might not want you to grow up and that I would not forgive you?

**P:** I feel just like a traitor. The other day I thought how much I loved Tom. Of course I do, because I know him and he loves me. –– I'll

469

never know. Of all the people that I made a relationship with, I've rejected them all as being parents. Tom's mother is the only one to accept me. She has hostility but she has accepted me. *My* mother hasn't. -- I remember the thought I had when I saw Tom standing in the doorway and I felt that I love Tom more than I love you, and I felt guilty. Not really, it's just. . . . . – I think about how much do you feel? I guess I've suppressed these thoughts but I've had them. I'm going to leave and you really get no thanks. I'm like all of your patients and we just leave and go happily on our way and you tackle another patient. I feel sorry for you. I know it's not reality, because this is your job. -- Jean was back over Christmas. She hurt Harris when she got married, but that's his fault for getting so involved. She didn't call him and she resents him and I can tell that. -- Is this all me and is it something that I wish? All I can

*Cry*  think is about my grandmother. She gave me so much and she gave me the ability to mature and to take that step and I should be thankful, but it's her that I hurt. It's like you. It's almost too much. I have guilt feelings and love feelings and hurt feelings and hostile feelings. I hope that I can control them all. But the worst is the hurt. What will I do when I pass this place? It's like a home to me. -- Now I think about those books. Why? -- I guess they are symbolic of you and your penis. I was thinking last night such weird thoughts about my body. I have the most beautiful one in the world and I wanted to show someone. It's so smooth. -- That's the basis of me, and that's the one thing that if I do it, I'll be all right, and that is to give up the idea of a penis. To me it's a sign of insecurity as if I'd die without it. -- Now I think about

*Cry*  Harris and I wonder why I think about him. When I had Carol he was
*Slightly*  so upset that I didn't call him. I never even thought about calling him. Why should I? I keep wondering if that's why he terminated me, because I'd never accept him as he wanted me to. It's a good thing that I didn't. I *know* that you'd never do that to me! I've *got* to go off on my own and I can't stay here forever. Only the child wants you as Daddy and the adult loves and wants Tom, and that's what I want to be. -- Where do you get guilt feelings? I want *no* guilt and not even that much. -- I *know* that your goal for two years is to make me an adult and to let me go. So *why* the guilt? It's happened all of my life and it's happened with everyone. I can say it about them now and it's just too bad if they don't want me an adult. But I *can't* say that about you. I just *can't*. I want this all clear. -- Maybe this just attaches me to you somehow. I go . . . . . I think about the recent holidays and I'd go for so long and not even think about you, and I'd feel so good. It was like last

Friday. I felt that Tom and I have *so* much. And I felt it with all of my friends. And then my mother called and it was late and I felt that she hates me for this, and she always will and that's when it started again. I was feeling guilty. She says that I booted her out of my life and so she'll do the same thing to me. Great! I just can't help it. – – – When I feel guilty, I feel hostile because it shows up how much I was rejected in my past or I wouldn't feel so guilty. – – – Now I feel like starting to hate you again. I feel it's all too much for me and all I can do is hate, and I have too many feelings and that's all I can do. I can't stand to leave here without any feelings but love. Because then there are no more strings attached, and that's the way I felt this morning. – – Now I have a horrible fear that you're not going to let me go. I'm scared to death that you won't let me go, or else that you'll make it hard for me. – – I guess it's easier to think that you're trying to hold on to me here. You can't, but maybe it would be easier if I thought that I was doing something that you didn't want me to. But I'd end up hating you then. – – There is *no* string that I can attach to you. I just can't believe it. There is no thought that I can have for you except love. – – It makes me mad! It depresses me! It does everything to me! – – –

**A:** For you to feel guilty about leaving or to think that I'm hurt or angry about your independence the way Harris was, is to try to keep your attachment here to me.

**P:** It would all be so much easier to feel that you are trying to hold me here and then I could say, no, that I'm ready to leave. That hurt isn't as bad as the other. But I *know* that it wouldn't be easier in the long run. – –

**A:** We'll stop here today.

At the door, the analyst gives her the bill for the previous month.

### Discussion

The patient is continuing to work through her feelings and conflicts about termination of her analysis. The sadness of affect and crying are in response to this, and at the beginning of the session she demonstrates the typical conflict of a patient at this stage of analysis. Initially she oscillates between her awareness of how good things are for her in her life at the present time, and her sense of depression at the recognition that because things are going well she is that much closer to termination of her relationship with me.

After she describes her murderous thoughts towards her husband and children and her attempts to analyze them herself, she begins to experience me in the transference as the grandmother. She attempts the defense of feeling the termination to be a rejection for her growing up, as occurred in the relationship with the grandmother, but almost immediately the adult self-observing ego indicates that "I know that it's not true." She then goes on to allude to her feeling of disloyalty to me for preferring her husband, followed again by the regressive wish to cling to me in the form of her jealousy of the new patient who will take her place.

The grandmother transference reaction and feeling of guilt for growing up are relatively new in the analysis and have not been fully explored or worked through. Therefore, in my first intervention of the session, I choose to interpret this material as a current transference experience. The patient's response is a further elaboration of feelings of being a traitor for preferring her husband to me, but followed by her realistic recognition of my professional role and her part in my life as a patient. She goes on then to experience another transference response to me as if I were her former therapist, whom she saw as resenting his patient's independence, and as part of this growing independence she alludes to her increased pleasure and satisfaction at being an adult sexual woman, and to the realistic need to give up the remaining phallic wishes. The conflict between the regressive wish to remain the child who is attached to me, as compared with the adult woman, is again elaborated, accompanied by feelings of guilt for her adult strivings which now emanate also from the transference to me as the mother. Subsequently she elaborates on this in the detail about the mother's call and the mother's angry response to the patient having separated herself. This in turn leads to the intensified transference experience of me as the mother towards whom she feels both guilt and hatred. But at the same time there is a spontaneous recognition that the hatred is a continuing form of attachment to me. This is followed by a brief defensive attempt to project on to me the thought that I will not let her go, but again this is promptly recognized spontaneously by her adult ego, with further consolidation regarding the reality of the situation between us. However, as she indicates, this is accompanied by a painful affective experience.

My next intervention in regard to her previous therapist and the transference from him to me is essentially a rephrasing of her own material and may well have been unnecessary. It is made in an attempt to highlight the projective defense that she had previously used, and thereby to make it easier for her adult integrative ego functions to cope with the conflict. Again her final response is an elaboration of both sides of this conflict, expressing the regressive wish to avoid the pain of voluntary renunciation of me as the infantile object, but also the recognition that in the long run facing and experiencing this pain will be more appropriate and effective.

In this session the patient illustrates the phenomenon of multiple transferences. She experienced me as grandmother, former therapist, and mother in rapid succession, but on the basis that all three of these important people had resented her attempts at growth and independence, and had reacted in ways to enhance her feelings of guilt.

---

## SESSION 322

Patient comes in, wearing eye-makeup for the first time. She hands the analyst her check for the previous month's bill, but it has not been endorsed properly and the analyst returns it to her.

**P:** – I'm sorry about the check. – – – I'm finally coming to the point where this is so hard for me and the answer is for me to get out. I think about this everyday frustration and I'm sure it can't be worse after I stop. But I have to come here every single day and I have to face a fact that I'm frustrated, and so it seems like the end of the world. That's tough, but I can take it. But this way, either I'm on the verge of tears or the feeling like I have a knife twisting in my heart or else I'm hostile and I'm fighting. This way I'm on a treadmill and I think I'll get nowhere until I get out of here. I think I'm facing the fact. – – When I left here Monday I hurt so badly. I was so depressed and I felt hostile. It comes out in little frustrations around the house, but at least then I didn't hurt. I draw inside of myself and I give nothing except hostility. It was that way all day Tuesday. Tom worked Tuesday night and I felt that I had nothing to live for. Yet I know that I have Tom and the children. But the analysis is so much a part of my life that it keeps me going and thinking. But it will all be gone, and what do I do then? I'm mad that you'll be in here and you'll be busy. Those thoughts to cut my wrists, I think I've figured it out finally that they really represent a tremendous love for Tom. That's the easier for me now, to feel love for Tom, and I can't stand being withdrawn into myself any more. I must decide that I'm the happiest at home with my children as a wife and a mother. But then I begin to wonder if I'm really nothing and if I'm just empty. I had wonderful warm and good dreams last night, but I can't remember them. I woke up feeling so good but when I really got up I was yelling. I had a dream on Monday that the world was coming to an end, and that the planet was crashing into something. I used to dream that all the time. But this one continued. It was about myself and my family. There was a dictator who came in and he controlled the place where I lived. He saw my daughter and I felt that he'd see how smart she is, and then he'd take her away. Instead, he wanted me and he wanted me as his wife, but he already had someone else. I felt as if he'd take me away from my children. I couldn't help it. I looked up and I could see the star and it hit the earth and that was the end of the world, but it was also the end of the dictator. Life went on and then someone wanted a doctor, and Tom took care of it. Life was going on and I was scared that it might end. We are looking for a house and life is going to go on and I'm unsure when it is going to end. I have such a horrible feeling in my stomach. I felt that I can't stand it, and yet I *am* standing it. – – The only time I can let myself go and stand the hurt is when I'm in here and I can't do it when I'm out of here. – – I have thoughts about people saying that the hardest part for mental patients is rehabilitation. I feel as if I'm on stilts that are a mile high and I'm unsure if I'll fall. Is it worth it? It's good that I have Tom and the children because they keep me going. I want to cry. If I make it through leaving here then I've got it made for life. And yet, I hear about patients and about never getting well. After all of the time and effort and money and frustration that I've put in here, I've *got* to make it. I've got to for Tom, too. He couldn't take it again. I've got to make it. – – I've got to decide whether . . . . . no, I'm not really there. Sometimes I feel as if I've got nothing to live for. And yet, deep within me I feel that my instinct to live is greater than my thoughts to die. The thoughts that I have of cutting my wrists is only wanting attention and saying that I'm a little girl and that I can't take care of myself. God-damn you bastard! If I ever do it, I'm lost and Tom and the children are lost. I must give up thinking about myself and think of other people. I *should* want this for myself. Now I can remember the dream that I had last night. It was about Maine and there was a lot of water, and we were living in an apartment. Our friends were around. There

*Cry!* were some new clerks and their wives. – – Suddenly I feel as if all of the fear and all of the hurt and all of the hostility have crashed in on me like a bomb. I'm defenseless and I can't do anything. It's like the star that hit the earth and shook it. That's me, because I'm hit, but I keep going. I hope to God I have the strength to do it, and I know that I've *got* to, I've just *got* to. That's another fact that I'm facing. I expected that it would be easy and that I'd be prepared to leave. I'm not, and it's the hardest thing in my life for me to do. I'm not. I not only have to leave you but I must face the facts of my childhood and say, "Goodbye and I can't change it." – – I not only have to feel the hurt of losing you, but it goes way back to the hurt when I was a little girl of losing my father or really of never having him. It means not having a father and facing it and *not* saying that I'll get him tomorrow or in some way or that I don't want him. The hardest part is just facing it. Also, not needing attention. I think about cutting my wrists. It's not the idea of dying, but of getting attention. I must not need or want any except what Tom gives me, and that's the adult's kind. He's the only one and I really don't need that attention. In that relationship I must give him attention and love, and I know that he needs to come home and heal his little wounds. I'm not getting it. We're a family and by giving love I get it. J must face it all. That's *all* that I'll get after I leave here. I've been getting so much attention here from you, and I'll not get that any more. – – I find myself to be the center of my family and I have to give and not expect anything. That's the way it has to be to be good. I can't expect anything from my children. When they give it, I love it, but I can't expect it. It's the same with Tom. When I'm upset and mad, Tom gets mad. No one gives in to me any more, nobody. That's the role that I'm used to, I'll tell you that. – – I always felt that my strength comes from somebody else. It always comes from mother or from Tom or Tom's mother or Mrs. Jones or Tom or Jean or you. Now I realize that it comes from me, and I don't know if there is any there. Where is it? I don't ever see it. – – – I can't believe that I'm through here and that I don't have a mother or a father any more to take care of me. I feel as if the door is closed. Did you close it, or did I close it? It's closed and it will never open again. I'll never be able to nurse. . . . . . Another thing I realize is that I must fight the defenses that I've had all of my life. I must fight the idea that I've got to have a man or that I want to take his penis or that I will need to have a nervous breakdown and be taken care of or that I'm going to be hostile and fight. I'm *not* going to give in to those things. I will not do them. – – – The only time I'm happy now is when I give up fighting. I can picture giving up fighting when I leave here and just loving. It's only when I let go and I'm loving, do I feel good and I'm happy. – – I'm sorry about the check. To me . . . . . that's it when I give you the check.

A: What's the detail of the feeling?

**P:** There's no more money in the bank. Oh, we can get more if it's necessary, but also I feel that I'm handing you everything that we ever wanted to hang onto, and it's just like saying goodbye. I know that I will. It's like saying, "I realize everything and I'll not hang on any more." But I *did* hang on, didn't I? Oh shit! – – I realize that it's not going to go on and on every month. – – I can't wait to get out of here and start over. I feel that only after I leave here will I really start growing. Tom's and my life is really just starting and I'm so scared! But I don't want to act crazy just because I'm scared, which is what I've always done before. – – I think of all of this that I've been through and there's nothing left for me but grief and fear. And I thought it would be like a fairytale and that I'd be happy and free of fear. – – My biggest fear is whether I'm going to make it. I know it's up to me, isn't it? I wish it weren't. – – I know what this is. In the past when I'm scared I can talk myself out of it by thinking that I can depend on someone. But I can't do that any more. And so I have a good reason for being scared.

**A:** We'll stop here for today.


D I S C U S S I O N

As in all patients who have experienced a full-blown regressive trans- ference neurosis, the resolution of this neurosis during the termination phase is a crucial factor in the ultimate success of the analysis, and there is an extensive working through of the ties to the analyst. Throughout this session, the patient again reworks these problems.

I might have inquired early in the session about her associations to the improperly endorsed check, since she did not immediately associate to it spontaneously. However, I want to observe whether or not she will come to it herself and whether or not she will be able to analyze the transfer- ence meaning of the incident. And toward the end of the session she does return to the issue of the check spontaneously and when I then ask her for the details of her feeling, she indicates her ability to analyze it on her own when she recognizes that it meant she did try to hold on to me through this symptomatic act. The ability to perform a piece of self- analysis such as this is another indicator of the success of the analysis to date, and of the appropriateness of termination in the near future. The same is true in regard to her attempts to understand better the impulse to cut her wrists, as well as the reference to her increasing ability genuinely to love her husband and children.

The mention of the dream about the dictator occurs in the sequence of thoughts regarding her role as wife and mother, and is immediately followed by a reference to the present situation of looking for a new house and of making plans for her realistic life in the immediate future. The dream itself is a recurrent one from childhood that has been mentioned many times earlier in the analysis. This time, however, the dream is completed and it involves the reworking of the oedipal theme. My own thoughts about it are that the patient is represented both by herself as an adult woman and also by her child and that the dictator represents me. This again is a working-through of the old conflict that has come up many times in the analysis as to whether I will accept her as a child or as an adult sexual woman, and in the dream the dictator already has someone else. The resolution in the dream, which parallels the current working-through process in the analysis, is that life goes on and that when someone needs a doctor her husband takes care of it.

However, the patient goes on to describe the continuing grief and mourning over the separation, and she also illustrates the characteristic uncertainty and anxiety of patients at this stage in analysis as to whether or not they will "make it." In the midst of this there is a breakthrough of the regressive yearning to be the child again and to get the attention she is seeking, accompanied by the outburst of anger when she calls me a bastard. This again is followed by the expression of her anxiety and uncertainty about the future, but also by her adult perception that leaving me also involves facing "the facts of my childhood and saying goodbye and I can't change it." With this there is a further elaboration of the recognition of her need voluntarily to renounce the oedipal wishes for the father and to do it without her old characteristic defenses and distortions. There is also an increasing and appropriate elaboration of her perception of her role of wife and mother. There is also a more solid recognition that dependency on others for her strength is inappropriate, and that it actually comes from within herself, as well as a realization that she feels good and happy when she is able to love and no longer has to fight for or demand the old infantile gratifications.

This session involves an elaboration of these themes, as well as a tacit recognition that the analysis is dissolving the fixations which previously had interferred with her maturation, and that this process of maturation, which should have occurred as she grew up, is now beginning and will probably continue after the analysis has terminated. It should be noted that throughout this entire session my only intervention is a single request for the details of her feelings about the check. The patient is demonstrating her increasing capacity for self-analysis.

## SESSION 323

The patient is five minutes late. She comes in with a new upswept hairdo and hands the analyst the check for the previous month's bill.

**P:** −−−−−− Why does being late bother me? I don't try to be late, but I find myself thinking, "Ha ha." −− I'm trying to convince myself that I hate you. −− Yesterday I cried most of the way home. For the first time it really hit me how much I'll miss you and miss this place. Every time I think about it, I start crying. I felt like it a lot of times before but I wouldn't. −−− This morning I feel there are two ways to feel. I can cry and feel sad and horrible, or else I can feel that I hate you and seduce you if I really wanted to.

**A:** Let's look at the details of both ways.

**P:** It's just a thought. I have no intention of trying it. It's all just a cycle. Yesterday I really felt that I'm leaving here and I love you and I love everything that you've done for me, and I think that you're a wonderful person. −− It hurt and I could cry. I know that I will cry if I talk about it. This morning I'm the bitchy person who could seduce every man and there's a wall in front of the scared little girl, but it gives her strength thinking about it. It starts with the grief and then it turns into fear and the fear turns into hate. I'm leaving here and I'm giving up all the chances of satisfying this need down in the core of me. It's childish and I don't need it as an adult, but I panic about giving it up and that it will never be satisfied in the way that I want. It's so basic. It's just like with my children. I can deprive them of something and then they want it more. It's all related to insecurity. I somehow think it will satisfy me to seduce a man. And the funny thing is that if I have such a desire for this, why didn't I marry a man like this, one I can hate, and one who is really a boy who just acts tough. It's ridiculous, because . . . . . big deal. −− It's funny how I can see how I work. I see the little girl making up fantasies of her life because I'm so scared. My children do it all of the time. As an adult, I know that I'm a woman and that's all. I don't *need* anything else and I can accept what I have here and I can love you. I don't have to be any more than that. −− But when I'm that way I lose you because I'm giving you up and that makes me feel wild. −−−−−−−−−− Now I get the sudden thought that I could kill you, and it scares me to death.

**A:** What's the detail of the thought?

**P:** I don't know. My mind was wandering, but suddenly I just had that thought. -- It's something I've thought about before. If I ever give up wanting you and wanting my father. . . . . then I 'd hate you so much because I might as well kill you because I don't need you or want you anyway. Now I think about cutting off your penis.

**A:** We've seen before that hating me and wanting to cut off my penis really represents a continuing tie and an attachment to me.

**P:** -- (Sigh.) --

**A:** And so you're still trying to avoid feeling the grief.

**P:** - I don't know *how* I think I could love anybody that just sits there and says things like nothing! Suddenly all I can think of you is as a father. You're so much like him. You're so analytic and you can reason everything. There's no emotion. There's none. You're saying, "Be a big girl and don't feel anything and don't ever cry." You're constantly telling me that I'm trying to attach myself to you. I know what I'm doing. When you say that you make me feel like I'm a child. I *know* that I'm trying to make you like my father. I don't need you to tell me anything. I have complete control of myself and I know everything that I do and why I do it. *[Cry, Anger Anger]*

**A:** The idea that I'm saying, "Be a big girl and don't feel anything and don't cry" is really part of the wish to make me like your father. In reality, I'm saying the opposite. I'm really saying that it's important to let yourself feel it, and to let yourself cry if you want to, and not to hide your feelings.

**P:** How much can I take? I get to feeling that and I can't stand it! I think that I'll love you when I get through, but not while I'm in here. I just can't stand it. It's really so frustrating. It starts welling up inside of me and it starts flowing out, and then I feel like I. . . . . I just don't want to feel anything. -- I can't see how I could possibly let all of my love out. It's so strong that I feel it is going to turn into something physical. I feel that I want to touch you, that's why it's so much easier for me to feel it when I'm out of here. I have a picture of myself opened up and it's all just flowing out and it all disappears. -- *[Cry]*

**A:** What's the detail of the thought that it's going to turn into something physical and that you want to touch me?

**P:** I don't know. My body just feels like it can't stand it. All I can think of is myself as a child and loving and loving and thinking that if I let it all out it's so strong that it's going to be physical. I think it's like my mother. It's going to turn into a penis and I'm going to make love to my mother! -- Or else, it's some kind of attachment between you and me.

A: We'll stop here for today.

## DISCUSSION

Although it was not directly commented upon in this session, the patient's new hair-do is an indication that she is taking greater pains to be more appropriately attractive and interested in her appearance than she has been previously in the analysis. Her anxiety about making herself more attractive had come up many months ago in connection with the last session before her trip to Florida, when she had made unusual efforts about her hair and clothing. The fact that she is doing it now without such a special occasion is a sign that she has a growing confidence in herself as a woman and in her ability consciously to control or deal with whatever sexual fantasies she may continue to have about me in the transference. It may also imply a growing sense of confidence in me and in my role as her analyst who will not be seduced by her oedipal transference demands and feelings toward me, and thereby, a more firm sense of differentiation between me and the original oedipal father. However, another possibility would be that she is making one last attempt at seduction, and at achievement of the infantile and childhood oedipal gratifica tions, stimulated now by the growing awareness of herself as a woman and the wish to provoke my interest and test my susceptibility to her feminine attractiveness. No one of these alternatives is clearly dominant in the patient's current material, nor is any one of them mutually exclusive of another. But since this is a new form of behavior, I choose not to confront her with it at the present moment, preferring instead to let her develop and elaborate upon such patterns of activity without undue self-consciousness for the present. My assumption is that if these various possible motivations are significant, this material will eventually find its way into her conscious associations and it can then be dealt with more effectively.

In the meantime, the patient's material indicates the continuing process of grief and mourning over the prospect of termination. Her initial and defensive attempt to convince herself that she hates me quickly gives way to her expression of grief, which she can experience chiefly when she is away from me but still not fully during the analytic sessions themselves.

She illustrates the conflict between her painful but conscious experience and elaboration of the grief, as compared with resorting to her old patterns of defense through hostility and/or seduction. Because this is such a crucial conflict and because of her continuing temptation to use outmoded mechanisms to deal with it, I ask her to focus on the details of the conflict. Her response involves continuing working over of this painful material, thus strengthening the mature and more effective functions of the ego and achieving gradual conscious mastery of the affects involved.

The indicator that she is moving in the direction of a voluntary renunciation of infantile wishes is in her statement, "I'm leaving here and I'm giving up all the chances of satisfying this need down in the core of me. It's childish and I don't need it as an adult but I panic about giving it up and that it will never be satisfied in the way that I want. It's so basic." A little while later she answers this saying, "As an adult I know that I'm a woman and that's all. I don't *need* anything else and I can accept what I have here and I can love you. I don't have to be any more than that. -- But when I'm that way I lose you because I'm giving you up and that makes me feel wild."

As she takes this step in the direction of maturation and renunciation of the childhood wishes, there is then a regressive return to the neurotic demands, and the experience of hostility and the wish to kill me and castrate me. This represents a continuing transference tie to the infantile object and her attempts to protect herself against the sadness and pain of voluntary renunciation. My interpretation of this wish to continue the attachment to me and to avoid the experience of grief at its frustration is an attempt to help her face this issue more clearly. Her response expresses the continuing transference to me as the father, along with an attempt at projection of her defense against affects by feeling that I'm saying she should not experience reactions about this. My interpretation of this projection and confrontation to her of the realistic necessity to experience the grief in consciousness blocks this defense and encourages her to experience her affects and drives directly.

In response to this she is again able, at the end of the session, to return to the primary process infantile fantasy of becoming a penis and thereby of maintaining an attachment to her mother. At this moment, under the impact of separation from me, the transference has become a maternal one, which is again characteristic of the transference oscillation that occurs in the termination phase of analysis where separation and loss is equated with the initial separation of self from mother in the early development of the child. However, regression to the maternal transference may also at times be used as a defense against the anxiety mobilized by conflicts from a more advanced level of psychosexual development.

---

## SESSION 324

Patient comes in with another new hair-do.

**P:** – – – – – – – – – – – – – – – Suddenly I'm suppressing my sexual feelings and I know that I'm having them. For some reason I feel as if they're wrong. Yesterday I wondered as I left if it's wrong. . . . . if it's wrong for me to have sexual feelings for you as a woman. It's happened. I suppressed them all the time, even with Tom, and I eat instead. I don't see why it should scare me. I just don't feel it's right. I guess I'm dividing love and sex again. If I love, then I love Tom and I love you and I don't trust the reasons why I have sexual feelings.

**A:** You mentioned that these are sexual feelings as a *woman* rather than as a little girl. What comes to your mind?

**P:** Yesterday before I left I said. . . . . I gave the idea that you were mother and I was a little girl. I knew that I said that to you because I was so afraid to say the other. I'm suddenly aware that I'm a woman and that you're a man; I'm *not* a little girl and it makes me so nervous! I don't understand why I'm so afraid! Yesterday as I was going home I felt that I could think about it as much as I want but that doesn't make it happen. If I accepted the fact that *you* are you, then I'd *know* that it's not going to happen. – – I feel that when I have sexual thoughts for you I'm afraid they're not real, and that it's just wanting my father again. But for once I feel that they *are* out of real love and it's *not* just sexual or physical, but I can't see that it's right for me to be sitting here having tremendous sexual feelings for you. – – I guess I'm blown up with the thought that sex is not right and that a man only has sex *outside* of marriage and a woman never enjoys it at all. This is the way it was with my parents. So the only way for me to have sex is to go outside of marriage. I don't like that idea at all! I want it to be with love! – – – – Who. . . . . – – I'm wondering why I can't have sexual feelings in marriage. There really is no reason that I shouldn't. – – I feel this is all something that I've learned and that I can't practice because the minute I have sexual feelings for you this other stuff comes back. It's easier not to have them,

because it reduces a lot of conflict and frustration and fear and anxiety. – –
It means completely unattaching myself from my parents. It's somehow
safe to identify with my family and to be the way they were, but I don't
want that. It means breaking away and saying that they were wrong.
They *are* wrong! And I can live a completely different life. – – I can't get
everything together because I have too many emotions and I can't control
them and they bombard me.

A: Let's look at the image you have of finding your own identity
which is different from your parents.

P: There's a tremendous love conflict. I'd be the type of woman that
my mother would think was horrible. – – I picture myself as being what
I've always wanted to be. Just a separate woman to be able to have sexual
feelings for anyone I feel like and for Tom. I have a terrible problem with
you and Tom and it drives me nuts. If I have sexual feelings for you then
I'm *bad* and I'm not a good mother or a good wife. And if I have them
for Tom, then I feel guilty about you. – – – –

A: Let's look at the detail of both alternatives and see what comes
to your mind.

P: I could just be so realistic and I guess I could realistic myself into
nothing. You've been a tremendous father image for me for two years.
How far away from that can I get? I have all of these sexual feelings and
they're natural about my love for you. Even the physical attraction I have
for you. I can't put them all together. I'll tell you that if I think of you
as my father. . . . . I find myself. . . . . thinking of you as a man. You are
very attractive and I'm attracted to you physically. But because you've
been a father, I can't take this, and it's hard and one leads to the other
and I can't do it. I guess if I could lose the father image then I'd be OK.
Can I love you in any other way? I guess it's right, because you're *not*
my father. I love you for what you've done, but you're a *man!* I can't do
it, I'm sorry, but I fall apart like right now. – – If I were a woman and I
didn't need you and I wasn't so emotionally involved with you, then I
could have sexual feelings and it would be all right. But I can't. I've had
too many feelings for you to just turn around and say, "It's all gone." – –
I guess I could, but I don't think that I want to. But it seems to follow
a pattern that I can't avoid. If I let my love out then my sexual feelings
follow, and then I see you as a man and not as a father. But then I'd
lose you forever if you became just a man. – – Then I'm afraid that my
sexual feelings will be this seductive thing, like for other men. – – – I'm
going nuts with this thought. My sexual feelings as a woman are very
physical and very strong. But then I keep remembering. . . . . I'm think-

*Upset,
Loud*

ing of the detail of my sexual thoughts for you, and then I think. . . . .
you're not my husband, so then where am I? I think about my father
and my uncle and because of the physical details I think more of my
uncle.

A: I think you may have had the fantasy that although you can't
have your father as a little girl, that when you grow up and become a
woman, maybe you can, and maybe he'll be waiting for you. I wonder
if maybe you don't have the same idea with me. Now that you've grown
up and you're ready to stop treatment and you're "cured," it means that
you are a woman and I wonder if it's possible that the fantasy is that
you can now have me.

P: (Laughs.) No, I don't want it and I couldn't stand it. I've got a
husband and that's the way it's going to be. I can't differentiate between
a wish and a fear. I may wish it in one sense but it keeps me from
letting my feelings out. I don't *want* it to happen, I really don't. And yet,
the feelings inside me are that I do! Christ! How much can a person take!
– – If I really let them out, they're so strong to me that I just don't. . . . .
I wonder how much can I expect from you? If I let *my* self go completely.
. . . . There are no defenses on my part. Do you know what I mean? – –
I'm realizing that all of my life I expected people to be perfect and to
be emotionless. I find out that they're not and they're imperfect as
humans just like I am.

A: I think behind this is the wonder whether I can control myself
sexually if you let your sexual feelings out. Can I control myself or will
I let go?

P: I'm sure that you wouldn't let go. All right, a man is a man! A
man is physical about sex and a woman depends more on emotions. I
could say that you don't love me but that makes no difference. You're
not a God and you're just a human being, you just are! – – – I don't want
to feel that you have to control yourself. – –

A: What's the detail?

P: The thoughts that I have, if I ever said them, are so sexual to me.
If I say them to any man they'd excite him and you are a normal man,
I guess. I've never been in your position, so maybe you *can* sit there day
after day and listen to women say things. But I can't imagine it. – –
Why is this such a big deal to me? I *know* that you're not going to act
out on anything. – – I guess that all I can do is do it. – – These are the
strongest feelings of my whole life. – –

A: We'll stop here for today.

### DISCUSSION

Once again in this session I do not comment upon the patient's attempts to make herself more attractive with a new hair-do, but her material indicates that this new attention to her physical appearance is the result of mounting sexual tension in the transference, and of a more firm perception of herself as an attractive young woman. This is a relatively new identity for her and it evokes conflict and anxiety from which she had apparently regressed yesterday at the end of the session when she had returned to the role of the little girl with her mother.

This relatively new and shaky perception of herself as a sexual woman now produces a conflict for her in the transference at a new and somewhat different level. Whereas previously as the little girl she had the same desires but had felt herself to be incapable of attracting and satisfying her father, she now, as a grown woman, has a greater sense of attractiveness, and with it a fantasy that she could now attract him to her. However, the persistence of the childhood perceptions in separating sexuality from love is illustrated by the fantasy that she has to go outside of her marriage in order to enjoy sex. This is followed immediately by the more mature perception that she doesn't like such an idea and wants it to be with love and with her husband. However, recognizing the reality that sexuality and love can and should go together, means further renunciation of parental values and models, and with this a further separation from and giving up of the childhood love objects. My intervention regarding her establishing an independent identity is an attempt to help her further highlight and clarify this conflict and the issues involved in emancipating herself from the childhood fixations and identifications.

Her subsequent associations develop her awareness of the conflict over the continuing oedipal attachment experienced toward me in the transference, where she has difficulty in separating her perception of me as the father from me as a man. To recognize and accept me as a man and to give up the attachment to me as the father is another step toward renunciation of the oedipal wish, something she is ambivalent at doing. This is illustrated by her statement, "But then I'd lose you forever if you became just a man."

My interpretation of the latent fantasy that when she grows up she will be able to close the generation gap between herself and her father, and that as a man her father will then find her to be an attractive woman, is an attempt to bring out this underlying fantasy implicit in the uncertainty as to whether I am continuing to be her father or am now a man for her. Her initial response to this is a defensive pseudo-maturity in which she uses the current reality of her husband to avoid the implications of the fantasy. But the confirmation of the interpretation comes in the recognition that "The feelings inside me are that I do!" followed by her anxiety lest her sexual feelings successfully excite and seduce me. Although this is expressed indirectly, my interpretation regarding the concern over my control helps her express this conflict more openly and directly. This now brings into full consciousness the patient's anxiety and conflict over possible *real* seduction. This conflict will have to be experienced and lived through consciously in the transference in order that comfortable mastery of it can eventually occur.

---

## SESSION 325

P: – – – I can't stand coming here every day. I just want to get out. Especially on Mondays. I've been gone for the weekend, and I'm full of hate and fear and everything this morning. I feel great. – – Tom worked last night and I felt that I can't stand it. I can't stand to be left alone. I was in bed and I had the thought of cutting my wrists but I know that I won't do it and that I have complete control. If I really want to kill myself I can find much better ways. I was mad that I had the thought. Then I was thinking about a girl who was killed in a car while we were in high school. She was sort of a prostitute and I went to her funeral and I remembered the coffin. I was suddenly scared last night. I wasn't at the time and I haven't thought of her in years. – – I feel like a caged animal and I want to strike out and I'm so scared that I don't know what to do with myself, so all I can do is strike back. Last night after Tom left, I felt scared. It was the same physical fear as when my parents would leave me. I had stomach cramps and my heart was beating fast and I felt that I'd literally die. – – There are times when I can't believe that I'm a woman. For instance, last night. I had the three children and the big house and I was all by myself. I kept wondering, how can I take care of them? It's such a shock to me. – – I'm beginning to feel that if I could just get away from you things would ease up 100 percent. I can't take coming here every morning. I feel that I'm constantly being pushed into asking for trouble. I can only think how much I hate you for putting me through all of this. I feel like a child who would lie in bed and think that I was a big monster. I'll sneak up and destroy you in the most painful, bloody, horrible way for doing this to me. – – – Now suddenly I wonder if this is the result of what we talked about on Friday. I feel as if I've regressed to two-years-old, and the warning signal has been sounded again.

**A:** Let's go back to Friday and to the feelings that you couldn't express that frightened you so much that you had to do this.

**P:** – (Sigh.) – – – . . . . . This is so crazy I can't believe it. I'm convinced that you're a complete bastard like my father. I'm sure that you run around with young blonde women and that you have no intention of marrying them and that you're just a playboy. – – I couldn't stand it. Even though deep inside of me I think it's an "in" for me, I still couldn't stand it. – – I can't get through this part of it. I haven't got what it takes.

**A:** I think the fantasy that I'm a playboy that runs around with blondes is part of your defense at the moment. The feelings on Friday were those of a woman who loves and is sexually aroused and attracted at the same time. It wasn't the bitch, but it was really the woman that frightened you on Friday.

**P:** It's all a vicious circle. As I get well, I realize that you're a human and you're not God. You have feelings and thoughts and a life. It's a defense to think that you *are* God and that you have no feelings or that you're just a machine. I've never let my sexual feelings out. . . . . . . . – – I started to say that I never let them out to a man that they haven't been responded to in some way. Except Tom's brother Frank. If at all, he responded with complete nervousness. I had a dream about Frank the other night. – – I wonder why I won't listen to the adult in myself. The adult knows that I could let *all* of my sexual feelings out in here and everything would be fine, so why don't I? It's the easiest way. But I never do. Instead, I jump up and down and beat my head against the wall and do anything instead. – – I'm asking you to tell me that I'm a child so that I need you and I still need to be in therapy. And yet, whenever you say it I get so mad that I could scream. – – – – –

**A:** Let's go back to what it is that keeps you from listening to the adult inside of yourself.

**P:** All I can think is why should Í let *all* of that out when I'm leaving here? By my termination I have such tremendous fears of death and I guess my love feelings originally were symbolic of death also. – – I can't picture how I'll stand it if I completely let myself go in here. I feel that I'll be draining myself of everything and there will be nothing left to stand up on when I leave. – – – – Somehow I've always thought of love . . . . . like I'm doing now, would be the end. – – – (Laughs.) – – – – – I'm having such a battle inside of myself, and I get more and more scared and

I just can't do it. – – If I could just *see* you. I can't stand this not seeing you. – – Oh, it would probably be worse. – – – It must be something else. If I think that you will act on my sexual feelings, it's a defense. I *know* that you're not going to, I just *know* it, so it must be something else.

**A:** If you listen to the adult inside yourself and really *feel* like her, then it takes you a step closer to termination.

**P:** A step closer! I'd be *terminated!* There's one thing that helps my decision. I *have* had these love and adult feelings and I love them and there's nothing better and it's the greatest thing in the world. All I can see is that if I let them out and really feel them, and don't let them frighten me then I'll really be ready to leave. – – It's only when I *am* loving and feeling like a woman, that's the only time in my life that I feel that I can handle anything. I feel so content with the world. – –

**A:** We'll stop here for today.

### DISCUSSION

The patient begins the session by describing the recurrence of some of her symptoms over the weekend, but this is accompanied by her conscious awareness that she is in control of herself. However, there is a continuing oscillation between the regressive return to experiences of childhood (as in her association between her husband leaving and her parents leaving as a child) and her awareness of herself as an adult. Part of this regressive experience is the expression of her transference fantasy of destroying me and getting revenge for causing her to feel pain. The likelihood is that this fantasy is one she used to have as a girl to help her cope with the feelings of helplessness she experienced.

This is followed, after a brief silence, by a piece of self-analysis in which she spontaneously recognizes that the regressive expression of symptoms is a response to the feelings and conflicts which emerged in the previous analytic session. My first intervention is an indirect confirmation that I agree with her hypothesis that the recurrence of symptoms is related to the transference conflict. This is followed by the transference experience of me as a philanderer like the father, thus giving her an opportunity to iden-tify with one of his mistresses, but accompanied simultaneously by the hope that I am not like the father. My understanding of this material is that the regressive return to the childhood transference experience of me as a philanderer is a defense against a more active and immediate current conflict about herself as an independent and adult woman who is now capable of fusing love and sexuality toward the same object. It is this line of reasoning that leads to my interpretation of her anxiety at becoming such a woman.

This interpretation brings her back to confronting her conflict and anxiety over becoming an adult woman who is free to experience her feelings fully, with confidence that she can manage and control the situation. And my suggestion that she associate further to the fear of listening to the adult within her helps her to experience and elaborate this conflict further.

The patient herself recognizes that her fantasy of my acting on her sexual feelings is a defense, and that therefore there must be other meanings in the situation. At this point I interpret her anxiety and defense against termination, and thereby bring into focus again the termination conflict, with its attendant need for working-through and for the acceptance of the grief that accompanies it. The patient's response at the end of the session indicates her recognition of the conflict over termination, but rather than face the sadness and renunciation that it entails, she instead emphasizes for herself the positive advantages of maturity. On the one hand, this mature awareness is a necessary experience for her in order to develop this new image and structure within her personality. However, this somewhat precocious emphasis on maturity serves simultaneously as a defense against the continuing necessity for the work of grief and mourning. But it is the end of the session, and therefore I am not in a position to interpret or deal with its defensive functions at this time.

---

## SESSION 326

P: – I'm really in a thing! I'm back to where I was a year ago. All I did was eat and run yesterday. I'm panicked. I'm just like a caged animal. I can only eat and sleep. I actually *want* to get fat and I know that now. – – I find myself hating anyone that I have sexual feelings for. It's like I can't stand it and I can't figure out why. – – – . . . . . I feel like I'm on a treadmill and I can't get off. I know what I'm doing, but I can't make the big jump. – – Under it all is the thought that if I let my love feelings go and have sexual feelings then I'm giving you up. *Then* I have to hurt like shit and I can't do it.

A: I wonder if you aren't confusing, "can't" with "don't want to"?

P: – (Sigh.) – – – After eating last night I finally went to bed to try to escape to sleep. The phone rang after about an hour and it woke me up and I started to have my feeling. I didn't have it but it started. And then I had a dream which was so obvious. I was with Tom and this was all about my future. I was all ready to leave. There was a little man in a house and he wouldn't let me go. He barred all the windows. I wanted to get out but I felt so sorry for the little man because he was sick and he was dying, so I let him kiss me, but it wasn't sexual. I was going to get what he had. I wanted to go with Tom so desperately, but I was so sorry for this little man who was going to die. – – I have complete control of my thoughts and

*Sadness* | actions, so why can't I break through? I just keep hanging on. – – I could either love you or hate you and either become a woman or stay a child. – – I think that my biggest fear. . . . . I don't know. I'm wondering that if I leave here without completely working through this last part, can I suppress it over a period of years? Which I did, and which Harris brought out. This would be the same thing. – – Unless I work through this last part the

*Cry* | analysis is not going to do me any good. This is the cause of my whole problem. It's related to my father and having to give him up and to face reality. I can't face it, so I eat or I think about cutting my wrists or I regress. I'm not giving up. I'm not going to face the fact that I can't ever have you. I picture myself as a child and facing the fact that I'm never going to have my father. As a child my only defense was to never face the facts. Life was so abnormal with my father. But it's *not* abnormal here, but I still must face it. I must let out all of those feelings that I never could let out, knowing. . . . . – My loving you and feeling myself a woman with sexual feelings for you is letting it out because then the hurt comes. It's giving up everything and it's realizing that I *am* a woman and I love *being* a woman. Which means that I'm giving up a lot of defenses and fantasies that I used to have which helped me over it. – – Up to now I have always thought that there was *something* between my father and me.

*Cry,* | I've been thinking. . . . . as a child I always felt, "It doesn't bother me that
*Anger* | my mother doesn't really love me and I don't care, because my father does." But it's not true. My mother loved me more. My father wished that none of us had been born and probably hates all of us more than he loves us. Jesus Christ! There's absolutely nothing there! I can't believe it. – – Now I'm so scared. I'm not going to get this from you either. If I face the

*Cry!!!* | fact then I feel out in the cold and I'll die and it *scares me!* – It's an empty part of my life but I always had dreams that I'll fill this up some day. And now I know that I'll never fill it. I must jump over it. It's always going to be empty. – – And I have to do the best I can with the relationship here. I have to forget my desires for you as a father or a husband or a lover to satisfy all of this. I have to say OK, that was as a child and now I don't need it. I can love you as a woman and appreciate you but I must love and appreciate Tom. But it's just an empty space. *Every* girl wants to replace their mother. How many have to face the fact that they never will? Every girl turns her husband into her daddy, and I can't even do that. Thank God, I can't. But I feel that everyone has something that I don't have and maybe when I grow up I'll get it. I have to face the fact that I won't. – – And that's why I run and hide and eat. – – Will I suppress this, or will I accept it? What do you do? What is the answer? It throws me, I don't know how to react or what to do. I can't make it go away.

*Sadness*

**A:** It's not an issue of "don't know." You *know* how to react, and how you feel and what to do, but you just don't want to do it.

**P:** Oh! – – Every time I love Tom and have sexual feelings for Tom and love my family I face this fact. It's the same with you, especially letting my sexual feelings out. – – – (Sigh.) – Every time that I'd be faced with this problem I have a childish fantasy that I'd become a man and have a woman, because a woman is motherly and secure. And I'd go back up inside my mother and never have been born, and none of this problem would ever have been. But I can't do that. – – Being a woman gives up any ideas about that. – – I can't believe that I have to say all of these things and accept them! They make me so scared! Everything is gone and my legs are knocked out from under! The *past* is what makes a person! I'm supposed to burn it all and still *be* somebody! – – – It seems that by accepting the fact that I'm a woman and loving you and all the phases of it that I'm really giving up..... everything..... about my past. – – – – –

*Cry,
Anger*

*Sadness*

**A:** What are your associations to the little old man wanting to keep you and barring the windows in the dream?

**P:** He wasn't old, and I'm sure that I just..... it's a desire on *my* part to stay with you and with my father. It was also guilt that I...... was letting you die. I feel guilty that I'm *not* fulfilling my father's wish in life, whatever it was. I always felt that I would fulfill it and I feel terribly bad that I'm not. He'll just die with it. – –

*Sadness,
Cry*

**A:** What was the fantasy of fulfilling his wish?

**P:** I love my father and I know that he has tremendous problems. He married my mother and my mother didn't give to him as he gave to her. He'd go out and he wouldn't find it and so he'd return to mother. I could give it to him as a woman because he really needs a mother who just gives to him without expecting him to give anything in return. I could be that to him as a woman but I won't. I'm not going to fulfill Daddy's needs and he'll die with a sickness and it will never be fulfilled. – – All of my life he has waited for me to grow up to fulfill this and I'm deserting him. But what else can I do? I know this is just inside of me. – – Maybe I feel guilty because I'm expressing my hostility by saying, "Ha, ha, you'll die and go to hell and I'm paying you back for everything that you never gave me." I procrastinated all my life. I always had the thought that when I'm a woman all of my problems will be solved. I can't face the fact that it's not so and they won't be. And that's why I can't become a woman.

A: We'll stop here for today.

## DISCUSSION

The patient's recurrence of symptoms since the last session is in response to my having focused on and thereby further mobilized her conflict about becoming the adult woman, and her recognition that to do so is to terminate the childhood transference relationship to me. She indicates that she has a conscious awareness of the sequence of events, and of the meanings of her behavior, and that the fear which prevents her from applying this insight to the control of her behavior is her anticipation of the intense grief and psychic pain in doing so. Her statement, "I actually *want* to get fat and I know that now," illustrates the theoretical concept that the patient's conscious symptom represents a compromised solution to an intrapsychic conflict, and as such is held on to by the patient in spite of conscious distress. In other words, although the conflict is conscious, there is still a good deal of working through that must be accomplished before a lasting change in behavior and structure will result. My initial intervention is an attempt to deal with one of the specific resistances against making this additional step, namely the avoidance of the particular painful affects involved, and the confrontation that she now has a greater degree of conscious control over these conflicts than she previously had.

The dream she reports represents a further elaboration of the conflict she is currently facing in the transference neurosis in regards to termination and her equation of termination with death. When she terminates her treatment and I am no longer an active person in her life, it will be as if I am dead for her, and she already has interpreted this general meaning of the dream for herself. Her subsequent references to the previous therapist and to the way in which she managed the termination of that treatment, are signs of her growing ego strength and capacity for self-observation, and are a recognition of the reality principle and a further acceptance of the realization that the reality principle requires her to face the pain involved in giving up the infantile and childhood neurotic attachments. She spontaneously goes on to the expression of her awareness that the relationship to me and also to the previous therapist are transferences from the child-

hood situation with her father, and with this comes the intense affective ac-
companiment as she relives the old conflict. In this material she demonstrates her insight and awareness of the pathological relationships from
childhood, and the recognition of their repetition in her current life.

At this point she begins to elaborate the childhood fantasy of a future
relationship with her father, which is the transference fantasy I had interpreted two sessions ago that when she was cured and was a woman she and
I would have a love relationship, accompanied by the reconstruction of the
childhood fantasy that when she grew up she could have her father and
close the generation gap. Now that fantasy emerges with anger and intense
affect as a combined recall of childhood experience and relationship and
current transference interaction with me. Accompanied by intense affect,
she expresses her adult recognition of the needs for voluntary renunciation
of the childhood wish, and the need for acceptance that she cannot go
back and fill in her past history as she would have wanted. She also demonstrates her recognition that the symptoms during the previous evening
represent a defense against the acceptance of this painful frustration.

My next intervention, that she knows what she must do but doesn't
want to do it, stimulates a further working-through and recognition of her
defensive retreat to regressive fantasies of becoming a man and having the
love of her mother, or the even more regressive fantasy of the intra-uterine
relationship with the mother. At the same time, the adult synthetic and
integrative ego functions are maintained as she recognizes the implications
of giving up the past by maturing, and becoming and feeling like an adult
woman. In this way she again demonstrates a basic psychoanalytic theoretical postulate that the neurosis represents a continuing effort in adult
life to achieve the gratifications of the childhood relationships and wishes.

In the dream reported earlier, one defensive element of the dream
work was the projection to the little old man (a representation of me in
the transference) of the wish to stay attached and to maintain the relationship. My choice at this point to return to her associations to this dream
element is based on an attempt more adequately to expose and work
through her continuing use of this mechanism. The immediate associations
indicate her own conscious recognition of the projective mechanism and
that the wish originates within herself, but it leads immediately into a
similar projective wish-fulfilling fantasy from childhood that her father
wanted and expected her to fulfill his life. The elements of this childhood
fantasy about the father's needs and wishes have been alluded to previously throughout the analysis, both directly and indirectly, but now under
the impact of the termination conflict it returns again.

My request for her to elaborate on the fantasy of fulfilling the father's needs and wishes brings another reworking of this fantasy of replacing mother in the oedipal triangle and of being able to satisfy and fulfill her father's needs better than the mother did. Again it must be pointed out that the feeling in the transference neurosis that she is deserting me and leaving me to die unfulfilled represents a repetition of this childhood fantasy. And even as she is experiencing this fantasy and the affects that accompany it, the self-observing adult ego functions indicate that "I know this is just inside of me."

In this session the termination conflict has been clarified and the process of working-through is going on effectively. The intense and sustained affective component is being consciously experienced and expressed as part of this working-through process. The expectation is that this material will have to be gone over again and again before the working-through process will have been completed.

---

## SESSION 327

Patient comes in with another new hair-do.

**P:** – – – I dreamed last night that you left town when I was through with my analysis. On the last day that I was here I came and you had everything packed up and I thought to myself, "He's had to leave town because he isn't any good." – – – – On the way home yesterday I was thinking that if I could accept this and let all of my love and my sexual feelings out, I'll never have the thought of cutting my wrists again. I don't know why, but it just. . . . . – – – – – Every morning I wake up and think, "I'll call Dr. Dewald and tell him that I can't come." If I could just leave now, I just can't take this frustration. It's just hell. I feel that my emotions are worn to a frazzle and I can't take much more. The minute I let my love feelings out, I. . . . . Oh God! and they're right here, up to the surface and I'm eating them away. They're right here, and I either have to let them out or I have to leave here. – –

**A:** What comes to your mind about that choice?

**P:** I'm trying to talk myself into letting them out, but it means. . . . .

*Cry*          I don't know what it means. It means that I have to accept an empty feeling and it's going to hurt like hell. – – – – – I've just rationalized it as much

*Sadness*      as I can and I can't do it any more. I know I'll be miserable and unhappy and it will be unprofitable for me to regress, and to hate my parents for what they did. It was fine as a child, but it's going to do no good as an adult. I can only be happy if I give up the past. And when I do and I'm a woman and an adult and a mother then I'm happier than I've ever been in my life. – – I can sit here and say it over and over but it does no good. – – I know that I can trust you to the hilt and I can say anything in here and it does't bother me. I'm sorry that I *can't* trust you. I eat like this and I get mad at you, but it's no good because it's not your fault. That's the whole damn trouble, I can't blame anyone! – – – Why do I think that I'm going to be fulfilled if I have a wild love affair outside of my marriage. I don't understand why. . . . . yes I do. – – Why do I still think that I want daddy? I don't understand this any more. I *know* this is ridiculous. It's just like a blind puppy looking for its mother's nipple. I'm not thinking or looking, I'm just blindly going because I feel. . . . . . –

A: What did you stop at?

P: I don't know what I was saying. I'm thinking that. . . . . I'm scared suddenly. Terminations throw me into a frenzy and I don't know what I'm doing and I'm acting on the impulses that I learned twenty-seven years ago. Which is so asinine that I can't believe it. – – Suddenly I realize that mamma's breast isn't there any more and no matter how hard I think about it, it isn't there. So I think I'll die. I feel absolutely hysterical. I've tried to fight it for years against looking at this fact. Now I see it and I'm absolutely hysterical! I've never looked before because I *know* how unreal it is and how unattainable it is. It's a closed door. – – I can see the whole pattern now. I start to have sexual feelings for a man and I can't take it, and so I run back to mamma and mamma isn't there any more and my God, I don't know what to do! – – – I can have my sexual thoughts right now and I can think them about you and about my father, but I think they're wrong! – – When I think about it I'm a woman! I'm *not* a child, and I'm a woman!! – *Anxiety*

A: And then?

P: – (Sigh.) – I think thoughts like I do with Tom when we have intercourse. It's like . . . . . – . . . . . Oh dead. I love you and right now I feel so womanly. I can satisfy you as a woman and I want to more than any-thing. I could satisfy you because I *love* you. – – Another thing that I have to accept is that you're *not* rejecting me and I still *am* a woman and I can still do this with Tom. – – I've always thought that any strong sexual and love feelings like I have for you *must* be fulfilled, and they won't be in here. But I'll have them coming out of my ears they're so strong! And I'll just have to have them and not feel rejected. Really, I don't think that I *do* feel rejected. I just feel sad!! – – – I think that's it. That's the biggest *Cry* thing I have to do. I have to let all my feelings out for you and I have to accept the frustration of not having them fulfilled because I don't care *how* well adjusted I am, I get *frustrated!!* − − − − − − It's this frustration that I can't take! I feel wild! I hate you! I'm never going to have sexual feelings again! (Laughs.) − − − − I feel desperate! Oh, I feel absolutely desperate! − −

A: What about the desperate feeling?

P: When I said that I'd *never* have sexual feelings again, I started having them. But they were more hostile. It was like I'd finally let some sexual feelings out and I was frustrated and so I got hostile and now I'm desperate. The reason that I never loved like this before is that I *know* that I'm going to be rejected! And I can't take it! I can't take it! − − It's amazing how one minute I can be such a woman and the next minute I'm a child! Just like that! Just like now. The woman *knows* that she hasn't been rejected. − − It's that feeling unfulfilled! It's empty and I've *got* to fill it up with eating or *something!* I just can't take it!

A: This phrase, "I can't take it," is a phrase that you've used a great deal here. What are your associations to it?

P: (Laughs.) Oh Jesus, all I can think of is that a long time ago in here I was referring to my father's penis, erected. I want it so badly, but . . . . . it will kill me. − − It's a ridiculous fear now. − − There's something so safe about being a little girl because you can have sexual thoughts about penises and nothing is going to happen. But as a woman, it's different, and I do have them. I have dreams about great big penises and I *love* them!

A: We'll stop here for today.

*Anxiety* (margin note)

## DISCUSSION

At the manifest level the patient's dream represents her continuing preoccupation with the termination conflicts and her attempts to master them. Although the dream itself was not subsequently analyzed during this session, it also has a number of latent and unconscious implications to it. Leaving town represents an allusion to the father who had to make several moves during his life because of the realistic difficulties which his extramarital affairs had created. The idea that I leave town when she is through with her analysis means that we would both be departing together, and in that sense it may represent a fantasy of continuing attachment to one another through the sharing of such an experience. The idea of death and/or departure may also at times be symbolically equated with orgasm, which might be another possible wish-fulfilling element in this dream. The [1] fense against grief over separation also occurs in the dream through the attempt to depreciate me as being no good, in order that she will not feel she is losing something of great value.

Although this understanding of its various possible meanings is clear to me as the patient tells the dream, my judgment is that the immediate conscious direct transference experiences will be more meaningful to her, in terms of the working-through process, than an attempt to use the dream for this purpose. In such situations the use of a dream may frequently permit the patient to use a maneuver of distancing herself from the material by virtue of the fact that it relates "only to a dream." In her subsequent associations the patient indicates that the feelings of love and the frustration of them, as well as her fears about them, are very much conscious to her in the transference at this moment. In one sense, none of this material is new, since throughout the analysis, almost from the very beginning there have been numerous references to her experiences of love and sexual arousal, as well as frustration of such wishes in the transference relationship to me. However, this material does illustrate that such experiences occur at differing levels of intensity and directness, and from her description, the current transference experiences stimulated by the anticipated termination are even more intense and direct than some of the earlier ones. It is in this phase of the analysis that the realistic threat and possibility of overt seduction often reaches its peak.

Although the issue of her choice whether to experience and express these things consciously, or to suppress them and defend against them in other ways, has come up many times before, it is part of the essence of the working-through process that it must be gone over again. It is the attempt to foster her further working-through of these conflicts that leads me to ask the somewhat banal question about her associations to the choice she must make. This immediately mobilizes the affective component of her response, which in turn is stimulated by her growing conscious ego recognition not only of the inevitability of frustration of these infantile yearnings, but also of the advantages to her in the long run from such a renunciation. Her statement of how unprofitable it would be to go on hating her parents for what they did represents a further sign of mastery and recognition, as well as a further coming-to-terms with them for their failures and their shortcomings.

One of the ultimate hallmarks of a successful analysis is the patient's ability to accept the parental frustrations and limitations without the continuing resentment and wish to blame them that are parts of the neurotic process itself. This same issue is repeated in the transference, where consciously she "knows" that she can trust me, and yet affectively feels that she cannot, but simultaneously recognizes that to continue to be angry at me will do no good since it is not my fault. She also demonstrates the need for further working-through when she speaks of her knowledge that to go on clinging to the father and the oedipal wishes is ridiculous, and yet she is still unable to prevent it affectively, and she uses the analogy of the blind puppy.

This same conflict between intellectual and cognitive awareness, as opposed to drives and affective experience, is illustrated by her sudden realization about the loss of the mother's breasts. There is simultaneously a recognition of the various defenses she has used in the past and a growing insight into the dynamic pattern of her own mental operations. She is gradually achieving a deeper level of understanding and integration, and as these affective experiences occur, anxiety is mobilized. Her emphasis that she is now a woman and no longer a child while experiencing her sexual drives is another allusion to the possibility of a real seduction here with me. My brief question, "And then?" is another attempt to help her consciously face her feelings and fantasies about such a possibility, and thereby achieve further mastery over them.

This leads her to the description of her current sexual feelings and to another step toward the healthy fusion of sexuality with love. Accompanying this is the simultaneous adult recognition that the frustration of these oedipal transference wishes does not in reality signify a rejection of her as a woman, although their frustration will lead to sadness and grief. At this point there is a brief regressive return to the use of hostility as a defense against the transference frustration, as well as her brief disclaimer that she will never again permit herself to have sexual feelings. Both of these are characteristic of the way in which she has handled this conflict in the past, but because of the analytic work which has taken place up to now, neither defense can be sustained and simultaneously her spontaneous laughter is the indicator of the adult self-observation that is occurring. As she elaborates on these mechanisms, there is again a return to the transference experience of rejection accompanied by anxiety, and yet at the same time, a continuing self-observation about her oscillations between being a child and being a woman.

The phrase, "I just can't take it," had caught my attention many times throughout the analysis, and at this moment my feeling is that it represents a defensive attempt to dramatize and exaggerate some of her current feelings. It is for this reason that I ask her about it, which stimulates her subsequent associations to the castration complex which had been previously brought up many times. This material is also an indicator of her increasing capacity for self-analysis, and of her increased ego acceptance into consciousness of what had previously been unacceptable and anxiety-provoking fantasies and drives. In other words, she can now more comfortably rely upon conscious controlling ego mechanisms, and therefore no longer needs to maintain energy in the unconscious repression of such impulses or fantasies.

## SESSION 328

P: – – Yesterday when I left here, revelations kept dropping on me! It was wild! I had the thought that I should write them down or I ll forget them. It was as if I was learning something for the first time in my life and yet, it's something that I've really known. There's one thing that I've known and you've told me it before. . . . . that my mouth and my vagina are the same to me. Suddenly it dawned on me why. It's crazy, and I can't even think of it. After I left I started having sexual thoughts about the penis. I realized that I think of it orally as a child and vaginally as an adult, and it's the same sexual feeling to me. – – As a child I can picture myself with my uncle and I'm having thoughts about my father and I could kiss the penis and play with it. I *couldn't* think about it in my vagina, I just couldn't! Now I *can*! And it's a very strong fulfilling thought! – – I also had a thought yesterday about my role in sex. My feelings are becoming very different. You, not even you, have ever been able to have this feeling that a woman has. I like that fact. I don't know why, but you've heard women talk and you read, and you've probably written and talked about it, but you'll never *know* about it. You have to *be* a woman to know, and this thought separates me from you and it makes me *somebody* without you. – – I feel that I worry all the time and I worry if I'm happy that I'll die, or if I love I'll die, or if I give in then I'm through. I'm so tired of all of this worry. This morning I had the thought, "Why do I think of all of these problems to bring in here, when I'd love to just let all of my sexual feelings go and be happy in here." – – And when I start thinking like this, then reality hits me that these will never be fulfilled with you and it makes me want to hold on to them. – – I start to have sexual and love feelings and I start feeling happy and then something stops me and it's frustrating. I do a complete about-face and I go back to mother. But mother means death. Yesterday I also had the thought, "I give my love to you and you disappear." I felt this morning, why don't I come in here and be happy and have my sexual feelings and let my love out and really there's no reason not to. I've always thought that it would be like jumping off a cliff. It would be like one moment of ecstasy and then you die and it's almost

*Excited*    worth it. – – I'll let all of my love and sexual feelings out and they'll be snapped off like that! There's nothing and it's like hitting a brick wall. – – I wonder what harm would it do if you *did* replace my father? – –

**A:** Let's go back to the fantasy of jumping off the cliff with the one moment of ecstasy. What comes to your mind?

**P:** – It's like. . . . . I don't know, but there's a damned good chance that I'll die. My logic says not and the only thing to do is jump. It's just like the first time on the diving board where either you are going to die or it's going to be fun. It took me an hour, but I finally did it. It's just like an orgasm. Sexual feelings are the strongest in the human, and I know and I've loved it more than anything! And so I want it! It would be much easier if I didn't know or didn't want it, because then I'd not be so tempted. What's going to happen? I don't know. I picture myself going down a drain and it's like dying and the end of the world. What I can't picture is

*Cry*    life going on afterwards in a normal way. – – – That thought to cut my wrists is in place of my sexual thoughts. To me, to let these thoughts go, all I can picture is my death and I'm bleeding and it's so violent and I want it so badly!

**A:** So you still fantasy that your vagina is a little girl's vagina and that your father's *big* penis would rip it and tear it and kill you.

**P:** It seems so silly now. But it's just like it was as a girl and I'd lie in

*Loud,*    bed and I'd think about it but I *knew* that it wouldn't happen. It makes
*Excited*    me so mad to think it. It's so stupid *now*. It's just like here if I let my thoughts go, I'll lose myself and it will actually happen because I'll think it all through, detail by detail. – – This is like the feeling that I had last night that my mind would blank out. – – Ha! It *is* like I still think of myself as a little girl and I'm looking at Daddy's penis and at mother. I think how wonderful it is and I want it so badly, but it's *not* for me and I'm a little girl and I can't do it. – – I can project myself into a woman as a little girl, but suddenly I realize that I *am* a woman and I don't need to project any more. This is fine and these are all of my dreams, but am I ready? It's fine to look and watch it and to dream about it. But to live it! It comes closer and closer to the surface. It's all right here and I want to let it out so badly! – – I always think of it in my mouth. That's not as bad either, but that's also like a little girl. – – – It all stems around thinking of myself as a child. That's why I have these fears. I *know* that I'm a woman and if I'd think of myself as a woman, I could let these out without the

fears. But it all goes back to my fears about leaving here. As a woman I can handle anything. It's like when Harris terminated me and all I could do was to be a child with childish sexual thoughts. That's another thing that I was thinking about yesterday. It's so *easy* to be a child because you can always find someone to take care of you. – – Before I went to see Harris my sexual thoughts were on an infantile level, and he brought them up a little bit, but I never knew what a woman's sexual thoughts were, and now I *really* know. – – –

**A:** So we can see that there is a conflict in you between being a woman with love and sexual feelings and freedom and satisfaction, but giving me up on one hand, as compared with being a child with all the sexual fears and misconceptions and the doubts about yourself and the symptoms, but being able to go on clinging to me on the other.

**P:** All of my life I've wanted to get away from my mother, but I couldn't turn my sexual thoughts to my father. That was too frightening. But you've let me have these sexual feelings and you've let me get away from mother, and now if you leave I don't have mother *or* you. – – If I could be a woman and have you forever I'd do it just like that. – – By being a child I can have you but being a woman, I lose you. The conflict is un-believable! There are so many reasons why I want to leave here that I can't count them all. And there are a few why I *don't* want to. The more that it comes to the surface, the more anxious and fearful I get. I'm in a twit! And I will be until I decide! If I react like a woman to this then I have to leave. If I'm a child, then I'm anxious and frustrated and miserable and I hate it. But if I'm a woman, I *know* that I have to leave. It's all in front of me and it gets bigger and bigger and bigger!! – – – – – – – – – I wonder where I'm going to get my feeling of confidence. I don't have any right now. I am *so scared* of leaving here. – – – –

*Loud, Excited*

**A:** We'll stop here for today.

## DISCUSSION

The patient's initial material indicates another characteristic of patients at this stage of analysis. By virtue of all the analytic work that has occurred up to this time, she is now ready consciously to accept and integrate at a deeper level some of the insights and awareness that have previously been discussed or interpreted. Her statement, "It was as if I was learning some-thing for the first time in my life and yet it's something that I've really known," is a confirmation of an observation in this regard made by Freud in one of his early papers. In the unconscious portion of the patient's mind there is a recognition and "knowledge" of the nature and dynamics of the neurotic process. But by virtue of the various unconscious defensive functions of the ego, this "knowledge" cannot be admitted into consciousness. The final effect is that the patient "knows" and yet at the same time "doesn't know" about himself and his symptoms. The material regarding her equation of the mouth with the vagina, and her linking this to the genetic material about the father and the uncle, illustrate this concept and although it was not directly commented upon in this session, the connection of this material to the symptom of bulimia is obvious. This material also illustrates the concept of the upward displacement of sexual drives which occurred in childhood, and the giving up of this mechanism as a result of analysis.

The material describing her pleasure that only a woman can experience a woman's sexual feeling and her satisfaction that I, as a man, will never directly know this, is part of her ongoing attempt to solidify her enjoyment in her new role and identity as a woman. However, this role is still impeded by neurotic and infantile fantasy, as in her material regarding the jumping from a cliff and the one moment of ecstasy followed by death. This equation of orgasm with death has not yet been worked through, although it has been interpreted and exposed to consciousness previously. Because this fantasy still serves as a force contributing to continuing inhibition of full sexual freedom, I choose to return to the image of jumping from the cliff and the moment of ecstasy. The patient's material confirms my own silent association to orgasm, and she begins to elaborate on her equation of orgasm with death.

At that point her associations shift to the symptom of her fantasy of cutting her wrists, which she spontaneously associates to sexuality and to the wish for and fear of such an experience. The connecting links in her associative train have been omitted and presumably occurred either consciously or unconsciously during the 1½ minutes of silence. In trying to fill that gap, my own associations had gone to the end of yesterday's session when the subject of the father's big penis had come up, and to the fact that this material was followed, while she was at home, by the sudden recognitions and awarenesses that she had reported earlier in the session. In the context of these thoughts I am struck by her description of violent death and bleeding, and it is this understanding which leads to my interpretation of the fantasy of the father's penis tearing and killing her.

This interpretation leads to her filling in the childhood experiences and fantasies, but accompanied by the adult secondary-process perceptions of the unreality of the child's primary-process fantasy. Her statement that

"It all goes back to my fears about leaving here" again illustrates how clinging to the neurotic distorted childhood fantasy represents the continuing
wish for infantile gratification and a defense against renunciation of these
longings. My interpretation of this conflict is an attempt to help her bring
it out more clearly, and to help the emerging adult ego become more
aware of the advantages in such a renunciation. The interpretation permits
her to respond by further working-through of this termination conflict.

My association to her statement, "It's all in front of me, and it gets
bigger and bigger and bigger!!" is that this is a reference not only to the
current termination conflict, but also to the uncle (father) and the oral
sexual episode in the cellar. However, since my tactical goal at the present
moment is to deal with the current termination conflict and the continuing conflict over her role as a woman, I decide not to make any attempt
at this time to go back to the childhood trauma, feeling that this would
distract her from the more pertinent conflict at this moment.

---

## SESSION 329

P: ------------ On the weekends reality comes through so
strong. I get here Monday and I hate it. I feel that you are a complete
stranger and I'm having all of these love and sexual feelings for a complete
stranger! It drives me nuts! --

A: You mentioned that reality comes through strong on the weekends.
What's the detail?

P: I kind of. . . . . it's the other way around. When I'm away from you
I can *feel*. It's all so unreal. I can love you and think about you and I can
think of termination and I can feel sad. But then I come in on Monday
and it throws me. When I don't see you, I can look at all of this. But when
I look at you, I know who you are! -- I feel that I *shouldn't* be having
these feelings. -- Saturday I was thinking. . . . . . - I cannot stand to think
about you as a human being! It's too much for me! Saturday I was think- *Anxiety*
ing. . . . . I'm *not* a dummy here and I'm alive and I'm a person, and you
know that. -- I've been thinking so hard about love and sexual feelings
and talking about it. I was wondering, "What does he do? Does he just
sit and think about something else while I'm talking?" These are *real* feelings that I have. They come from love. Other men may be physically
attracted to me but I don't know or love them and so there's nothing there.
I swear that Tom is the only other person that I ever felt this way about,
and now suddenly I'm feeling this way about you. -- I've had this fantasy

all of my life about a man with feelings. He loves me. I never could figure this out before. He *feels*. I've always said to myself, "If I could just find a man like this." And suddenly it dawns on me that Tom is a man like this, and he loves me in the way that I've always wanted to be loved. I used to put him out. – Push him away, and not think about him. I also realized that I like to be hurt by a man. I enjoy it. I've had dreams that I'm in love with a man and he shits on me and leaves me, but he always comes back. It's always so exciting. It's so obvious now that I can't believe it. I now realize that I *enjoyed* the ideas of Tom's affairs. I'd convince myself of it and I'd cry and be upset and be worried but I loved it! He always comes back to me. That's the most exciting part of it, better than the man who doesn't go out on her. Why didn't I marry a man like that? I *couldn't* have married anyone more different.

A: What comes to your mind about that?

P: I don't know. I'm thinking about my uncle. Tom is like a mother and I'm really so safe. He's so stable and responsible and he would never do that to me. I try to think what it is. There *must* be a reason. I guess it's. . . . .

A: What did you stop at?

P: I've analyzed Tom down to nothing. He's identified with his mother beautifully, and yet he also is a man. Tom is the only man for me. When I met him I *knew* that he was the man for me and I could trust him

*Cry* | and he'd take care of me, and he was what I needed, and yet, he's adjusting to the *new* me, a person who doesn't need him in this same way. – – – Sometimes I think that a long time ago that I had a feeling for my uncle, that I never had before or again. Maybe I saw this in Tom. It's not all the reason. – – I couldn't have taken anyone like my father, because I'm not strong enough. And yet, it makes me so sad to think that I didn't. I wonder why I didn't. I knew about my father and I saw him as a child and I saw him needing someone desperately. That's exactly the type of man that Carol married. I've felt it all of my life, this urge to take my father and *help* him and *be* my mother and be different! I guess I didn't grow up that far to do it. – – I think about my parents and sometimes I say something and then I think, "That sounds just like your mother," or else I say to myself, "Mother would never feel or do this." It's with handling children, or with Tom, or either when I'm making love with Tom that I think of this. I say to myself, "Oh, they never felt this way." – – Sometimes I feel that I react just as my father does, and that's when I'm yelling at my children. – – I think about what I have to do here and I get so nervous. I really have to realize that you are *not* my father. Every day it comes closer.

When I finally realize that you're not, then I realize that the analysis has not given me a father, and that scares me. You're not my father and you never were. But to have sexual feelings for you and to look at you, that's the way I must feel. – – I feel as if I'm being squeezed and torn and I can hardly take it. The minute I accept you as Dr. Dewald, is the minute I give up my father and realize that I'll never have a father. I give up the dreams and fantasies that I've had that have kept me going in life and gave me something to live for. – – I've always thought of myself as a little girl and a child, and I've always thought, "I want to grow up so badly I can't wait to be an adult." Suddenly I realize that's what I am. – – I used to *love* feelings of grief and think that they were wonderful. Suddenly I'm feeling them for *real* and they're *not* so wonderful. – – Off and on, it hits me that I'm not a little girl and I'm a woman and I have absolutely noth ing to fear and no reason to be anxious or scared. It's so clear an outsider could say, "Of course." – – – –

A: Let's go back to the feeling that you enjoyed being hurt, and that you enjoyed the feeling of grief. What comes to your mind?

P: They made me an adult and that was the way I'd think of myself as a woman. I think of myself being hurt and then being loved. As a child . . . . . a child doesn't feel that way. I don't like to think of myself as a child thinking these things. As a child I was helpless. I never thought directly about my father. I always projected them to the future, and I'd think, "When I'm a woman," or "I'll dream about a woman going through this." – – It makes me feel that I'll go crazy thinking about that little girl lying in bed thinking. I could never face the fact that this was *my* family, and so I'd make up fantasies. I was a woman or an adult, and the woman always got him back and the child didn't. I begin to feel how helpless I'd feel. The child *is* helpless about its parents. The adult isn't. My mother as a woman could always get daddy back, or else she could go get a man. I couldn't as a child. Only a woman could do that, and so I'd just lie in bed and think I was going to die, night after night. It scares me that all of my life I lived on the thought that when I was a woman I'd have a man. Now I *am* a woman and I realize that I'll never have *that* man. It doesn't bother the woman much, but it scares the little girl to death. – – – I don't think that my mind would ever snap or lose track of reality. Only an adult mind can. I was a baby and I cried and cried and someone would eventually answer. Even though my problem is that I never matured, I never really would snap. – – Someone would always pity me and that's the way I made it. I'd get a glimpse of the adult world and I'd cry and some- one would pat me on the back and say, "You poor little thing, I'll take

*Sadness, Cry*

care of you." I never got past that stage. – – I wonder sometimes if nobody does that and I look at life, will I still go crazy? I know that I must do what I never did as a child and that is to look at reality. – – There's one advantage now. As a child, without parents, I'd have died and I'd have been wandering around in the cold. But I know that that's not true *now*.
– – –

A: We'll stop here for today.


## Discussion

The patient begins the session by talking about her perceptions of reality and of me as a stranger, and in this way she is illustrating another step toward the resolution of the transference neurosis. The perception and experience of me as if I were her father, and the regressive transference responses to me in that role, are increasingly recognized by her as unreal and as continuing attempts to cling to an old fantasy, and as a result the more mature and integrative ego perceptions of me as a human being who is her analyst are gradually becoming stronger and more structured for her. Along with this there is a new and more solid perception of her husband as he really is, which parallels the growing more realistic perceptions of me. Both of these sets of perceptions are results of her decreasing need to look for and "see" her father in the current male figures in her life, and therefore a diminished tendency to distort her perceptions in keeping with the old childhood wishes.

In her statement, "I also realized that I like to be hurt by a man," she again is reaching a new level of insight and self-awareness, and shows a realization that one of her important presenting symptoms (jealousy of her husband and the painful obsessional preoccupation with his possibly having affairs with other women) was in fact a disguised wish-fulfilling perception of her husband in the role of her father. Her comments about the dreams in which she loves a man who leaves, but always comes back, are clearly references to the father and the childhood relationship to him, and the exciting feeling that accompanies them represents one of the affects she would have experienced if the childhood wishes had been fulfilled. Her statement, "It's so obvious now that I can't believe it," indicates her recognition and personal insight about these persistent childhood wishes.

Her spontaneous question of how she happened to marry the man she did, and her own recognition that her husband was an object for feelings once held toward her uncle, are further indicators of her increased capacity for self-analysis and self-observation. The same is true of her increasingly realistic perceptions of the father, of her awareness of the identification with her mother, and of her spontaneous movement toward renunciation of me as the transference father. On her own she recognizes that the resolution of the transference neurosis involves seeing me for who I am, rather than a continuing perception of me as her father, and this is accompanied by her realization that analysis will not provide her with the father she has wanted for so long. Her statement, "It's so clear an outsider could say: 'Of course,' " is an important reference to the difference between emotional and personal insight, as compared with purely intellectual awareness. It has taken a great deal of analytic work for her to become aware of these issues on a personal and emotional level, even though an outsider, observing the patterns of her behavior, could easily have constructed an accurate formulation of these issues long before this.

Because I want to explore further the masochistic elements in these responses, I return to the question about her enjoyment of being hurt. In response to this she is able to reconstruct, and at the same time partially experience, the childhood feelings of helplessness and of identification with her mother's pain, while at the same time she can take distance from the past and recognize that the adult is not helpless in the same way. This reality-oriented perception of the greater ability of an adult to cope with conflict which was for the child an overwhelming and threatening experience is one of the important factors in the therapeutic process. The psychic reality of the child involves his own feelings of helplessness in the face of his various primary process fantasies, as well as the various realistic interactions between himself and his environment. The "reality" of this for the child evokes so much anxiety and painful affect that the entire issue is repressed and/or otherwise defended against and therefore, being now unconscious, is no longer subject to learning or to maturing reality-testing capacities. It is only through the analytic process, when these previously threatening or overwhelming "danger situations" are brought to conscious awareness and experienced again by the patient, that the more mature integrative and synthetic ego functions can consciously observe and ultimately resolve these pre-existing conflicts from the point of view of *adult* reality and secondary-process thought.

The more that the patient herself is able to analyze, experience, and recognize the old conflicts and the contrast to current reality, and the more that she herself works toward a spontaneous and voluntary renunciation of infantile and childhood drives and fantasies, the more effective will be the ultimate therapeutic outcome. Since the patient is demonstrating her abilities to do this, there is little need for me to do anything more in this session than listen, continue to serve as the transference object that must be given up, and occasionally focus her attention toward some particular aspect of these problems. In this session I made just four interventions, each of which was merely a request for associations or elaboration of issues that she herself had raised.

---

## SESSION 330

P: – – – – More things have happened to me since I was here, and more thoughts have come to me. I'm realizing that I really don't have any reason to come down here any more, except to work through the rest of this. It scared me and it depressed me, because I'll never get what I thought I always wanted. – – Last night I had the wildest dreams. When I suppress my sexual feelings then I have orgasms in my dreams. I never dream anything but I just have orgasms. Last night I felt as if I was pregnant and I was eating carrots and tuna fish and I know that I'm not pregnant, but in the dream the orgasm was like when I am pregnant. The uterus clamps down and it hurts like hell, and then I dreamt about my mother (laughs) at the bottom of a huge cliff. There were some silly men with wheelbarrows running straight up and down the cliffs. Then we were in the house and my mother said, "I am going to go to Mrs. Jones for Christmas and I'm going to leave your father and I'll show him." The whole dream was a situation that I've lived. My father was in the background and my mother was trying to get back at my father. And she hurt Sally to do it. I screamed at my mother, "I've had to have two years of analysis because of you!" I was furious at my mother's selfishness. And then I walked to the sink to wash my face. By screaming this at mother I'd realized something that I never could admit. It was a fear and a horror to see it all with my family as being so empty and that it never was there and never will be there. I was really upset about it. – – I've been fine. It's hard to take, but I can do it. The hardest thing is to stay a woman when I leave here. I'm not afraid of anything any more and I'm very capable. But it's such a problem to think of myself as a woman. (Elaborates.) I can't figure out why I was mad at my mother and not at my father in the dream. It was daddy who left me, not mother. It's you I'm separating from, and not mother. I guess I never *had* daddy and so I don't have to give him up. It's mother. I never did get daddy and so I'd fall back on mother. So it's not daddy I give up, it's mother. I'm used to not getting daddy and I'm used to that frustration. It's not going back to mother that I'm *not* used to and I'm giving mother up. – – – There was a dream that I didn't tell you about. I have a tooth with the nerve out, and that time that I was so upset it was really about that. It's not healing. I dreamed that I lost this tooth and that it came out. It doesn't bother me as I was before and I'm not frightened about my appointments with the dentist as I used to be. I have one this week and another one in a month. I think this tooth is my illness. In the dream I didn't lose it and it was hanging on by a thread. I wondered, should I yank it out? And I woke up before I did anything. I know that's what it is. – – I'm thinking. . . . . I'm having such feelings of love for you and I'm trying to avoid them. I'm so tired of this other shit, which is not the future or the present. It's no fun! I want to forget it and concentrate on you, but I can't. I'm afraid. I'm afraid of going home after doing it. – –

**A:** What's the detail?

**P:** All I can think is to do it and then go home. I don't know what I think will happen. I guess it's *the end*. Something is going to be empty. I have a weird fantasy that my love is physical. If I give it to you, I'll never have it back. I can't picture having it at home and all I can picture is emptiness and death. And yet I *know* that if I let my love out I'll carry it home with me. That's what's so sad. It's not losing you but losing my love feelings, because I don't think I can take them home with me. I have two choices and they're both sad. I can keep my love inside and be miserable or else I can give it to you without having it back. But I want to. That *is* love. Love is giving, even if it's just an emotion that you give. – – It soothes me to think that you will be alive after I leave and you'll go on and do what you do and you'll be here and it's not for *my* sake, but for *your* sake. It's comforting for me to know that you're not *really* going to die. – – Now I can understand why children have such problems when a parent dies when they're young. Even without the guilt which I've worked through. You give love which is so precious to you and they take it with them and all you have is grief, and it's not worth it. – – – I think about when my grandmother died. She and I had a *thing* going when I was little. Then I broke it off and I stopped giving my love later on. I think maybe it was a good thing that I did, because when she died I didn't feel the grief. – – –

**A:** What are your associations to the silly men with wheelbarrows in that other dream?

*Sadness, Cry*

*Sadness, Cry*

*Cry!*

**P:** When I said it I thought that that's what my father has been doing. They were little boys and they were trying to show off and to do something spectacular and they were just being stupid. It's like I've suddenly realized. . . . . I don't know. . . . . that I really don't. . . . . I can't stand to say it. I want to hang onto my old feelings about my father, but as an adult and a woman, my father means nothing to me, just nothing! The few feelings that I had for him as a child were warm and wonderful, but no more. There's no use to hang onto them. I don't want to talk about this. It seems that my father doesn't bring out anything in me any more. It's not hate or love, and I'm just sorry for him. He's lived his life and it's over and all he can do is the best that he can. He's a little boy and he runs up and down that cliff and he falls on his nose and mother picks him up and he sits around. He's really nothing and he has no security and if I don't hate him or don't love him, then there's nothing there.

**A:** So the tooth hanging by a thread is also your father.

*Sadness,*
*Cry*

**P:** You would think that I'd jump for joy, but I don't feel like jumping for joy. It's like a death that's sad, but doesn't effect me too much. The only problem is guilt. And yet there's no reason for guilt and it's only an attachment to him. I don't want to love a boy. I want to love a man, and so I can't attach myself to my father that way because he's not a man and he never was. Tom is so much more of a man than my father. –– Ha! I was just struck by a bolt of lightning! –– This is the point where I run back to my mother. I don't want to do it. –– My adult mind says that there's no use getting upset about it because it is, and it *has* been and I'm fortunate to have a person like Tom. (Laughs.) But the child says, "God-damn my parents, I'll kill them for this because I'm so mad at them." –– This suddenly places you so differently in my mind! You're over here away from them! I'm so shook! –– I feel as if I've just gone through one of the spells that I used to have that would leave me shaking. ––– Now I have the most ridiculous thought! I don't bring my purse in here any more. I think I'm afraid that I'll leave it and I don't want to leave anything in here. –––– Now suddenly I feel *sick*. ––

**A:** What's the detail?

**P:** For the first time in the analysis I've been able to lie here and *not* look at you, and still know who you are. And when I see you it will be verified. I feel as if I *have* been sick and I've thrown up on the floor. I don't have the desire to turn around and cling to you any more and that makes me sick. I'm suddenly in that wide, bright, open light. I was always afraid of it before. Now I'm there and I will stay in it. I'm not able to get away and it makes me sick to my stomach. –– I have such a fear that I'll die the minute I walk out of this door. It's a fear that I've had all of my life and it really scares me. – – –

A: We'll stop here for today.

## Discussion

In the first part of this session the patient again indicates the continuing integration that is taking place within her in response to the impending termination of her treatment and the reworking of conflict that this produces. There is an increasing awareness that fulfillment of the fantasies she has clung to was really never possible even in childhood, and that it will never be possible for her in the future either. And this is accompanied by her statement that she is increasingly confident and capable as an adult in her life outside.

Again her capacity for self-analysis is illustrated by her own question as to why she was angry at her mother in the dream rather than at her father, which is followed immediately by associations which help her to conceptualize for herself the regressive attachment to the mother in response to the frustrations in the relationship with her father. There is a recognition that not only must she relinquish the childhood ties to the father, but also that she must give up the attachments to her mother.

This conceptualization leads to the recall of the tooth dream. Among her associations to it is the rather casual remark, made in passing, of how she is now able to go to the dentist without the neurotic anxiety that this situation once produced for her. This kind of casual mention of the relief of a particular neurotic symptom is another indicator of conflict resolution, and of underlying structural change as the result of analysis. In the context of the analytic work that has been done, the relief of this particular phobic symptom suggests that the underlying conflict, which in the past had produced the symptom, has now been at least partially resolved. Therefore, the derivative expression of this conflict is no longer activated by the situation of the dentist's office.

The patient goes on again to work through, with accompanying affect of sadness and crying, her reactions to the termination of the analysis. This leads to another primary-process fantasy that love is like a physical substance which can be taken away, leaving the individual empty and drained. This type of fantasy may well have had its origins in the early nursing experience, where love is in part expressed and received through a physical substance (milk) with quantitative limitations. But there is also a recognition that termination does not really mean my death, even though in the transference she may experience it as such. This material leads to a further recall and integration of the experience of her relationship to the grandmother and to the grandmother's death, where she apparently used the mechanism of denial of her grief.

Throughout the session, up to this point, I have been curious about the dream element of the men with wheelbarrows to which she had not spontaneously associated. After a brief interval of silence, I therefore choose to ask her about it. The patient's response, "When I said it, I thought that that's what my father has been doing," illustrates that when a patient is associating freely in analysis, there may be multiple associations that occur simultaneously or in very rapid fashion, and that even without any conscious attempt at resistance or withholding, it is not possible for the patient to say everything as it occurs in his mind. Inevitably there is a selective process by the patient as to which of the multiple associations he will be able to express verbally, and in the usual situation the pressure of the currently activated conflict, in the absence of other resistances, will determine what material is verbally presented.

However, as in this instance, more than one important conflict may exist simultaneously, and my question serves to bring the omitted elements back into focus. Accompanied by crying and genuine affect, it leads to the current adult perception of the father's immaturity and of the continuing decathexis of him as a result of the analytic work. This material illustrates the concept that when the unconscious childhood cathexis of the parental object has been resolved, the patient then can perceive the parent in a more realistic light and without intense disturbing affect. She describes how he means increasingly less to her, either in positive or negative terms, and therefore it becomes more likely that she will be able to relate to him on a reality basis as an adult today, recognizing his limitations as well as his assets. When an analysis has been successful, a patient should be in a position to relate to parental objects without the fantasy or infantile and childhood expectations that the neurosis had involved, and therefore no longer carry unrealistic feelings of hatred, frustration, disappointment, or idealization that are among the hallmarks of an active neurotic process.

My interpretation at this point, based on the patient's associations to her new perception of the father, that the tooth hanging by a thread represents him, again stimulates the affect of sadness at her renunciation of him as her chief libidinal object. The recognition of his limitations, and of the fact that her husband is more mature as a man than her father, are part of her recognition of the need for voluntary renunciation of father. At this point the patient has a sudden affective deepening of awareness as she describes being struck by a bolt of lightning, and recognizes that rather than face the sadness of the renunciation of the father in the past, she would regress to the attachment to the mother. This insight in regard to the parents leads to an immediate separation experience from me, in which the perception of me is strengthened as someone different from both of them. She feels "shook" by this recognition, and herself equates it with one of her anxiety episodes that she once had as part of her symptom picture. Her sudden feeling of being sick at this point represents a conversion symptom, in which the psychic conflict is being expressed through a somatic discharge. My asking her for the details of the somatic feeling returns it to the focus of a psychic experience that she now attempts to verbalize.

The patient's statement, "For the first time in the analysis I have been able to lie here and *not* look at you, and still know who you are," is something of a surprise to me, but it and the subsequent associations clarify the meaning of the conversion symptom. The early psychic mode of attachment to the mother is through the psychological mechanism of incorporation by introjection of the loved object, so that the object is retained inside as a part of the self. Feeling sick as if she had just vomited represents the reverse of this process and the externalization of the object through the mechanism of projection, based on the mode of vomiting. In other words, as the transference object I am at this moment no longer "inside," but instead have been extruded by her as part of the process of separation. Although the prototype of this transference experience is probably a maternal relationship, in this case her oedipal attachment to the father (and uncle) had so many oral components and experiences that it probably simultaneously also represents the psychic extrusion of the father. This experience may also have connections to the dream of extruding the tooth, but that particular connection did not occur to me at the time.

---

## SESSION 331

P: ---------- I can't figure out how I feel this morning. I thought that I want to come in here and bitch and bitch. I'm mad. I'm not scared of anything. I feel mad and yet I'm not really. I was depressed yesterday and I ate last night. I have no sexual feelings and no love feel- | *Tense, Angry* ings. I want to say that I can't take it. (Laughs.) – – I don't even want to cry. – – I feel like absolutely hell and I hate all of this that I have to face. I hate it and I feel it's shitty and that's what it is! – – I don't want to be a big girl, and I don't want to accept this at all. – – – – I feel that I could so easily pick myself up. I've been really hurt. I could say to hell with men and that I don't hate or love them and that I could get through life without them. I don't feel like a warm woman with so much love. That's what hurts. I say to myself, "What's the use." I could cry about it, but I don't want to. I want to tell you that I feel like hell and that the world is shitty and I'm mad. But it's not, and my parents. Then who? I'm just *Sadness,* mad. I don't love or hate because hate is no good and I don't love. I can *Angry* just sit here and be a void. It's just like last night when I ate and I felt that I was incapable of functioning as a human being and I was just a void. – – I have no reason to be a woman and I don't even care what I look like and I say to myself, why should I bother, so I let my hair down and become a slob and why should I even take a bath? And yet, I do. – – I feel like all of my. . . . . warm, feminine, lovely feelings have been completely rejected. There's no reason for them.

A: What's the detail of feeling that they have been rejected?

P: I don't know, but I feel that there's no reason for them. If I can't. . . . . I don't know. There's no reason to be a woman or pretty or to attract other men or to be fun or happy or to laugh, there's just no reason. It's natural to me but I don't want to feel that way.

A: So you still prefer to think of me as *actively* rejecting you rather than to accept the reality of the situation of this as inevitable and not an active rejection.

P: That makes it worse. The rejection I could do something about. *Sadness* Reality, I can't. I feel like the world is closing in on me. I know I must accept reality, but I don't want to. (Elaborates.) If only I could change reality, but I can't. I wish I could escape without facing it. If I could just hate you or hurt you or something. – – I wonder what it would be like to accept the fact and be able to love you anyway, and to have those warm feminine wonderful feelings again. I don't really feel. . . . . – – I can visualize what I want and it makes me happy but I just don't do it and I don't want to do it either. – – I feel like a little girl and I see myself as an adult but I'm not quite there. I can see myself loving you and having my warm wonderful feelings about you and then I leave here and I go with Tom and I start over and I have my warm wonderful feelings about him. I see no big problems ahead and our future is wonderful, and yet I stay here unhappy. – – I always pictured adult life as full of problems. It bothers me that I can't see any problems ahead. I just *can't*. – – My whole life is becoming new. I had a dream about Sally last night. (Laughs.) Every two years, and the two years was up and she was being taken away from me. How it hurt! It was absolutely horrible! My whole life is changing and we are going to leave the office and Tom is going to start practice and we're going to be in a different world and in a new house with new friends and all kinds of wonderful things. Everything in the past is being taken from me. Not only analysis. It's great! Most people are *never* this fortunate. It's great and yet, I don't want it. I do. – – When I left here yesterday I had a funny sensation as if I'd started to bleed or as if I'd been wounded and it was as if I'd been castrated. That's the way I think of my menstrual periods, that it's as if I'd been castrated every month. It's God's gift to woman and we call it the curse! I want to be negative, and to hate everything that I have and I wish that I didn't have anything and I didn't have a wonderful husband and three wonderful children and a wonderful house and a wonderful future and a wonderful body and a wonderful face and I hate it all!! – – – What do I want? I want to be ugly. I want to be. . . . . I guess I'm trying to say that I want to be a man and I want to be a little boy.– –

*Cry*

*Cry!*

**A:** I think you want to be able to go on saying that life is shitty. But when you have all of the positive things that you just described, you feel that there is no reason to go on feeling that way any more.

**P:** – – – – – – I'm so used to feeling hurt and unhappy and to have people to feel sorry for me. I have *no* reason to feel sorry for myself. But that's not me! I'm scared to death, God-damn it! If I want to, I could be happy and I could do it. There's absolutely no reason to be afraid except that I am.

**A:** You'd like to feel that you've gotten a series of shitty deals. The first one was that your mother didn't give you a penis. The next one was that your father didn't give you his. And in your life, this went on and on. And the final one now is that the analysis hasn't given you one either. Instead, you find out that you don't need one and that you can be happy without having one. I think you are scared to give up the final wish still to have a penis.

**P:** – – I can't imagine *not* being afraid to give it up. I'm (gestures with her fingers) this close to it and I back down. Like right now. I'm having such wonderful feelings about being a woman and I feel the sexual side of being a woman is wonderful, and then I back down. – – I see now why I want to leave here before I let go of all of my love feelings. If I do I let go of all desires for a penis. You bring this out in me and Tom does. I want to leave before it comes out.

A: And this is like the dream of the tooth. The tooth also represents the penis, but we'll stop here for today.

### DISCUSSION

The patient begins the session by describing her symptom recurrence in response to the transference experience of further separation here yesterday. The depression, anger, retreat from femininity, and the recurrence of eating represent regressive attempts to undo the process of extrusion and separation which had occurred yesterday in the conversion reaction at the end of the session. This progression of symptoms with the recurrence of the eating represents a reenactment of the conflict she had recognized in the "bolt of lightning," during the session, where frustration by the father stimulated a regressive recathexis of the mother. However, during the session itself I was not consciously aware of these specific connections to the conversion reaction, and my handling of the material indicates the failure specifically to make this connection. Her feeling of being "just a void" demonstrates how tenaciously she clings to the old oral fantasies of being empty if she gives up the childhood objects, and it is also a response to her awareness that doing so will result in ultimate transference frustration.

Once again she regressively experiences the situation between us as an active frustration and rejection by me of her femininity, and my interpretation of this transference experience of me as actively rejecting her femininity helps her to face this problem more clearly in the light of reality. But facing this reality evokes the sadness that accompanies the mourning process, although simultaneously she is able to see and anticipate the realistic pleasures and satisfactions that her life can offer if she voluntarily accepts the frustrations involved in renunciation of the childhood objects.

The dream about her daughter being taken away after two years represents losing the little girl in herself after the two years in analysis. But the same projective defense is manifest in the dream work as was used in her feeling that I am *actively* rejecting her because of her femininity. In the dream the little girl is being actively taken away from her, presumably by someone else. She goes on to illustrate further the ambivalent conflict between the wish for health and the transference resistance of remaining with me.

In response to the felt rejection of herself as a woman, the old wish for the penis and wish to have been a boy had been mobilized yesterday, along with a clearer recognition that the analysis is not going to provide one for her either. Her feeling as if she had started to bleed after the session and her equation of menstruation with castration are part of a total reaction condensed in the feeling of vomiting, and all this material is associated to the old fantasy stimulated by the sexual experience with the uncle that she had actually orally incorporated his penis. In this context the sensation of vomiting is likewise an expression of the defensive wish to get rid of the incorporated penis, but this also produces an intensification and regressive reactivation of the wish still to acquire it or to hold on to it. This sequence of material demonstrates how, in the termination phase, there occurs the need again to work through a conflict which had apparently been settled long ago in the analysis.

My first confrontation of her own realization that she has no rational justification to go on believing that life is "shitty" is focused at the level of her healthy ego in her attempts to free herself from the neurotic process. She goes on to elaborate on her realistic perceptions of this situation, and this permits me to make the rather lengthy interpretation of her continuing neurotic wish still to acquire a penis. Her response indicates her awareness of this continuing wish and at the same time, a recognition that she doesn't need it in order to be satisfied. It also demonstrates her wish to hold on to this fantasy and possibly leave the analysis before that complex is completely resolved. My recognition of this wish still to cling to the old fantasy leads me to remind her of the tooth dream from yesterday in which the tooth was hanging by a thin thread, and she was unsure whether or not to pull it out completely.

---

## SESSION 332

P: ------- I'm so nervous this morning that I can hardly swallow. I've been having my moods and if I'm not depressed then I'm nervous. I run and run and run and I'm scared to death. -- It's generally when I'm trying to act out on my adult feelings. I feel as if I'm *straining* out of a hole and I'm pulling myself out and it's making me so nervous. -- Last night I decided that this hanging on to being a child was for the birds. I really wanted to be an adult, to be a woman. It starts to come naturally and then I get scared. --- Last night Tom and I made love and all the time I went back and forth feeling like a chilo and feeling like a woman.

I'd start to relax and enjoy it and then the thought would come to my mind that my father and mother never enjoyed this. I'd feel bad about it and I'd feel guilty and then I'd try to talk myself out of it. Why would I think those ridiculous thoughts about my father? — — I think I figured it out. As a little girl, and I think this is true for all girls, your father is the only man in your life. You feel such love and sexual feelings and naturally they'd go to your father. But they must be channeled by your father to the right direction. I want to love daddy and be his wife and please him and to do things for him and to have him love me. Your father should let you know that you can't be, but that he loves you anyway. I feel guilty to put all of these feelings onto Tom. I feel bad to think that I'm crossing out my parents completely. I feel guilty to enjoy it with Tom, and then I feel hostile and I can't stand him. But I *will not* let these hostile feelings out on him. — — I figured out that one reason that I'm so upset about my sexual feelings for other men and theirs for me is that I had such a tremendous desire for my father and I felt that they'd replace him. But if I have no desire for my father then I don't have to worry and I can let my feelings out because I'll not act on them, and I don't really want to. But I'm still afraid of that in here. — — — I know that the minute that I accept the fact that you're not my father. . . . . Oh! . . . . . There will just be no reason to hate you. — — I don't know why I can't simply relax and have sexual feel-ings for you, but I can't. It's all so clear to me and the other is really so

*Excited* | ridiculous. It's just a beat around the bush and jump up and down and you're all upset and nervous for no reason at all. — — It's also admitting that I don't need you and that I'm as capable as you are to help myself. And it's not even sad. It's happy. But I can't take it. The woman I want to be wants to look at you and say that I have sexual feelings, but so what. It's like it would be with a man at a cocktail party but it will go no further. I *want* to kiss you goodbye and leave here and move into a new house and start my life. (Elaborates.) But I haven't reached that point yet. It's not even sad, and there's no reason why I should feel sad. — — It's all a vicious

*Sadness* | circle. Only when I admit who you are can I help myself. If I don't let my sexual and love feelings out then I can hang onto you. But if I left here like that, I would say to myself, "He's still my father and I still need

*Excited* | him." — — I think of you as the man and the symbol of my life. You who were so important to me! I can't imagine you *not* being important to me any more. You're just the past! You will not be important to me at all!

*Sadness* | I've outgrown you. — — — — If I sit here and concentrate on who you are, I *can* love you and have sexual feelings for you. I can just completely let them out. There's no reason for me to be scared or embarrassed. — — — — — —

It's so easy to do this outside of here and yet, I *can't* do it. It's too precious
to me and its *so* precious to me, it's *the* most precious thing in my life! --
Now I have gotten to the point that my sexual feelings aren't too physically
based any more. -- It means *much* more to me, *much* more.

*Upset*

A: What's the detail?

P: They're. . . . . for the first time I've let them be based on love. My
love feelings cause sexual feelings. That makes me vulnerable. The physical
feelings are safe. I don't care about them so much any more and they're
not that important to me. But with you and Tom they're based on love and
they are very precious to me. -- I'm trying to figure out how I can have
sexual *and* love feelings for Tom *and* for you and still keep them precious,
because they are. I feel they're very sacred things. For some reason, because
I *have* them for you, I feel that I *shouldn't*. -- I guess it's not wrong to
have them for you.

A: Any more than it was wrong for you to have had them for your
father as a little girl.

P: -- (Sigh.) – I can't decide if this is an excuse or if I'm honestly
afraid that you'll act on them. I think of myself as a girl with sexual feelings,
and I think that my father wasn't bothered, but he *was* bothered by them
as I grew up. And then there was my uncle! I enjoyed it, but l let myself go!
I don't think it's dirty or bad, but I just don't want it to happen! If I can
keep you in your place then I'm not scared. It's just when I turn you into a
father and an uncle that I get scared. I'm running back to being a little
girl again and I'm saying, "I'm just a little girl so you couldn't possibly have
sexual feelings for me." It's as if I'm asking you to let me be a woman. ---
I don't think that my fear is of you being like my father. It's in you *not*
being my father. That scares the hell out of me. It means that I *can* let
them all out. I *know* that you're not like my father. -- It's like trying to
believe in. . . . . I don't know what! I never experienced it before! I'm
scared to death! ---- I know there's absolutely *no* reason that I should
be scared of you. *Absolutely none.* ----------

*Anxiety*

A: We'll stop here for today.

### DISCUSSION

The patient begins the session by describing her anxiety at the prospect
of the realistic pleasures and satisfactions that an adult identity can offer,
and of her continuing oscillation between the progressive wishes toward
maturity and the regressive wishes to cling to the outmoded neurotic fantasies and objects. This is part of the working-through process and is a

continuation of work on the conflicts that had been further stimulated in yesterday's session. This material also illustrates the common neurotic occurrence of guilt feelings when the child experiences pleasures or successes which he feels the parents could never enjoy. Her generalized formulation of the oedipal phase of development and its healthy resolution represents another integrative step, in that she can see herself as having had conflicts about it which are not too dissimilar from those experienced by all girls. Although there are resistant elements in this, since it permits her to take greater distance from the immediacy of her own feelings, it is nevertheless also helpful in her movement toward mastery of these conflicts. She gives up the intellectualizing defense spontaneously as she indicates her own self-analysis of the sexual feelings toward other men and the fear that they would replace her desire for the father.

This material about the father leads to the immediacy of the transference feelings and the fear and guilt she still has at accepting her sexuality and desires toward me. Again she illustrates the ambivalence between the wish to renounce me as the transference object, and thereby move into her new life, as contrasted with the continuing wish to hold on to her childhood sexual fantasy in the transference. During this she alternates between excitement and sadness as the process of working-through goes on, and in the transference she experiences toward me the shift in our relationship that is simultaneously going on in her relationship to the father. In other words, as she described it earlier, the father is the most important male figure in a young girl's life, but in normal development this must gradually be changed and another man must eventually become more important to her as her chief libidinal object. The same is true in the analytic experience, and the idea that I will not be important to her in the future and that she will have outgrown me brings with it a sense of sadness illustrated by her affective response as she describes how precious these feelings are to her.

At this point she also describes a new level of integration and maturity as she indicates that sexuality is no longer primarily a physical experience for her, but that instead it is now increasingly based on and associated with love for the same object. However, there is still a lingering sense of guilt for these oedipal transference feelings which she tries to offset by her statement, "I guess it's not wrong to have them for you." My response, which interprets them in the context of the original, normal oedipal feelings, is an attempt to foster her efforts to dissolve these residual guilt feelings.

The effect of this interpretation is that she again works through the differentiation of me from her father and uncle, recognizing that whereas there were realistic possibilities of seduction in childhood, these are not present in the analytic situation. When she says, "It's as if I'm asking you to let me be a woman," she is referring to an important experience that she missed as a girl. She should have had the opportunity to experience her full sexual fantasy and love for the father without having to face a realistic possibility that such wishes would be overtly gratified. But because of the nature of her relationship to the father and uncle, experiencing her sexuality fully would lead her toward a dangerous and guilt-producing situation. And since the child had not yet matured enough to develop effective conscious controlling and integrative psychological mechanisms, she had to avoid the danger and guilt through the use of unconscious ego defenses such as repression, displacement, and regression.

My permitting her to have these kinds of experiences, drives, and feelings in the transference neurosis without a realistic risk that they would be gratified allows her sexuality to return to consciousness, to mature, and to become an acceptible part of herself, without needs for the previous unconscious defense mechanisms to cope with them. In other words, these experiences in the transference situation permit her to become increasingly confident of her conscious and rational controls and integrative mechanisms as a means of dealing with her sexuality, while at the same time accepting love and sexuality as an integral part of herself. The reality perception that there is now no reason for her to be scared of me is part of this process of strengthening her confidence in herself and her own controls.

## SESSION 333

P: – – – – – – – – I feel that I've been driven into a corner and I can't get out, and I can't take it. I just eat and eat until I stop feeling and thinking. If I'd just stop feeling and thinking I'd be so happy. I don't know what I'm afraid of. – – – – If I could get out of here I could make it regardless of whether I'm well or not. I just want to get out of here. I can't believe that this termination is scaring me this much, or whether my sexual feelings for you scare me this much that I'm just wild! Friday night I had a dream that was horrible. I was riding around in a car with Tom and I was driving. We passed an accident in the street. Because I was driving I had to look and I couldn't look away. There was a white car with a child, or maybe some children, in it and they were dead. – – – I don't know yesterday what happened to me. I woke up and I felt happy and good after five hours of sleep. I was so relaxed and Tom took the children to the office for a while. (Elaborates.) I enjoyed myself away from the children. I felt great and I

*Tense*

*Sadness, Cry*

*Anxiety*

felt all beautiful and I loved the world. And then Tom and I wanted to make love but we couldn't because of the children. I looked at Tom and his face looked so big! And then I started eating and I didn't stop. I ate and ate and ate!! – – If I could just think of something to relieve myself! I can't think of anything. – –

A: You mentioned that Tom's face looked so big. What are your associations?

*Upset,*
*Cry*

P: I don't know. It scared me. . . . . It was like. . . . . I was a child suddenly and he was a man. . . . . that's why that deal with my uncle scared me. I've been thinking so much about that lately. I just can't stand it and I think I will lose my mind. I can't *stand* to think! – –

A: What about the deal with your uncle?

*Anxiety,*
*Cry*

P: Do you know what it is? As a child I was rejected by my father and so I went to my uncle. Now I'm rejected here and I go to my husband. I can't stand it. I feel horrible! – – I'm so scared I feel I'll die and I can't breathe! – – The child is *scared* out of her mind. The only way to keep from going crazy is to realize that I'm an adult and that I have no reason for fear and I can control my life. That's fine and it takes care of the scared child, but then something else happens that scares me. . . . . last night we were watching TV and something there was bringing out my emotions. It was

*Cry*

about a girl who loved her father so much, but she had to tell her father goodbye. He was hurt, but he let her go. I cried and cried and I felt horrible and my body felt dead and it was awful. I stopped eating then. I had such a fear that I'd lose my mind and that I wasn't thinking right. It's so much easier to get mad and to say, "Go to hell, I hate you," and just walk out. It would be much easier for me and I don't know why. – – That's what I dreamed last night. There was a man who was a music instructor and he was so damned bossy. He controlled everything. There were all girls around and I was not in it, but I was watching and the girls were terrified. In the dream I felt that I'd tell him to go to hell and that I'd not take all that guff from the bastard. But all through it I had a headache and I couldn't get rid of it. I tried sleeping pills for it in the dream and it was all going on in a basement. – – I feel that if I don't decide on something soon I'll lose my mind. I keep thinking about my uncle and my father and that's all I can see. I even called Tom "Daddy." It's horrible! – –

A: On the one hand you say that you can't believe that the termination and your sexual feelings for me could cause all of this. And yet, we can see that these are the central issues in almost all of your thoughts at the moment.

*Tense*

P: – As long as I can get scared, I can think of myself as a child in here.

But I'll tell you one thing, and that is, that when I think of myself as a woman, it means not being afraid, because a woman isn't afraid and there's no reason to be. But I *am* and it bothers me and I don't want you to see me as a woman. – –

A: Why not?

P: I'm afraid that you're *not* very strong. Maybe I conjure it all up in my mind, but that's what I'm afraid of. I picture *myself* always having to be strong. But if I let myself go I *can't* be strong. All I know is that my father and my uncle and my husband and every man that I ever had sexual feelings for always responds! Even the ones I *don't* have sexual feelings for! – – – And if I try it and find that you don't respond then I'm absolutely facing the fact that you're not my father. On the one hand that looks nice to me and yet it scares the *hell* out of me because I know that's what's going to happen here. – – –

A: And when that happens, then it's time to say goodbye, because the child in you is gone. I think this is like the dead child in the dream. -

P: That makes me feel hysterical and I feel frantic!! – - I feel I have nothing to hold on to. – – All of my defenses scare me. That's wonderful! – – The more I think about it, the more I see the reason *for* my love feelings is the reason for my grief. If I hated you, I wouldn't be sad about leaving. If I thought that you weren't nice, I wouldn't be sad. It's funny but I've said that over and over and now suddenly I *believe* it. That's why I see you as my father or someone like him. I can hate and hate and say that you're horrible and stay here. Now I see you for what you *really* are and I have to leave. – –

A: And I think this is what you were trying to do in the dream last night. You attempted to avoid the grief by seeing the music teacher who represents me as someone who is mean and horrible and you don't want anything to do with him.

P: – – – – (Laughs.) – – –

A: We'll stop here for today.

## DISCUSSION

Once again the patient begins the session with a description of the recurrence of her symptom of bulimia as a means of coping with the affects which are part of her response to the termination conflict. This affective component is a mixture of anxiety and grief, and her wish, "To get out of here," whether she has resolved her problems or not, is a manifestation of the reluctance fully to experience and work-through the grief response. At the same time, however, this is not a serious prospect since in her healthy integrative functions she recognizes the needs to complete the analysis.

After mentioning the dream, she goes on to describe her relief of symptoms when she is able to experience herself as a more mature wife. The still tentative and temporary quality of this self-image is demonstrated by the fact that when in the real life situation this adult sexual response was frustrated, there was a regression indicated by the perceptual distortion of her husband's face. This in turn was followed by the symptom of eating, with the inability to alleviate her anxiety, as a symptomatic response to the emergence of the regressive conflict. The occurrence of a perceptual distortion such as her image of the husband's face is an indicator of a threatened emergence of an unacceptable drive, and therefore I choose to focus on this with my question about the husband appearing so large.

The patient shows that she understands that the distortion in size represents a return to a previous discrepancy in size relating to herself as a child, and she then indicates that the conflict over the sexual experience with the uncle has not yet been fully resolved. The return of this conflict at this time is again characteristic of the pattern during the termination phase of analysis when old conflicts must again be reworked and further resolved. Her response to this is a wish to continue the repression and suppression of this material, but my question about her associations to the situation with her uncle interferes with this defense. The patient is able to recognize the displacement that occurred in childhood from the father to the uncle, and the reexperiencing of this particular conflict and defense in the current transference relationship toward me, with a similar use of the husband as an object for displacement. At the same time the self-observing ego functions are manifest in her recognition that if she can continue to perceive herself as an adult, the anxiety and conflict that originated in the childhood seduction situation will be controlled, since as an adult it is no longer appropriate.

A derivative of the conflict over termination and the renunciation of the oedipal ties to me occurs in her response to the television program which has a clearly oedipal theme. When her grief was experienced consciously in the crying, the eating (as the previous defense against grief) apparently stopped. But then a new set of defenses to cope with this affective component is instituted by her mobilization of hostility and aggression against me. This new level of defense in turn leads to the recall of another dream about the music instructor, which is a similar representation of her conflict over loss of the object, using aggression as the defense against grief. The manifest dream also contains a reference to the uncle, in that it occurred in a basement. Another derivative of the same conflict occurs in her description of the slip in which she calls her husband, "Daddy."

Early in the session the patient had attempted a defense against the full impact of the termination conflict when she said, "I can't believe that this termination is scaring me this much." This resistance is a form of ego-splitting and isolation, in which the affective components and the cognitive understanding are not in keeping with one another. My tactical aim is to interfere with this defense, and therefore I remind her of her earlier statement and contrast it to the material that has emerged subsequently. This intervention has the desired effect of mobilizing her conflict more directly, accompanied by a significant increase in the intensity of her tension and anxiety. It then leads her to face and further work through the conflict over the reality of a sexual seduction if she permits herself to experience womanly feelings here. Even though this material has been gone over many, many times in the analysis, it still returns at this point and once again she has difficulty in differentiating me from the father and the uncle. As she herself says, the wish to maintain the transference fantasy that I will attempt a seduction of her represents the defense against "absolutely facing the fact that you are not my father."

This issue of the renunciation of the oedipal father through full recognition and acceptance that I am not he is the chief remaining therapeutic task in the analysis, and it is with this in mind that I point out to her how such a recognition means the end of her childhood. I choose to relate this back to the dream of the dead child, feeling that even though they were not specifically labeled as such, most of the patient's associations in this session are connected to that "horrible" dream. One could argue that there had as yet been no specific associations to the other dream elements such as the fact that she was driving, or the fact that the other car was white, and it is possible that had I chosen to focus on these elements, other conflicts might have been elucidated. However, it was my feeling that at this moment the termination conflict was the major one and there was a need for reworking of the oedipal wishes, and therefore I chose to handle it as I did.

Her response again indicates both the mobilization of conflict and also the recognition that resolution of the transference neurosis and renunciation of the oedipal attachments to me is not a personal rejection by me, but instead something which is inevitable and ultimately in her own best interest. She illustrates the deepening level of her awareness when she says, "I've said that over and over, and now suddenly I *believe* it." She also demonstrates that the transference distortion of me as father represents the wish still to hold on to him, whereas a recognition of me in reality represents giving him up. My final interpretation in regard to the dream of the music teacher is an attempt to illustrate this same mechanism from another perspective, and thereby again to show her that depreciation of a love object is partly a defense against separation and grief. The patient's laugh during the period of silence suggests that the interpretation is successful and that ego integration of these issues is occurring.

---

## SESSION 334

*Tense*

**P:** – – – – – – – – – – – I feel like my feelings are right up on my nose this morning. I'm so nervous! (Elaborates.) I wish my mind would just blank out. I wish I had the nerve just to get up and walk out of here! – – – – – – – – – – – – – I have a picture of myself letting these sexual feelings out and. . . . . – – – – I hate this! I don't want to go through this! I don't think I can! These sessions here are hell now and I hate them! It's honestly something that I don't want to do. – – When I'm thinking about you as someone else it's not so hard. But when I realize who you are, it's. . . . . Oh. . . . . –

**A:** Let's look at the detail of the difference.

**P:** I'm used to handling other situations. If I think of you as mother, it's easy, and if I think of you as my father then I'm hostile. And as my uncle, I can handle you. But if I think of you as you, I could fall apart and I just want to cry and I can't handle it. You sit there and are you and I'm

*Tense, Loud*

here and I'm me. You're *not* my father, you're not my husband, you're not my uncle, you're not my mother. It makes me feel . . . it makes me *me*. It draws me out from being a child and a patient. It makes me a woman and it makes me me. – – I've had sexual feelings for you before but they haven't ever bothered me this much. Nothing in my life ever has. I'm so nervous at home. I think of dying and I think of someone coming in and raping me and I think I could go crazy and I can't breathe and I have all kinds of symptoms. (Elaborates.) I'd rather think of *all* of these things than to think about my sexual feelings for you! – – – – – – – – – – – – – –

**A:** What are your associations to all of the silences today?

**P:** I don't have anything to say. – – All I want to talk about are my sexual feelings and I can't. So I have nothing. Now I'm mad that I can't and that I'm not allowed to.

**A:** What's the detail?

**P:** It's just a feeling. I'm seeing a picture and it's like a dream that I'm doing it. I let it all out and you accept them. I'm expressing my sexual feelings and my love for you. But I can't do it, because it's only a dream and I've gone this far before. – – – I start to have sexual feelings and they seem natural and they start to come out and I can't let them and so I get depressed and frustrated and mad. – – –

**A:** You have the feeling that you're not allowed to let them out. What are your associations?

**P:** I've had them before for my father. I can remember sitting there and looking at him and boring a hole in him with these feelings. That's as far as I ever got. – – As a little girl I took his embarrassment and his getting up and walking out of the room as rejection. I felt like a dunce. That's the way I feel right now. It's like I'm feeling, "Who am I to have these feelings for you?" – – And then there's my uncle. Frankly I can't take either one of them again. – – And I know you won't react either way, and that's the most frightening of all.

**A:** Let's see what makes it the most frightening.

**P:** Because I don't know how to handle it. When I let go, I let go! I can just picture it. – – It all boils down to the question, can you handle it? If I let go, I *can't* handle it. I'll let go and I know I'm supposed to and so it's all up to you and I just wonder how much you realize that? – – – – – – – – – – *Anxiety*

**A:** We'll stop here for today.

## DISCUSSION

Once again the patient illustrates the mobilization of conflict over experiencing her sexual drives, accompanied by mounting anxiety and the defensive wish to walk out of here in order not to face them. My matter-of-fact question interferes with her defenses and tacitly encourages her to try to face the conflicts more directly. Still accompanied by anxiety, she again goes over material which has been so frequently brought up in the transference perception of me, as compared with the recognition of reality which forces her to face herself in the adult role as an independent, adult sexual woman. Again she illustrates how, in the working-through process, the intensity of the sexual drives and her conflicts over them is greater during the termination phase than it was earlier in the analysis. She also illustrates how the exacerbation of her various psychological and somatic symptoms represents a defense against these underlying sexual conflicts. Painful as these symptoms are, they are nevertheless preferred over experiencing the full impact of her sexual drives.

My understanding of the lengthy silences is that she is struggling over the conflict between the psychic forces pushing toward maturation (which involve experiencing the full impact of her feminine sexuality), and the continuing regressive transference wishes and fantasies of me as father or uncle (which involve a continuing attachment to the oedipal object, but with the expression of such fantasies in an attenuated and childlike form). In an attempt to bring this conflict to greater conscious expression, I therefore choose to ask her about the silences themselves. In response to this she indicates the pressure of her sexual drives, but she also attempts the defensive projection to me that I do not allow her to express them here. My question about her not being allowed to do so here is an attempt to block the use of this projective defense mechanism, and it results in the elaboration of her memory of the intensity of sexual fantasy about the father, and of his embarrassed rejection of those feelings. Again she seeks to see me in the transference role as father rejecting her overtures, or uncle responding to them with sexual seduction, but this is immediately followed by the more reality-oriented perception of me as not reacting in either way. And when I focus on why this should frighten her so much, I encourage her to face a relatively new situation of conflict in which she permits herself to experience her drives fully and to rely on me and my controls in this situation, leading to an acceptance of her sexual feelings without a seductive acting-out response. Facing the possibility of seduction in the analytic situation is accompanied by heightened anxiety, but the working-through process requires that she cope with such a conflict directly and openly.

This current conflict over the possibility of realistic seduction again illustrates how important it is that the analyst maintain a situation of transference abstinence for the patient. In spite of the intensity of her transference wishes, it is only the realistic perception of me as an analyst in control of myself and the situation, and the expectation that I will *not* respond to her at a direct sexual level, that permits her the full range of experience of her own sexuality. Earlier in the analysis, if I had been overtly seductive, or if I had gratified some of her transference demands, this realistic perception of me and my role would not be possible, and the anxiety and guilt over real sexual seduction would have prevented her from experiencing her full sexual desire and drives. It would therefore have made it necessary for her to maintain the various repressive, displacement, projective, etc., defenses against her sexuality, and as a result the significant conflicts over these issues would not have been resolved.

---

There is a severe snow storm with hazardous driving conditions and cars are stuck with long delays and traffic tieups. The patient calls about forty minutes after her hour was to have started to say that she had tried to come but was unable to get through the traffic and apologizes for not being able to get in for her hour.

---

## SESSION 335

**P:** – – I'm so depressed today and I'm so tired of all of this that I just can't stand it. You know and I know, and I just know. It hits me like a ton of bricks that I'm giving up and that I'll never have what I dreamed of getting as a child and those are my fantasies about my father. – – Every time I do this I get depressed, and I'm so tired of acting like a child and I don't want to act that way any more and it gets me nowhere. – – But I *feel* like a child and I feel like stamping my feet and yelling, and I'm so God-damned mad about it that I can't stand it! – – I'm so tired of trying to see this and to react to it in an adult way! I can't! It makes me madder than shit and it always will! – – – – – – – – – Every time I come in here I'm faced with this fact and I'll never be happy about it. As much as you've done for me. . . . . I'll never be happy about it and I'll never be. . . . . . – – I feel that I want to hurt you the way that you've hurt me. – – But when I start thinking of hurting you and getting back at you, I realize how stupid it is. You haven't really hurt me, not you. And then I don't know *what* to do! Shit! – – When I start being happy and appreciating everything that I have and thinking why should I go on beating my head against the wall, something inside of me says, "Don't give up, don't ever give in to your father. It's for his sake and not mine that I'm miserable." It's a battle. If I give up then I'm saying, "It's all right. You've hurt me and you took knives and drilled them into me ten times a day, so it's all right." The only way that I can ever do that is not to care and to not need you.

**A:** Let's look at the detail of the thought that it's for *my* sake that you don't give up and that you're miserable.

**P:** I don't know. Suddenly my mind is a blank and I can't even think.

*Sadness*

*Angry*

*Cry*
*Sadness*

*Loud*

*Cry*

*Cry!*

*Sadness*

I don't want to be unhappy. I hate this, but I think about being happy. . . . . and I feel like I'm. . . . . I think. . . . . if I'm happy then I'm giving in to you and I'm letting you get by with all of this shit that you dumped all over me. Then I stop and think. . . . . I don't know, good God! It's not really there, it's not really *there* any more. So why am I making myself miserable? I don't know. I *know* that you're not my father, so why don't I take advantage of all that you've done for me? You've brought out feelings in me that are wonderful and that were never there before, and that can let me live. So it doesn't matter that you're not my father. But I can't give up because then I have no purpose with my father any more and I can't cure him and I can't help him and there's nothing. It's the stupidest fantasy that I've ever had. -- The only way I could keep you my father is to get mad at you and leave here mad, but I can't, because I love you and you've brought out many wonderful feelings in me. So I have to give up my father. I feel like I'm losing my father and it's killing me. I'm losing my parents! They are just people. That's all they are. I'm losing everything, and it's hurting me and it kills me! I've already lost my parents and my past and I've lost everything, and now I'm going to lose you. They're all dead! That's the way I want them. I don't want to bring any of this stuff up again. I'm so tired of it! -- But it's all gone and I'll leave here and never get any of it back, but I don't want it back! I can't believe it! I can't believe that I'm losing you! -- You've given me so much and now you're leaving. Sometimes I wonder if I wanted it in the first place knowing that I'd lose you. --

**A:** I wonder if you have the feeling that to grow up and to be happy with Tom is to be disloyal to me, or to be ungrateful to me?

**P:** – Even though I know that you don't hold me, that's true, and there is some feeling there. Even though I know that you want me to be happy, it's like you're old and you've lived your life. I feel that I'm young. . . . . not only have you brought me love in here, but what goes with you is analysis, and I don't want any more analysis. It's the most unpleasant experience in my life. But I love you. -- Oh God, I hope that doesn't hurt you! But that's your job, and it *is* unpleasant to your patients. -- I can't imagine leaving you here to do this to another patient. I love you and I want to take you with me with my love. I feel like I'm leaving you here with the analysis I went through which is all *blackness*. And *I'm* going off lighthearted and happy. The other I want to leave here, but the love I don't want to leave. --- When you love someone you want to please them. If I can't be remaking your life and making you happy, then the way I can is to leave and to make *my* life happy and to build on what you've given me. And I'm not doing it to make you love me. I'm doing it because I love you. -- Suddenly you seem like 180 to me, and I'll be so shocked when I look at you. --

**A:** You haven't said anything yet about your feelings when you couldn't get here yesterday.

**P:** I felt as if I'd failed and as if I'd done something that I wanted to do. I did it all day. I was not going to drag three children to the club There comes a time when you *must* think of yourself. I'm sorry! I'm sorry! That really upsets me.

**A:** What's the detail of the upset?

**P:** That I put my life and myself ahead of you and the analysis. I put myself before other people. There's no reason that I *should* feel that I've failed, but I felt, "It's just too much and it's too much trouble to get there." I tried. -- You've given me a lot of strength and so now I'll leave you and I wonder if you will dissolve and fall apart because I've taken you with me and I've taken all of the *good* parts of you. Sometimes I feel that it would be better if *I* died because I'm afraid that this will kill you. --- I wonder if I'll ever come to the point where I realize that I don't need you and that you don't need me? Just what is really real in here? --- Now I have a sudden thought that I can love you and have sexual feelings for you and be happy in my life and love other people. It's the greatest feeling in the world! -- It's like I'm so happy to have known and loved you and I want to take advantage of it. ---

**A:** We'll stop here for today.

### DISCUSSION

Once again, with affective accompaniments, the patient returns to the ambivalent conflict over termination, and her recognition of the requirement of giving up the cherished infantile and childhood fantasies that she has sustained for so long. She manifests both the sadness and the angry wish to have a temper-tantrum and to hurt me in the transference. And at the same time, there is the adult recognition of the unreality of these reactions, but followed immediately by the return of the wish not to give up. Implied in these adult recognitions is the necessity to give up her transference wish for revenge, and the need for acceptance of the fact that although she was hurt in childhood, it is now too late to do anything about it.

As she is presenting this material, I am struck by her statement, "It's for his sake and not mine that I'm miserable," and I feel that this passing comment might be an indicator of a still-unresolved fantasy keeping her attached in the oedipal relationship. In order to explore and elaborate upon this, I ask my question, interpreting it directly into the transference relationship to me as the father. Initially her response is the defensive one of being blank, but this is followed by the transference experience of the need for giving up the wish for revenge upon me, which is accompanied by sadness and grief. Although she attempts to recognize the reality of the situation between us, and of what has been done for her in the analysis, the fantasy of curing her father emerges more clearly, and the idea of giving up this fantasy again represents losing him to the past. She is ambivalent about this, oscillating between the adult recognition that continuing to relive her childhood is not appropriate, and the childhood wish to cling to me (father) and thereby make up for past disappointments and frustrations.

Her description of her sense of continuing responsibility for the father and his welfare, which is repeated in the transference, suggests to me that this unrealistic sense of obligation to him is not only a continuing wish to maintain the attachment to him, but is also a source of some ambivalence for her. The tactical issue is to help the healthy and integrative elements of her personality to recognize the unreality of such a sense of responsibility for me (father), and thereby to foster movement in the direction of maturation. It is this reasoning which leads me to make the interpretation regarding her feeling of disloyalty to me if she were to grow up. Her response is to elaborate on this feeling of guilt at the thought of leaving me and at the thought that I am now old, whereas she is in the prime of her adult life. Another derivative of this transference conflict is the fantasy of leaving me with the blackness of her analysis, while she leaves happy and free.

Her statement, "I'm not doing it to make you love me, I'm doing it because I love you," is a highly significant one. "Doing it" in order for me to love her would be a form of transference resistance in which she would be relinquishing a particular form of attachment in order to achieve the underlying infantile gratification in the transference. "Doing it" independently of my love and for herself because it is the appropriate thing to do represents a more mature, and therefore more lasting, kind of motivation.

Because she has not yet mentioned it spontaneously, and because I anticipate she would have reactions to the missed session yesterday (since this is so unusual for her), I choose to point out her omission of any mention of it. Her response is a mixed one, reflecting a sense of guilt and fear that she has disappointed me, and at the same time a healthy form of narcissism and need to do what is appropriate and best for herself, even if this runs the risk of disappointing the love object.

At the end of the session she again experiences a transference to me as the father toward whom she feels a guilty obligation, when she fantasies that I may "dissolve and fall apart" because she is leaving me. But this is spontaneously followed by the adult perception of the reality situation and her further recognition of us as two separate individuals. "I wonder if I'll ever come to the point where I'll realize that I don't need you and that you don't need me?" Having recognized this, she can then go on to a positive adult experience and feeling about herself. Her final statement, "It's like I'm so happy to have known and loved you and I want to take advantage of it," is analogous to the healthy adult recognition of the importance of the role of the parents in growing up, accompanied by the acceptance of the fact that parental influence and importance gradually fade as the child matures and finally a new kind of peer-like relationship must take its place. In this sense the process of termination is also somewhat analogous to the phase of normal adolescent emancipation and separation from old parental ties.

# 13

# THE TWENTY-FOURTH MONTH

## SESSION 336

**P:** – – – – – – I keep wondering if normal people ever get just plain scared like I do. I sit and suddenly get so frightened that I can't think and I feel my mind will blank out and I'll get hysterical. That's the way I've been all week. – – I break through one emotion and there's another huge one facing me. I guess that's the way it's always going to be. – – – I had the funniest dream. I went to a party and I was in a long ball gown. I looked beautiful and I walked into the room and there were millions of people around. I was stuck talking to one person all night long. I wanted to leave and I had a strong desire to, and so I did. And then I was walking with some children and we were poor and we were on a long road and we had no shoes. I knew that if we went on and got there we'd be all right. There were others with us who wouldn't make it, like Helen. I was sorry for them, but I couldn't stop to help. I had enough to do to handle my own problems. I had the three children with me. I was wheeling the buggy and Sally was walking in my shoes. I was afraid that she'd never make it. And then there were two men and they were huge, and my fear was that they were going to kill me. But I said to myself, "I have to go on and face them." One was a Negro and he couldn't speak English, but then we were walking together and I felt, "Why was I ever afraid, because we're going to the same place." He said that he was bleeding and I was too, but I forgot to use anything to stop it. I said, "There are only two more hours and I'll make it." – – – – I could figure it all out except for the bleeding and the man bleeding, I can't understand. – – – All weekend long I had periods of hours that I'd feel so happy and content with my family and it was wonderful, and then my mind would snap as if I'd just come back from being crazy or as if I'd lost my mind. Then I'd snap out of it and then I'd eat and then I wouldn't eat. – – Friday I felt like something had been taken off of me and I felt that I'd burst through a door that I'd been trying to get in. – – It was like suddenly I see this whole situation for what it is. – – When I think about letting you down it's so different from what I used to be. It's *not* a torrid, passionate love affair. I think you're so nice and I love you and I feel so soft and warm about you. Occasionally I think how nice it would be to be your wife, but it's just a thought and I really don't want to be because it's just not the right situation. I feel separate from you and I have my life to lead and it's separate from yours, and yet I still love you very much and I still love to feel like a woman around you. – – I feel like I'm going out on my own to sink or swim and I can never come back to you. – – I'm scared! God, I can't tell you how scared I am. – – – The biggest fear with leaving here is that I. . . . . it brings up the old fear that I used to have of losing my father and losing the penis and I have nothing and I'm just going to die. – – If I talk to myself I know that's *not* what's really happening. – – –

**A:** You mentioned that you understood everything about the dream except the bleeding. What are your associations to that bleeding?

**P:** For myself I'm doing it now. It's always been such a *thing* with me. – –

**A:** What's the detail?

**P:** I think about the first time that I started, and I was so proud and I wanted the world to know but no one cared. So I turned it to something bad. I used to have cramps and I'd stay home and I'd vomit. My father would come up each time to see me about my appendix and he'd punch my stomach. I wanted to think that I hated it, but really I loved it. It's important to me that I love being a woman now and that I leave you wanting to be a woman. But about the man, I don't know. I wonder where was he bleeding from? Had I hurt him? – – I don't know who the man was. It wasn't Tom, because I was going to Tom. And it wasn't you, because I'd left you. It was just a man, a sexual man. But why was he bleeding? It's like Tom, and I think of him as my mother at times and. . . . . – It didn't bother me too much in my dream. – – I suddenly think about a TV show that I saw and Oliver Wendell Holmes. It came to my mind yesterday and I got so depressed. I *don't* want to think of you as an old man because that will not help me. I must think that men are men and I'll be attracted to them and they to me and that's that! There's no need for it to cause all of these emotions in me! I can't castrate every man I see just so that he's not dangerous. – – – –

**A:** And what are your associations to Sally walking in your shoes in the dream?

**P:** – – Was I thinking that it was me? I don't think so, because *I* was there. It's the way I. . . . . the heels are a sign of being grownup. – – I can put myself in her place now and she does try to be grownup so often and to wear my shoes and to do what I do. I got the feeling. . . . . why should she pretend? She has her own shoes to wear, so why should she wear mine and make it twice as difficult to walk? But she'd rather pretend and have trouble walking. -- God, I don't know. -- Suddenly I feel 100 years old. I'm not decrepit but I'm mature and adult. I look at my daughter and I say, "I know exactly how you feel. You want to be an adult but you're still a little girl and you have plenty of time, so don't sweat it." -- That's the way I feel here. No matter how old I am or how adult, I still have these love and these sexual feelings for you. It's me, just me, Betty Ann. It's not as a mother or a wife or a little girl. It's just *me*. That's all. --- I've been thinking that I have to be so much older than I am for you. And now I suddenly don't *have* to be. I'm young. -- I'm so scared! I don't really care about all of this other. I'm *me* and I love you and I'll miss you something terrible but I'm not going to try to be anything else. -- Now I feel that I can't *stand* the thought of leaving here. It's going to be horrible. -- I don't understand it but I feel as if I've taken off this huge *mask* of a woman and yet I'm *not* a little girl. I don't care. -- I feel absolutely *wide open*. --- Suddenly I feel like a little tiny child and I'm scared! ------- I feel as if for the first time the real *me* has said, "I love you," and I mean you. Not my father or my mother or my uncle or anyone else, and it's the real *me*, and I'm scared.

> **Cry**

**A:** We'll stop here for today.

At the door the analyst gives the patient the bill for the previous month.

### Discussion

Once again the patient begins the session with a description of symptoms that are now intermittently recurring during the termination phase. After the brief silence, she goes on to describe a rather lengthy dream, the manifest content of which partly involves feelings of confidence in herself and in her ability to do what she wants; the capacity to leave someone with whom she has been talking for a long time; the ability to face a situation which momentarily evokes anxiety for her; and a generalized sense of confidence that she will be able to get where she was going. Her statement that she could figure it all out except for the element of bleeding is another indicator of her capacity at least to try to analyze her own dreams. There is a strong likelihood that she is not able fully to understand all the latent dream thoughts and unconscious dream meanings, but inasmuch as she is currently making the effort to analyze herself on her own, and to establish herself as an independent individual who is separate from me, I feel that it would be inappropriate to challenge her understanding of the dream at this time. To do so would be to emphasize her continuing needs for me and my help in dream interpretation, whereas not to challenge her would reflect my acceptance of her growing independence from me.

After a brief silence she again describes the oscillation between her progressive achievement of maturity with the satisfactions that accompany it, and the regressive return of symptoms. She refers back to the transference experience in last Friday's session, where she had taken a further conscious step towards separation and individuation of herself from me, indicating that she had felt relieved by it and that her capacity to see and feel the reality of our relationship is increasing. She describes her increasing ability to see me as separate from herself, and yet still to have generally positive, though not such intense, feelings about me. Her statement, "Occasionally I think how nice it would be to be your wife, but it's just a thought and I really don't want to be because it's just not the right situation," is a sign of the gradual dissolution of the oedipal attachment in the transference neurosis. The fantasy is still there, but its intensity is diminishing, and the perception of the reality situation is increasing, with recognition of the needs for renunciation without a personal sense of rejection, but also without a sense of guilt for the occurrence of these feelings. This is followed almost immediately by a brief regressive return of her anxiety about taking such a maturing step, and to the fantasies that she will have nothing. But again the progressive and integrative mechanisms take over, although she still needs conscious and self-conscious awareness and talking to herself to maintain the difference between reality and the transference.

At this point I feel that she is generalizing, and to reduce this defense I therefore choose to focus on the specific dream elements which she herself said she had not been able to understand. Once again her response is a generalized one, but my request for details easily overcomes this resistance so that she is now able to fill in a bit more about her specific experiences with her menstrual periods. This material also supports the analogy, mentioned in the discussion of the last session, between termination and the psychic changes that occur during adolescence. The ego capacity now to tolerate what were previously unacceptable impulses and drives is illustrated by her statement, "I wanted to think that I hated it, but really I loved it," in reference to the father's "punching" her stomach as a disguised sexual acting-out.

She continues to associate to the element of the man who was bleeding by asking herself a number of pertinent questions about it, thereby illustrating her capacity to carry on the work of analysis on her own. The meaning of this dream element becomes clear with the sudden apparently random association to the TV show, which then permits her spontaneously to analyze the dream as involving the defensive wish to see me as sexually nonthreatening. However, she is able immediately to recognize the defensive nature of this and to accept in consciousness the possibility that she may have sexual fantasies about other men without the need for anxiety, or the need to act on such feelings, or the defensive need symbolically "to castrate every man I see."

My question in regard to the dream element of her daughter walking in the patient's shoes elicits another indication of the changes that are occurring within her. Her associations demonstrate an increasing capacity for empathy with her child and a willingness to accept the child's feelings and motivations, while at the same time maintaining her perspective as an adult and not overly identifying with the child. Following this there is an acceptance of the generation difference between us, but with a continuing perception of herself as an adult woman, and a further expression of her capacity now to accept herself as she is. This is followed almost immediately by the realization that such an acceptance of herself signifies the approaching end of the analysis, and of the relationship to me, and this mobilizes the affect of sadness which accompanies such a realization.

After the relatively long silence, she is able to express directly the fact that she has permitted herself the significant emotional experience of feeling love for me without defensive or regressive distortion or undoing. This experience still mobilizes anxiety for her, but it is tolerable and she is able to master the anxiety through conscious ego controls. This reaction is the result of the internal psychic changes that have been progressively taking place, but it also serves as a prototype for the development of new psychic structures for adaptation to such experiences in the future.

---

## SESSION 337

Patient gives the analyst the check which is signed with her husband's signature for the first time in the analysis.

**P:** – – – I feel on top of the world! What's wrong? It's so great I feel like shouting! It's as if I've just waked up from a terrible dream. It scares me. But for the first time I know who you are, and that you're *not* my father. I think I put the puzzle together and I've figured out the whole thing. Before the analysis I was in a constant fight to have my father. If I didn't eat, then I could be my father's mistresses, and it was all sexual. But I had my children, so by eating I suppressed my sexual feelings and I was still trying to have my father. I must give up my father and then I don't have to eat *or* be a bitch. Tom is *not* my father and if I eat it is not the same thing as going back to my mother. But I don't have to do either one if I don't want my father! – – I *feel* such a sense of relief! It all has to do with giving up my father. I've spent my whole life trying to get my father. I tried to do it through eating. I tried it through the ideas of sex outside of marriage, but having children interfered with all of this and I couldn't take it. I couldn't stand *not* having my father, so I'd return to my mother. Monday, after I left here, it dawned on me that you are *you*. I was sick and really scared at first. – – I guess it happens to every person who becomes an adult. For instance, you go to college or you get married and you leave home, and you must break away. This is what I want and I know that it will lead to happiness and that it's right and it's good. But the temptation stays so great! But everyone does it. It will be a struggle for a while, but I know it's right. I don't really *want* to, but I know that I *have* to do it or else I'll *never* be happy and grownup and be the things that I want to be. I have a *lot* of growing up *still* to do but I can't stay still or I'll regress. All of my dreams have been about climbing hills or walking long distances, but I know I'll make it, but it's harder than hell. – – – – – Yesterday I wondered if it would be wrong of me . . . . . to adopt you as a father, and use you as a backboard for my emotions. I mean as I remember you. I guess that's the way I *do* look at you. I still have a little trouble placing my sexual feelings. I see you as someone I have all of these feelings for to the ultimate, but that's that and that's as far as it goes. I have no tremendous desire to *have* you or to seduce you. – – I have to face the fact that you're a man and I'm a woman. – – I have all the warm wonderful womanly love for you and then my sexual feelings come in and I don't know what they are exactly. But I'm losing the feeling that I have to act out on them with you. I know that this belongs to Tom and I. – – About my father, it bothers me to realize . . . . . that if you're *not* my father, then no one is. It scares me. I'm at the end, and I can go no further. If I can't get it from you then I'm not going to get it from anyone and I'll accept that fact, but then who do I cling to when I'm scared? I feel that I love you as you, because you've done *so* much for me and you're such a good therapist and you've let all of these new feelings come out which I never had before. But I can't depend on you for all of that awful old stuff any more. I have to depend on myself. I've tried the religion bit and it doesn't work and I've gone as far as I can medically. I must now depend on myself. – – I think of you as being you and I feel desperate and I have a fear of cutting my wrists. It bugs me! But it's like if I do, maybe my father will pop up somewhere! – – – Oh shit! So what! God! It's up to me. I either make it now, or I don't make it. – – I feel as if I've been living with my father up to now and I'm not going to from now on. I don't know what it's like. – – – – – – It's all so easy to say and to figure out. I guess I just have to *live* with it for a long time. I *know* that I don't need a father or need a penis. I have everything in the world that I need, and I have strength. I know all of these things but it still makes me hysterical. – –

**A:** You mentioned that you'd like to adopt me as a father after you leave, and as you remember me. What comes to your mind about this?

**P:** I think of you with love and as someone I loved very much. You made me happy and even if I never see you again I can think back on this and it helps me. Is that wrong? – – It's so much better than hating you. I don't think that I *can* hate you. It's a feeling I never had for my father.

*Cry* | But I *do* now. I can think of the times that he loved me, but he hurt me and so it's not totally. You've *never* hurt me. – – I *don't* want to leave here. If I do I want to love you and profit from what you've done and *not* regress and hate and act like a child as I always used to. You've given me no cause to hate you. You just have been honest with me and helped me as a doctor. Others have. Even Tom does sometimes. – – I feel it's secure leaving someone like that. But it's so unnatural here. You're not allowed to have human emotions like a real father would. – – It dawns on me that I have accepted the fact that there has been no interacting of emotions between us and that you're not secretly hating me or secretly loving me. – – I can't tell you how nervous I am! I *want* to do it. My thoughts to kill myself and go crazy can go to hell. I *want* to be an adult and to be happy. Those thoughts are my past and I *don't* need them. – – I'm scared to death to love and to accept life and what it gives, but I'm going to do it and I will live through the fear and eventually it will go away. Because realistically there's nothing to fear. It's just what I've lived through. – – – But I'll not charge out of here and live through my life like a big, strong Amazon. I just can't do it. – – It's not as if the hate has gone. This thought to cut my wrists is suppressed hate. I can't do anything about it. It will not help me and there's no *real reason* to hate you. I may feel it some-

*Cry* | times but I don't want it to grow. – – Now I think how *sad* it is that I
*Softly* | have to leave here, but I *do* have to leave. And I know what I have to do. – – I've been walking around wide open with my backbone showing. Now

I want to close it up because I'm tired of it. But when I do, I close you up too. It's frightening and sad but I *want* to. The only way I can is to remember you the way I want to. – – The way I'm going to remember you is as someone that I've loved very much. I'm all soft inside as I think of it. You're someone I idolize and someone I admire and you let me do all of this and you're so strong. It's sad that I can't live with you forever, but I can't. We all must face it some time, and I know I can't ever pay you back. – – Even though you've never said anything, I feel that you accept me as a person and as a woman and just as I am. You believe in me. – – I think you do. – – – – – –

A: We'll stop here for today.

## DISCUSSION

Throughout this session the patient expresses and elaborates upon the emotional transference experience that occurred at the end of the last session. In this she demonstrates that she has achieved a new and deeper level of emotional awareness and synthesis, and with this a further development of the new psychic structures that are taking the place of the old maladaptive structures which had evolved out of the oedipal fixation. The emotionally meaningful insight that she has worked to achieve is now being put to effective use and helps her in the structural reorganization of personality that is occurring, and permits the resumption of psychic development that was partially fixated at the time of the childhood oedipal phase.

Her description of the analytic work she has done between sessions again reveals the extent of her psychological growth and ego-capacity now to accept consciously the previously unacceptable oedipal drives. Her recognition that she doesn't really want to give up the father, and yet knows that she has to do so in order to be happy as a grownup, reflects the growing voluntary acceptance of the oedipal renunciation. And the dreams of climbing hills or walking for long distances but knowing that she will succeed indicate her growing confidence in herself and in her own integrative capacities. That this is not a flight into health is indicated by her acceptance of the continuing uncertainty about her sexuality. The oedipal wishes persist but in a weakened and much attenuated intensity. This reduction in the intensity of her oedipal drives reflects an economic as well as structural change occurring with the dissolving of the oedipus complex. The sexual drives themselves have been freed from repression and/or other unconscious defensive adaptations, and there is now developing an increasing structural reorganization and capacity for conscious and voluntary control, and for age-appropriate full drive discharge. Less of her psychic energy is now bound in defensive functions.

There is an increasingly solid perception of me as her therapist, and a sense of past dependency upon me, but an increasing recognition of her own capacities and of her needs to depend upon herself. Her statement that "You've let all of these new feelings come out which I never had before" is a reference to one of the important factors in the therapeutic process. I have permitted her to use me as a transference object, and have accepted the various regressive manifestations of her unconscious psychic life. I have been able to maintain the therapeutic and analytic situation and atmosphere in spite of the transference provocations, and have been able through interpretations to help her increase her confidence in her own ability to deal with her inner psychic drives. And as a result, the old drives, which previously had evoked anxiety and guilt accompanied by multiple unconscious defensive maneuvers, could now gradually return from repression and be experienced by her in consciousness as an integral part of herself. This experience in the transference relationship, supported by my analytic activity and attitude, permits her in an affective way to become conscious of the important element in her psychic life from which she was previously cut off by the neurotic unconscious defense mechanisms. Through repeated transference experiences she is able, as if for the first time, to accept her sexuality as a part of herself, and to experience her own capacities to control these drives and their objects through conscious integrative and synthetic ego-activity. As a result of these experiences, what was once a fantasied and reality danger can now be tolerated in consciousness because the developing of new structures means that this situation is no longer the danger situation that it once was.

However, this forward progress is not made without a brief reexperiencing of conflict and temptation toward regression, as in her statement about cutting her wrists, accompanied by the fear and sense of desperation at giving up the neurotic attachment. There is a brief fantasy that if she cuts her wrists, "Maybe my father will pop up somewhere," but again this is brief and is quickly overcome by the maturing ego acceptance of reality.

My one intervention during the entire session is to focus on the comment made in passing that she wants to adopt me as a father after the analysis. The reasoning behind this is that I need to assess to what extent she anticipates some type of continuing relationship with me after termination of her treatment, either in fantasy or in reality. One sign of an incomplete resolution and dissolution of the transference neurosis is a patient's continuing expectation, wish, or fantasy that after the analysis has been terminated, some type of ongoing relationship with the analyst may then be possible. Her response suggests that her expectation is not that of an ongoing active relationship, but rather of remembering someone who in the past had once been important in one's life. In this way it is similar to the normal adult, who though now mature and able to function independently, will still retain a memory of parental and other important figures in his life who have helped him to mature and develop, and for whom there will always be a fond affection. But for the mature person, such past figures are no longer an active, dynamically necessary force in the individual's psychic experience. Another characteristic feature is that as she resolves this issue with me and permits me to fade into the past as someone who once was important in her life, she is then able to do somewhat the same thing in regard to the true father. "It's a feeling I never had for my father. But I *do* now."

Another interesting phenomenon is the fact that in spite of all the pain, rejection, frustration, rage, and other unpleasant affects she has experienced in the transference neurosis, she is still able to say, "You've *never* hurt me." This reflects the fact that in spite of the intensity of her transference experience, there is and has been sufficient self-observing reality-oriented ego function to permit a recognition and acceptance of the fact that my aim has been therapeutic and not aggressive or personal. This perception would be analogous to the professional, realistic necessity for a surgeon to inflict pain on his patient as part of the process of appropriate treatment. The same observational capacity is reflected in her statement that she is now increasingly accepting of the fact that there has not been a real emotional interaction between us, and that I do not have secret affective responses toward her.

Again the healthy maturing forces and functions help her assess the needs for continuing working-through, as in her statement, "I will live through the fear and eventually it will go away." But there is also a healthy acceptance of some persistent anxiety and symptomatology which will only gradually subside. This is again followed by a return to the experience and working-through of the grief reaction of sadness at leaving. But during this she makes the significant statement, "I've been walking around wide open with my backbone showing. Now I want to close it up because I'm tired of it. But when I do I close you up too. It's frightening and sad, but I *want* to." Here she is alluding to a characteristic phenomenon that after the analysis is terminated, there is often a gradual tendency toward repression of the analysis itself, with reduction of the self-conscious awareness and need to analyze all mental functions in detail, and often resulting in large amnesic gaps for the patient regarding the analysis and the process by which change took place. However, the intensity and the nature of the experiences that are again repressed, and the intensity of the conflicts about them, has been permanently modified and this form of repression is analogous to the existence of unconscious mental forces as they occur in "normal" individuals.

The patient's final remarks about my accepting her as a person and as a woman, "just as I am," indicate that although I have not commented about such issues overtly during the analysis, my continuing analytic interest, neutrality, and acceptance has been appreciated by her. It is difficult to assess how important a factor this is, and it is likely that this element has been underestimated in many discussions of the analytic process. The constancy of the analyst's interest in his patient, his attention to her and her material, and his general suspension of moralistic judgment, as well as his willingness to tolerate without impatience the patient's faltering steps toward maturity, are all important elements in the development and maintenance of an analytic situation. It is likely that the patient then introjects this set of attitudes as part of the basis for a new identification and sense of self.

---

## SESSION 338

**P:** I felt so great all day yesterday and this morning. Until I thought, "What am I doing?" I've been feeling this for two days in a row, and then I began to feel like shit. I thought to myself, "I'm leaving here and so I have no reason to be happy." It makes me so mad. I'm so scared of you. I had it all figured out. I felt so good! – – – What did it? I *did* think this morning that it bothered me that I felt so good, and it was all so great and I was ready to leave here to go ahead and . . . . – I was thinking about Tom and I realized that not only am I in love with him but I'm *physically* attracted to him, too. That sounds crazy after seven years of marriage. I thought to myself, "I love to kiss him." – – And then I thought about you and your mustache and I thought, "He couldn't be married, because his wife couldn't stand it." That's when it happened! I thought, "What do I have to be happy about? I hate him." – – I felt that I was giving in to you and it made me mad. I know that I wasn't and I didn't feel it yesterday or even this morning. – – – It makes me so damned mad that I still do this. It's so silly, but I can't help it, I do it. – – I can't leave here and I can't lose you and it makes me desperate and I couldn't live.

A: I think that one of the things to make you mad is that you can't even believe *that*, any more.

P: I think so much about leaving and what it's going to be like. I wish I'd never started. I've been so involved and you're really a part of me. My whole life revolved around this for two years. And suddenly it's gone and there's nothing and it's like a part of me is taken away. I had myself convinced yesterday that it's like dying. Sure it hurts and there's fear that goes with it, but you get over it and you have to, it's just life. – – – I can't imagine leaving here and forgetting about you. – – But that's what will happen. Ten years from now you'll be just a little tiny spot in my mind, I'm afraid. – – – – It's only when I'm happy like yesterday that I can honestly think about leaving here and what it will be like, and then it throws me into this. – – I keep thinking . . . . . there's . . . . . oh crap, I can't talk about it. There's not much more that I can do here. I must work on leaving. I can't work in here any more and I've got to work *out* of here. – –

A: Try to elaborate on that.

P: There's not anything else to work on in here. I want to leave and start working on living by myself. It will be hell, but I want to get it over. It makes it worse every day coming here. If I leave now or three months from now it's not going to make any difference. So I might just as well get started. I can't stand coming every day and knowing that I have to leave. I just can't leave yet! You just can cry so long over something that is gone. You must finally get away. And the only way is to break away. If I could see you every day from now on, I'd be happy but to come and realize that I'll *never* see you again tears me up inside!! – – I also feel that as long as I stay, I'll not start growing. I'm not going to start growing until I get out of here. Is the end result worth all of this? It's like trying to believe in God. There's nothing that you can see. – – – I feel like I'm *wide* open, and I'm completely opened up. You can see straight through me and that's no way to live. I must close up again and I can't until I leave, but I will after I do and I know I'm going to slowly close up. Much as I love you and love being here, I can't take it much longer. It's fruitless now. I have a life outside and I want to live it and I can't while I'm still here and it's already started. And it *kills* me to leave here and I can't *tell* you how badly! – – – – – – Suddenly I feel like you can't wait for me to get out of here. – – |

A: What's the detail of that feeling?

P: – – I don't know. Except that . . . . . (sigh) – I've been figuring

*Excited*

*Sadness, Cry*

*Cry!*

*Quiet*

that this would be the last month that I'd be here. I've also been . . . . .
thinking that . . . . . – – Oh, I don't know. – – – One part of me wants to
leave as soon as I can for financial reasons. Of course, the other would
like to stay here forever. I suddenly feel that I'm apologizing to you for
wanting to leave.

**A:** Let's look at the detail of the feeling that you *have* to apologize.

**P:** I don't know, but I'm doing it. It's for *your* benefit that I said,
"The other part of me would like to stay here." – – Do I feel guilty for
leaving you? Do I want to stay a child? I'm not sure if I'd stay a child for
*your* sake or *my* sake. I think about all of the people in my life that I've
interacted with. They all wanted me as a child. Is this in me? Is it in the
people that I choose? But the minute I'm an adult, then bam! – – Sometimes I'd like to stand up and say to you that I'm an adult and a mature
woman and that's it. I'm not going to kid any longer and I'm *not* a child.
– – Suddenly that brings in my sexual feelings. It's like I'm saying, "All
right, I can take your sexual feelings." – –

**A:** Try to follow your associations there.

**P:** Well, . . . . . I think that . . . . . I see Tom and my children or any
father when his daughter grows up and she's beautiful he *could* have sexual
feelings for her. I guess it's normal, although I don't know, but why
wouldn't it be? I have a horrible feeling that I'm going to . . . . . – that I'm
not going to care about your sexual feelings and then I don't need them.
But as a woman, I'm naturally going to get them. I wonder if I blow up
sexual feelings too much.

**A:** I think you are feeling guilty that you prefer Tom to me. He's
young and vigorous and in your image of me I'm old, and so you'd rather
have Tom as a lover than me now.

**P:** – Oh Jesus! Why can't you ever be mean? I can't *stand* it when
you're nice. That's ridiculous. Because just because you're nice doesn't
mean that I'm hurting you or letting you shrivel up and die. I just can't
believe that you could be so understanding. – – Suddenly I see you being
so mad! – – It's like I can't stand you understanding this. I may feel it

*Anger*  . . . . . it's so final. You're saying that it's all right and I'm not sure that it
is. I can't stand to think of you as someone I'd prefer someone else to! I
can't let you gently drift away! I prefer to scream and yell, and to do it
violently and to tell you to go to hell! – – That's so silly that I'd rather
have you mad at me for taking Tom than to be nice about it. It throws me
for a loop. I guess because that's the last string to cut. – – – –

**A:** We'll stop here for today.

## DISCUSSION

In spite of the progressive movement yesterday, the old neurotic attachments have still not been fully dissolved, and with each step she takes toward maturity there is a temptation to regress and remain attached to me. This is illustrated in her description of the onset of her symptoms, and of the persistent oedipal attachment expressed as a derivative in the fantasy about me kissing my wife. With this there is a momentary upsurge of the oedipal drives, followed by a recognition of this as a persistence of her neurosis which now interferes with the new ego-ideal of herself as a mature woman.

She expresses the regressive wish to remain attached to me and the feeling that she cannot leave as if it were a need, and my first intervention is an attempt to strengthen the healthier forces of maturity and her own recognition of her power and control over the residual neurotic elements. This intervention leads to her description of the fact that she has internalized me, and that I have become, through the process of identification, a part of her. This is again like the relationship to a parent, where the early identifications are indelible and where even though the individual may mature, change, and grow, residues of the early relationships with parents are never completely eradicated. The idea of losing me again evokes the grief response, with the equation of termination with death, and with her own anticipation that my importance for her will gradually fade in the coming years. Throughout this material the work of grief and mourning continues with her affective response to the impending termination.

She verbalizes again the conflict between the wish for independence, emancipation, and her recognition that this will lead to further maturation and growth, as compared with her continuing wish to cling as a defense against the grief over separation and loss. And she refers again to the upcoming process of gradual repression after the analysis terminates, when she talks about "closing up again." The anticipation of her new maturity is expressed in her statement, "I have a life outside and I want to live it, and I can't while I'm still here and it's already started." But this is followed, after a silence, by a projective defense in which she feels that I am impatient for her to leave. My neutral request for details again interferes with this defense, and after several hesitations the underlying feeling of guilt for her wish to be independent begins to emerge again as a transference response. This conflict has been worked over before, but its reemergence in this form now, where she feels it necessary to apologize for wanting to leave, indicates that it has not been fully worked through, and therefore needs more analytic attention.

My request for details leads into the residual transference reactions to me, in which she sees me as wanting her to remain a child as others in her life have done, but simultaneously she is observing herself in this thought and asking whether this is a conflict within herself, or whether there is something in herself that leads her to choose this type of person. Once again the new adult sense of self and of her identity as an adult woman emerges, which brings with it the still not completely resolved issue of her sexual attraction to me as a woman. Because this is still not fully resolved, I ask for her associations and this in turn leads to her accurate perception of a father's oedipal sexual attraction to his daughter. This brings into focus the issue of herself as an attractive, sexual, adult woman, who may become the recipient of sexual attraction from an adult man.

My interpretation of her continuing sense of guilt that she now prefers her husband to me as a lover is partly based on her description early in the session of her sexual attraction to her husband, as well as on her statement hat she doesn't need my sexual feelings any more. The interpretation also serves as an indirect indication that I can accept her sexuality fully, but that even if I were to have sexual fantasy and attraction to her, I have sufficient strength and willingness to accept the reality of the situation that I can permit her to enjoy herself sexually with another man. This attitude is part of the dissolution of the oedipus complex that must occur in the course of normal development where the father must accept without jealousy (or the multiple defenses against it) the fact that his daughter will eventually enjoy sexuality with someone else. The fact that I indicate my acceptance of this in the transference makes her own needs voluntarily to renounce her attachment to me that much more difficult, and tacitly helps her accept the idea that I am satisfied with my own life as it is, and that I do not need her as she (rightly or wrongly) perceives that her father did and/or does. She attempts to deny this by the perception of me as being "mad," but this mechanism is not sustained and she again returns to the mourning process accompanied by the anger at the recognition that it is up to her to cut the last strings.

This session again illustrates how the process of integration that occurs during the termination phase of the analysis involves an intermittent oscillation between the progressive and regressive forces of the personality. The conflicts return again and again in a variety of forms, and the working-through process goes on. However, in the total picture the progressive and maturing forces are gradually more and more in the ascendancy, while the regressive attachments and symptomatic behavior resulting from them are less intense, last for shorter times, and are more readily apparent to the patient herself even without the analyst's active intervention.

---

## SESSION 339

**P:** — — — — — I had a dream that this man was chasing me. I kept trying to get away from him. It was icy and snowy and I couldn't quite make it. I finally ran into this house and ran upstairs. I looked down the stairwell and there was his face at the bottom. He said that he had to measure something or to calculate. I just gave up and went with him. — — I think that was you, and the basement meant with my uncle. It all started in the basement but in the end I was in the dark and in a hall, and I could see the light and I went into the light. — — I'm so hostile this morning. I woke up with such a fear and I felt just like a baby and I have a feeling of absolute helplessness. — — — I got the feeling that I don't want to leave here and yet I *know* that there's no sense getting hysterical about it. But I just don't want it to happen to me as it did after Harris terminated me. I tell myself that it won't but I keep remembering it. — — It seems that there are two ways that I could act. Sometimes I want to get mad as hell about leaving here, and then the other is wanting to leave and wanting to start growing and to live with my family. — —

**A:** So the question is do you leave here because you're being kicked out, the way you felt with Harris, or is it because you're ready to and you yourself *want* to go?

**P:** Both of them are there. I know the reality, but sometimes I can't help it and I feel the other. It's so basic with me.

**A:** What are your associations to the man measuring something or calculating something in the dream?

**P:** It has something to do with me. — — It was like he was measuring something . . . . . that I already knew. — — (Sigh) – Suddenly now all I can think of is . . . . . the hole was the vagina and the man was the penis. I had the feeling being inside there that I wasn't sure that this could get in or not. That's why I came out. I solved the problem. — — It might have had something to do with . . . . . . – Now I remember! When I ran into the house I was dressed up like an eleven-year-old girl! And I was scared that this man would realize that I wasn't an eleven-year-old girl! Uhm! I had heels on and bobby-sox. As I was running up the stairs he'd just discovered that I was trying to fool him. — — Uhm! – It seems so silly to dream something like that. – – – For the past few days I've been feeling . . . . . it hits me that I'm a woman and it surprises me. – – I guess when I feel like a little girl I feel I'm much too small for a man. – –

**A:** What are your associations to an *eleven*-year-old girl?

**P:** I don't know. – – – Except at first I thought that's when I started having my periods, but that isn't when I started my periods. – – My room-mate in college told me that that's when she started hers. I thought it was pitiful for a girl to have the body of a woman and the mind of a child. – – Now suddenly I feel so depressed! I feel like a girl looking at daddy and saying that I'd love to have it but I'm too small and when I get big, then I'll have it. It's depressing that I still think of myself as a girl. Now I'm big and I still don't have it. – –

**A:** I think what's depressing is that now that you're big you don't really want it any more .

**P:** Last night Tom and I made love and I realized for the first time how wonderful and sexual the part of a woman is in love-making. And then I do this! I have to slap myself across the face every time I'm happy about something. – –

**A:** What was the detail about this realization last night?

**P:** I realized that I love being a woman, and that it's so wonderful to be made the way I am so that a man can enter me and get so much satis-faction from it. I was *not* afraid that I was too small. For the first time I *knew* that I'm not and that's what I'm *for* and that's what makes *me* happy and it makes Tom happy. – – The same thing happened the other night after we were making love. I thought to myself, "I give it all to Tom and I wonder, can he take it?" I give up all of my wishes to be a man and I just want to be a woman and be happy at home with my children and let Tom take over the finances and his professional life and make the living. I used to worry so much about his work and stuff like that. He al-ways thought that I was crazy. I felt as if I snapped when I decided it. It's as if that's *my* part of being masculine and I decided that I'd *not* do it any longer. Tom is perfectly capable of handling that part of our life. At least, I hope he is. These thoughts bother me. – – – When I have thoughts like that I completely let go of my father. It's my father who couldn't take it. He could never stand a woman like me. He would have completely crum-pled to the ground, just completely. – – I act out on these feelings and I go ahead and I *do* them and yet, I'm so scared that I get as stiff as a board and that's the way I am right now. I hope that will go away because it's *Excited,* better to do it and to go ahead and *feel* the way I want to feel. I can't *Angry* believe that I'm doing all of this for your benefit. What I *really* feel like saying is that *I* am a woman and I love it and you can go to hell if you don't like it! I love *all* of those feelings! But I put myself through torture just for your sake. I do it just to leave an opening in case you don't like it. – – – I work you into my father again so that I can hate you because you don't like me the way I am. – – It's just so that I won't have to feel the guilt and grief. – –

    **A:** What's the detail about the guilt?

    **P:** I'll be a woman in spite of you. I don't feel guilty at all. I like it! If you liked it too, then I'd stay with you. That God-damn grief! I start thinking of you as you *are* and I can't take it! Maybe it's because I felt so much happiness with Tom last night, and so I built up this wall again. I drive myself nuts. – – I can't fool myself very well any more. – – I suddenly realize why should I stay here and have all of my sexual feelings here? They'll never be satisfied in here. All I can do is love you, but I *can* with Tom. – – – – That's the way it is. I want Tom instead of you. – –

    **A:** We'll stop here for today.

*Quiet*

*Angry*
*Cry!*

*Quiet*

## DISCUSSION

Once again the patient demonstrates that the working-through process involves oscillation between progressive integration of her new self-image, with gratification in the role of an adult woman, and symptomatic regressive attempts to maintain the image of a little girl, and thereby achieve gratification of the oedipal wishes. In the first description of the dream she projects the regressive wish to me, in that I am chasing her while she tries to get away from me. However, the dream has a more progressive resolution since she is in the dark, but could see the light, "And I went into the light."

But upon awakening, the symptomatic regressive wishes are experienced and lead to the dominating current conflict over termination. The deeper meaning of this behavior and of the dream only becomes clear later in the session after she describes the successful sexual experience as an adult woman with her husband the night before. At this point in the session, however, that experience is not yet known to me, and therefore I can only follow the patient's own associations, which are to the termination of her previous treatment and her reactions to it. In my own associations to the dream I was struck by her movement out into the light, and therefore in my first confrontation I choose to clarify for her the fact that she increasingly is experiencing a voluntary wish for renunciation of the childhood object in the transference. Her response merely confirms the existence of this as a conflict, and at the moment she does not bring up any new or affectively significant response to it.

I am also puzzled by the dream element in which the man is measuring or calculating something, and my own associations are that the man, representing myself, was measuring or calculating how close she is to being ready to terminate. In my request for her associations in regard to this dream element I hope it might be the stimulus for exploration of further elements in the current termination conflict. Her own associations to the vagina and the penis, with the question as to whether the vagina would be large enough, are a surprise to me, but this material is followed by her reporting the previously repressed portion of the dream. The implications of this sequence are that the previously repressed portion of the dream, and the conflict that it expresses, evokes more anxiety than the patient is capable of tolerating at the moment, and hence the defense of repression is used. After part of the conflict is exposed to consciousness (by the association of the vagina and penis), rational ego processes can function more effectively and the previously anxiety-provoking conflict becomes somewhat less intense. As a result, the needs for repression of that dream element are reduced, thus permitting the conscious recall of the conflict derivative expressed in the forgotten dream fragment.

At this point I am struck by her emphasis on the specific age of the girl and I wonder if this might represent a particular incident or conflict in her life. It is this reasoning that leads me to ask for her associations to the age, which brings to consciousness the characteristic fantasies of the prepubescent girl who has an intellectual knowledge of bodily penetration, but who is still emotionally frightened at the prospect, and experiences the typical concerns about the size of her genitals and the fantasies about painful penetration.

My interpretation that her depressed feeling results from the fact that part of her no longer wants the childhood object is based on my awareness of growth reflected in recent sessions, as well as my own associations throughout the current session. There had been the dream in which she went out into the light, and there was the repressed dream element that she was fooling the man, as well as the expression of the prepubescent (rather than directly oedipal) girl's orientation and fantasy. And I feel that some of the continuing regressive behavior represents an attempt to "fool" me. Her response indicates the correctness of my reasoning, and for the first time in the session she mentions the gratifying sexual experience last night, and her pleasure in the adult sexual role. Her statements ". . . I realized for the first time how wonderful and sexual the part of a woman is . . ." and later, "for the first time I *knew* that I'm not (too small) . . ." are indications of the new level of emotional awareness and integration she is achieving. In the conscious portion of her mind she has "known" this for many years. But the previous repression of childhood sexuality and fantasy has meant that she continued to behave as if her fantasies were real, and that she was unable to apply her conscious knowledge to change them. As a result of the analytic work, she can now apply the conscious learning, thereby dissolving the childhood fantasies, and then come to "know" about her sexual self in a new and more unified way.

In order to foster and strengthen these progressive forces and to help her further establish them as new structures within herself, I ask her for the details about this new and more mature experience. This adult sexual experience proves to be the crucial element in this session, and she is able now to elaborate upon it with obvious pleasure and satisfaction. The occurrence of maturing and gratifying experiences such as this paradoxically mobilize her anxiety and grief over separation, since they bring her closer to termination of the relationship to me. She describes this process and reaction when she says, "When I have thoughts like that I completely let go of my father." And subsequently she describes her anxiety, in spite of conscious recognition of the advantages of her new maturity.

At this point she repeats in the transference this same sequence of psychic events, again regressively perceiving me as the father, and in an excited angry way feeling that I am trying to hold on to her, and that like the father, I do not want her to be a mature and feminine woman, and that she must oppose me in order to grow up. "What I *really* feel like saying is that *I* am a woman and I love it, and you can go to hell if you don't like it!" After this recurrence of the transference experience, there is a spontaneous recognition of it as a transference, resulting in a reduction of affect that permits her to observe herself and to verbalize its meaning as a defense against guilt and grief.

The issue of her guilt for growing up and leaving me has been brought into the analysis previously, but apparently has not been fully resolved, and therefore my question is an attempt once more to help her expose this component and further work it through. Again there is a mixture of transference and self-observation occurring simultaneously, with further recognition and acceptance within herself that she now prefers her husband to me.

It should be noted that most of the analytic work is being done by the patient, and that she is increasing her capacity simultaneously to experience the transference reactions and at the same time observe herself and recognize the reality of the situation. Integration of her new perceptions of herself is occurring steadily, with a deeper and more gratifying set of experiences and attitudes as an adult woman in relationship to her husband. This deeper and more sustained level of integration also provides more effective and satisfying personal and self-sufficient reinforcement in her new role, and hence is another force in helping her to accept the voluntary renunciation of the childhood drives.

---

## SESSION 340

Patient is four or five minutes late.

**P:** – Now the fear is gone and the hostility is coming out. I'd forgotten how horrible it is. – – My only consolation last night after two days of lovely (sarcasm) thoughts was that I realized that they are unreal about Tom and even about you. It's the *child* wanting to kill her father and it's past. I'm not that child any more. Good God! Which is worse, the feeling of wanting to kill someone or wanting to kill yourself? Or the feeling that everything is closing in on me? I had them all this weekend. It really wasn't so bad this weekend, but it was just the one about killing Tom. It helps to realize that it's the little girl's thoughts of wanting to take a knife and stab him. Still they scare me. I *know* that I'm not mad at Tom, he's the last person that I'm mad at. These are like the thoughts to cut my wrists. The thoughts plague me and I know that I won't do it, and I don't want to, but they come to mind just to drive me nuts. – – – Really, it doesn't bother me that much. Tom is much bigger than I am. Last night he fell asleep and I let him sleep for two hours. I went in and turned on the light and he jumped. He didn't know where he was and I thought to myself, "God, he's completely helpless and just like a baby." – – Why do I have these thoughts? I know that anger is natural, but how many adults think like this? It's the childish part of me that wants to regress and stay here. I want to tell you that I can't stand leaving. I want you to get mad, and I want you to say, "You're just as normal as anyone else and you're on your own, so get out." When I'm on my own, then I'm at my best. It's like some of the thoughts that I have while we were in church. I was having self-pity thoughts about my past, and it was like the church that we went to as children, and I felt that everyone knows about me and pities me and is sorry for me. It's a kind of negative attention. If people say, "You're big, so don't sweat it and you can take care of yourself," then I can do it. I hate those self-pitying thoughts. They got me in here in the first place. – – – Every weekend I say in my mind that I'm terminating and that I'm not going to come back here. I'm really *living* this. – – – Saturday night Tom left around 10:30 to go to work. I was really scared, and I fantasied that I was going to kill myself because I couldn't take it by myself and I was scared to death. He left and I watched TV for about thirty minutes and then I got to feeling all right. I went to bed and I slept fine and I knew there was nothing I could do about it. I had a wild dream about you. You were just like my father. I was here in the analysis and I thought that you were pushing me away. I had to wait and then you went out and I came in here, but it was like a motel room. There was a woman lying in a bed, and on the bed was the stuff that a man ejaculates. How familiar it is to me. I thought that if he could make love to that woman, why won't he make love to me? I wondered whether the woman was a patient or was she just a woman? But I felt that she was familiar and somehow this was right, and it had to be accepted by me. I think about that stuff on the bed. Ugh! It's like it's the very essence of a man. – – –

A: What other associations do you have to this?

P: It's so obvious what I'm thinking. I hope that the woman on the bed was my mother or your wife. But I'm not sure. Just like about my father. I didn't like it and I felt rejected but as long as it was mother I felt it's all right, and this is the way it should be. – – I feel as if it's actually happened. That stuff is so familiar to me! I've seen it before! That white cloudy stuff! It shouldn't matter to me at all! It should be *in* a woman and not on the bed. – –

*Anxiety*

A: What are your associations to your feeling of familiarity with it?

P: I don't know! It's like a long time ago, it's a thought from a long time ago. – – I wasn't afraid of it, but I could see it so clearly and I know exactly what it looks like. Only once have I ever seen Tom's. But it's further back than that. It shouldn't matter. It doesn't surprise me and I know how it feels and I know it's what makes babies. – –

A: You mentioned that only once have you ever seen Tom's. What are your associations?

P: It was when I was pregnant with Carol. I couldn't stand sex but I couldn't stand Tom being mad at me. I was around eight months. I told Tom that I'd masturbate him and I wanted to do it and I talked him into it. – – But it's so much further back than that. There's something about this stuff. – I *was* thinking, either before or after the dream, how if you look at my father's affairs on the surface, it's really not *that* bad, that it's really not death. But if you analyze and think of that stuff going into

*Cry!*

another woman! I can't stand it! It's so final! – – It hurt like hell to have the man have affairs, and I can think of all of the parts but that. But once he's given that part to another woman, that's it, and I can't think about it and it's final and there's nothing left. It's a part that you don't usually think of. It's life itself, and it's so intimate to me, and so sacred. – – I don't know why this matters so much. It's a part of you that I have to think about and accept too. It means that part of you will always go to someone else. A woman can have intercourse out of, or before, marriage and it's not so detrimental unless she has a baby. But when a man, once he's put that stuff into another woman, God damn it, that's it! I used to love the thought of Tom putting his in me. I loved it. – –

A: I wonder if this expresses a wish that I'd give you a baby and impregnate you before you leave here?

P: – Maybe I do have that wish, because it means that you're giving me part of you. But then something else in me. . . . . keeps it from being so sacred. This is something that a man gives a woman in love. – – That stuff is something that I love, and it's like an old friend, and it doesn't regurgitate me like it does to some women. It's silly.

A: How do you mean silly?

*Cry!*

P: I don't know! It's just silly! To talk about something so. . . . . I don't know. – – I just. . . – I find it hard to believe that I could love you as I do Tom, and have these deep thoughts about you. Even though I've made my choice and I know what I want, it doesn't wash them away. I found someone that I love and could be happy with. But since I can't ever have him I *have* someone that I *can* have and love and fulfill *all* of these thoughts with. – – It bugs me to think about loving you as a woman, and I could do it if there were different circumstances. And I know. . . . . – that if it really were possible I wouldn't want it, even though I have these feelings. – –

A: We still don't understand the feeling of familiarity you had about that stuff on the bed in the dream.

P: (Sigh.) – I can't help thinking that it had something to do with my uncle. One reason that I don't like to think about my uncle is. . . . .

*Cry*

it's something that I'd like to forget. It wasn't normal and it wasn't love. It was love on my part. It's so hard to be realistic and to say, all right, it happened and I was a little girl and I was loving. But that doesn't make it right and it doesn't keep it from being detrimental. And my grandmother

*Angry,*
*Upset*

was so horrible to me. It was only through that that I realized how stupid it was. I realized that my uncle was a sick little boy and it meant nothing to him. It's like with my periods. They're a part of me and that's wonderful and I love them and I don't care *what* the world thinks. This is part of a man and it's wonderful and it's love. I think it's wonderful! It's mine! My uncle gave it to me! I can't look at it any other way! I can't say it's gone and it's all past. My uncle failed me but he gave it to me. It's a bond between a man and a woman and it's a way of saying, "You *are* a woman, and I love you." But it hurts me. It's like the girl who gets pregnant before she gets married. She never gets over it. I don't want it to bother me or to make me feel guilty or bad or dirty or hateful. I'm still looking for an answer to this situation. I'm thinking about *my* feelings which are so wonderful and loving, but my uncle is so ashamed and afraid, and my grandmother is saying, it's so awful and so *dirty*. And everyone else is not saying a word! They're all thinking, "Don't look at her because she's a witch and she's terrible."

A: We'll stop here for today.

## DISCUSSION

The pleasurable and mature sexual experiences with her husband described in the last session, and the working-through toward voluntary renunciation of me in the transference, have again mobilized and stimulated the regressive wishes still to hold on to the past objects and not to give up the yearnings for oedipal gratification. As a result, there is an exacerbation of her symptoms over the weekend. But at the same time she shows an increasing capacity, even as the symptoms are occurring, to distinguish between the childhood fantasies and the current reality and to recognize her displacements of drive and affect, and she feels a sense of confidence in her ability to control and deal with these conflicts. Even during the experience of symptoms at home she was able, after a relatively brief time, to control these regressive forces and to respond more appropriately in accordance with the reality situation. Throughout this she was also living through the termination reaction, thereby further desensitizing herself to it, and at the same time, achieving mastery over it.

The dream represents another elaboration of the persistent oedipal triangular relationship in the transference, but a new component is her description and reaction to the seminal ejaculation, and it is this emphasis in her presentation that leads me to ask for her further associations to it.

Initially her associations lead to the normal situation in which the resolution of the oedipus complex ordinarily can occur in childhood. In the healthy family situation, the frustration of the oedipal wish toward the father is more easily tolerated if the father can accept the girl's sexuality without seductive response, and instead can focus his sexual interest on the mother. This permits the girl the experience of seeing that love, marriage, and sexuality can be fused toward one object, and also encourages and enhances the girl's tendency toward identification with the mother as the object of the father's love and sexuality. In this context she can more readily accept her feminine yearnings, and postpone for adult life the gratification of these drives, while gradually accepting the idea that when she is an adult she can have a relationship with a man similar to the relationship her mother has with the father. However, where the father's sexual interest is toward women other than the mother, the girl's jealousy and resentment is likely to be enhanced, and the identification with the mother in a feminine role is less gratifying and more difficult. If the father can have sex with these other women, the fantasies as to why he can't have it with the daughter tend to be reinforced by the realities of the father's behavior. This is condensed in her statement, "I didn't like it and I felt rejected, but as long as it was mother I felt it's all right and this is the way it should be."

However, the unsettled issue about the seminal fluid again presses toward expression, accompanied by the affective experiences of anxiety and familiarity, thus indicating a persistent and unresolved component in her sexual conflict and orientation. It is this that leads me to ask for her associations to the familiar feeling itself. Her response indicates her own awareness that this conflict about seminal fluid has roots in her childhood, but that it is still active in her adult sexual relations with her husband. Her statement that she had only seen her husband's semen once is an indication of an inhibition of freedom in their sexual relations. Since this is a current and therefore conscious experience, I feel it will be easier to begin the approach to this material at that level, rather than to press for details about something vague which she feels is "farther back than that," but which at the moment is still repressed. It is this reasoning that leads me to inquire first about the current experiences with her husband.

Her associations immediately go to the eighth month of her second pregnancy, at which time she actively persuaded her husband to permit her to make him ejaculate through masturbation. It should be remembered that the time of onset of her acute neurotic decompensation was in the eighth month of a pregnancy, and that earlier in the analysis the issue of the sexual seduction by the uncle had been analyzed as involving the fantasy that she had swallowed the uncle's penis and that it was still inside of her. At that time we had also worked out the connection that when she was told in the eighth month of her first pregnancy that delivery would be by Caesarean section, there had been the unconscious fantasy that in opening her abdomen the doctor would find the uncle's penis still there. Although this material does not consciously and clearly come to her mind (or to mine) at this moment, there is the spontaneous recognition that "It's so much further back than that."

Once again the affective component of her association is related to the father giving his semen to another woman, which represents the typical oedipal wish to be impregnated by the father. She spontaneously brings this into the transference when she says, "It's a part of you that I have to think about and accept too. It means that part of you will always go to someone else." It is these references to the oedipal wish for impregnation and their repetition in the transference that lead to my direct interpretation at this point of her wish and fantasy that I would impregnate her before she terminates.

Her response to my interpretation is a tentative and rather remote one, but this is quickly replaced by her continuing preoccupation with the semen itself, accompanied by a defensive avoidance through the thought, "It's silly." My questioning this defense mobilizes again the affective response, and again the issue of not receiving my semen becomes part of the termination conflict, with feelings of disappointment that she has to give up this idea in the relationship to me (father).

Earlier in the session I had been struck by her emphasis on the feelings of familiarity in regard to semen, but when I previously inquired about it, the associations had been rather sparse and limited, and had not produced any definitive insights. I still feel that this is an important clue and therefore again choose to focus on the feeling of familiarity. At this point, accompanied by an intense affective experience, she once again returns to the sexual trauma with the uncle, and further working-through and mastery of the event and its repercussions now takes place. As she develops this material there is an increasing regression and reexperiencing of the little girl's perception that the uncle has given her his semen, that it is hers, and that the sexual seduction itself is a positive, pleasurable, loving, and gratifying experience for her, which only subsequently evoked guilt, shame, and a feeling of being rejected for her sexuality. In summary, the little girl in that situation had experienced pleasure and pride in her sexuality, and had experienced the capacity to have love and sexual feeling toward the same object. However, because of the traumatic nature of the situation, and of her fantasies, and the traumatic effects of the response by others in the environment (with its effects on superego development) her sexuality had to be repressed as unacceptable, intolerable, and threatening to any feelings of love, resulting in the arrest of her psychosexual development at that level.

The latter material in this session again illustrates how conflicts, traumatic events, or old memories, which had been largely worked through much earlier in the analysis, are again revitalized and worked through under the impact of the termination phase. In this terminal reworking of conflicts, and as a result of the overall maturation and ego development that has occurred, a more definitive and integrative type of resolution can now take place.

---

## SESSION 341

**P:** – – – – – – I've decided this morning that you can go straight to hell! I've been totally rejected in here regardless of any circumstances and situations, and it makes me mad! – – – – – – – – – – – – – – – I can't believe that you were actually just going to let me go. – – I feel that I'm dying inside and you don't even care and no one even knows it. – – I'm hurting and hurting, and I'm supposed to pick myself up and walk out of here as though nothing is wrong. I can't. I don't want you or need you! You can

*Scream* | go to hell! I'll hate you for the rest of my life. – – I don't like to be hurt like this. No one does. – – – I can't make you do anything! You just sit there! Isn't there *something* that I could do to make you mad? I can't

*Cry* | make you *love* me and I can't make you *hate* me! – – – I just want once to make you hurt, just once! That's all I want. I don't have to walk around here and hurt every day and feel like I have five tons of bricks on my head. I don't have to. I can hate you and feel fine. But I want some revenge, just

*Anger* | a little bit for making me hurt like this! – – – I don't need you and I don't want you! I honestly don't! – – But I'm sick and tired of all this hurt. I've had it! I don't *need* to hurt! I don't need *you!* – – – – – – – – – – I sud-

*Loud,* | denly realized that no one will *ever* give me what I want. Nobody. And I

*Anger* | hate everybody for it! – – – I hate you for making me realize that I don't want or need anything. You're a man who showed me that I don't need a penis or a father or any man but Tom. And I hate you for it! You've shown me that what I've always wanted from women and from my father and from men is no good and it's useless. (Elaborates.) Even that stuff that comes from a man's penis. It will *not* stay with me or make me a man! And I don't need yours! I can kid myself as much as I want to, but it's nothing. It's just a physical thing that disappears. – – – No man is going

*Anger* | to totally give himself to me and get inside me and live. I'm never going

to be a man! – – – When I came to analysis, I thought that it would give me something. It's failed completely to give me what I thought it would! What it has given me or will give me, I don't know, and I don't know if I'll ever see any results. But about what I thought it would give me it's failed! – – – (Laughs.) – – I've got to wipe the slate clean completely, because nothing does any good. There's no way that I can get what I want. No one can give it to me. Not you, or mother or father or Tom or men or children or anything. And I can't say that I didn't want it. I did. It was what I wanted! I wanted you and now I know that I wanted your penis. | *Loud,*
And I can't get it even if you'd give it to me! I can't go back to mother | *Anger*
and be reborn. There's nothing. There's no hope. I'm not sure I can ever be satisfied with what I have. (Elaborates.) All right, so I don't *need* it. Big deal! That makes me want to throw up! – – – – – How do I walk out | *Cry!!*
of here without defenses against this hurt? Are you going to tell me? How do I take that huge hurt? I feel as if I'm the one who is dying and not you. It's huge and black and it weights me down. How can I walk out of here and feel that? – – – –

A: I think your wish is to feel that *I* am inflicting this hurt on you. But what we have to see is that because you're clinging to wishes from the past that you no longer really want, you're inflicting this hurt on yourself from now on.

P: Ha! I can't believe that!

A: You don't want to believe it because if it's true then it means that I don't even have to feel guilty about your being hurt.

P: All I can think of is my parents. They think that they're getting by | *Anger,*
with this, and if you think that you will, you're crazy as hell! To think that | *Cry*
I'll just give up! And love you. Just for a few times. You shit all over me. I'm going in circles. I'm scared to leave here and I hang on as long as I can whether I torture myself or not! That's the truth. I know when I leave here I'll pick myself up and be fine. So why can't I do it before I leave? – – I want someone to pat me on the head and say, "You poor thing, your childhood was hell and I know how you're hurting." I want *you* to say that. And yet on Sunday I wanted that and it scared me. Then I wanted you to say, "Listen, kid, you don't get any pity because you don't deserve it." – – I feel that everyone knows that I'm terminating and no one acknowledges that I'm going through hell. They feel I'll just walk around and be just fine. – – I guess I think that by failing in here I'll pay you back. It gives me an inner satisfaction to make myself miserable because it's directed against you in a round-about way. – –

A: What's the detail of the picture of failing in here?

**P:** Being scared, or having thoughts to kill myself or being frigid or being a child and kicking and screaming. That's the way I feel. It's funny that I can't say things to hurt you directly. I have the urge to call you a dried up old man, and to say that I couldn't ever have sexual feelings for you even if I wanted to, and I don't even know you. But I don't want to hurt you that way. I'd rather hurt myself than you. That's silly. I must still feel that I need you or else it wouldn't matter if I hurt you or if I left here. – – –

**A:** We'll stop here for today.


### DISCUSSION

The patient indicates immediately that she is continuing to experience the transference conflicts that had been exposed and elaborated in the previous session. In the transference I represent the father and uncle by whom she feels rejected for her sexuality and for her loving attachment and wishes, and towards whom she ever since has harbored intense feelings of rage and the wish for revenge. But the wish for revenge is frustrated in the transference by the fact that I do not respond personally or defensively to her provocations. It is possible for an analyst to maintain his relative neutrality and his analytic posture by fully understanding the meaning of the patient's transferences. Both the idealized love and the depreciating hostility are drives which originate within the patient independent of the analyst as a real person, and as long as he does not interfere with their development, such drives will be manifest no matter what his personal characteristics may be. Therefore, it is possible to accept the patient's positive and negative reactions without personal anxiety or challenge, and to appreciate their expression as a sign of analytic progress and as a step toward ultimate success in the analysis.

The present upsurge of these transferences is the result of my interpretation in the previous session concerning her wish to be impregnated by me before she terminates. In the woman with strong phallic strivings the baby is often a substitute for the desired penis, and in the normal development of the girl, this equation helps in her resolution of the phallic conflict and in the establishment of her feminine identification. But at this point, the interpretation has pushed her to the adult realization that no one will ever give her what she has wanted for so long, and has fostered an adult recognition of the irrationality of the forces that have driven her in her life. With anger, pain, and frustration she must now face the final realization that analysis will not make her over into a man.

In this material she demonstrates the typical unconscious wish and motivation of many women who enter analysis with the unconscious fantasy that the analysis will magically provide them with the missing phallus that they have yearned for since childhood. Successful analysis means a disillusionment of this wish and a final recognition and acceptance of its inevitable frustration. "It was what I wanted! I wanted you, and now I know that I wanted your penis. And I can't get it even if you'd give it to me!" From the point of view of the child, she feels that this frustration means there will be nothing for her in her life, whereas simultaneously from the point of view of the adult she recognizes that she doesn't need a penis and yet feels hurt and resentful that she has to face this reality.

The hurt and anger toward me for making her face this realization still includes the defense mechanism of projection, with the childhood feeling that this is all my fault. My interpretation that she is now doing this to herself is simultaneously an attempt to point out the existence of this projective mechanism, and also to remind her of the healthy forces within herself which recognize the pleasures and satisfactions she can achieve by accepting herself as a woman. Her response that she can't believe it is an attempt to cling to this projective defense. My next interpretation is partly determined by my own response of sympathy for the intensity of her acute distress and pain. As a result of this response within myself, I have an intuitive hunch that she wants me to feel guilty and feel that I am causing the pain she is experiencing. The interpretation of this wish has the desired effect of helping her to recognize and verbalize the wish for revenge against both parents and in the current transference reactions toward me. This is followed by her recognition of her wish for sympathy, and then by the fantasy of revenge on me through her transference resistance of maintaining the neurosis and failing to complete her analysis. In this material she is masochistically turning her aggression inward against herself, and toward the end of the session this mechanism is illustrated even more directly when she has the urge to express derogatory and depreciatory remarks toward me, but instead recognizes that she would rather hurt herself.

It should be noted that there are more than forty minutes of silence in this session, and although it was not directly interpreted, the likelihood is that the silence itself may represent some of the same wishes to withhold herself and her feelings from me, as an indirect means of expressing the anger and the wish for revenge.

## SESSION 342

Patient is four or five minutes late.

P: – – – – – I'm so nervous this morning. I just can't run down. – – – It's because I'm having love feelings this morning which always lead to sexual feelings and I don't want to have them. I started to yesterday. – – In the back of my mind I always think. . . . . you're getting by with something. It's ridiculous and I know that it's not true, but I think it. – – That's the reason I can't show my love. At times I've had tremendous love for people who made me so mad! But I can't show it because it's not real. How can you hate and love somebody at the same time? They say that that's normal. – – I started having love feelings for you yesterday because even though you were not giving me what I wanted, you know what's best and you're my therapist and of course you'll not give in to me. It's just like every girl with her father. She wants him and she stamps her feet, but she knows that she can't. It's best and that's the way it is, but I still want to keep stamping my feet. – – I had a dream of our house in Evanston and I had to completely redecorate it inside. I woke up in a bad mood about it. – – – I know that I could make all of these decisions and I could give up my father and have love for you and accept the real situation in here and love my children and love my husband. But it doesn't last always, and I could go, bing, and fall on my nose. – – It will be hell when I leave here. I'm sure I'll be all right if I want to be, but I keep thinking about never seeing you again. You're just my therapist and I didn't know you two years ago, and there's no *real* interaction and relationship here between us. It's all been on *my* part and so theoretically there can be no feeling there. But there *is*. And I can't talk to anyone about it. It's just something I carry around inside of me. – – – I picture myself as someone whose parents have died, or else there's a close death and it takes a while to get over and it's hell and it hurts and it's sad and it's frightening. I've never had anyone

*Cry* disappear out of my life just like that, like you're going to. – – – You know I love you and I feel that you've held me like this (gestures with her hands) for this whole time and you've kept me from *really* being hurt. And now you're not holding me up any more and no one is keeping me from being hurt. – – – There's nothing more that I can do and you know it. – – – When I leave I *want* to feel like this, because eventually it will grow into *not* crying or feeling sad, but still loving. But I always build up those

damned walls! – – I feel that as long as I can love you and remember you
as wonderful and nice, then nothing can touch me and nothing can *really*
hurt me. Because I don't *need* anything else except Tom who doesn't
usually hurt me. – – This week every day I've been different and I've had
completely different feelings every day that I've been here. Today I feel,
why should I bother. I get tired of it, and I'm tired of building up defenses
and I'm tired of analyzing. – – I decided yesterday. . . . . as I left here, I
felt, "I'm so glad that *he* didn't let me feel self-pity." And then it made
me mad. I don't need you to tell me that I don't need self-pity. I don't
need to lean against you and have you stand me up because that's kind
of what it was. – – – – It's funny how I identify loving with giving in and
with being. . . . . shit on it, I always say. – – – I know how my feelings
about you are. Just like now. I think that you're. . . . . a very nice person.
I wish that I really *knew* you so that I'd know if that was true or not. But
it wouldn't make any difference if I didn't know you because I'd look at
you as I want to, I guess. – – – I sit here and want to talk about leaving
and how it's all right to go and how I love you. But I'll go home and I'll
think about this and I'll get so mad! – – – Now I'm thinking that I haven't
really tried you to the fullest. I wonder what would happen if I stood up
and asked you to make love to me? – – –

**A:** Try to carry through the fantasy. What comes to your mind?

**P:** (Laughs.) I'm never sure. I think one thing but I don't really know
you and I never *really* tested you as far as I can go. You'd sit and ask me
some psychological question or else you'd get embarrassed or else you'd
do it. – – I know what you could do. I just must be sure so that after I
leave I won't think, "What if I had done that?" And then I wonder why
I want you to. – – I sometimes think that underneath it all you *are* very
weak. Just like my uncle on Monday. I got out of here and I felt, "Thank
God." I was expecting you to react like my uncle. I was testing you as far
as I could. – – I begin to realize why my sexual feelings for men scare me
so. There were two weak men about that thing in my life and it's hard for
me to believe that *all* men aren't that way. Now a new idea comes to my
mind. So there are sexual feelings between a man and a woman, that
doesn't mean that something will happen. So you see an attractive man
and you're attracted to him but that's all. Nothing needs to happen from
it. I always before this felt that it would. I feel this about you. But love is
involved too. – – – I guess that's it. I come here every day and have such
sexual feelings and love and I sit and look at you and I think you're the
best-looking man and how much I'd like to make love to you, and nothing's going to happen. – – Oh! – – You said once that I didn't want to find

a man who wouldn't have sexual feelings for me, but who I didn't have sexual feelings for. That's partly true. But now I'm having sexual feelings and I want it and yet really I *don't* want it to be, and I must be sure. I feel as if I'm talking like an idiot. – –

**A:** I wonder if you aren't asking, is it possible to be fully aware of your own feelings and still not to have to act on them?

**P:** I think that's what I was asking. Because I do have them a lot, and not just for you or for Tom. It's just completely physical. – – I've always made such a strong line between sexual feelings and being a mother. I can't do it any more. We go out with men and I have sexual feelings and it's great. And then I feel, how can I also be a wife and a mother? So, I think that I have to eat and get fat. I've a fear that I'll turn into one big sexual feeling and go crazy. I used to lie in bed and think about this. – – The act of love is so explosive to a child if she has normal feelings, and it looks so wild. I'd hear my parents making love and I knew it was wild and I could see my father's penis and it's so big and then it's small and it explodes. That's what I'd think, and I'd be lying there writhing with sexual feelings just like now and feel very explosive. – – – Yesterday I wondered why I feel so. . . . . funny around you. It dawned on me that there's no reason I should. – –

**A:** We'll stop here for today.

### DISCUSSION

The intense transference experience in yesterday's session is followed today by indications of her further integration and acceptance of the transference frustration, and the resulting gradual renunciation of the childhood oedipal wishes. She expresses an increasing conscious acceptance and tolerance for her own sexual impulses, and a growing capacity to experience them in the presence of the object without undue anxiety or fears over loss of control. She also indicates her recognition that these feelings are part of the normal developmental sequence, and she shows the capacity to understand the oedipal wishes of the little girl, and at the same time the awareness that she cannot in reality have her father.

The brief dream of redecorating the inside of the old house is a reference to herself, to the internal changes that have occurred and that will continue after termination, as well as to the "bad mood" about having to do so. She also elaborates on the reality perception that what has occurred in the analysis has been chiefly a series of intrapsychic processes, and that the realistic components of our interaction have been of relatively minor importance. However, it must be emphasized that it was the reality factors and behavior in her role as patient and my role as analyst that set the stage to permit these intrapsychic experiences and changes to occur.

She equates the termination with death and the necessity for grief and mourning, but expresses the knowledge that once the mourning process has been completed and the pain experienced, reorganization and resumption of living will occur. Her statement, "You've kept me from *really* being hurt," is a tacit recognition again that even though she has experienced intense psychic pain here as a result of the analysis, she has been aware that my motives have not been hostile or punitive, but have been part of an attempt to help her in a therapeutic way. There is also an increasing confidence in herself as an independent and separate individual who no longer needs to lean up against me for support.

This movement toward integration and maturity is briefly interrupted by the regressive fantasy that she really has not tested me to the fullest, and that she still anticipates the possibility that she could seduce me if she chose. My simple intervention of asking her to elaborate on the fantasy indicates once again that I accept the fantasy and feelings, but that I am not threatened by this possibility, and that it is safe for her to experience the full intensity of her sexual drives toward me. Initially she deals with this at the level of the reality of my role as her analyst, but subsequently the residual transference to me as the uncle is expressed in her reference to the Monday session, and the sexual testing of me in connection with her fantasies about the semen and the issues of pregnancy. Her reaction, "Thank God," as she left without overt seduction reveals again how in spite of the intensity of the patient's sexual transference drives and demands, there is reassurance and relief that the analyst does not respond to them. This issue has particular relevance today in view of the so-called therapies now being promulgated which encourage various forms of overt physical and/or sexual contacts. In this context she is able cognitively to recognize how she has displaced the fantasies and perceptions about the uncle and father to all subsequent men in her life, and how only after the repetitive experiences in the transference is she now able to separate feelings and thoughts from the needs to act on them.

My intervention about the difference between feeling and acting is an attempt further to strengthen this recognition and awareness, and it leads her to express her growing capacity to accept the fact that she may have sexual feelings toward realistically inappropriate objects without undue guilt, and that she can maintain control of such drives at the conscious level of thinking and of voluntary renunciation. This capacity to accept the occurrence of such feelings without undue neurotic guilt is a reflection of structural changes that have occurred. In terms of superego functions, there is now a more realistic modulation and acceptance of sexuality as part of human existence without fear of punishment or loss of love. Changes in ego functions include greater confidence in herself and in her conscious voluntary controls to the point that there is no longer the previously experienced fear of being overwhelmed by her instinctual strivings. Sexuality is no longer associated with the various primary-process fantasies of danger, and the resolution of the oedipal attachment permits her to make an age-appropriate and stable object choice for the discharge of sexual drives.

This current material again leads back genetically in her associations to the primal scene experiences in childhood, which occurred at a time when ego controls were not as effectively established as at present, when superego threats were more primitive and severe, when the fantasies accompanying the sexual arousal and the primal scene experiences involved a sense of personal danger and destruction, and when the capacity to deal with all this at conscious integrative levels was limited. Her final statement that it has dawned on her that there is no need to feel anxious and "funny" in the situation with me is an indicator of this now-matured ego capacity for regulation, control, and discharge of the sexual drives.

Once again it is clear from the material of this session that the patient is doing almost all the analytic work herself, and that she hardly needs me any more to prompt her associations or to interpret the material for her. She is continuing the working-through process on her own, and shows the capacity for self-analysis.

---

## SESSION 343

**P:** – – – – All of a sudden. . . . . . – I've decided it's time for me to leave. – – I feel there is nothing more I can do in here. I know. . . . . you can talk just so much and then you must act on it. I come here and one day I love you and the next day I've regressed to being a child. I guess it's natural. I may do it when I leave, but I'll come out of it. I know what I'm doing. Last night I realized how I'd run. . . . . I used to get a release from a book or a movie about a man and a woman. It was very satisfying. But I don't get it any more. I must face the facts. All the ways that I act in here are attempts to stay a child and I'm *not* any more. – – – – I was thinking about it last night. I never before just sat and kept feeling it and realized that none of this will get me my father. Not reading a book or watching television or acting out on all of this. . . . . and then I'd get the thought to cut my wrists. I hate to have it, and I don't want it or plan to do it. I know now that it's a mechanism that I use and I use it on myself and on you or on Tom. It's funny but it doesn't scare the adult, but it scares the hell out of the child. – – – When you leave someone that you love very much, it's natural to think that you will want to die too. People tell me that. But it's a thought and it won't happen and I will get over it. And to cut my wrists is violent and hostile, and to want to claw your face and see the blood. If I ever did, I'd give up. It's like dying, and it would be stupid and childish and not thinking and I'd ruin my life. After all, I'm seeking happiness and not death. It also dawns on me that I have no reason for these thoughts now, and that Tom is *not* going out with women. (Elaborates.) They all belong to the past. (Elaborates.) All I have to do is accept it and accept the fact that Tom loves me and that there is absolutely nothing wrong with me. – – – Thinking like this really bothers me. I'm thinking that. . . . . there's nothing here for me. You're a doctor and you've treated a patient. And I love you for it but I'm in complete control of myself and I don't *need* you. – – All good things have to come to an end and they can't go on forever. The only good thing is my love feelings for you because they can't grow any more and they can't go any further. It's such a strain to think these things, but I want to. I can regress and act like a child all that I want, but it's no good. – – – – I also decided that I can just hate for so long. I have nothing to hate now because all that I hated is in the past. I could carry it on my back for so long and it's just ridiculous. – – – – – I can't believe it! Am I wrong? – –

A: What was going through your mind?

P: – I actually want to leave and I actually want to leave today. – – It makes me so sad that I can't. . . . . I can't believe it. – – I can't believe that I'm thinking this. (There is a knock on the door and the analyst goes to the door briefly and then returns to his chair.) – – Last night I kept thinking. . . . . that I'd ask you and set a time. And then I thought that between today and the time there would be nothing to do in here. I'm really scared. It's just like the first time on the diving board. I want to do it so badly, but I can't believe that it's me doing it. – – – *Cry*

A: What was the detail of the thought that there would be nothing to do between today and the time that you set?

P: I thought. . . . . about coming in and telling you what you thought about a week from Monday. I thought about a week from today as the last day. And then I thought, "But then what?" I've been doing everything I *Cry*

probably would do. How much. . . . . so I act out childishly and it's still
an act. If I tell you to go to hell and I hit you, it's not real. I love you. So
I cry about it. But why come every day and cry? I know I'm sad. Or else
I'll tell you how scared I am. But I know I'm scared. I feel like I've been
through it all. – – I can't sit and talk to you intelligently because. . . . . I
just can't. I don't know whether to come back on Monday or what. I didn't
plan this at all, and I can't believe that I'm thinking this. It just hit me
last night. – – I always thought that I'd get up and say goodbye and thank
you and feel like a million dollars. But I'm scared and I'm shaking all over
and I think that I would be if I left a month from now. – – –

**A:** It's usually best in analysis to set a date sometime in advance as to
when you are actually going to stop.

**P:** – – – I guess I'll plan to leave a week from today, then. – – – (Sigh.)
– I keep thinking that I'm kidding myself and that I can't be anxious to
leave. I feel like I'm starting a race and I'm waiting for them to yell start.
I *feel* it and I feel that I'm ready to leave. But then I wonder if I'm kidding
myself, and am I really incapable? But I know it's not true and I can do
it now just as well as any other time. – – This is a very odd feeling for me
that I have complete control of my life. – – – I feel like I'm leaving you
nothing but the satisfaction of knowing that I love you. – –

**A:** What's the detail?

*Quiet*
*Sadness*

**P:** I just get the thought. . . . . I hate to leave you with problems and
I wonder about yours. But it's your life. I can't solve your problems for
you. It's just another way of trying to wriggle my way into your life and
I don't really want to. I think of all that you've done for me and I'm just
going to walk out. It's a way of holding on. It's your job and you don't
need me. It doesn't matter if I walk out. That's all that I can do. – – If
you think about it hard enough you'll realize that my love is just an emotion. Because I don't really know you. There's no interacting. – – – I'm
taking it with me and you're not getting any of it. I guess it doesn't matter.
I keep forgetting that you don't need it. – – Regardless of anything, I still
love you. You're an awfully nice person. – – – – – – –

**A:** We'll stop here for today.

## DISCUSSION

Throughout the first portion of this session the patient again elaborates
upon her growing awareness of herself, her sense of confidence and control,
her identity as a woman, and her realization of the irrational and unfulfill-
ing character of her regressive oscillations. There is a growing recognition

of the reality of my role, and further evidence of her having increasingly resolved the transference neurosis. In contrast to earlier times during the termination phase, this material comes out with a quiet sincerity and earnestness, and without major affective storm or explosion.

Her feeling of sadness is again experienced in response to my question of what was going through her mind when she asked if she were wrong. This question is prompted by the fact that I do not know what she is referring to, and it leads to her recognition and expression of a positive wish on her part now to leave.

The setting of the termination date is a significant event during the termination phase, since it brings with it an increased recognition of the time limits of the analysis, and an increasing reality perception of its finality. From the very beginning of the analysis, the patient "knows" that one day it will end, and that it cannot be a permanent relationship. After the working-through of infantile conflicts in the transference neurosis, and the beginning introduction of the termination phase, the patient more forcefully recognizes that the analysis will end, and much of the termination conflict and its elaboration during this phase is then stimulated. However, when a definite date is finally established as the last session, the reality of this experience is increasingly brought home to the patient and there is often a final flurry and upsurge of conflict in response to this. It is the anticipation of this final upsurge and the affects that will accompany it that leads the patient to manifest the typical resistance and defense that there will be nothing to do between the time that the date is set and the actual termination. My question about this is an attempt to highlight and clarify this defensive resistance.

Her response indicates the anticipation that she will be angry again or that she will cry and experience sadness daily, and that she will be frightened at the prospect of termination. She briefly manifests another typical resistance of patients at this point in analysis in the wish to terminate immediately and thereby avoid the time interval up to the final session. This is expressed in her statement "I don't know whether to come back on Monday or what." And this wish for immediate termination is rationalized by her partly realistic statement that it would be the same if she left a month from now.

In order to block this resistance, I make the generalized suggestion that she set a date sometime in advance, but I deliberately do not suggest when it should be. Actually the termination phase has been going on for more than the last four months, and in this time there has been a great deal of working-through of the typical termination conflicts. A good deal of structural change has been occurring with significant maturation and consolidation of her identity as an adult woman, and an increased confidence in herself, her own judgment, and her own capacities for control. In view of all this, I feel that for me actively to participate in the setting of the termination date would be to depreciate this new identity and concept of herself, and it would be a way of indirectly saying that she still needs me to guide her, and to help her make important decisions. Since most of the work of termination has already been accomplished, I feel it will make relatively little difference in the final outcome whether she were to remain in analysis for a short time, or for a longer interval of another month or so. Therefore, when she herself immediately and spontaneously decides to terminate a week from today, I remain silent, thereby acknowledging my confidence in her to make this decision.

Having made this decision, she almost immediately begins to express the typical anxiety and doubts that all patients experience at such a time, but these are accompanied by the adult recognition of her growth and her own capacities.

The final material of the session involves another reworking of the transference fantasies about the father and his needs for her, but this time from a more adult and reality-oriented perspective, with the spontaneous recognition that it represents the continuing wish to remain attached to me. This is accompanied by a quiet and reflective sense of sadness as she comments upon the reality of our respective positions. Different from many patients in analysis for whom the analyst must point out issues such as this, the fact that this patient does it on her own and with a voluntary sense of renunciation is a sign of the extent of the working-through that has occurred, and the completeness with which the transference neurosis is being resolved. In resolving the attachment to me and giving me up in the transference, she is simultaneously at last giving up the final neurotic attachments to the father of her childhood.

---

## SESSION 344

Patient is five minutes late.

P: – – – – – – – – – We went to visit my parents this weekend, and it's so hard not to get caught up in their emotions. It's so hard not to do it after a while. I found myself doing it. I must set myself aside from them and tell myself that it has no effect on me any more. But it's hard as hell.

What do people do if they live in the same town. How do they ever get over it? – – – I feel as if I'm walking around in a daze and nothing affects me. I can think of leaving and being gone from here. It seems natural to see myself in that position of not coming here. I can see that I'll be all right, and yet I had a cold fear and a sense of terror and I wanted to cry hysterically all weekend when I'd think about it. But the best thing is that I remember how nice you've been to me and it helps. Every time that I've hurt myself, you've said. . . . . "there's no reason to." – – And I have very open thoughts now because I'm used to not suppressing things. It's almost as if I was a child. I guess these are the thoughts that everyone has that they automatically suppress. I had open sexual thoughts about my father. They weren't generated by anything and they were just there. Once I had the fear that something happened to mother and it scared me. And then I felt, "That's what the child is thinking." These are thoughts that caused terror in me and they're natural, I guess. I didn't act out on it and it went away. It was all a battle inside. Each time I have these thoughts I strain as hard as I can and I finally get out of it. – – – It's funny what little things bother me. I saw a movie and Judy Garland was in it. She's so sick and she's an alcoholic and she's cut her wrists and she's made a mess of her life. I guess I identify with her and I'm hysterical. Rose called me on Friday and she reminds me of myself when I was having such problems.

**A:** What were some of the details about Judy Garland and Rose?

**P:** I don't know. Rose calls when she has problems and not when she doesn't. She has the same problems that I do, but much worse. She's done things that I wouldn't do. I just listen to her talk. She goes to see Harris and I wonder does it do her any good? She's not getting anywhere. It's just like Judy Garland who had therapy and went to a hospital but got nowhere. This bothers me. – – I know that my problems are not as bad as theirs. It's silly, but they scare me and they make me feel, "Oh." – – So few people that I know have been in therapy and I can't say that any of it has worked. Oh, it's worked and it's helped them a little, but I want mine to *cure* me! Is that asking too much? I want to go home and be a wife and a mother and not be pressured into going outside the home. – – I guess I'll find out. I *am* the way I am. I feel occasionally that people don't like me this way, but it doesn't really bother me. I think about my father's crack at me about me having no brains and it was really very hostile but it rolled off my back. Why? And my sister's crack that I don't do things for people. And Tom's comment about me as a bad mother. I'm doing the best that I can for the three children and myself and that's all I can do. I can't also go around being a good Samaritan to everyone else. (Elaborates.) If people don't like me this way, it's tough, because no one else is in my position and so they can't say what they'd do. – – I feel that leaving here makes me feel very insecure and any of these things bothers me. But I'm not going to change. Analysis has given me my security and I've fallen back on it. Really it's you who has. I felt that I could take anything and not fall apart. And now I don't have you to fall back on and I'm going to do it for myself. And I *do* get it. – – These are all things that I have to accept and not let them bother me. – – – It's surprising how much it helps just to talk about things. And then I realize how ridiculous they are. – – I feel like a child crying on your shoulder, and telling you all of the bad things that happen. I grab at you frantically. You caused me to. That's the rule of my life that you've always been and that's why I won't grow until I get out of here. – – – Now I feel absolutely frantic and I don't know why. Except that I don't want to look at something. – –

A: What comes to your mind?

P: I don't know. Is it an idea or a thing? I'm having both thoughts. I'm having the old ones to grab your penis and take it with me or eat you and keep you inside of me. I don't want to let you go. – – In here you're the biggest person, and the strongest and you're my parent. And when I'm *not* in here then *I'm* the biggest and no one else can do things for me and I'm going to have to leave here. But that in itself is what gives me my strength. – – I'm terribly anxious to try my own wings and I get excited to think about it. But then I'll never ever see someone that I love very much again. Never! Ever! And then I think to myself, "Oh, I'm going to stay a child." – –

A: I think that this is one component of the frantic feeling that you had. I mean that you're excited and you're anticipating and you're secretly glad that you're going to try your own wings.

P: – I'm *very* optimistic. I know that I'll regress occasionally but I feel that I'll make it. But then I wonder *how* do I know? – – – Something says to me that I have complete control of myself and that if I want to, I can make it with a breeze. It's not even going to be as hard as I think it is. – – – – – – – – – – – – – – – – – – –

A: We'll stop here for today.

## DISCUSSION

Once again the patient indicates the growing capacity for integration, confidence, and control at the level of action, while at the same time accepting the fact that at times she will have unwelcome fantasies. However, the fact that she can accept them without automatic defenses, and can analyze them as they occur, and thereby control them without undue anxiety is a further sign of her growth and her increased ego-capacity for integration. Her reference to Judy Garland and her unsuccessful treatment, as well as her friend's problems, suggests to me that she has a continuing uncertainty and fear about the success of her own treatment, and of how permanent the changes would be. In asking her about the details of this, I am attempting to get her to elaborate on her own fears of a recurrence of her illness after leaving the treatment.

After elaborating on the emotional difficulties of these two women and their unsuccessful treatment, the patient then begins to expose her own concerns, and her wish to be sure that she has been cured. Her statement, "I guess I'll find out," again reflects her growing sense of confidence in herself, and in her capacity to face whatever is in store for her, while at the same time recognizing that realistically speaking there can be no guarantee at this time about the question of "cure." However, she follows this with a number of incidents which reveal her increasing capacity to tolerate other people's disapproval or criticism without undue distress, but also accompanied by a realistic appraisal of her own limitations.

In describing her feeling that it is I who have given her a sense of security which she can now maintain for herself, she is condensing a psychic process that has been occurring throughout the course of the analysis in the transference neurosis, and is also describing a process which occurred only incompletely and inadequately during her original development. This involves a partial identification with and internalization of the parental object, resulting in a nucleus for the further internal development of the sense of self, the sense of identity, and the establishment of comfortably integrated ego-functions. However, to continue or intensify this type of identification and internalization beyond the optimal degree and level is to hamper the child's growth to reach his own individual potential, and is to limit him to the range of possible identifications with the parent, and not permit him his own further independent freedom to develop in his own ways. She indicates a perception of this when she says, "That's why I won't grow until I get out of here."

However, this image of taking what she has received here and building upon it in accordance with her own talents, wishes, and abilities evokes in her an immediate sense of anxiety, accompanied by a transient regression and wish to acquire my penis or else incorporate me orally as a defense against the impending separation. At this point the patient illustrates the typical adolescent-level conflict in which the child is eager to leave the parent and go out on his own and live in the adult world, and at the same time is still anxious and has tendencies toward regression to the previously gratifying dependent status.

My intervention pointing to my recognition of the secret pleasure she has at the anticipation of "trying your own wings" is an attempt to foster and strengthen this component, and again to permit her the recognition that her previous transference fantasies of my wanting to cling to her and not let her grow up are distorted perceptions that do not correspond to the reality of our relationship. Her response is again to emphasize the optimism and her growing sense of confidence in her own abilities. This is analagous to the normal late adolescent who leaves home for college or marriage with a sense of uncertainty and regret, and yet a genuine sense of pleasurable anticipation of the unknown life ahead.

---

## SESSION 345

P: – – – The past two days have been horrible. Monday I ate so much! And Tuesday I was in a black cloud all day! I felt like a child who'd been weaned and I couldn't stand it. Well, I could. But it was as if I was dying inside. I had dreams of bathrooms and of worms and Maine and the house in Evanston. They are always the same old dreams. – – I'm mad! And yet I don't know what I'm mad about. I know that I can't go on forever like this and I don't *want* to! – – – – – – – – I get to feeling frustrated. I *know* that I can take care of myself. And I know after all that I've looked at here that I can't do anything else. So I can't figure out why I act this way.

A: What comes to your mind?

P: It's the old feeling I can't believe I could get through this without much trouble. It would be as if I'm dead. I *know* that I can, and I will do it. I have nothing to fear and I don't need anybody. – – But I'm so afraid to come in here and be happy, or to be as happy as I can be. This is not easy to do. But it's as if I'm determined to make it as hard on myself as I can. And yet, all through this I have the feeling that I don't need to act this way. – – Yesterday I had the thought that maybe if I got sick for the rest of this week then I could come next week. – –

A: What was the detail?

P: I can't remember how I thought I'd get sick. When I eat a lot I get in a mood and I feel physically sick the next day, as if I'm getting flu or something. – – – I feel so. . . . . when I know I'm coming here I can act so beautifully. I feel so adult and secure and happy and I love my family and I love being a woman. – – And then, I realize that I'll not be here and I feel that it's all being taken away from me. It's so easy to do it with support. But without support. . . . . . – – I go back to the same old thing. I'm afraid to be happy. Why? All I think is. . . . . I get absolutely no attention.

A: Let's go back to why it is that you feel that if you want to come here next week too, that you have to be sick in order to ask. And let's look at what it means that you couldn't just ask to come if you wanted to.

P: I don't know. . . . . . I would feel that I'd failed.

A: In what way?

P: I have a horrible fear of. . . . . I'd ask for next week and then the next week and the next week. I don't want to do that. It's not a matter of *really* wanting to come. If it was, I think I'd come in here and get hysterical and say I just can't leave. – – – I think that if I asked you I'd be more afraid of you saying, yes, that I can come back, than of you saying, no, you don't need to come back. – – It would be like throwing my whole need onto you and have you gobble it up and I just disappear. – – There's a part in me that says that I would like to stay in here forever. If I let it go I'd get nowhere. It's a part of all children. Part wants to stay under their parents' wings. But they fight it somehow and they go off and they marry and they overcome it. – – I know that I'm scared and I know that you know that I'm scared, but I can't give in to all of these things and I'm not going to get sick. – – – The main thing I have to do is give up my father and any desire of ever having my father, and I have to keep that in the past. (Sigh.) – And when I give up my father I'd have to not try to go back to mother. – – – I feel that this is do or die! I can't come back here! If I ever. . . . . if I ever! . . . . . I either get out of here and keep going, or else if I ever come back, I'll come back and back and back, and I don't want that. I don't want to live off of someone else for the rest of my life. I know it happens that some people haven't worked through everything, and they *do* need to come back occasionally, but I don't want to. Maybe that's wrong and maybe I should accept the idea that I might need more therapy some time. But why should I? Damn it, I'm supposed to be well. – – – I don't know. I don't know how to think about this. The feeling I have now is that I want to forget it and make it a void in my life and be able to pick up my living. – – I'll always love you for what you've done for me, but I don't want to hang on to analysis. I'll not go around and talk about it, or analyze other people or stuff like that. I want to forget the whole psychiatric field of medicine. --- . . . . . . -- I just can't keep myself wide open when I leave here. I'm too soft inside. I don't think it's humanly possible and I don't want to think every day of my life how much I'm going to miss you and how much I love you. --- I don't want to hate

*Cry* analysis or hate you, but I don't want to put you in front of myself every night and say that I still want you. If you can't have something in life you must overcome it. There *was* a time when I wanted you and needed you and needed help. I still love you but that was in the past now. --- I don't know whether this is wrong or right, but it's the only way that I can do this. I can't take something that I love very much and spend the rest of my life wanting it. I know logically and reasonably all the reasons why I don't want you, but I love to work at it. When you love someone

*Cry* you want them around all the time, and that's natural. But I also realize that I can't live a full mature life *with* this feeling. -- Do you see what I mean? -

**A:** What comes to your mind that you feel I might *not* see what you mean?

**P:** Again I feel that I'm apologizing to you. This is the hardest thing in my life. I have to choose the lesser of the two evils and I have to choose the one that's best for me. It will come easy but I'll never be able to say that I never loved you.

**A:** It was once appropriate to want your father as a little girl and during the analysis to want me. But now both your childhood and the analysis are in the past and so this situation changes.

**P:** It's not that I don't want you. But I'm choosing something instead of you because it's the best. I guess it's accepting my love for you without ever having you. --- I don't have to act out on it or to fulfill it, but it's there and it always will be but I don't have to live it. I'll be living a completely different life. -- It's just soaked in on me what you said, the meaning of it. My wanting and loving my father as a child was very natural then, but not now. It's natural *not* to now. But you don't forget it. It's still part of you and it's a thought that will stay in your mind forever. --- It's so funny because you've said that to me lately but I never realized it. Now I do, and it makes me feel better. I feel relieved, that I can keep it in the past and it will not be detrimental to anyone. What went on was natural then and what's going on now is natural. -- It's frustrating to me to find for the first time a love that I've never seen before and then to have to detour it immediately. I wish I could take years to outgrow it. ----

**A:** We'll stop here for today.

DISCUSSION

The affects connected with the resolution and termination of the transference relationship to me still predominate in the patient's psychic life, although the conflict over termination is gradually being resolved. Although there still is sadness, pain, and anger associated to the idea of separation from me, she has actually resolved her conflict about leaving through making the conscious decision to do so, aided by her increasing recognition of the advantages in termination, as well as her growing capacity to tolerate and deal with the painful affects involved.

She also illustrates the awareness that her anticipation of pain and distress is actually greater than the reality event itself would justify or involve. As she says, "It's as if I'm determined to make it as hard on myself as I can. And yet, all through this I have the feeling that I don't need to act this way." Following this there is a transient regressive fantasy of getting sick in order to extend our contact, thereby resorting to a now out-moded means of coping with her distress.

This fantasy of using sickness as a means of prolonging our relationship is a complex one involving a number of issues. As mentioned above, it represents a continuing use of an archaic and now out-moded means of adaptation and gratification, similar to the times in childhood when she would complain of being sick and her father would come to examine her. It also reflects a current fear of asking directly for something she wants or feels she needs, as well as a fantasy that since she has set a termination date, it must remain immutable and that she cannot change her mind or ask me directly that it be postponed. This is part of a continuing pattern to deny any "normal" dependency needs or wishes, and as such, it probably reflects a projection to me of the father's attitude and demands that she be strong, never have doubts or fears, and never admit or express them if she does. It is in order to explore these latter implications behind this fantasy that I ask her to associate to the fantasy itself and to the hesitation about asking directly for what she wants.

Her response that it would mean she had failed, and her continuing fear about the intensity of the regressive pull, are part of the old transference patterns which she simultaneously recognizes are no longer really applicable. There are elements in her response that indicate the uncertainty she feels in her new adult identity, in whether or not it is ever appropriate to ask for help, and in the continuing fear that if she does so she will lose herself. On her own she begins to take some distance from this, recognizing that others may at times need to return for further therapy, and that perhaps she should accept this within herself. But at the same time she dismisses and depreciates this possibility for herself. In her material she indicates a recognition of the need to let the transference be resolved and fade into the past as a once important but no longer significant experience. In passing she refers to a mechanism which many patients use to avoid breaking the final ties to their analyst, by continuing to "talk about it, or analyze other people, or stuff like that." For many patients such behavior represents an identification with the aggressor, or a continuing defense against separation and loss.

She goes on to refer to her progressive feelings of independence and resolution of the attachment to me, with further consolidation of her recognition that only through such a resolution can she live a full and satisfying life. However, there is still a momentary sense of guilt at leaving me and a regression to the fantasy that I will not accept her wish for independence, expressed in her question as to whether I can understand her. It is to block the implications of this fantasy that I ask about her question that I might not see what she meant.

Her response again elaborates upon the sense of guilt over choosing reality instead of me, and her statement, ". . . I'll never be able to say that I never loved you," implies a feeling that she should not have experienced the kinds of transference reactions that she has had. My intervention in regard to having once wanted the father during childhood, and having experienced similar wishes toward me during the analysis, is an attempt to help her more effectively integrate these experiences as important *past* relationships which she will never forget, but for which any continuing sense of guilt would now be inappropriate.

The oedipal phase of development, with the various wishes, drives, and fantasies that accompany it, is part of the normal process of growth and maturation, and it is important for the formation of psychic structures within the individual. As part of normal healthy development, it *should* be present, and its failure to develop would be a sign of psychological arrest with significant later pathological repercussions. However, as childhood proceeds, healthy maturation requires that the oedipus complex should be dissolved and gradually replaced by other age-appropriate heterosexual object-relationships, and once fully resolved, there should then be no persistent guilt for its having at one time been present. In other words, the ideally healthy resolution of the oedipus complex involves a child's acceptance of the drives and fantasies that accompany it, followed by renunciation of the parental objects, and thus leading to ultimate relief from the conflict and guilt that may have been engendered at its height.

In a parallel way, the same is true in regard to the transference neurosis during the course of psychoanalysis. The transference neurosis is an important and major therapeutic tool through which psychic conflicts are mobilized, experienced, and ultimately resolved, and these transference phenomena are a necessary part of the analysis. During the height of the transference neurosis various pleasurable and painful drives and affects will be evoked, but as the transference neurosis is finally resolved during the termination phase of the analysis (analagous to the resolution of the oedipus complex during normal psychosexual development) these drives and affects are no longer appropriate, and can be gradually given up and disappear. In other words, when the transference objects have been renounced by the patient, and when the patient is now capable of achieving mature and age-appropriate gratifications with realistic objects in his life, there can and should be an acceptance of the transference neurosis as a "normal" phase of psychological development during analysis. Therefore, the fact of its having occurred should no longer evoke feelings of guilt, shame, or disloyalty to other people after the analysis is terminated.

Parenthetically, it is not uncommon for the spouse of a patient to feel left out, resentful, or jealous of the patient's transference relationship to the analyst. But as long as the analyst uses the transference neurosis for the patient's therapy and does not respond with countertransference needs of his own, these reactions in the spouse would be analogous to similar feelings toward the parents in the original oedipal relationship.

It is to these issues that my intervention about the appropriateness of her oedipal and transference feelings is focused, accompanied by the statement that since both her childhood and analysis are now in the past, the situation about such matters is changed. The patient's response indicates her recognition of these issues and her statement, ". . . It's there and it always will be, but I don't have to live it. I'll be living a completely different life," is a reflection of this kind of acceptance. It implies that the memories of the transference neurosis and its implications (analogous to the memories of the oedipal relationship and its implications) should and will always be a part of the patient's life, but will not be a currently active and significant one, and will become one of the background experiences that now permits full and healthy development and maturity. She goes on to elaborate these issues, indicating how something which has been said before "just soaked in on me," thereby achieving a deeper and more integrated recognition and awareness. This new level of recognition and awareness permits a more appropriate judgment by her, and thereby also permits a relief of the inappropriate guilt feelings that had accompanied it, so that she now feels better. "I feel relieved that I can keep it in the past and it will not be detrimental to anyone. What went on was natural then, and what's going on now is natural."

This session illustrates that significant and deepening insights may still occur in the very last stages of an analysis, and that the working-through process can be maintained, both by the patient and by the analyst, right up to the end of the treatment.

---

## SESSION 346

**P:** I can't believe that I'm leaving here. Tomorrow's my last day. — — I've been dreaming wildly all night long, dream after dream. — — I dreamt of four girls and one of them was myself from high school, we're waiting for a bus for a big basketball game. We were standing in line and there were two girls ahead of me. I was mad because they wouldn't wait. They'd saved me a seat but I refused to sit with them. It was an air-conditioned bus and I sat in the other seat. Then I had that feeling of claustrophobia. (Elaborates.) I was playing with a red shoe with a loop in the back. I looked out the window and I saw my ex-husband, but I'd not ever been married to him. I felt, "That's the way life is, but why doesn't it hurt?" And then I thought, "You can remember the old times, but gosh it doesn't hurt and I'm accepting it." I couldn't believe that it was me. I was dressed in rags. There was a girl with my ex-husband who was in a beautiful formal dress. — — And then I was with Tom in bed and we were trying to make love, but my father and sister kept coming in and we'd go to answer the door. Then I had a dream that I was a young boy and I was fighting with a man and I killed him and I was happy because I knew that I'd be killed. — — — — I've depended on others to tell me that I'm not sick or that I have minor problems and stuff. I don't know how I'm supposed to be when I'm leaving. Am I supposed to worry? Am I supposed to be afraid that I'll regress? Or, is it all normal? Or, is it up to me? — — I'm afraid that I'll fly out of here in a cloud as I did with Harris and then bang! I'll have it hit like hell. I know that it's a completely different situation here but I can't help thinking about it. — — Yesterday I had a repetitive thought that got me so excited, but I can't remember it. – – When I left here, I was thinking. . . . . when I feel love for you, I feel love for others, and when I feel love for other people I remember my love for you. – – I just hope that six months from now I'm still loving you. I know that realistically I have absolutely no reason to hate you. – – – – –

**A:** What are your associatitns to the red shoes in the dream?

**P:** – (Laughs.) I don't know. I can only think that one shoe was all right and one wasn't. – Suddenly it's like Tom and I, and I'm the shoe that's all right, and he's the shoe that isn't. I was trying to fix it. The loop was a hole in the shoe. To me, a hole is symbolic of the vagina, and the red is always a sexual symbol to me, but I don't know why. Tom is not going to bowl into this hole and I was trying to make a woman out of him. He's changed a lot since the analysis. He doesn't baby me any more. I married him to have him take care of me but now he doesn't, and it's really the other way around. He gets upset and I take care of him. I'll never be able to go back to the other. But it *should* be this way. I have a horrible vision of leaving here and floundering and grasping every straw that I can find and there not being any straws. – – It's like the dream about the man. I'm very capable of living now and I have none of the frantic periods as I used to have, but I can still remember them. If I didn't I wouldn't realize how weak I used to be. Two years ago I was so weak! And now I'm not. I don't understand how this can be. – – – Except that I've gone over and over everything that bothered me and learned that it doesn't need to bother me any more. I haven't lived it yet, and I have lived the other. – – In the face of frustration and anxiety like I'm feeling now, I can't come back to nursing. I want to, but I know that I can't, but it's what caused my problems. But now I have another road to go on and one that I couldn't see the other way. – – – I think I want you to tell me that I'm all right, and that I'm well. I know that people don't always get well. – – But if you did, I'd know that you don't know. No one knows but me. You know what you think, but. . . . . – – – – – – – – I try to think why sex with Tom would throw me into these things, or any kind of sexual feelings. I never could let them out with my father and I went back to mother. So outside of marriage it was easier to let them out because it represented my father. But *in* marriage I was giving up *both* mother *and* father. That sounds so simple. – – – It's funny all that hell that I went through in here last year when I thought that I was around three weeks old. I can't remember any of that very well, but what has evolved from all that is this simple little conclusion I've come to. – – – – – – – Suddenly I'm feeling all of these wonderful feelings | *Sad* about you. But they're so final. I feel like a woman and yet I feel like your daughter, and I feel so grateful for what you've done for me. You're absolutely the nicest person I've ever met. – – – – I've heard that this is the

*Cry*
*Quietly*

way you feel regardless of who your analyst is, but I feel that this is different, because I feel that you really *are* this way. – – – – – – It takes so much more effort when I like you. – – It makes me so happy to think

*Sad*

that I can have these feelings about you. I can have them for the rest of my life every time I think of you. The other day I thought that I wanted to bury all of these feelings, but I don't. – – – – It really is a *terribly* sad thing to me that I have to leave here. – – (Sigh.) – – – – – – (Sigh.) – – – –

A: We'll stop here for today.

At the door the analyst gives the patient her bill for the current month, including tomorrow's session.

### Discussion

The patient's dreams are rather complex and from their manifest content, they apparently involve the continuing reworking of conflict as the analysis comes to an end. My own associations are that the four girls represent the four analytic sessions per week, and that the two who were in front of her, represent the remaining sessions of the analysis. I feel that the ex-husband to whom she had never really been married represents me, and that the feelings she had about him represent her further acceptance of the termination. There is a continuing reworking of the oedipal theme when the father comes in on the love-making. And there is also the last gasp of her masculine protest and herself as a boy, who fights with a man whom she finally kills (probably me) and then is happy because she knows that this part of herself (the wish to be the boy) will also be killed.

However, the patient does not spontaneously attempt to analyze the dreams, and instead her associations are driven by the uncertainty and doubt over herself, her new capacities, her reactions to the termination, and her questions about the future.

After the silence, I ask about the dream element of the shoes, since to me this is the least clear. Her own association of the shoes representing herself and her husband is a surprise to me. But when she describes in passing how the husband has changed in his attitudes and expectations toward her, and how he no longer feels it necessary to gratify her neurotic demands, she illustrates another criterion of structural change as the result of analysis. The patient's more mature level of integration now elicits greater freedom of response from others in the environment, who recognize the patient's increased capacity to tolerate stress and can therefore make appropriate mature demands on the patient.

This shift in the dynamics of the marriage relationship is another characteristic feature of a successful analysis, which in this instance has occurred gradually and without disruptive effect. In other situations, where the spouse may have unconscious neurotic needs to adapt to or to maintain the patient's neurotic behavior, this can be more disruptive of the marital situation. When the spouse has a significant neurosis of his own and therefore cannot tolerate the patient's maturation and development of more healthy modes of behavior and adaptation, it can produce significant conflict between them, and at times can be disruptive to the psychic equilibrium of the spouse. In such situations, it is not infrequently necessary for the spouse also to seek therapy, in order to be able to accept the patient's more mature behavior and expectations.

The patient now begins to reflect, somewhat remotely, upon the nature of the therapeutic process itself, and she then develops the concise formulation regarding the dynamics of her neurotic problems. Her statement about the hell that she went through here, the fact she no longer remembers it very well, "But what has evolved from all of that is this simple little conclusion I have come to," is another characteristic feature of the analytic process. Much of the material that is brought up and worked-through during an analysis is subsequently again repressed and often not immediately accessible to conscious recall. However, this form of repression is usually different from that which existed prior to the analysis, in that there is less anxiety and conflict about such material, and having once been exposed, it could now be recovered from repression more easily if this would become necessary in the future. Patients looking back on their analysis after a significant time interval frequently have "forgotten" many of the day-to-day experiences, associations, fantasies, dreams, etc., that have been so significant for them at the time they came up in the analysis.

Her statement about the "simple little conclusion" also warrants comment. This type of formulation and conclusion was made at the time of the initial diagnostic interviews, and has been apparent throughout most of the analysis. However, to have formulated the conflict to the patient in this way earlier in the analysis would not have produced any significant therapeutic benefit since it is therapeutically necessary for the patient to go through "all that hell" in order for such a formulation ultimately to have genuine synthetic and emotionally significant meaning.

At this point she again experiences the sadness of the termination, but again from a different perspective and with a different intensity than at the height of her transference reaction, or at the height of the working-through of the termination phase. The sense of quiet sadness that accompanies these associations is characteristic for this stage of the process, and is significantly different from the major affective working-through and genuine depression that occurred earlier. It is the sign that the work of successful grief and mourning has been largely accomplished, and that in the months ahead, these residual affective reactions will gradually subside.

---

## SESSION 347

Patient pays her final bill.

P: ————— I felt so good this morning before I got here. I thought to myself that this will be a breeze, and then I got in that waiting room and I felt hysterical and I can't stand it and I'll be all alone now. —— I haven't needed you for weeks now. I just liked being here. ————— When I'm afraid then I'm not sad. I now realize that I have nothing to be afraid of, and I'm a big girl and I can take care of myself and so I feel like crying. You know, it's sad. —— Regardless of how sad it is, I'm also

*Cry*  realizing that I really *want* it this way. —— I feel like I've been to school and now I'm graduating. ——— This is such a free kind of sadness. It's the same feeling and yet I feel free from it. I've had the same feelings before but now somehow it's without all the depression and hostility and fear. —— What scares me is that it's all up to me. You are totally free. You've done your very best for me. —————— Something else has dawned on me. You've done a wonderful thing for me. You've completely opened up my life for me and my children's lives and my husband's. But I also realize that Tom should get the credit. *He* made it all possible, because without him I never could have done this. —— I wonder if it's wrong for me to have just a tiny bit of hostility for having to leave. It's my choice and I know that. I could flounder around in psychiatry if I had to. I can't help but feel, God-damn it, why do I have to go through all of this.

*Sad,*  My only consolation is that it's my life and I'll eventually benefit, and I
*Cry*  might even be better off than most people. —— It's the hardest to admit
*Softly*  that I'm sad about leaving and that I love you and yet, I'm going. And

that this is one part of life that I'll say goodbye to. You taught me a tremendous lesson, but now I leave and that's it and it doesn't go on and on. I've never experienced anything like this before. -- I feel that I have to muster all of the courage I have. -- I thought that I should come in and tell you how happy I am. I'm sorry, but I just can't, and I've decided that I'll not dump it on anyone else after I leave. I'll tell *you* how sad I am because I don't want to have to tell anyone else. --- I feel as if I've experienced my first love feelings and my first sexual feelings with you but they can't be fulfilled with you. It's sad because they were my first ones. I'm so grateful for them, but Tom is going to benefit from them. ----- Damn! Every time I start feeling happy, I feel like crying! One minute I feel young and I have my whole life ahead and how happy it will be and then I think of how sad it is! --------- It really is so frustrating but I guess it's part of the therapy that I feel I want to *do* something *for* you, to let you know how much I love you. But you already know so all I can do is accept the fact that I can't do anything for you. I can't even touch you! Someone who has done so much for me! ----- Now I try to talk myself into thinking that I'm mad because you won't give in to me, not even one little bit, not even when I'm leaving. You're going to stay the therapist. --

**A:** What's your feeling about it?

**P:** I think about what a good therapist you are. It's been my salvation in here. If you were all emotional, it would ruin me. Not really. But that's what has been so good about it. -- I guess I'm still hanging on to the end. --- One minute I feel like a child and I want to throw my arms around you and say, "Thank you," but I realize that I can't, because I'm a woman and you know that I thank you. -- I know how sad I am and you know how sad I am, but I'm *not* going to go home and cry and cry and cry. --- Now I feel as if I'm wasting time. I feel that I have nothing more to say here or do in here. ---

**A:** How do you mean that you're *wasting* time?

**P:** I'd like to get up and leave. --- And, I'm not going to. ---- I feel sad but I feel excited too, because I have so much that I didn't have before and that I didn't let out. I know that I'll live my life completely without you, but it's *because* of you, and it's challenging, and I'm *not* alone because I have lots of friends. I *love* being a woman and feeling mature and it's *fun* to be that way. Now I'm sad again! While I'm sure the sadness will disappear. -- As far as I'm concerned, you're the most wonderful person in the world and you always will be. -----------

**A:** We'll stop here.

*Cry!*

At the door, I say, "Goodbye and good luck. I hope your life is satisfying and fulfilling." The patient looks directly at me as I say this and she answers, "Thank you, Dr. Dewald," and turns around and leaves.

### DISCUSSION

At the end of the previous session I had given the patient her final bill, which included today's last session. Although it is not the end of the month, and it therefore represents a departure from the standard analytic procedure, I did it in order that the final ties between us would be cut today. Not infrequently patients delay paying their final bill beyond the time of the actual last session, and this is often used by them as a means of psychically holding on and maintaining an attachment to the analyst. Therefore the handling of the last bill by the patient can be another indicator of the extent to which this tie has been given up and the transference neurosis resolved. In this instance the patient pays the bill in full at the beginning of the session, thereby indicating that she does not have a psychological need to make use of such a mechanism.

In this last session the patient again experiences the sadness and uncertainty over leaving. However, her description of this as "a free kind of sadness," is significant of the degree to which the work of mourning has progressed. "I've had the same feelings before but now somehow it is without all of the depression and hostility and fear."

She also makes another important observation of the role that her husband has played during the analysis, although for the most part it has been a silent one. The role of a spouse is not easy when a patient is in analysis and is in the midst of a significant transference neurosis. Not infrequently the spouse feels left out of the situation, and frequently is jealous of the fact that the patient can confide to the analyst many things that he has been unable to say to his spouse. And the fact that in analysis it is best if the patient does not discuss the analyst or the analytic sessions with anyone outside the analysis at times intensifies this conflict for the spouse. Furthermore, during the height of a transference neurosis, the patient will experience a variety of intense affective attachments to the analyst, and this may at times detract from his capacities also to relate himself to his spouse, who in turn may feel a sense of alienation from the patient, and respond with anger or jealousy. There are also times during analysis when the patient may need extra amounts of reassurance or support from the spouse, particularly if painful and anxiety-provoking conflicts are being mobilized, and this at times may put an added burden on the marriage relationship and on the role that the spouse is expected to play. The spouse has also frequently had his own childhood voyeuristic concerns about secrets and the primal scene, and frequently equates the relationship between the patient and the analyst in such a form and feels excluded from it. Throughout all this the spouse must accept the financial drain that analysis causes, and also consciously continue to encourage the patient's participation and continuation of the analysis. And, as mentioned earlier, the spouse may also have to undergo internal modification of his own behavior or perceptions as the patient changes under the impact of the analytic process. In all these ways the spouse plays an important, silent role in the success of the analysis, and the patient's spontaneous acknowledgment of this is an indicator of her growing realistic appreciation of her husband and of his healthy and mature qualities.

As the session continues, she again experiences the same sadness described before, again with the growing sense of acceptance of its inevitability, but also with growing confidence that these responses will be limited in time and intensity.

Again it is important to point out the patient's current attitudes about my having remained the therapist throughout her analysis, and about my not having become emotionally involved, or gratifying her in the transference. In spite of all the affective storms earlier in the analysis in regard to my frustration of her demands and wishes, she is now able to recognize that only this attitude by me permits the analysis to be successfully conducted.

In the final minutes of the session, she again returns to her anticipation of the life that is waiting for her, and thereby illustrates the new sense of confidence in herself that has developed as a result of the analytic process. The analysis has freed her from the unconscious childhood fixations and conflicts which had prevented her from spontaneously developing into a mature personality. By resolving these conflicts, the patient is now able to resume her psychological development without the neurotic distortions that had occurred earlier and thereby it should permit her to make use of herself, her affective life, her drives and her various talents in keeping with reality and to the fullest extent possible for her. In other words, the analysis has now set in motion a process of psychological maturation and development which the patient can continue on her own after the treatment itself has been terminated.

Termination of the analysis also presents a psychological task for the analyst, who must do his own work of mourning and separation. For two years I had invested myself and my talents in her and in her treatment.

She was an apt and responsive patient, and someone whom I liked and enjoyed working with. Watching her grow and develop had been professionally gratifying and had provided me with narcissistic reinforcement and satisfaction. She would now be leaving my life and if the analysis was truly successful I would probably never see her again. The analyst's gratifications in having his patient develop and grow into a strong and mature person are analogous to those of a parent with his child. When the time comes for the child to leave home, the parent also feels a sense of sadness at the departure and must work through and accept the grief involved, regardless of how proud he may be. As I said goodbye at the door, it was with a lump in my throat and my own needs to work the feelings through were settled only after some time of self-analysis.

Analysis is a long-term intensive and major treatment undertaking, and frequently the criticism is made that "it takes so long." In one sense this is true, and cannot be minimized. However, if one considers that in this case the total analysis required approximately 347 treatment hours, this is the equivalent of fifteen elapsed days in her life. Considering the extent of the changes that have taken place up to now, this is a remarkably short time.

# Perspectives

# *14*
# SYNTHESIS

As mentioned in the introduction, the analysis of any single patient will provide information and understanding primarily applicable to the specific case involved. However, while some of the material is highly idiosyncratic, other elements of the primary data are applicable on a more general level, and may be used to illustrate theoretical concepts of psychodynamics and psychopathology, as well as factors and forces in the general understanding of the therapeutic process. In this chapter an attempt will be made to synthesize the material of the whole analysis from both of these points of view.

It should be apparent that the voluminous amounts of primary data resulting from a psychoanalytic experience can be studied from a variety of perspectives, and at many different levels of depth and detail. For example, one might choose to trace the origins, vicissitudes, and modifications of a particular drive or defense; one might study in depth the changing nature and functions of the analyst's interpretations; one might follow the nature and changes in the patient's dreams; one might make statistically manipulable estimates of particular aspects in the psychopathological or therapeutic processes; one might attempt to quantify the relative activity of analyst and patient and correlate it with the various phases of the analysis; etc.

The possible uses of these data are essentially limitless, and a choice of a particular focus and approach must be made. My approach will be an essentially macroscopic one, attempting to use the data to illustrate some generally accepted conceptualizations about psychopathology and the therapeutic process.

It should be emphasized again that for reasons to be discussed below this case was unusual in many respects. Her personality organization was such that she was able to make particularly effective use of the analytic opportunity and virtually every session involved large concentrations of emotionally significant material. For many other patients analysis is a much slower, less concentrated, less consistently meaningful experience, and therapeutic progress is commensurately delayed, intermittent, and less obvious. This patient was able to develop a full-blown regressive transference neurosis, while for other patients the transference experiences are more dilute and more dependent upon reconstruction and interpretive inferences. And her character structure permitted the analytic process to continue steadily with minimal disruption by conscious resistances. In many other patients the occurrence of massive and disruptive resistances (both conscious and unconscious) may delay analytic progress for extended periods of time, and make it a more uncertain and at times tedious procedure.

The fact that this was a relatively brief analysis and that the patient made rapid and at times dramatic progress will allow a more clear-cut and definitive isolation of therapeutic factors than is usually possible in slower and more difficult cases. The fact that this case required few parameters also permits the view of it as a relatively uncommon paradigm of uncontaminated psychoanalysis. This is analogous to the use of phase cinematography where the viewing of a natural process (i.e., the growth and blossoming of a plant) appears speeded up to the viewer and thus dramatically illustrates the naturally slow processes involved.

## Initial Formulation

The material emerging during the course of the analysis confirmed the initial diagnostic and prognostic formulations. The analysis demonstrated that the patient did suffer from a mixed psychoneurosis with the major level of fixation and disturbance in the oedipal phase conflict over her relationship to her father. The analysis also demonstrated significant preoedipal conflicts, but that these were not the major source of her psychopathology. She was able to establish a meaningful therapeutic relationship, to develop a classical transference neurosis, and her ego functions were sufficiently developed and integrated to permit its ultimate resolution. She was therapeutically suitable for psychoanalysis and obtained a significant therapeutic result.

However, the initial formulation, although correct in a general way, offered only a bare skeleton of the patient and her problems, and could not provide the full, detailed, and rich picture of the patient and her conflicts and life experiences as these emerged during the course of the treatment. Nor can an initial formulation provide a specific understanding of the multiple levels of psychic meaning; the detailed patterns of interaction between drives, superego functions, and defenses; the interrelationships between intrapsychic fantasy life and current external reality; or even the detailed elucidation of her presenting symptoms.

But it is significant to note that the dream which she presented in her first diagnostic interview contained multiple allusions to the major sexual conflict and to the sexually traumatic event which fixated her neurosis. None of these references were accessible to the patient or to me at the time, but it is interesting to review that dream in the light of the material of the analysis.

A crazy man was loose and I was afraid that he was going to break into the house. I was worried he would do something to my child. I went down into the basement and there I saw a toilet and I thought I saw my husband's arm in the toilet. I thought my husband was dead and was very upset. I ran back upstairs and told someone about it. They said to me that it was not my husband, but that it was just worms and I woke up.

The crazy man refers to both the father and the uncle and to their inability to control instinctual drives, and on several occasions during the analysis each was referred to by the patient as being "sick" or "crazy." The fear that he was going to break into the house is a reference to her ideas of violence in the sexual act derived from the primal scene experiences, and a house is a common symbolic reference to the patient's own body.

The patient's fear that he would do something to her child represents an unconscious awareness of the fact that the traumatic event occurred in childhood. It also indicates her identification with her own children, a reaction which emerged on a number of occasions during the analysis. Frequently the introduction to her own childhood sexual memories would be via her current impressions and fantasies about her children and their reactions to sexual situations. And going down into the basement is a reference to the fact that the traumatic event actually occurred in the basement of her grandmother's home.

Seeing her husband's arm in the toilet is a condensed derivative expression of the unconscious central organizing fantasy that she had swallowed the uncle's penis (arm) and that it was to be extruded from the body as a fecal product. Thinking that her husband was dead and being very upset about it refers to the fantasy that she had destroyed her uncle by the sexual act, and to the guilt she had experienced over this fantasy ever since. Going back upstairs and telling someone about it expresses the fact of the discovery by the grandmother when the patient came back upstairs at the time of the original incident. Being told that it was just worms is a reference to the screen memory of the childhood infestation by worms. It was the recovery of this screen memory of the worms which led to the full return from repression of the sexual incident itself.

The presentation of this dream in the first diagnostic session illustrates the general concept that at an unconscious level the patient "knows" about the conflicts and disturbances which produced and sustained the neurosis. This is expressed in the frequently quoted aphorism that full analysis of the first dream will reveal the core of the neurosis, and therefore the importance of the first dream. However this knowledge is inaccessible to consciousness by either the patient or the analyst at that time. In essence much of the analytic work is a preparation for the return to consciousness of this knowledge and of the conflicts which it represents.

## Final Formulation

A retrospective synthesis of the material disclosed by the analysis permits the following understanding and formulation of her psychopathology. She was born at a time when the parents were having marital difficulties and when the mother was significantly depressed over the possible breakup of her marriage and loss of her husband. The analytic material emerging in the primitive maternal transference and relating to the oral triad suggests a significant degree of conflict and disturbance during the oral incorporative phase of development, in terms of both libidinal and aggressive drives. Material emerging in the maternal transference and in subsequent recall was strongly suggestive that weaning from the breast had been abrupt and traumatic for her, thus further fostering a partial psychic fixation at that point. Accompanying this was a partial interference of optimal ego development in terms of separation and individuation of self from mother, resulting in a significant degree of primitive oral organization of subsequent development and personality structure. This was partially offset by her loving, supportive, and gratifying attachment to the grandmother. But the latter relationship had conflictual elements in that the grandmother attempted in derivative ways to maintain the patient's passive, dependent, oral attachment, and thus made it more difficult for the patient to emancipate herself from this level of psychic function and development.

However, after a relatively unconflicted anal phase, significant developmental energies and drive capacities were still available so that she was able to enter into a fully developed oedipal phase with its triadic level of conflict and object relatedness. This phase took the form of the classical oedipal triangle, with rivalry toward the mother as well as the various mistresses to whom the father went for his love and sexual gratification. Accompanying this disturbed relationship were significant and repeated sexual traumata, including multiple early exposures to the primal scene (with the various fantasied distortions involved), as well as considerable unconscious seductiveness on the part of the father toward the patient. In this conflict there were also elements of the negative oedipus complex in which the father was seen as a rival for the love and attention of the mother, and in which there was a significant identification with him (and his penis) as an attempted solution of conflicts, thus stimulating further sexual demands and desires toward the mother. There was also a significant and intense phallic-level conflict with penis envy, feelings of phallic inferiority, and an aggressive castrating wish toward men in a fantasied attempt to undo the supposed phallic inferiority, and to punish the father for the oedipal frustrations. As part of this conflict, the mother represented a poor object for satisfactory feminine identification, thus further strengthening the patient's ambivalence over the image of herself in the feminine role. Within the feminine role there was intense conflict between identifying with the mother and with the father's mistresses.

As part of her attempt to resolve the frustrating oedipal conflict, the patient displaced many of her positive, loving, and sexual feelings to the uncle as a substitute object for the inaccessible father. In this context there occurred the major traumatic sexual seduction by the uncle, with her accompanying fantasies of having orally incorporated and destroyed the uncle's penis, as well as the fantasy of retaining it inside and of its ultimate elimination as part of the fecal products. This intolerable fantasy evoked intense guilt, anxiety and shame, and led to the repression of the entire infantile neurosis with the establishment of multiple ego defenses against the reemergence of such conflictual material into consciousness. This repressed and now unconscious fantasy and its accompanying affects was a central organizing unconscious factor in her subsequent psychic life and development, with significant impact upon superego structure expressed by a continuous feeling of being bad, criticized, looked at, and hated. In addition, the impact upon ego development was reflected by her subsequent neurotic choice of objects, her various inhibitions particularly in terms of sexual function, the unconscious equation of mouth with vagina, the fantasy of the vagina as an incorporating and castrating organ, and the necessity to maintain multiple ego defenses against awareness of these fantasies with significant investment of psychic energy involved in doing so.

It is probable that the oral fixation and the oral organization of basic personality described earlier were influential in providing the *anlage* for the development of this specific organizing fantasy at the phallic and oedipal levels, resulting finally in a significant fixation of psychological development at that point. Another incident which may have been significant in forming a background for the development of the specific unconscious organizing fantasy was recovered in memory long after the incident with the uncle had emerged. Between age two and three the patient had swallowed a coin. She was taken to a hospital where unsuccessful efforts were apparently made to recover the coin from her gastro-intestinal tract. Eventually the coin was passed in her feces and found there by her grandmother.

Up to now in this discussion the emphasis has been on the psychopathological developments in her life experience and character structure. It must also be pointed out, however, that many of her early relationships, experiences, and reactions to them were positive and satisfactory, so that there was a simultaneous development of healthy, relatively mature, and effective aspects in her personality. The capacity for intense object relatedness was present at the time that she began analysis. In spite of her repeated emphasis on the idea of not trusting me in the transference, she nevertheless did enter into an analytic relationship quickly and easily, and in her behavior she did manifest a significant element of basic trust. The capacity for intense drive experience, both libidinal and aggressive, was likewise present from the outset of the analysis, as were her intelligence, ability to introspect and experience her own affective life, and her tolerance of anxiety and depression without paralyzing decompensation. In other words, in spite of the severity of her psychopathology, there were also a number of positive and healthy aspects to her basic development and personality structure.

Following the repression of the infantile neurosis there was a time of relative quiescence during latency. However, some of the pathological and now unconscious conflicts were reinforced by repetitive experiences with the father and his behavior in the extramarital situations, as well as by the mother's attitudes toward men and her attempts to foster a hostile and negative attitude toward the father in the three children.

In the adolescent period there was a significant upsurge of conflict, this time manifested in an adolescent rebellion with considerable displacement and sexual acting-out, and intensified identification with the various mistresses in the father's life. This was also a time of considerable reality stress, in that the father's affairs required a family move with reorientation to the external life situation. During this time the parents were sufficiently preoccupied with their own difficulties so that they were unable to meet the patient's latent, unverbalized, but nevertheless important, requests for guidance, control, and family structure.

Another manifestation of the healthier components of her personality was that although there was considerable rebellion and acting-out during adolescence, this never reached truly major proportions and she did maintain herself in the school and college situations without major self-destructive behavior. Another sign of strength was her choice of a husband, and it appears that in spite of her neurosis she was able to select a man with many positive healthy supporting attributes. However, there was another upsurge of neurotic symptomatology with anxiety, depression, and significant bulimia in the time interval shortly before the marriage itself, thus indicating the existence of significant neurotic conflict at the prospect of marriage.

Following the marriage her major symptom was a pathological jealousy of her husband, with multiple fantasies that he was engaged in various extramarital sexual affairs, which has obvious implications in terms of her unconscious identification of husband and father in a reinactment of the conflict with the father and his affairs from childhood.

There followed again a period of relative quiescence until the eighth month of her first pregnancy, at which time two significant precipitating events occurred concurrently. The first was her husband's joking statement that she was "getting fat," which had significant unconscious connections to the basic conflicts and fantasies underlying the oral organization of her personality structure. The second and major precipitant was her obstetrician's decision to deliver the child by Caesarean section. This evoked the specific idea connected with the unconscious organizing fantasy, that in opening her abdomen they would there find the uncle's incorporated phallus. It was in this specific setting with these particular connections to the central organizing unconscious fantasy that anxiety was mobilized, followed by significant regression and the onset of the acute neurosis which ultimately led to her seeking treatment.

## Specific Neurotic Symptoms

A review of some of the specific neurotic symptoms of which the patient complained indicates the characteristic pattern that each of them is a compromised attempt at the resolution of preexisting unconscious intrapsychic conflicts, with elements of the drives being gratified in derivative or fantasied forms, and elements of the prohibiting or controlling factors likewise present in the manifest symptom. Study of these manifest symptoms in the light of the analytic material and process also demonstrates the principle of multiple function and the concept of multiple simultaneous levels of psychic meaning.

## BULIMIA

One of her important symptoms was the bulimic overeating. By the act of eating, drives and their associated fantasies relating to the oral phase conflicts over the wishes for gratification by incorporation of the mother's breast were partially discharged. The oedipal phase fantasies involving oral incorporation of the phallus were also expressed in the act of eating. Other oedipal drives and fantasies were also expressed in disguised form through the equation of mouth and vagina, utilizing the mechanism of upward displacement. As a result, eating at times represented the use of oral incorporation to discharge heterosexual drive tensions.

The prohibitions against the direct expression of these drives were manifest in their displacement to food, and by the intense anxiety, guilt, and shame which accompanied the eating episodes, as well as in her feelings that overeating interfered with her consciously desired feminine attractiveness and body image. Repeatedly throughout the analysis eating could also be seen as a reaction to separation and loss, and as a defense against the depression associated with such loss, particularly as manifested in her transference behavior. Food provided her with a substitute object she could keep, manipulate, and control, and to this extent made her less dependent on the human object who was disappointing her at the time. Food and eating also expressed in a symbolic and displaced way her wishes for pregnancy, supported by the fantasy of oral impregnation. At the same time, she used obesity and her subjectively disturbed body image as a defense against the various conflicts evoked in potentially sexual situations.

## THE DISTURBED MARRIAGE

In her marital relationship the patient in many ways re-created the childhood family situation under the impact of the repetition compulsion, and through the mechanism of neurotic identifications. She equated her husband with her father, and in spite of the conscious anger, depression, and distress provoked by her thoughts of his infidelities, the existence of such fantasies provided a partial unconscious gratification for the wish finally to have her father in a marital and sexual situation. She also resented the role of woman and housewife, thereby manifesting her partial identification with the depreciated mother in seeing herself as dowdy, unfulfilled, and unattractive. By identifying with the mother, however, she was again unconsciously expressing the fantasy of replacing her mother, with the father as a husband. She also equated her children with her siblings, even to the point of giving both daughters the same first name as her sisters. Her hostility and resentment toward the children was partly a function of rivalry and envy based upon this neurotic equation, thereby further recreating the original family situation. In psychically repeating in the present the pathological family situations of childhood, she was unconsciously reexperiencing the old situation again in a variety of roles, with the unconscious wish this time to achieve the gratifications she had failed to obtain as a girl.

## SEXUAL DYSFUNCTION

Although her libidinal drives and sexual potential were high, the patient experienced varying degrees of sexual frigidity throughout most of her adult life and primarily in her marriage. This symptom related to her unconscious equation of husband with father, and therefore sexual activity was accompanied by unconscious guilt-provoking prohibitions against the gratification of incestuous feelings and wishes. The sexual inhibition also reflected her phallic and competitive strivings, manifested by fantasies of destroying men as a mean of revenge on father for his failure to gratify her oedipal yearnings. Inability to enjoy sexuality in the feminine role was also related to her phallic identification with the father in the negative oedipal conflict.

Another effect of her fantasies of oral incorporation was the equation of the vagina with the mouth, and therefore a fear of carrying through her castrating fantasies toward men if she were to give up conscious control and fully express her sexual drives. At the same time, however, she used her sexual provocativeness and flirtatiousness with men as a means of symbolically castrating them by exciting their interest and attention and then refusing them any gratification. In this behavior she was also reversing the childhood role in which she was passively stimulated and then frustrated, and converting it to an active one in which she became the one who frustrates.

As illustrated in her behavior and associations in the transference neurosis during the termination phase, to enjoy adult sexuality with her husband meant painful renunciation of the various infantile and childhood drives and objects. This involved accepting the frustration of positive and negative oedipal wishes, phallic competition and strivings, and the pre-phallic oral attachments to the mother.

## FEARS OF DYING

Her fears of dying, choking, being unable to breathe, and her fear of going to sleep were derivative manifestations of the oral conflicts with the unconscious equation of each of these activities with suckling at the breast and the various fantasied dangers elaborated as part of the oral triad. In these various symptomatic experiences she was unconsciously gratifying the fantasy of nursing and of being devoured by the breast, while at the same time experiencing this as a dangerous and anxiety-provoking situation and as an ego-alien fear which interfered with normal functions. In the fear of death she was also unconsciously equating orgasm with dying, so that this fear also had meaning for her as a defense against the prohibited oedipal sexual gratification.

## OTHER PHOBIAS

In the various phobias about being alone, having men break into the apartment, being attacked, etc., she was unconsciously expressing the fantasy of violent sexual assault which was part of her sexual orientation resulting from the fantasies connected with the multiple primal scene experiences of childhood. In those fantasies she was at times the woman being attacked and assaulted, and at other times she was identified with the man (and the penis) who was the active assailant and destroyer. Once again, however, these unconsciously fantasied gratifications were experienced consciously as punitive, unpleasant, and evoking of intense anxiety and distress.

## DEPRESSION

The recurrent depressive mood experiences, frequently accompanied by fantasies of slashing her wrists and committing suicide, were sometimes responses to the threat of separation from significant objects, while at other times they were attempts at manipulation of the person involved, and demands for control by him. They also represented the expression of her own unconscious aggression against these objects, by turning the aggression against herself. On a number of occasions the blood that would result from the slashing of her wrists was equated with menstruation and with the idea of experiencing herself as a woman. The depression was also the result of the inevitable frustration of her childhood fantasies and yearnings, particularly those related to her phallic wishes and those connected to the demands for oedipal and pre-oedipal satisfactions. These depressive responses to infantile and childhood frustration were particularly manifest in the transference neurosis during the termination phase of the analysis.

### FREE-FLOATING ANXIETY

Her intermittent episodes of acute anxiety were repeatedly manifest in her responses to the transference neurosis. On those occasions there was the stimulation of an unacceptable drive or drive-derivative which was accompanied by a fantasy of danger or punishment, and for which no other secondary defensive mechanisms were suitable or available at the moment. In such episodes both the drive and the anticipated danger or punishment were experienced in fantasy at unconscious levels.

## Specific Therapeutic Factors in This Patient

In this case, a number of specific factors were important in terms of the rapidity with which the analysis progressed, and the relative success of the outcome.

She had a well-developed capacity for intense object relationships and therefore for the development of a meaningful transference relationship, beginning the analysis with these capacities manifest. This was illustrated by her intense emotional relationships to the husband and parents, as well as her reported response to her previous psychotherapist. Her potential for the development of a transference neurosis was illustrated in the material from the social worker's contacts, which indicated that she had already begun to experience an essentially positive attachment and trust in me prior to the beginning of her analysis. This capacity for the development of an intense and emotionally meaningful relationship to the therapist is a positive prognostic sign, suggesting that a transference neurosis is potentially possible. However, such intense transference potentials must be differentiated from situations in which patients will develop anaclitic forms of a relationship where expectations of being passively cared for and supported predominate. In this instance her capacity to continue to function in spite of her symptoms, her ability to tolerate the abrupt termination of her previous treatment, and her motivation for psychoanalysis indicated her workable transference potential.

As illustrated by the material from the diagnostic as well as the therapeutic sessions, the patient had a conscious awareness of her drive levels, thus further indicating the potential that if properly dealt with these drives and their derivatives would be experienced in the analytic situation. In individuals with minimal or reduced drive elements consciously available, a good deal of analytic time and effort must be initially devoted to their mobilization so that they can become manifest in the analytic situation of the transference neurosis. Such analytic work was not necessary in this patient.

Throughout the course of her analysis the patient manifested a ready availability of affective experience, with a wide range of emotions consciously available to her. This is in contrast to isolated, intellectualized, or rigidly controlled patients in whom affective experience and expression are a source of great conflict and anxiety, and in whom these character defenses must first be analyzed before their emotional life becomes available for analysis. In this latter type of case the analytic process is frequently a much longer, less dramatic, less intensive, and therefore less effective procedure.

From the beginning of the analysis the patient demonstrated a capacity for introspection, which in turn is a basic tool for developing the function of free association and the ability for direct and active communication with the analyst. This is in contrast to those patients who have difficulty in introspection or in meaningful communication with the analyst, and who thus have major inhibitions in the development of their capacity for effective free association. In analysis, the primary mode of communication and interaction is at a verbal level, and patients who have difficulty with this form of communication will require proportionately longer treatment, and much of the analytic work will have to be devoted to the relief of these specific inhibitions.

In spite of symptomatic suffering this patient also showed a considerable capacity for tolerance of anxiety and depression without need for disruptive acting-out of conflicts or interference with the analytic situation and process. Patients who lack this capacity frequently tend to withdraw from the analytic process, or at times manifest disruptive forms of acting-out in which the search for displaced gratification of transference demands

may interfere with the analysis and the introspective elaboration of unconscious psychic forces.

The patient also demonstrated a significant capacity for effective
therapeutic regression, thus permitting the relatively rapid development
of the transference neurosis and remobilization of early childhood conflicts
and experiences. This is in contrast to those patients for whom regression
per se mobilizes intense anxiety, and in whom there may be multiple character defenses erected against the experiencing of earlier ego, drive, and
superego states. Such patients frequently manifest much more intense
defenses against the development and conscious emergence of a transference neurosis, and hence the total analytic process is more difficult and
delayed.

At most times throughout the treatment this patient maintained a
high degree of motivation for analysis based on a number of factors. These
included her significant degree of symptomatic disturbance and psychic
pain, with optimally intense symptomatology. Furthermore, she had tried
to utilize religion, acting-out of her conflicts, and her previous partially
effective psychotherapy, but none of them had been effective or successful.
She began analysis already recognizing that other less intensive forms of
treatment would not be fully successful. Another factor was the financial
outlay, which was a significant one for her family, and which fostered
optimal use of the analytic situation. Again this is in contrast to patients in
whom motivation is mixed or ambivalent, and who may maintain conscious reservations against their needs for analysis; or those for whom the
financial outlay is an insignificant element in their life situation and who
thus have fewer conscious pressures pushing them to make optimal use of
the therapeutic time.

This patient's reality situation was optimal for psychoanalysis in that
her husband was a warm, essentially healthy, supportive individual, capable
of psychological change and adaptation to the patient's personality modifications resulting from her analysis. Her reality situation was relatively
stable, with minimal contribution to her neurotic suffering from external
conflicts, and with minimal resistance to intrapsychic change among her
current objects. This must be contrasted to those patients with severely
disturbed or basically neurotic marital or other life situations, in whom
psychic change in the patient threatens the neurotic interaction in the
marriage or reality situation, thereby enhancing the external resistances to
change. The essentially positive elements of this patient's current life situation also meant that with renunciation of the infantile and childhood
demands she could move into realistically fulfilling and satisfying adult

relationships, again minimizing her external reluctance and resistance to give up archaic objects or modes of gratification. The therapeutic situation is far more difficult when patients have little or no possibility of realistic satisfactions and fulfillment in exchange for renouncing their childhood wishes.

In this instance there seems to have been a particularly good "fit" between patient and analyst. For the most part I was able empathically to understand and work with her, and countertransference interferences seem to have been minimal. This is in contrast to certain types of analytic situations in which the patient and analyst seem unable to establish a workable situation between them, or analytic situations in which countertransference forces within the analyst preclude his ability to work effectively with the patient.

## The Clinical Theory of the Therapeutic Process

The clinical material in this case permits a conceptualization of psychoanalysis as a process occurring between patient and analyst in a specifically structured situation and relationship which is in many of its aspects unique in human experience. Although a continuing interaction between them occurs, and each is acutely sensitive and responsive to the reactions of the other, the primary focus of their efforts is on the mental life of the patient. Their goal is to set in motion a process of internal change in the patient's mental and emotional life leading toward psychological development and maturation.

To accomplish this goal, the relationship is used by both participants in a specific way in order to promote the development of a transference neurosis which becomes the central *sine qua non* of classical psychoanalysis. This transference neurosis in turn becomes the vehicle by which there is a gradual and progressive mobilization and revitalization of unconscious intrapsychic conflicts from the infantile, childhood, and later stages of the individual's development. These conflicts are experienced by the patient in the current interactional process as related to the analyst and the analysis, and thus they achieve a sense of psychic reality and emotional impact for him. The reexperiencing of early psychic conflicts in the transference neurosis is the first step toward ultimate recovery in conscious memory of the original psychic events and associated fantasies.

As the various components of these conflicts are experienced in the transference neurosis *as if* they were the original childhood pathogenic disturbances, they are simultaneously subjected to the patient's mature secondary-process reasoning and reality-testing. Because of the chronological development and maturation that has taken place in the patient since the original conflicts occurred, as an adult he is now less helpless and less limited in his potential solutions than he was as a child. The focusing of these conflicts and their various derivative effects into the transference neurosis offers the patient another chance to resolve them or achieve mastery over them, thereby dispelling or diminishing their pathogenic influence. The process of interaction between patient and analyst is used to develop, explore, and ultimately resolve the transference neurosis, and thus to dissipate the developmental and maturational arrest resulting from the infantile and childhood conflicts which are repeated in the psychoanalytic situation. The ultimate internal resolution and renunciation by the patient of the transference attachments represents the active giving up of those infantile and childhood wishes and objects which had unconsciously promoted and maintained the existence of the neurosis and neurotic personality organization.

## Structure of the Psychoanalytic Situation

The psychoanalytic situation provides a unique and well-defined structure as background for the interactions between patient and analyst, which in turn will allow the emergence of the therapeutic alliance and the transference neurosis. The structure of this situation is established chiefly by the analyst, and is communicated to the patient as he sets up and explains the "ground rules" at the beginning of the analysis. Although the patient accepts the various elements in the structure consciously, he usually has little understanding of their implications at the outset.

However, the patient himself also contributes to the situation in that he is someone who is at least partially disabled and in need of professional assistance to achieve his personal goals. As such, he is more or less willing consciously to accept the role of patient in this situation (although unconsciously he will have many conflicts and ambivalent reactions to this role). He is also presumably willing consciously to accept the analyst as a professionally qualified person who has the necessary training and skill to provide the services that are needed, and he has acknowledged a willingness to try psychoanalysis as a therapeutic modality. In this frame of mind he is usually willing to accept the procedural recommendations offered by the analyst, although he may object and protest against them as the analysis proceeds. However, from the outset some patients will object strenuously to one or more of the components in the situation, and the way in which the analyst deals with these issues will be important in whether or not an analytic situation can be established.

The factors in the analyst which determine the structure of the situation are a function of his professional identity and integration, as well as his more specifically technical training and experience.

The analyst must be willing to make a professional commitment of his skills and efforts in behalf of the welfare and progress of his patient. He need not necessarily like him as a person, but the analyst must feel a sense of respect for his patient as an individual and for the validity and significance of the patient's neurotic disturbances. The analyst must accept the limitation that his own personal gratification will come chiefly from the use and further development of his professional skills, and from the financial remuneration for his work. He must accept the principle that he will not use the patient or the analysis to gratify his own personal emotional needs, and, if he finds such uses occurring, that he will make whatever efforts are necessary to deal with such forces within himself analytically.

In addition the analyst accepts the burden of maintaining a relatively constant attitude toward his patient, as well as a relative personal anonymity, all occurring within a narrow range of variance and hopefully without personal rigidity of character structure.

The technically determined elements of the psychoanalytic situation are a product of general experience and training, and are established as parts of the initial therapeutic agreement. By virtue of his general knowledge and experience, the analyst can anticipate a number of frequently occurring behavior patterns in patients, and he thus establishes the structure of the psychoanalytic situation to be able effectively to deal with them if they do occur in the particular case in question.

The analytic appointments must occur frequently enough to provide continuity from one session to the next, and to provide an optimal intensity of exposure between patient and analyst in order to provide a setting for the development of the analytic relationship. In classical psychoanalysis four or five sessions a week is considered ideal in providing this continuity and in offering the patient the supporting reassurance of being able to see the analyst soon if distressing or anxiety-provoking material emerges. If the patient must wait for significantly longer time intervals between sessions, he is left alone in coping with the conflicts mobilized by the analysis, and is therefore frequently increasingly reluctant to permit the emergence of distressing material. Although interruptions in the scheduled sessions are inevitable during the course of an analysis (i.e., for vacations, holidays, meetings, etc.) the analyst seeks to minimize these in order to maintain the constancy and structure of the analytic situation.

In scheduling the times of the individual sessions, the analyst tries wherever possible to minimize the disruptive effects upon the patient's external life situation (i.e., the patient with fixed job hours, the housewife with young children, etc.), thereby reducing the likelihood of the patient using such external problems as a rationalization for resistances.

The usual analytic session lasts for forty-five or fifty minutes and this length of time is designed to permit the patient the opportunity to undergo the necessary regression and exploration of his mental contents which analysis entails. Brief sessions, which may be appropriate in other forms of psychotherapy, would be ineffective in analysis in that they would not permit the time sufficient to develop and then explore the regressive experiences and their multiple manifestations.

Within general limits the analyst attempts to keep the duration of each session relatively constant, beginning and ending on time. This is done so that the patient is neither punished nor rewarded for the material he is discussing, and also in order to maintain the relative constancy of the situation. In that way, patients' reactions to it can more readily be demonstrated to them as originating intrapsychically and not in response to various deviations introduced by the analyst.

During the session the analyst also attempts to minimize interruptions such as telephone calls, not only because he wants to give the patient his full attention, but also because such interruptions inevitably interfere with the analytic process occurring in the patient during the session. Furthermore, if the patient observes the analyst in other forms of interaction, the ideal of personal anonymity is interfered with.

The analyst can anticipate that the conscious and unconscious issues involved in the financial payment for his services will become increasingly significant as the transference neurosis develops. Therefore, as part of the structure of the psychoanalytic situation he arranges to set and collect the fee directly with and from the patient, thus assuring that it will remain a potentially active issue throughout the duration of the analysis.

Although Freud initially introduced the couch because he objected to having patients look at him all day long, it has remained in use because it adds specific elements to the structure of the analytic situation. The use of the reclining position promotes relaxation and regression in the patient, and other things being equal, it thus promotes the type of introspective communication which is necessary to the analytic process. Analogous to the situation in dreaming, the use of the couch also inhibits motility in the patient, thereby making it easier for him to express impulses and fantasies which might be considerably more threatening for the patient if there were more ready access to motility.

In the classical analytic situation the analyst sits out of the direct line of sight and usually behind the patient, in order to reduce feedback to the patient regarding his communications. Positive, negative, or even neutral facial expressions by the analyst would have a directing or contaminating effect on the patient's free flow of associations. Patients try to compensate for this lack of visual feedback by sensitizing themselves to other cues such as movement, restlessness, breathing, tone of voice, or the brief glimpses of facial expression which they can get when coming in or leaving the session, but by sitting behind the patient the analyst deliberately attempts to minimize the impact of these cues. Furthermore, as the transference neurosis develops the opportunity for the patient to experience regressive projected transference distortions of the analyst is enhanced if such distortions are not immediately correctible by visual reality perception or confrontation.

Another element in structuring the psychoanalytic situation is the agreement, usually requested at the beginning of treatment, that the patient make no major life-changing decisions until they have been fully discussed and understood analytically. The analyst can anticipate that frequently, under the impact of the transference neurosis and the mobilization of unconscious conflicts, patients may experience transient pressures toward impulsive acting-out of conflicts. Such an agreement reduces the risks of self-defeating or neurotic action, and makes it easier for both patient and analyst fully to explore the meanings of the proposed decision while it is still at the level of thought.

## The Therapeutic Alliance

As a result of the structured psychoanalytic situation and of the developing interactions between patient and analyst, an essential facilitating aspect of the total relationship is the establishment and subsequent maintainence of a therapeutic alliance. This term refers to that aspect of the analyst-patient relationship in which the two of them cooperate in the analytic process, aligning themselves against the unconscious neurotic elements in the patient's mental life, with the mutual goal of bringing the analysis to a successful conclusion. On the part of the analyst this partnership involves his theoretical and technical skills, his devotion and dedication to the patient and to the unfolding and resolution of the neurotic processes, his capacity for empathy, communication, and understanding, and his maintenance of the therapeutic situation for the primary benefit of the patient. From time to time forces within the analyst may interfere with this optimal level of functioning, in which case they are recognizable as countertransference factors which tend to disrupt or interfere with the maintenance of the therapeutic alliance.

From the standpoint of the patient, his contributions to the therapeutic alliance include his conscious motivations for analysis, his capacity to tolerate anxiety or other unpleasurable affects in the service of the therapeutic task, his willingness to reexperience the archaic and childhood conflicts with the ultimate goal of their resolution, his capacity for self-observation and integration of the material as it unfolds, and his capacity to make use of the analyst as a helping instrument and to understand and integrate the analyst's interventions.

The establishment and maintenance of the therapeutic alliance is a necessary precondition for the full development of a workable regressive transference neurosis, which then becomes the vehicle of theraputic understanding and change. If the therapeutic alliance should not develop adequately, either the patient may fail to develop a transference neurosis, or he may develop a transference neurosis which is no longer readily manageable, becomes disruptive of psychic equilibrium, and no longer has therapeutic potentials. Where the transference neurosis is not perceived by the patient in the context of its therapeutic necessity and where its "as if" characteristics are not accepted, the patient may be described as manifesting a transference psychosis. In such situations the demands and expectations of realistic gratification of infantile strivings take such precedence over the therepeutic goals that the patient is no longer able to use the transference experiences as a vehicle towards resolution or mastery of the conflicts they represent.

Although the development of a workable and effective therapeutic alliance is largely a function of characteristics which the patient brings to the analytic situation, the analyst's activities may either foster or hamper the establishment of such an alliance. Typical specific techniques and technical maneuvers used by the analyst to foster such an alliance were described in the discussions of the various individual sessions. Essentially they require his recognition of the priority for the development of this aspect of the total relationship. This involves such things as his ability to maintain a therapeutic and analytic atmosphere; his capacity to encourage the patient's participation in it; his capacity for empathy, understanding, and analytic insight; his nonjudgmental attitude and orientation; his ability to present the painful interpretations which he must make in a tactful and analytically appropriate fashion; and his ability to use himself as an analytic instrument without major contamination by countertransference forces. As a result of the analyst's interventions, one essential aspect in developing the therepeutic alliance is the patient's gradually increasing capacity to identify himself partially with the analyzing functions of the analyst, thereby fostering the therapeutic ego split into experiencing as compared with self-observing functions.

Although the major emphasis and attempts at establishing a therapeutic alliance occur in the earlier phases, its maintenance and at times its reestablishment must be an important consideration for the analyst throughout the total course of the analysis. As illustrated repeatedly in this patient's material, maintenance of the therapeutic alliance was of vital importance in permitting her the full experience and resolution of the transference neurosis.

## The Transference Neurosis

As described earlier, the structuring of the psychoanalytic situation provides the setting in which the interactions between patient and analyst can lead to the progressive development of the total therapeutic relationship. One of the major components of this relationship has been elucidated as the therapeutic alliance. The other major line of development in the relationship involves the transference component. As mentioned previously, the hallmark of classical psychoanalysis is the progressive establishment, elaboration, and ultimate resolution of a transference neurosis. Given the progressive development of the therapeutic alliance, a number of other factors in the analytic process contribute to full and workable transference development.

### FACTORS IN THE PATIENT

1. One important issue is the patient's spontaneous capacity for object-relationships. The greater the patient's capacity for basic trust of human beings and for establishing emotionally meaningful and significantly lasting

ties to them, the more readily and rapidly will he be able to repeat this process toward the analyst. If he experiences a major sense of mistrust and distancing, or other types of defensiveness against establishment of emotionally meaningful object-relationships, he will more likely repeat these patterns with the analyst and thus delay the establishment of a regressive transference neurosis. In other words, his transference behavior toward the analyst will consist largely of his defenses against emotional involvement, and the analytic management of these forms of transference reactions is often slow and difficult.

2. The degree of conscious awareness in the patient of drives and affects will also directly influence the rate of establishment of a transference neurosis. If these are readily consciously available in the patient's previous life situations, the likelihood is they will also become manifest in the analytic situation. In those instances where experiences of drives and affects are heavily and rigidly defended against in life situations, the same defensiveness is likely to occur in the relationship to the analyst, and hence the development of a full-blown transference neurosis will be delayed at least until the defenses are dealt with in the analytic work.

3. Another factor determining the rate of development of the transference neurosis is the extent and effectiveness to which the patient can follow the basic analytic rule of free association. The method of free association requires that the patient suspend his usual conscious editing processes and that he learn to express verbally the thoughts, feelings, sensations, wishes, fantasies, and images which are ordinarily subjected to the rules of secondary-process logic before being verbalized in customary social interchange. Although this results in an apparently structureless and random flow of material, the general tendency in the absence of defensive editing will be toward the progressively direct expression of those psychic forces and conflicts which have the greatest intensity and meaning for the patient, in keeping with the general concept of psychic determinism.

Most patients in analysis learn the technique of free association only gradually, and usually the best examples of effective free association occur in the middle and late phases of analytic treatment. In essence, the form and content of mental functioning manifest in an on-going pattern of free association tends to be increasingly regressive in the direction of the primary-process mode of thinking, and hence tends further to foster the process of regression in the service of the ego.

4. The capacity for regression in the service of the ego and of the therapeutic task is another important factor determining the rate and extent to

which the transference neurosis will develop. By virtue of the regression and/or fixation which are part of the psychopathology, the patient enters analysis manifesting a type of fixed regressive behavior in which there will be a tendency to displace to the analyst the same unconscious drives, fantasies, expectations, and defenses which are the roots of the neurosis and which are already being experienced toward other objects in his daily life situation.

However, another form of further regression is specifically induced as part of the analytic process. This results from the various elements in the structure of the analytic situation, the participation by the patient in the therapeutic alliance, the use of the method of free association, and the role of the analyst (to be discussed shortly). This latter form of regression in the service of the ego and of the therapeutic task is ideally induced during the analytic sessions, reversed when the patient leaves, and becomes increasingly manifest in the patient-analyst relationship. It is an important dimension for the development and elaboration of a full-blown regressive transference neurosis.

## THE ROLE OF THE ANALYST

1. As much as possible the analyst attempts to maintain his personal anonymity to the patient, not revealing his life experiences, emotions, attitudes, or reactions to the patient's material, in order that positive or negative feedback and influence upon the patient's material can be minimized. In this way transference distortions in the patient's perceptions or reactions to the analyst can be more readily demonstrated as arising from intrapsychic forces rather than in response to realistic provocations or reactions in the analyst. This type of anonymous neutrality cannot be perfectly maintained and the patient will frequently become sensitive to subtle and at times nonverbal clues which the analyst is unable to avoid giving. However, within a reasonable range the analyst attempts to maintain a situation of relative constancy and lack of personal response in order to help promote the development of the transference neurosis.

2. As part of his therapeutic activity, the analyst deliberately permits himself to be used by the patient as a readily available current object toward whom the patient can displace and project intrapsychic drives, fantasies, wishes, fears, expectations, and defenses. The analyst accepts this role as much as possible without defensiveness or personal needs to correct the patient's distortions of him. By accepting such distortions and not directly or immediately correcting them, the analyst tacitly encourages the

patient to permit such transference reactions and the affective experiences that accompany them to occur.

3. The analyst's interventions are an important factor in helping the patient to establish and develop a transference neurosis. His acceptance of the patient's material during free association and his interventions at points where the process of free association is interfered with foster and encourage this regressive mode of communication. The analyst's interpretations of the various defenses or resistances within the patient against the emergence of a transference relationship tend to encourage the patient to reduce the intensity and use of such mechanisms and thus permit the underlying transference drives and fantasies to emerge more closely into consciousness.

At other times he may interpret the content of transference feeling or fantasy, as well as the other elements of the conflict associated with the transference, thereby increasingly focusing the patient's attention upon himself and the interactions which occur between them. These types of intervention acknowledge tacitly to the patient the therapeutic importance of this relationship, and accompanied by the analyst's nonjudgmental acceptance of the transference distortions as they occur, encourage the patient to explore these component responses more fully.

4. The analyst's maintenance of transference abstinence as this relationship develops and evolves is another important factor in the ultimate elaboration of the transference neurosis. When drive derivatives remain unfulfilled and ungratified, drive tension tends to intensify and press for expression in increasingly direct fashion. As the transference drives become increasingly direct and compelling toward gratification by the object, and as the analyst increasingly is invested with these yearnings and their multiple derivatives, their intensity is enhanced, substitute objects are less gratifying, and the final result is an increased tendency toward conscious awareness of their existence and multiple manifestations toward the analyst.

Simultaneously, the state of transference abstinence permits the patient to separate thought from action, and this makes the analytic situation "safe" for the verbal expression of such drives or fantasies. Most neurotic patients can only express the full intensity of their transference wishes and fantasies if they know that they will not be held personally accountable by the analyst, that the situation will remain controlled, and that direct action between patient and analyst will not be forthcoming. In situations where derivative drive gratification is forthcoming from the analyst, the patient will frequently be unable to express deeper and more directly primitive drives lest they too be satisfied. In terms of the transference demands, abstinence by the analyst evokes frustration in the patient; but in terms of the therapeutic alliance, abstinence permits the patient to explore his transference demands more fully.

5. Another factor in promoting the transference neurosis is the analyst's capacity to tolerate anxiety within himself and ambiguity in regard to the patient's material without undue discomfort and without the necessity for premature closure. The analyst must be capable of tolerating the intense drives, affects, and conflicts which the patient experiences at the height of a transference neurosis, and he must be capable of accepting the fact he may not always clearly or fully understand the meanings of the patient's communications in this situation. By this type of nonverbal attitude and response to the patient's material, the analyst establishes a model of an analytic attitude with which the patient can identify in the therapeutic alliance as he simultaneously experiences the various transference phenomena. This attitude in the analyst helps the patient to maintain the therapeutic alliance in the face of the intense transference demands and conflicts, and it is the maintenance of the therapeutic alliance which encourages the patient to accept and continue experiencing the transference conflicts and phenomena. In other words, although the phenomena of the transference neurosis have a quality of immediate psychic reality and experience for the patient, they can be therapeutically useful only if they are simultaneously perceived by both the patient and the analyst as part of a therapeutic process and as a vehicle for uncovering the inner psychic life of the patient. The transference neurosis remains an artificially induced, primarily fantasied, and unreal "as if" component in the overall therapeutic relationship.

6. The analyst's suspension of moralizing judgment, advice, or participation in the patient's reality life situations further fosters the transference elements and experiences, and permits the patient's superego functions also to become part of the transference relationship. In the absence of specific feedback in regard to moral values and critical judgments, the patient involved in a transference neurosis projects to the analyst those fantasies, ideals, judgments, and expectations of punishment or reward which were internalized during psychological development, and which now compromise his superego functions. The patient now projects to the analyst his own superego functions, thus experiencing them again as external phenomena relating to infantile and childhood objects and fantasies. Having projected these superego functions to the analyst, the patient now anticipates reward and punishment as coming from external sources analogous to his experience as a child, with the difference that he now is an adult who can

judge more rationally and in accordance with secondary-process reasoning the reality and validity of such values, fantasies, and expectations.

# Significance of the Transference Neurosis

In summary, the development, exploration, and elaboration of the transference neurosis occurs in the analytic situation as the result of the combined effects of the various factors described above. These combine to induce a type of regression in the service of the ego and of the therapeutic task which increasingly occurs in the analytic situation itself. Since this form of regression occurs chiefly during the analytic sessions when in the presence of the analyst, and since it is reversed when the patient leaves the session, the analyst becomes the object toward whom the patient experiences the earlier drives and the conflicts associated with them. As the regression is further confined to the analytic situation, the analyst becomes increasingly important to the patient as the object of his infantile and childhood drives and conflicts. And concomitantly there occurs a relative decrease in the use of other objects for these purposes.

In these regressive states there is an artificial, fantasied reexperiencing and repetition toward the analyst of all the elements of psychic conflict from earlier in the patient's life. During these periods of regression in the analysis (when adult self-observation, reality-testing, and integration are temporarily reduced) the patient experiences toward the analyst the spectrum of his infantile and childhood instinctual drives and their derivitives in roughly the same proportion and intensity as occurred during the original developmental stages. Simultaneously accompanying the experience of these drives forces or derivatives, there occur the phase-appropriate and linked superego experiences, likewise projected to the analyst. Also accompanying these earlier forms of psychic conflict are the various previously experienced ego states, defensive processes, and levels of reality-testing which existed at the time when these various internal conflicts originally occurred. Thus, what is transferred and reexperienced in the analytic situation are the various component psychic functions making up the states of conflict from infancy and early childhood, currently experienced toward the analyst in an active form as a psychic reality. As these experiences are repeated in the transference neurosis, there occurs an associated reduction in the strength of the repressive forces, and a resulting conscious recall of the infantile and childhood memories and experiences. This lifting of the infantile and childhood amnesia allows a conscious recollection of the details of the patient's external and intrapsychic life from those periods.

However, the difference between the analytic situation and the original developmental stages is that in spite of the psychic reality of the transference experiences, these are occurring in an individual who has subsequently undergone considerable maturation, development, and growth during the intervening years. These regressive transference reactions are occurring in an individual who can simultaneously (or at least in alternation), observe himself in this relationship, take psychic distance from it, and recognize the artificial "as if" character of these experiences.

These latter ego functions and self-observations thus permit the possibility that the patient can now subject his infantile and childhood memory, fantasy, and experience to the scrutiny and impact of subsequent secondary-process learning, reality-testing, and maturation. Additionally, as an adult he presumably has a greater number of options and potential solutions to the conflicts which he was unable to resolve as a child. In childhood his potential for individual and independent adaptation, adjustment, or conflict resolution was significantly limited by his real relationships to his parents and by the immaturity of his ego development.

In other words, the transference neurosis becomes the vehicle by which there is a return to consciousness, in a psychically active form, of previously repressed conflicts; there is an associated remembering and recall of the important childhood fantasies, memories, and relationships; and there is thus an opportunity for a second chance at resolution and mastery of previously unsolved pathogenic conflicts. As Freud's aphorism states, "One cannot slay a dragon in absentia."

## Impact of the Reality Situation

The nature of the patient's current reality situation and object relationships will be an important factor in the rate and completeness with which therapeutic changes occur. The more that the patient's current objects (i.e., spouse, family, community, occupation, etc.) are healthy and provide the possibilities for realistic gratifications and reduction of conflict, the more readily can the patient renounce the infantile objects in the transference neurosis in favor of the realistically more gratifying reality objects and patterns of drive discharge. If current object relationships have been highly neurotic and are dependent on continuing patterns of infantile gratification, or if the current objects are unable to modify their expectations and demands of the patient in keeping with his new development and maturation, the more difficult will be the renunciation of the infantile and childhood fixations. In essence, the patient can more easily give up the neurosis in favor of gratifying and successful object relationships in an adult and secondary-process sense in the former situation, whereas if there are few realistic gratifications and adult relationships potentially available to him, he is in essence being asked to give up his old neurotic attachments without anything more gratifying in a realistic sense to replace them in the current situation. Such forces can produce important resistances to change and can reduce the patient's motivations toward elimination of the neurosis.

## Support in the Analytic Relationship

The analytic relationship offers the patient a type of support and encouragement which is in many ways unique in his life experience. The frequency of analytic sessions means that ordinarily the patient does not go for extended periods of time without the benefits of contact with the analyst. The analyst accepts the patient and his neurosis with respect for the individual, and without making demands for direct or immediate behavioral change. He indicates by his therapeutic interest and attitude that he takes the patient's complaints seriously, and that he recognizes them as outside the patient's voluntary control at the moment. The analyst makes the patient the chief focus of interest in their interactions, and aside from the financial obligation he makes no other direct demands upon the patient in terms of a give-and-take concern for himself.

Furthermore, the analytic situation offers the patient an opportunity to talk about himself and be listened to intently and with concern, without demands that the patient in his turn listen to the analyst. In other words, the reciprocal demands which occur in usual realistic external object relationships are suspended during the analytic process. And in facing the mobilization of his preexisting unconscious conflicts, the patient has someone with him who can empathically share the experience and provide a sense of presence which offsets the isolation and loneliness which the patient experienced in childhood in his initial attempts to cope with the conflicts resulting from his developmental vicissitudes.

These characteristics of the analytic situation provide a matrix within which the patient can also experience unconscious gratification of so-called basic or primal transference fantasies toward an all-knowing and ever-understanding primal parent. Although these fantasies are ultimately explored and analyzed (particularly during the termination phase), their gratification during earlier phases of the analysis provide an important support to the patient during much of the therapeutic process.

## The Role of Suggestion

Although the analyst scrupulously attempts to avoid direct suggestion in regard to behavior or thought processes, he nevertheless exerts a considerable indirect force of suggestion upon the patient. One basic suggestion resulting from the analyst's total behavior is his assumption that facing psychic truth, difficult and painful as this may be, will ultimately result in more effective and mature resolution or adaptation to psychological conflicts and current life situations.

Another function through which suggestion is manifest is the selectivity which the analyst exercises as he listens to the patient's associations and chooses the material about which he will intervene. As mentioned previously, the relative lack of feedback by the analyst results in an increasing sensitivity by the patient to various clues regarding the analyst's feelings, opinions, and thoughts. One way in which the analyst may manifest these is in his choice of those elements in the patient's random and free associations about which he intervenes in some form. By his intervention he is indirectly suggesting to the patient that this particular psychic component is of relatively greater interest to him than other elements in the patient's associations about which he did not intervene. Patients are frequently acutely sensitive to the subject matter or patterns influencing the analyst's interventions, and depending upon the state of the transference they may use these as either positive or negative suggestions to elaborate upon the material in question.

The analyst attempts as much as possible to offset this effect by making sure that he intervenes in an equally frequent pattern in regard to all the various component elements in the patient's conflicts and the material which is expressed. But if, for example, the analyst remains silent during most of an analytic session and intervenes only a few times in response to the patient's associations, the patient will frequently infer that the material which led to these interventions was "more important" than the material which was not responded to overtly. This reaction may occur even if the analyst's decision on whether or not to intervene was made on the basis of factors other than the psychological importance of the particular issue.

By virtue of his clinical experience, theoretical knowledge, and emotional neutrality, the analyst can frequently recognize derivatives of specific unconscious conflicts long before the patient develops such recognition. By emphasizing these elements unduly he might thus through indirect suggestion to a significant extent focus the patient's interest and attention in the directions which he sees as most significant in terms of his theoretical understanding. Although his clinical and theoretical understanding will cause the analyst to exercise selectivity in his interactions with the patient, he must be aware of the potency of this form of indirect suggestion. Otherwise he may find himself in the situation of unconsciously suggesting material to the patient, and then, hearing it repeated back to him, mistake this for a spontaneous confirmation of his ideas.

## The Role of Abreaction

As pathogenic conflicts or traumatic experiences are recovered, (either as transference responses or as memories), the affects associated with them are likewise reexperienced in the current analytic situation. This discharge of "strangulated affect," which Freud initially thought was the curative process in psychoanalysis, is one necessary precursor to the ultimate resolution of conflict. By the repeated discharge of unpleasant affects associated with a particular conflict, relationship, or traumatic event, the memory becomes less distressing or painful to the patient's recall and thus can be accepted in consciousness more fully and with less accompanying psychic pain. As a result, the capacity of the patient to retain in consciousness the memory and understanding of the situation in question is enhanced, and having become conscious this material can now be subjected to new and more effective integrative and synthetic ego functions.

In other words, abreaction is part of a process of desensitization to core conflicts, fantasies, experiences, or relationships which, because of their previously associated intensely painful affects, could not be accessible to conscious recognition and awareness and hence could not be resolved. In one sense this process is analogous to desensitization procedures employed in behavior modification therapies. But in the latter forms of treatment the desensitization process is applied only to the conscious derivatives of the unconscious conflicts, whereas in psychoanalysis it occurs at the level of the pathogenic unconscious conflicts themselves as a partial step towards

ultimate resolution. Abreaction is also an important element in the working-through process, a topic to be discussed shortly.

As illustrated in this case, the early recoveries of material concerning
the primal scene and the uncle's seduction were accompanied by intensely
painful, threatening, and anxiety-provoking affects. Only after the affective
charge associated with these experiences had been reduced by the repeated
abreactions could the patient clearly remember and retain them in consciousness. And retention in consciousness was another precursor toward
eventual resolution of the danger situations and the conflicts previously
associated with these experiences.

## The Role of Insight

An erroneous idea that is frequently expressed, particularly by critics
of psychoanalysis, is that *insight per se* is the goal and the curative factor
in psychoanalytic treatment. In adhering to this misconception these critics
set up a straw man which they then attack with arguments to demonstrate
that insight alone does not produce therapeutic change.

Most experienced analysts readily agree that insight alone is not curative, and that the mistaken notion that it is represents a carryover from the
early topographic theoretical hypothesis in which the goal of therapy was
"to make the Unconscious Conscious." The impact of the developments in
ego psychology upon the theory of the therapeutic process lead to the conceptualization that insight is a means rather than an end in itself. It represents a complex and important tool which the patient acquires during
analysis and which he then must put to use in his efforts at resolution of
his previously unconscious neurotic conflicts.

The development of insight is a gradual process, occurring throughout
the course of the analysis, by which the patient's own understanding of
himself, his mental life, and the role of his psychic conflicts is progressively
deepened and expanded as the result of a number of factors. These include
the therapeutic alliance and the accompanying split into observing and experiencing ego functions, and the patient's identification with the analyzing functions of the analyst. In this context, the developing and deepening
regressive transference neurosis, with its attendant mobilization of unconscious conflicts, becomes the vehicle by which the patient simultaneously
becomes aware of and reexperiences the pathogenic infantile and childhood
situations and conflicts. At the same time in the therapeutic alliance he

achieves cognitive and conscious awareness of their existence, impact, and derivative effects on his psychic life. An important component in this process is the patient's capacity for psychological introspection and effective free association, which provide the raw data from which the analyst can make his various interpretations and reconstructions, each of which ideally adds a small increment of expanded awareness for the patient.

The analyst's attention and interest are focused with equal intensity upon the drives and their various derivatives, the superego processes and expectations of punishment or reward, and the integrative, defensive, and adaptive ego processes established by the patient as his characteristic means and methods of coping with conflict. The analyst is also interested in the mutual interactions between the patient's inner psychic life (as both child and adult), and his current external reality situation, object relationships, experiences, and events with which he must cope in his everyday life situation. In this context, there develops a further elaboration and understanding of the ways in which the patient's past life experiences and conflicts are being repeated in the present, and the ways in which he is using current objects and situations to gratify infantile and childhood wishes. The analyst's understanding and conceptualizations are shared with the patient when deemed appropriate, thus extending the patient's own conscious awareness and recognition about his psychic experience, and further extending his understanding of how past and present are interrelated, and of how his mind functions.

Included in this acquisition of insight is a gradual expansion of the patient's conscious awareness of his own primary-process mental functioning and the nature of his repressed infantile and childhood fantasy life, as well as the major contributions that these primary-process fantasies make to his current psychic adaptation. The various fantasied danger situations, whether due to primitive superego expectations or ideals, or due to misperceptions of reality by the immature and undeveloped infantile and childhood ego, are likewise exposed and explored during this process of acquisition of insight.

Another dimension of insight occurs along a continuum, ranging from cognitive and primarily intellectual awareness to a deeply personal, emotionally experienced, immediate understanding which bears a subjective sense of truth and conviction for the patient. It is the latter level of insight which is sought in psychoanalysis.

This gradual acquisition of emotionally meaningful insight in all its various dimensions and patterns of functioning represents an important

component of analysis, and is a necessary prerequisite for the actual curative processes to occur as these insights are progressively applied to the
goal of resolution of infantile and childhood conflicts.

For the purposes of this exposition, the acquisition of insight and its
application in the working-through process have been somewhat artificially
separated. In the actual clinical situation these two facets of the therapeutic process are intimately interrelated. Small incremental extensions of
insight are applied in small increments of working-through, which in turn
set the stage for further acquisition of deeper or more extensive insight.

## The Role of Working-Through

It is the repeated application by the patient of the painfully acquired
insights to the task of resolution of infantile and childhood conflict which
produces the curative changes in psychoanalysis. This application of insights occurs repetitively in the interactions involved in the transference
neurosis, in the recall and return from repression of the infantile and
childhood phases of development, and in the dynamic understanding of
interactions in the patient's current life situation. And this repetitive application of understanding to the various areas of function and the changes
which this produces are known as the process of working-through.

As the name implies, and as this case demonstrates, working-through
involves multiple repetitions in the application of insight regarding any
particular core conflict or its many derivatives. A single interpretation of
any psychic element rarely, if ever, produces lasting change. Interpretations
must be made again and again, from varying points of view, in various
situations of conflict, and in a variety of forms before the working-through
process can be effective in producing lasting change.

As described in the discussion of the transference neurosis, the patient
in analysis consciously reexperiences the original infantile and childhood
drives, fantasies, ego-states, and superego expectations, but simultaneously
the maturation and development which has occurred in the interim permits the patient's now partially adult ego to observe these phenomena and
their dynamic implications from the current rational viewpoint. He does
so in the current analytic edition of these old conflicts, supported by the
interpretive help, understanding, and tacit encouragement of the analyst
in his attempts to face and resolve them. The application of secondary
process reasoning to the previously pathogenic primary-process fantasies
permits the patient to recognize in the current situation the irrationality

and unreality of the situations which previously had been unconsciously experienced as dangerous.

As a result of this repeated exposure to rational perception and conscious integration, the patient is now less threatened by the conflicts, and therefore the anxiety, guilt, shame, etc., previously evoked by the fantasied danger situations, are gradually reduced and ultimately eliminated. As a result of the gradual dissolution of the danger situations through application of secondary-process reasoning, and the concomitant reduction of the painful associated affects, the previously unconscious needs for specifically structured and automatic defensive responses to such situations is likewise reduced. The patient can then make trial-and-error attempts at new modes of adaptation, of object choice and relatedness, of more satisfying drive discharge, and of new integrative and synthetic patterns. The net result is a reduction in the intensity of the previously established unconscious defenses, with an increased acceptance of the previous conflicts into consciousness, and thus a greater capacity to master them effectively through conscious adaptive ego mechanisms. This, in turn, results in a freeing of the energy previously bound in the fixed defensive processes, which energy is now freely available for other uses.

The same type of process occurs concomitantly in relationship to the unconscious and previously automatic superego responses, in terms of fantasied expectations of punishment and reward. In the working-through process, these previously unconscious superego responses are projected to the analyst as a component part of the transference neurosis, but when the analyst does not react with the expected responses, it forces the patient to reevaluate his anticipations in the context of the reality principle and secondary process. This, in turn, provides the patient with an opportunity gradually to establish for himself a more rational and personally selected system of values, rewards, and punishments which he can then reinternalize as newly developed superego functions. These will be based on adult perceptions of the conflict situations, on a firm differentiation between thought and action, on a realization of the "normality" of his drives and their derivatives, and on his current level of maturation, all of which now permit greater independence from the environmental objects in terms of these functions.

Another aspect of the working-through process is the patient's gradual recognition, by virtue of the transference abstinence, of the advantages of secondary-process and reality-oriented functioning to achieve satisfactory and gratifying drive discharge. The patient can become increasingly consciously aware of the inevitable frustration which is inherent in his tendency to cling to his infantile drives, objects, and demands for gratification, particularly as these are reexperienced in the transference neurosis. This aspect of the working-through process is particularly highlighted during the termination phase of the analysis, in which the therapeutic goal is the eventual voluntary renunciation of the infantile objects and demands for drive gratification by them in the transference neurosis. In this termination phase there is a reworking of the emotional investments in infantile and childhood objects and fantasies of gratification, and as the patient faces and deals with the ultimate frustration of these relationships and derivative gratifications in the transference resolution, there is an increasing cathexis of available current reality objects and situations. Ideally, the maturational processes instituted by the analytic experience permit the establishment of age-appropriate and reality-oriented modes of drive discharge and object relationships, without substitution by other displaced infantile and childhood strivings or relationships.

Throughout the course of analysis and particularly in the working-through process, the analyst's model of an anxiety-free, tolerant, repetitive search for more basic issues and understanding permits the patient to identify with this attitude, thereby strengthening his capacity to cope with these forces in conscious awareness and encouraging the acceptance of psychic truth. In this way the analyst's responses and behavior provide a significant element of support to the patient during periods in the analysis when the spontaneously occurring wish to avoid unpleasurable and painful affects would lead the patient again to institute the unconscious automatic ego defense and adaptive mechanisms which result in the neurotic symptomatology.

By virtue of his interventions, the analyst indirectly suggests to the patient that facing the truth and psychic reality of his own mental life will ultimately result in more effective, comfortable, and gratifying adaptation than could exist in the previous unconscious modes of adjustment to conflicts. This model also serves an important function in preparing the patient to continue the introspective analytic process after the formal analysis has terminated. The maintenance of ideal emotional maturity after completion of an analysis involves the patient's capacity for continuing self-analysis as he deals with the inevitable conflicts and vicissitudes of his life. The techniques of self-analysis have been developed during the analytic process itself, and are partially a reflection of the patient's healthy identification with the analyzing functions and attitudes of the analyst. The application and use of self-analysis in dealing with subsequent inevitable psychological conflicts represents the patient continuing the working-through process on his own.

# The Metapsychology of Structural Change

In the development of psychoanalysis, the technique and clinical findings of therapy and the elaboration of metapsychological theory have had a reciprocal influence upon one another. These historical developments of metapsychology and of the theory of psychoanalytic technique have been well presented in the psychoanalytic literature and need not be repeated here. In essence, however, when the topographic theory was the predominant line of psychoanalytic thinking, the therapeutic goal was "to make the Unconscious Conscious," with important repercussions on analytic technique.

The introduction of the structural theory produced a profound modification in psychoanalytic thinking, leading to the major revisions and elaborations of ego and superego psychology. The impact of these theoretical developments upon the technique of psychoanalysis and the data derived from the new technical approaches and their influence upon subsequent theory building and model construction have again been documented. These developments meant that the new goal of psychoanalytic technique and treatment became the production of structural change and structural reorganization of the personality.

The psychic structures represent an abstraction based upon a generally accepted set of definitions and a conceptual grouping of mental functions in a particular way. Psychic structures have *no real existence*, despite the anthropomorphism that occurs in clinical or theoretical discourse on the subject. Psychic structures represent only an acceptable shorthand for discussing groups of mental functions which have certain common characteristics and which tend to be persistent or repetitive, relatively automatic, predictable, and to have a slow rate of change.

The major psychic structures (id, ego, and superego) have their own independent and yet interrelated lines of development and their own internally consistent characteristics which make it possible to define them in a usefully consistent fashion. These are known as the macrostructures of the personality, each of which refers to a group of psychic functions organized in such a way as to permit a conceptualization of the inevitable states of intrapsychic conflict between one group of functions and another.

The particular development, mutual characteristics, levels of consciousness, and interactions between these groupings is a well-known and accepted part of psychoanalytic theory and need not be expanded here. These particular conceptual abstractions of the macrostructures permit a metapsychological understanding of so-called intersystemic conflicts.

More recently there has been introduced the concept of intrasystemic conflict, stemming from the recognition that within any one of the macrostructural groups there may occur conflicts and incompatibilities between the individual psychic functions which compose that group. Specific instinctual drives may be in conflict with each other, as may the various superego demands or values, as well as particular individual ego functions. This concept of intrasystemic conflict represents an attempt to extend metapsychological understanding to account for the complexities of psychic life as revealed in the clinical situation.

The overall therapeutic goal of structural change within the personality therefore refers to the production of lasting change in the individual specific microstructures (the individual mental functions which comprise the macrostructures) and thus to a permanent reorganization of the characteristic and automatic modes of function of the macrostructures within themselves and also vis-à-vis their relationships to the other macrostructures. Structural change may thus involve modification of the individual functions vis-à-vis one another, change in the organization of the individual functions which comprise the macrostructures, change in the relationship between one macrostructure and another, elimination of specific pathogenic structures, or the establishment and development of new mental structures (functions). The degree and rate of change in the dissolution of old structures or relationships between them, or the degree of development of new mental structures, is variable from patient to patient, and within the individual patient may vary considerably from one function or set of functions to another.

As the result of psychoanalytic observations, there is a general conceptual agreement among psychoanalysts that the basic elements of personality structure are established during the infantile and childhood years, and that core development of id, ego, and superego has taken place by the time of the original resolution of the oedipal phase and the onset of latency. In keeping with the genetic hypothesis, subsequent psychological development during latency, adolescence, and adulthood consists of an evolutionary change and development of structural elements derived from the basic core structures. These later developing components are known as "derivative structures."

As a result of repression of the infantile and earliest childhood phases of development, and of their inaccessibility to full consciousness, the psychic structures developed and established to adapt to the inevitable internal and external conflicts of those periods remain unconscious and therefore largely resistant to basic change. Their continued existence is inferred on the basis of their derivative effects and organizing influences upon the later conscious and preconscious behavior of the individual, and the interrelationship between external and intrapsychic forces in the subsequent development of derivative character structure.

During infancy and early childhood the maturational and sequential experiencing of the various drives become associated with and expressed by a variety of wishes and primitive fantasies. There also develop a group of automatically associated primitive superego fantasies and expectations which increasingly accompany the psychic experiencing of the drives. By virtue of the immaturity of the developing child's ego, a variety of fantasied danger situations also become associated with these drives and superego forces, organized in the mode of the primary process. These patterns of association and relationship among the psychic functions become increasingly automatic, and repetitive (and therefore structured) sequences of mental processes in response to the stimulation, intensification, or threatened emergence of the particular drive in question.

Accompanying these automatically associated phenomena are the various affective responses appropriate to the infant or child's perceptions and anticipations in these psychological sequences. In an effort to avoid these painful, threatening, and disruptive affective experiences and the danger situation they represent, the child develops a series of increasingly automatic, stereotyped, and repetitive ego adaptive responses and defense mechanisms whose function it is to cope with these unpleasurable states. As psychological development continues, these various adaptive mechanisms become increasingly complex, with a developing potential for multiple ways and means by which the conflict situations are adapted to or controlled. The principle of economy in the maintenance of these adaptations and controls involves an increasingly automatic, stereotyped, and characteristic mode and method of adaptation and integration.

With the repression of the entire infantile and childhood phase, these automatically associated elements of intrapsychic conflicts and the stereotyped modes of adaptation are applied to later occurring situations, relationships, and states of conflict which in one way or another have an associated relationship to the now repressed infantile and childhood conflicts. The final effect is a series of structured, sequential responses to the various situations derived from the basic core conflicts, with the result that there is developed a mode and pattern of adaptation which is characteristic for the particular individual and which has a relatively slow rate of change.

Because of the nature of the therapeutic process and limitations inherent in nonpsychoanalytic approaches, most other forms of psychiatric treatment are focused therapeutically at the level of the derivative structures and their effects upon the individual's behavior and experience. As long as the core structures established during infantile and early childhood phases of development remain inaccessible to consciousness, their therapeutic modification remains negligible. Their effects upon the behavior and experience of the patient may be modified by changes in the derivative ways by which they are manifested, but the component core psychic structures will remain essentially unchanged.

As described in the section on the clinical theory of the therapeutic process, the psychoanalytic situation and the interactional processes between patient and analyst are specifically designed to enhance the possibility of making these infantile and early childhood core structures available to conscious awareness through the vehicle of the regressive transference neurosis. Conscious awareness of the infantile and core psychic structures provides the setting and capability by which the patient can effect change of these components through application of the insight by the more mature elements of his personality in the working-through process.

In essence, in the situation of the infantile and childhood regressive transference neurosis, the drives, wishes, fantasies, expectations, affects, and behavior experienced by the patient toward the analyst represent automatic, stereotyped, repetitive responses which occur without realistic stimulation by the analyst. The partial psychic regression of the established transference neurosis means that core structures from infancy and early childhood become part of the patient's manifest behavior in the total sense, including subjective experience. In other words, the transference neurosis in all its "inappropriate" aspects represents the final common pathway in the expression of all the core psychic functions (structures) as they were developed and existed during the earliest phases of psychological development. As such, the regressive transference behavior and experiences serve as prototypes for the examination and ultimate modification of these psychic structures. They reflect the patient's stereotyped, repetitive, unconscious, and automatic responses to conflict situations in the absence of specific stimulation by the analyst, and represent the simultaneous interaction of the various core structural components of the personality.

Given this organization of the personality and its repetition in the transference situation, there are a number of points at which therapeutic structural change becomes potentially possible. This potential for change arises from the fact that the regressive transference phenomena occur in an individual who simultaneously maintains adult, rational, self-observing, reality-oriented and integrative ego functions which he can apply to the resolution of the transference conflicts and experiences. This application has been previously described in the discussion of the repetitive use of insight in the working-through process.

The instinctual drives themselves cannot be qualitatively changed, but a quantitative redistribution of their relative importance may occur. As there occurs an exploration of the various archaic superego fantasies and expectations, and as these are subjected to secondary-process awareness and judgments, a change in the nature and intensity of these component forces becomes possible. The same process of judgment and reality-testing may be applied to the various nonmoralistic ego perceptions of childhood danger situations, with resulting modification in the degree to which they are now perceived as dangerous and therefore in their impact upon the personality. This same type of change may also occur in the ego's scanning of the environment for objects upon whom drives can be discharged, with a more conscious and rational selection of age-appropriate conflict-free objects, thereby again modifying stereotyped unconscious object-choices.

Another potential for change is an increased tolerance of unpleasurable affects such as anxiety, depression, guilt, shame, etc., thereby reducing the immediate and unconsciously automatic use of defense mechanisms to eliminate these affective signals. The patient can also increase his tolerance to frustration of ungratified instinctual drives, thereby reducing the automatically impelling and motivating power that such forces induce. And, finally, another potential point of change is in the choice of defensive and adaptive ego-mechanisms used by the individual to cope with unpleasurable affect states, replacing them by consciously selected ones in keeping with the secondary process and the reality principle. Such a shift of defensive, integrative, and synthetic mechanisms can permit more effective and less disabling states of adaptation to irresolvable conflict.

The opportunity for the patient to achieve an increment of structural change in basic personality forces exists as a result of the modification of any one of the various elements in the automatic, previously unconscious sequence described above. In the more effective analytic situations, modification occurs in several or all elements in the structured sequence, although the degree of change may vary from one to another. The analyst's equal interest in promoting therapeutic change in all the different component elements of these structured responses encourages the patient to try to achieve a maximal degree of modification as he applies his deepening insight in the working-through process.

During the process of therapy it is frequently necessary that one structural element be modified (i.e., a defensive function of the ego) as a prerequisite step before change in another component function in the sequence can occur (i.e., the emergence into consciousness of an unconscious fantasy of a danger situation which can then be dissolved by the process of adult reality-testing). In some instances change results from the reduction or elimination of the intensity of one or more elements in the structured sequence of responses. In other instances, old structures are not only reduced or resolved, but they may be replaced by new, more mature, and more effective structured sequences and responses. Such change may be reflected in a particular or specific area of function, but in other cases the change may be more global in the total integration of characteristic behavior patterns, states of consciousness, or modes of conflict resolution.

During the analysis itself, analyst and patient are primarily occupied with attempts at modifying the specific individual microstructures which comprise the stereotyped sequential elements related to any one particular psychic conflict. As a result of the cumulative effect of work focused at the level of particular microstructures, there occurs a corresponding modification in the organization of the various macrostructures as well.

Structural change of the id is reflected by the degree to which previously unavailable drive energies are mobilized, the extent to which genital primacy is established, the degree of fusion of libidinal and aggressive drives, and the fate of pregenital strivings. As mentioned above, the drives themselves are not altered, but the objects of the drives and the conflict-determined inhibitions, deviations, or distortions which had previously blocked the patient from spontaneous maturation toward genital primacy are modified. In other words, qualitatively the drives remain essentially the same but their quantitative distribution is altered by the reorganization of the intrapsychic management of drive discharge. Such apparent changes in the structure of the id are actually a reflection of changing patterns of function within the ego and superego in relationship to the id drives, and the establishment of more mature defensive and adaptive ego functions involved in their control, modulation, and expression.

Structural changes in the superego are reflected in the replacement of primitive- and primary-process introjects by more reality-oriented, personally developed, secondary-process systems of moral values and ideals. This includes a modification of the ego-ideal, with development of a consciously selected, secondary-process set of goals which take realistic account of the patient's potentialities and limitations.

Structural change within the ego involves the degree to which pathological structured ego responses are dissolved and replaced by more effective and adaptive functions which now permit the individual to tolerate situations of conflict or stress without resorting to his previous pathological patterns. Change in ego structure is also reflected in the degree to which the reality principle replaces the pleasure principle, and the freeing of previously impaired ego functions from intrapsychic conflict and their establishment as secondarily autonomous capacities. It also involves the stability of the patient's sense of self and sense of identity, with decrease in preexisting intrasystemic conflict in regard to these issues. The flexibility and appropriateness of the newly integrated defense systems, the stability and effectiveness of sublimations developed to manage pregenital drive discharge, the age-appropriateness and constancy of object choices, and the functional capacity to use them for effective and gratifying drive discharge are also manifestations of structural change within the ego. Implied also is the degree to which there is a renunciation of inappropriate infantile and childhood objects for such drive discharge, and the functional capacity to tolerate frustration and anxiety without defensive regression or a reinstituted search for displaced infantile or childhood objects. Structural change is also reflected in the degree to which the patient can tolerate in conscious awareness those previously unconscious residual drives and fantasies which heretofore had evoked the neurotic structured responses. He can accept such drives and fantasies as a part of the self, with a firm differentiation between thought and action and thus a capacity to tolerate their existence without undue anxiety or needs for neurotic and unconscious defensive adaptations. This capacity is reflected in his ability to continue the work of self-analysis.

In terms of the total integrated functioning of the personality, structural change may be manifested in the patient's overall capacity for more effective and gratifying integration and adaptation, and an ability to cope with stressful situations effectively, along with a qualitatively different awareness of himself, his relationships, and his internal and external environments. This is frequently reflected in the patient's increasing subjective sense of richness, depth, sensitivity, and responsiveness in his life and relationships.

It should be obvious from this study that classical psychoanalysis is a method of treatment ideally applicable to only a relatively small number of psychiatrically ill patients. It cannot be conceived of as a generally applicable method of treatment for the mass of the mentally ill. In well-selected cases it can produce major therapeutic change which for the individual involved makes the time, effort, and expense worthwhile. But its major usefulness and impact arise from its unique position as a methodology for the extensive exploration and study of the complexities and interrelationships of conscious and unconscious functioning of the human mind. Therein lies its most important contribution to the advancement of scientific knowledge, and thus to the welfare of humanity.

# Epilogue

# 15

# FOLLOW-UP by
# E. JAMES ANTHONY, M.D.
## (St. Louis)

---

The first reevaluation of an analysis (modestly entitled "a postscript") took place in the spring of 1922 some seventeen years after Freud had concluded the treatment of Little Hans with the feeling of satisfaction that the child had recovered from his phobic illness and had established a fearless and trustful relationship with his father. Even a chance encounter of this kind, solicited by the patient himself, was characteristically seized upon by Freud to reflect on the outcome of therapy and lay down a few ground rules for assessment. It was not until many years later that his daughter's conception of diagnostic profiles provided us with a more precise and comprehensive instrument for estimating change.

There were roughly four areas covered in the reevaluation, all of which are pertinent to the present study:

1. The current mental health. (The young man was "perfectly well" and free from troubles and inhibitions.)
2. The response to subsequent stress. ("His emotional life had successfully undergone one of the severest of ordeals"—the divorce of his parents and the consequent separation from his much loved sister.)
3. The aftermath of the analysis itself. (No detrimental consequences as a result of opening up the "unconscious" mind. The uncovered events had undergone rerepression and the analysis itself had been "overtaken by amnesia" apart from a "glimmering recollection.")
4. Further development. (He had traversed the pitfalls of puberty "without any damage" and any unfinished business in the analysis had procured its own resolution.) No analyst is ever completely satisfied at termination and Freud was no exception in this case. If it had been left to him, he would have given Hans further sexual enlightenment on copulation and the existence of the vagina, and so "further diminished his unsolved residue," but clearly further development had taken care of this untouched remnant. Analysts today are more content not to

analyse "everything," relying on the self-analytic momentum generated by the analysis.

In these hyperscientific times, one might discount Freud's precursory effort at evaluation as possibly biased, and there is certainly something to be said in favor of having the assessment carried out "blindly" by an independent judge less likely to be influenced by preconceptions, wishful thinking, and subtle countertransference effects. This latter course was followed in the present circumstance, although the judging analyst was also given an opportunity to reconsider his appraisal later in the light of reading the full analytic text. There were, therefore, several stages in the process of evaluation that can be summarized under the following headings:

1. Without any prior communication or exchange of knowledge, apart from the fact that she was an analytic patient and that an account of her treatment was being prepared for publication, an appointment was set up directly with her. She missed this because of some apparent confusion in the arrangement, but kept a subsequent one. The session was conducted in a face-to-face situation and was as nondirective as possible. What she discussed was, therefore, largely of her own choosing; no special effort was made to extract detailed information about the analysis and her current reaction to it. What she discussed was either what she considered significant and important or what she felt was relevant to the purpose of the visit, a purpose that she understood quite well. She was consciously cooperative although a little anxious about the "examination." My assessment of her current mental health, her response to subsequent stress, the effect of the analysis, and her continuing development was chiefly based on comments and nonverbal cues spontaneously expressed.
2. I then regarded this interview material in terms of my own expectation of how a successfully analysed patient should behave in an analytically-oriented examination.
3. Some time later, I read the complete account of her analysis and compared the analytic with the postanalytic picture of the patient.
4. Having learned something about her preanalytic life and her preanalytic therapy, I was confronted with the additional fact that her analysis had been completed in two years, or approximately 347 hours which is the equivalent of 14½ days. Her analyst pointed out that considering the extent of the changes that had taken place, "this is a remarkably short time." It is, and the question here is, why?

5. Finally, I deal with the assessor's overall reaction to the total experience as outlined above.


# 1. The "Blind" Interview

The patient is a young looking, attractive, tall but well-built woman. Her face is rounded and her coloring healthy. She was simply dressed and seemed fairly at her ease, although, later in the session, she confessed to some initial nervousness. I will describe the session more or less as it progressed.

She informed me that her treatment with Dr. Dewald had lasted about two years. She was twenty-seven years old when it began. Her last child was born six months ago, and it was a boy. She now had two girls and two boys.

I asked her to tell me something about how her trouble had started, and she immediately launched into a very detailed and acrimonious account of her preanalytic therapy or counseling (she was not sure exactly what to call it) which had lasted for one year. It terminated, somewhat abruptly, when her therapist recommended that she should have an analysis, and shortly after, informed her that he himself would not be able to treat her any longer. She returned to the subject of her treatment by this therapist over and over again during the session, expressing a great deal of anger and resentment at him. Eventually she did approach the Psychoanalytic Foundation with the idea that she might be accepted as a control case. This was turned down, and Dr. Dewald, who had interviewed her for this purpose, offered to see her himself when he found time. She had applied for clinic treatment because of the expense.

Looking back now, she felt that her preanalytic therapist had gone far beyond his role in his treatment of her. He got overinvolved and caught up with things that he really, she said, did not know how to cope with. He was even more deeply involved with a friend of hers, also a patient of his, from whom she learned a great deal about the therapist. She sensed that he had problems when she brought up the subject of her sexual feelings toward him. This really seemed to shake him. On one occasion, she recalled, he moved from his chair to sit next to her, and then, in "a very mechanical way" put his arm around her shoulder. On another occasion, he took hold of her hand and this made her feel extremely nervous. She did not now regard these maneuvers as seductive, but it irritated her to think that he used them simply as a technical procedure and not because he had any real feelings about her. She looked upon him as a weak and incompetent man, and she was relieved to find out that he worked under supervision. Her dreams were not about the therapist but his supervisor. She had actually seen the supervisor on several occasions when the therapist was away and she felt that he knew his business and was competent. Later she had the same feeling about Dr. Dewald. She imagined that the supervisor had advised the therapist to refer her to the clinic of the Psychoanalytic Foundation because the situation had gone too deep for him to handle.

At this point, she confessed to feeling very nervous talking about this previous therapist, and exclaimed, in a somewhat agitated way: "This man is not even a doctor. He would laugh at some of the things I said, sensitive things!" She described him as a man of about thirty-five whom she did not find at all attractive physically. "I tried very hard because I knew that one is supposed to feel such things." She did realize, however, that she had been very jealous of his relationship with his other patient, her girl friend. One interpretation that occurred to her regarding his termination of her treatment was that he had become aware that she and her friend talked together far too much about their respective experiences in therapy and that he did not like this. (The intimate relationship with the friend had broken off soon after she left psychotherapy and she had seen little of her since although they did correspond a little.)

She still feels that this therapist hurt her "tremendously," aggravating all her problems by adding to them his own incompetent treatment of her. If only he had said to her: "I think that you should go to analytic treatment because I think we have gone as far as we can, and you need more help," she would have understood, "but he simply threw me out just like my father."

It was difficult for her to shake off the experience even though it seemed to distress her. He had laughed at her when she had told him that her husband had been so upset with her that they had not had sexual intercourse for a month. He said that her husband could not have been too upset or else he would not have gone that long. He also speculated on the idea that her husband probably had difficulties with his masculinity; this she had found very objectionable. "I did not realize at the time how hostile I felt toward him. All I would do was cry, and he would say to me: 'All you can do is to cry like a baby.'"

"I don't think I ever told Dr. Dewald about his touching me, and putting his arm around me, and holding my hand. I *never* had the feeling that he would ever do that with me. I'm not sure why I didn't tell him. I think it was because I thought he was hostile to him. He always referred to him by his surname without his title."

She had entered therapy suffering from acute anxiety, but only later did she learn that this was what it was. At the time, her hands shook and her pupils were dilated. Unknown to her, her husband had discussed her state with a psychiatrist and had been informed that this was anxiety. The condition developed during the last month of her first pregnancy. She had become very angry with her husband because he had remarked that she looked fat. Her anger turned into anxiety which she felt was due to the suppression of the hostility, but at the time she did not know of what she was afraid. She would become anxious especially if left alone, or if left alone with the baby after the birth. When she finally got into treatment, her therapist had helped her to pinpoint some of the sources of her anxiety such as her sexual feelings for any goodlooking man who came along and her suppressed hostile feelings. She had always liked men with good looks who were quiet and tender. Her therapist reminded her of one of those big football players who were so unsure of themselves and had to parade their masculinity.

In her analysis with Dr. Dewald, she had begun to learn a great deal about the origins of her anxiety. He did not interpret to her at the beginning except to point out that she desired a penis and was consequently envious of men. Toward the end of the analysis, however, she became aware *that she wanted her father's penis as a pretext for getting back inside her mother*. A little later, just before the end, she realized the extent of her hostile feelings toward her younger sister *who had been inside her mother while she herself was out*. This understanding came like *a tremendous revelation* as if she had struggled out of a small aperture into a very brightly lit room, which made her think of *the birth process*.

During childhood, she had had a good relationship with her older sister who, although only a year ahead, was mature and motherly and substituted for her mother. The younger sister, four years her junior, was very bright, petite and beautiful, and only later did she get to know how hostile she felt toward her.

This consideration seemed to trigger off her smoldering resentment against the therapist. He had primed her to such an extent that she began talking all over the place, especially to her mother-in-law, about her feelings for her father. She could not stop herself thinking how her father had hurt and rejected her. In this sense particularly, both father and therapist had treated her alike. Her father had been rather undemonstrative, and

although like the therapist he was weak, he was also "very deep" and had
a mind that she admired. In any case, he did not crumble like her mother
who was incapable of thinking things out. She felt that her younger sister
had rather a masculine streak and identified herself with the father. She
had organized a nursery school and had taught.

"I had, perhaps, the most feeling of the three girls, but we were all
blessed with good looks like my mother, although later she put on a lot of
weight."

She had spent four years at college, but was not at all interested in
learning and had been unable to decide whether to major in sociology or
English.

Her life had not been by any means an easy one. Her parents had
quarreled a lot and were frequently on the verge of divorce. Twice her
father had left home and twice he had come back. She had resonated to
this and everything else. "I suppose that all children have the sort of feelings that I had, but perhaps I just had more of them. I can see the same
sort of feelings in my own children but I try not to interpret to them."

She realized what a great change had taken place in her with her
analysis. She had no more of the anxiety attacks and felt much more sure
of herself. If people did not like her, she no longer considered it an overwhelming problem.

A new note now crept into the interview as she turned from reminiscing
with feeling about the past to her current life situation. All her babies had
been born by Caesarian section, and at the last one the obstetrician had
found fibroids in the uterus and had recommended hysterectomy. No one,
including her husband, wanted her to have any more children and usually
this entailed no more than the tying of the tubes; but having an hysterectomy at this early age seemed a dreadful thing. She had begun to feel very
anxious when the obstetrician left town or when her husband was not
around. She had also had very hostile feelings toward me when I had
"messed up" the first appointment and she had gone to the wrong place.
This was the first time in the interview that her affects had been overtly
directed toward me and it seemed to be connected to the anxiety generated
by the thought of losing her womb.

She was obviously quite distressed possibly by the turn the interview
was taking, but insisted that everyone had been so surprised that she had
been able to cope with such a severe stress without relapsing into her
previous nervous state. It was a terrible thing for a young woman of thirty-
two to undergo. "Just as I had begun to accept and appreciate what it was

to be a woman, it was taken away from me. I went through all the feelings that women who go through a change of life experience even though I had my hormones working for me. I was sad that I was not going to have any more kids, and I really began to feel and behave as if I was fifty. I was psychologically fifty."

There was a short silence during which she seemed to be pulling herself together and succeeding. Eventually she said: "I'm sure I'll get through it. I often think that things are better when they are really bad than when they are only a little bad." She had recovered her poise and we were able to continue the session on a more even keel.

She returned once again to the matter of her first therapist. He had come to her recently asking for financial support for a special treatment project in which he was involved. The idea had made her very angry and she wanted to prevent other people from going to him and being made to suffer in the way she had. She was glad that he had been turned out of his job and that his association did not support him.

She seemed to want me to recognize her greater resilience. She said she was surprised herself how well she had gone through this major crisis without having to lean on her husband's shoulder nor he on hers. All in all, she felt that she owed a great deal to Dr. Dewald. When she had received his letter asking whether she would agree to come and see me, she had cried. He was like a loving father who had died and had come back. She had learned in analysis that he was not God but just a man, and a man who did not love her even though she loved him. "What he did for me was so marvelous that I wish other people could have it as well."

We discussed the reluctance she expressed at coming for another session. She said that talking about her previous therapist had made her feel extremely nervous, and she worried about coming again and getting upset. I assured her that this was completely up to her and that the assessment was a voluntary act on her part for which Dr. Dewald and I were both very appreciative. However, if she did not feel inclined to take on another session and reactivate all these feelings once again, I would quite understand. She said that she did not mind talking about the present but it was talking about the past that worried her. I pointed out that the task of evaluation made it inevitable for cross-references between the present and the past, both the immediate past of her analysis as well as the remote past of her childhood, to occur. She should know this and appreciate it before making up her mind about a second session. She said, without too much enthusiasm, that she would come again but not the following week when she would be out of town, but the week after. I remarked that although I appreciated this decision, I would still like her to feel perfectly free to cancel the appointment should she not feel up to it.

She cancelled the appointment and that was the last I heard from her. I made no further effort to get in touch with her for reasons I shall presently discuss.

## 2. The Assessor's Reaction to the Interview

The elements in the interview that were salient in my mind were: the angry preoccupation with the previous therapist; her response to post-analytic stresses; her capacity for almost "instant" transference reactions and the matrix of transference in which she involved people; her appreciation of the sharp contrast in style and management of therapist and analyst; and, finally, her complex response to me, the interviewer.

Why the spontaneous attack on the therapist? On the basis of the interview material, a number of possible causes suggested themselves. In the first place, it seemed as if the patient was looking past her successful analysis at an experience that she had come to regard as predominantly traumatic. The transference neurosis generated by the analysis must have been systematically interpreted and resolved without an itching residue, whereas from the evidence, however distorted, offered by the patient, it would appear that the transference developments in the therapy had been misunderstood, at times misused, and generally mismanaged to the point of artful manipulation as when her wish for closeness was actually gratified in the name of technique—the most generous interpretation of what took place. The lack of resolution would be reinforced by the abrupt termination.

Secondly, judging from her remarks alone, the internal representation of the therapist became in time a much closer replica of the primary object (the father) than the image of the analyst, not only because of an obvious failure in correcting the transference distortions but also as a result of the therapist to a large extent falling a passive victim of the transference. He was perceived as weak, hurtful, and rejecting "just like my father," and insensitive to her very vulnerable narcissism.

Thus, whereas the analysis like the analysed dream is "overtaken by amnesia" (although certainly not to the degree that occurred with the

grownup Hans), the therapy persists as a traumatic memory still provocative of angry affect and anxiety.

The situation was also highly conducive to the mechanism of splitting
as became increasingly clear in the latter part of the interview. The legiti-
mate doctor-analyst was seen as strong, efficient, sensitive, self-sufficient,
impervious to seduction—just like my good father; the therapist, "not even
a doctor" had become the embodiment of weakness, incompetence, in-
sensitivity, susceptibility, and in need of support himself—just like my bad
father. She was unable to shake off her preoccupation with the bad father
and her wish to help, support, and protect him, as well as destroy him.
She did not want to expose him to the wrath of the good father by reporting his misdemeanors and although openly hostile to him herself, she did
not relish the idea of exposing him (and the part of her identified with
him) to the hostility of others.

Her enhanced capacity to bear stress was very much in evidence when
she discussed her hysterectomy, emerging from the rush of anxiety with a
composure that the interviewer found admirable. It was the "really bad"
things that stimulated her coping abilities and made her confident that
she would "get through it." This was both in spite of and because of a good
analytic understanding of what the situation entailed. "Just as I had begun
to accept and appreciate what it was to be a woman, it was taken away
from me." She had developed a pride in this newly found mastery over
anxiety and felt that it was important for me to appreciate it as part of the
change. Yet, she was realistic enough not to want to push herself need-
lessly into a testing circumstance. It was for this reason too that I refrained
from pressing her for a second interview. She had every right, having undergone a successful analysis, to have both the uncovered material and the
analytic process itself relegated comfortably to the background, having
achieved their purpose. Not only is the relative amnesia seemingly inevitable, as pointed out by Freud, but also necessary to the maintenance of
psychic balance.

Her analysis might undergo suppression and repression but not her
capacity for self-analysis which revealed itself in various parts of the session.
Apart from the splitting tendency already noted and fostered in large part
by the circumstance, I was struck by the perceptiveness with which she
appraised her therapist and analyst, her interest in protecting others from
incompetent therapy and sharing with them a "marvelous" experience,
her ability to extract goodness out of badness (the therapist did help her
to pinpoint some of the sources of her anxiety), her generous expression of

thankfulness for what she owed to analysis and her analyst who had returned from the grave (amnesia) like a loving father to show she was neither rejected nor forgotten, and her acceptance of the final reality—he was not God but a man who had done a "marvelous" professional job on her but could not be expected to love her although she loved him.

Her analytic awareness manifested itself in her sophisticated and subtle analysis of the transference constellation that had dominated her treatment: the trauma of the oedipal rejection by the father (repeated by the therapist but skillfully avoided by the analyst); the pre-oedipal tie to the mother in the context of which her wish for a penis and her hostility toward her younger sister are reinterpreted at this psychosexual level as variants of a deep uterine fantasy; the older sister seen as a pre-oedipal mother substitute, and the younger sister as both a pre-oedipal and oedipal rival. The "tremendous revelation" during analysis had to do with the pre-oedipal components of her total psychopathology as conceptualized in the birth trauma. The oedipal wishes and phallic strivings on the other hand seemed "old familiars" to her as if she had lived closely with them all her life and was constantly poised for the "return of the unconscious." The analytic task would consist of making this quasi-intellectual awareness an affective experience of the transference neurosis so that her insightfulness possessed the quality of the "depth" characteristic of those who have undergone a therapeutic regression. It was because of this that she could deal with the reactivated castration anxieties occasioned by the discussion of her hysterectomy during the interview, and it was because of this that she could remark with analytic equanimity that now if people did not like her, she no longer considered it an overwhelming problem.

Her reaction to me fluctuated during the course of the session. She had come somewhat enraged by "the mess" I had made of the arrangements, and also a little nervous. While she reported past events, she remained at first fairly comfortable, but as the past began to reopen, she became more involved in the interview and more angry with her recollections. Eventually her proclivity for "instant" transference asserted itself and some of the irritability started to focus on me as she saw me more and more as a prying provocateur, not too sensitive to the anxieties I was rousing. I wondered at the time whether her perceptiveness made her realize, with anger, that I ascribed her interview distress more to her castration anxieties, reactivated by the hysterectomy which she judged she was coping with very well, than by the recollection of the rejection trauma by the therapist. I did not say anything, of course, to this effect, but I detected a growth of negative feeling which led to the cancellation of the second appointment. Despite this, I was left with a wholly positive feeling for her and somewhat saddened by the thought that after a great comeback following a disturbing and disturbed childhood, she had been unfairly exposed to "too searching a fate."

The interview, and the comments that followed, understandably reflect my expectations of analysis and my image of the well-analysed person. I would expect the postanalytic identity to display among other things a sense of historical continuity, an acceptance of sexual and reproductive role appropriate to the individual, a well-differentiated personality, an executive competence reflected in everyday organization and orientation, responsibility for one's own action, activity and initiative on one's own behalf, and an overall capacity to form good and enduring relationships with others.

I would expect the postanalytic outlook to be objective with regard to outside perceptions, realistically oriented to both internal and external worlds, psychologically minded and insightful, "in touch with the unconscious," empathic with respect to others, fair and honest in judgments, open to new experiences and ideas, flexible in the alteration of attitude, and generally, to view reality (in Schafer's terms) ironically and tragically, but not without a leavening of humor and romance.

I would expect the postanalytic responsiveness of the patient to include a better-than-before capacity to master anxiety, tolerate stress, react with less guilt and shame, masochism, depression and grandiosity, feel safer, and altogether to be less hysterically miserable even if ordinarily unhappy. There is a capacity to suffer and be depressed but not overwhelmed. An important part of this responsiveness is based on the new realization of the extent to which one brings about one's own suffering.

Whether penis envy (in the woman) and the hankering after fusion with the pre-oedipal mother (in both sexes) remains after all else is analysed is still a moot question, but there is no doubt that these basic regressive pulls contribute to the brute fact that every (analytic) advance is only "half as great as it appears to be at first" (Freud).

The analyst must, therefore, be realistic in his expectations of outcome, especially if fate, in the guise of some overpowering catastrophe aimed at the most vulnerable section of the ex-patient, takes an unfair hand. Schafer has this reassuring comment to offer: "Who among the reasonably well-analysed patients is invulnerable to a painful stirring up of his pre-oedipal and oedipal conflicts by, for example, his children—their birth, their infancy, their instinctual moving away during adolescence? Who is immunized by his analysis against neurotically coloured responses to the advance of age, the disharmonies of marriage, the death of parents, and the limits of career?" Who indeed?

It is often said, with some justification, that the analytic style is the man and that therefore the account of an analysis is as recognizable as a fingerprint. What about the analysed patient? Does she display in any way the analyst who analysed her? If Loewald is correct in his view that some sort of internalization of the analyst as analyst into the patient's ego and ego-ideal organization takes place in analysis and accounts for the self-analytic propensity, and Piers has spoken of the identification with the analyst in his analytic role, then it should be possible to detect the analyst at work when interviewing the postanalytic patient if one knows the analyst. What I detected in the interview was a careful, *systematic* approach to her self-analysis, for the most part objectively and neutrally expressed, and couched in the careful, precise language that I have come to associate with Dr. Dewald. I experienced almost a déjà vu sensation as I heard the patient systematically unfold her evaluation of her own psychopathology (and it must be remembered that this was done with minimal interruption from me). She first reviewed her relationship with her first therapist, her earliest symptoms in her first pregnancy, the first interpretation in analysis (of penis envy); her gradual realization in transference that the desire for the penis was a pretext to fuse with her mother and her hostility toward her sister was an envy of her fused state with the mother. Finally came the "tremendous revelation" that her anxiety was in essence a separation anxiety and associated with the birth trauma. From dealing with the remote past and the analytic past, she progressed very logically to considering her postanalytic resilience in the light of her womb loss and the effect of this on her analytic gains. She terminated the interview with a fine postanalytic appraisal of her analyst.

Although one could deduce the "grey eminence" of the analyst behind the postanalytic adjustment of the patient—in the manifold evidence she gave of being an historically continuous person, a woman (and mother) now in her own right, a multilayered personality, a self-reliant individual, "in touch with her unconscious," empathic with regard to others, realistic and fair-minded, and capable of handling her anxiety, her guilt, her shame, her narcissism and her masochism—one must admit that she came into analysis already endowed with analytic potential for transference, introspection, empathy, articulateness, and what she especially admired in her father —brightness and depth. She was, therefore, a "good" analytic patient with a good analytic prognosis, and well prepared to respond to a good analyst.

## 3. Some Reconsiderations after Reading the Analytic Protocol

After reading through the full analytic account of the patient, I reconsidered my postanalytic assessment. I was especially pleased at the nearness to which I had been able "blindly" to reconstruct for myself the "natural history" of her analysis. The unfolding of the transference neurosis under the aegis of the analyst was magisterial in its sureness and a model for what can and should take place in every classical analysis.

What struck me especially (with my weather eye open for it) was the extent of the pre-oedipal pathology in a classically phobic patient manifesting a typical oedipal conflict with as much fixation as regression to account for it. The traumatic undertones that pervade both the analysis and my interview with her seem to relate to both pregenital as well as genital trauma. She oscillates constantly from one to the other; at the genital level, she turns repetitively to the missing penis, the disappointing father, the phallic mother, the primal experience, the menstrual "shock," and the relinquishing of aggressiveness (oral castrating) for the passive-masochistic position; at the pregenital level, she is a "displaced" child, an abandoned infant, perpetually haunted by a sense of emptiness and a great fear of loneliness. The sequela to the later trauma lies in the seductive, castrating wishes, and to the earlier trauma in the hostile-dependent relationship to the mother, the bad image of herself as a mother, the occasionally murderous impulses toward her children and the powerfully persistent rage against her younger sister. ("I hate my mother—bitch—want to kill her— stab her with a knife—hurt her by killing myself—that's what she wanted in the beginning—unwanted child—mother wished I was dead. . . ." "I'm really a bad mother and I hate my children, and I want to kill them just as my mother hated me, resented me, didn't want me, and wanted to kill me. . . ." "I can remember my mother putting her [the younger sister] down in the middle of the bed. I felt she didn't want me anymore. My sister was squirting my mother with urine. She was blonde and beautiful. My mother loves her much more than she does me. . . . They just don't want me anymore. I'm nothing and I'm not even there and my mother just loves this baby. . . . It hurt like hell, it really does.") This is what Odier described as "the neurosis of abandonment" and what Erikson referred to as "the center of despair" within the "inner space" of the woman. Over and over again, one gets the feeling that when this patient speaks of her "emptiness," she is talking not only of her sense of phallic nothingness but of that emptiness that is, says Erikson, "the female form of perdition ... to be left, for her, means to be left empty, to be drained of the blood of the body, the warmth of the heart, the sap of life. How a woman thus can be hurt in depth is a wonder to many a man, and it can arouse both his empathic horror and his refusal to understand. Such hurt can be re-experienced in each menstruation; it is crying to heaven in the mourning over a child; and it becomes a permanent scar in the menopause ... the very existence of the inner productive space exposes women early to a specific sense of loneliness, to a fear of being left empty or deprived of treasures, of remaining unfulfilled and of drying up."

The trauma of losing her womb and developing symptoms of an artificial menopause can therefore be understood on both these levels, as too her effort to synthesize her psychopathology—that her wish for her father's penis was a pretext for getting back inside her mother and her hatred for her younger sister stemmed from the fact that she was inside mother while she was outside.

The intensity and vividness of the oral imagery is constantly reactivated during the analysis, although clearly muted by the strength of the father transference later in the treatment. ("My mother is feeding me. She hates me and hates my dependency on her. I can't do it, not even for milk and food. I need it and she won't give it to me. . . . When mother fed me, I had a feeling she'd laugh and say: I'll either kill you or save you. . . . A woman is trying to devour me and kill me [feeling in my mouth] . . . .)

It is not surprising that in a dream she screams at her mother: "I've had to have two years of analysis because of you," and adds, in her associations that she cannot figure out why she was mad at her mother and not her father (which suggests that this may have been the latent content of the dream. Both parents disappointed her at the different levels, but both therapist and analyst reinforced the father disappointment, giving it thereby greater significance during the treatment. It is possible that a woman analyst may have effected a different unconscious influence).

The bias at work here is that of a child analyst confronted with adult material and therefore hyperconscious as one always is in child analysis of pre-oedipal propensities. My experience to date has led me to believe that frequently behind the anxious, phobic, hysterical woman patient with strong phallic strivings that respond well to analysis of the oedipal feelings for the father is a somewhat dependent, insecure, and immature female with a pregenital tie to the mother and an unconscious hostile identification with her, so that she is constantly struggling with the need to feel and behave differently from the mother. Whether the pre-oedipal section of the analysis succeeds as well as the oedipal section, only time will tell. In the case of Dr. Dewald's patient, the current state of both sections looked reasonably good and I did not feel that she required further analysis, which suggests that in many cases that if you do a competent job with the oedipal complex, the pre-oedipal components will, with a little help, look after themselves.

Analysts who read this protocol will undoubtedly be impressed by the controlled analytic mind at work and the way in which the analysis of the patient, the analysis of the process, and the analysis of the analyst himself all proceed "with the inevitability of gradualism" as someone once termed it. They might disagree with some elements of the general strategy and because of the complex nature of the process involved this is to be expected. There are innumerable factors influencing the analyst's technique and as many having their effect on the patient's response, so differences there will be. As Schafer has summarized it, one cannot do better than quote what he has to say on the matter:

... notwithstanding his close adherence to classical and well-founded principles of technique, he (the analyst) remains the tool of his own work and so can analyse only in his own way. His use of the established principles and his way of recognizing and verbalizing fundamental trends in the analytic material ought to be not too different from the next analyst's, and so the insights and changes achieved during the analysis ought not to be too different from what one would expect them to be if the next analyst had this case. *But differences there will be.** These differences exist partly because analysts differ among themselves in their life histories, their talents and training, and their id, ego and superego organizations. . . . (The analyst) is, for example, attempting to clarify and account for very particular definitions of danger, defences, shifts of level, preferred shades of feeling, interests and values. Each analyst's sensitivities, interests and cultural scope are bound to influence his exploration and comprehension of the material. . . . Thus it is a necessary part of the analyst's vision of his work to recognize that no matter how objectively he carries out his analyses, no matter how far above reproach by his colleagues the essentials of his technique may be, and no matter how satisfactory the results, each of his analyses will bear his trademark or one of his several trademarks. (Page 292.)

# 4. The Responsiveness of the Patient

This patient was analysed, by present-day criteria, in "a remarkably short time" (two years: 347 hours: 14½ days!), and the question that arises is, what made this possible? With regard to the phenomenon of

* My italics.

shortening, two separate issues need to be considered: rapidity in adopting the analytic posture (becoming an analytic patient) and the unusual acceleration of the analytic process (the development and resolution of the transference neurosis).

I was struck, in the interview, how rapidly and systematically she got down to the business of self-evaluation and I ascribed this at least in part to the self-analytic skills she had developed as a result of her analysis. Later, I began to feel that this was only partly true and that she was to a great extent a "born patient," that is, she came with certain facilitating attributes into treatment. Her dependency, her masochism, and her narcissism allowed her to assume the patient posture more "naturally" and this was further helped by her previous therapeutic experience. Her brightness, her intuitiveness, and her eagerness to please quickly alerted her to what was expected of an analytic patient; and finally, her empathy, her sensitivity to interpersonal feelings made it possible for her to enter, without inordinate mistrustful questioning, into a therapeutic alliance.

Her "transference potential" was evident in the interview where I found myself rapidly drawn into a transference situation. She had been kept waiting for her first interview with Dr. Dewald and had become very angry as a result. A woman social worker had stood between her and her high expectations from analysis. Her first interview with me had been delayed because I, or a secretary, had "messed it up" and she was very angry about it. Being a man, I was inevitably destined to make her suffer, frustrate, and disappoint her and she was ready to hate me for it.

In addition to this propensity, she had an insightfulness derived from the actualization of fantasy during childhood, from repeated emotional traumata, from open seductiveness, from vivid dreaming and daydreaming, so that her oedipal wishes and fears were never far away from consciousness. There are sensitive and sensitized individuals like this who "discover" the oedipus complex for themselves because of the pressure of these several factors. Freud would be one of these, Stendhal another. Here she is describing her "primal" experience:

When my parents made love it was as if the whole world ceased. It was so sick. If I could only get it cleared and if it didn't panic me and make me sick or hysterical, or make me want to scream or beat my head against the wall. I can see it. That was the stupidest thing they ever did. I used to lie in my room and put my pillow over my head. . . . But there was nothing more horrible than that as a child.

She adds later that "my mother, my sisters, and myself all shared my father's sexuality."

Compare this with Stendhal's description of his relationship with his mother written almost a hundred years before the "official" recognition of the oedipus complex and by someone without the benefit of analysis:

My mother was a charming woman and I was in love with my mother. I was perhaps six years old when I fell in love with her but my character was exactly the same as when I was thirty-nine and madly in love with Alberthe. As far as the physical side of love was concerned . . . I wanted to cover my mother with kisses and for her to have no clothes on. She loved me passionately and often kissed me and I returned her kisses with such fire that she often had to leave me. I abhorred my father when he came and interrupted our embraces. I always wanted to kiss my mother on the throat. . . . Chance never brought together two beings who were more fundamentally antipathetic to each other than my father and I. (In my dreams I always referred to him as "the bastard.") At the age of seven, my mother died and at that point my moral life began.

There is every reason to believe that patients with this almost unrepressed understanding of the infantile nuclear complex may not only face the analytic process less defensively but also develop extremely intense transference neuroses to an almost delusional degree. The enhancement of the transference tendency can be at times tantamount to pleasure-seeking. The analyst, in resolving the transference neurosis, is attempting to attenuate the general transference proclivity to which the patient is addicted. While the immediate outcome and early outcome of this analysis are excellent, it will be the remote outcome, ten years on, from which we will learn something about the long-term stability of the "accelerated" analytic process.

# 5. The Overall Assessment

This is not only an unusual undertaking but an unusual undertaking very well done. The honesty and courage involved are very much in keeping with the historical tradition in psychoanalysis that dared to publish case material antipathetic to the culture. There have been no verbatim accounts of a complete analysis depicting its unfolding through various stages. Generally highlights are given or selections appertaining to theory. Even in this case study, sessions have had to be omitted or summarized for the sake of economy.

To what extent does the reporting of a verbatim account distort the veridical nature of the process being observed? Freud in 1912 proscribed any note taking during the analytic hour on the grounds that this conscious, secondary-process activity interfered with the proper analytic stance of evenly hovering attention that was the counterpart of the patient's free association. It could also deflect the analyst from attending fully to his task of interpretation. The avoidance of note taking helps, in addition, to ensure privacy and confidentiality or at least may remind the patient that his rights are being safeguarded. Certain of the charges of incompleteness and distortion are applicable to process notes, since, even with the best intentions, there is a selective sampling of the "universe of events" taking place during a session. Wallerstein and Sampson point to some of the advantages: the notes are "a permanent, and 'public' record of a systematic series of observations by a highly trained participant observer" and therefore do allow for "independent and concurrent observation and study"; they are obtained "with relatively little special effort and with minimal disruption of the natural analytic situation"; and finally, there is an enormous gain in having a relatively brief account of a long analytic treatment which "the human mind can process so that large sweeps of material, disclosing major configurations and sequences of change can be encompassed." (It should be remembered that process note taking involves a fifty-fold reduction of material obtained from tape typescripts. However, in the latter, what is missing is any account of nonverbal behavior and the unspoken thoughts and feelings of the analyst.) Bion has suggested that the sessional notes may be "far from a record of what took place: yet near to the anticipation of a future development." The images evoked in the analyst related to events still to come. The notes would become a repository of creative ideas to be used in the service of the treatment. The combination evolved by Dr. Dewald of process and commentary would seem to represent the best of all procedural worlds and the nearest we can get to date of "what actually happens." More than any account I have read, it conveys not only the excitement entailed in the gradual exposure of the internal world within us all but also the hard creative work done by the analyst, in conjunction with the patient to bring it about. We get to know the analytic patient in a way that we never get to know another human being. It should convince all students of psychotherapy that their efforts can become as creative in the fullest meaning of the term. In the words of Bergson:

If then the triumph of life is expressed by creation, ought we not to think that the ultimate reason of human life is a creation which, in distinction from that of the artist or man of science, can be pursued at every moment and by all men alike: I mean the creation of self by self, the continual enrichment of personality by elements which it does not draw from outside but causes to spring forth from itself!

This is what psychoanalysis is ultimately about, and this is what we learn from this enthralling illustration of its process.

# References

BERGSON, H. *Creative Evolution.* New York: Modern Library, 1944.

BION, W. R. *Second Thoughts: Selected Papers on Psycho-Analysis.* London: Heinemann, 1967.

FREUD, S. "Analysis of a Phobia in a Five-year-old Boy" (1909). *Collected Papers,* Vol. 3. New York: Basic Books, 1959.

SCHAFER, R. "The Psychoanalytic Vision of Reality," *International Journal of Psychoanalysis* 51, no. 3 (1970): 279–298.

STENDHAL. *La vie de Henri Brulard.* New York: French and European Publication.

WALLERSTEIN, R. S. and SAMPSON, H. "Issues in Research in the Psychoanalytic Process." *International Journal of Psychoanalysis.* 52, no. 1 (1971): 11–50.

# INDEX

abandonment: fear of, 389; and repression of love feelings, 393

abreaction: role of, 621–622

acting-out, 162, 163, 204, 276, 604

adolescent emancipation: compared to termination of analysis, 533, 537, 575–576

adult identity: and termination of analysis, 464–465; and wish to remain child, 472, 477, 488–489, 492–493, 498, 502–503

affective experience: availability of, 604, 613

affective responses: and adaptive mechanisms, 629

aggression: as defense against grief, 524; defenses against, 134, 321–322, 331, 383, 384; defensive function of, 67, 72, 97; displacement of, 156, 330, 352; fantasied as destruction, 157; and helplessness, 322

anal sadism, 90

analysis, 59; and acceptance of parental limitations, 497, 512–513; anxiety about, 25, 38, 44–45, 67, 85, 90; length of, 590; and marriage, 585, 588–589; as nursing situation, 198; and pregnancy, 62–63; resistance to, 274; see also termination of analysis, transference neurosis

analyst, 3, 544, 608; compared to parent, 590; establishing trust in, 49; identification with, 50–51, 101–102; individuality of, 648, 651; and negative transference, 334–335; neutrality of, 71–72, 562, 589, 614; and note taking, 654; and transference

**DATE DUE**